MERGERS, ACQUISITIONS, AND OTHER RESTRUCTURING ACTIVITIES

SEVENTH EDITION

Praise for *Mergers, Acquisitions, and Other Restructuring Activities*

"DePamphilis has masterfully covered in one book all relevant managerial, strategic, financial, accounting, legal and tax aspects of M&A in an easily understood road map for any M&A transaction, large or small. With totally up-to-date material, he provides the crucial information that is necessary in today's rapidly changing M&A world."
—**Lloyd Levitin,** Professor of Clinical Finance and Business Economics, University of Southern California

"Mergers, Acquisitions, and Other Restructuring Activities, Sixth Edition, delivers an essential understanding of the corporate restructuring processes by combining insights from many case studies with academic rigor. The book points out how M&A can create value as well as the ways it can lead to value destruction. In addition to the state-of-the-art valuation techniques, it also explains the regulatory corporate governance framework for both the United States and Europe. It's an excellent text, and I highly recommend it."
—**Luc Renneboog,** Professor of Corporate Finance, Tilburg University

"Great textbook that in a simple and straightforward manner combines the latest insights from academia with contemporary industry practices. It fits perfectly in a class of MBA students or executives. I will for sure use it next time I teach M&A."
—**Karin Thorburn,** DnB Nor Professor of Finance, Norwegian School of Economics and Business Administration

"Mergers, Acquisitions, and Other Restructuring Activities is quite simply an outstanding text. Don DePamphilis delivers a comprehensive guide to the M&A process from start to finish....In sum, this book is a comprehensive, up-to-date, outstanding text."
—**Scott C. Linn,** R.W. Moore Chair in Finance and Economic Development, University of Oklahoma

"I am happy to recommend the fifth edition of *Mergers, Acquisitions, and Other Restructuring Activities*. Having used prior editions of Don DePamphilis's text, I can affirm that this edition builds on a firm foundation of coverage, real-world examples, and readability. My students have consistently responded favorably to prior editions of the book. In this edition, I was delighted to discover that Don is expanding his coverage of family-owned businesses, already a strength in his earlier editions that were distinguished by their coverage of the valuation of privately held businesses. Additional attention is paid to restructuring, bankruptcy, and liquidation as well as risk management, which are clearly topics of interest to every business person in today's economic climate."
—**Kent Hickman,** Professor of Finance, Gonzaga University

"The fifth edition is one of the most comprehensive books on mergers and acquisitions. The text combines theories, valuation models, and real-life cases to give business students an overall insight into the M&A deal process. The up-to-date real-life examples and cases provide opportunities for readers to explore and to apply theories to a wide variety of scenarios such as cross-border transactions, highly levered deals, firms in financial distress, and family-owned businesses. The chapter on restructuring under bankruptcy and liquidation both inside and outside the protection of the bankruptcy court is timely and most useful in light of today's economic crisis. Overall, this is an excellent book on mergers, acquisitions, and corporate restructuring activities."
—**Tao-Hsien Dolly King,** Rush S. Dickson Professor of Finance, Associate Professor, Department of Finance, Belk College of Business, The University of North Carolina at Charlotte

"Mergers, Acquisitions, and Other Restructuring Activities is an interesting and comprehensive look at the most important aspects of M&A and corporate restructuring—from strategic and regulatory considerations and M&A deal process, through several chapters on M&A valuation and deal structuring, to other types of restructuring activities. It not only provides a road map for the M&A and other corporate restructuring transactions, but also highlights the key things to watch for. The book is clearly written with extensive but easy-to-follow case examples and empirical findings and cases to illustrate the points in the text. It is a book by an expert, and for M&A instructors and students as well as practitioners."
—**Qiao Lui,** Faculty of Business and Economics, The University of Hong Kong

"I am delighted with Don DePamphilis's *Mergers, Acquisitions, and Other Restructuring Activities, Fifth Edition*. It is a clear, comprehensive, and thorough discussion of the issues involving all restructuring activities. The use of mini-cases throughout each chapter both highlights and clarifies key elements of aspects of the decision-making process. The end-of-chapter discussion questions are ideally complemented with the problem set questions to challenge readers' understanding of the covered concepts. I am impressed with the current reflection of market conditions throughout the text and the extent of the recent changes to provide greater understanding for students. I expect to find that students are also impressed with its clarity and structure when I introduce this edition to my course. I recommend it to any professor covering mergers, acquisitions, bankruptcies, or other restructuring ... to cover limited topics, or as a text for a complete course on restructuring."

—John F. Manley, Professor of Finance, Hagan School of Business, Iona College

"Mergers and acquisitions continue to be amongst the preferred competitive options available to the companies seeking to grow and prosper in the rapidly changing global business scenario. In the fifth edition of his path-breaking book, the author and M&A expert Dr. DePamphilis illustrates how mergers, acquisitions, and other forms of restructuring can help a company grow and prosper in the highly complex and competitive corporate takeover marketplace. Interspersed with most relevant and up-to-date M&A case studies... this book deals with the multifarious aspects of corporate restructuring in an integrated manner...a lucid style... Every effort has been made to deal with the intricacies of the subject by offering comprehensive coverage of the latest methods and techniques... of both public and private companies.

The book provides practical ways of dealing with M&As even in an economic downturn with a chapter on corporate restructuring under bankruptcy and liquidation. With the greatly enlarged and up-to-date material on varied aspects of the subject, the book provides a plethora of real-world examples which will go a long way in making the subject easy, stimulating, and interesting to both academicians and practitioners alike."

—Donepudi Prasad, ICFAI Business School, Hyderabad, India

"Professor DePamphilis has made significant, important, and very timely updates in the fifth edition of his text. He incorporates contemporary events such as the credit crunch and the latest accounting rules in the West, plus M&A issues in emerging markets including family businesses. He also readdresses corporate governance, a topic that will become increasingly important in business schools the world over in M&A. This text has become, and will increasingly become, the definitive comprehensive and thorough reference on the subject."

—Jeffrey V. Ramsbottom, Visiting Professor, China Europe International Business School, Shanghai

"I think the fifth edition of *Mergers, Acquisitions, and Other Restructuring Activities* does a comprehensive job of covering the M&A field. As in the previous edition, the structure is divided into five parts. These are logical and easy to follow, with a nice blend of theory, empirical research findings, and practical issues. I especially like two chapters—the chapter on bankruptcy and liquidation is extremely relevant in today's economic conditions; and the chapter on private equity and hedge funds is interesting because M&A activities by these players are not well-documented in the literature. Overall, I believe that MBA students would find the book useful both as a textbook in class and as a reference book for later use."

—Raghavendra Rau, Purdue University and Barclays Global Investors

"This book is truly outstanding among the textbooks on takeovers, valuation, and corporate restructuring for several reasons: the DePamphilis book not only gives a very up-to-date overview of the recent research findings on takeovers around the world, but also offers nearly 100 recent business cases. The book treats all the valuation techniques in depth and also offers much institutional detail on M&A and LBO transactions. Not just takeover successes are analyzed, but also how financially distressed companies should be restructured. In short, the ideal textbook for any M&A graduate course."

—Luc Renneboog, Professor of Corporate Finance, Tilburg University, The Netherlands

"The fifth edition of *Mergers, Acquisitions, and Other Restructuring Activities* by Professor Donald DePamphilis is an excellent book. Among its many strengths, I could easily identify three features that stand out. First, it is up-date, covering the recent knowledge published in most of the academic journals. Second, it offers comprehensive coverage of the subject matter, including chapters on the U.S. institutional, legal, and accounting environment; on technical aspects; valuation techniques; and strategic issues. Third, it is practical by including Excel spreadsheet models and a large number of real cases. These three aspects along with the…end-of-chapter discussion and review questions, problems, and exercises make this book one of the best choices for the subject."

—**Nickolaos G. Travlos,** The Kitty Kyriacopoulos Chair in Finance, and Dean,
ALBA Graduate Business School, Greece

"It is difficult to imagine that his fourth edition could be improved on, but Dr. DePamphilis has done just that. This edition is clearer, better organized, and contains a wealth of vitally important new material for these challenging times. I especially recommend the new chapter on liquidation for members of boards of directors who face extreme circumstances. This is a remarkably useful book for readers at any level—students, instructors, company executives, as well as board members. Bravo Don!"

—**Wesley B. Truitt,** Adjunct Professor, School of Public Policy, Pepperdine University

"The book is an excellent source for both academicians and practitioners. In addition to detailed cases, it provides tools contributing to value creation in M&A. A must-read book for an M&A course."

—**Vahap Uysal,** Assistant Professor of Finance, Price College of Business, University of Oklahoma

"An impressive detailed overview of all aspects of mergers and acquisitions. Numerous recent case studies and examples convince the reader that all the material is very relevant in today's business environment."

—**Theo Vermaelen,** Professor of Finance, Insead

MERGERS, ACQUISITIONS, AND OTHER RESTRUCTURING ACTIVITIES

AN INTEGRATED APPROACH TO PROCESS, TOOLS, CASES, AND SOLUTIONS

SEVENTH EDITION

Donald M. DePamphilis, Ph.D.

College of Business Administration
Loyola Marymount University
Los Angeles, California

End-of-chapter Questions © 2011. CFA Institute, reproduced and republished with permission from CFA Institute. All rights reserved.

Questions 7.14, 18.11 and 18.12 taken from: SOLNIK, RUNO; MCLEAVEY, DENNIS, GLOBAL INVESTMENTS, 6th Edition, © 2009. Reprinted by permission of Pearson Education, Inc., Upper Saddle River, NJ.

AMSTERDAM • BOSTON • HEIDELBERG • LONDON
NEW YORK • OXFORD • PARIS • SAN DIEGO
SAN FRANCISCO • SINGAPORE • SYDNEY • TOKYO
Academic Press is an imprint of Elsevier

ELSEVIER

Academic Press is an imprint of Elsevier
525 B Street, Suite 1800, San Diego CA 92101, USA
225 Wyman Street, Waltham, MA 02451, USA
The Boulevard, Langford Lane, Kidlington, Oxford, OX5 1GB, UK

Sixth edition 2012
Seventh edition 2014

Notices
Knowledge and best practice in this field are constantly changing. As new research and experience broaden our understanding, changes in research methods, professional practices, or medical treatment may become necessary.

Practitioners and researchers must always rely on their own experience and knowledge in evaluating and using any information, methods, compounds, or experiments described herein. In using such information or methods they should be mindful of their own safety and the safety of others, including parties for whom they have a professional responsibility.

To the fullest extent of the law, neither the Publisher nor the authors, contributors, or editors, assume any liability for any injury and/or damage to persons or property as a matter of products liability, negligence or otherwise, or from any use or operation of any methods, products, instructions, or ideas contained in the material herein.

Library of Congress Cataloging-in-Publication Data
Application submitted.

British Library Cataloguing-in-Publication Data
A catalogue record for this book is available from the British Library.

ISBN: 978-0-12-385487-2

For information on all Academic Press publications
visit our Web site at *www.elsevierdirect.com*

Printed in the United States

14 15 16 17 18   10 9 8 7 6 5 4 3 2 1

I extend my heartfelt gratitude to my wife, Cheryl, and my daughter, Cara, without whose patience and understanding this book could not have been completed; and to my brother, Mel, without whose encouragement this book would never have been undertaken.

Contents

I

THE MERGERS AND ACQUISITIONS ENVIRONMENT

1. An Introduction to Mergers, Acquisitions, and Other Restructuring Activities

2. The Regulatory Environment

3. The Corporate Takeover Market

II

THE MERGERS AND ACQUISITIONS PROCESS: PHASES 1–10

4. Planning: Developing Business and Acquisition Plans

5. Implementation: Search Through Closing

6. Postclosing Integration: Mergers, Acquisitions, and Business Alliances

III

MERGERS AND ACQUISITIONS VALUATION AND MODELING

7. Mergers and Acquisitions Cash Flow Valuation Basics

IV

DEAL-STRUCTURING AND FINANCING STRATEGIES

V
ALTERNATIVE BUSINESS AND RESTRUCTURING STRATEGIES

Contents of the Companion Website

1. Student Chapter PowerPoint Presentations' Folder
   a. Chapter 1: Introduction to Mergers, Acquisitions, and Other Restructuring Activities
   b. Chapter 2: The Regulatory Environment
   c. Chapter 3: The Corporate Takeover Market: Common Takeover Tactics, Anti-Takeover Defenses, and Corporate Governance
   d. Chapter 4: Planning—Developing Business and Acquisition Plans Phases 1 & 2 of the Acquisition Process
   e. Chapter 5: Implementation—Search Through Closing Phases 3–10 of the Acquisition Process
   f. Chapter 6: Postclosing Integration—Mergers, Acquisitions, and Business Alliances
   g. Chapter 7: Merger and Acquisition Cash Flow Valuation Basics
   h. Chapter 8: Relative, Asset-Oriented, and Real Option Basics
   i. Chapter 9: Applying Financial Models To Value, Structure, and Negotiate Mergers and Acquisitions
   j. Chapter 10: Analysis and Valuation of Privately Held Companies
   k. Chapter 11: Structuring the Deal: Payment and Legal Considerations
   l. Chapter 12: Structuring the Deal: Tax and Accounting Considerations
   m. Chapter 13: Financing the Deal: Private Equity, Hedge Funds, and Other Sources of Funds
   n. Chapter 14: Highly Leveraged Transactions: LBO Valuation and Modeling Basics
   o. Chapter 15: Business Alliances: Joint Ventures, Partnerships, Strategic Alliances, and Licensing
   p. Chapter 16: Alternative Exit and Restructuring Strategies: Divestitures, Spin-Offs, Carve-Outs, Split-Ups, and Split-Offs
   q. Chapter 17: Alternative Exit and Restructuring Strategies: Bankruptcy Reorganization and Liquidation
   r. Chapter 18: Cross-Border Mergers and Acquisitions: Analysis and Valuation
2. Student Chapter Summaries and Practice Questions and Answers Folder
   a. Chapter 1: Introduction to Mergers, Acquisitions, and Other Restructuring Activities
   b. Chapter 2: The Regulatory Environment
   c. Chapter 3: The Corporate Takeover Market: Common Takeover Tactics, Anti-Takeover Defenses, and Corporate Governance

Students, for free supporting materials please visit the Companion website: http://booksite.elsevier.com/9780123854872

Instructors, for tutor support materials, please visit: http://textbooks.elsevier.com/web/Manuals/9780123854872

Please note – tutors must be registered users at: www.textbooks.elsevier.com to access these ancillary materials

Preface to the Seventh Edition

TO THE READER

Despite an upsurge in certain types of corporate restructuring activity, the outlook remains challenging for dealmakers at the time of this writing. Uncertainty surrounding economic growth in Europe, the United States, and China continues to weigh on the willingness of firms to undertake mergers and acquisitions (M&A), despite holding record levels of cash. Against this backdrop, this book attempts to bring clarity to what can be an exciting, complex, and sometimes-frustrating subject. Intended to help the reader think of the activities involved in mergers, acquisitions, business alliances, and corporate restructuring in an integrated way, M&A activities are discussed in the context in which they occur and how they interact.

This book is unique in that it is the most current, comprehensive, and cutting-edge text on M&A and corporate restructuring available. It is *current* in that it includes the most up-to-date and notable transactions (e.g., Facebook's takeover of Instagram, LinkedIn's IPO, and the Kodak bankruptcy), regulations (e.g., Dodd-Frank Act of 2010 and the JOBS Act of 2012), trends (e.g., the increasing role of emerging country acquirers in global M&As), and tactics (e.g., "top-up" options and "cash-rich" split-offs) employed in M&As. More than 85%

of the 54 integrative case studies are new for this edition and involve transactions that have been announced or completed since 2010. It is *comprehensive* in that nearly all aspects of M&As and corporate restructuring from takeovers to spin-offs to reorganizations are explored. It is *cutting edge* in that conclusions and insights are anchored by the most recent academic research, with references to more than 170 empirical studies published in leading peer-reviewed journals just since 2010. And the substantially updated content is illustrated with numerous practical exhibits, case studies involving diverse transactions, easy-to-understand numerical examples, and hundreds of discussion questions and practice exercises. The current edition also includes a new chapter on how deals are financed.

The highlights of the new edition are:

- **New Chapter:** The current edition contains a new Chapter 13, which details how deals are financed with particular emphasis on the role of private equity investors and hedge funds in financing transactions. Highly leveraged transactions, typically referred to as *leveraged buyouts* (LBOs), are discussed in the context of a financing strategy. This chapter also describes the changing nature of LBOs, their impact on innovation, firm performance, and employment, as well as factors contributing to their success; typical deal and capital structures; and the pitfalls of improperly structured LBOs.

- **New Cases:** The forty-six new case studies involving transactions announced or completed during the last three years represent friendly, hostile, highly leveraged, and cross-border deals in nine different industries, involving public and private firms as well as firms experiencing financial distress. All case studies begin with a "Key Points" section indicating what the student should learn from the case study and include discussion questions and solutions available in the online instructors' manual.

- **Latest Research:** This edition focuses on the most recent and relevant academic studies, some of which contain surprising insights changing the way we view this subject matter. This recent research has significant implications for academicians, students, and M&A practitioners, shedding new light on current developments and trends in the ever-changing mergers and acquisitions market. The market for corporate control and corporate restructuring strategies are constantly changing, reflecting the ongoing globalization of both product and capital markets, accelerating technological change, escalating industry consolidation, changing regulatory practices, and intensifying cross-border competition. While continuing to be relevant, empirical research covering the dynamics of the M&A markets of the 1970s, 1980s, and

1990s, may be less germane in explaining current undercurrents and future trends.

- **Chartered Financial Analyst (CFA) Sample Exam Questions:** The CFA Institute awards the Chartered Financial Analyst designation to those having passed the CFA exam series. Among the most widely recognized designations in the financial industry worldwide, the CFA program includes a series of three exams that must be passed sequentially as one of the requirements for earning a CFA Charter. Most of the chapters contain sample test questions extracted from recent CFA exams. Each question tests how well the student understands the chapter's content.

- **New in Chapters 1–10:** Chapter 1 contains the latest empirical research pertaining to the success rates among mergers and acquisitions. Chapter 2 discusses the impact of the JOBS Act of 2012 on emerging companies and the implications of the Dodd-Frank Act for M&As. Chapter 3 provides the latest research on the increasing effectiveness of activist investors in promoting good governance, especially when the threat of a takeover exists. This chapter also contains an expanded discussion of differential voting rights and capital structures and their impact on corporate governance and firm value and as takeover defenses. Chapter 5 contains a more detailed discussion of the purpose of legal documents commonly used in M&A process. Estimates of firm size premiums and their applications have been updated in Chapter 7 along with a more detailed discussion of the "bottoms-up" approach to estimating firm betas. Chapter 8 now includes a discussion of how to address the unique challenges of valuing financial services firms and more detailed examples of how to determine the breakup value of a firm. Chapter 10 includes a more detailed discussion of the buildup method for estimating a discount rate for private firms and how to estimate the total beta used for estimating the cost of equity for a private firm whose owner's net worth is not well diversified. In addition to explaining how to determine the appropriate tax rate for valuation purposes, the chapter provides alternative ways of adjusting firm value to reflect the value of control as well as liquidity and minority discounts, either by adjusting firm value directly or by adjusting the firm's discount rate to reflect these factors.

- **New in Chapters 11–18:** Chapter 11 discusses the increasing use of "top-up" options to complete short-form mergers and other novel deal strategies. Chapter 12 has been substantially rewritten to illustrate more taxable and tax-free deal structures and how they are used to meet the requirements of different negotiated outcomes between buyers and sellers. The chapter also discusses the use of master limited partnerships in deal structuring and provides a more detailed explanation of when and why recapitalization accounting is used. How LBOs create value and how such transactions are financed (including illustrations) are discussed in greater detail in Chapter 13. Chapter 14 outlines alternative ways of valuing LBOs and provides a useful approach to modeling leveraged buyouts. Chapter 15 includes an expanded discussion of alternative structures employed in creating business alliances. Chapter 16 includes a discussion of the increasingly popular "cash-rich" split-off restructuring strategy and a more thorough discussion of the selling process. Chapter 17 contains a detailed discussion of the role of hedge funds in Chapter 11 reorganizations and in valuing distressed securities. Reflecting the increasing importance of cross-border transactions, Chapter 18 has been expanded to include a more detailed discussion of emerging country transactions, reflecting the growing importance of developing nations in cross-border deals.

- **Updated Ancillary Materials:** Both student and instructor PowerPoint slide presentations have been updated to reflect recent research, trends, and new chapter content. Located below each slide, instructor PowerPoint presentations also contain suggested topics and key points to be made by the instructor for each slide. The student PowerPoint slides are structured to serve as student study guides.

The textbook contains more than 300 end-of-chapter discussion and review questions, problems, and exercises that give readers the opportunity to test their knowledge of the material.

Many of the exercises enable students to find their own solutions based on different sets of assumptions, using Excel-based spreadsheet models available on the companion site to this textbook. Solutions to all questions, problems, and exercises are available on the expanded Online Instructor's Manual, available to instructors using this book. The online manual now contains more than 1,600 true/false, multiple-choice, and short essay questions as well as numerical problems. In addition to Excel-based customizable M&A and LBO valuation and structuring software; PowerPoint presentations; and due diligence materials; the companion site also contains a Student Study Guide and models for estimating a firm's borrowing capacity and adjusting a firm's financial statements and numerous illustrations of concepts discussed in the book.

This book is intended for students in courses on mergers and acquisitions; corporate restructuring; business strategy; management; and entrepreneurship. This book works well at both the undergraduate and graduate levels. The text also should interest financial analysts, chief financial officers, operating managers, investment bankers, and portfolio managers. Others who may have an interest include bank lending officers, venture capitalists, government regulators, human resource managers, entrepreneurs, and board members. Hence, from the classroom to the boardroom, this text offers something for anyone with an interest in mergers and acquisitions, business alliances, and other forms of corporate restructuring.

TO THE INSTRUCTOR

This text is an attempt to provide organization to a topic that is inherently complex due to the diversity of applicable subject matter and the breadth of disciplines that must be applied to complete most transactions. Consequently, the discussion of M&A is not easily divisible into highly focused chapters. Efforts to compartmentalize the topic often result in the reader's not understanding how seemingly independent topics are integrated. Understanding M&A involves an understanding of a full range of topics, including management; finance; economics business law; financial and tax accounting; organizational dynamics; and the role of leadership.

With this in mind, this book provides a new organizational paradigm for discussing the complex and dynamically changing world of M&A. The book is organized according to the context in which topics normally occur in the M&A process. As such, the book is divided into five parts: M&A environment; M&A process; M&A valuation and modeling; deal-structuring and financing strategies; and alternative business and restructuring strategies. Topics that are highly integrated are discussed within these five groupings. See Exhibit 1 for the organizational layout of the book.

This book equips the instructor with the information needed to communicate effectively with students having different levels of preparation. The generous use of examples and contemporary business cases makes the text suitable for distance learning

EXHIBIT 1   COURSE LAYOUT: MERGERS, ACQUISITIONS, AND OTHER RESTRUCTURING ACTIVITIES

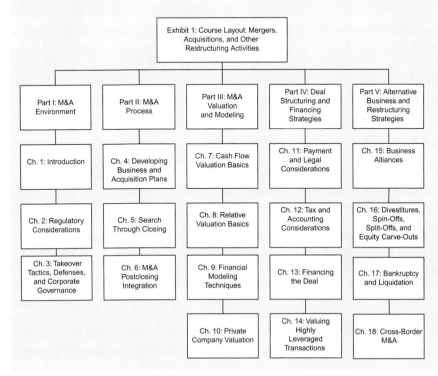

and self-study programs as well as for large, lecture-focused courses. The extensive use of end-of-chapter discussion questions, problems, and exercises (with answers available in the Online Instructor's Manual) offer instructors the opportunity to test the students' progress in mastering the material. Prerequisites for this text include familiarity with basic accounting, finance, economics, and management concepts.

ONLINE INSTRUCTOR'S MANUAL

The manual contains PowerPoint presentations (including instructor commentary for most slides) for each chapter (completely consistent with those found on the companion site), suggested learning objectives, recommended ways to teach the materials, and detailed syllabi for both undergraduate- and graduate-level classes, and an exhaustive test bank. The test bank contains more than 1,600 test questions and answers (including true/false, multiple choice, short essay questions, case studies, and computational problems) and solutions to end-of-chapter discussion questions and end-of-chapter business case studies in the book. The online manual also contains, in a file folder named "Preface to the Online Instructor's Manual and Table of Contents," suggestions on how to teach the course to both undergraduate and graduate classes.

Please e-mail the publisher at textbook@elsevier.com (within North America) and emea.textbook@elsevier.com (outside of North America) for access to the online manual. Please include your contact information (name, department, college, address, e-mail, and phone number) along with your course information, including course name and number, annual enrollment, ISBN, book title, and author. All requests are subject to approval by the company's representatives. For instructors who have already adopted this book, please go to www.textbooks.elsevier.com (Elsevier's instructors' website) and click on the button in the upper left-hand corner entitled "Instructors' Manual." You will find detailed instructions on how to gain access to the online manual for this book.

STUDENT STUDY GUIDE

The guide contained on the companion site to this book includes chapter summaries highlighting key learning objectives for each chapter as well as true/false, multiple-choice, and numerical questions and answers to enhance the student's learning experience.

MANY PRACTICAL, TIMELY, AND DIVERSE EXAMPLES AND CURRENT BUSINESS CASES

Each chapter begins with a vignette intended to illustrate a key point or points described in more detail as the chapter unfolds. Hundreds of examples, business cases, tables, and figures illustrate the application of key concepts. Many exhibits and diagrams summarize otherwise-diffuse information and the results of numerous empirical studies substantiating key points made in each chapter. Each chapter concludes with a series of 10 discussion questions and recent integrative end-of-chapter business cases intended to stimulate critical thinking and test the reader's understanding of the material. Many chapters also include a series of practice problems and exercises to facilitate learning the chapter's content.

COMPREHENSIVE YET FLEXIBLE ORGANIZATION

Although the text is sequential, each chapter was developed as a self-contained unit to enable adaptation of the text to various teaching strategies and students with diverse backgrounds. The flexibility of the organization also makes the material suitable for courses of various lengths, from one quarter to two full semesters. The amount of time required depends on the students' level of sophistication and the desired focus of the instructor. Undergraduates have consistently demonstrated the ability to master eight or nine chapters of the book during a typical semester, whereas graduate-level students are able to cover effectively 12 to 14 chapters during the same period.

Students, for free supporting materials please visit the Companion website: http://booksite.elsevier.com/9780123854872

Instructors, for tutor support materials, please visit: http://textbooks.elsevier.com/web/Manuals/9780123854872

Please note – tutors must be registered users at: www.textbooks.elsevier.com to access these ancillary materials

Acknowledgments

I would like to express my sincere appreciation for the many helpful suggestions received from a number of anonymous reviewers and the many resources of Academic Press/Butterworth-Heinemann/Elsevier. Specifically, I would like to thank Alan Cherry, Ross Bengel, Patricia Douglas, Jeff Gale, Jim Healy, Charles Higgins, Michael Lovelady, John Mellen, Jon Saxon, David Offenberg, Chris Manning, Maria Quijada, Warren Miller, Jillian Jaccard, Janet Torres and Chris Kohler for their constructive comments. I would also like to thank Scott Bentley, Executive Editor at Academic Press/Butterworth-Heinemann/Elsevier, for his ongoing support and guidance, as well as Production Project Manager Pauline Wilkinson.

About the Author

Dr. Donald DePamphilis has managed through closing more than 30 transactions, including acquisitions, divestitures, joint ventures, minority investments, licensing, and supply agreements in a variety of different industries. These industries include financial services, software, metals manufacturing, business consulting, healthcare, automotive, communications, textiles, and real estate. He earned a B.A. in economics from the University of Pittsburgh and an M.A. and Ph.D. in economics from Harvard University.

He is currently Clinical Professor of Finance at Loyola Marymount University in Los Angeles, where he teaches mergers and acquisitions; corporate restructuring; dealmaking; finance; micro- and macroeconomics (to both business and nonbusiness majors); leadership and corporate governance to undergraduate, MBA, and executive MBA students. He is also an instructor in the Loyola Marymount University International Executive Education Program, teaching corporate restructuring tactics and strategies in a global context. He has served as chair of the Student Investment Fund at Loyola Marymount University's College of Business and is a member of the graduate business program curriculum committee. Dr. DePamphilis also is the recipient of the Loyola Marymount University Executive MBA Leadership Achievement Award.

Dr. DePamphilis has lectured on M&A and corporate restructuring, finance, and economics at the University of California, at Irvine, Chapman University, and Concordia University. As a visiting professor, he taught mergers and acquisitions, and corporate restructuring strategies at the Antai School of Management, Shanghai Jiao Tong University, in Shanghai, China.

Dr. DePamphilis has more than 25 years' of experience in businesses ranging in size from small, privately owned firms to Fortune 100 companies in various industries and with varying degrees of responsibility. Previously, he served as Vice-President of Electronic Commerce for Experian Corporation; Vice-President of Business Development at TRW Information Systems and Services; Senior Vice-President of Planning and Marketing at PUH Health Systems; Director of Corporate Business Planning at TRW, and Chief Economist for National Steel Corporation.

He also served as Director of Banking and Insurance Economics for Chase Econometric Associates, and as an economic analyst for United California Bank, where he developed a complex, interactive econometric forecasting model of the U.S. economy, which was used in both internal and external bank forecasts. Dr. DePamphilis has also spoken to numerous industry trade associations and customer groups and to Los Angeles community and business groups. He is a graduate of the TRW and National Steel Corporation Executive Management Programs.

Dr. DePamphilis has authored numerous articles, chapters in books, and books on the topic of M&A; business planning and development; marketing; and economics, in both peer-reviewed academic journals and trade publications. His books include *Mergers and Acquisitions Basics: All You Need to Know*; and *Merger and Acquisition Basics: Negotiation and Deal Structuring*.

Mergers, Acquisitions, and Other Restructuring Activities has been translated into Chinese and Russian and is used in universities worldwide.

Dr. DePamphilis serves as a consultant in product and personal liability; patent infringement; and business valuation litigation, including but not limited to providing expert analysis and depositions in cases primarily related to mergers and acquisitions. He also offers target selection, negotiation support, and business valuation services.

Please forward any comments you may have about this book to the author at ddepamph@lmu.edu. Your suggestions about ways in which this text may be improved are welcome.

THE MERGERS AND ACQUISITIONS ENVIRONMENT

"I've come up with our new logo, JB."

From www.CartoonStock.com; BMA239-MR.

The lingering effects of the 2008–2009 recession and Europe's sovereign debt crisis crippled the confidence of company executives, despite cash-laden balance sheets and continued low interest rates. Corporate restructuring activity in recent years was largely initiated by buyers seeking to strengthen their core businesses and sellers attempting to increase their product and market focus. Financial buyers, those using high amounts of leverage to finance transactions, were largely on the sidelines, with the volume of highly leveraged transactions having peaked in 2007, prior to the economic downturn.

The popular media tends to use the term *corporate restructuring* to describe actions taken to expand or contract a firm's basic operations or fundamentally change its asset or financial structure. Corporate restructuring runs the gamut from reorganizing business units to takeovers, from joint ventures to divestitures, spin-offs and equity carve-outs. Consequently, virtually all of the material covered in this book can be viewed as part of the corporate restructuring process. Part I discusses the contexts in which mergers, acquisitions, and corporate restructuring occur, including factors often beyond the control of the participants in the M&A process.

Chapter 1 provides an overview of mergers and acquisitions by discussing basic vocabulary; the most common reasons why M&As happen; how such transactions occur in a series of somewhat predictable waves; and participants in the M&A process, from investment bankers to lenders to regulatory authorities. The chapter also addresses whether M&As benefit shareholders, bondholders, and society, with conclusions based on recent empirical studies. The labyrinth of regulations that impact the M&A process are addressed in Chapter 2, including U.S. federal and state securities and antitrust laws as well as environmental, labor, and benefit laws that add to the increasing complexity of such transactions. The implications of cross-border transactions, which offer an entirely new set of regulatory challenges, also are explored. Viewed in the context of a market in which control transfers from sellers to buyers, Chapter 3 addresses common takeover tactics employed as part of an overall bidding strategy, the motivation behind such tactics, and the defenses used by target firms to deter or delay such tactics. Bidding strategies are discussed for both friendly and unwanted or hostile business takeovers. In hostile transactions, the corporate takeover is viewed as a means of disciplining underperforming management, improving corporate governance practices, and reallocating assets to those who can use them more effectively.

The reader is encouraged to read about deals currently in the news and to identify the takeover tactics and defenses employed by the parties to the transactions. One's understanding of the material can be enriched by attempting to discern the intentions of both the acquiring and target firms' boards and management, if the proposed business combination makes sense, and thinking about what you might have done differently to achieve similar goals.

An Introduction to Mergers, Acquisitions, and Other Restructuring Activities

If you give a man a fish, you feed him for a day. If you teach a man to fish, you feed him for a lifetime. —**Lao Tze**

INSIDE M&A: BRAND MANAGEMENT—V.F. CORP. BUYS TIMBERLAND

KEY POINTS

- Acquisitions are often used to change a firm's product focus rapidly.
- Acquisitions of direct competitors often represent significant revenue growth and cost-saving opportunities.
- The timely realization of synergies is critical to recovering purchase price premiums.

Widely recognized in the United States and Europe as a maker of rugged outdoor apparel, Timberland (TBL) had stumbled in recent years. Its failure to turn around its money-losing Yellow Boot brand, the limited success of its advertising campaign to encourage consumers to think of Timberland apparel as a year-round brand, and overly ambitious expansion plans in China caused earnings to deteriorate. Despite annual revenues growing to more than $1.6 billion in fiscal year 2011, the firm was losing market share to such competitors as the Gap and Sears Holdings. Timberland's share price declined as investor confidence in management waned when the firm failed to meet its quarterly earnings forecasts. Timberland was ripe for takeover.

With annual revenue of $7.7 billion, apparel maker V.F. Corporation (VFC), owner of such well-known brands as The North Face, Wrangler, and Lee, was always on the prowl for firms that fit its business strategy. VFC has grown historically by adding highly recognizable brands with significant market share. The strategy has been implemented largely through acquisition rather than through partnering with others or developing its own brands. Furthermore, the firm was shifting its product offering toward the rapidly growing outdoor-apparel business.

With its focus on outdoor apparel, Timberland became a highly attractive target, especially as its share price declined. VFC pounced on the opportunity to add the highly recognizable Timberland trademark to its product portfolio. On June 13, 2011, VFC announced that it had reached an agreement to pay TBL shareholders $43 per share in an all-cash deal, a 43% premium over the prior day's closing price. The deal valued TBL at about $2 billion.

Including the Timberland acquisition, VFC's outdoor and action sports product lines were expected to contribute about one-half of the firm's total annual revenue in 2012, ultimately rising by more than 60% by 2015. In buying Timberland, VFC gained access to new retail outlets and the opportunity to better position TBL as a lifestyle brand in the apparel and accessories market. VFC also hoped to use TBL's rapidly growing online business to help it achieve its online sales goal of more than $400 million by 2015, more than three times their 2011 total. VFC hoped to accelerate the growth in TBL product sales by expanding their availability through its own e-commerce site and through its international operations. Likewise, VFC expected to achieve substantially larger discounts on raw material purchases than TBL because of its larger bulk purchases and to reduce overhead expenses by eliminating redundant positions.

CHAPTER OVERVIEW

Although corporate restructuring is discussed throughout this book, the focus in this chapter is on M&As, why they happen, and why they tend to cluster in waves. You will also be introduced to a variety of legal structures and strategies that are employed to restructure firms. A firm that attempts to acquire or merge with another company is called an *acquiring company, acquirer,* or *bidder*. The target company or target is the firm being solicited by the acquiring company. *Takeovers* and *buyouts* are generic terms for a change in the controlling ownership interest of a corporation. A review of this chapter (including practice questions and answers) is available in the file folder entitled Student Study Guide on the companion site for this book (http://booksite.elsevier.com/9780123854872).

WHY MERGERS AND ACQUISITIONS HAPPEN

The reasons M&As occur are numerous, and the importance of factors giving rise to M&A activity varies over time. Table 1.1 lists some of the more prominent theories about why M&As happen. Each theory is discussed in greater detail in the remainder of this section.

Synergy

Synergy is the value realized from the incremental cash flows generated by combining two businesses. That is, if the market value of two firms is

TABLE 1.1   Common Theories of What Causes Mergers and Acquisitions

Theory	Motivation
Operating Synergy • Economies of Scale • Economies of Scope	Improve operating efficiency through economies of scale or scope by acquiring a customer, supplier, or competitor
Financial Synergy	Lower Cost of Capital
Diversification • New Products/Current Markets • New Products/New Markets • Current Products/New Markets	Position the firm in higher-growth products or markets
Strategic Realignment • Technological Change • Regulatory and Political Change	Acquire capabilities to adapt more rapidly to environmental changes than could be achieved if they were developed internally
Hubris (Managerial Pride)	Acquirers believe their valuation of the target is more accurate than the market's, causing them to overpay by overestimating synergy
Buying Undervalued Assets (Q-Ratio)	Acquire assets more cheaply when the equity of existing companies is less than the cost of buying or building the assets
Managerialism (Agency Problems)	Increase the size of a company to increase the power and pay of managers
Tax Considerations	Obtain unused net operating losses and tax credits and asset write-ups, and substitute capital gains for ordinary income
Market Power	Actions taken to boost selling prices above competitive levels by affecting either supply or demand
Misvaluation	Investor overvaluation of acquirer's stock encourages M&As

$100 million and $75 million, respectively, and their combined market value is $200 million, then the implied value of synergy is $25 million. The two basic types of synergy are *operating* and *financial*.

Operating Synergy

Operating synergy consists of both economies of scale and economies of scope, which can be important determinants of shareholder wealth creation.[1] Gains in efficiency can come from either factor and from improved managerial operating practices.

Economies of scale refers to the reduction in average total costs for a firm producing a single product for a given scale of plant due to the decline in average fixed costs as production volume increases. Scale is defined by such fixed costs as depreciation of equipment and amortization of capitalized software, normal maintenance spending, and obligations such as interest expense, lease payments, long-term union, customer, and vendor contracts, and taxes. These costs are *fixed* since they cannot be altered in the short run. *Variable* costs are those that change with output levels. Consequently, for a given scale or amount of fixed expenses, the dollar value of fixed expenses per unit of output and per dollar of revenue decreases as output and sales increase.

To illustrate the potential profit improvement from economies of scale, consider the merger of Firm B into Firm A. Firm A has a plant producing at only one-half of its capacity, enabling Firm A to shut down Firm B's plant that is producing the same product and move the production to its own, underutilized facility. Consequently, Firm A's profit margin improves from 6.25% before the merger to 14.58% after the merger because of the higher profit margin associated with the additional output from Firm B, which adds nothing to Firm A's fixed costs (Table 1.2).[2]

Economies of scope refers to the reduction in average total costs for a firm producing two or more products, because it is cheaper to produce these products in a single firm than in separate firms. Economies of scope may reflect *both* declining average fixed and variable costs. Common examples of overhead- and sales-related economies of scope include having a single department (e.g., accounting and human resources) support multiple product lines and a sales force selling multiple related products rather than a single product. Savings in distribution costs can be achieved by transporting a number of products to a single location rather than a single product. Additional cost savings can be

---

[1] Houston et al., 2001; DeLong, 2003

[2] The profit improvement is overstated because of the simplifying assumption that variable costs per unit are constant at $2.75. In reality, average variable costs rise as output increases, reflecting equipment downtime due to necessary maintenance, increased overtime pay, additional shifts requiring hiring new and often less productive employees, and disruptions to production resulting from the logistical challenges of maintaining adequate supplies of raw materials.

TABLE 1.2   Economies of Scale

Period 1: Firm A (Premerger)	Period 2: Firm A (Postmerger)
ASSUMPTIONS:	ASSUMPTIONS:
• Price = $4 per unit of output sold • Variable costs = $2.75 per unit of output • Fixed costs = $1,000,000 • Firm A is producing 1,000,000 units of output per year • Firm A is producing at 50% of plant capacity	• Firm A acquires Firm B, which is producing 500,000 units of the same product per year • Firm A closes Firm B's plant and transfers production to Firm A's plant • Price = $4 per unit of output sold • Variable costs = $2.75 per unit of output • Fixed costs = $1,000,000

Profit = price × quantity − variable costs
      − fixed costs
   = $4 × 1,000,000 − $2.75 × 1,000,000
      − $1,000,000
   = $250,000
	Profit = price × quantity − variable costs
	      − fixed costs
	   = $4 × 1,500,000 − $2.75 × 1,500,000 − $1,000,000
	   = $6,000,000 − $4,125,000 − $1,000,000
	   = $875,000[1]

Profit margin (%)[2] = $250,000/$4,000,000 = 6.25%	Profit margin (%)[3] = $875,000/$6,000,000 = 14.58%
Fixed costs per unit = $1,000,000/$1,000,000 = $1.00	Fixed cost per unit = $1,000,000/1,500,000 = $.67

[1]Contribution to profit of additional units = $4 × 500,000 − $2.75 × 500,000 = $625,000.
[2]Margin per unit sold = $4.00–$2.75–$1.00 = $.25.
[3]Margin per unit sold = $4.00– $2.75–$.67 = $.58. Note that this illustration does not reflect any costs incurred in closing Firm B's plant.

realized using a specific set of skills or an asset currently employed in producing a specific product to produce multiple products. Procter & Gamble, the consumer products giant, uses its highly regarded consumer-marketing skills to sell a full range of personal care as well as pharmaceutical products. Honda employs its proprietary know-how (an intangible asset) to enhance internal combustion engines to manufacture, in addition to cars, motorcycles, lawn mowers, and snow-blowers.

Financial Synergy

Financial synergy refers to the reduction in the acquirer's cost of capital due to a merger or acquisition. This could occur if the merged firms have cash flows that are relatively uncorrelated, that realize cost savings from lower securities' issuance and transactions costs, or that result in a better matching of investment opportunities with internally generated funds.[3]

[3]Furfine and Rosen (2011) argue that M&As may increase default risk (and the cost of capital), particularly for acquirers whose prior stock performance has been poor and whose CEOs have large option-based compensation, which drives them to excessive risk taking.

TABLE 1.3   The Product–Market Matrix

Products	Markets Current	New
Current	Lower Growth/Lower Risk	Higher Growth/Higher Risk (Related Diversification)
New	Higher Growth/Higher Risk (Related Diversification)	Highest Growth/Highest Risk (Unrelated Diversification)

Diversification

Buying firms beyond a company's current lines of business is called *diversification*. Diversification may create financial synergy that reduces the cost of capital, or it may allow a firm to shift its core product lines or target markets into ones that have higher growth prospects, even ones that are unrelated to the firm's current products or markets. The product–market matrix illustrated in Table 1.3 identifies a firm's primary diversification options.

A firm facing slower growth in its current markets may accelerate growth through related diversification by selling its current products in new markets that are somewhat unfamiliar and, therefore, more risky. Such was the case in 2012 when IBM acquired web-based human resource software maker Kenexa to move its existing software business into the fiercely competitive but fast-growing market for delivering business applications via the web.

A firm may also attempt to achieve higher growth rates by acquiring new products with which it is relatively unfamiliar and then selling them in familiar and less risky current markets. Retailer J. C. Penney's $3.3 billion acquisition of the Eckerd Drugstore chain (a drug retailer) in 1997 and Johnson & Johnson's $16 billion acquisition of Pfizer's consumer healthcare products line in 2006 are examples of such related diversification. In each instance, the firm assumed additional risk by selling new product lines, but into markets with which it had significant prior experience: J.C. Penny in consumer retail markets and J&J in retail healthcare markets.

There is considerable evidence that acquisitions resulting in unrelated diversification frequently result in lower financial returns when they are announced than nondiversifying acquisitions.[4] Firms that operate in a number of largely unrelated industries, such as General Electric, are called *conglomerates*. The share prices of conglomerates often trade at a discount to shares of focused firms or to their value if broken up.[5] This markdown is called a *conglomerate* or *diversification discount*.[6] Investors often perceive conglomerates as riskier because management has difficulty understanding these firms and outside investors may have trouble

[4] Akbulut and Matsusaka, 2010

[5] Berger and Ofek, 1995; Lins and Servaes, 1999; Khorana et al., 2011; Ammann et al., 2012

[6] Some researchers argue the magnitude of the discount is overstated (Campa and Simi, 2002; Hyland and Diltz, 2002), while others say it reflects sample bias (Villalonga, 2004; Graham, Lemmon, and Wolf, 2002).

in valuing the various parts of highly diversified businesses.[7] Investors may also be reluctant to invest in firms whose management appears intent on diversifying to build "empires" rather than to improve firm performance;[8] moreover, such firms often exhibit poor governance practices.[9]

Other researchers find evidence that the most successful mergers in developed countries are those that focus on deals that promote the acquirer's core business, largely reflecting their familiarity with such businesses and their ability to optimize investment decisions.[10] Related acquisitions may even be more likely to generate higher financial returns than unrelated deals,[11] since related firms are more likely to realize cost savings due to overlapping functions.[12]

Strategic Realignment

Firms use M&As to make rapid adjustments to changes in their external environment such as regulatory changes and technological innovation. Those industries that have been subject to significant deregulation in recent years—financial services, healthcare, utilities, media, telecommunications, defense—have been at the center of M&A activity,[13] because deregulation breaks down artificial barriers and stimulates competition. Technological advances create new products and industries. The smartphone spurred the growth of handheld telecommunications devices while undercutting the point-and-shoot camera industry and threatening the popularity of wristwatches, alarm clocks, and MP3 players. Tablet computers reduced the demand for desktop and notebook computers, while e-readers reduced the popularity of hardback books.

Hubris and the "Winner's Curse"

Acquirers overpay for targets when they overestimate synergies due to excessive optimism. Competition among bidders is also likely to result in the winner's overpaying because of hubris, even if significant synergies are present. CEOs with successful acquisition track records may pay more than the target is worth due to overconfidence.[14] Acquirers overpaying for a target firm may feel remorse at having done so—hence what has come to be called the "winner's curse."

[7] Morck, Schleifer, and Vishny, 1990; Best and Hodges, 2004

[8] Andreou et al., 2010

[9] Hoechle et al., 2012

[10] Harding and Rovit, 2004; Megginson et al., 2003

[11] Singh and Montgomery, 2008

[12] Diversified firms in developing countries having limited capital market access may sell at a premium since they may use cash generated by mature subsidiaries to fund those with higher growth potential (Fauver et al., 2003).

[13] Mitchell and Mulherin, 1996; Mulherin and Boone, 2000

[14] Billet and Qian, 2008; Malmendier and Tate, 2008.

Buying Undervalued Assets: The q-Ratio

The q-ratio is the ratio of the market value of the acquirer's stock to the replacement cost of its assets. Firms can choose to invest in new plant and equipment or obtain the assets by buying a company with a market value of less than what it would cost to replace the assets (i.e., a market-to-book or q-ratio that is less than 1). This theory is useful in explaining M&A activity when stock prices drop well below the book value (or historical cost) of many firms.

Managerialism (Agency Problems)

Agency problems arise when the interests of current managers and the firm's shareholders differ. Managers may make acquisitions to add to their prestige, build their spheres of influence, or augment their compensation or for self-preservation.[15] Such mismanagement can persist when a firm's shares are widely held, since the cost of such negligence is spread across a large number of shareholders. Acquisitions often take place to pressure managers to take actions to raise the share price or become the target of acquirers, who perceive the stock to be undervalued.

Tax Considerations

Acquirers of firms with accumulated losses and tax credits may use them to offset future profits generated by the combined firms. However, the taxable nature of the transaction often plays a more important role in determining whether a merger takes place than do any tax benefits accruing to the acquirer. The seller may view the tax-free status of the transaction as a prerequisite for the deal to take place. A properly structured transaction can allow the target shareholders to defer any capital gain until the acquirer's stock received in exchange for their shares is sold.

Market Power

Despite little empirical support, the market power theory suggests that firms merge to improve their ability to set product prices at levels not sustainable in a more competitive market. Many recent studies conclude that increased merger activity is much more likely to contribute to improved operating efficiency of the combined firms than to increased market power (see the section of this chapter entitled "Do Mergers Pay Off for Society?"). There is, however, evidence that increased industry concentration can force suppliers to lower their selling prices.[16]

[15] Masulis, Wang, and Xie, 2007

[16] Bhattacharyya et al., 2011

Misvaluation

Absent full information, investors may periodically over- or undervalue a firm.[17] Acquirers may profit by buying undervalued targets for cash at a price below their actual value or by using overvalued equity (even if the target is overvalued), as long as the target is less overvalued than the bidding firm's stock.[18] Overvalued shares enable the acquirer to purchase a target firm in a share-for-share exchange by issuing fewer shares, reducing the dilution of current acquirer shareholders in the combined companies.[19] The effects of misvaluation tend to be short-lived, since the initial overvaluation of an acquirer's share price is reversed in one to three years as investors' enthusiasm about potential synergies wanes.[20]

HISTORICAL DEVELOPMENTS IN MERGERS AND ACQUISITIONS

M&As cluster in waves, with public firms more active buyers than private firms due in part to their greater access to financing and their more liquid stock.[21] Insights gained by analyzing these waves help buyers to understand when to make and how to structure and finance deals.

Why M&A Waves Occur

M&As in the United States have tended to cluster in six multiyear waves since the late 1890s. There are two competing explanations for this phenomenon. One argues that merger waves occur when firms react to industry "shocks,"[22] such as from deregulation, the emergence of new technologies, distribution channels, substitute products, or a sustained rise in commodity prices. Such events often cause firms to acquire either all or parts of other firms.[23] The second argument is

---

[17] Edmans et al., 2012

[18] Ang et al. (2006) and Dong et al. (2006)

[19] Consider an acquirer who offers the target firm shareholders $10 for each share they own. If the acquirer's current share price is $10, the acquirer would have to issue one new share for each target share outstanding. If the acquirer's share price is valued at $20, only 0.5 new shares would have to be issued, and so forth. Consequently, the initial dilution of the current acquirer's shareholders' ownership position in the new firm is less the higher the acquirer's share price compared to the price offered for each share of target stock outstanding.

[20] Petmezas (2009) and Akbulut (2013)

[21] Maksimovic et al., 2013; Gugler et al., 2012

[22] Martynova and Renneboog, 2008A; Brealey and Myers, 2003; Mitchell and Mulherin, 1996

[23] According to Netter et al. (2011), the existence of merger waves in industries subject to shocks is less apparent in larger data samples than in smaller. M&A activity that includes small deals and private acquirers is much smoother and less wavelike than patterns observed with only public acquirers and large deals.

based on misvaluation and suggests that managers use overvalued stock to buy the assets of lower-valued firms. For M&As to cluster in waves, goes the argument, valuations of many firms must increase at the same time. Managers whose stocks are believed to be overvalued move concurrently to acquire firms whose stock prices are lesser valued.[24] For this theory to be correct, the method of payment would normally be stock. In fact, the empirical evidence shows that less stock is used to finance takeovers during merger waves.

Since M&A waves typically correspond to an improving economy, managers confident about their stocks future appreciation are more inclined to use debt to finance takeovers,[25] because they believe their shares are currently undervalued. Thus, the shock argument seems to explain M&A waves better than the misevaluation theory.[26] However, shocks alone, without sufficient liquidity to finance deals, will not initiate a wave of merger activity. Moreover, readily available, low-cost capital may cause a surge in M&A activity even if industry shocks are absent.[27]

While research suggests that shocks drive merger waves within industries, increased M&A activity within an industry contributes to additional M&A activity in other industries as a result of customer–supplier relationships.[28] For example, increased consolidation among computer chip manufacturers in the early 2000s drove an increase in takeovers among suppliers of chip manufacturing equipment to accommodate growing customer demands for more complex chips.

The First Wave (1897–1904): Horizontal Consolidation

M&A activity reflected a drive for efficiency, lax enforcement of the Sherman Anti-Trust Act, migration, and technological change. Mergers were largely between competitors and resulted in increased concentration in primary metals, transportation, and mining. Fraudulent financing and the 1904 stock market crash ended the boom.

The Second Wave (1916–1929): Increasing Concentration

Activity during this period was a result of the entry of the United States into World War I and the postwar economic boom. Mergers also tended to be horizontal and further increased industry concentration. The stock market crash of 1929 and the passage of the Clayton Act that further defined monopolistic practices brought this era to a close.

---

[24] Rhodes-Kropf and Viswanathan, 2004; Schleifer and Vishny, 2003

[25] Malmendier et al., 2011

[26] Garcia-Feijoo et al., 2012

[27] Harford, 2005

[28] Ahern and Harford, 2010

The Third Wave (1965–1969): The Conglomerate Era

Firms with high P/E ratios learned to grow earnings per share (EPS) through acquisition rather than reinvestment by buying firms with lower P/E ratios but high earnings growth to increase the EPS of the combined companies. This in turn boosted the share price of the combined companies—as long as the P/E ratio applied to the stock price of the combined companies did not fall below the P/E ratio of the acquiring company before the deal. To maintain this pyramiding effect, though, target companies had to have earnings growth rates that were sufficiently attractive to convince investors to apply the higher multiple of the acquiring company to the combined companies. In time, the number of high-growth, relatively low P/E ratio companies declined, as conglomerates bid up their P/E multiples. The higher prices paid for the targets, coupled with the increasing leverage of the conglomerates, caused the "pyramids" to collapse.

The Fourth Wave (1981–1989): The Retrenchment Era

The 1980s was characterized by the breakup of many major conglomerates by so-called corporate raiders using hostile takeovers and leveraged buyouts (LBOs). LBOs involve the purchase of a company financed primarily by debt. Conglomerates began to divest unrelated acquisitions made in the 1960s and early 1970s. For the first time, takeovers of U.S. companies by foreign firms exceeded in number and dollars the acquisitions by U.S. firms of foreign companies. Foreign buyers were motivated by the size of the market, limited restrictions on takeovers, the sophistication of U.S. technology, and the weakness of the dollar against major foreign currencies. Toward the end of the 1980s, the level of merger activity tapered off in line with a slowing economy and widely publicized LBO bankruptcies.

The Fifth Wave (1992–1999): The Age of the Strategic Mega-Merger

The longest economic expansion and stock market boom in U.S. history was powered by a combination of the information technology revolution, continued deregulation, reductions in trade barriers, and the global trend toward privatization. Both the dollar volume and number of transactions continued to set records through the end of the 1990s before contracting sharply when the Internet bubble burst, a recession hit the U.S. in 2001, and global growth weakened.

The Sixth Wave (2003–2008): The Rebirth of Leverage

United States financial markets, especially from 2005 through 2007, were characterized by a proliferation of highly leveraged buyouts and complex securities collateralized by pools of debt and loan obligations of varying levels of risk. Much of the financing of these deals, as well as mortgage-backed security issues, has taken the form of syndicated debt (i.e., debt purchased by underwriters for resale to the investing public). Lenders have an incentive to increase the volume of lending to generate fee income by accepting riskier loans.[29] Once

---

[29] Brunnermeier, 2009.

loans are sold to others, loan originators are likely to reduce the monitoring of such loans. These practices, coupled with exceedingly low interest rates (which substantially underpriced risk) made possible by a world awash in liquidity and highly accommodative monetary policies, contributed to excessive lending and encouraged acquirers to overpay significantly for target firms. However, limited credit availability, as banks attempted to rebuild their capital following substantial asset write-downs, not only affected the ability of private equity and hedge funds to finance new or refinance existing transactions but also limited the ability of other businesses to fund operations. These conditions were exacerbated by European sovereign debt concerns and escalating oil prices that triggered a global economic downturn in 2008 and a listless recovery through 2012. Mirroring the global malaise, M&A activity languished during this period.

Similarities and Differences among Merger Waves

Mergers commonly occur during periods of sustained high rates of economic growth, low or declining interest rates, and a rising stock market. Historically, each merger wave has differed in terms of a specific development (such as the emergence of a new technology), industry focus (such as rail, oil, or financial services), degree of regulation, and type of transaction (such as horizontal, vertical, conglomerate, strategic, or financial, discussed in more detail later in this chapter). Table 1.4 compares the six U.S. merger waves. Merger waves are also present in cross-border M&As, with European waves following those in the United States with a short lag.[30]

Why it is Important to Anticipate Merger Waves

The stock market rewards firms acting early and punishes those that merely imitate. Firms pursuing attractive deals early pay lower prices for targets than followers. Late in the cycle, purchase prices escalate as more bidders enter the takeover market, leading many buyers to overpay.[31] Reflecting this "herd mentality," deals completed late in M&A waves tend to show lower acquirer returns than those announced prior to an upsurge in deal activity.[32]

UNDERSTANDING CORPORATE RESTRUCTURING ACTIVITIES

Corporate restructuring is often broken into two categories. *Operational restructuring* entails changes in the composition of a firm's asset structure by

[30] Brakman et al., 2005; Gugler et al., 2012

[31] McNamara et al., 2008; Gell et al., 2008

[32] Duchin et al., 2013

TABLE 1.4 U.S. Historical Merger Waves

Time Period	Driving Force(s)	Type of M&A Activity	Key Impact	Key Transactions	Factors Contributing to End of Wave
1897–1904	Drive for efficiency Lax antitrust law enforcement Westward migration Technological change	Horizontal consolidation	Increasing concentration: Primary metals Transportation Mining	U.S. Steel Standard Oil Eastman Kodak American Tobacco General Electric	Fraudulent financing 1904 stock market crash
1916–1929	Entry into WWI Post-WWI boom	Largely horizontal consolidation	Increased industry concentration	Samuel Insull builds utility empire in 39 states called Middle West Utilities	1929 stock market crash Clayton Antitrust Act
1965–1969	Rising stock market Sustained economic boom	Growth of conglomerates	Financial engineering leading to conglomeration	LTV ITT Litton Industries Gulf and Western Northwest Industries	Escalating purchase prices Excessive leverage
1981–1989	Rising stock market Economic boom Underperformance of conglomerates Relative weakness of U.S. dollar Favorable regulatory environment Favorable foreign accounting practices	Retrenchment era Rise of hostile takeovers Corporate raiders Proliferation of financial buyers using highly leveraged transactions Increased takeover of U.S. firms by foreign buyers	Breakup of conglomerates Increased use of junk (unrated) bonds to finance transactions	RJR Nabisco MBO Beecham Group (U.K.) buys SmithKline Campeau of Canada buys Federated Stores	Widely publicized bankruptcies 1990 recession
1992–1999	Economic recovery Booming stock market Internet revolution Lower trade barriers Globalization	Age of strategic megamerger	Record levels of transactions in terms of numbers and prices	AOL acquires Time Warner Vodafone AirTouch acquires Mannesmann Exxon buys Mobil	Slumping economy and stock market in 2001–2002 Escalating terrorism
2003–2008	Low interest rates underpricing risk Rising stock market Booming global economy Globalization High commodity prices	Age of cross-border transactions, horizontal megamergers, and growing influence of private equity investors	Increasing synchronicity among world's economies	Mittal acquires Arcelor P&G buys Gillette Verizon acquires MCI Blackstone buys Equity Office Properties	Loss of Confidence in global capital markets Economic slowdown in industrial nations

acquiring new businesses or by the outright or partial sale or spin-off of companies or product lines. Operational restructuring could also include downsizing by closing unprofitable or nonstrategic facilities. *Financial restructuring* describes changes in a firm's capital structure, such as share repurchases or adding debt either to lower the company's overall cost of capital or as part of an antitakeover defense. The focus in this book is on business combinations and breakups rather than on operational downsizing and financial restructuring. Business combinations can be known as *mergers, consolidations, acquisitions,* or *takeovers* and can be characterized as friendly or hostile.

Mergers and Consolidations

Mergers can be described from a legal perspective and an economic perspective.

A Legal Perspective

A *merger* is a combination of two or more firms, often comparable in size, in which all but one ceases to exist legally. A *statutory* or *direct merger* is one in which the acquiring or surviving company assumes automatically the assets and liabilities of the target in accordance with the statutes of the state in which the combined companies will be incorporated. A *subsidiary merger* involves the target's becoming a subsidiary of the parent. To the public, the target firm may be operated under its brand name, but it will be owned and controlled by the acquirer. A *statutory consolidation*—which involves two or more companies joining to form a new company—is technically not a merger. All legal entities that are consolidated are dissolved during the formation of the new company, which usually has a new name, and shareholders in the firms being consolidated typically exchange their shares for shares in the new company.

An Economic Perspective

Business combinations may also be defined depending on whether the merging firms are in the same (horizontal) or different industries (conglomerate) and on their positions in the corporate value chain (vertical). Figure 1.1 illustrates the different stages of a value chain. A simple value chain in the basic steel industry may distinguish between raw materials, such as coal or iron ore; steel making, such as "hot metal" and rolling operations; and metals distribution. Similarly, a value chain in the oil and gas industry would separate exploration activities from production, refining, and marketing. An Internet value chain might distinguish between infrastructure providers such as Cisco, content providers such as Dow Jones, and portals such as Google. In a vertical merger, companies that do not own operations in each major segment of the value chain "backward integrate" by acquiring a supplier or "forward integrate" by buying a distributor. When paper manufacturer Boise Cascade acquired Office Max, an office products distributor, the $1.1 billion transaction

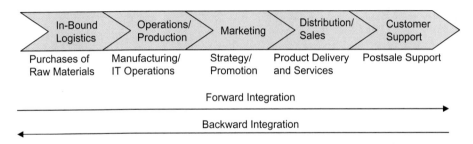

FIGURE 1.1   The corporate value chain. *Note: IT stands for to information technology.*

represented forward integration.[33] PepsiCo backward integrated through a $7.8 billion purchase of its two largest bottlers to realize $400 million in annual cost savings.

Acquisitions, Divestitures, Spin-Offs, Carve-Outs, and Buyouts

An *acquisition* occurs when a company takes a controlling interest in another firm, a legal subsidiary of another firm, or selected assets of another firm, such as a manufacturing facility. They may involve the purchase of another firm's assets or stock, with the acquired firm continuing to exist as a legally owned subsidiary. In contrast, a *divestiture* is the sale of all or substantially all of a company or product line to another party for cash or securities. A *spin-off* is a transaction in which a parent creates a new legal subsidiary and distributes shares in the subsidiary to its current shareholders as a stock dividend. An *equity carve-out* is a transaction in which the parent issues a portion of its stock or that of a subsidiary to the public (see Chapter 15). Figure 1.2 provides a summary of the various forms of corporate restructuring.

ALTERNATIVE TAKEOVER STRATEGIES

The term *takeover* is used when one firm assumes control of another. In a *friendly takeover*, the target's board and management recommend shareholder approval. To gain control, the acquiring company usually must offer a premium to the current stock price. The excess of the offer price over the target's premerger share price is called a *purchase premium* or *acquisition premium* and varies widely by country,[34] reflecting the perceived value of obtaining a controlling interest (i.e., the ability to direct the activities of the firm) in the target, the

---

[33] According to Gugler et al. (2003), horizontal, conglomerate, and vertical mergers accounted for 42%, 54%, and 4%, respectively, of the 45,000 transactions analyzed between 1981 and 1998.

[34] United States merger premiums averaged about 38% between 1973 and 1998 (Andrade, Mitchell, and Stafford, 2001). Rossi and Volpin (2004) document an average premium of 44% during the 1990s for U.S. mergers and find premiums in 49 countries ranging from 10% for Brazil and Switzerland to 120% for Israel and Indonesia.

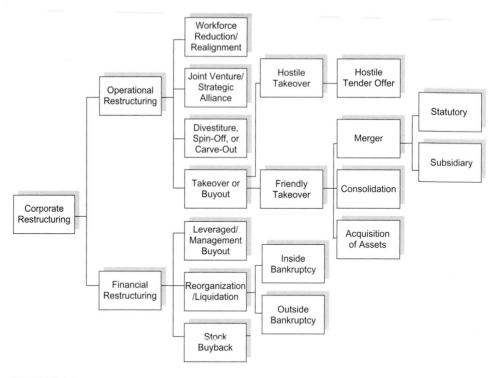

FIGURE 1.2   The corporate restructuring process.

value of expected synergies (e.g., cost savings) resulting from combining the two firms, and any overpayment for the target firm. Overpayment is the amount an acquirer pays for a target firm in excess of the present value of future cash flows, including synergy.[35] The size of the premium fluctuates widely from one year to the next. During the 30-year period ending in 2011, U.S. purchase price premiums averaged 43%, reaching a high of 63% in 2003 and a low of 31% in 2007.[36] The premium size also varies substantially across industries, reflecting their different expected growth rates.[37]

---

[35] Analysts often attempt to determine the premium paid for a controlling interest (i.e., *control premium*) and the amount of value created due to operating synergies. An example of a pure control premium is a conglomerate willing to pay a price above the prevailing market price for a target to gain a controlling interest, even though operating synergies are limited. The acquirer believes it will recover the control premium by making better management decisions for the target firm. What is often called a "control premium" in the popular press is actually a purchase or acquisition premium that includes both a premium for synergy and a premium for control.

[36] *FactSet Mergerstat Review*, 2011

[37] Madura, Ngo, and Viale, 2012

A formal proposal to buy shares in another firm made directly to its share-holders, usually for cash or securities or both, is called a *tender offer*. Tender offers most often result from friendly negotiations (i.e., negotiated tender offers) between the boards of the acquirer and the target firm. Cash tender offers may be used because they could represent a faster alternative to mergers.[38] Those that are unwanted by the target's board are referred to as *hostile tender offers*. *Self-tender offers* are used when a firm seeks to repurchase its stock.

A *hostile takeover* occurs when the offer is unsolicited, the approach was con-tested by the target's management, and control changed hands. The acquirer may attempt to circumvent management by offering to buy shares directly from the target's shareholders (i.e., a *hostile tender offer*) and by buying shares in a pub-lic stock exchange (i.e., an *open market purchase*). Friendly takeovers are often con-summated at a lower purchase price than hostile deals, which may trigger an auction for the target firm. Acquirers often prefer friendly takeovers because the postmerger integration process is usually more expeditious when both parties are cooperating fully and customer and employee attrition is less. Most transac-tions tend to be friendly.

THE ROLE OF HOLDING COMPANIES IN MERGERS AND ACQUISITIONS

A *holding company* is a legal entity having a controlling interest in one or more companies. The key advantage is the ability to gain effective control[39] of other companies at a lower overall cost than if the firm were to acquire 100% of the target's shares. Effective control sometimes can be achieved by owning as little as 30% of the voting stock of another company when the firm's bylaws require approval of major decisions by a majority of votes cast rather than a majority of the voting shares outstanding. This is particularly true when the target com-pany's ownership is highly fragmented, with few shareholders owning large blocks of stock. Effective control generally is achieved by acquiring less than 100% but usually more than 50% of another firm's equity. Because it can gain effective control with less than 100% ownership, the holding company is left with minority shareholders, who may not always agree with the strategic direc-tion of the company. Implementing holding company strategies may become

---

[38]Speed is important to acquirers if there are other potential bidders for the target firm. Cash tender offers may be completed more rapidly than mergers since no target shareholder meeting is required and the length of time regulators have to review tender offers is less than for mergers (Offenberg and Pirinsky, 2012).

[39]One firm is said to have effective control when control has been achieved by buying voting stock, it is not likely to be temporary, there are no legal restrictions on control (such as from a bankruptcy court), and there are no powerful minority shareholders.

very contentious. Also, holding company shareholders may be subject to an onerous tax burden.[40]

THE ROLE OF EMPLOYEE STOCK OWNERSHIP PLANS (ESOPS) IN MERGERS AND ACQUISITIONS

An ESOP is a trust fund that invests in the securities of the firm sponsoring the plan. Designed to attract and retain employees, ESOPs are defined contribution[41] employee pension plans that invest at least 50% of the plan's assets in the sponsor's common shares. The plans may receive the employer's stock or cash, which is used to buy the sponsor's stock. The sponsor can make tax-deductible contributions of cash, stock, or other assets into the trust.[42] The plan's trustee is charged with investing the trust assets, and the trustee can often sell, mortgage, or lease the assets. Stock acquired by the ESOP is allocated to accounts for individual employees based on some formula and vested over time. ESOP participants must be allowed to vote their allocated shares at least on major issues, such as selling the company. However, there is no requirement that they be allowed to vote on other issues such as choosing the board of directors.

ESOPs may be used to restructure firms. If a subsidiary cannot be sold at what the parent firm believes to be a reasonable price and liquidating the subsidiary would be disruptive to customers, the parent may divest the subsidiary to employees through a shell corporation. A *shell corporation* is one that is incorporated but has no significant assets. The shell sets up the ESOP, which borrows the money to buy the subsidiary; the parent guarantees the loan. The shell operates the subsidiary, whereas the ESOP holds the stock. As income is generated from the subsidiary, tax-deductible contributions are made by the shell to the ESOP to service the debt. As the loan is repaid, the shares are allocated to employees who eventually own the firm. ESOPs may also be used by employees in leveraged buyouts to purchase the shares of owners of privately held firms. This is particularly common when the owners have most of their net worth tied up in their firms. ESOPs also provide an effective antitakeover defense, since employees who are additionally shareholders tend to vote against bidders for fear of jeopardizing their jobs.

[40]Subsidiaries of holding companies pay taxes on their operating profits. The holding company then pays taxes on dividends it receives from its subsidiaries. Finally, holding company shareholders pay taxes on dividends they receive from the holding company. This is equivalent to triple taxation of the subsidiary's operating earnings.

[41]Employee contributions are set as a percentage of salary, while the value of their pensions depends on the performance of the sponsoring firm's shares.

[42]Cash contributions made by the sponsoring firm for both interest and principal payments on bank loans to ESOPs are tax deductible by the firm. Dividends paid on stock contributed to ESOPs are also deductible if they are used to repay ESOP debt. The sponsoring firm could use tax credits equal to 0.5% of payroll if contributions in that amount were made to the ESOP. Finally, lenders must pay taxes on only one-half of the interest received on loans made to ESOPs owning more than 50% of the sponsoring firm's stock.

BUSINESS ALLIANCES AS ALTERNATIVES TO MERGERS AND ACQUISITIONS

In addition to mergers and acquisitions, businesses may combine through joint ventures (JVs), strategic alliances, minority investments, franchises, and licenses. The term *business alliance* is used to refer to all forms of business combinations other than mergers and acquisitions. See Chapter 15 for more details.

Joint ventures are business relationships formed by two or more separate parties to achieve common objectives. While the JV is often a legal entity such as a corporation or partnership, it may take any organizational form desired by the parties involved. Each JV partner continues to exist as a separate entity; JV corporations have their own management reporting to a board of directors. A *strategic alliance* generally does not create a separate legal entity and may be an agreement to sell each firm's products to the other's customers or to co-develop a technology, product, or process. Such agreements may be legally binding or largely informal. *Minority* investments, those involving less than a controlling interest, require little commitment of management time. A company may choose to assist small companies in the development of products or technologies it finds useful, often receiving representation on the board in exchange for the investment. *Licenses* enable firms to extend their brands to new products and markets by licensing their brand names to others or to gain access to a proprietary technology through the licensing process. A *franchise* is a specialized form of a license agreement that grants a privilege to a dealer from a manufacturer or franchise service organization to sell the franchiser's products or services in a given area. Under a franchise agreement, the franchiser may offer the franchisee consultation, promotional assistance, financing, and other benefits in exchange for a share of the franchise's revenue. Franchises represent a low-cost way for the franchiser to expand.[43]

The major attraction of these alternatives to outright acquisition is the opportunity for each partner to gain access to the other's skills, products, and markets at a lower overall cost in terms of management time and money. Major disadvantages include: limited control, the need to share profits, and the potential loss of trade secrets and skills to competitors.

PARTICIPANTS IN THE MERGERS AND ACQUISITIONS PROCESS

In addition to the acquirer and target firms, the key participants in the M&A process can be categorized as follows: providers of specialized services, regulators, institutional investors and lenders, activist investors, and M&A arbitrageurs. Each category plays a distinctly different role.

---

[43]Franchising has been limited to industries such as fast-food services and retailing, in which a successful business model can be easily replicated.

Providers of Specialized Services

The first category includes investment banks, lawyers, accountants, proxy solicitors, and public relations personnel. Not surprisingly, the number and variety of advisors hired by firms tends to increase dramatically with the increasing complexity of the deal.[44]

Investment Banks

Investment banks provide advice and deal opportunities; screen potential buyers and sellers; make initial contact with a seller or buyer; and provide negotiation support, valuation, and deal structuring guidance. The "universal or top-tier banks" (e.g., Goldman Sachs) also maintain broker-dealer operations, serving wholesale and retail clients in brokerage and advisory roles to assist with the complexity and often-huge financing requirements of megatransactions.[45]

Investment bankers derive significant income from writing so-called *fairness opinion letters*—written and signed third-party assertions that certify the appropriateness of the price of a proposed deal involving a tender offer, merger, asset sale, or leveraged buyout. They are often developed as legal protection for members of the boards of directors against possible shareholder challenges of their decisions.[46] Researchers have found that fairness opinion letters reduce the risk of lawsuits associated with M&A transactions and the size of the premium paid for targets if they result in acquirers' performing more rigorous due diligence and deal negotiation.[47]

In selecting an investment bank, the average size of financial returns on announcement dates for those deals for which they serve as an advisor is far more important than the investment bank's size or market share.[48] Smaller advisors may generate higher returns for their clients than the mega-investment banks because of proprietary industry knowledge and relationships. However, reputation does matter in certain situations. Contrary to earlier studies that report a negative or weak relationship between bidder financial advisor reputation and bidder returns,[49] bidders using top-tier investment banks as advisors

---

[44] DeMong et al., 2011

[45] For a career guide to investment banking, see T. Lott (2007).

[46] Typically limited to "change of control" transactions, fairness opinions include a range of values for a firm. The proposed purchase price is considered "fair" if it falls within the range. Problems with fairness opinions include the potential conflicts of interest with investment banks that generate large fees. In many cases, the investment bank that brings the deal to a potential acquirer is the same one that writes the fairness opinion (Henry, 2003). Acquirers using one firm to write the fairness opinion for a fixed fee and a different firm in an advisory capacity for a contingent fee to close the deal show higher abnormal positive returns than those that do not (Chen, 2010).

[47] Kisgen et al., 2009

[48] Bao et al., 2011

[49] Rau, 2000; Hunter and Jagtiani, 2003; and Ismail, 2010

report on average a 1% improvement in returns in deals involving public targets.[50] Top-tier investment banks are better able to assist in funding large transactions, which typically involve public companies, because of their current relationships with lenders and broker networks. Public takeovers are often more complex than private takeovers due to their greater bargaining power, need for greater disclosure, and regulatory issues. Targets, having long-standing relationships with investment banks, are more likely to hire M&A advisors[51] and to benefit by receiving higher purchase price premiums.[52]

Lawyers

Lawyers help structure the deal, evaluate risk, negotiate the tax and financial terms, arrange financing, and coordinate the sequence of events to complete the transaction. Specific tasks include drafting the purchase agreement and other transaction-related documentation, providing opinion of counsel letters to the lender, and defining due diligence activities.

Accountants

Accountants provide advice on financial structure, perform financial due diligence, and help create the optimal tax structure for a deal. Income tax, capital gains, sales tax, and sometimes gift and estate taxes are all at play in negotiating a merger or acquisition. In addition to tax considerations, accountants prepare financial statements and perform audits. Many agreements require that the books and records of the acquired entity be prepared in accordance with Generally Accepted Accounting Principles (GAAP).

Proxy Solicitors

Proxy contests are attempts to change the management control or policies of a company by gaining the right to cast votes on behalf of other shareholders. In contests for the control of the board of directors of a target company, it can be difficult to compile mailing lists of stockholders' addresses. The acquiring firm or dissident shareholders hire a proxy solicitor to obtain this information. The target's management may also hire proxy solicitors to design strategies for educating shareholders and communicating the reasons why they should support the board.

Public Relations Firms

Such firms are often hired to ensure that a consistent message is communicated during a takeover attempt or in defending against takeovers. In initiating a hostile takeover attempt, the message to target shareholders must be that the acquirer's plans for the company will increase shareholder value more than the plans of incumbent management. Often, the target company's management will hire a private investigator to develop detailed financial data on the company

[50]Golubov et al., 2011; Bao et al., 2011

[51]Forte et al., 2010

[52]Wen et al., 2012

and do background checks on key personnel, later using that information in the public relations campaign in an effort to discredit publicly the management of the acquiring firm.

Regulators

Regulations that affect M&A activity exist at all levels of government and involve security, antitrust, environmental, racketeering, and employee benefits laws. Others are industry specific, such as public utilities, insurance, banking, broadcasting, telecommunications, defense contracting, and transportation. State antitakeover statutes place limitations on how and when a hostile takeover may be implemented. Moreover, approval at both the state and federal levels may be required for deals in certain industries. Cross-border transactions may be even more complicated, because it may be necessary to obtain approval from regulatory authorities in all countries in which the acquirer and target companies do business.

Institutional Investors and Lenders

These financial intermediaries pool funds provided by others and invest or lend those funds to finance the purchase of a wide array of assets, from securities to real property to corporate takeovers. Such organizations include insurance companies, pension funds, and mutual funds; private equity, hedge funds, and venture capital funds; sovereign wealth funds; and angel investors. Commercial banks are also prominent intermediaries; however, under recent legislation their role is relegated primarily to lending rather than investing money deposited with the bank.

Insurance, Pension, and Mutual Funds

Relatively risk averse and subject to substantial regulation, these institutions invest mostly in assets whose risk and return characteristics match their obligations to their customers. For example, an insurance company offers to mitigate risk for its customers in exchange for an insurance premium. The main source of profit for insurance companies is the sale of insurance products, but they also make money by investing premium income. Employers establish pension funds to generate income over the long term to provide pensions for employees when they retire. Typically, pension funds are managed by a financial advisor for the company and its employees, although some larger corporations operate their pension funds in-house. Mutual funds are pools of money professionally managed for the benefit of investors. A mutual fund's portfolio is structured and maintained to match the investment objectives stated in its prospectus.

Commercial Banks

Traditionally, commercial banks have accepted checking, savings, and money market accounts and would lend these funds to borrowers. This model has evolved into one in which banks sell many of the loans they originate to others for whom buying, selling, and collecting on loans is their primary business. Commercial banks also derive an increasing share of their profits from fees charged for various types of services offered to depositors and fees charged for underwriting and other investment banking services. The Dodd-Frank bill, passed in 2010, is intended to limit the riskiness of bank lending and to severely restrict the types of investments that can be made.

Hedge, Private Equity, and Venture Capital Funds

These funds assume higher levels of risk than other types of institutional investors and usually are limited partnerships in which the general partner has made a substantial personal investment. They are distinguished by their investment strategies, lockup periods (i.e., the length of time investors are required to commit funds), and the liquidity of their portfolios. Hedge fund investment strategies include trading a variety of financial instruments—debt, equity, options, futures, and foreign currencies—as well as higher-risk strategies, such as corporate restructurings (e.g., LBOs) and credit derivatives (e.g., credit default swaps). Because of their shorter lockup periods, hedge funds focus on investments that can be readily converted into cash. In contrast, private equity funds often make highly illiquid investments in private companies and hold such investments for five years or more; they attempt to control risk by being actively involved in managing the firm in which they have invested. Venture capitalists are a significant source of funds for financing both start-ups and acquisitions.

Sovereign Wealth Funds

Sovereign wealth funds are government-backed or -sponsored investors whose primary function is to invest accumulated foreign currency reserves. Countries with huge quantities of U.S. dollars would, through such funds, often reinvest the money in U.S. Treasury securities. Recently, these funds have begun to grow and are increasingly taking equity positions in foreign firms, often making high-profile investments in public companies.

Angel Investors

Angel investors are wealthy individuals who band together in "investment clubs" or networks to identify deals, pool money, and share expertise. Some angel groups imitate professional investment funds, some affiliate with universities, while others engage in for-profit philanthropy.

Activist Investors

Institutions often play the role of activist investors to affect the policies of companies in which they invest and especially to discipline corporate management.

Mutual Funds and Pension Funds

Institutional ownership of public firms increased substantially in recent decades. While regulations restrict the ability of institutions to discipline corporate management, institutional investors with huge portfolios can be very effective in demanding governance changes.[53] These organizations may challenge management on such hot-button issues as antitakeover defenses, CEO severance benefits, and employee stock option accounting. Voting against management, though, can be problematic, since some mutual funds manage retirement plans and, increasingly, provide a host of outsourcing services—from payroll to health benefits—for their business clients. Mutual funds may own stock, on behalf of their clients, in these same firms.

Pressure from institutional activists may account for the general decline in the number of executives serving as both board chairman and CEO of companies.[54] Sometimes, CEOs choose to negotiate with activists rather than face a showdown at an annual shareholders meeting. Activists are also finding that they may avoid the expense of a proxy fight simply by threatening to vote in certain ways on supporting a CEO or a management proposal. This may mean a "no" vote, although in some instances the only option is to vote in the affirmative or abstain. Abstaining is a way to indicate dissatisfaction with a CEO or a firm's policy without jeopardizing future underwriting or M&A business for the institution.

Hedge Funds and Private Equity Firms

Hedge funds and private equity firms have had more success as activist investors than other institutional investors. They are successful about two-thirds of the time in their efforts to change a firm's strategic, operational, or financial strategies, often generating attractive financial returns for shareholders.[55] They seldom seek control (with ownership stakes averaging about 9%) and are most often nonconfrontational. Their success as activists can be attributed to their managers, who direct large pools of relatively unregulated capital and who are highly motivated by financial gain. Because hedge funds are not subject to the same regulations governing mutual funds and pension funds, they can hold concentrated positions in a small number of firms. Moreover, they are not limited

[53] Mutual funds, to achieve diversification, are limited in the amount they can invest in any one firm's outstanding stock. State regulations often restrict the share of a life insurance or property casualty company's assets that can be invested in stock to as little as 2%.

[54] Goyal and Park, 2002. The number of executives serving in both positions of their companies declined from about 91% during the 1980s to 58% during the 1990s (Kini, Kracaw, and Mian, 2004).

[55] Brav et al. (2006) argue that activist hedge funds occupy a middle ground between internal monitoring by large shareholders and external monitoring by corporate raiders. Clifford (2007) and Klein and Zur (2009) found that hedge fund activism generates an approximate 7% abnormal financial return to shareholders around the announcement that the hedge fund is initiating some form of action.

by the same conflicts of interests that afflict mutual funds and pension funds. Hedge funds tend to have the greatest impact on shareholder returns when they prod management to sell a company, but their impact dissipates quickly if the sale of the company is unsuccessful.[56] Firms once targeted by activists are more likely to be acquired.

M&A Arbitrageurs (Arbs)

When a bid is made for a target firm, the target's stock price often trades at a small discount to the actual bid—reflecting the risk that the deal may not be completed. *Merger arbitrage* refers to an investment strategy that attempts to profit from this spread. Arbs buy the stock and make a profit on the difference between the bid price and the current stock price if the deal is completed. Others may "short" the stock once it increases, betting that the proposed merger will not be completed and the target's share price will drop to its premerger announcement level. Assume a target firm's shares are selling at $6 per share and an acquirer announces an offer to pay $10 per share. Because the outcome is uncertain, the target's share price will rise to less than $10, assume $9.[57] Other investors may bet the merger will not be completed and sell the stock short (i.e., sell borrowed shares—paying interest to the share owner based on the value of the shares when borrowed—hoping to buy them back at a lower price) at $9 and buy it back at $6.

Hedge fund managers, playing the role of arbs, may accumulate a substantial percentage of the stock held outside of institutions so that they can be in a position to influence the outcome of the takeover attempt. If other offers for the target firm appear, arbs approach institutional investors with phone calls and through leaks to the media, attempting to sell their shares to the highest bidder. Acquirers making a hostile bid often encourage hedge funds to buy as much target stock as possible so that they can gain control of the target later by buying the stock from the hedge funds.

Arbs also provide market liquidity during transactions. In a cash-financed merger, arbs seeking to buy the target firm's shares provide liquidity to the target's shareholders that want to sell on the announcement day or shortly thereafter. Arbs may actually reduce liquidity for the acquirer's stock in a share for share merger because they immediately "short" the acquirer shares. The downward pressure that arb short-selling puts on the acquirer's share price at the time the deal is announced makes it difficult for others to sell without incurring a loss from the premerger announcement price. Merger arbitrage short-selling may account for about one-half of the downward pressure on acquirer share prices

---

[56] Greenwood and Schor (2007) found that under such circumstances, there is little change in the firm's share price during the 18 months following the sale of the company, even if the firm follows the activist's recommendations and buys back shares or adds new directors.

[57] The target's share price would rise by $4 to $10 if investors were certain the deal get done. Because it rises only to $9, investors are implicitly stating that there is a 75% (i.e., $3/$4) probability that the merger will be completed.

around the announcement of a stock-financed merger.[58] Merger arbitrage has the potential to be highly profitable.[59]

THE IMPLICATIONS OF MERGERS AND ACQUISITIONS FOR SHAREHOLDERS, BONDHOLDERS, AND SOCIETY

The outdated notion that most M&As fail in some substantive manner is not supported by recent evidence. On average, the sum of target and acquirer shareholders' gains around the deal's announcement date is positive and statistically significant. While most of the gain accrues to target shareholders, acquirer shareholders often experience financial gains in excess of what would have been realized in the absence of a takeover.[60] However, in the three to five years after a takeover, it is less clear if shareholders continue to benefit from the deal. As time passes, other factors impact performance, making it increasingly difficult to determine the extent to which a change in performance is attributable to an earlier acquisition.

Researchers use a wide variety of approaches to measure the impact of takeovers on shareholder value.[61] What follows is a discussion of the results of the two most common types of analyses of pre- and postmerger returns. The "event study" examines abnormal stock returns to the shareholders of both acquirers and targets around the announcement of an offer (the "event"). Empirical studies of postmerger returns use accounting measures to gauge the impact on shareholder value following the announcement date.

Premerger Returns to Shareholders

Positive *abnormal* or *excess* shareholder returns may be explained by such factors as improved efficiency, pricing power, and tax benefits. They are abnormal in that they exceed what an investor would normally expect to earn for accepting a certain level of risk. If an investor expects to earn a 10% return on a stock but actually earns 25% due to a takeover, the abnormal or excess return to the shareholder would be 15%.[62]

---

[58] Mitchell, Pulvino, and Stafford, 2004

[59] Such arbitrage generates financial returns ranging from 4.5% to more than 100% in excess of what would be considered normal in a highly competitive market (Jindra et al., 1999; Mitchell et al, 2001).

[60] Ahern, 2012

[61] In an analysis of 88 empirical studies between 1970 and 2006, Zola and Meier (2008) identify 12 different approaches to measuring the impact of takeovers on shareholder value. Of these studies, 41% use the event study method to analyze premerger returns and 28% utilize long-term accounting measures to analyze postmerger returns.

[62] Abnormal returns are calculated by subtracting the actual return from a benchmark indicating investors' required returns, often the capital asset pricing model or the S&P 500 stock index.

Returns High for Target Shareholders

Average abnormal returns to target shareholders during the 2000s averaged 25.1% as compared to 18.5% during the 1990s.[63] This upward trend may reflect a tendency by bidders to offer a substantial premium in friendly takeovers to preempt other possible bidders and the potential for revising the initial offer because of competing bids. Other contributing factors include the increasing sophistication of takeover defenses and federal and state laws requiring bidders to notify target shareholders of their intentions before completing the deal. Returns from hostile tender offers generally exceed those from friendly mergers, which are characterized by less contentious negotiated settlements and the absence of competing bids.

Returns to Acquirer Shareholders Generally Favorable

Recent research involving large samples over lengthy time periods involving U.S., foreign, and cross-border deals (including public and private firms) shows that returns to acquirer shareholders are generally positive except for those involving large public firms and those using stock to pay for the deal.[64] Unlike earlier results, these studies document that acquirer shareholders earn positive abnormal returns of about 1 to 1.5%. While earlier studies show such returns to be zero or negative, they fail to explain why the number and size of M&As continues to grow globally, implying that managers do not learn from past failures. Earlier studies may understate average acquirer returns because they are based on relatively small samples of mostly public firms, employ problematic methodologies, fail to capture the preannouncement rise in acquirer share prices,[65] and fail to adjust for distortions of a few large transactions.[66] Further, they do not view M&As in the context of a larger business strategy[67] and do not account for the beneficial impact of defensive acquisitions.[68]

Postmerger Returns to Shareholders

The objective of examining postmerger accounting or other performance measures such as cash flow and operating profit, usually during the three- to five-year period following closing, is to assess how performance changed. The evidence, however, is conflicting about the long-term impact of M&A activity. In a review of 26 studies of postmerger performance during the three to five years after the merger, Martynova and Renneboog (2008a) found that 14 showed a decline in

[63] See Table 11 in Netter et al. (2011).

[64] Netter et al., 2011; Ellis et al., 2011

[65] Cornet et al., 2011, and Cai et al., 2011

[66] Moeller et al., 2005

[67] Barkema and Schijven, 2008

[68] Bidders may rationally overpay when the cost of overpaying is less than the cost incurred in losing the target to a competitor (Akdogu, 2011).

operating returns, 7 provided positive (but statistically insignificant) changes in profitability, and 5 showed a positive and statistically significant increase in profitability.[69] The inability to determine the long-term impact of M&As appears to be affected by methodological issues and the failure to distinguish among alternative situations in which M&As occur. The longer the postmerger period is analyzed, the greater the likelihood that other factors, wholly unrelated to the merger, will affect financial returns. Moreover, these longer-term studies are not able to compare how well the acquirer would have done without the acquisition.

Acquirer Returns Vary by Characteristics of Acquirer, Target, and Deal

Abnormal returns to acquirer shareholders are largely situational, varying according to the size of the acquirer, the type and size of the target, and the form of payment (See Table 1.5).

Smaller Acquirers Tend to Realize Higher Returns

Managers at large firms tend to overpay more than those at smaller firms, since large-firm executives may have been involved in more deals and be overconfident. Incentive systems at larger firms may also skew compensation to reflect more the overall size of the firm than its ongoing performance. Finally, managers of large firms may pursue larger, more risky investments (such as unrelated acquisitions) in an attempt to support the firm's overvalued share price. Regardless of the reason, for the 20-year period ending in 2001, researchers found that large firms destroyed shareholder wealth, while small firms created wealth.[70]

Acquirer Returns Often Positive for Privately-Owned or Subsidiary Targets

United States acquirers of private firms or subsidiaries of publicly traded firms often realize positive abnormal returns of 1.5 to 2.6%.[71] Acquirers pay

---

[69] The disagreement about postmerger returns may be the result of sample and time selections, methodology employed in the studies, or factors unrelated to the merger, such as a slowing economy (Fama, 1998; Lyon et al., 1999). Dutta and Jog (2009) do not find evidence of any systematic long-term deterioration in acquirer financial performance and attribute findings of such deterioration to the choice of benchmarks, differing methodologies, and statistical techniques.

[70] Regardless of how they were financed (i.e., stock or cash) or whether they were public or private targets, acquisitions made by smaller firms had announcement returns 1.55% higher than a comparable acquisition made by a larger firm (Moeller et al., 2004).

[71] Moeller et al., 2005; Fuller et al., 2002; and Ang and Kohers, 2001. Similar results were found in an exhaustive study of U.K. acquirers (Draper and Paudyal, 2006) making bids for private firms or subsidiaries of public firms, where the positive abnormal returns were attributed to the relative illiquidity of such businesses.

TABLE 1.5   Acquirer Returns Differ by Characteristics of the Acquirer, Target, and Deal

Characteristic	Empirical Support
TYPE OF TARGET	
Acquirer returns are often positive when the targets are privately owned (or are subsidiaries of public companies) and slightly negative when the targets are large publicly traded firms (i.e., so-called "listing effect"), regardless of the country.	Netter et al. (2011) Capron and Shen (2007) Faccio et al. (2006) Draper and Paudyal (2006) Moeller et al. (2005)
FORM OF PAYMENT	
• Acquirer returns on equity-financed acquisitions of large public firms often *less than* cash-financed deals in the United States.	Schleifer and Vishny (2003) Megginson et al. (2003) Heron and Lie (2002) Linn and Switzer (2001)
• Acquirer returns on equity-financed acquisitions of public or private firms frequently *more than* all-cash-financed deals in European Union countries. • Acquirer returns on equity-financed acquisitions of private firms (or subsidiaries of public firms) often exceed significantly cash deals.	Martynova and Renneboog (2008) Chang (1998) Officer et al. (2009) Netter et al. (2011)
ACQUIRER/TARGET SIZE	
• Smaller acquirers often realize higher returns than larger acquirers. • Relatively small deals often generate higher acquirer returns than larger ones. • Acquirer returns may be lower when the size of the acquisition is large relative to the buyer (i.e., more than 30% of the buyer's market value).	Moeller et al. (2004) Moeller et al. (2005) Offenberg (2009) Gorton et al. (2009)[a] Hackbarth et al. (2008) Frick and Torres (2002) Rehm et al. (2012)

[a]*Size is measured not in absolute but relative terms compared to other firms within an industry*

less for private firms or subsidiaries of public companies due to the limited availability of information and the limited number of bidders for such firms. Since these targets may be acquired at a discount from their true value, acquirers are able to realize a larger share of the combined value of the acquirer and target firms.

Relatively Small Deals May Generate Higher Returns

High-tech firms realize attractive returns by acquiring small, but related, target firms to fill gaps in their product offerings.[72] Larger deals tend to be riskier for acquirers[73] and experience consistently lower postmerger performance, possibly reflecting the challenges of integrating large target firms and realizing projected synergies. There are exceptions: Firms making large acquisitions show less negative or more positive returns in slower-growing than in faster-growing sectors.[74] In slow-growth industries, integration may be less disruptive than in faster-growing industries, which may experience a slower pace of new product introductions and upgrade efforts.

Form of Payment Impacts Acquirer Returns

Returns to acquirer shareholders often are negative when the acquirer and target are publicly traded and the form of payment consists mostly of stock. For publicly traded firms, managers tend to issue stock when they believe it is overvalued. Investors treat such decisions as signals that the stock is overvalued and sell their shares when the new equity issue is announced, causing the firm's share price to decline. Bidding firms that use cash to purchase the target firm exhibit better long-term performance than do those using stock.[75] However, equity-financed transactions in the European Union often display higher acquirer returns than those using cash, due to the existence of large-block shareholders, whose active monitoring tends to improve the acquired firm's performance. Such shareholders are less common in the United States.[76]

Announcement-period gains to acquirer shareholders tend to dissipate within three to five years, even when the acquisition was successful, when stock is used to acquire a large public firm.[77] These findings imply that shareholders, selling around the announcement dates, may realize the largest gains from either tender offers or mergers.

Payoffs for Bondholders

M&As have little impact on abnormal returns either to the acquirer or to the target bondholders, except in special situations. The limited impact on bondholder wealth is due to the relationship between leverage and operating

---

[72]For the 10-year period ending in 2000, high-tech companies, averaging 39% annual total return to shareholders, acquired targets whose average size was about 1% of the market value of the acquiring firms (Frick et al., 2002).

[73]Hackbarth and Morellec, 2008; Alexandridis et al., 2011

[74]Rehm et al., 2012

[75]Akbulut, 2012; Schleifer et al., 2003; Megginson et al., 2003; Heron et al., 2002; Linn et al., 2001

[76]Martynova and Renneboog, 2008a

[77]Alexandridis et al., 2011; Deogun and Lipin, 2000; Black et al., 2000

[78]Renneboog and Szilagyi, 2007

performance.[78] How M&As affect bondholder wealth reflects, in part, the extent to which an increase in leverage that raises the potential for default is offset by the discipline imposed on management to improve operating performance.[79] Other things being equal, increasing leverage will lower current bondholder wealth, while improving operating performance will improve bondholder wealth. Target firm bondholders, whose debt is below investment grade, experience positive abnormal returns if the acquirer has a higher credit rating.[80] Further, when loan covenant agreements for firms that are subject to takeovers include poison puts that allow bondholders to sell their bonds back to the company at a predetermined price, bondholders experience positive abnormal returns when a change of control takes place.[81]

Payoffs for Society

Most empirical studies show that M&As result in improved operating efficiencies and lower product prices than would have been the case without the deal. Gains in aggregate shareholder value are attributed more to the improved operating efficiency of the combined firms than to increased market or pricing power.[82] That is, many M&As create value when more productive firms acquire less productive ones.[83]

SOME THINGS TO REMEMBER

M&As represent only one way of executing business plans. Alternatives include "go it alone" strategies and the various forms of business alliances. Which method is chosen depends on management's desire for control, willingness to accept risk, and the range of opportunities present at a particular moment in time. M&As generally reward target and, with some exceptions, acquirer shareholders.

[79] The empirical evidence is ambiguous. A study by Billett et al. (2004) shows slightly negative abnormal returns to acquirer bondholders regardless of the acquirer's bond rating. However, they also find that target firm holders of below-investment-grade bonds earn average excess returns of 4.3% or higher around the merger announcement date, when the target firm's credit rating is less than the acquirer's and when the merger is expected to decrease the target's risk or leverage. Maquierira et al. (1998) show positive excess returns to acquirer bondholders of 1.9% and .5% for target bondholders, but only for nonconglomerate transactions. A study of European deals finds positive returns to acquirer bondholders of .56% around the announcement date of the deal (Renneboog et al., 2006).

[80] Kedia and Zhou, 2011

[81] Billet et al., 2010

[82] Shahrur, 2005; Ghosh, 2004; Song and Walking, 2000

[83] Maksimovic and Phillips, 2001 and Maksimovic et al., 2013

DISCUSSION QUESTIONS

1.1 Discuss why mergers and acquisitions occur.

1.2 What is the role of the investment banker in the M&A process?

1.3 In your judgment, what are the motivations for two M&As currently in the news?

1.4 What are the arguments for and against corporate diversification through acquisition? Which do you support, and why?

1.5 What are the primary differences between operating synergy and financial synergy?

1.6 At a time when natural gas and oil prices were at record levels, oil and natural gas producer Andarko Petroleum announced the acquisition of two competitors, Kerr-McGee Corp. and Western Gas Resources, for $16.4 billion and $4.7 billion in cash, respectively. The acquired assets complemented Andarko's operations, providing the scale and focus necessary to cut overlapping expenses and concentrate resources in adjacent properties. What do you believe were the primary forces driving Andarko's acquisition? How will greater scale and focus help Andarko cut costs? What are the assumptions implicit in your answer to the first question?

1.7 Mattel, a major U.S. toy manufacturer, virtually gave away The Learning Company (TLC), a maker of software for toys, to rid itself of a disastrous acquisition. Mattel, which had paid $3.5 billion for TLC, sold the unit to an affiliate of Gores Technology Group for rights to a share of future profits. Was this a related or unrelated diversification for Mattel? Explain your answer. How might your answer to the first question have influenced the outcome?

1.8 AOL acquired Time Warner in a deal valued at $160 billion. Time Warner was at the time the world's largest media company, whose major business segments included cable networks, magazine publishing, book publishing, direct marketing, recorded music and music publishing, and film and TV production and broadcasting. AOL viewed itself as the world leader in providing interactive services, web brands, Internet technologies, and electronic commerce services. Would you classify this business combination as a vertical, horizontal, or conglomerate transaction? Explain your answer.

1.9 Pfizer, a leading pharmaceutical company, acquired drug maker Pharmacia for $60 billion, betting that size is what mattered in the new millennium. Pfizer was finding it difficult to sustain the double-digit earnings growth demanded by investors due to the skyrocketing costs of developing and commercializing new drugs. Expiring patents on a number of so-called blockbuster drugs intensified pressure to bring new drugs to market. In your judgment, what were the primary motivations for Pfizer's wanting to acquire Pharmacia? Categorize these in terms of the primary motivations for mergers and acquisitions discussed in this chapter.

1.10 Dow Chemical, a leading chemical manufacturer, acquired Rohm and Haas Company, a maker of paints, coatings, and electronic materials, for $15.3 billion. While Dow has competed profitably in the plastics business for years, this business has proven to have thin margins and to be highly cyclical. As a result of the acquisition, Dow would be able to offer less cyclical and higher-margin products. Would you consider this related or unrelated diversification? Explain your answer. Would you consider this a cost-effective way for the Dow shareholders to achieve better diversification of their investment portfolios?

Answers to these Chapter Discussion Questions are available in the Online Instructor's Manual for instructors using this book.

QUESTIONS FROM THE CFA CURRICULUM

1.11 If the technology for an industry involves high fixed capital investment, then one way to seek higher profit growth is by pursuing:
    a. Economies of scale.
    b. Diseconomies of scale.
    c. Removal of features that differentiate the product or service provided.
  Source: CFA Institute, 2011, Introduction to Industry and Company Analysis, Reading 59, question 18.

 **CFA Institute**

Answers to questions from the CFA curriculum are available in the Online Student Companion site to this book in a file folder entitled CFA Curriculum and Solutions.

CASE STUDY 1.1
Google Acquires Motorola Mobility in a Growth-Oriented as well as Defensive Move

Key Points

- The acquisition of Motorola Mobility positions Google as a vertically integrated competitor in the fast-growing wireless devices market.
- The acquisition also reduces their exposure to intellectual property litigation.

By most measures, Google's financial performance has been breathtaking. The Silicon Valley-based firm's revenue in 2011 totaled $37.9 billion, up 29% from the prior year, reflecting the ongoing shift from offline to online advertising. While the firm's profit growth has slowed in recent years, the firm's 26% net margin remains impressive. About 95% of the firm's 2011 revenue came from advertising sold through its websites and those of its members and partners.[84] Google is channeling more resources into "feeder technologies" to penetrate newer and faster-growing digital markets and to increase the use of Google's own and its members' websites. These technologies include the Android operating system, designed to power wireless devices, and the Chrome operating system, intended to attract Windows- and Mac-based computer users.

Faced with a need to fuel growth to sustain its market value, Google's announcement on August 15, 2011, that it would acquire Motorola Mobility Holdings Inc. (Motorola) underscores the importance it places on the explosive growth in wireless devices. The all-cash $12.5 billion purchase price represented a 63% premium to Motorola's closing price on the previous trading day. Chicago-based, Motorola makes cellphones, smartphones, tablets, and set-top boxes; its status as one of the earliest firms to develop cellphones and one of the leading mobile firms for the past few decades meant that it had accumulated approximately 17,000 patents, with another 7500 pending. With less than 3% market share, the firm had been struggling to increase handset shipments and was embroiled in

multiple patent-related lawsuits with Microsoft.

As Google's largest-ever deal, the acquisition may be intended to transform Google into a fully integrated mobile phone company, to insulate itself and its handset-manufacturing partners from patent infringement lawsuits, and to gain clout with wireless carriers, which control cellphone pricing and distribution. Revenue growth could come from license fees paid on the Motorola patent portfolio and sales of its handsets and by increasing the use of its own websites and those of its members to generate additional advertising revenue.

Google was under pressure from its handset partners, including HTC and Samsung, to protect them from patent infringement suits based on their use of Google's Android software.[85] Microsoft has already persuaded HTC to pay a fee for every Android phone manufactured, and it is seeking to extract similar royalties from Samsung. If this continues, such payments could make creating new devices for Android prohibitively expensive for manufacturers, forcing them to turn to alternative platforms like Windows Phone 7. With a limited patent portfolio, Google also

[84] Google views its members (customers) as the over 1 million businesses that post advertisements on its websites; partners consist of website publishers on whose sites Google posts advertisements and with whom Google shares revenue from those advertisements. At 69% of total Google revenue, advertising revenue from Google websites grew at 34% in 2011, while advertising revenue from its members contributed 27% of total and grew by 18%.

[85] Apple, Microsoft, and Oracle accused Google or the companies that use its Android operating system in the handsets they manufacture, such as Motorola and HTC, a Taiwan handset maker, of infringing on their patents. Each has filed its own patent infringement lawsuit. In late 2012, Apple won its U.S. patent case against Samsung.

was vulnerable to lawsuits against its Android licenses.

Innovation in information technology usually relies on small, incremental improvements in software and hardware, which makes it difficult to determine those changes covered by patents. Firms have an incentive to build up their patent portfolios, which strengthens their negotiating positions with firms threatening to file lawsuits or demanding royalty payments. Historically, firms have simply cross-licensed each other's technologies; today, however, patent infringement lawsuits create entry barriers to potential competitors, as the threat of lawsuits may discourage new entrants. It now pays competitors to sue routinely over alleged patent infringements.

Risks associated with the deal include the potential to drive Android partners such as Samsung and HTC to consider using Microsoft's smartphone operating system, with Google losing license fees currently paid to use the Android operating system. The deal offers few cost savings opportunities due the lack of overlap between Google, an Internet search engine that also produces Android phone software, and handset manufacturer Motorola. Google is essentially becoming a vertically integrated cellphone maker. Furthermore, when the deal was announced, some regulators expressed concern about Google's growing influence in its served markets. Finally, Google's and Motorola's growth and profitability differ significantly, with Motorola's revenue growth rate less than one-third of

Google's and its operating profit margin near zero.

Samsung, HTC, Sony Ericsson, and LG are now both partners and competitors of Google. It is difficult for a firm such as Google to both license its products (Android operating system software) and compete with those licensees by selling Motorola handsets at the same time. Nokia has already aligned with Microsoft and abandoned its own mobile operating system. Others may try to create their own operating systems rather than become dependent on Google. Samsung released phones in 2011 that run on a system called Bada; HTC has a team of engineers dedicated to customizing the version of Android that it uses on its phones, called HTC Sense.

Motorola Mobility's shares soared by almost 57% on the day of the announcement. Led by Nokia, shares of other phone makers also surged. In contrast, Google's share price fell by 1.2%, despite an almost 2% rise in the S&P 500 stock index that same day.

Discussion Questions

1. In what sense is Motorola Mobility's role in this transaction unclear? Identify sources of synergy between Google and Motorola Mobility. What factors are likely to make the realization of this synergy difficult? Be specific.
2. Using the motives for mergers and acquisitions described in Chapter 1, which do you think apply to Google's acquisition of Motorola Mobility? Be specific.

3. Speculate as to why the share price of Motorola Mobility did not increase by the full extent of the premium and why Google's share price fell on the day of the announcement.

4. Speculate as to why the shares of other handset manufacturers jumped on the announcement

that Google was buying Motorola Mobility. Be specific.

5. How might the growing tendency for technology companies to buy other firms' patents affect innovation? Be specific.

Answers to these questions are found in the Online Instructor's Manual available to instructors using this book.

CASE STUDY 1.2
Lam Research Buys Novellus Systems to Consolidate Industry

Key Points

- Industry consolidation is a common response to sharply escalating costs, waning demand, and increasing demands of new technologies.
- Customer consolidation often drives consolidation among suppliers.

Highly complex electronic devices such as smartphones and digital cameras have become ubiquitous in our everyday lives. These devices are powered by sets of instructions encoded on wafers of silicon called *semiconductor chips* (*semiconductors*). Consumer and business demands for increasingly sophisticated functionality for smartphones and cloud computing technologies require the ongoing improvement of both the speed and the capability of semiconductors. This in turn places huge demands on the makers of equipment used in the chip-manufacturing process.

To stay competitive, makers of equipment used to manufacture

semiconductor chips were compelled to increase R&D spending sharply. Chip manufacturers resisted paying higher prices for equipment because their customers, such as PC and cell-phone handset makers, were facing declining selling prices for their products. Chip equipment manufacturers were unable to recover the higher R&D spending through increasing selling prices. The resulting erosion in profitability due to increasing R&D spending was compounded by the onset of the 2008–2009 global recession.

The industry responded with increased consolidation in an attempt to cut costs, firm product pricing, and gaining access to new technologies. Industry consolidation began among chip manufacturers and later spurred suppliers to combine. In February 2011, chipmaker Texas Instruments bought competitor National Semiconductor for $6.5 billion. Three months later, Applied Materials, the largest semiconductor chip equipment manufacturer, bought Varian

Semiconductor Equipment Associates for $4.9 billion to gain access to new technology. On December 21, 2011, Lam Research Corporation (Lam) agreed to buy rival Novellus Systems Inc. (Novellus) for $3.3 billion. Lam anticipates annual cost savings of $100 million by the end of 2013 due to the elimination of overlapping overheads.

Under the terms of the deal, Lam agreed to acquire Novellus in a share exchange in which Novellus shareholders would receive 1.125 shares of Lam common stock for each Novellus share. The deal represented a 28% premium over the closing price of Novellus's shares on the day prior to the deal's public announcement. At closing, Lam shareholders owned about 51% of the combined firms, with Novellus shareholders controlling the rest.

In comparison to earlier industry buyouts, the purchase seemed like a good deal for Lam's shareholders. At 2.3 times Novellus's annual revenue, the purchase price was almost one-half the 4.5 multiple paid by industry leader Applied Materials for Variant in May 2011. The purchase premium paid by Lam was one-half of that paid for comparable transactions between 2006 and 2010. Yet Lam shares closed down 4%, and Novellus' shares closed up 28% on the announcement date.

Lam and Novellus produce equipment that works at different stages of the semiconductor-manufacturing process, making their products complementary. After the merger, Lam's product line would be considerably broader, covering more of the semiconductor-manufacturing process. Semiconductor-chip manufacturers are inclined to buy equipment from the same supplier due to the likelihood that the equipment will be compatible. Lam is also seeking access to cutting-edge technology and improved efficiency. Technology exchange between the two firms is expected to help the combined firms to develop the equipment necessary to support the next generation of advanced semiconductors.

Customers of the two firms include such chip makers as Intel and Samsung. By selling complementary products, the firms have significant cross-selling opportunities as equipment suppliers to all 10 chip makers globally. Together, Lam and Novellus are able to gain revenue faster than they could individually by packaging their equipment and by developing their technologies in combination to ensure they work together. Lam has greater penetration with Samsung and Novellus with Intel.

Lam also stated on the transaction announcement date that a $1.6 billion share repurchase program would be implemented within 12 months following closing. The buyback allows shareholders to sell some of their shares for cash such that, following completion of the buyback, the deal could resemble a half-stock, half-cash deal, depending on how many shareholders tender their shares during the buyback program. The share repurchase will be funded out of the firms' combined cash balances and cash flow. Structuring the deal as an all-stock purchase at closing allows Novellus shareholders to have a tax-free deal.[86]

Discussion Questions

1. Why did Lam's shares close down 4% on the news that Lam would buy Novellus? Why did Novellus' shares close up 28%?
2. Speculate why Lam used stock rather than some other form of payment?
3. Describe how market pressures on semiconductor manufacturers impact chip-equipment makers and how this merger will help Lam and Novellus better serve their customers.
4. How do the high fixed costs in the cyclical chip-equipment-manufacturing industry encourage consolidation?
5. Is this deal a merger or a consolidation from a legal standpoint?
6. Is this deal a horizontal or a vertical transaction? Why is this distinction significant?
7. What are the motives for the deal? Discuss the logic underlying each motive you identify.
8. How are Lam and Novellus similar and how are they different? In what way will their similarities and differences help or hurt the long-term success of the merger?
9. Speculate as to why Lam announced a $1.6 billion share repurchase program at the same time it announced the deal.
10. Do you believe this transaction would help or hurt competition among semiconductor-equipment manufacturers?

Answers to these questions are found in the Online Instructor's Manual available to instructors using this book.

---

[86] When target firm shareholders receive primarily acquirer company stock in exchange for their stock, the transaction is tax free to the target firm's shareholders. That is, they do not have to pay tax on any gain until they decide to sell their stock. This may be more appealing to target shareholders, because it gives them the choice of holding stock to defer tax payments on any gains realized when the shares are sold or taking cash by selling shares during the firm's buyback program.

The Regulatory Environment

Character is doing the right thing when no one is looking. —**J. C. Watts**

INSIDE M&A: AT&T/T-MOBILE DEAL SHORT-CIRCUITED BY REGULATORS

KEY POINTS

- Regulators often consider market concentration when determining whether an M&A will drive up prices and reduce consumer choice and product/service quality.
- What is an acceptable level of concentration is often difficult to determine.
- Concentration may be an outgrowth of the high capital requirements of the industry.
- Attempts to limit concentration may actually work to the detriment of some consumers.

United States antitrust regulators have moved aggressively in recent years to block horizontal mergers (i.e., those involving direct or potential competitors) while being more lenient on vertical deals (i.e., those in which a firm buys a supplier or distributor). These actions foreshadowed the likely outcome of the deal proposed by telecommunications giant AT&T to acquire T-Mobile for $39 billion in cash in early 2011. Despite the unfavorable regulatory environment for horizontal deals, AT&T expressed confidence that it could get approval for the deal when it accepted a sizeable termination fee as part of the agreement if it did not complete the transaction by March 2012. However, the deal would never be completed, as U.S. antitrust regulators made it clear that a tie-up between number two, AT&T (behind Verizon), and number four, T-Mobile (behind Sprint), would not be permitted.

41

On December 20, 2011, AT&T announced that it would cease its nine-month fight to acquire T-Mobile. AT&T was forced to pay T-Mobile's parent, Deutsche Telekom, $3 billion in cash and a portion of its wireless spectrum (i.e., cellular airwaves) valued at as much as $1 billion. T-Mobile and AT&T did agree to enter into a seven-year roaming agreement[1] that could cost AT&T another $1 billion. The announcement came shortly after AT&T had ceased efforts to fight the Justice Department's lawsuit filed in August 2011 to block the merger. The Justice Department would not accept any combination of divestitures or other changes to the deal, arguing that the merger would raise prices to consumers and reduce both choice and service quality. Instead, the Justice Department opted to keep a "strong" fourth competitor rather than allow increased industry concentration.

But T-Mobile's long-term viability was in doubt. The firm's parent, Deutsche Telekom, had made it clear that it wants to exit the mature U.S. market and that it has no intention of investing in a new high-speed network. T-Mobile is the only national carrier that does not currently have its own next-generation high-speed network. Because it is smaller and weaker than the other carriers, it does not have the cash or the marketing clout with handset vendors to offer exclusive, high-end smartphones to attract new customers. While competitors Verizon and AT&T gained new customers, T-Mobile lost 90,000 customers during 2011.

In response to these developments, T-Mobile announced a merger with its smaller rival MetroPCS on October 3, 2012, creating the potential for a stronger competitor to Verizon and AT&T and solving regulators' concerns about increased concentration. However, it creates another issue by reducing competition in the prepaid cell phone segment. MetroPCS's low-cost, no-contract data plans and cheaper phones brought cellphones and mobile Internet to millions of Americans who could not afford major-carrier contracts. While T-Mobile announced the continuation of prepaid service, it has an incentive not to make it so attractive as to cause its own more profitable contract customers to shift to the prepaid service as their contracts expire. While T-Mobile also announced plans to develop a new high-speed network, it will be late to the game.

Some industries are more prone to increasing concentration because of their high capital needs. Only the largest and most financially viable can support the capital outlays required to support national telecom networks. While the U.S. Justice Department has sent a clear signal that mergers in highly concentrated industries are likely to be disallowed, it is probable that the U.S. cellular industry will become increasingly concentrated despite disallowing the AT&T/T-Mobile merger due to the highly capital-intensive nature of the business.

CHAPTER OVERVIEW

This chapter focuses on the key elements of selected federal and state regulations and their implications for M&As while providing only an overview of the

---

[1] Roaming agreements are arrangements between wireless companies to provide wireless service to each other's subscribers in areas where a carrier's coverage is spotty.

labyrinth of environmental, labor, benefit, and foreign laws that affect M&As. Table 2.1 provides a summary of applicable legislation. A review of this chapter is available (including practice questions and answers) in the file folder entitled Student Study Guide contained on the companion site to this book (http://book-site.elsevier.com/9780123854872).

TABLE 2.1   Laws Affecting M&A

Law	Intent
FEDERAL SECURITIES LAWS	
Securities Act (1933)	Prevents the public offering of securities without a registration statement; defines minimum data requirements and noncompliance penalties
Securities Exchange Act (1934)	Established the Securities and Exchange Commission (SEC) to regulate securities trading. Empowers the SEC to revoke the registration of a security if the issuer is in violation of any provision of the 1934 Act
Section 13	Defines content and frequency of SEC filings as well as events triggering them
Section 14	Defines disclosure requirements for proxy solicitation
Section 16(a)	Defines what insider trading is and who is an insider
Section 16(b)	Defines investor rights with respect to insider trading
Williams Act (1968)	Regulates tender offers
Section 13D	Defines disclosure requirements
Sarbanes-Oxley Act (2002)	Initiates reform of regulations governing financial disclosure, governance, auditing, analyst reports, and insider trading
FEDERAL ANTITRUST LAWS	
Sherman Act (1890)	Made "restraint of trade" illegal; establishes criminal penalties for behaviors that limit competition unreasonably
Section 1	Makes mergers creating monopolies illegal
Section 2	Applies to firms already dominant in their served markets to prevent them from "unfairly" restraining trade
Clayton Act (1914)	Outlawed such practices as price discrimination, exclusive contracts, and tie-in contracts, and created civil penalties for illegally restraining trade
Celler-Kefauver Act of 1950	Amended the Clayton Act to cover asset as well as stock purchases
Federal Trade Commission Act (1914)	Established a federal antitrust enforcement agency; made it illegal to engage in deceptive business practices

(Continued)

TABLE 2.1   (Continued)

Law	Intent
Hart-Scott-Rodino Antitrust Improvement Act (1976)	Requires a waiting period before a transaction can be completed, and sets regulatory data-submission requirements
Title I	Defines what must be filed
Title II	Defines who must file and when
Title III	Enables state attorneys general to file triple damage suits on behalf of injured parties

OTHER LEGISLATION AFFECTING M&AS

Law	Intent
Dodd-Frank Wall Street Reform and Consumer Protection Act (2010)	Reforms executive compensation; introduces new hedge/private equity fund registration requirements; increases Federal Reserve and SEC regulatory authority; gives the government authority to liquidate systemically risky firms; enables government regulation of consumer financial products; and makes it illegal for federal employees and regulators to engage in insider trading
State Antitakeover Laws	Define conditions under which a change in corporate ownership can take place; may differ by state
State Antitrust Laws	Similar to federal antitrust laws; states may sue to block mergers, even those not challenged by federal regulators
Exon-Florio Amendment to the Defense Protection Act of 1950	Establishes authority to review the impact of foreign direct investment (including M&As) on national security
U.S. Foreign Corrupt Practices Act	Prohibits payments to foreign government officials in exchange for obtaining new business or retaining existing contracts
Regulation FD (Fair Disclosure)	All material disclosures of nonpublic information made by public corporations must be disclosed to the general public
Industry-Specific Regulations	Banking, communications, railroads, defense, insurance, and public utilities
Environmental Laws (federal and state)	Define disclosure requirements
Labor and Benefit Laws (federal and state)	Define disclosure requirements
Applicable Foreign Laws	Cross-border transactions subject to jurisdictions of countries in which the bidder and target firms have operations

UNDERSTANDING FEDERAL SECURITIES LAWS

Whenever the acquirer or target is publicly traded, the firms are subject to the substantial reporting requirements of the current federal securities laws. Passed in the 1930s, these laws reflected the loss of confidence in the securities markets following the 1929 stock market crash.

Securities Act of 1933

This legislation requires that securities offered to the public be registered with the government to protect investors by making issuers disclose all material facts regarding the issue. Registration requires, but does not guarantee, that the facts represented in the registration statement and prospectus are accurate. The law makes providing inaccurate or misleading statements in the sale of securities to the public punishable with a fine, imprisonment, or both. The registration process requires a description of the company's properties and business, a description of the securities, information about management, and financial statements certified by public accountants.

Securities Exchange Act of 1934

The Securities Exchange Act extends disclosure requirements stipulated in the Securities Act of 1933 to include securities already trading (so-called seasoned or secondary issues) on the national exchanges. The Act also established the Securities and Exchange Commission (SEC), whose purpose is to protect investors from fraud by requiring full and accurate financial disclosure by firms offering stocks, bonds, and other securities to the public. In 1964, coverage was expanded to include securities traded on the Over-the-Counter (OTC) Market. The Act also covers proxy solicitations (i.e., mailings to shareholders requesting their vote on a particular issue) by a company or shareholders. The 2010 Dodd-Frank Wall Street Reform and Consumer Protections Act (Dodd-Frank Act) strengthened the SEC enforcement powers by allowing the commission to impose financial penalties against any person, rather than against just regulated entities.

Reporting Requirements

Companies required to file annual and other periodic reports with the SEC are those for which any of the following are true: The firm has assets of more than $10 million and whose securities are held by more than 499 shareholders; it is listed on any of the major U.S. or international stock exchanges; or its shares are quoted on the OTC Bulletin Board. Even if both parties to a transaction are privately owned, an M&A transaction is subject to federal securities laws if a portion of the purchase price is going to be financed by an initial public offering of securities.

Section 13: Periodic Reports

Form 10K documents the firm's financial activities during the preceding year. The four key financial statements that must be included are the income statement, the balance sheet, the statement of retained earnings, and the statement of cash flows. Form 10K also includes a relatively detailed description of the business, the markets served, major events and their impact on the business, key competitors, and competitive market conditions. Form 10Q is a highly succinct quarterly update of such information. If an acquisition or divestiture is deemed significant,[2] Form 8K must be submitted to the SEC within 15 days of the event. Form 8K describes the assets acquired or disposed, the type and amount of consideration (i.e., payment) given or received, and the identity of the person (or persons) for whom the assets were acquired. In an acquisition, Form 8K must also identify who is providing the funds used to finance the purchase and the financial statements of the acquired business.

Section 14: Proxy Solicitations

Where proxy contests deal with corporate control, the act requires materials containing the names and interests of all participants to be filed with the SEC in advance of voting to comply with disclosure requirements. If the deal involves either acquirer or target shareholder approval, any materials distributed to shareholders must conform to the SEC's rules for proxy materials.

Insider Trading Regulations

Insider trading involves individuals who buy or sell securities based on knowledge that is not available to the general public. Despite the recent success of high-profile cases such as the sentencing of Galleon hedge fund manager, Raj Rajaratnam, to 12 to 24 years in prison in 2011, there is widespread evidence that insider trading is rampant.[3] Historically, insider trading has been covered under the Securities and Exchange Act of 1934. Section 16(a) of the act defines "insiders" as corporate officers, directors, and any person owning 10% or more of any class of securities of a company. The Sarbanes-Oxley Act (SOA) of 2002 amended Section 16(a) of the 1934 act by requiring that insiders disclose changes in ownership within two business days of the transaction, with the SEC posting the filing on the Internet within one business day after the filing is received.

The SEC is responsible for investigating insider trading. Regulation 10b-5, issued by the SEC, prohibits the commission of fraud in relation to securities transactions. Regulation 14e-3 prohibits trading securities in connection with a tender offer based on information that is not available to the general public. Individuals found guilty of engaging in insider trading may be subject to substantial penalties and forfeiture of any profits.[4] In 2010, the Dodd-Frank Act granted the Commodity Futures Trading Commission authority to investigate insider trading in commodities used in interstate commerce and made it illegal

---

[2] Acquisitions and divestitures are usually deemed significant if the equity interest in the acquired assets or the amount paid or received exceeds 10% of the total book value of the assets of the registrant and its subsidiaries.

[3] Barrett et al., May 11, 2011

[4] According to the Insider Trading Sanctions Act of 1984, those convicted of engaging in insider trading are required to give back their illegal profits and to pay a penalty three times the amount of such profits. A 1988 U.S. Supreme Court ruling gives investors the right to claim damages from a firm that falsely denied it was involved in negotiations that subsequently resulted in a merger.

for federal employees to engage in insider trading. The Act also allows the SEC to compensate those providing original information on insider trading activities (so-called whistleblowers) up to 30% of the damages assessed in the successful prosecution of insider trading cases.

The effectiveness of insider trading legislation is limited, due to the difficulty in defining such activity. While the rate at which insiders buy target firm shares slows prior to takeover announcement dates, they reduce the pace at which they sell shares by even more, such that their actual holdings increase.[5] Such activity is most common in deals where there is less uncertainty about their completion, that is, friendly deals and those with a single bidder. The magnitude of the increase in the dollar value of insider share holdings is about 50% higher than levels normally found in the six months prior to announcement dates.[6]

Jumpstart Our Business Startups Act (JOBS Act)

Passed on April 12, 2012, the JOBS Act is intended to reduce reporting requirements for so-called "emerging companies," those with less than $1 billion in annual revenue in their most recent fiscal year and fewer than 2000 shareholders. To qualify for the lighter disclosure requirements, the firm must have issued new securities after December 8, 2011. For qualifying firms, the SEC requires only two years of audited financial statements in its IPO registration documents, a less detailed disclosure of executive compensation, and no requirement for Sarbanes-Oxley Act Section 404(b), which deals with internal controls and financial reporting.

The Williams Act: Regulation of Tender Offers

Passed in 1968, the Williams Act consists of a series of amendments to the Securities Act of 1934 intended to protect target shareholders from fast takeovers in which they do not have enough time to assess adequately the value of an acquirer's offer. This protection was achieved by requiring more disclosure by the bidding company, establishing a minimum period during which a tender offer must remain open, and authorizing targets to sue bidding firms. The disclosure requirements of the Williams Act apply to anyone, including the target, asking shareholders to accept or reject a takeover bid. The major sections of the Williams Act as they affect M&As are in Sections 13(D) and 14(D). The Williams Act requirements apply to all types of tender offers, including those negotiated with the target firm (i.e., negotiated or friendly tender offers), those undertaken

---

[5]If insiders normally buy 100 shares and sell 50 shares each month, the normal increase in their holdings would be 50. However, if their purchases drop to 90 and sales to 30 each month, their holdings rise by 60 shares.

[6]Agrawal and Nasser, 2012

by a firm to repurchase its own stock (i.e., self-tender offers), and those that are unwanted by the target firm (i.e., hostile tender offers).[7]

Sections 13(D) and 13(G): Ownership Disclosure Requirements

Section 13(D) of the Williams Act is intended to regulate "substantial share" or large acquisitions and provides an early warning for a target company's shareholders and management of a pending bid. Any person or firm acquiring 5% or more of the stock of a public firm must file a Schedule 13(D) with the SEC within 10 days of reaching that percentage threshold.[8] Section 13(D) also requires that derivatives, such as options, warrants, or rights convertible into shares within 60 days, must be included in determining whether the threshold has been reached. Schedule 13(D) requires the inclusion of the identities of the acquirer, their occupation and associations, sources of financing, and the purpose of the acquisition. If the purpose of buying the stock is to take control of the target firm, the acquirer must reveal its business plan for the target firm. The plans could include the breakup of the firm, suspending dividends, a recapitalization of the firm, or the intention to merge it with another firm. Otherwise, the purchaser of the stock could indicate that the accumulation was for investment purposes only.

Under Section 13(G), any stock accumulated by related parties, such as affiliates, brokers, or investment bankers working on behalf of the person or firm, are counted toward the 5% threshold. This prevents an acquirer from avoiding filing by accumulating more than 5% of the target's stock through a series of related parties. Institutional investors, such as registered brokers and dealers, banks, and insurance companies, can file a Schedule 13(G)—a shortened version of Schedule 13(D)—if the securities were acquired in the normal course of business.

Section 14(D): Rules Governing the Tender Offer Process

Although Section 14(D) of the Williams Act relates to public tender offers only, it applies to acquisitions of any size. The 5% notification threshold also applies.

Obligations of the Acquirer. An acquirer must disclose its intentions, business plans, and any agreements between the acquirer and the target firm in a Schedule 14(D)-1. The schedule is called a *tender offer statement*. The commencement date of the tender offer is defined as the date on which the tender offer is

---

[7]The Williams Act is vague as to what is a tender offer so as not to construe any purchase by one firm of another's shares in the open market as a tender offer. The courts have ruled that a tender offer is characterized by a bidder's announcing publicly the intent to purchase a substantial block of another firm's stock to gain control or the actual purchase of a substantial portion of another firm's shares in the open market or through a privately negotiated block purchase of the firm's shares.

[8]The permitted reporting delay allows for potential abuse of the disclosure requirement. In late 2010, activist hedge fund investor William Ackman and real estate company Vornado Realty Trust surprised Wall Street when they disclosed that they had acquired nearly 27% of megaretailer J.C. Penney's outstanding shares. Once the investors exceeded the 5% reporting threshold, they rapidly accumulated tens of millions of shares during the ensuing 10-day period, driving J.C. Penney's share price up 45%.

published, advertised, or submitted to the target. Schedule 14(D)-1 must contain the identity of the target company and the type of securities involved; the identity of the person, partnership, syndicate, or corporation that is filing; and any past contracts between the bidder and the target company. The schedule must also include the source of the funds used to finance the tender offer, its purpose, and any other information material to the transaction.

Obligations of the target firm. The management of the target company cannot advise its shareholders how to respond to a tender offer until it has filed a Schedule 14(D)-9 with the SEC within 10 days after the tender offer's commencement date. This schedule is called a *tender offer solicitation/recommendation statement*.

Shareholder rights: 14(D)-4 to 14(D)-7. The tender offer must be left open for a minimum of 20 trading days. The acquiring firm must accept all shares that are tendered during this period. The firm making the tender offer may get an extension of the 20-day period if it believes that there is a better chance of getting the shares it needs. The firm must purchase the shares tendered at the offer price, at least on a pro rata basis, unless the firm does not receive the total number of shares it requested under the tender offer. The tender offer may also be contingent on attaining the approval of the Department of Justice (DoJ) and the Federal Trade Commission (FTC). Shareholders have the right to withdraw shares tendered previously as long as the tender offer remains open. The law also requires that when a new bid for the target is made from another party, the target firm's shareholders must have an additional 10 days to consider the bid.

The "best price" rule: 14(D)-10. To avoid discrimination, the "best price" rule requires that all shareholders holding the same class of security be paid the same price in a tender offer. Consequently, if a bidder increases what it is offering to pay for the remaining target firm shares, it must pay the higher price to those who have already tendered their shares.

Court rulings in the mid-1990s indicated that executive compensation such as golden parachutes, retention bonuses, and accelerated vesting rights triggered whenever a change in control occurred should be counted as part of the compensation they received for their shares. These rulings significantly reduced the use of tender offers, due to concerns that all shareholders would have to receive payment for their shares comparable to what executives had received following a change in control. The "best price" rule was clarified on October 18, 2006, to exclude executive compensation following a change in control from the price paid for their shares. The rule changes make it clear that the "best price" rule applies only to the consideration (i.e., cash, securities, or both) offered and paid for securities tendered by shareholders.[9] This clarification contributed to the recovery in the use of

---

[9] Acquirers often initiate two-tiered tender offers, in which target shareholders receive a higher price if they tender their shares in the first tier than those submitting shares in the second tier. The "best price" rule simply means that all shareholders tendering their shares in the first tier must be paid the price offered for those shares in the first tier, and those tendering shares in the second tier are paid the price offered for second-tier shares unless precluded by state law.

tender offers in recent years. Having fallen to 3.2% of total deals in 2006, tender offers accounted for about one-fifth of deals in recent years.[10]

The Sarbanes-Oxley Act (SOA) of 2002

The SOA was signed in the wake of the egregious scandals at such corporate giants as Enron, MCI WorldCom, ImClone, Qwest, Adelphia, and Tyco and has implications ranging from financial disclosure to auditing practices to corporate governance. Section 302 of the act requires quarterly certification of financial statements and disclosure controls and procedures for CEOs and CFOs. Section 404 requires most public companies to certify annually that their internal control system is operating successfully. The legislation, in concert with new listing requirements at public stock exchanges, requires a greater number of directors on the board who do not work for the company (i.e., so-called independent directors). The act also requires board audit committees to have at least one financial expert, while the full committee must review financial statements every quarter after the CEO and chief financial officer certify them. The SOA also provides for greater transparency, or visibility into a firm's financial statements and greater accountability. However, the flagrant practices of some financial services firms (e.g., AIG, Bear Stearns, and Lehman Brothers) in recent years cast doubt on how effective the SOA has been in achieving its transparency and accountability objectives.

The costs associated with implementing the SOA have been substantial. As noted in a number of studies (see Chapter 13), there is growing evidence that the monitoring costs imposed by Sarbanes-Oxley have been a factor in many small firms' going private since the introduction of the legislation. The overall costs of corporate boards soared post-SOA due to sharply higher director compensation.[11] However, shareholders of large firms that are required to overhaul their existing governance systems under Sarbanes-Oxley may in some cases benefit as new shareholder protections are put in place.[12] Moreover, the run-up in target share prices before they are publicly announced has decreased significantly since the SOA's introduction, perhaps reflecting improved accountability and regulatory oversight of bidder managers and boards involved in deals.[13] To reduce some of SOA's negative effects, the SEC allowed foreign firms to avoid having to comply with the reporting requirements of the act.

New York Stock Exchange listing requirements far exceed the SOA's auditor-independence requirements. Companies must have board audit committees consisting of at least three independent directors and a written charter describing its

[10] Offenberg et al., 2012

[11] Link et al. (2009)

[12] Chaochharia and Grinstein (2007) conclude that large firms that are the least compliant with the rules around the announcement dates of certain rule implementations are more likely to display significantly positive abnormal financial returns. In contrast, small firms that are less compliant earn negative abnormal returns.

[13] Brigida and Madura, 2012

responsibilities in detail. Moreover, the majority of all board members must be independent, and nonmanagement directors must meet periodically without management. Board compensation and nominating committees must consist of independent directors. Shareholders must be able to vote on all stock option plans.

The SOA also created a quasi-public oversight agency, the Public Company Accounting Oversight Board (PCAOB). The PCAOB is charged with registering auditors, defining specific processes and procedures for compliance audits, quality control, and enforcing compliance with specific SOA mandates.

UNDERSTANDING ANTITRUST LEGISLATION

Federal antitrust laws exist to prevent individual corporations from assuming so much market power that they can limit their output and raise prices without concern for any significant competitor reaction. The DoJ and the FTC have the primary responsibility for enforcing federal antitrust laws. The FTC was established in the Federal Trade Commission Act of 1914 to enforce existing antitrust laws, such as the Sherman, Clayton, and Federal Trade Commission Acts.

National laws usually do not affect firms outside their domestic political boundaries. There are two exceptions: antitrust laws and laws applying to the bribery of foreign government officials.[14] Outside the United States, antitrust regulation laws are described as competitiveness laws, which are intended to minimize or eliminate anticompetitive behavior. The European Union antitrust regulators were able to thwart the attempted takeover of Honeywell by General Electric—two U.S. corporations with operations in the European Union. Remarkably, this occurred following the approval of the proposed takeover by U.S. antitrust authorities. The other exception, the Foreign Corrupt Practices Act, is discussed later in this chapter.

The Sherman Act

Passed in 1890, the Sherman Act makes illegal all contracts, combinations, and conspiracies that restrain trade "unreasonably." Examples include agreements to fix prices, rig bids, allocate customers among competitors, or monopolize any part of interstate commerce. Section I of the Sherman Act prohibits new business combinations resulting in monopolies or in a significant concentration of pricing power in a single firm. Section II applies to firms that already are dominant in their targeted markets. The act applies to all transactions and businesses involved in interstate commerce or, if the activities are local, all transactions and business "affecting" interstate commerce. Most states have comparable statutes.

The Clayton Act

Passed in 1914, the Clayton Act was created to outlaw certain practices not prohibited by the Sherman Act and to help government stop a monopoly before it

---

[14]Truitt, 2006

developed. Section 5 of the act made price discrimination between customers illegal, unless it could be justified by cost savings associated with bulk purchases. Tying of contracts—in which a firm refuses to sell certain important products to a customer unless the customer agrees to buy other products from the firm—was also prohibited. Section 7 prohibits one company from buying the stock of another company if their combination results in reduced competition. Interlocking directorates were also made illegal when the directors were on the boards of competing firms.

Unlike the Sherman Act, which contains criminal penalties, the Clayton Act is a civil statute. The Clayton Act allows private parties that were injured by the antitrust violation to sue in federal court for three times their actual damages. State attorneys general may also bring civil suits. If the plaintiff wins, the costs must be borne by the party that violated the prevailing antitrust law, in addition to the criminal penalties imposed under the Sherman Act. Acquirers soon learned how to circumvent the original statutes of the Clayton Act of 1914, which applied to the purchase of stock. They simply would acquire the assets, rather than the stock, of a target firm. In the Celler-Kefauver Act of 1950, the Clayton Act was amended to give the FTC the power to prohibit asset as well as stock purchases.

The Federal Trade Commission Act of 1914

This act created the FTC, consisting of five full-time commissioners appointed by the president for a seven-year term and supported by a staff of economists, lawyers, and accountants to assist in the enforcement of antitrust laws.

The Hart-Scott-Rodino (HSR) Antitrust Improvements Act of 1976

Acquisitions involving companies of a certain size cannot be completed until certain information is supplied to the federal government and a specified waiting period has elapsed. The premerger notification allows the FTC and the DoJ sufficient time to challenge acquisitions believed to be anticompetitive before they are completed. Once the merger has taken place, it is often difficult to break it up. Table 2.2 provides a summary of prenotification filing requirements.

Title I: What Must Be Filed?

Title I of the act gives the DoJ the power to request internal corporate records if it suspects potential antitrust violations. Information requirements include background data on the "ultimate parent entity"[15] of the acquiring and target parents, a description of the deal, and all background studies relating to the transaction.

Title II: Who Must File and When?

Title II addresses the conditions under which filings must take place. As of January 10, 2013, to comply with the size-of-transaction test, transactions in which the buyer purchases voting securities or assets valued in excess of $70.9 million

---

[15]The ultimate parent entity is the firm at the top of the chain of ownership if the actual buyer is a subsidiary.

TABLE 2.2   Regulatory Prenotification Filing Requirements.

	Williams Act	**Hart-Scott-Rodino Act**
Required filing	1. Schedule 13(D) within 10 days of acquiring 5% stock ownership in another firm 2. Ownership includes stock held by affiliates or agents of the bidder 3. Schedule 14(D)-1 for tender offers 4. Disclosure required even if 5% accumulation not followed by a tender offer	HSR filing is necessary when:[a] 1. Size-of-transaction test: The buyer purchases assets or securities > $70.9 million or 2. Size-of-person test:[b] Buyer or seller has annual sales or assets ≥ $141.8 million and any other party has sales or assets ≥ $14.2 million 3. If the acquisition value > $283.6, a filing is required regardless of whether (2) is met. Thresholds in (1) to (3) are adjusted annually by the increase in gross domestic product.
File with whom	Schedule 13(D) 1. 6 copies to SEC 2. 1 copy via registered mail to target's executive office 3. 1 copy via registered mail to each public exchange on which target stock is traded Schedule 14(D)-1 1. 10 copies to SEC 2. 1 copy hand-delivered to target's executive offices 3. 1 copy hand-delivered to other bidders 4. 1 copy mailed to each public exchange on which the target stock is traded (each exchange must also be phoned)	1. Premerger Notification Office of the Federal Trade Commission 2. Director of Operations of the DoJ Antitrust Division
Time period	1. Tender offers must stay open a minimum of 20 business days 2. Begins on date of publication, advertisement, or submission of materials to target 3. Unless the tender offer has been closed, shareholders may withdraw tendered shares up to 60 days after the initial offer	1. Review/waiting period: 30 days (15 days for cash tender offers) 2. Target must file within 15 days of bidder's filing 3. Period begins for all cash offers when bidder files; for cash/stock bids, period begins when both bidder and target have filed 4. Regulators can request a 20-day extension

[a]Note that these are the thresholds as of January 10, 2013.
[b]The "size of person" test measures the size of the "ultimate parent entity" of the buyer and seller. The ultimate parent entity is the entity that controls the buyer and seller and is not itself controlled by anyone else.

must be reported under the HSR Act. However, according to the size-of-person (a reference to the acquirer and target firms) test, transactions valued at less than this figure may still require filing if the acquirer or the target firm has annual net sales or total assets of at least $141.8 million and the other party has annual net sales or total assets of at least $14.2 million. These thresholds are adjusted upward by the annual rate of increase in gross domestic product. A filing is required if the transaction value exceeds $283.6 without regard to whether the size-of-person test is met.

Bidding firms must execute an HSR filing at the same time as they make an offer to a target firm. The target firm is also required to file within 15 days following the bidder's filing. Filings consist of information on the operations of the two companies and their financial statements. The waiting period begins when both the acquirer and the target have filed. Either the FTC or the DoJ may request a 20-day extension of the waiting period for transactions involving securities and 10 days for cash tender offers. If the acquiring firm believes there is little likelihood of anticompetitive effects, it can request early termination. In practice, only about 20% of transactions require HSR filings; of these only about 4% are challenged by the regulators.[16]

If the regulatory authorities suspect anticompetitive effects, they will file a lawsuit to obtain a court injunction to prevent completion of the proposed transaction. Although it is rare for either the bidder or the target to contest the lawsuit, because of the expense involved, and even rarer for the government to lose, it does happen.[17] If fully litigated, a government lawsuit can result in substantial legal expenses as well as a significant cost in management time. Even if the FTC's lawsuit is overturned, the benefits of the merger often have disappeared by the time the lawsuit has been decided. Potential customers and suppliers are less likely to sign lengthy contracts with the target firm during the period of trial. New investment in the target is likely to be limited, and employees and communities where the target's operations are located would be subject to uncertainty. For these reasons, both regulators and acquirers often seek to avoid litigation.

How Does HSR Affect State Antitrust Regulators?

Title III expands the powers of state attorneys general to initiate triple-damage suits on behalf of individuals in their states injured by violations of the antitrust laws.

---

[16] In 2007, there were 2,201 HSR filings with the FTC (about 20% of total transactions), compared to 1,768 in 2006 (Barnett, 2008). Of these, about 4% typically are challenged and about 2% require second requests for information (Lindell, 2006). About 97% of the 37,701 M&A deals filed with the FTC between 1991 and 2004 were approved without further scrutiny (BusinessWeek, 2008).

[17] Regulators filed a suit on February 27, 2004, to block Oracle's $26-per-share hostile bid for PeopleSoft on antitrust grounds. On September 9, 2004, a U.S. District Court judge denied a request by U.S. antitrust authorities that he issue an injunction against the deal, arguing that the government failed to prove that large businesses can turn to only three suppliers (i.e., Oracle, PeopleSoft, and SAP) for business applications software.

Procedural Rules

When the DoJ files an antitrust suit, it is adjudicated in the federal court system. When the FTC initiates the action, it is heard before an administrative law judge at the FTC, whose ruling is subject to review by FTC commissioners. Criminal actions are reserved for the DoJ, which may seek fines or imprisonment for violators. Individuals and companies may also file antitrust lawsuits. The FTC reviews complaints that have been recommended by its staff and approved by the commission. The commission then votes whether to accept or reject the hearing examiner's findings. The decision of the commission then can be appealed in the federal circuit courts. As an alternative to litigation, a company may seek to negotiate a voluntary settlement of its differences with the FTC. Such settlements usually are negotiated during the review process and are called consent decrees. The FTC then files a complaint in the federal court along with the proposed consent decree. The federal court judge routinely approves the consent decree.

The Consent Decree

A typical consent decree may consist of both structural and behavioral remedies. Structural remedies generally require the merging parties to divest overlapping businesses. In late 2011, VeriFone Systems, the second-largest maker of electronic payment systems in the United States, reached a settlement with the U.S. Justice Department to acquire competitor Hypercom Corp on the condition it sold Hypercom's U.S. point-of-sale terminal business. Without the sale, the combined firms would control more than 60% of the U.S. market for terminals used by retailers. The regulators reasoned the sale would create a significant independent competitor. Behavioral remedies require the combining firms to agree to adopt a set of practices designed to lessen potentially anticompetitive policies. As a condition of approving the January 2011 acquisition of NBC Universal (NBCU) by Comcast, Comcast agreed to arbitrate disputes with other cable systems concerning their access to NBCU's cable channels. In addition, Comcast assured regulators that it would adhere to so-called "net neutrality" conditions by licensing its content to competing Internet sites at competitive rates.

If a potential acquisition is likely to be challenged by the regulatory authorities, an acquirer may seek to negotiate a consent decree in advance of the deal. In the absence of a consent decree, a buyer often requires that an agreement of purchase and sale must include a provision that allows the acquirer to back out of the transaction if it is challenged by the FTC or the DoJ on antitrust grounds. There is evidence that consent decrees to limit potential increases in business pricing power following a merger have proven successful by creating viable competitors.[18]

---

[18] In a report evaluating the results of 35 divestiture orders entered between 1990 and 1994, the FTC concluded that the use of consent decrees to limit market power resulting from a business combination has proven to be successful by creating viable competitors (Federal Trade Commission, 1999b).

Antitrust Merger Guidelines for Horizontal Mergers

Understanding an industry begins with understanding its market structure. Market structure may be defined in terms of the number of firms in an industry; their concentration, cost, demand, and technological conditions; and ease of entry and exit. Intended to clarify the provisions of the Sherman and Clayton Acts, the DoJ issued largely quantitative guidelines in 1968, presented in terms of specific market share percentages and concentration ratios, indicating the types of M&As it would oppose. Concentration ratios were defined in terms of the market shares of the industry's top four or eight firms. Because of their rigidity, the guidelines have been revised to reflect the role of both quantitative and qualitative data. Qualitative data include factors such as the enhanced efficiency that might result from a combination of firms, the financial viability of potential merger candidates, and the ability of U.S. firms to compete globally.

In 1992, both the FTC and the DoJ announced a new set of guidelines indicating that they would challenge mergers creating or enhancing market power, even if there are measurable efficiency benefits. *Market power* is defined as a situation in which the combined firms will be able profitably to maintain prices above competitive levels for a significant period. The 1992 guidelines were revised in 1997 to reflect the regulatory authorities' willingness to recognize that improvements in efficiency over the long term could more than offset the effects of increases in market power. On August 19, 2010, the guidelines were updated to give regulators more leeway to challenge mergers than previously. However, they also raised the thresholds for determining if a merger would cause anticompetitive concentration.

The 2010 guidelines express a clear commitment to more aggressive horizontal-merger enforcement, rely much less on formulas than the earlier guidelines, and reflect heightened concern about unilateral effects (i.e., firms achieving such market power that they can unilaterally raise prices above competitive levels). The new guidelines also closely resemble the European Union's antitrust guidelines.[19] In general, horizontal mergers are most likely to be challenged by regulators. Vertical mergers—those involving customer–supplier relationships—are considered much less likely to result in anticompetitive effects, unless they deprive other firms access to an important resource. As part of the review process, regulators consider customers and the prospect for price discrimination, market definition, market share and concentration, unilateral effects, coordinated effects, ease of entry, realized efficiencies, potential for business failure, and partial acquisitions. These factors are considered next.

Targeted Customers and the Potential for Price Discrimination

Price discrimination occurs when sellers can improve profits by raising prices to some targeted customers but not to others. For such discrimination to exist there must be evidence that certain customers are charged higher prices even

[19]Horton, 2011

though the cost of doing business with them is no higher than selling to other customers, who are charged lower prices. Furthermore, customers charged higher prices must have few alternative sources of supply.

Market Definition

Markets are defined by regulators solely in terms of the customers' ability and willingness to substitute one product for another in response to a price increase. The market may be geographically defined, with scope limited by such factors as transportation costs, tariff and nontariff barriers, exchange rate volatility, and so on.

Market Share and Concentration

The number of firms in the market and their respective market shares determine market concentration. Such ratios measure how much of the total output of an industry is produced by the "n" largest firms in the industry. To account for the distribution of firm size in an industry, the FTC measures concentration using the Herfindahl-Hirschman Index (HHI), which is calculated by summing the squares of the market shares for each firm competing in the market. For example, a market consisting of five firms with market shares of 30, 25, 20, 15, and 10%, respectively, would have an HHI of 2,250 ($30^2 + 25^2 + 20^2 + 15^2 + 10^2$). Note that an industry consisting of five competitors with market shares of 70, 10, 5, 5, and 5%, respectively, will have a much higher HHI score of 5075, because the process of squaring the market shares gives the greatest weight to the firm with the largest market shares.

The HHI ranges from 10,000 for an almost pure monopoly to approximately 0 in the case of a highly competitive market. The index gives more weight to the market shares of larger firms to reflect their relatively greater pricing power. The FTC developed a scoring system, described in Figure 2.1, as one factor in determining if the FTC will challenge a proposed deal.

Unilateral Effects

A merger between two firms selling differentiated products may reduce competition by enabling the merged firms to profit by unilaterally raising the price of

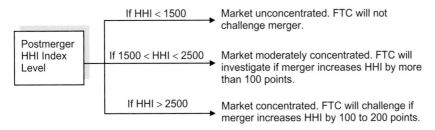

FIGURE 2.1 FTC actions at various market share concentration levels. HHI, Herfindahl-Hirschman Index. *Source: FTC Merger Guidelines, www.ftc.gov.*

one or both products above the premerger level. Further, a merger between two competing sellers prevents buyers from negotiating lower prices by playing one seller against the other. Finally, in markets involving undifferentiated products, a firm, having merged with a large competitor, may restrict output in order to raise prices.

Coordinated Effects

After a merger with a competitor, a firm may coordinate its output and pricing decisions with the remaining firms in the industry. Such actions could include a simple understanding of what a firm would do or not do under certain circumstances. If the firm with dominant market share were to reduce output, others may follow suit, with the implied intent of raising product prices.

Ease of Entry

Ease of entry is defined as entry that would be timely, likely to occur, and sufficient to counter the competitive effects of a combination of firms that temporarily increases market concentration. Barriers to entry—such as proprietary technology or knowledge, patents, government regulations, exclusive ownership of natural resources, or huge investment requirements—can limit the number of new competitors that enter a market. Excessive entry barriers may hinder innovation because of a reduced need to do so due to the limited threat of competition.[20] However, defining what is excessive is highly subjective.

Efficiencies

Increases in efficiency that result from a merger or acquisition can enhance the combined firms' ability to compete and result in lower prices, improved quality, better service, or innovation. However, efficiencies are difficult to measure and verify, because they will be realized only after the merger has taken place. An example of verifiable efficiency improvements would be a reduction in the average fixed cost per unit of output due to economies of scale.

Alternative to Imminent Failure

Regulators also consider the likelihood that a firm would fail if not allowed to merge with another firm. The regulators must weigh the potential cost of the failing firm, such as a loss of jobs, against any potential increase in market power resulting from a merger.

Partial Acquisitions

Regulators may also review acquisitions of minority positions involving competing firms if it is determined that the partial acquisition results in the effective control of the target firm. A partial acquisition can lessen competition by giving the acquirer the ability to influence the competitive conduct of the target firm, in that the acquirer may have the right to appoint members of the board of

[20] Park and Sonenshine, 2012

directors. Furthermore, the minority investment may also blunt competition if the acquirer gains access to non–publicly available competitive information.

Antitrust Guidelines for Vertical Mergers

Vertical mergers may become a concern if an acquisition by a supplier of a customer prevents the supplier's competitors from having access to the customer. Alternatively, the acquisition by a customer of a supplier could become a concern if it prevents the customer's competitors from having access to the supplier. Vertical mergers are more likely to result in regulatory review when firms that are dominant in their respective markets integrate vertically.[21]

Antitrust Guidelines for Collaborative Efforts

Collaborative efforts are horizontal agreements among competitors, including joint ventures, strategic alliances, and other competitor agreements. Regulators are less likely to find a collaborative effort to be anticompetitive if (1) the participants have continued to compete through separate, independent operations or through participation in other collaborative efforts; (2) the financial interest in the effort by each participant is relatively small; (3) each participant's ability to control the effort is limited; (4) effective safeguards prevent information sharing; and (5) the duration of the collaborative effort is short.

THE IMPLICATIONS FOR M&A OF THE DODD-FRANK WALL STREET REFORM AND CONSUMER PROTECTION ACT

Comprehensive in scope, the Dodd-Frank Act (the Act) substantially changed federal regulation of financial services firms as well as some nonfinancial public companies. The Act's objectives include restoring public confidence in the financial system and preventing future financial crises that threaten the viability of financial markets. Its provisions range from giving shareholders a say on executive compensation to greater transparency in the derivatives markets to new powers granted to the Federal Deposit Insurance Corporation (FDIC) to liquidate financial firms whose failure would threaten the U.S. financial system (i.e., systemic risk).

While the implications of the legislation are far reaching, the focus in this book is on those aspects of the Act impacting corporate governance directly; the environment in which M&As and other restructuring activities take place; and participants in the restructuring process. The Act's provisions having the greatest impact on the subject matter addressed in this book are summarized in Table 2.3 according to the categories *governance and executive compensation, systemic regulation and emergency powers, capital markets*, and *financial institutions*. These provisions are discussed in more detail in the chapters in which they are most applicable.

[21] Kedia et al., 2011

TABLE 2.3   Selected Dodd-Frank Act Provisions

Provision	Requirements
GOVERNANCE AND EXECUTIVE COMPENSATION[a]	
Say-on-Pay	In a nonbinding vote on the board, shareholders may vote on executive compensation packages every two or three years.
Say on Golden Parachutes	Proxy statements seeking shareholder approval of acquisitions, mergers, or sale of substantially all of the company's assets must disclose any agreements with executive officers of the target or acquiring firm with regard to present, deferred, or contingent compensation.
Institutional Investor Disclosure	Institutional managers (e.g., mutual funds, pension funds) must disclose annually their position on pay and on golden parachutes voting records.
Clawbacks	Public companies are required to develop and disclose mechanisms for recovering incentive-based compensation paid during the three years prior to earnings restatements.
Broker Discretionary Voting	Public stock exchanges are required to prohibit brokers from voting shares without direction from owners in the election of directors, executive compensation, or any other significant matter as determined by the SEC.
Compensation Committee Independence	SEC to define rules requiring stock exchanges to prohibit listing any issuer that does not comply with independence requirements governing compensation of committee members and consultants.
SYSTEMIC REGULATION AND EMERGENCY POWERS	
Financial Stability Oversight Council	To mitigate systemic risk, the Council, which consists of ten voting members and is chaired by the Secretary of the Treasury, monitors U.S. financial markets to identify domestic or foreign banks and some nonbank firms whose default or bankruptcy would risk the financial stability of the United States.
New Federal Reserve (Fed) Bank and Nonbank Holding Company Supervision Requirements	Bank and nonbank holding companies with consolidated assets exceeding $50 billion must: • Submit plans for their rapid and orderly dissolution in the event of failure • Provide periodic reports about the nature of their credit exposure. Limit their credit exposure to any unaffiliated company to 25% of its capital • Conduct semiannual "stress tests" to determine capital adequacy • Provide advance notice of intent to purchase voting shares in financial services firms
Limitations on Leverage	For bank holding companies whose assets exceed $50 billion, the Fed may require the firm to maintain a debt-to-equity ratio of no more than 15-to-1.
Limits on Size	The size of any single bank cannot exceed 10% of deposits nationwide. The limitation does not apply for mergers involving troubled banks.
Capital Requirements	Bank capital requirements are to be left to the regulatory agencies and should reflect the perceived risk of bank or nonbank institutions.
Savings and Loan Regulations	Fed gains supervisory authority over all savings and loan holding companies and their subsidiaries.

(Continued)

TABLE 2.3   (Continued)

Provision	Requirements
Federal Deposit Insurance Corporation (FDIC)	The FDIC may guarantee obligations of solvent insured depository institutions if the Fed and the Systemic Risk Council determine that financial markets are illiquid (i.e., investors cannot sell assets without incurring an unusual and significant loss).
Orderly Liquidation Authority	The FDIC may seize and liquidate a financial services firm whose failure threatens the financial stability of the United States, to ensure the speedy disposition of the firm's assets and to ensure that losses are borne by shareholders and bondholders while losses of public funds are limited.[b]

CAPITAL MARKETS

Provision	Requirements
Office of Credit Ratings	Proposes rules for internal controls, independence, transparency, and penalties for poor performance, making it easier for investors to sue for "unrealistic" ratings. Office to conduct annual audits of rating agencies.
Securitization	Issuers of asset-backed securities must retain an interest of at least 5% of any security sold to third parties.
Hedge and Private Equity Fund Registration	Advisers to private equity and hedge funds with $100 million or more in assets under management must register with the SEC as investment advisers; those with less than $100 million will be subject to state registration. Registered advisors to provide reports and be subject to periodic examinations.
Clearing and Trading of Over-the-Counter (OTC) Derivatives	Commodity Futures Trading Commission (CFTC) and SEC to mandate central clearing of certain OTC derivatives on a central exchange and the real-time public reporting of volume and pricing data as well as the parties to the transaction.

FINANCIAL INSTITUTIONS

Provision	Requirements
Volcker Rule	Prohibits insured depository institutions and their holding companies from buying and selling securities with their own money (so-called proprietary trading) or sponsoring or investing in hedge funds or private equity funds. Underwriting and market-making activities are exempt. Proprietary trading may occur outside the United States as long as the bank does not own or control the entity. *Sponsoring private funds* is defined as serving as a general partner or in some way gaining control of such funds.
Consumer Financial Protection Bureau	Creates an agency to write rules governing all financial institutions offering consumer financial products, including banks, mortgage lenders, and credit card companies as well as pay day lenders. The authority will apply to banks and credit unions with assets over $10 billion and all mortgage-related businesses. While institutions with less than $10 billion will have to comply, they will be supervised by their current regulators.
Federal Insurance Office	Monitors all aspects of the insurance industry (other than health insurance and long-term care), coordinates international insurance matters, consults with states regarding insurance issues of national importance, and recommends insurers that should be treated as systemically important.

[a]*See Chapter 3 for more details.*
[b]*See Chapter 17 for more details.*

STATE REGULATIONS AFFECTING MERGERS AND ACQUISITIONS

State regulations affecting takeovers often differ from one state to another, making compliance with all applicable regulations a challenge.

State Antitakeover Laws

With almost one-half of U.S. companies incorporated in Delaware, Delaware corporate law has a substantial influence on publicly traded firms. Delaware corporate law generally defers to the judgment of business managers and board directors in accordance with the "business judgment rule," except in change-of-control situations. In takeover situations, managers are subject to an enhanced business judgment test. This requires a target board to show that there are reasonable grounds to believe that a danger to corporate viability exists and that the adoption of certain defensive measures is reasonable. While Delaware law is the norm for many companies, firms incorporated in other states are often subject to corporate law that may differ significantly from Delaware law. What follows is a discussion of commonalities across the states.

States regulate corporate charters. *Corporate charters* define the powers of the firm and the rights and responsibilities of its shareholders, boards of directors, and managers. However, states are not allowed to pass any laws that impose restrictions on interstate commerce or conflict in any way with federal laws. State laws affecting M&As tend to apply only to firms incorporated in the state or that conduct a substantial amount of their business within the state. These laws often contain *fair price provisions*, requiring that all target shareholders of a successful tender offer receive the same price as those tendering their shares. In an attempt to prevent highly leveraged transactions, some state laws include *business combination provisions*, which may specifically rule out the sale of the target's assets for a specific period. By precluding such actions, these provisions limit LBOs from using asset sales to reduce indebtedness.

Other common characteristics of state antitakeover laws include cash-out and control-share provisions. *Cash-out provisions* require a bidder whose purchases of stock exceed a stipulated amount to buy the remainder of the target stock on the same terms granted to those shareholders whose stock was purchased at an earlier date. By forcing the acquiring firm to purchase 100% of the stock, potential bidders lacking substantial financial resources effectively are eliminated from bidding on the target. *Share-control provisions* require that a bidder obtain prior approval from stockholders holding large blocks of target stock once the bidder's purchases of stock exceed some threshold level. The latter provision can be troublesome to an acquiring company when the holders of the large blocks of stock tend to support target management.

State Antitrust and Securities Laws

As part of the Hart-Scott-Rodino Act of 1976, the states were granted increased antitrust power. The state laws are often similar to federal laws. Under federal law, states have the right to sue to block mergers, even if the DoJ or FTC does not challenge them. State "blue sky" laws are designed to protect individuals from investing in fraudulent security offerings. State restrictions can be more onerous than federal ones. An issuer seeking exemption from federal registration will not be exempt from all relevant registration requirements until a state-by-state exemption has been received from all states in which the issuer and offerees reside.

RESTRICTIONS ON DIRECT FOREIGN INVESTMENT IN THE UNITED STATES

The Committee on Foreign Investment in the United States (CFIUS) operates under the authority granted by Congress in the Exon-Florio amendment (Section 721 of the Defense Production Act of 1950). CFIUS includes representatives from many government agencies to ensure that all national security issues are identified and considered in the review of foreign acquisitions of U.S. businesses. The president can block the acquisition of a U.S. corporation based on recommendations made by CFIUS if there is credible evidence that the foreign entity exercising control might take action that threatens national security.[22]

THE U.S. FOREIGN CORRUPT PRACTICES ACT

The Foreign Corrupt Practices Act prohibits individuals, firms, and foreign subsidiaries of U.S. firms from paying anything of value to foreign government officials in exchange for obtaining new business or retaining existing contracts. Even though many nations have laws prohibiting bribery of public officials, enforcement tends to be lax. Of the 38 countries that signed the 1997 Anti-Bribery Convention of the Organization for Economic Cooperation and Development, more than one-half of the signatories have little or no enforcement mechanisms for preventing the bribery of foreign officials, according to a 2010 study by Transparency International. The U.S. law permits "facilitation payments" to foreign government officials if relatively small amounts of money are required to expedite goods through foreign custom inspections or to gain

---

[22] In 2008, CFIUS was amended to cover investments involving critical infrastructure. The intention is to cover cross-border transactions involving energy, technology, shipping, and transportation. Some argue that it may also apply to large U.S. financial institutions, in that they represent an important component of the U.S. monetary system.

approval for exports. Such payments are considered legal according to U.S. law and the laws of countries in which such payments are considered routine.[23]

FAIR DISCLOSURE (REGULATION FD)

The U.S. Securities and Exchange Commission adopted this regulation on August 15, 2000, to address concerns about the selective release of information by publicly traded firms. The rule aims to promote full and fair disclosure. Regulation FD requires that a publicly traded firm that discloses material nonpublic information to certain parties, such as stock analysts and individual shareholders, must release that information to the general public.

Rather than less information about stock prices provided by managers concerned about litigation, there are indications that there has been an increase in voluntary disclosure following the adoption of Regulation FD. In theory, an increase in the availability of such information should reduce earnings' "surprises" and lower stock price volatility. However, studies provide conflicting results, with one study reporting an increase in share price volatility and another showing no change following the implementation of Regulation FD.[24]

Consistent with the trend toward increased voluntary disclosure of information, the fraction of U.S. acquirers disclosing synergy estimates when announcing a deal has increased from 7% in 1995 to 27% of total transactions in 2008, with much of the increase coming since the introduction of Regulation FD. Some researchers argue that public disclosure of synergy can help the acquirer communicate the potential value of the deal to investors lacking the same level of information available to the firm's board and management, enabling investors to make more informed decisions.[25] Others contend that disclosing such information is self-serving, since it helps the acquirer's board and management gain shareholder support for the transaction.[26]

SPECIFIC INDUSTRY REGULATIONS

In addition to the DoJ and the FTC, a variety of other agencies monitor activities (including M&As) in certain industries, such as commercial banking, railroads, defense, and cable TV.

---

[23] Truitt, 2006

[24] All studies show an increase in voluntary disclosure by firms (e.g., Heflin et al., 2003; Bailey et al., 2003; and Dutordoir et al., 2010). However, Bailey et al. (2003) reports an increase in the variation of analysts' forecasts but no change in the volatility of share prices following the introduction of Regulation FD. In contrast, Heflin et al. (2003) finds no change in the variation of analysts' forecast but a decrease in share price volatility.

[25] Dutordoir et al., 2010

[26] Ismail, 2011

Banking

Currently, three agencies review banking mergers. The Office of the Comptroller of the Currency has responsibility for transactions in which the acquirer is a national bank. The FDIC oversees mergers where the acquiring bank or the bank resulting from combining the acquirer and the target will be a federally insured state-chartered bank that operates outside the Federal Reserve System. The third agency is the Board of Governors of the Federal Reserve System (the Fed). It has the authority to regulate mergers in which the acquirer or the resulting bank will be a state bank that is also a member of the Federal Reserve System.

The Dodd-Frank legislation eliminated the Office of Thrift Supervision and transferred the responsibility for regulating savings and loan associations, credit unions, and savings banks (collectively referred to as *thrift institutions*) to other regulators. Specifically, the Fed will supervise savings and loan holding companies and their subsidiaries; the FDIC will gain supervisory authority of all state savings banks; and the Office of the Comptroller of the Currency will supervise all federal savings banks.

M&A transactions involving financial institutions resulting in substantial additional leverage or in increased industry concentration will also come under the scrutiny of the Financial Stability Oversight Council created by the Dodd-Frank Act to monitor systemic risk. The council is empowered, among other things, to limit bank holding companies with $50 billion or more in assets or a nonbank financial company that is regulated by the Federal Reserve from merging with, acquiring, or consolidating with another firm. The council may require the holding company to divest certain assets if the company is deemed to constitute a threat to the financial stability of U.S. financial markets. Under the new legislation, the size of any single bank or nonbank cannot exceed 10% of deposits nationwide. However, this constraint may be relaxed for mergers involving failing banks.

Communications

The Federal Communications Commission (FCC) is charged with regulating interstate and international communication by radio, television, wire, satellite, and cable. The FCC is responsible for the enforcement of such legislation as the Telecommunications Act of 1996, intended to reduce regulation while promoting lower prices and higher-quality services.

Railroads

The Surface Transportation Board (STB), the successor to the Interstate Commerce Commission (ICC), governs mergers of railroads. Under the ICC Termination Act of 1995, the STB determines if a merger should be approved by assessing the impact on public transportation, the areas currently served by the carriers involved in the proposed transaction, and the burden of the total fixed charges resulting from completing the transaction.

Defense

During the 1990s, the U.S. defense industry underwent consolidation, consistent with the Department of Defense's (DoD's) philosophy that it is preferable to have three or four highly viable defense contractors than a dozen weaker firms. Although defense industry mergers are technically subject to current antitrust regulations, the DoJ and FTC have assumed a secondary role to the DoD. As noted previously, efforts by a foreign entity to acquire national security–related assets must be reviewed by the Council on Foreign Investment in the United States.

Other Regulated Industries

Historically, the insurance industry was regulated largely at the state level. Under the Dodd-Frank Act, the Federal Insurance Office was created within the U.S. Treasury to monitor all non-healthcare-related aspects of the insurance industry. As a "systemic" regulator, its approval will be required for all acquisitions of insurance companies whose size and interlocking business relationships could have repercussions on the U.S. financial system. The acquisition of more than 10% of a U.S. airline's shares outstanding is subject to approval of the Federal Aviation Administration. Public utilities are highly regulated at the state level. Like insurance companies, their acquisition requires state government approval.

ENVIRONMENTAL LAWS

Failure to comply adequately with environmental laws can result in enormous potential liabilities to all parties involved in a transaction. These laws require full disclosure of the existence of hazardous materials and the extent to which they are being released into the environment. Such laws include the Clean Water Act (1974), the Toxic Substances Control Act of 1978, the Resource Conservation and Recovery Act (1976), and the Comprehensive Environmental Response, Compensation, and Liability Act (Superfund) of 1980. Additional reporting requirements were imposed in 1986 with the passage of the Emergency Planning and Community Right to Know Act (EPCRA). In addition to EPCRA, several states also passed "right-to-know" laws, such as California's Proposition 65.

LABOR AND BENEFIT LAWS

A diligent buyer must also ensure that the target is in compliance with the labyrinth of labor and benefit laws. These laws govern such areas as employment discrimination, immigration law, sexual harassment, age discrimination, drug testing, and wage and hour laws. Labor and benefit laws include the

Family Medical Leave Act, the Americans with Disabilities Act, and the Worker Adjustment and Retraining Notification Act (WARN). WARN governs notification before plant closures and requirements to retrain workers.

Employee benefit plans frequently represent one of the biggest areas of liability to a buyer. The greatest potential liabilities are often found in defined pension benefit plans, postretirement medical plans, life insurance benefits, and deferred compensation plans. Such liabilities arise when the reserve shown on the seller's balance sheet does not accurately indicate the true extent of the future liability. The potential liability from improperly structured benefit plans grows with each new round of legislation, starting with the passage of the Employee Retirement Income and Security Act of 1974. Laws affecting employee retirement and pensions were strengthened by additional legislation, including the Multi-Employer Pension Plan Amendments Act of 1980, the Retirement Equity Act of 1984, the Single Employer Pension Plan Amendments Act of 1986, the Tax Reform Act of 1986, and the Omnibus Budget Reconciliation acts of 1987, 1989, 1990, and 1993. Buyers and sellers must also be aware of the Unemployment Compensation Act of 1992, the Retirement Protection Act of 1994, and Statements 87, 88, and 106 of the Financial Accounting Standards Board.[27]

The Pension Protection Act of 2006 places a potentially increasing burden on acquirers of targets with underfunded pension plans. The legislation requires employers with defined benefit plans to make sufficient contributions to meet a 100% funding target and erase funding shortfalls over seven years. Furthermore, the legislation requires employers with so-called "at-risk" plans to accelerate contributions. At-risk plans are those whose pension fund assets cover less than 70% of future pension obligations.

CROSS-BORDER TRANSACTIONS

Transactions involving firms in different countries are complicated by having to deal with multiple regulatory jurisdictions in specific countries or regions, such as the European Union. More antitrust agencies mean more international scrutiny, potentially conflicting philosophies, and substantially longer delays in completing all types of business combinations. According to the International Competition Network (ICN), an organization of competition regulators around the globe, efforts to harmonize international antitrust review processes have been mixed. By 2011, 87 of the ICN's members had merger-control laws in place, but most conflict with some aspect of the ICN recommendations.[28] Antitrust law can also restrict the formation of other types of business combinations, such as joint ventures, when the resulting entity is viewed as limiting competition. Despite the potential for huge cost savings, regulators would not approve the creation of a mammoth joint venture (JV) between BHP Billiton and Rio Tinto in 2010.

[27] Sherman, 2006
[28] *The Deal*, May 2011, p. 30

SOME THINGS TO REMEMBER

Current laws require that securities offered to the public must be registered with the government and that target firm shareholders receive enough information and time to assess adequately the value of an acquirer's offer. Federal antitrust laws exist to prevent individual corporations from assuming too much market power. Numerous state regulations affect M&As, such as state anti-takeover and antitrust laws. A number of industries are also subject to regulatory approval at the federal and state levels. Finally, gaining regulatory approval in cross-border transactions can be nightmarish because of the potential for the inconsistent application of antitrust laws as well as differing reporting requirements, fee structures, and legal jurisdictions.

DISCUSSION QUESTIONS

2.1   What factors do U.S. antitrust regulators consider before challenging a transaction?

2.2   What are the obligations of the acquirer and target firms according to the Williams Act?

2.3   Discuss the pros and cons of federal antitrust laws.

2.4   When is a person or firm required to submit a Schedule 13(D) to the SEC? What is the purpose of such a filing?

2.5   Give examples of the types of actions that may be required by the parties to a proposed merger subject to an FTC consent decree.

2.6   Ameritech and SBC Communications received permission from the FCC to combine to form the nation's largest local telephone company. The FCC gave its approval, subject to conditions requiring that the companies open their markets to rivals and enter new markets to compete with established local phone companies, in an effort to reduce the cost of local phone calls and give smaller communities access to appropriate phone service. SBC had considerable difficulty in complying with its agreement with the FCC. Over an 18-month period, SBC paid the U.S. government $38.5 million for failing to provide rivals with adequate access to its network. The government noted that SBC failed to make its network available in a timely manner, meet installation deadlines, and notify competitors when their orders were filled. Comment on the fairness and effectiveness of using the imposition of heavy fines to promote government-imposed outcomes rather than free market–determined outcomes.

2.7   In an effort to gain approval of their proposed merger from the FTC, top executives from Exxon Corporation and Mobil Corporation argued that they needed to merge because of the increasingly competitive world oil market. Falling oil prices during much of the late 1990s put a squeeze on oil industry profits. Moreover, giant state-owned oil companies pose a competitive threat because of their access to huge amounts of capital. To offset these factors, Exxon and Mobil argued that they had to combine to achieve substantial cost savings. Why were the Exxon and Mobil executives emphasizing efficiencies as a justification for this merger?

2.8 How important is properly defining the market segment in which the acquirer and target companies compete in determining the potential increase in market power if the two firms are permitted to combine? Explain your answer.

2.9 Comment on whether antitrust policy can be used as an effective means of encouraging innovation. Explain your answer.

2.10 The Sarbanes-Oxley Act has been very controversial. Discuss the arguments for and against the Act. Which side do you find more convincing, and why?

Answers to these Chapter Discussion Questions are available in the Online Instructor's Guide for instructors using this book.

QUESTIONS FROM THE CFA CURRICULUM

2.11 Which of the following is most likely a characteristic of a concentrated industry?
 a. Infrequent, tacit coordination.
 b. Difficulty in monitoring other industry members.
 c. Industry members attempting to avoid competition on price.

Source: 2011 Introduction to Industry and Company Analysis, Reading 59, question 22.

Answers to questions from the CFA curriculum are available in the Online Student Companion site to this book in a file folder entitled CFA Curriculum Questions and Solutions.

CASE STUDY 2.1
Regulatory Challenges in Cross-Border Mergers

Key Points

- Such mergers entail substantially greater regulatory challenges than domestic M&As.
- Realizing potential synergies may be limited by failure to receive support from regulatory agencies in

the countries in which the acquirer and target firms have operations.

European Commission antitrust regulators formally blocked the attempted merger between the NYSE Group and Deutsche Borse on February 4, 2012, nearly one year after the exchanges first announced the deal. The stumbling block appeared to be the inability of the parties involved to reach agreement on divesting their derivatives trading markets. The European regulators argued that the proposed merger would result in the combined exchanges obtaining excessive pricing power without the sale of the derivatives trading markets. The disagreement focused on whether the exchange was viewed as primarily a European market or a global market.

The NYSE Group is the world's largest stock and derivatives exchange, as measured by market capitalization. A product of the combination of the New York Stock Exchange and Euronext NV (the European exchange operator), the NYSE Group reversed the three-year slide in both its U.S. and European market share in 2011. The slight improvement in market share was due more to an increase in technology spending than any change in the regulatory environment. The key to unlocking the full potential of the international exchange remained the willingness of countries to harmonize the international regulatory environment for trading stocks and derivatives.

Valued at $11 billion, the mid-2007 merger created the first transatlantic stock and derivatives market. Organizationally, the NYSE Group operates as a holding company, with its U.S. and European operations run largely independently. The combined firms trade stocks and derivatives through the New York Stock Exchange, on the electronic Euronext Liffe Exchange in London, and on the stock exchanges in Paris, Lisbon, Brussels, and Amsterdam.

In recent years, most of the world's major exchanges have gone public and pursued acquisitions. Before this 2007 deal, the NYSE merged with electronic trading firm Archipelago Holdings, while NASDAQ Stock Market Inc. acquired the electronic trading unit of rival Instinet. This consolidation is being driven by declining trading fees, improving trading information technology, and relaxed cross-border restrictions on capital flows and in part by increased regulation in the United States. U.S. regulation, driven by increased Sarbanes-Oxley reporting requirements, contributed to the transfer of new listings (IPOs) overseas. The strategy chosen by U.S. exchanges for recapturing lost business is to follow these new listings overseas.

Larger companies that operate across multiple continents also promise to attract more investors to trading in specific stocks and derivatives contracts, which could lead to cheaper, faster, and easier trading. As exchange operators become larger, they can more easily cut operating and processing costs by eliminating redundant or overlapping staff and facilities and, in theory, pass the savings along to investors. Moreover, by attracting more buyers and sellers, the gap between prices at which investors are willing to buy and sell any given stock (i.e., the bid and ask prices) should narrow. The presence of more traders means more people are bidding to buy and sell any given stock. This results in prices that more accurately reflect the true underlying value of the security because of more competition. The cross-border mergers should also make it easier and cheaper for individual investors to buy and sell foreign shares.

Before these benefits can be fully realized, numerous regulatory hurdles have to be overcome. Even if exchanges merge, they must still abide by local government rules when trading in the shares of a particular company, depending on where the company is listed. Companies are not eager to list on multiple exchanges worldwide because that subjects them to many countries' securities regulations and a bookkeeping nightmare. At the local level, little has changed in how markets are regulated. European companies list their shares on exchanges owned by the NYSE Group. These exchanges still are overseen by individual national regulators. In the United States, the SEC still oversees the NYSE but does not have a direct say over Europe, except in that it would oversee the parent company, the NYSE Group, since it is headquartered in New York. EU member states continue to set their own rules for the clearing and settlement of trades. If the NYSE and Euronext are to achieve a more unified and seamless trading system, regulators must reach agreement on a common set of rules. Achieving this goal seems to remain well in the future. Consequently, it may be years before the anticipated synergies are realized.

Discussion Questions

1. What key challenges face regulators resulting from the merger of financial exchanges in different countries? How do you see these challenges being resolved?
2. In what way are these regulatory issues similar to or different from those confronting the SEC and state regulators and the European Union and individual-country regulators?
3. Who should or could regulate global financial markets? Explain your answer.
4. In your opinion, would the merging of financial exchanges increase or decrease international financial stability? Explain your answer.

Solutions to these case study questions are found in the Online Instructor's Manual available to instructors using this book.

CASE STUDY 2.2
The Importance of Timing: The Express Scripts and Medco Merger

Key Points

- While important, industry concentration is only one of many factors antitrust regulators use in investigating proposed M&As.
- The timing of the proposed Express Scripts–Medco merger could have

been the determining factor in its receiving regulatory approval.

Following their rejection of two of the largest M&As announced in 2011 over concern about increased industry concentration, U.S. antitrust regulators approved on April 2, 2012, the proposed takeover of pharmacy benefits manager Medco Health Solutions Inc. (Medco) by Express Scripts Inc., despite similar misgivings by critics. Pharmacy benefit managers (PBMs) are third-party administrators of prescription drug programs responsible for processing and paying prescription drug claims. More than 210 million Americans receive drug benefits through PBMs. Their customers include participants in plans offered by Fortune 500 employers, Medicare Part D participants, and the Federal Employees Health Benefits Program.

The $29.1 billion Express Scripts–Medco merger created the nation's largest pharmacy benefits manager administering drug coverage for employers and insurers through its mail order operations, which could exert substantial influence on both how and where patients buy their prescription drugs. The combined firms will be called Express Scripts Holding Company and will have $91 billion in annual revenue and $2.5 billion in after-tax profits. Including debt, the deal is valued at $34.3 billion. Together the two firms controlled 34% of the prescription drug market in the first quarter of 2012, processing more than 1.4 billion prescriptions; CVS-Caremark is the next largest, with

17% market share. The combined firms will also represent the nation's third-largest pharmacy operator, trailing only CVS Caremark and Walgreen Co.

The Federal Trade Commission's approval followed an intensive eight-month investigation and did not include any of the customary structural or behavioral remedies that accompany approval of mergers resulting in substantial increases in industry concentration. FTC antitrust regulators voting for approval argued that the Express Scripts–Medco deal did not present significant anticompetitive concerns, since the PBM market is more susceptible to new entrants and current competitors provide customers significant alternatives. Furthermore, the FTC concluded that Express Scripts and Medco did not represent particularly close competitors and that the merged firms would not result in monopolistic pricing power. In addition, approval may have reflected the belief that the merged firms could help reduce escalating U.S. medical costs because of their greater leverage in negotiating drug prices with manufacturers and their ability to cut operating expenses by eliminating overlapping mail-handling operations. The FTC investigation also found that most of the large private health insurance plans offer PBM services, as do other private operators. Big private employers are the major customers of PBMs and have proven to be willing to switch PBMs if another has a better offer. For example, Medco lost one-third of its business during 2011, primarily to CVS Caremark.

In addition, to CVS Caremark Corp, PBM competitors include UnitedHealth, which has emerged as a recent entrant into the business. Having been one of Medco's largest customers, UnitedHealth did not renew its contract, which expired in 2012, with Medco, which covered more than 20 million of its pharmacy benefit customers. Other competitors include Humana, Aetna, and Cigna, all of which have their own PBM services competing for managing drug benefits covered under Medicare Part D. With the loss of UnitedHealth's business, Express Script–Medco's share dropped from 34% in early 2012 to 29% at the end of that year.

Critics of the proposed merger argued that smaller PBM firms often do not have the bargaining power and data-handling capabilities of their larger competitors. Moreover, benefit managers can steer health plan participants to their own pharmacy-fulfillment services, and employers have little choice but to agree, due to their limited leverage. Opponents argue that the combination will reduce competition, ultimately raising drug prices. As the combined firms push for greater use of mail-ordering prescriptions instead of local pharmacies, smaller pharmacies could be driven out of business, for mail-order delivery is far cheaper for both PBMs and patients than dispensing drugs at a store.

Discussion Questions

1. Why do you believe that U.S. antitrust regulators approved the merger despite the large increase in industry concentration?
2. Did the timing of the proposed merger between Express Scripts and Medco help or hurt the firms in obtaining regulatory approval? Be specific.
3. Speculate as to how the Express Scripts–Medco merger might influence the decisions of their competitors to merge? Be specific.

Solutions to these case study questions are found in the Online Instructor's Manual available to instructors using this book.

The Corporate Takeover Market

Common Takeover Tactics, Antitakeover Defenses, and Corporate Governance

Treat a person as he is, and he will remain as he is. Treat him as he could be, and he will become what he should be. —**Jimmy Johnson**

INSIDE M&A: LINKEDIN IPO RAISES GOVERNANCE ISSUES

KEY POINTS

- Various antitakeover defenses raise shareholder rights issues.
- Critics argue such measures entrench existing management.
- Firms employing such measures argue that they allow the founder to retain control, attract and retain key managers, and enable the firm to continue its business strategy.

Investors often overlook governance structures when the prospect of future profits is high. This may have been the case when Internet social media company LinkedIn completed on May 9, 2011, the largest IPO since Google's in 2004. With 2010 revenues of $243 million and net income of $15 million, the eight-year-old firm was valued at $8.9 billion, nearly 600 times earnings.

Investors in the IPO received Class A shares, which have only one vote, while LinkedIn's pre-IPO shareholders hold Class B shares, entitled to ten votes each. The dual share structure guarantees that cofounder and CEO, Reid Hoffman, will own about 20% of LinkedIn and, in concert with three venture capital firms, will have a controlling interest. In contrast, public shareholders will have less than 1% of the voting power of the firm. Different classes of voting stock allow the founder's family to preserve and protect their desired corporate culture, to preserve continuity of policies and practices, to attract and retain key managers, and to enable the current board and management to look beyond quarterly earnings pressures. The dual structure also allows founders to cash out without losing control of the companies they started.

LinkedIn also adopted a staggered board, which effectively requires at least two years before a majority of the firm's current board can be replaced. To make it more difficult to eliminate the staggered board defense, LinkedIn shareholders must vote to change the firm's certificate of incorporation after the board recommends such a vote. Once the recommendation is made, all LinkedIn shares (Class A and Class B) have only one vote. However, the removal of the staggered board is still unlikely, because the firm's certificate of incorporation requires that more than 80% of all shareholders approve changes in the staggered board structure.

The firm also added bylaw notice provisions—to discourage shareholder activists—more onerous than would be required in SEC filings, when a shareholder has more than 5% ownership interest in a public firm. If it is later determined that the shareholder has misstated the facts in any manner, LinkedIn's bylaws allow the board to disqualify the proposal or nomination. Finally, according to LinkedIn's charter, any shareholder lawsuits must be litigated in the state of Delaware, where the laws are particularly favorable to corporations.

These measures raise questions about the rights of pre-IPO investors versus those of public shareholders. Do they allow the firm to retain the best managers and to implement fully its business strategy? Do they embolden management to negotiate the best deal for all shareholders in the event of a takeover attempt? Or do they entrench current management intent on maintaining their power and compensation at the expense of other shareholders?

CHAPTER OVERVIEW

While not the only means, corporate takeovers represent a common way to transfer control of a firm from ineffective to effective management. The *corporate takeover market* in which control is transferred serves two important functions in a free market economy: the allocation of resources to sectors in which they can be used most efficiently and as a mechanism for disciplining failing corporate managers. By replacing such managers through hostile takeover attempts or proxy fights, the corporate takeover market can help to promote good *corporate governance*, which in turn can improve corporate financial performance.

Corporate governance refers to the rules and processes by which a business is controlled, regulated, or operated. There is, though, no universally accepted goal for corporate governance. Traditionally, the goal has been to protect shareholder rights. More recently, this has expanded to encompass additional corporate stakeholders, including customers, employees, the government, lenders, communities, regulators, and suppliers. For our purposes, corporate governance is about leadership and accountability, and it involves all those factors internal and external to the firm that interact to protect the rights of corporate stakeholders. Figure 3.1 illustrates the range of factors affecting corporate governance, including the corporate takeover market. A chapter review (including practice questions) is available in the file folder entitled Student Study Guide contained on the companion site to this book (http://booksite.elsevier.com/9780123854872).

CORPORATE GOVERNANCE

Where capital markets are liquid, investors discipline bad managers by selling their shares (i.e., the market model). Where capital markets are illiquid, bad managers are disciplined by those owning large blocks of stock in the firm (i.e., the control model). Table 3.1 summarizes the characteristics of these two common models. The following sections describe those factors internal and external to the firm, including M&As, impacting corporate governance.

Internal Factors

Corporate governance is affected by the effectiveness of the firm's board, internal controls and incentive systems, takeover defenses, and corporate culture. These factors are discussed next.

The Board of Directors/Management

The board hires, fires, sets CEO pay and is expected to oversee management, corporate strategy, and the firm's financial reports to shareholders. Some board members may be employees or founding family members; others may be affiliated with the firm through a banking relationship, a law firm retained by the firm, or someone who represents a customer or supplier. Such members may be subject to conflicts of interest causing them to act in ways not in the shareholders' best interests. This has led some observers to argue that boards should be composed primarily of independent directors and that different individuals should hold the CEO and board chairman positions. Studies show that firm performance is improved by more independent boards and the separation of the CEO and board positions.[1] Board structure has been moving in this direction. In the early 1990s, about 40% of boards were composed of senior corporate managers or individuals affiliated with the corporation. However, in recent years, more than 90% of boards have only one or two nonindependent directors.[2]

---

[1] Byrd and Hickman (1992), Shivdasani (1993), and Yermack (1996) find that firm value is positively influenced by outsider-dominated boards.

[2] Gordon, 2007

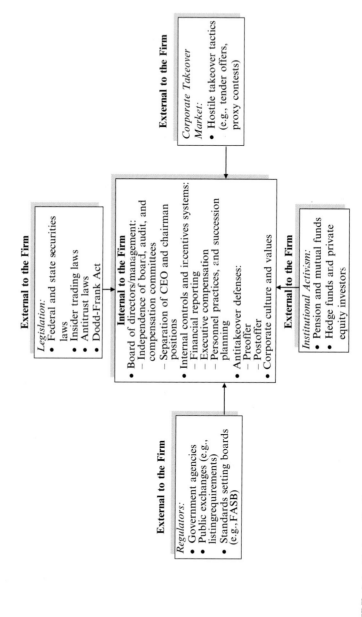

External to the Firm

Legislation:
- Federal and state securities laws
- Insider trading laws
- Antitrust laws
- Dodd-Frank Act

Internal to the Firm
- Board of directors/management:
  – Independence of board, audit, and compensation committees
  – Separation of CEO and chairman positions
- Internal controls and incentives systems:
  – Financial reporting
  – Executive compensation
  – Personnel practices, and succession planning
- Antitakeover defenses:
  – Preoffer
  – Postoffer
- Corporate culture and values

External to the Firm

Corporate Takeover Market:
- Hostile takeover tactics (e.g., tender offers, proxy contests)

External to the Firm

Institutional Activism:
- Pension and mutual funds
- Hedge funds and private equity investors

External to the Firm

Regulators:
- Government agencies
- Public exchanges (e.g., listing requirements)
- Standards setting boards (e.g., FASB)

FIGURE. 3.1 Factors affecting corporate governance.

TABLE 3.1 Alternative Models of Corporate Governance

Market Model Applicable When:	Control Model Applicable When:
Capital markets are highly liquid.	Capital markets are illiquid.
Equity ownership is widely dispersed.	Equity ownership is heavily concentrated.
Board members are largely independent.	Board members are largely "insiders."
Ownership and control are separate.	Ownership and control overlap.
Financial disclosure is high.	Financial disclosure is limited.
Shareholders focus more on short-term gains.	Shareholders focus more on long-term gains.

Today, boards average about 10 members, about one-half of their average size during the 1970s. There is evidence that smaller boards tend to be more effective, since each member can wield more influence, thereby effectively reducing the power of the CEO. Smaller boards are also more likely to replace a CEO due to poor performance.[3] However, more complicated firms may benefit from larger boards capable of providing a broader range of advice to the CEO.[4]

Internal Controls and Incentive Systems

Internal controls are critical in preventing fraud as well as ensuring compliance with prevailing laws and regulations. Financial and legal auditing functions, as well as hiring and firing policies within the firm, are examples of internal controls. Compensation, consisting of base pay, bonuses, and stock options, underpins incentive systems used to manage the firm in the manner the board deems appropriate. To rectify abuses, the Dodd-Frank Act of 2010 gives shareholders of public firms the right to vote on executive compensation. Under the new rules, such votes must occur at least once every three years. The Dodd-Frank Act also requires publicly traded firms to develop mechanisms for recovering compensation based on executive misconduct.

Managerial and shareholder interests can be aligned in other ways. Option strike prices (i.e., prices at which options can be converted into company shares) can be linked to the firm's share price performance relative to the stock market, ensuring that increases in the stock market do not benefit managers whose companies are underperforming. Another way is for managers to own a significant portion of the firm's outstanding stock or for the manager's ownership of the firm's stock to comprise a substantial share of his or her personal wealth. An alternative to concentrating ownership in management is for one or more shareholders who are not managers to accumulate a large block of voting shares. So-called "blockholders" may be more aggressive in monitoring management and more receptive to takeovers, thereby increasing the risk to managers that they will be ousted for poor performance.

[3] Yermack, 1996

[4] Coles et al., 2008

Antitakeover Defenses

A firm's board and management may employ defenses to negotiate a higher purchase price with a bidder or to solidify their current position within the firm. The range of defensive actions is detailed later in this chapter.

Corporate Culture and Values

Good governance also depends on an employee culture instilled with appropriate values and behaviors. Setting the right tone comes from the board of directors' and senior management's willingness to behave in a manner consistent with what they demand from other employees.

Bond Covenants

Legally binding on both the bond issuer and the bond holder, covenants forbid the issuer from undertaking certain activities, such as dividend payments, or require the issuer to meet specific requirements, such as periodic information reporting. Strong covenants can motivate managers to pursue relatively low-risk investments, such as capital expenditures, and avoid higher-risk investments, such as research and development spending.[5]

Factors External to the Firm

Federal and state legislation, the court system, regulators, institutional activists, and the corporate takeover market all play an important role in maintaining good corporate governance practices.

Legislation and the Legal System

The 1933 and 1934 Securities Acts underlie U.S. securities legislation and created the Securities and Exchange Commission, charged with writing and enforcing securities' regulations. The U.S. Congress has since transferred some enforcement tasks to public stock exchanges operating under SEC oversight.[6] Under the Sarbanes-Oxley Act of 2002, the SEC oversees the Public Company Accounting Oversight Board, whose task is to develop and enforce auditing standards. State legislation also has a significant impact on governance practices by requiring corporate charters to define the responsibilities of boards and managers with respect to shareholders

Regulators

The SEC, Federal Trade Commission, and Department of Justice can discipline firms through formal investigations and lawsuits. In 2003, the SEC approved new listing standards that would put many lucrative, stock-based pay plans to a

---

[5]King and Wen, 2011

[6]The SEC itself has delegated certain responsibilities for setting accounting standards to the not-for-profit Financial Accounting Standards Board (FASB).

shareholder vote. In 2007, additional disclosure requirements for CEO compensation exceeding $10,000 were implemented. The 2010 Dodd-Frank Act requires listed firms, through new rules adopted by the stock exchanges, to have fully independent compensation committees, based on new standards that consider the source of compensation for the director and whether the director is affiliated with the company.

Institutional Activists

Pension funds, hedge funds, private equity investors, and mutual funds have become increasingly influential in affecting the policies of companies in which they invest. Shareholders of public firms may submit proposals to be voted on at annual meetings, but such proposals are not binding, in that the firm's board can accept or reject the proposal even if approved by a majority of shareholders. Only 30% of proposals receiving majority support are implemented within one year of the vote.[7] Nonbinding proposals approved by shareholders pertaining to takeover defenses, executive compensation, etc., are more likely to be implemented if there is an activist investor likely to threaten a proxy fight.[8] When nonbinding votes are too close to call, there is evidence that firm value can increase by as much as 1.8% on the day of the vote if it passes and as much as 2.8% if it is later adopted by the firm's board. The impact on shareholder value is even greater for firms with a substantial number of takeover defenses in place.[9]

The Corporate Takeover Market

Changes in corporate control can occur because of a hostile or friendly takeover or because of a proxy contest initiated by shareholders. When a firm's internal management controls are weak, the takeover market acts as a "court of last resort" to discipline bad management behavior.[10] Strong internal governance mechanisms, by contrast, lessen the role of the takeover threat as a disciplinary factor. However, the disciplining effect of a takeover threat on a firm's management can be reinforced when it is paired with a large shareholding by an institutional investor.[11] Larger firms are more likely to be the target of disciplinary takeovers than smaller firms, and their CEOs are more likely to be replaced following a series of poor acquisitions.[12]

Several theories attempt to explain why managers resist a takeover attempt. The *management entrenchment theory* suggests that managers use takeover defenses to ensure their longevity with the firm. While relatively rare in the

[7]Ertimur et al., 2010

[8]Levit et al., 2012

[9]Cunat et al., 2012

[10]Kini, Kracaw, and Mian, 2004

[11]Cremers and Nair, 2005

[12]Offenberg, 2009

United States,[13] hostile takeovers or the threat of such takeovers have historically been useful for maintaining good corporate governance by removing bad managers and installing better ones.[14] Indeed, there is evidence of frequent management turnover even if a takeover attempt is defeated, since takeover targets are often poor financial performers.[15] An alternative viewpoint is the *shareholder interest's theory*, which suggests that management resistance to takeovers is a good bargaining strategy to increase the purchase price to the benefit of the target's shareholders.[16]

Proxy contests are attempts by a group of shareholders to gain representation on a firm's board or to change management proposals by gaining the support of other shareholders. While those that address issues other than board representation do not bind the board, boards are becoming more responsive—perhaps reflecting fallout from the Enron-type scandals in 2001 and 2002.[17] Even unsuccessful proxy contests often lead to a change in management, a restructuring of the firm, or investor expectations that the firm ultimately will be acquired.

UNDERSTANDING ALTENATIVE TAKEOVER TACTICS

Implementing a friendly takeover is described briefly in the next section and in considerable detail in Chapter 5. Hostile-takeover tactics are described extensively in the following sections.

The Friendly Approach in the Corporate Takeover Market

In friendly takeovers, a negotiated settlement is possible without the acquirer's resorting to aggressive tactics. The potential acquirer initiates an informal dialogue with the target's top management, and the acquirer and target reach an agreement on the key issues early in the process, such as the long-term business strategy, how they will operate in the short term, and who will be in key executive positions. Often, a *standstill agreement* is negotiated in which the acquirer agrees not to make any further investments in the target's stock for a specific period. This compels the acquirer to pursue the acquisition on friendly terms, at least for the period covered

---

[13] According to Dealogic, the number of annual hostile bids for U.S. firms between 2000 and 2012 has averaged 31. Of these, less than one-third have been successful. The rarity of such deals reflects the substantial flexibility target boards have in defending against hostile bids as well as their potential to increase bid premiums and to retard postclosing integration.

[14] Morck, Schleifer, and Vishny, 1988

[15] Economic Report to the President, 2003, p. 81

[16] Franks and Mayer, 1996; Schwert, 2000

[17] According to Ertimur (2010), boards implemented 41% of nonbinding shareholder proposals for majority voting in 2004, versus only 22% in 1997. A board was more likely to adopt a shareholder proposal if a competitor had adopted a similar plan.

by the agreement, and permits negotiations without the threat of more aggressive tactics, such as those discussed in the following sections.

The Hostile Approach in the Corporate Takeover Market

If initial efforts to take control of a target firm are rejected, an acquirer may choose to adopt more aggressive tactics, including the bear hug, the proxy contest, and the tender offer.

The Bear Hug: Limiting the Target's Options

A *bear hug* is an offer to buy the target's shares at a substantial premium to its current share price and often entails mailing a letter containing the proposal to the target's CEO and board without warning and demanding a rapid decision. It usually involves a public announcement, to put pressure on the board. Directors voting against the proposal may be subject to shareholder lawsuits. Once the bid is made public, the company is likely to attract additional bidders. Institutional investors[18] and arbitrageurs add to the pressure by lobbying the board to accept the offer. By accumulating target shares, they make purchases of blocks of stock by the bidder easier, for they are often quite willing to sell their shares.

Proxy Contests in Support of a Takeover

Activist shareholders often initiate a proxy fight to remove management due to poor performance, to promote the spin-off of a business unit or the outright sale of the firm, or to force a cash distribution to shareholders.[19] Proxy fights enable such shareholders to replace board members with those more willing to support their positions. Proxy contests are a means of gaining control without owning 50.1% of the voting stock, or they can be used to eliminate takeover defenses, as a precursor of a tender offer, or to oust recalcitrant target-firm board members. In late 2010, Air Products & Chemicals, after being rejected several times by Airgas Inc., succeeded in placing three of its own nominees on the Airgas board and, in doing so, voted to remove the chairman of Airgas, who had led the resistance to the Air Products' offer.

Implementing a Proxy Contest

When the bidder is also a shareholder, the proxy process may begin with the bidder's attempting to call a special shareholders meeting. Alternatively, the bidder may put a proposal to replace the board at a regularly scheduled

---

[18]Institutional investors include insurance companies, retirement or pension funds, hedge funds, banks, and mutual funds and account, on average, for more than two-thirds of the shareholdings of publicly traded firms (Bogle, 2007).

[19]Faleye, 2004

shareholders meeting. Before the meeting, the bidder opens an aggressive public relations campaign, with direct solicitations sent to shareholders and full-page advertisements in the press to convince shareholders to support the bidder's proposals. The target often responds with its own campaign. Once shareholders receive the proxies, they may choose to sign and send them directly to a designated collection point, such as a brokerage house or a bank.

SEC regulations cover proxy solicitations under Section 14(A) of the Securities Exchange Act of 1934. All materials distributed to shareholders must be submitted to the SEC for review at least ten days before they are distributed. The party attempting to solicit proxies from the target's shareholders must file a *proxy statement* and Schedule 14(A) with the SEC and mail it to the target's shareholders. Proxy statements may be obtained from the companies involved and on the SEC's website, and they are excellent sources of information about a proposed transaction.

The Impact of Proxy Contests on Shareholder Value

Despite a low success rate, proxy fights often result in positive abnormal returns to target shareholders regardless of the outcome.[20] The reasons include the eventual change in management at firms embroiled in proxy fights, the tendency for new management to restructure the firm, investor expectations of a future change in control, and special cash payouts made by firms with excess cash holdings. However, when management wins by a wide margin, shareholder value often declines, since little changes in how the firm is managed.[21]

The Hostile Tender Offer

A *hostile tender offer* circumvents the target's board and management to reach the target's shareholders directly with an offer to purchase their shares. While boards often discourage unwanted bids initially, they are more likely to relent to a hostile tender offer.[22] Such offers are undertaken for several reasons: (1) as a last resort if the bidder cannot get the target's board and management to relent, (2) to preempt another firm from making a bid for the target, and (3) to close a transaction quickly if the bidder believes that time is critical. A common hostile-takeover strategy involves the bidder's acquiring a controlling interest in the target and later completing the combination through a merger. This strategy is described in detail later in this chapter.

---

[20] In studies of proxy battles during the 1980s through the mid-1990s, abnormal returns ranged from 6 to 19%, even if the activist shareholders were unsuccessful in the proxy contest (Mulherin and Poulsen, 1998; Faleye, 2004).

[21] Listokin, 2009

[22] In a study of 1018 tender offers in the United States between 1962 and 2001, Bhagat et al. (2005) found that target boards resisted tender offers about one-fifth of the time. In a study of 49 countries, Rossi and Volpin (2004) found that only about 1% of 45,686 M&A deals between 1990 and 2002 were opposed by target firm boards.

Pretender Offer Tactics: Toehold Bidding Strategies

Bidders may purchase stock in a target before a formal bid to accumulate stock at a price lower than the eventual offer price. Such purchases are secretive to avoid increasing the average price paid. The advantage to the bidder is the potential leverage achieved with the voting rights associated with the stock it has purchased. The bidder can also sell this stock if the takeover attempt is unsuccessful. Once a toehold position has been established, the bidder may attempt to call a special stockholders' meeting to replace the board of directors or remove takeover defenses.[23] While rare in friendly takeovers, these actions are commonplace in hostile transactions, comprising about one-half of all such takeovers. In friendly deals, bidders are concerned about alienating a target firm's board with such actions; however, in hostile situations, the target firm would have rejected the initial bid under any circumstances. On average, toehold positions represent 20% of the target's shares in hostile transactions and 11% in friendly takeovers. The frequency of toehold bidding has declined since the early 1990s in line with the widespread adoption of takeover defenses and a decline in the frequency of hostile deals.[24]

Implementing a Tender Offer

Tender offers can be for cash, stock, debt, or some combination. Unlike mergers, tender offers frequently use cash as the form of payment. Securities transactions involve a longer period to complete because of the need to register with the SEC, to comply with state registration requirements, and, if the issue is large, to obtain shareholder approval. If the offer involves a share-for-share exchange, it is referred to as an *exchange offer*. Whether cash or securities, the offer is made to target shareholders, is extended for a specific period, and may be unrestricted (any-or-all offer) or restricted to a certain percentage or number of the target's shares.

Tender offers restricted to purchasing less than 100% of the target's outstanding shares may be oversubscribed. Because the Williams Act of 1968 requires equal treatment of all shareholders tendering shares, the bidder may either purchase all of the target stock that is tendered or purchase only a portion of the tendered stock. For example, if the bidder has extended a tender offer for 70% of the target's outstanding shares and 90% of the target's stock actually is offered, then the bidder may choose to prorate the purchase of stock by buying only 63% (i.e., 0.7×0.9) of the tendered stock from each shareholder. If the bidder chooses to revise the tender offer, the waiting period is automatically extended. If another bid is made, the waiting period must also be extended by another ten days.

---

[23] The conditions under which such a meeting can be called are determined by the firm's articles of incorporation, governed by the laws of the state in which the firm is incorporated. A copy of a firm's articles of incorporation can usually be obtained from the Office of the Secretary of State of the state in which the firm is incorporated.

[24] Betton, Eckbo, and Thorburn, 2009

Once initiated, tender offers for publicly traded firms are usually successful, although the success rate is lower if it is contested.[25]

Federal securities laws impose reporting, disclosure, and antifraud requirements on acquirers initiating tender offers. Once the tender offer has been made, the acquirer cannot purchase any target shares other than the number specified in the offer. Section 14(D) of the Williams Act requires that any individual or entity making a tender offer resulting in owning more than 5% of any class of equity must file a Schedule 14(D)-1 and all solicitation materials with the SEC.

Multitiered Offers

A bid can be either a one- or two-tiered offer. In a *one-tier offer*, the acquirer announces the same offer to all target shareholders, which offers the potential to purchase control of the target quickly and discourage other potential bidders from attempting to disrupt the deal. In a *two-tiered offer*, the acquirer offers to buy a number of shares at one price and more at a lower price at a later date. The form of payment in the second tier may be less attractive, consisting of securities rather than cash. The intent of the two-tiered approach is to give target shareholders an incentive to tender their shares early in the process to receive the higher price. Since those shareholders tendering their shares in the first tier enable the acquirer to obtain a controlling interest, their shares are worth more than those who may choose to sell in the second tier.

Once the bidding firm accumulates enough shares to gain control of the target (usually 50.1%), the bidder may initiate a so-called *back-end merger* by calling a special shareholders meeting seeking approval for a merger, in which minority shareholders are required to accede to the majority vote. Alternatively, the bidder may operate the target firm as a partially owned subsidiary, later merging it into a newly created wholly owned subsidiary. Many state statutes require equal treatment for all tendering shareholders as part of two-tier offers and give target shareholders *appraisal rights* that allow those not tendering shares in the first or second tier to ask the state court to determine a "fair value" for the shares.[26] State statutes may also contain *fair-price provisions*, in which all target shareholders, including those in the second tier, receive the same price and redemption rights, enabling target shareholders in the second tier to redeem their shares at a price similar to that paid in the first tier.

There are disadvantages to owning less than 100% of the target's voting stock. These include the potential for dissatisfied minority shareholders owning significant blocks of stock to disrupt efforts to implement important management decisions and the cost incurred in providing financial statements to both majority and minority shareholders.

---

[25] According to FactSet Mergerstat, the success rate of total attempted tender offers between 1980 and 2000 was more than 80%, with the success rate for uncontested offers more than 90% and for contested offers (i.e., by the target's board) slightly more than 50%.

[26] The minority shares may be subject to a "minority discount," since they are worth less to the bidder than those acquired in the process of gaining control.

WHAT MAKES THE AGGRESSIVE APPROACH SUCCESSFUL?

Successful hostile takeovers depend on the size of the offer price premium, the board's composition, and the makeup, sentiment, and investment horizon of the target's current shareholders. Other factors include the provisions of the target's bylaws and the potential for the target to implement additional takeover defenses.

The target's board will find it more difficult to reject offers exhibiting substantial premiums to the target's current share price. The composition of the target's board also influences what the board does because one dominated by independent directors may be more likely to negotiate the best price for shareholders by soliciting competing bids than to protect itself and current management.[27] The final outcome of a hostile takeover is also dependent on the composition of the target's ownership, how shareholders feel about management's performance, and how long they intend to hold the stock. Firms held predominately by short-term investors (i.e., less than four months) are more likely to receive a bid and exhibit a lower average premium of as much as 3% when acquired; researchers speculate that firms held by short-term investors have a weaker bargaining position with the bidder due to the limited loyalty of such shareholders.[28]

To assess these factors, an acquirer compiles (to the extent possible) lists of stock ownership by category: management, officers, employees, and institutions such as pension and mutual funds. This information can be used to estimate the target's *float*—total outstanding shares less shares held by insiders. The larger the share of stock held by corporate officers, family members, and employees, the smaller the number of shares that are likely to be easily purchased by the bidder, since these types of shareholders are less likely to sell their shares.

Finally, an astute bidder will always analyze the target firm's bylaws for provisions potentially adding to the cost of a takeover.[29] Such provisions could include a staggered board, the inability to remove directors without cause, or supermajority voting requirements for approval of mergers. These and other measures are detailed later in this chapter.

OTHER TACTICAL CONSIDERATIONS

To heighten the chance of a successful takeover, the bidder will include provisions in a *letter of intent* (LOI) to discourage the target firm from backing out of

---

[27] The shareholder gain from the inception of the offer to its resolution is 62.3% for targets with an independent board, as compared with 40.9% for targets without an independent board (Shivdasani, 1993).

[28] Gaspara and Massa, 2005

[29] Unlike charters, which are recorded in the Office of the Secretary of State in the state in which the firm is incorporated, corporate bylaws are generally held by the firm along with other corporate records and may be available through the firm's website or by requesting a copy directly from the firm.

any preliminary agreements. The LOI is a preliminary agreement between two companies intending to merge stipulating areas of agreement between the parties as well as their rights and limitations. It may contain a number of features protecting the buyer; among the most common is the *no-shop agreement*, prohibiting the target from seeking other bids or making public information not currently readily available.

Contracts often grant the target and acquirer the right to withdraw from the agreement. This usually requires the payment of *breakup or termination fees*, sums paid to the acquirer or target to compensate for their expenses. Expenses could include legal and advisory expenses, management time, and the costs associated with opportunities that may have been lost to the bidder while involved in trying to close this deal.[30] Termination fees are used more frequently on the target side than on that of the acquirer because targets have greater incentives to break contracts and seek other bidders. Such fees give the target firm some leverage with the bidder. Averaging about 3% of the purchase price and found in about two-thirds of all M&A deals, such fees tend to result in an approximately 4% higher premium paid to target firms. The higher premium represents the amount paid by the bidder for "insurance" that it will be compensated for expenses incurred if the transaction is not completed and for motivating the target to complete the deal.[31] Low or moderate-size fees do not discourage postannouncement competing bids.[32]

Breakup fees paid by the bidder to the target firm are called *reverse breakup fees*, and they have become more common in recent years as buyers, finding it difficult to finance transactions, have opted to back out of signed agreements. The *stock lockup*, an option granted to the bidder to buy the target firm's stock at the first bidder's initial offer, is another form of protection for the bidder. It is triggered whenever the target firm accepts a competing bid. Because the target may choose to sell to a higher bidder, the stock lockup arrangement usually ensures that the initial bidder will make a profit on its purchase of the target's stock. The initial bidder may also require that the seller agree to a *crown jewels lockup*, in which the initial bidder has an option to buy important strategic assets of the seller, if the seller chooses to sell to another party.

DEVELOPING A BIDDING STRATEGY

The tactics used in a bidding strategy represent a series of decision points, with objectives and options well understood before a takeover is initiated. A poorly thought-out strategy can result in unsuccessful bidding for the target firm, which

---

[30] Hotchkiss et al. (2004) found a target termination or breakup fee included in the initial agreement in 55% of all deals, while in 21% of the deals both target and acquirer termination fees were included.

[31] Officer, 2003

[32] Jeon et al., 2011

can be costly to CEOs, who may lose their jobs.[33] Common bidding-strategy objectives include winning control of the target, minimizing the control premium, minimizing transaction costs, and facilitating postacquisition integration.

If minimizing the purchase price and transaction costs while maximizing cooperation between the two parties is critical, the bidder may choose the "friendly" approach. This minimizes the loss of key personnel, customers, and suppliers while control is changing hands. Friendly takeovers avoid an auction environment, which may raise the target's purchase price. Moreover, amicable deals facilitate premerger integration planning and increase the likelihood that the combined firms will be integrated quickly. If the target is unwilling to reach a negotiated settlement, the acquirer is faced with the choice of abandoning the effort or resorting to more aggressive tactics. Such tactics are likely to be less effective because of the extra time they give the target's management to put additional takeover defenses in place. In reality, the risk of loss of surprise may not be very great because of the prenotification requirements of current U.S. law.

Reading Figure. 3.2 from left to right, we see that the bidder initiates contact informally through an intermediary (sometimes called a *casual pass*) or through a more formal inquiry. If rejected, the bidder's options are either to walk away or to become more aggressive. In the latter case, the bidder may undertake a simple bear hug, hoping that pressure from large institutional shareholders and arbs will nudge the target toward a negotiated settlement. If that fails, the bidder may accumulate enough shares in the open market from institutional investors to call a special shareholders' meeting or initiate a proxy battle to install new board members receptive to a takeover or to dismember the target's defenses. While generally less expensive than tender offers (which include a premium to the target's current share price), proxy campaigns are expensive, with an average cost of $6 million, not including possible litigation costs.[34] If the target's defenses are weak, the bidder may forego a proxy contest and initiate a tender offer for the target's stock. If the target's defenses appear formidable, the bidder may implement a proxy contest and a tender offer concurrently; however, the exorbitant cost makes this option uncommon.

Litigation is often used to pressure the target's board to relent to the bidder's proposal or remove defenses and is most effective if the firm's defenses appear to be especially onerous. The bidder may initiate litigation that accuses the target's board of not giving the bidder's offer sufficient review, or the bidder may argue that the target's defenses are not in the best interests of the target's shareholders. Table 3.2 summarizes common bidder objectives and the advantages and disadvantages of the various tactics that may be employed to achieve these objectives.

[33] In a sample of 714 acquisitions between 1990 and 1998, Lehn and Zhao (2006) found that 47% of acquiring firm CEOs were replaced within five years. Moreover, top executives are more likely to be replaced at firms that have made poor acquisitions some time during the previous five years.

[34] Gantchev, 2013

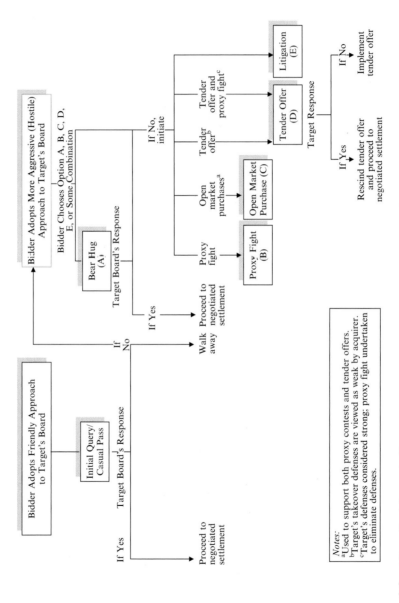

FIGURE. 3.2   Alternative takeover tactics.

TABLE 3.2 Advantages and Disadvantages of Alternative Takeover Tactics

Common Bidder Strategy Objectives

- Gain control of target firm
- Minimize the size of the control premium
- Minimize transactions costs
- Facilitate postacquisition integration

Tactics	Advantages	Disadvantages
Casual Pass (i.e., informal inquiry)	May learn target is receptive to offer	Gives advance warning
Bear Hug Offer (i.e., letter to target board forcefully proposing takeover)	Raises pressure on target to negotiate a deal	Gives advance warning
Open Market Purchases (i.e., acquirer buys target shares on public markets)	• May lower cost of transaction • Creates profit if target agrees to buy back bidder's toehold position • May discourage other bidders	Can result in a less than controlling interest Limits on amount one can purchase without disclosure Some shareholders could hold out for higher price Could suffer losses if takeover attempt fails Could alienate target management and make a friendly takeover more difficult
Proxy Contest (i.e., effort to obtain target shareholder support to change target board)	Less expensive than tender offer May obviate need for tender offer	Relatively low probability of success if target stock widely held Adds to transactions costs
Hostile Tender Offer (i.e., direct offer to target shareholders to buy shares not supported by the target's board or management)	Pressures target shareholders to sell stock Bidder not bound to purchase tendered shares unless desired number of shares tendered	Tends to be most expensive tactic Disruptive to postclosing integration due to potential loss of key target management, customers, and suppliers
Litigation (i.e., lawsuits accusing target board of improper conduct)	Puts pressure on target board	Expense

UNDERSTANDING ALTERNATIVE TAKEOVER DEFENSES

Takeover defenses are designed to slow down an unwanted offer or to force a suitor to raise the bid to get the target's board to rescind the defense. They can be grouped in two categories: those put in place before receiving an offer (preoffer) and those implemented after receipt of an offer (postoffer). Table 3.3 shows the most commonly used pre- and postoffer defenses.

Preoffer Defenses

Preoffer defenses are used to delay a change in control, giving the target firm time to erect additional defenses after the unsolicited offer has been received. Such defenses generally fall into three categories: poison pills,[35] shark repellents, and golden parachutes. Table 3.4 summarizes the advantages and disadvantages of preoffer defenses.

Poison Pills

A poison pill involves a board's issuing rights to current shareholders, with the exception of an unwanted investor, to buy the firm's shares at an exercise price well below their current market value. Because they are issued as a dividend and the board usually has the exclusive authority to declare dividends, a pill can be adopted without a shareholder vote and implemented either before or after a hostile bid. If a specified percentage (usually 10–20%) of the target's common stock is acquired by a hostile investor, each right entitles the holder to purchase common stock or some fraction of participating preferred stock[36] of the target firm (*a flip-in pill*). If a merger, consolidation, sale of at least some percentage (usually 50%) of the target's assets, or announced tender offer occurs, the rights holder may purchase acquirer common shares (*a flip-over pill*). Both the flip-in and flip-over pills entitle their holders, upon paying the exercise price, to buy shares having a market value on the date the pill is triggered equal to some multiple (often two times) the right's exercise price.[37] Rights are redeemable at any time by the board, usually at $.01 per right, expire after some period (sometimes up to ten years), and trade on public exchanges.

The flip-in pill discourages hostile investors from buying a minority stake in the firm because it dilutes their ownership interest in the firm as more target

[35] Poison pills could be viewed as postoffer defenses, since they can be implemented after an offer has been made.

[36] The fraction of a preferred share is intended to give the shareholder about the same dividend, voting, and liquidation rights as would one common share and should approximate the value of one common share.

[37] The exercise price is determined by estimating the long-term trading value of the company's common shares during the life of the plan. The greater the exercise price relative to the market value of the firm's share price, the greater the number of new shares a rights holder can buy once he or she pays the exercise price.

TABLE 3.3 Alternative Preoffer and Postoffer Takeover Defenses

Preoffer Defenses	Postoffer Defenses

Poison Pills:[a]
   Flip-Over Rights Plans
   Flip-In Rights Plans
   Blank Check Preferred Stock Plans
	Greenmail (bidder's investment purchased at a premium to what bidder paid as inducement to refrain from any further activity)

Shark Repellents (Implemented by Changing Bylaws or Charter):
   Strengthening the Board's Defenses
     Staggered or Classified Board Elections
     "For Cause" Provisions
   Limiting Shareholder Actions
     Calling Special Meetings
     Consent Solicitations
     Advance Notice Provisions
     Supermajority Rules
   Other Shark Repellents
     Antigreenmail Provisions
     Fair-Price Provisions
     Dual Class Recapitalization
     (supervoting stock)
     Reincorporation
	Standstill Agreements (often used in conjunction with an agreement to buy bidder's investment)

Golden Parachutes (Change of Control payments)	White Knights Employee Stock Ownership Plans Leveraged Recapitalization Share Repurchase or Buyback Plans Corporate Restructuring Litigation

[a]*While many different types of poison pills are used, only the most common forms are discussed in this text. Note also that the distinction between pre- and postoffer defenses is becoming murky as increasingly poison pill plans are put in place immediately following the announcement of a bid. Pills can be adopted without a shareholder vote because they are issued as a dividend and the board has the exclusive authority to issue dividends.*

shares are issued. For example, if the hostile investor buys a 20% interest in the firm and the number of target shares doubles, the investor's ownership stake is reduced to 10%. Further, the value of the investor's investment also decreases as other shareholders buy more shares at a deeply discounted price. Efforts by the hostile investor to sell shares at what he or she paid are thwarted by the willingness of other shareholders, having acquired shares at a much lower price, to sell below the price paid by the hostile investor. Finally, the total cost of completing the takeover increases as the number of shares that must be acquired in a cash offer or the number of acquirer shares issued in a share exchange increases, diluting current acquirer shareholders. Similarly, the flip-over poison pill dilutes the acquirer's current shareholders and depresses the value of their investment as more acquirer shares are issued at below their current market value.

Netflix adopted a poison pill, having both flip-in and flip-over rights, on November 2, 2012, in response to a 9.98% investment stake in the firm by

TABLE 3.4   Advantages and Disadvantages of Preoffer Takeover Defenses

Type of Defense	Advantages for Target Firm	Disadvantages for Target Firm
POISON PILLS: RAISING THE COST OF ACQUISITION		
Flip-Over Pills (rights to buy stock in the acquirer, activated with 100% change in ownership)	Dilutes ownership position of current acquirer shareholders Rights redeemable by buying them back from shareholders at nominal price	Ineffective in preventing acquisition of ‹100% of target (bidders could buy controlling interest only and buy remainder after rights expire) Subject to hostile tender contingent on target board's redemption of pill Makes issuer less attractive to white knights
Flip-In Pills (rights to buy target stock, activated when acquirer purchases < 100% change in ownership)	Dilutes target stock regardless of amount purchased by potential acquirer Not given to investor who activated the rights Rights redeemable at any point prior to triggering event	Not permissible in some states due to discriminatory nature No poison pill provides any protection against proxy contests
SHARK REPELLENTS: STRENGTHENING THE BOARD'S DEFENSES		
Staggered or Classified Boards	Delays assumption of control by a majority shareholder	May be circumvented by increasing size of board, unless prevented by charter or bylaws
Limitations on When Directors Can Be Removed	"For cause" provisions narrow range of reasons for removal	Can be circumvented unless supported by a supermajority requirement for repeal
SHARK REPELLENTS: LIMITING SHAREHOLDER ACTIONS		
Limitations on Calling Special Meetings	Limits ability to use special meetings to add board seats, remove or elect new members	States may require a special meeting if a certain percentage of shareholders requests a meeting
Limiting Consent Solicitations	Limits ability of dissident shareholders to expedite a proxy contest process	May be subject to court challenge
Advance-Notice Provisions	Gives board time to select its own slate of candidates and to decide an appropriate response	May be subject to court challenge

(Continued)

TABLE 3.4   (Continued)

Type of Defense	Advantages for Target Firm	Disadvantages for Target Firm
Supermajority Provisions	May be applied selectively to events such as hostile takeovers	Can be circumvented unless a supermajority of shareholders is required to change provision

OTHER SHARK REPELLENTS

Antigreenmail Provision	Eliminates profit opportunity for raiders	Eliminates greenmail as a takeover defense
Fair-Price Provisions	Increases the cost of a two-tiered tender offer	Raises the cost to a White Knight, unless waived by typically 95% of shareholders
Dual Class Recapitalization/ Supervoting Stock	Concentrates control by giving "friendly" shareholders more voting power than others	Difficult to implement because requires shareholder approval and only useful when voting power can be given to pro-management shareholders
Reincorporation	Takes advantage of most favorable state antitakeover statutes	Requires shareholder approval; time consuming to implement unless subsidiary established before takeover solicitation
Gaolden Parachutes	Emboldens target management to negotiate for a higher premium and raises the cost of a takeover to the hostile bidder	Negative public perception; makes termination of top management expensive; cost not tax deductible; subject to nonbinding shareholder vote

investor Carl Icahn. Each shareholder, except Icahn, received a right for each common share held as of November 12, 2012, to buy one one-thousandth of a new preferred share at an exercise price of $350 per right if an investor acquires more than 10% of the firm without board approval. If triggered, each flip-in right entitled its holder to purchase by paying the right's exercise price a number of shares of Netflix common stock having a market value of twice the exercise price (i.e., $700). At the time of the issue, Netflix common stock traded at $76 per share. Each right would be convertible into 9.2 common shares [i.e., (2 × $350)/$76] if the pill were triggered. If the firm were merged into another firm or it were to sell more than 50% of its assets, each flip-over right would entitle the holder to buy a number of common shares of the acquirer at the then-market value at twice the exercise price following payment of the $350 exercise price.

Poison pill proponents argue that it prevents a raider from acquiring a substantial portion of the firm's stock without board permission. Since the board generally has the power to rescind the pill, bidders are compelled to negotiate with the target's board, which could result in a higher offer price. Pill defenses may be most effective when used with staggered board defenses, because a raider would be unable to remove the pill without winning two successive elections. This increases the likelihood of the target's remaining independent.[38] Detractors argue that pill defenses simply entrench management and encourage disaffected shareholders to litigate.

Shark Repellents

Shark repellents are takeover defenses achieved by amending either a *corporate charter* or the *corporation bylaws*.[39] They predate poison pills as a defense, and their success in slowing down takeovers and making them more expensive has been mixed. Today, shark repellents have largely become supplements to poison pill defenses. Their primary role is to make it more difficult to gain control of the board through a proxy fight at an annual or special meeting. In practice, shark repellents necessitate a shareholder vote because they require amendments to the firm's charter. Although there are many variations of shark repellents, the most typical are staggered board elections, restrictions on shareholder actions, antigreenmail provisions, differential voting rights shares, and debt-based defenses.

Strengthening the Board's Defenses

Corporate directors are elected at annual shareholder meetings by a vote of the holders of a majority of shares who are present and entitled to vote. The mechanism for electing directors differs among corporations, with voting shares being cast either through a straight vote or cumulatively. With *straight voting*, shareholders may cast all their votes for each member of the board of directors, thereby virtually ensuring that the majority shareholder(s) will elect all of the directors. For example, assume that a corporation has four directors up for election and has two shareholders, one owning 80 shares (i.e., the majority shareholder) and one owning 20 shares (i.e., the minority shareholder). With each share having one vote, the majority shareholder will always elect the director for whom he or she casts his or her votes. In *cumulative voting* systems, the number of votes each shareholder has equals the number of shares owned times the

---

[38] Bebchuk et al., 2002

[39] The charter gives the corporation its legal existence and consists of the *articles of incorporation,* a document filed with a state government by the founders of a corporation, and a *certificate of incorporation,* a document received from the state once the articles have been approved. The corporation's powers thus derive from the laws of the state and from the provisions of the charter. Rules governing the internal management of the corporation are described in the corporation's bylaws, which are determined by the corporation's founders.

number of directors to be elected. The shareholder may cast all of these votes for a single candidate or for any two or more candidates. With cumulative voting, all directors are elected at the same time. Using the same example, the majority shareholder will have 320 votes (80 × 4), and the minority shareholder will have 80 votes (20 × 4). If the minority shareholder casts all of her votes for herself, she is assured of a seat, since the majority shareholder cannot outvote the minority shareholder for all four board seats.[40]

In states where cumulative voting is mandatory, companies sometimes distribute the election of directors over a number of years to make it harder for a dissatisfied minority shareholder to gain control of the board. This makes it more difficult for the minority shareholder to elect a director when there is cumulative voting because there are fewer directors to be elected at one time. This so-called *staggered* or *classified board election* involves dividing the firm's directors into a number of different classes. Only one class is up for reelection each year. A 12-member board may have directors divided into four classes, with each director elected for a four-year period. In the first year, the three directors in what might be called "Class 1" are up for election; in the second year, "Class 2" directors are up for election; and so on. This means that a shareholder, even one who holds the majority of the stock, would have to wait for three election cycles to gain control of the board. Moreover, the size of the board is limited by the firm's bylaws to preclude the dissident shareholder from adding board seats to take control of the board.

For-cause provisions specify the conditions (e.g., fraud, noncompliance with prevailing regulations) for removing a member of the board of directors. This narrows the range of permissible reasons and limits the flexibility of dissident shareholders in contesting board seats.

Limiting Shareholder Actions

The board can also reinforce its control by restricting shareholders' ability to gain control of the firm by bypassing the board. Limits can be set on their ability to call special meetings, engage in consent solicitations, and use supermajority rules (explained later). Firms frequently rely on the conditions under which directors can be removed (i.e., the "for cause" provision discussed earlier) and a limitation on the number of board seats as defined in the firm's bylaws or charter.

In some states, shareholders may take action—without a special shareholders meeting—to add to the number of seats on the board, remove specific board members, or elect new members. These states allow dissatisfied shareholders to obtain support for their proposals simply by obtaining the written consent of shareholders under what is known as *consent solicitation*, a process that

---

[40]While there are many possible combinations, if the majority shareholder were to cast 81 votes for each of three seats, he would have only 77 votes remaining (i.e., 320–243) for the last seat. As the number of directors increases, it becomes easier for the minority shareholder to win a seat (or seats), since the majority shareholder's votes must be spread over more directors to block the minority shareholder.

still must abide by the disclosure requirements applicable to proxy contests. The process circumvents delays inherent in setting up a meeting to conduct a shareholder vote.[41] Corporate bylaws may include *advance-notice provisions* requiring shareholder proposals and board nominations to be announced well in advance, sometimes as long as two months, of an actual vote, to buy time for management. *Supermajority rules* require a higher level of approval than is standard to amend the charter for transactions such as a merger or acquisition. Such rules are triggered when an "interested party" acquires a specific percentage of the ownership shares (e.g., 5 to 10%). Supermajority rules may require that as much as 80% of the shareholders must approve a proposed merger or a simple majority of all shareholders except the potential acquirer.

Other Shark Repellents

Other shark repellent defenses include antigreenmail provisions, fair-price provisions, differential voting rights shares, reincorporation, and golden parachutes. These are discussed next.

Antigreenmail Provisions

During the 1980s, bidders profited by taking an equity position in a firm, threatening takeover, and subsequently selling their shares back to the firm at a premium over what they paid for them. The practice was dubbed "greenmail." Many firms have since adopted charter amendments, called *antigreenmail provisions*, restricting the firm's ability to repurchase shares at a premium.

Fair-Price Provisions

Requirements that any acquirer pay minority shareholders at least a fair market price for their stock are called *fair-price provisions*. The fair market price may be expressed as some historical multiple of the company's earnings or as a specific price equal to the maximum price paid when the buyer acquired shares in the company.[42]

Dual Class Recapitalization

A firm may create more than one class of stock to separate the performance of individual operating subsidiaries, compensate subsidiary operating management, maintain control, or prevent hostile takeovers. The process of creating another class

---

[41] Whereas the winning vote in a proxy fight is determined as a percentage of the number of votes actually cast, the winning vote in a consent solicitation is determined as a percentage of the number of shares outstanding. A dissatisfied shareholder may find it easier to win a proxy contest because many shareholders simply do not vote.

[42] In two-tiered tender offers, the fair-price provision forces the bidder to pay target shareholders who tender their stock in the second tier the same terms offered to those tendering their stock in the first tier.

of stock is called a *dual class recapitalization* and involves separating shareholder voting rights from cash flow rights. Voting rights indicate the degree of influence shareholders have over how a firm is managed, while cash flow rights are rights to receive dividends. Shares with different voting rights are called *differential voting rights* (DVR) shares and may have multiple voting rights (so-called supervoting shares), fractional voting rights, or no voting rights. DVR shares may have ten to 100 times the voting rights of another class of stock or a fraction of a voting right per share (e.g., a shareholder might be required to hold 100 DVR shares to cast one vote). Shares without voting rights but having cash flow rights may pay a dividend higher than those with voting rights. Once approved by shareholders, the new class of stock is issued as a pro rata stock dividend or an exchange offer, in which the new class of stock is offered for one currently outstanding.

Dual class structures tend to concentrate voting power as supervoting shares are issued as a pro rata dividend; later, shareholders are given the option of exchanging their supervoting shares for shares offering higher dividends, with managers retaining their supervoting shares. How this increased concentration impacts the value of the firm is unclear. Some studies find that firm value is reduced as controlling shareholders erect excessive takeover defenses and avoid higher risk value-enhancing investments.[43] Other studies document an increase in firm value when the firm moves from a single to a dual class capital structure. By enabling controlling shareholders to diversify their net worth by selling a portion of their equity in the firm, insiders may be more inclined to pursue higher-risk, higher-return investments to improve corporate performance.[44] Dual class IPOs may be particularly appropriate for firms in which the founding family or founding entrepreneur(s) are widely viewed as critical to the firm's long-term performance.[45] Examples include Mark Zuckerberg of Facebook and Larry Page and Sergey Brin of Google.

Reincorporation

A potential target may change the state within which it is incorporated to one where the laws are more favorable for implementing takeover defenses by creating a subsidiary in the new state and later merging with the parent. Several factors need to be considered in selecting a state, such as how the state's courts have ruled in lawsuits alleging breach of corporate director fiduciary responsibility in takeovers as well as the state's laws pertaining to certain takeover tactics and defenses. Reincorporation requires shareholder approval.

Golden Parachutes (Change-of-Control Payouts)

Employee severance packages, triggered whenever a change in control takes place, are called *golden parachutes*. These arrangements typically cover only a few

[43]Gompers et al., 2010; Lins, 2003; Claessens et al., 2002
[44]Baugess et al., 2012; Ferreira et al., 2010
[45]Chemmanur et al., 2012

dozen employees, who are terminated following the change in control. They are designed to raise the bidder's cost of the acquisition rather than to gain time for the target board. Such severance packages may also serve the interests of shareholders by making senior management more willing to accept an acquisition. There is evidence that golden parachutes benefit target shareholders by increasing the likelihood deals will be completed, but often at a lower purchase-price premium.[46] Actual payouts to management, such as accelerated equity awards, pensions, and other deferred compensation following a change in control, may significantly exceed the value of the so-called golden parachutes.[47] Tax considerations and recent legislation affect corporate decisions to implement such compensation packages.[48]

Postoffer Defenses

Once an unwanted suitor has approached a firm, a variety of additional defenses can be introduced. These include greenmail to dissuade the bidder from continuing the pursuit; defenses designed to make the target less attractive, such as restructuring and recapitalization strategies; and efforts to place an increasing share of the company's ownership in friendly hands by establishing employee stock ownership plans (ESOPs) or seeking white knights. Table 3.5 summarizes the advantages and disadvantages of these postoffer defenses.

Greenmail

Greenmail (introduced earlier) is the practice of paying a potential acquirer to leave you alone. It consists of a payment to buy back shares at a premium price in exchange for the acquirer's agreement not to initiate a hostile takeover. In exchange for the payment, the potential acquirer is required to sign a *standstill agreement*, which specifies the amount of stock, if any, the investor can own and the circumstances under which the raider can sell such stock.[49]

White Knights

A target may seek a *white knight*: another firm that is considered a more appropriate suitor. The white knight must be willing to acquire the target on terms

---

[46] Fich et al., 2013

[47] Offenberg et al., 2012

[48] The 1986 Tax Act imposed penalties on these types of plans if they create payments that exceed three times the employee's average pay over the previous five years and treats them as income and thus not tax-deductible by the paying corporation. More recently, the Dodd-Frank bill of 2010 gives shareholders the opportunity to express their disapproval of golden parachutes through a nonbinding vote.

[49] Courts view greenmail as discriminatory because not all shareholders are offered the opportunity to sell their stock back to the target firm at an above-market price. Nevertheless, courts in some states (e.g., Delaware) have found it appropriate if done for valid business reasons. Courts in other states (e.g., California) have favored shareholder lawsuits, contending that greenmail breaches fiduciary responsibility.

TABLE 3.5 Advantages and Disadvantages of Postoffer Takeover Defenses

Type of Defense	Advantages for Target Firm	Disadvantages for Target Firm
Greenmail	Encourages raider to go away (usually accompanied by a standstill agreement)	Reduces risk to raider of losing money on a takeover attempt; unfairly discriminates against nonparticipating shareholders; generates litigation; triggers unfavorable tax issues and bad publicity
Standstill Agreement	Prevents raider from returning for a specific time period	Increases amount of greenmail paid to get raider to sign standstill; provides only temporary reprieve
White Knights	May be preferable to the hostile bidder	Involves loss of target's independence
ESOPs	Alternative to white knight and highly effective if used in conjunction with certain states' antitakeover laws	Employee support not guaranteed; ESOP cannot overpay for stock because transaction could be disallowed by federal law
Recapitalizations	Makes target less attractive to bidder and may increase target shareholder value if incumbent management motivated to improve performance	Increased leverage reduces target's borrowing capacity
Share Buyback Plans	Reduces number of target shares available for purchase by bidder, arbs, and others who may sell to bidder	Cannot self-tender without SEC filing once hostile tender under way; reduction in the shares outstanding may facilitate bidder's gaining control
Corporate Restructuring	Going private may be an attractive alternative to bidder's offer for target shareholders and for incumbent management	Going private, sale of attractive assets, making defensive acquisitions, or liquidation may reduce target's shareholder value vs. bidder's offer
Litigation	May buy time for target to build defenses and increases takeover cost to the bidder	May have negative impact on target shareholder returns

more favorable than those of other bidders. Fearing a bidding war, the white knight often demands some protection in the form of a lockup. This may involve giving the white knight options to buy stock in the target that has not yet been issued at a fixed price or to acquire specific target assets at a fair price. Such lockups usually make the target less attractive to other bidders. If a bidding war does ensue, the knight may exercise the stock options and sell the shares at a profit to the acquiring company.

Employee Stock Ownership Plans

ESOPs are trusts that hold a firm's stock as an investment for its employees' retirement program. They can be quickly set up, with the firm either issuing shares directly to the ESOP or having an ESOP purchase shares on the open market. The stock held by an ESOP is likely to be voted in support of management in the event of a hostile takeover attempt (see Chapter 1 for more detail).

Leveraged Recapitalization

A firm may recapitalize by assuming substantial amounts of new debt either to buy back stock or to finance a dividend payment to shareholders. The additional debt reduces the firm's borrowing capacity and leaves it in a highly leveraged position, making it less attractive to a bidder that may have wanted to use that capacity to help finance a takeover. Moreover, the payment of a dividend or a stock buyback may persuade shareholders to support the target's management in a proxy contest or hostile tender offer.[50] Recapitalization may require shareholder approval, depending on the company's charter and the laws of the state in which it is incorporated.[51]

Share Repurchase or Buyback Plans

Firms repurchase shares to reward shareholders, signal undervaluation, fund ESOPs, adjust capital structure, and defend against takeovers.[52] When used as a takeover defense, share buybacks reduce the number of shares that could be purchased by the potential buyer or by arbitrageurs who will sell to the highest bidder. What remains are shares held by those who are less likely to sell. So for a hostile tender offer to succeed in purchasing the remaining shares, the premium offered would have to be higher, thereby discouraging some prospective bidders. There is considerable evidence that buyback strategies are an effective deterrent.[53] However, the buyback may reduce the number of shares outstanding, making it easier for the bidder to gain control because fewer shares have to be purchased to achieve a controlling interest.

[50] The primary differences between a leveraged recapitalization and a leveraged buyout are that the firm remains a public company and that management does not take a significant equity stake in the firm.

[51] Shareholders will benefit from the receipt of a dividend or from capital gains resulting from a stock repurchase. The increased interest expense shelters some of the firm's taxable income and may encourage management to improve the firm's performance. Thus, current shareholders may benefit more from this takeover defense than from a hostile takeover of the firm.

[52] According to Billett and Xue (2007), firms frequently increase their share repurchase activities when confronted with an imminent takeover threat.

[53] Potential acquirers are less likely to pursue firms with substantial excess cash, which could be used to adopt highly aggressive share repurchase programs (Harford, 1999; Pinkowitz, 2002; Faleye, 2004).

Corporate Restructuring

Restructuring may involve taking the company private, selling attractive assets, undertaking a major acquisition, or even liquidating the company. "Going private" typically involves the management team's purchase of the bulk of a firm's shares. This may create a win–win situation for shareholders, who receive a premium for their stock, and management, who retain control. Alternatively, the target may make itself less attractive by divesting assets the bidder wants, with the proceeds financing share buybacks or payment of a special stockholder dividend. A target company may also undertake a so-called *defensive acquisition* to draw down any excess cash balances and to exhaust its current borrowing capacity. A firm may choose to liquidate the company, pay off outstanding obligations to creditors, and distribute the remaining proceeds to shareholders as a *liquidating dividend*. This makes sense only if the liquidating dividend exceeds what the shareholders would have received from the bidder.

Litigation

Lawsuits may involve alleged antitrust concerns, violations federal securities laws, undervaluation of the target, inadequate disclosure by the bidder as required by the Williams Act, and fraudulent behavior. Targets often seek a court injunction to stop a takeover until the court has decided the merits of the allegations. By preventing a bidder from buying more stock, the target firm is buying more time to erect additional defenses. While litigation is seldom successful in preventing a takeover, it may uncover additional information about the bidder through the ensuing discovery, or fact-finding, process that leads to more substantive lawsuits. Bidders may sue targets to obtain shareholder mailing lists or to have arguably unreasonable takeover defensives removed. While the probability of completing deals embroiled in litigation falls by about 8%, the takeover premium for those deals that are completed increases by about 30%.[54]

THE IMPACT OF TAKEOVER DEFENSES ON SHAREHOLDER VALUE

Empirical evidence suggests that on average takeover defenses have a slightly negative impact on firm value, while those instituted prior to an IPO or during the early stages of the firm's development can increase shareholder value.

Takeover Defenses and Target Firm Shareholder Financial Returns

Early empirical studies provide inconsistent results. Some empirical studies suggest that takeover defenses in general have virtually no statistically

---

[54]Krishnan et al., 2012

significant impact on shareholder returns.[55] Other studies point to poison pills having a positive impact.[56] Studies that find a positive return seem to support the idea that incumbent management acts in the best interests of shareholders (the shareholders'-interests hypothesis), while those studies that find a negative return seem to support the notion that incumbent management acts in its own interests (the management-entrenchment hypothesis). Overall, the earlier research suggests that takeover defenses have a slightly negative impact on target shareholder returns.[57]

Recent research provides more consistent evidence that takeover defenses destroy shareholder value. For instance, the creation of a detailed "management entrenchment index" revealed that during the 1990s, firms scoring lower on the index (i.e., exhibiting lower levels of entrenchment) had larger positive abnormal returns than firms with higher scores.[58] In other words, firms with a management team that acted not in its own best interest but more for the interest of the shareholders performed better. However, the close correlation between a firm's entrenchment and abnormal returns disappeared in the 2000s, since investors had already bid up the prices of those firms that had removed takeover defenses in the 1990s and penalized those that had not.[59] Another large study concludes that managers at firms protected by takeover defenses are less subject to takeover and are more likely to engage in "empire building" acquisitions that destroy firm value.[60] Firm value may also be reduced because managers shielded from the threat of a hostile buyout may be under less pressure to innovate.[61] Still another study found that firms moving from staggered board elections to annual elections of directors experience a cumulative abnormal

---

[55] Karpoff and Walkling (1996); Field and Karpoff (2002)

[56] Comment and Schwert (1995) found that poison pills have a positive impact on shareholder returns if investors believe a takeover is imminent or that the firm's management would use such a defense to improve the purchase price during negotiation. Several studies suggest that investors will react positively to the announcement of the adoption of takeover defenses if the firm's management interests are viewed as aligned with those of shareholders and will react negatively if management is viewed as seeking to entrench itself (Boyle et al., 1998; Malekzadeh et al., 1998).

[57] Comment and Schwert (1995) conducted a comprehensive review of previous studies and found that most takeover defensives resulted in a slightly negative decline in shareholder returns of about 0.5%.

[58] Bebchuk et al. (2005) created a management entrenchment index in an effort to assess which of 24 provisions tracked by the Investor Responsibility Research Center (IRRC) had the greatest impact on shareholder value. The index, which is negatively correlated with firm value between 1990 and 2003, includes staggered boards, limits to shareholder bylaw amendments, supermajority requirements for mergers, supermajority requirements for charter amendments, poison pills, and golden parachutes.

[59] Bebchuk, Cohen, and Wang, 2010

[60] Masulis et al., 2007

[61] Atanassov, 2012

return of 1.8%, reflecting investor expectations that the firm is more likely to be subject to a takeover.

Takeover defenses can have subtle wealth-creating effects for target firm shareholders. Takeover defenses reduce the likelihood of a bid but not the success of a bid once it is made. That is, formidable defenses discourage opportunistic bidders seeking buyouts at "bargain" prices. Therefore, the bids that are received by target firms with defenses in place are likely to be higher than they would have been had the firm been defenseless.[62] Studies also show that staggered boards can be effective in helping a firm lower its cost of debt[63] and enable management to focus on longer-term value-enhancing investments such as R&D.[64]

Takeover Defenses and Public Offerings

There is evidence that takeover defenses create firm value at the very point the firm is formed (i.e., an IPO) if they help the firm attract, retain, and motivate effective managers and employees. Furthermore, such defenses give the new firm time to implement its business plan fully and to invest in upgrading the skills of employees.[65] There is also evidence that investors may prefer the adoption of takeover defenses during the early stages of a firm's development.[66]

SOME THINGS TO REMEMBER

Corporate takeovers facilitate the allocation of resources and promote good governance by disciplining underperforming managers. Other factors external to the firm—such as federal and state legislation, the court system, regulators, and institutional activism—also serve important roles in maintaining good governance practices. Governance is also affected by the professionalism of the firm's board of directors as well as by the effectiveness of the firm's internal controls and incentive systems, takeover defenses, and corporate culture.

---

[62] Goktan et al., 2012

[63] Chen (2012) argues that by reducing concern over takeovers, managers are less inclined to engage in high-risk strategies and engage in more detailed financial disclosure. Both activities aid bondholders.

[64] Duru et al., 2012

[65] Stout, 2002

[66] This is suggested by the finding of Coates (2001) that the percentage of IPO firms with staggered boards in their charters at the time of the initial public offering rose from 34% in the early 1990s to 82% in 1999.

DISCUSSION QUESTIONS

3.1 What are the management-entrenchment and the shareholders'-interests hypotheses? Which seems more realistic in your judgment? Explain your answer.

3.2 What are the advantages and disadvantages of the friendly versus hostile approaches to a corporate takeover? Be specific.

3.3 What are the primary advantages and disadvantages of commonly used takeover defenses?

3.4 How may golden parachutes for senior management help a target firm's shareholders? Are such severance packages justified in your judgment? Explain your answer.

3.5 How might recapitalization as a takeover defense help or hurt a target firm's shareholders?

3.6 Anheuser-Busch (AB) rejected InBev's all-cash offer price of $65 per share, saying it undervalued the company, despite the offer's representing a 35% premium to AB's preannouncement share price. InBev refused to raise its offer while repeating its strong preference for a friendly takeover. Speculate as to why InBev refused to raise its initial offer price. Why do you believe that InBev continued to prefer a friendly takeover? What do you think InBev should have done to raise pressure on the AB board to accept the offer?

3.7 What do you believe are the primary factors a target firm's board should consider when evaluating a bid from a potential acquirer?

3.8 If you were the CEO of a target firm, what strategy would you recommend to convince institutional shareholders to support your position in a proxy battle with the bidding firm?

3.9 Anheuser-Busch reduced its antitakeover defenses in 2006, when it removed its staggered board structure. Two years earlier, it did not renew its poison pill provision. Speculate as to why the board acquiesced in these instances. Explain how these events may have affected the firm's vulnerability to a takeover.

3.10 In response to Microsoft's efforts to acquire the firm, the Yahoo! board adopted a "change in-control" compensation plan. The plan stated that if a Yahoo! employee's job is terminated by Yahoo! without cause (i.e., the employee is performing his or her duties appropriately) or if an employee leaves voluntarily due to a change in position or responsibilities within two years after Microsoft acquires a controlling interest in Yahoo!, the employee will receive one year's salary. Yahoo! notes that the adoption of the severance plan is an effort to ensure that employees are treated fairly if Microsoft wins control. Microsoft views the tactic as an effort to discourage a takeover. With whom do you agree, and why?

Answers to these Chapter Discussion Questions are available in the Online Instructor's Manual for instructors using this book.

QUESTIONS FROM THE CFA CURRICULUM

3.11 Which of the following is an example of a conflict of interest that an effective corporate governance system would mitigate or eliminate?

    a. A majority of the board is independent of management.

    b. Directors identify with managers' interests rather than those of the shareholders.

    c. Directors have board experience with companies regarded as having sound governance practices.

Source: CFA Institute, 2011 Corporate Governance, Reading 32, question 2

3.12 Which of the following best describes the corporate governance responsibilities of members of the board of directors?

    a. Establish long-term strategic objectives for the company.

    b. Ensure that at board meetings everything can be discussed and dissent is regarded as an obligation.

    c. Ensure that the board negotiates with the company over all matters such as compensation.

Source: CFA Institute 2011 Corporate Governance, Reading 32, questions 3.

Answers to questions from the CFA curriculum are available in the Online Student Companion site to this book in a file folder entitled CFA Curriculum Questions and Solutions.

CASE STUDY 3.1
Teva Acquires Cephalon in a Hostile Takeover

Key Points

- Friendly approaches are most commonly employed in corporate takeovers.
- Hostile takeovers may be employed by the bidder to break an impasse.
- Unplanned events are often a deciding factor in the timing of takeovers and the magnitude of the winning bid.

Discussions about a possible merger between Israel's mega generic-drug maker Teva Pharmaceutical Industries Ltd. (Teva) and a specialty drug firm, Cephalon Inc. (Cephalon), had been under way for more than a year. However, they took on a sense of heightened urgency following an unexpected public announcement on March 29, 2011, of an unsolicited tender offer for U.S.-based Cephalon by Canada's Valeant Pharmaceuticals International Ltd. (Valeant). The Valeant offer was valued at $5.7 billion, or $73 per Cephalon share. Cephalon had already rebuffed several friendly merger proposals made privately from Valeant earlier in 2011. Valeant, known for employing aggressive takeover tactics, decided to break the impasse in its discussions with Cephalon's board and management by taking its offer public.

Valeant argued publicly that their offer was fair and that the loss of patent protection for Cephalon's top-selling sleep-disorder drug, Provigil, in 2012 and the tepid adoption of a new version of the drug called Nuvigil would make it difficult for Cephalon to prosper on its own. Cephalon responded that the Valeant offer had undervalued the company. Valeant coupled its hostile offer with the mailing of a proposal to Cephalon shareholders to replace Cephalon's board with its own chosen directors and to have the new board rescind Cephalon's shareholder rights plan. Shareholders only had to sign and return a response card to Valeant giving the firm the right to vote their shares in support of the proposal to change the composition of the Cephalon board. Cephalon distributed their own candidates for the Cephalon board to the shareholders.

Valeant had a reputation for aggressive cost cutting and improving earnings performance by paring back its own internal R&D activities and acquiring new drugs through the acquisition of other pharmaceutical companies. This was in marked contrast to the more traditional approach taken by many pharmaceutical companies, which involved heavy reinvestment in internal research and development to develop new drugs.

Valeant's approach has been to cut R&D costs ruthlessly, seek undervalued targets, set aggressive timeframes for integrating acquisitions, and to use cash rather than equity. This set Valeant apart from many other pharmaceutical firms, which have commonly used equity to make acquisitions, despite the research showing that equity-financed deals tend to underperform those in which the purchase price was mainly cash.

Given its reputation, attempts to get an agreement between Valeant and Cephalon were in trouble from the outset. Valeant was not interested in Cephalon's oncology products and even proposed buying only the firm's non-oncology drugs. Cephalon's board and management showed little interest in dismembering the firm and proceeded to acquire U.S.-based Gemin X Pharmaceuticals Inc. for $225 million on March 21, 2011, and to buy up the outstanding shares of ChemGenex Pharmaceuticals Ltd of Australia for $175 million. The use of cash for these purposes substantially reduced the firm's cash balances.

Teva had significantly greater appeal to the Cephalon board, since it had expressed interest in the entire company. Teva was also willing to pay a substantially higher purchase price because of the greater perceived synergy between the two companies. To understand the source of this synergy it is important to recognize that Teva has historically been viewed by investors as primarily a manufacturer of low-margin pharmaceuticals. Profit margins on such drugs tend to be substantially less than those of branded drugs and were likely to continue to decline due to increased competition and government and insurance company pressure to reduce selling prices. Teva did have its own blockbuster branded drug, Copaxone, which accounted for 21% of the firm's $16.1 billion in 2010. However, the drug was going to lose patent protection in 2014.

Teva needed to achieve a better balance between branded and generic products. Acquiring Cephalon, with its strong drug pipeline and fast-growing cancer drug Treanda and pain medicine Fentora, offered the potential for offsetting any loss of Copaxone revenue and of expanding Teva's offering of high-margin branded drugs. These drugs would complement Teva's own portfolio of drugs, serving therapeutic areas ranging from central nervous system disorders to oncology to pain management, that generated $2.8 billion in 2010. With Cephalon, branded drugs would account for 36% of the combined firms' revenue. Together, the combined firms would have 30 pharmaceuticals at least at the mid-development stage. Teva believed the deal would be accretive immediately, with $500 million in annual cost savings and synergies realized within three years. Although the deal did offer cost-cutting opportunities, the ability to broaden the firm's product offering was a far greater attraction.

With this in mind, Teva lost little time in exploiting Cephalon's efforts to ward off Valeant's March 29 unwanted takeover bid by moving aggressively to trump Valeant's offer. Teva's all-cash bid of $81.50 per share represented an approximate 12% premium to Valeant's $73 per share offer and a 39% premium to Cephalon's share price the day after Valeant's announced its bid. The deal, including the conversion of its convertible debentures and stock options, is worth $6.8 billion to Cephalon's shareholders. The purchase agreement included a breakup fee of $275 million, about 4% of the purchase price.

Having publicly stated that they thought their offer fully valued the business, Valeant withdrew its offer after the joint Cephalon–Teva announcement on May 2, 2011. Valeant could not continue to pursue Cephalon unless it was willing to run the risk of being publicly perceived as overpaying for the target. Investors reacted favorably, with Cephalon's stock and Teva's rising 4.2% and 3.5%, respectively, on the announcement. Expressing their disappointment, investors drove Valeant's share price down by 6.5%. Valeant would still profit from the 1 million Cephalon shares it had acquired prior to Teva's and Cephalon's public announcement of their agreement. These shares had been acquired at prices below Teva's winning bid of $81.50 per share.

The acquisition of Cephalon marks the third major deal for Teva in four years as it continues to implement its business strategy of broadening its product portfolio by diversifying between generic-drug offerings and higher-margin branded offerings through acquisitions. This strategy is designed to reduce the firm's reliance on any single drug or handful of drugs.

Discussion Questions

1. What were the motivations for Valeant and Teva to be interested in acquiring Cephalon?
2. Identify the takeover tactics employed by Valeant and Teva. Explain why each was used.
3. What alternative strategies could Valeant and Teva have pursued?
4. Identify the takeover defenses employed by Cephalon. Explain why each was used.
5. What does the reaction of investors tell you about how they valued the combination of either Valeant or Teva with Cephalon? Be specific.
6. Why do the shares of acquiring companies tend to perform better when cash is used to make the acquisition rather than equity?

Solutions to these questions are found in the Online Instructor's Manual available to instructors using this book.

CASE STUDY 3.2
Balancing Board and Shareholder Rights: Air Products Aborted Takeover of Airgas

Key Points

- Defining the right balance of power between corporate boards and shareholders remains elusive.
- The Delaware court has ruled that a board can take as long as necessary to consider a bid and can prevent shareholders from voting on takeover bids.
- Activist investors are increasingly urging shareholders to pressure firms to drop staggered boards because of the potential to entrench management.

When, if ever, is it appropriate for a board to agree to a current bid to buy the firm if it, in good faith, believes that the bid undervalues the firm based on the board's knowledge of the long-term outlook for the firm? When, if ever, is it appropriate for a board to prevent shareholder votes on such matters? The answers to these questions are rooted in whether boards are perceived to be acting in the interests of all shareholders or simply attempting to entrench themselves and current management. How these questions are answered will determine whether the board or shareholders will have leverage in hostile takeover negotiations. What follows is a discussion of what is an important judicial precedent pertaining to board and shareholder rights.

The unsolicited offer by Air Products for Airgas on February 2, 2010, has been one of the longest-running hostile bids in U.S. history. After having revised up its offer twice, Air Products sought to bring this process to a close when it asked the Delaware Chancery Court to invalidate Airgas's poison pill. On February 15, 2011, the court ruled that the board has the right to prevent shareholders from voting on the takeover offer as long as it is acting in good faith. In the wake of the court's ruling, Air Products withdrew its bid.

The court argued that the Airgas board determined, using a good-faith effort, that the Air Products offer of $70 per share was inadequate and allowed Airgas to use a poison pill to defeat the hostile bid by Air Products. A firm is believed to have undertaken a good-faith effort when it has exhausted all reasonable means of resolving an issue. Airgas's board had demanded a bid of $78 per share. Because the Air Products bid was viewed as inadequate, the court ruled that Airgas could keep the poison pill in place against the will of the shareholders. The court also argued that the poison pill was not preventing Air Products from changing the composition of the board but, rather, extending the amount of time required to do so. The court also ruled that directors have the right to prevent shareholder votes if they believe that shareholders would accept a bid that undervalued the firm out of ignorance of the firm's true value.

In practice, the additional time that would have been required to change the composition of the board when the board is classified, as was the case with Airgas, is usually enough to force the bidder to walk away. Once an unsolicited bid is initiated, the composition of a target firm's shareholders moves from its long-term investors, who often sell when the offer is announced, to arbitrageurs and hedge funds, seeking to profit from temporary differences in the offer price and the target's short-term share price. From their perspective, the faster a deal is done, the greater their return on investment. Reflecting the change in composition of their shareholder base, target boards come under intense pressure to sell. However, the fiduciary responsibility of boards is to ensure that any bids are in the best interests of their shareholders; takeover defenses in the view of the board give them more time to evaluate the initial offer and to hold out for higher bids.

The court's decision illustrates how a poison pill can work in concert with a classified or staggered board, in which directors are elected one-third at a time. Bidders must therefore wait two years to elect a majority of the total board and force the poison pill to be rescinded. This combination has proven to be a highly potent anti-takeover defense. Air Products' bid for Airgas highlights the challenges of attempting to take control of another firm's board. Even if Air Products had been successful in electing a majority of board members, there was no assurance the new board would have supported the $70 Air Products bid. The Airgas rejection of their bid came after three new directors nominated by Air Products had been elected to the Airgas board in 2009. Instead of campaigning for a sale, the three new directors joined the rest of the Airgas board in demanding a higher price from Air Products.

The outcome of the court's ruling has implications for future hostile takeovers. The ruling upholds Delaware's long tradition of respecting managerial discretion as long as the board is found to be acting in good faith and abiding by its fiduciary responsibilities to the firm's shareholders. The ruling allows target firm boards to use a poison pill as long as the board deems justified, and it is far-reaching because Delaware law governs most U.S. publicly traded firms.

Discussion Questions

1. Do you believe that shareholders should always have the right to vote on a sale of the firm under any circumstances? Explain your answer.
2. Do you agree with the Delaware Chancery Court's ruling? Explain your answer.
3. Under what circumstances does the combination of a poison pill and a staggered board make sense for the target firm's shareholders? Be specific.
4. How might this court ruling impact the willingness of acquirers in the future to undertake hostile takeovers?

Solutions to these discussion questions are available in the Online Instructor's Manual for instructors using this book.

THE MERGERS AND ACQUISITIONS PROCESS

Phases 1–10

"The take-over seems to be going smoothly enough."

Part II views mergers and acquisitions not as business strategies but, rather, as a means of implementing business strategies. Business strategies define a firm's vision and long-term objectives and how it expects to achieve these ends. M&As simply represent one means of implementing the business strategy. The firm may choose from a range of reasonable alternative implementation strategies, including going it alone, partnering, and acquiring another firm.

Chapters 4 through 6 discuss the various activities often undertaken in M&As. These activities comprise the 10 phases of an M&A process. While not all mergers and acquisitions unfold in exactly the same way, the process outlined in this section serves as a roadmap for executing such transactions. This process is sufficiently flexible to be applicable to alternatives to M&As, such as business alliances, which are discussed in detail in Chapter 15.

Chapter 4 focuses on how to develop a business plan or strategy and, if an acquisition is viewed as the best way of realizing the business strategy, how to develop an acquisition plan. Chapter 5 deals with identifying, making initial contact with the potential target, and developing the necessary legal documents prior to beginning due diligence and formal negotiations. While initial valuations provide a starting point, the actual purchase price is determined during the negotiation period. If agreement can be reached, planning the integration of the target firm begins between the signing of the purchase agreement and the closing. The motivation for each phase of the process is discussed in detail.

Chapter 6 discusses the role of pre-integration planning and the common obstacles arising during the post-closing integration effort and how to overcome such challenges. While each phase of the M&A process represents a critical step in completing a transaction, integration often is viewed as among the most important. It is only after the target and acquiring firms have been combined successfully that the anticipated value of the transaction is realized.

Planning: Developing Business and Acquisition Plans
Phases 1 and 2 of the Acquisition Process

*If you don't know where you are going, any road will get you there. —**Lewis Carroll,** Alice's Adventures in Wonderland*

INSIDE M&A: FROM A SOCIAL MEDIA DARLING TO AN AFTERTHOUGHT—THE DEMISE OF MYSPACE

KEY POINTS

- It is critical to understand a firm's competitive edge and what it takes to sustain it.
- Sustaining a competitive advantage in a fast-moving market requires ongoing investment and nimble and creative decision making.
- In the end, Myspace appears to have had neither.

A pioneer in social networking, Myspace started in 2003 and reached its peak in popularity in December 2008. According to ComScore, Myspace attracted 75.9 million monthly unique visitors in the United States that month. It was more than just a social network; it was viewed by many as a portal where people discovered new friends and music and movies. Its annual revenue in 2009 was reportedly more than $470 million.

Myspace captured the imagination of media star, Rupert Murdoch, founder and CEO of media conglomerate News Corp. News Corp seemed to view the firm as the cornerstone of its social networking strategy, in which it would sell content to users of social networking sites. To catapult News Corp into the world of social networking, Murdock acquired Myspace and its parent firm, Intermix, in 2007 for an estimated $580 million. But News Corp's timing could not have been worse. Between mid-2009 and mid-2011, Myspace was losing more than

1 million visitors monthly, with unique visitors in May 2011 about one-half of their previous December 2008 peak. Advertising revenue swooned to $184 million in 2011, about 40% of its 2009 level.[1]

In the wake of Myspace's deteriorating financial performance, News Corp initiated a search for a buyer in early 2011. The initial asking price was $100 million. Despite a flurry of interest in social media businesses such as LinkedIn and Groupon, there was little interest in buying Myspace. In an act of desperation, News Corp sold Myspace to Specific Media, an advertising firm, for only $35 million in mid-2011 as the value of the MySpace brand plummeted.

What happened to cause Myspace to fall from grace so rapidly? A range of missteps befuddled Myspace, including a flawed business strategy, mismanagement, and underinvestment. Myspace may also have been a victim of fast-moving technology, fickle popular culture, and the hubris that comes with rapid early success. What appeared to be an unimaginative strategy and underinvestment left the social media field wide open for new entrants, such as Facebook. Myspace may also have suffered from waning interest from News Corp's top management. As consumer interest in Myspace declined, News Corp turned its attention to its acquisition of the *Wall Street Journal*. Culture clash may also have been a problem when News Corp, a large, highly structured media firm, tried to absorb the brassy startup. With a big company, there are more meetings, more reporting relationships, more routine, and more monitoring by senior management of the parent firm. Myspace managers' attention was often diverted in an effort to create synergy with other News Corp businesses.

In the new era of social media, the rapid rise and fall of Myspace illustrates the ever-decreasing life cycle of such businesses. When News Corp bought Myspace, it was a thriving online social networking business. Facebook was still contained primarily on college campuses. However, it was not long before Facebook, with its smooth interface and broader offering of online services, far outpaced Myspace in terms of monthly visitors. Myspace, like so many other Internet startups, had its "fifteen minutes of fame."

CHAPTER OVERIVEW

A poorly designed business strategy is among the reasons commonly given when mergers and acquisitions fail to satisfy expectations. Too often, the overarching role planning should take in conceptualizing and implementing business combinations is ignored. Some companies view mergers and acquisitions as a business growth strategy. Here, in accord with the view of many successful acquirers,[2] M&As are not considered a business strategy but rather a means of implementing a business strategy. While firms may accelerate overall growth in the short run through acquisition, the higher growth rate is often not sustainable

---

[1]Gillette, *Bloomberg BusinessWeek*, July 3, 2011, pp. 54–57.
[2]Palter and Srinivasan, 2006

without a business plan—which serves as a road map for identifying additional acquisitions to fuel future growth.

This chapter focuses on the first two phases of the acquisition process—building the business and acquisition plans—and on the tools commonly used to evaluate, display, and communicate information to key constituencies both inside the corporation (e.g., board of directors and management) and outside (e.g., lenders and stockholders). Phases 3–10 are discussed in Chapter 5. Subsequent chapters detail the remaining phases of the M&A process. A review of this chapter (including practice questions and answers) is available in the file folder entitled Student Study Guide and a listing of Common Industry Information Sources are contained on the companion site to this book (http://booksite.elsevier.com/9780123854872).

THE ROLE OF PLANNING IN MERGERS AND ACQUISITIONS

The acquisition process envisioned here can be separated into two stages. The *planning* stage comprises developing business and acquisition plans. The *implementation* stage (discussed in Chapter 5) includes the search, screening, contacting the target, negotiation, integration planning, closing, integration, and evaluation activities.

Key Business Planning Concepts

A planning-based acquisition process starts with both a business plan and a merger/acquisition plan, which drive all subsequent phases of the acquisition process. The *business plan* articulates a mission or vision for the firm and a *business strategy* for realizing that mission for all of the firm's stakeholders. *Stakeholders* are constituent groups, such as customers, shareholders, employees, suppliers, lenders, regulators, and communities. The business strategy is oriented to the long term and usually cuts across organizational lines to affect many different functional areas. Typically, it is broadly defined and provides relatively little detail.

With respect to business strategy, it can be important to distinguish between corporate-level and business-level strategies. *Corporate-level strategies* are set by the management of a diversified or multiproduct firm and generally cross business unit organizational lines. They entail decisions about financing the growth of certain businesses, operating others to generate cash, divesting some units, and pursuing diversification. *Business-level strategies* are set by the management of a specific operating unit within the corporate organizational structure and may involve a unit's attempting to achieve a low-cost position in the markets it serves, differentiating its product offering, or narrowing its operational focus to a specific market niche.

The *implementation strategy* refers to the way in which the firm chooses to execute the business strategy. It is usually far more detailed than the business strategy. The *merger/acquisition plan* is a specific type of implementation strategy and describes in detail the motivation for the acquisition and how and when it will be achieved. *Functional strategies* describe in detail how each major function within the firm (e.g., manufacturing, marketing, and human resources) will support the business strategy. *Contingency plans* are actions that are taken as an alternative to the firm's current business strategy. The selection of which alternative action to pursue may be contingent on the occurrence of certain events called *trigger points* (e.g., failure to realize revenue targets or cost savings), at which point a firm faces a number of alternatives, sometimes referred to as *real options*. These include abandoning, delaying, or accelerating an investment strategy. Unlike the strategic options discussed later in this chapter, real options are decisions that can be made after an investment has been made.

THE MERGER AND ACQUISITION PROCESS

An M&A process is the series of activities culminating in the transfer of ownership from the seller to the buyer. Some individuals shudder at the thought of following a structured process because they believe it may delay responding to opportunities, both anticipated and unanticipated. Anticipated opportunities are those identified as a result of the business planning process: Understanding the firm's external operating environment, assessing internal resources, reviewing a range of reasonable options, and articulating a clear vision of the future of the business and a realistic strategy for achieving that vision. Unanticipated opportunities may emerge as new information becomes available. Having a well-designed business plan does not delay pursuing opportunities; rather, it provides a way to evaluate the opportunity, rapidly and substantively, by determining the extent to which the opportunity supports realization of the business plan.

Figure 4.1 illustrates the 10 phases of the M&A process described in this and subsequent chapters. These phases fall into two distinct sets of activities: pre- and postpurchase decision activities. Negotiation, with its four largely concurrent and interrelated activities, is the crucial phase of the acquisition process. The decision to purchase or walk away is determined as a result of continuous iteration through the four activities comprising the negotiation phase.

The phases of the M&A process are summarized as follows:

Phase 1: Business Plan—Develop a strategic plan for the entire business.
Phase 2: Acquisitions Plan—Develop the acquisition plan supporting the business plan.
Phase 3: Search—Search actively for acquisition candidates.
Phase 4: Screen—Screen and prioritize potential candidates.
Phase 5: First Contact—Initiate contact with the target.
Phase 6: Negotiation—Refine valuation, structure the deal, perform due diligence, and develop the financing plan.
Phase 7: Integration Plan—Develop a plan for integrating the acquired business.
Phase 8: Closing—Obtain the necessary approvals, resolve postclosing issues, and execute the closing.

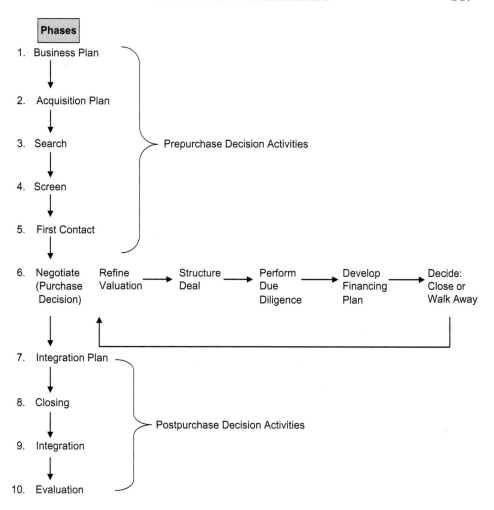

FIGURE 4.1   Flow diagram for the acquisition process.

Phase 9: Integration—Implement the postclosing integration.
Phase 10: Evaluation—Conduct the postclosing evaluation of acquisition.

PHASE 1: BUILDING THE BUSINESS PLAN

A well-designed business plan results from eight key activities, summarized next. The process of developing a business plan can be facilitated by addressing a number of detailed questions corresponding to each of these activities.[3]

[3]Extensive checklists can be found in Porter (1985). Answering these types of questions requires gathering substantial economic, industry, and market information.

The first activity is the *external analysis* to determine where to compete—that is, which industry or market(s)—and how to compete—that is, how the firm can most effectively compete in its chosen market(s). This is followed by the *internal analysis,* or self-assessment, of the firm's strengths and weaknesses relative to its competition. The combination of these two activities—the external and internal analyses—is often called *SWOT analysis* because it determines the strengths, weaknesses, opportunities, and threats of a business. Once this analysis is completed, management has a clearer understanding of emerging opportunities and threats to the firm and of the firm's primary internal strengths and weaknesses. Information gleaned from the external and internal analyses drives the development of business, implementation, and functional strategies.

The third activity is to define a *mission statement* that summarizes where and how the firm has chosen to compete, based on the external analysis, as well as management's basic operating beliefs and values. Fourth, *objectives* are set, and quantitative measures of financial and nonfinancial performance are developed. Having completed these steps, the firm is ready to *select a business strategy* likely to achieve the objectives in an acceptable period, subject to constraints identified in the self-assessment. The business strategy defines, in general terms, how the business intends to compete (i.e., through cost leadership, differentiation, or increased focus).

Next, an *implementation strategy* is selected that articulates how to implement the business strategy from among a range of reasonable options. The firm may choose to act on its own, partner with others, or acquire/merge with another firm. This is followed by development of a *functional strategy* that defines the roles, responsibilities, and resource requirements of each major functional area within the firm needed to support the business strategy.

The final step is to establish *strategic controls* to monitor actual performance to plan, implement incentive systems, and take corrective actions as necessary. They may involve establishing bonus plans and other incentive mechanisms to motivate all employees to achieve their individual objectives on or ahead of schedule. Systems are also put in place to track the firm's actual performance to plan. Significant deviations from the implementation plan may require switching to contingency plans. Let's look at each of these steps in greater detail.

External Analysis

The external analysis involves developing an understanding of the business's customers and their needs, the market/industry competitive dynamics or factors determining profitability and cash flow, and emerging trends that affect customer needs and industry competition. This analysis begins with answering two basic questions: where to compete and how to compete. The output of the external analysis is the identification of growth opportunities and competitive threats.

Determining Where to Compete

There is no more important activity in building a business plan than deciding where a firm should compete. It begins with identifying the firm's current and potential customers and their primary needs, and it is based on the process of market segmentation, which involves identifying customers with common characteristics and needs. For example, a firm may segment markets until it finds customers whose buying decisions are based on price, quality, or service. In determining where to compete, the firm is identifying where it will concentrate its resources. Frequently, firms lose sight of what has made them successful in the past, in a vain hope of accelerating earnings growth. In 2011, Cisco Systems Inc. sold or closed its consumer business, eliminating hundreds of millions of dollars spent on acquisitions. The company stated publicly that it had strayed from its core market, making networking equipment for business customers.

Whether it is made up of individual consumers or other firms, collections of customers comprise *markets*. A collection of markets is said to comprise an *industry*—for example, the automotive industry, which comprises the new and used car markets as well as the after-market for replacement parts. Markets may be further subdivided by examining cars by makes and model years. The automotive market could also be defined regionally (e.g., New England, North America, Europe) or by country. Each subdivision, whether by product or geographic area, defines a new market within the automotive industry.

Identifying a target market involves a three-step process. First, the firm establishes evaluation criteria to distinguish the attractiveness of multiple potential target markets. These criteria may include: market size and growth rate, profitability, cyclicality, the price sensitivity of customers, the amount of regulation, degree of unionization, and entry and exit barriers. The second step is to subdivide industries and the markets within these industries repeatedly and to analyze the overall attractiveness of these markets in terms of the evaluation criteria. For each market, each of the criteria is given a numerical weight (some even at zero) reflecting the firm's perception of their relative importance as applied to that market. Higher numbers imply greater perceived importance. The markets are then ranked from one to five according to the evaluation criteria, with five indicating that the firm finds a market to be highly favorable in terms of a specific criterion. In the third step, a weighted average score is calculated for each market, and the markets are ranked according to their respective scores. For an illustration of this process, see the document entitled *An Example of a Market-Attractiveness Matrix* on the companion site to this book.

Determining How to Compete

Determining how to compete requires a clear understanding of the factors that are critical for competing successfully in the targeted market. This outward-looking analysis applies to the primary factors governing the firm's external environment. Understanding the market/industry competitive dynamics (i.e., how profits and cash flow are determined) and knowing the areas in which the firm must excel in comparison to the competition (e.g., high-quality or low-cost products) are crucial if the firm is to compete effectively in its chosen market.

Market profiling entails collecting sufficient data to assess and characterize accurately a firm's competitive environment within its chosen markets. Using

Michael Porter's well-known "Five Forces" framework, the market or industry environment can be described in terms of competitive dynamics, such as: the firm's customers, suppliers, current competitors, potential competitors, and product substitutes.[4] The determinants of the intensity of competition in an industry include competition among existing firms, the threat of entry of new firms, and the threat of substitute products. While the degree of competition determines the potential to earn abnormal profits (i.e., those in excess of what would be expected for the degree of assumed risk), the actual profits are influenced by the relative bargaining power of the industry's customers and suppliers.

This framework may be modified to include other factors that determine actual industry profitability and cash flow, such as the severity of government regulation and the impact of global influences such as fluctuating exchange rates. Labor costs may also be included. While they represent a relatively small percentage of total expenses in many areas of manufacturing, they frequently constitute the largest expense in the nonmanufacturing sector. The analysis should also include factors such as the bargaining power of labor.

Figure 4.2 brings together these competitive dynamics. The data required to analyze industrially competitive dynamics include: the types of products and services; market share (in terms of dollars and units); pricing metrics; selling and distribution channels and associated costs; type, location, and age of the production facilities; product quality metrics; customer service metrics; compensation by major labor category; research and development (R&D) expenditures; supplier performance metrics; and financial performance (in terms of growth and profitability). These data must be collected on all significant competitors in the firm's chosen markets.

Determinants of the Intensity of Industry Competition

The overall intensity of industry competition reflects different factors in several categories. The first category includes the industry growth rate, industry concentration, degree of differentiation and switching costs, scale and scope economies, excess capacity, and exit barriers, which all affect the intensity of competition among current industry competitors. If an industry is growing rapidly, existing firms have less need to compete for market share. If an industry is highly concentrated, firms can more easily coordinate their pricing activities; in contrast, this is more difficult in a highly fragmented industry, in which price competition is likely to be very intense.

If the cost of switching from one supplier to another is minimal because of low perceived differentiation, customers are likely to switch based on relatively small differences in price. In industries in which production volume is important, companies may compete aggressively for market share to realize economies of scale. Moreover, firms in industries exhibiting substantial excess capacity

[4]Porter, 1985

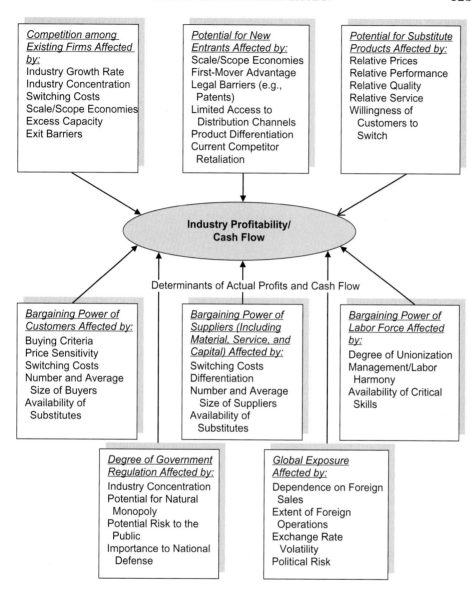

FIGURE 4.2   Defining market/industry competitive dynamics. Adapted from Palepu, Healy, and Bernard (2004).

often reduce prices to fill unused capacity. Finally, competition may be intensi-fied in industries in which it is difficult for firms to exit due to high exit barriers, such as large unfunded pension liabilities and single-purpose assets.

The second category is the potential for new entrants offering products similar to those provided by current competitors in the industry. Current com-petitors within an industry characterized by low barriers to entry have limited pricing power. Attempts to raise prices resulting in abnormally large profits will attract new competitors, thereby adding to the industry's productive capacity. In contrast, high entry barriers may give existing competitors significant pricing power. Barriers to new entrants include situations in which the large-scale operations of existing competitors give them a potential cost advantage due to economies of scale. The "first-mover advantage"—that is, being an early competitor in an industry—may also create entry barriers because first-movers achieve widespread brand recognition, establish industry standards, and/or develop exclusive relationships with key suppliers and distributors. Finally, legal constraints, such as copyrights and patents, may inhibit the entry of new firms.

The third category includes the potential for substitute products. The selling price of one product compared to a close substitute—called the *relative price*—determines the threat of substitution, along with the performance of competing products, perceived quality, and the willingness of the customer to switch. Potential substitutes could come from current or potential competitors and include those that are substantially similar to existing products and those performing the same function—for example, a tablet computer rather than a hardcover book.

Determinants of Actual Profits and Cash Flow

The bargaining powers of customers, suppliers, and the labor force are all important factors that affect profits and cash flow. Others include the degree of government regulation and global exposure. The relative bargaining power of buyers depends on their primary buying criteria (i.e., price, quality/reliability, service, convenience, or some combination), price sensitivity or elasticity, switching costs, and their number and size as compared to the number and size of suppliers. A customer whose primary buying criterion is product quality and reliability may be willing to pay a premium for a BMW because it is perceived to have higher relative quality. Customers are more likely to be highly price sensitive in industries characterized by largely undifferentiated products and low switching costs. Finally, buyers are likely to have considerable bargaining power when there are comparatively few large buyers relative to the number of suppliers. The relative leverage of suppliers reflects the ease with which customers can switch suppliers, perceived differentiation, their number, and how critical they are to the customer. Switching costs are highest when customers must pay penalties to exit long-term supply contracts or when new suppliers would have to undergo an intensive learning process to meet the customers' requirements. Moreover, reliance on a single or a small number of suppliers shifts pricing power from the buyer to the seller. Examples include Intel's global dominance of the microchip market and Microsoft's worldwide supremacy in the market for personal computer operating systems.

Work stoppages create opportunities for competitors to gain market share. Customers are forced to satisfy their product and service needs elsewhere. Although the loss of customers may be temporary, it may become permanent if the customer finds that another firm's product or service is superior. Frequent work stoppages may also have long-term impacts on productivity and production costs as a result of a less motivated labor force and increased labor turnover. Governments may choose to regulate industries that are heavily concentrated, are natural monopolies (e.g., electric utilities), or provide a potential risk to the public. Regulatory compliance adds significantly to an industry's operating costs. Regulations also create barriers to both entering and exiting an industry. Global exposure is the extent to which participation in an industry necessitates having a multinational presence. The automotive industry is widely viewed as a global industry in which participation requires having assembly plants and distribution networks in major markets worldwide. Global exposure introduces the firm to the impact of currency risk on profit repatriation and political risk such as the confiscation of the firm's properties.

Internal Analysis

The primary output of internal analysis is to determine the firm's strengths and weaknesses. What are they compared to the competition? Can the firm's critical strengths be easily duplicated and surpassed by the competition? Can they be used to gain advantage in the firm's chosen market? Can competitors exploit the firm's key weaknesses? These questions must be answered as objectively as possible for the information to be useful in formulating a viable strategy.

Ultimately, competing successfully means doing a better job than the competitors of satisfying the needs of the firm's targeted customers. A self-assessment identifies those strengths or competencies—so-called *success factors*—necessary to compete successfully in the firm's chosen or targeted market. These may include: high market share compared to the competition, product line breadth, cost-effective sales distribution channels, age and geographic location of production facilities, relative product quality, price competitiveness, R&D effectiveness, customer service effectiveness, corporate culture, and profitability.

Recall that the combination of the external and internal analyses just detailed can be done as a SWOT analysis; it determines the strengths, weaknesses, opportunities, and threats of a business. Table 4.1 illustrates a hypothetical SWOT analysis for Amazon.com. It suggests that the firm sees becoming an online department store as its greatest opportunity, while its greatest threat is the growing online presence of sophisticated competitors. The SWOT analysis then summarizes how Amazon.com might perceive its major strengths and weaknesses in the context of this opportunity and threat. This information helps management set a direction in terms of where and how the firm intends to compete, which is then communicated to the firm's stakeholders in the form of a mission/statement and a set of quantifiable financial and nonfinancial objectives.

Defining the Mission Statement

In 2009, Apple Computer's board and management changed the way they wished to be perceived by the world by changing their company name to Apple Inc. The change was intended to be transformative, reflecting the firm's desire

TABLE 4.1　Hypothetical Amazon.com SWOT Matrix

	Opportunity	Threat
	To be perceived by Internet users as the preferred online "department store" to exploit accelerating online retail sales	Wal-Mart, Best Buy, Costco, and so on are increasing their presence on the Internet
Strengths	• Brand recognition • Convenient online order entry system • Information technology infrastructure • Fulfillment infrastructure for selected products (e.g., books)	• Extensive experience in online marketing, advertising, and fulfillment (i.e., satisfying customer orders)
Weaknesses	• Inadequate warehousing and inventory management systems to support rapid sales growth • Limited experience in merchandising noncore retail products (e.g., pharmaceuticals, sports equipment) • Limited financial resources	• Substantially smaller retail sales volume limits ability to exploit purchase economies • Limited financial resources • Limited name recognition in selected markets (e.g., consumer electronics) • Retail management depth

to change from being a computer hardware and software company to a higher-margin, faster-growing consumer electronics firm characterized by iPod- and IPhone-like products. In other words, the firm was establishing a new corporate mission. In 2011, Starbucks dropped the word *coffee* from its logo and acquired upscale juice maker Evolution Fresh in an effort to transform itself from a chain of coffee shops into a consumer products firm selling products outside of its stores.

A mission statement describes the corporation's purpose for being and where it hopes to go. The mission statement should not be so general as to provide little practical direction. A good mission statement should include references to the firm's targeted markets, reflecting the fit between the corporation's primary strengths and competencies and its ability to satisfy customer needs better than the competition. It should define the product offering relatively broadly to allow for the introduction of new products that might be derived from the firm's core competencies. Distribution channels—how the firm chooses to distribute its products—should be identified, as should the customers targeted by the firm's products and services. The mission statement should state management beliefs with respect to the firm's primary stakeholders; these establish the underpinnings of how the firm intends to behave toward those stakeholders.

Setting Strategic or Long-Term Business Objectives

A business objective is what must be accomplished within a specific period. Good business objectives are measurable and have a set time frame in which to be realized. They include revenue growth rates, minimum acceptable financial returns, and market share; these and several others are discussed in more detail later. A good business objective might state that the firm seeks to increase revenue from the current $1 billion to $5 billion by a given year. A poorly written objective would simply state the firm seeks to increase revenue substantially.

Common Business Objectives

Corporations typically adopt a number of common business objectives. For instance, the firm may seek to achieve a rate of *return* that will equal or exceed the return required by its shareholders, lenders, or the combination of the two (cost of capital) by a given year. The firm may set a *size* objective, seeking to achieve some critical mass, defined in terms of sales volume, to realize economies of scale by a given year.

Several common objectives relate to *growth*. Accounting-related growth objectives include seeking to grow earnings per share (EPS), revenue, or assets at a specific rate of growth per year. Valuation-related growth objectives may be expressed in terms of the firm's price-to-earnings ratio, book value, cash flow, or revenue. *Diversification* objectives are those where the firm desires to sell current products in new markets, new products in current markets, or new products in new markets. For example, the firm may set an objective to derive 25% of its revenue from new products by a given year. It is also common for firms to set *flexibility* objectives, aiming to possess production facilities and distribution capabilities that can be shifted rapidly to exploit new opportunities as they arise. For example, major automotive companies have increasingly standardized parts across car and truck platforms to reduce the time required to introduce new products, giving them greater flexibility to facilitate a shift in production from one region to another. *Technology* objectives may reflect a firm's desire to possess capabilities in core technologies. Microchip and software manufacturers as well as defense contractors are good examples of industries in which keeping current with, and even getting ahead of, new technologies is a prerequisite for survival.

Selecting the Appropriate Corporate, Business, and Implementation Strategies

Each level of strategy serves a specific purpose. Implementation strategies, necessarily more detailed than corporate-level strategies, provide specific guidance for a firm's business units.

Corporate-Level Strategies

Corporate-level strategies may include all or some of the business units that are either wholly or partially owned by the corporation. A *growth strategy* focuses on accelerating the firm's consolidated revenue, profit, and cash-flow growth and may be implemented in many different ways, as is discussed later in this chapter. A *diversification strategy* involves a decision at the corporate level to enter new businesses. These businesses may be related to the corporation's existing businesses or completely unrelated. Relatedness may be defined in terms of the degree to which a target firm's products and served markets are similar to those of the acquiring firm. An *operational restructuring strategy,* sometimes called a *turnaround or defensive strategy,* usually refers to the outright or partial sale of companies or product lines, downsizing by closing unprofitable or nonstrategic facilities, obtaining protection from creditors in bankruptcy court, or liquidation. A *financial restructuring strategy* describes actions by the firm to change its total debt and equity structure. The motivation for this strategy may be better utilization of excess corporate cash balances through share-repurchase programs, reducing the firm's cost of capital by increasing leverage or increasing management's control by acquiring a company's shares through a management buyout.

Business-Level Strategies

A firm should choose the business strategy from among the range of reasonable options that enables it to achieve its stated objectives in an acceptable period, subject to resource constraints. These include limitations on the availability of management talent and funds. Business strategies fall into one of four basic categories: price or cost leadership; product differentiation; focus or niche strategies; and hybrid strategies.

Price or Cost Leadership

The price or cost leadership strategy reflects the influence of a series of tools, including the experience curve and product life cycle, introduced and popularized by the Boston Consulting Group (BCG). This strategy is designed to make a firm the cost leader in its market by constructing efficient production facilities, controlling overhead expenses tightly, and eliminating marginally profitable customer accounts.

The *experience curve* states that as the cumulative historical volume of a firm's output increases, cost per unit of output decreases geometrically as the firm becomes more efficient in producing that product. The firm with the largest historical output should also be the lowest-cost producer. This implies that the firm should enter markets as early as possible and reduce product prices aggressively to maximize market share. The experience curve seems to work best for largely commodity-type industries, in which scale economies can lead to reductions in per-unit production costs, such as PC or cellphone handset manufacturing. The strategy of continuously driving down production costs makes most sense for the existing industry market share leader, since it may be able to improve its cost advantage by pursuing market share more aggressively through price-cutting. For an illustration of how to construct an experience curve, see the Word document entitled *Example of Applying Experience Curves* on the companion site to this book.

BCG's second major contribution is the *product life cycle,* which characterizes a product's evolution in four stages: embryonic, growth, maturity, and decline. Strong sales growth and low barriers to entry characterize the first two stages. Over time, however, entry becomes more costly as early entrants into the market accumulate market share and experience lower per-unit production costs as a result of the effects of the experience curve. New entrants have poorer cost positions thanks to their small market shares compared with earlier entrants, and they cannot catch up to the market leaders as overall market growth slows. During the later phases, characterized by slow market growth, falling product prices force marginal firms and unprofitable firms out of the market or force them to consolidate with other firms. Knowing the firm's stage of the product life cycle can help project future cash flow growth, which is necessary for valuation purposes. During the high-growth phase, firms in the industry normally have high investment requirements and operating cash flow is normally negative. During the mature and declining growth phases, investment requirements are lower, and cash flow becomes positive.

Product Differentiation

Differentiation encompasses a range of strategies in which the product offered is perceived by customers to be slightly different from other product offerings in the marketplace. Brand image is one way to accomplish differentiation. Another is to offer customers a range of features or functions. For example, many banks issue MasterCard or Visa credit cards, but each bank tries to differentiate its card by offering a higher credit line or a lower interest rate or annual fee or with awards programs. Apple Computer has used innovative technology to stay ahead of competitors selling MP3 players, most recently with cutting-edge capabilities of its newer iPads. Providing alternative distribution channels is another way to differentiate—for example, giving customers the ability to download products from online sites. Other firms compete on the basis of consistent product quality by providing excellent service or by offering customers outstanding convenience.

Focus or Niche Strategies

Firms adopting focus or niche strategies tend to concentrate their efforts by selling a few products or services to a single market, and they compete primarily by understanding their customers' needs better than does the competition. In this strategy, the firm seeks to carve out a specific niche with respect to a certain group of customers, a narrow geographic area, or a particular use of a product. Examples include the major airlines, airplane manufacturers (e.g., Boeing), and major defense contractors (e.g., Lockheed-Martin).

Hybrid Strategies

Hybrid strategies involve some combination of the three strategies just discussed (Table 4.2). For example, Coca-Cola pursues both a differentiated and highly market-focused strategy. The company derives the bulk of its revenues by focusing on the worldwide soft drink market, and its main product is differentiated, in that consumers perceive it to have a distinctly refreshing taste. Fast-food industry giant McDonald's pursues a focused yet differentiated strategy, competing on the basis of providing fast food of a consistent quality in a clean, comfortable environment.

TABLE 4.2   Hybrid Strategies

	Cost Leadership	Product Differentiation
Niche focus approach	Cisco Systems	Coca-Cola
	WD-40	McDonald's
Multimarket approach	Wal-Mart	America Online
	Oracle	Microsoft

Implementation Strategies

Once a firm has determined the appropriate business strategy, it must decide the best means of implementation. Typically, a firm has five choices: implement the strategy based solely on internal resources (the solo venture, go it alone, or build approach); partner with others; invest; acquire; or swap assets. There is little evidence that one strategy is consistently superior to another. In fact, failure rates among alternative strategies tend to be remarkably similar to those documented for M&As;[5] this should not be surprising in that if one strategy consistently outperformed alternative approaches all firms would adopt a similar growth strategy. Table 4.3 compares the advantages and disadvantages of these options.

In theory, choosing among alternative options should be based on discounting projected cash flows to the firm resulting from each option. In practice, many other considerations are at work, such as intangible factors and the plausibility of underlying assumptions.

The Role of Intangible Factors

Although financial analyses are conducted to evaluate the various strategy implementation options, the ultimate choice may depend on the senior manager's risk profile, patience, and ego. The degree of control offered by the various alternatives is often the central issue senior management must confront as this choice is made. Although the solo venture and acquisition options offer the highest degree of control, they can be the most expensive, although for very different reasons. Typically, a build strategy will take considerably longer to realize key strategic objectives, and it may have a significantly lower current value than the alternatives—depending on the magnitude and timing of cash flows generated from the investments. Gaining control through acquisition can also be very expensive because of the substantial premium the acquirer normally has to pay to gain a controlling interest in another company. The joint venture may be a practical alternative to either a build or acquire strategy; it gives a firm access to skills, product distribution channels, proprietary processes, and patents at a lower initial expense than might otherwise be required. Asset swaps may be an

---

[5] A.C. Nielsen (2002) estimates the failure rate for new product introductions at well over 70%. Failure rates for alliances of all types exceed 60% (Ellis, 1996; Klein, 2004).

TABLE 4.3   Strategy Implementation

Basic Options	Advantages	Disadvantages
Solo venture or build (organic growth)	Control	• Capital/expense[a] requirements • Speed
Partner (Shared growth/shared control) • Marketing/distribution alliance • Joint venture • License • Franchise	• Limits capital and expense investment requirements • May be precursor to acquisition	• Lack of or limited control • Potential for diverging objectives • Potential for creating a competitor
Invest (e.g., minority investments in other firms)	• Limits initial capital/ expense requirements	• High risk of failure • Lack of control • Time
Acquire or merge	• Speed • Control	• Capital/expense requirements • Potential earnings dilution
Swap assets	• Limits use of cash • No earnings dilution • Limits tax liability if basis in assets swapped remains unchanged	• Finding willing parties • Reaching agreement on assets to be exchanged

[a]*Expense investment refers to expenditures made on such things as application software development, database construction, research and development, training, and advertising to build brand recognition, which (unlike capital expenditures) usually are expensed in the year in which the monies are spent.*

attractive alternative to the other options, but in most industries they are generally very difficult to establish unless the physical characteristics and use of the assets are substantially similar and the prospects for realizing economies of scale and scope are attractive.[6]

Analyzing Assumptions

Financial theory suggests that the option with the highest net present value is generally the preferred strategy. However, this may be problematic if the premise on which the strategy is based is questionable. Therefore, it is critical to understand the key assumptions underlying the chosen strategy, as well as those

---

[6]In 2005, Citigroup exchanged its fund management business for Legg Mason's brokerage and capital markets businesses, with the difference in the valuation of the businesses paid in cash and stock. In 2007, British Petroleum swapped half of its stake in its Toledo, Ohio, oil refinery for half of Husky Energy's position in the Sunrise oil sands field in Alberta, Canada. In 2011, Starbucks assumed 100% ownership of restaurants in major Chinese provinces from its joint venture partner, Maxim's Caterers, in exchange for Maxim's assuming full ownership of the JV's restaurants in Hong Kong and Macau.

underlying alternative strategies. This forces senior management to make choices based on a discussion of the reasonableness of the assumptions associated with each option rather than simply the numerical output of computer models.

Functional Strategies

Functional strategies focus on short-term results and generally are developed by functional areas. These strategies result in a series of concrete actions for each function or business group, depending on the company's organization. It is common to see separate plans with specific goals and actions for the marketing, manufacturing, R&D, engineering, and financial and human resources functions. Functional strategies should include clearly defined objectives, actions, timetables for achieving those actions, resources required, and identifying the individual responsible for ensuring that the actions are completed on time and within budget.

Specific functional strategies might read as follows:

- Set up a product distribution network in the northeastern United States that is capable of handling a minimum of 1 million units of product annually by 12/31/20XX. (Individual responsible: Oliver Tran; estimated budget: $5 million.)
- Develop and execute an advertising campaign to support the sales effort in the northeastern United States by 10/31/20XX. (Individual responsible: Maria Gomez; estimated budget: $0.5 million.)
- Hire a logistics manager to administer the distribution network by 9/15/20XX. (Individual responsible: Patrick Petty; estimated budget: $250,000.)
- Acquire a manufacturing company with sufficient capacity to meet the projected demand for the next three years by 6/30/20XX at a purchase price not to exceed $250 million. (Individual responsible: Chang Lee.)

Perhaps an application software company is targeting the credit card industry. Here is an example of how the company's business mission, business strategy, implementation strategy, and functional strategies are related.

- *Mission*: To be recognized by our customers as the leader in providing accurate, high-speed, high-volume transactional software for processing credit card remittances by 20XX.
- *Business Strategy:* Upgrade our current software by adding the necessary features and functions to differentiate our product and service offering from our primary competitors and satisfy projected customer requirements through 20XX.
- *Implementation Strategy:* Purchase a software company at a price not to exceed $400 million that is capable of developing "state-of-the-art" remittance processing software by 12/31/20XX. (Individual responsible: Daniel Stuckee.)

Functional Strategies to Support the Implementation Strategy.

- *Research and Development:* Identify and develop new applications for remittance processing software.

- *Marketing and Sales:* Assess the impact of new product offerings on revenue generated from current and new customers.
- *Human Resources:* Determine appropriate staffing requirements.
- *Finance:* Identify and quantify potential cost savings generated from improved productivity as a result of replacing existing software with the newly acquired software and from the elimination of duplicate personnel in our combined companies. Evaluate the impact of the acquisition on our combined companies' financial statements.
- *Legal:* Ensure that all target company customers have valid contracts and that these contracts are transferable without penalty. Also, ensure that we will have exclusive and unlimited rights to use the remittance processing software.
- *Tax:* Assess the tax impact of the acquisition on our cash flow.

Strategic Controls

Strategic controls include both incentive and monitoring systems. *Incentive systems* include bonus, profit sharing, or other performance-based payments made to motivate both acquirer and target company employees to work to implement the business strategy for the combined firms. Typically, these would have been agreed to during negotiation. Incentives often include *retention bonuses* for key employees of the target firm if they remain with the combined companies for a specific period following completion of the transaction. *Monitoring systems* are implemented to track the actual performance of the combined firms against the business plan. They may be accounting-based and monitor financial measures such as revenue, profits, and cash flow, or they may be activity-based and monitor variables that drive financial performance such as customer retention, average revenue per customer, employee turnover, and revenue per employee.

THE BUSINESS PLAN AS A COMMUNICATION DOCUMENT

The business plan is an effective means of communicating with key decision makers and stakeholders. A good business plan should be short, focused, and well documented. There are many ways to develop such a document. Exhibit 4.1 outlines the key features that should be addressed in a good business plan—one that is so well reasoned and compelling that decision makers accept its recommendations. The executive summary may be the most important and difficult piece of the business plan to write. It must communicate succinctly and compellingly what is being proposed, why it is being proposed, how it is to be achieved, and by when. It must also identify the major resource requirements and risks associated with the critical assumptions underlying the plan. The executive summary is often the first and only portion of the business plan that is read by a time-constrained CEO, lender, or venture capitalist. As such, it may represent the first and last chance to catch the attention of the key decision maker. Supporting documentation should be referred to in the business plan text but presented in the appendices.

EXHIBIT 4.1   TYPICAL BUSINESS UNIT–LEVEL BUSINESS PLAN FORMAT

1. **Executive summary**. In one or two pages, describe what you are proposing to do, why, how it will be accomplished, by what date, critical assumptions, risks, and resource requirements.

2. **Industry/market definition**. Define the industry or market in which the firm competes in terms of size, growth rate, product offering, and other pertinent characteristics.

3. **External analysis**. Describe industry/market competitive dynamics in terms of the factors affecting customers, competitors, potential entrants, product or service substitutes, and suppliers and how they interact to determine profitability and cash flow (e.g., Porter 5 forces model; see Figure 4.2). Discuss the major opportunities and threats that exist because of the industry's competitive dynamics. Information accumulated in this section should be used to develop the assumptions underlying revenue and cost projections in building financial statements.

4. **Internal analysis**. Describe the company's strengths and weaknesses and how they compare with the competition. Identify those strengths and weaknesses critical to the firm's targeted customers, and explain why. These data can be used to develop cost and revenue assumptions underlying the businesses' projected financial statements.

5. **Business mission/vision statement**. Describe the purpose of the corporation, what it intends to achieve, and how it wishes to be perceived by its stakeholders. An automotive parts manufacturer may envision itself as being perceived by the end of the decade as the leading supplier of high-quality components worldwide by its customers and as fair and honest by its employees, the communities in which it operates, and its suppliers.

6. **Quantified strategic objectives** (including completion dates). Indicate both financial goals (e.g., rates of return, sales, cash flow, share price) and nonfinancial goals (e.g., market share; being perceived by customers or investors as number 1 in the targeted market in terms of market share, product quality, price, innovation).

7. **Business strategy**. Identify how the mission and objectives will be achieved (e.g., become a cost leader, adopt a differentiation strategy, focus on a specific market, or some combination of these strategies). Show how the chosen business strategy satisfies a key customer need or builds on a major strength possessed by the firm. A firm whose customers are highly price sensitive may pursue a cost leadership strategy to enable it to lower selling prices and increase market share and profitability. A firm with a well-established brand name may choose a differentiation strategy by adding features to its product that are perceived by its customers as valuable.

8. **Implementation strategy**. From a range of reasonable options (i.e., solo venture, or "go it alone" strategy; partner via a joint venture or less formal business alliance, license, or minority investment; or acquire–merge), indicate which option would enable the firm to best implement its chosen business strategy. Indicate why the chosen implementation strategy is superior to alternative options. An acquisition strategy may be appropriate if the perceived "window of opportunity" is believed to be brief. A solo venture may be preferable if there are few attractive acquisition targets or the firm believes it has the resources to develop the needed processes or technologies.

9. **Functional strategies**. Identify plans and resources required by major functional areas, including manufacturing, engineering, sales and marketing, research and development, finance, legal, and human resources.

10. **Business plan financials and valuation**. Provide projected annual income, balance sheet, and cash flow statements for the firm, and estimate the firm's value based on the projected cash flows. State key forecast assumptions underlying the projected financials and valuation.

11. **Risk assessment**. Evaluate the potential impact on valuation by changing selected key assumptions one at a time. Briefly identify contingency plans (i.e., alternative ways of achieving the firm's mission or objectives) that would be undertaken if critical assumptions prove inaccurate. Identify specific events that would cause the firm to pursue a contingency plan. Such "trigger points" could include deviations in revenue growth of more than x percent or the failure to acquire or develop a needed technology within a specific period.

PHASE 2: BUILDING THE MERGER-ACQUISITION IMPLEMENTATION PLAN

If a firm decides to execute its business strategy through an acquisition, it will need an acquisition plan. Here, the steps of the acquisition planning process are discussed, including detailed components of an acquisition plan.[7] The acquisition plan is a specific type of implementation strategy that focuses on tactical or short-term issues rather than strategic or longer-term issues. It includes: management objectives, a resource assessment, a market analysis, senior management's guidance regarding management of the acquisition process, a timetable, and the name of the individual responsible for making it all happen. These and the criteria to use when searching acquisition targets are codified in the first part of the planning process; once a target has been identified, several additional steps must be taken, including contacting the target, developing a negotiation strategy,

---

[7]Note that if the implementation of the firm's business strategy required some other business combination, such as a joint venture or a business alliance, the same logic of the acquisition planning process described here would apply.

determining the initial offer price, and developing both financing and integration plans. These activities are discussed in Chapter 5.

Development of the acquisition plan should be directed by the "deal owner"—typically a high-performing manager. Senior management should, early in the process, appoint the deal owner to this full- or part-time position. It can be someone in the firm's business development unit, for example, or a member of the firm's business development team with substantial deal-making experience. Often, it is the individual who will be responsible for the operation and integration of the target, with an experienced deal maker playing a supporting role. The first steps in the acquisition planning process are undertaken prior to selecting the target firm and involve documenting the necessary plan elements before the search for an acquisition target can begin.

Plan Objectives

The acquisition plan's objectives should be consistent with the firm's strategic objectives. Financial and nonfinancial objectives alike should support realization of the business plan objectives. Moreover, as is true with business plan objectives, the acquisition plan objectives should be quantified and include a date when such objectives are expected to be realized.

Financial objectives could include a minimum rate of return or operating profit, revenue, and cash flow targets to be achieved within a specified period. Minimum or required rates-of-return targets may be substantially higher than those specified in the business plan, which relate to the required return to shareholders or to total capital. The required return for the acquisition may reflect a substantially higher level of risk as a result of the perceived variability of the amount and timing of the expected cash flows resulting from the acquisition.

Nonfinancial objectives address the motivations for making the acquisition that support achieving the financial returns stipulated in the business plan. They could include obtaining rights to specific products, patents, copyrights, or brand names; providing growth opportunities in the same or related markets; developing new distribution channels in the same or related markets; obtaining additional production capacity in strategically located facilities; adding R&D capabilities; and acquiring access to proprietary technologies, processes, and skills.[8] Because these objectives identify the factors that ultimately determine whether a firm will achieve its desired financial returns, they may provide more guidance than financial targets. Table 4.4 illustrates how acquisition plan objectives can be linked with business plan objectives.

Resource/Capability Evaluation

Early in the acquisition process, it is important to determine the maximum amount of the firm's available resources senior management will commit to

[8]DePamphilis, 2001

TABLE 4.4   Examples of Linkages between Business and Acquisition Plan Objectives

Business Plan Objective	Acquisition Plan Objective
Financial: The firm will	*Financial returns:* The target firm should have
• Achieve rates of return that will equal or exceed its cost of equity or capital by 20XX • Maintain a debt/total capital ratio of x%	• A minimum return on assets of x% • A debt/total capital ratio $\leq y$% • Unencumbered assets of $z million • Cash flow in excess of operating requirements of $x million
Size: The firm will be the number one or two market share leader by 20XX • Achieve revenue of $x million by 20XX	*Size:* The target firm should be at least $x million in revenue
Growth: The firm will achieve through 20XX annual average • Revenue growth of x% • Earnings-per-share growth of y% • Operating cash flow growth of z%	*Growth:* The target firm should • Have annual revenue, earnings, and operating cash flow growth of at least x%, y%, and z%, respectively • Provide new products and markets resulting in $z by 20?? • Possess excess annual production capacity of x million units
Diversification: The firm will reduce earnings variability by x%	*Diversification:* The target firm's earnings should be largely uncorrelated with the acquirer's earnings
Flexibility: The firm will achieve flexibility in manufacturing and design	*Flexibility:* The target firm should use flexible manufacturing techniques
Technology: The firm will be recognized by its customers as the industry's technology leader	*Technology:* The target firm should own important patents, copyrights, and other forms of intellectual property
Quality: The firm will be recognized by its customers as the industry's quality leader	*Quality:* The target firm's product defects must be less than x per million units manufactured
Service: The firm will be recognized by its customers as the industry's service leader	*Warranty record:* The target firm's customer claims per-million units sold should be not greater than x
Cost: The firm will be recognized by its customers as the industry's low-cost provider	*Labor costs:* The target firm should be nonunion and not subject to significant government regulation
Innovation: The firm will be recognized by its customers as the industry's innovation leader	*R&D capabilities:* The target firm should have introduced new products accounting for at least x% of total revenue in the last two years

a deal. This information is used when the firm develops target selection criteria before undertaking a search for target firms. Financial resources that are potentially available to the acquirer include those provided by internally generated cash flow in excess of normal operating requirements plus funds from the equity and debt markets. In cases where the target firm is known, the potential financing pool includes funds provided by the internal cash flow of the combined companies in excess of normal operating requirements, the capacity of the combined firms to issue equity or increase leverage, and proceeds from selling assets not required to execute the acquirer's business plan. Financial theory suggests that an acquiring firm will always be able to attract sufficient funding for an acquisition if it can demonstrate that it can earn its cost of capital. In practice, senior management's risk tolerance plays an important role in determining what the acquirer believes it can afford to spend on a merger or acquisition. Risk-averse managers may be inclined to commit only a small portion of the total financial resources that are potentially available to the firm.

Three basic types of risk confront senior management who are considering an acquisition. How these risks are perceived will determine how much of potential available resources management will be willing to commit to making an acquisition. *Operating risk* addresses the ability of the buyer to manage the acquired company. Generally, it is perceived to be higher for M&As in markets unrelated to the acquirer's core business. *Financial risk* refers to the buyer's willingness and ability to leverage a transaction as well as the willingness of shareholders to accept dilution of near-term earnings per share (EPS). To retain a specific credit rating, the acquiring company must maintain certain levels of financial ratios, such as debt-to–total capital and interest coverage. A firm's incremental debt capacity can be approximated by comparing the relevant financial ratios to those of comparable firms in the same industry that are rated by the credit-rating agencies. The difference represents the amount the firm, in theory, could borrow without jeopardizing its current credit rating.[9] Senior management could also gain insight into how much EPS dilution equity investors may be willing to tolerate through informal discussions with Wall Street analysts and an examination of comparable deals financed by issuing stock. *Overpayment risk* involves the dilution of EPS or a reduction in its growth rate resulting from paying significantly more than the economic value of the acquired company. The effects of overpayment on earnings dilution can last for years.[10]

---

[9]Suppose the combined acquirer and target firms' interest coverage ratio is three and the combined firms' debt-to–total capital ratio is 0.25. Assume further that other firms within the same industry with comparable interest coverage ratios have debt-to–total capital ratios of 0.5. Consequently, the combined acquirer and target firms could increase borrowing without jeopardizing their combined credit rating until their debt-to–total capital ratio equals 0.5.

[10]To illustrate the effects of overpayment risk, assume that the acquiring company's shareholders are satisfied with the company's projected increase in EPS of 20% annually for the next five years. The company announces it will be acquiring another firm and that "restructuring" expenses will slow EPS growth next year to 10%. Management argues that savings resulting from merging the two companies will raise the combined EPS growth rate to 30% in the second through fifth year of the forecast. The risk is that the savings cannot be realized in the time assumed by management and the slowdown in earnings extends well beyond the first year.

Management Guidance

To ensure that the process is managed in a manner consistent with management's risk tolerance, management must provide guidance to those responsible for finding and valuing the target as well as negotiating the deal. Upfront participation by management will help dramatically in the successful implementation of the acquisition process. Senior management frequently avoids providing input early in the process, inevitably leading to miscommunication, confusion, and poor execution later in the process. Exhibit 4.2 provides examples of the more common types of management guidance that might be found in an acquisition plan.

Timetable

A properly constructed timetable recognizes all of the key events that must take place in the acquisition process. Each event should have beginning and ending dates and milestones along the way and should identify who is responsible for ensuring that each milestone is achieved. The timetable of events should be aggressive but realistic. The timetable should be sufficiently aggressive to motivate all involved to work as expeditiously as possible to meet the plan's

EXHIBIT 4.2   EXAMPLES OF MANAGEMENT GUIDANCE PROVIDED TO ACQUISITION TEAMS

1. Determining the criteria used to evaluate prospective candidates (e.g., size, price range, current profitability, growth rate, geographic location, and cultural compatibility).
2. Specifying acceptable methods for finding candidates (e.g., soliciting board members; analyzing competitors; contacting brokers, investment bankers, lenders, law firms, and the trade press).
3. Establishing roles and responsibilities of the acquisition team, including the use of outside consultants, and defining the team's budget.
4. Identifying acceptable sources of financing (e.g., equity issues, bank loans, unsecured bonds, seller financing, or asset sales).
5. Establishing preferences for an asset or stock purchase and form of payment.
6. Setting a level of tolerance for goodwill (i.e., the excess of the purchase price over the fair market value acquired assets less assumed liabilities).
7. Indicating the degree of openness to partial rather than full ownership.
8. Specifying willingness to launch an unfriendly takeover.
9. Setting affordability limits (which can be expressed as a maximum price to after-tax earnings, earnings before interest and taxes, or cash flow multiple or maximum dollar amount).
10. Indicating any desire for related or unrelated acquisitions.

management objectives, while also avoiding overoptimism that may demotivate individuals if uncontrollable circumstances delay reaching certain milestones. Exhibit 4.3 recaps the components of a typical acquisition-planning process. The first two elements were discussed in detail in this chapter; the remaining items will be the subject of the next chapter.

EXHIBIT 4.3   ACQUISITION PLAN FOR THE ACQUIRING FIRM

1. *Plan objectives:* Identify the specific purpose of the acquisition. This should include what specific goals are to be achieved (e.g., cost reduction, access to new customers, distribution channels or proprietary technology, expanded production capacity) and how the achievement of these goals will better enable the acquiring firm to implement its business strategy.
2. *Timetable:* Establish a timetable for completing the acquisition, including integration if the target firm is to be merged with the acquiring firm's operations.
3. *Resource/capability evaluation:* Evaluate the acquirer's financial and managerial capability to complete an acquisition. Identify affordability limits in terms of the maximum amount the acquirer should pay for an acquisition. Explain how this figure is determined.
4. *Management guidance:* Indicate the acquirer's preferences for a "friendly" acquisition; controlling interest; using stock, debt, cash, or some combination; and so on.
5. *Search plan:* Develop criteria for identifying target firms, and explain plans for conducting the search, why the target ultimately selected was chosen, and how you will make initial contact with the target firm. See Chapter 5.
6. *Negotiation strategy:* Identify key buyer/seller issues. Recommend a deal structure addressing the primary needs of all parties involved. Comment on the characteristics of the deal structure. Such characteristics include the proposed acquisition vehicle (i.e., the legal structure used to acquire the target firm), the postclosing organization (i.e., the legal framework used to manage the combined businesses following closing), and the form of payment (i.e., cash, stock, or some combination). Other characteristics include the form of acquisition (i.e., whether assets or stock are being acquired) and tax structure (i.e., whether it is a taxable or a nontaxable transaction). Indicate how you might "close the gap" between the seller's price expectations and the offer price. These considerations will be discussed in more detail in Chapter 5.
7. *Determine initial offer price:* Provide projected five-year income, balance sheet, and cash flow statements for the acquiring and target firms individually and for the consolidated acquirer and target firms with and without the effects of synergy. (Note that the projected forecast period can be longer than five years if deemed appropriate.) Develop a preliminary minimum and maximum purchase price range for the target. List key forecast assumptions. Identify an initial offer price, the composition (i.e., cash, stock, debt, or some combination) of the offer price, and

why you believe this price is appropriate in terms of meeting the primary needs of both target and acquirer shareholders. The appropriateness of the offer price should reflect your preliminary thinking about the deal structure. See Chapters 11 and 12 for a detailed discussion of the deal-structuring process.

8. *Financing plan:* Determine if the proposed offer price can be financed without endangering the combined firm's creditworthiness or seriously eroding near-term profitability and cash flow. For publicly traded firms, pay particular attention to the near-term impact of the acquisition on the earnings per share of the combined firms. See Chapter 13.

9. *Integration plan:* Identify integration challenges and possible solutions. See Chapter 6 for a detailed discussion of how to develop integration strategies. For financial buyers, identify an "exit strategy." Highly leveraged transactions are discussed in detail in Chapters 13 and 14.

SOME THINGS TO REMEMBER

The success of an acquisition depends on the focus, understanding, and discipline inherent in a thorough and viable business plan that addresses four overarching questions: Where should the firm compete? How should the firm compete? How can the firm satisfy customer needs better than the competition? Why is the chosen strategy preferable to other reasonable options? An acquisition is only one of many options available for implementing a business strategy. The decision to pursue an acquisition often rests on the desire to achieve control and a perception that the acquisition will result in achieving the desired objectives more rapidly than other options. Once a firm has decided that an acquisition is critical to realizing the strategic direction defined in the business plan, a merger/acquisition plan should be developed.

DISCUSSION QUESTIONS

4.1 How does planning facilitate the acquisition process?

4.2 What is the difference between a business plan and an acquisition plan?

4.3 What are the advantages and disadvantages of using an acquisition to implement a business strategy compared with a joint venture?

4.4 Why is it important to understand the assumptions underlying a business plan or an acquisition plan?

4.5 Why is it important to get senior management involved early in the acquisition process?

4.6 In your judgment, which of the elements of the acquisition plan discussed in this chapter are the most important, and why?

4.7 After having acquired the OfficeMax superstore chain, Boise Cascade announced the sale of its paper and timber products operations to reduce its dependence on this cyclical business. Reflecting its new emphasis on distribution, the company changed its name to OfficeMax, Inc. How would you describe the OfficeMax mission and business strategy implicit in these actions?

4.8 Dell Computer is one of the best-known global technology companies. In your opinion, who are Dell's primary customers? Current and potential competitors? Suppliers? How would you assess Dell's bargaining power with respect to its customers and suppliers? What are Dell's strengths and weaknesses versus those of its current competitors?

4.9 Discuss the types of analyses inside GE that may have preceded GE's 2008 announcement that it would spin off its consumer and industrial business to its shareholders.

4.10 Ashland Chemical, the largest U.S. chemical distributor, acquired chemical manufacturer Hercules Inc. for $3.3 billion. This move followed Dow Chemical Company's purchase of Rohm & Haas. The justification for both acquisitions was to diversify earnings and offset higher oil costs. How will this business combination offset escalating oil costs?

Answers to these discussion questions are found on the online instructors' site available for this book.

QUESTIONS FROM THE CFA CURRICULUM

1. A company that is sensitive to the business cycle would most likely:
  a Not have growth opportunities.
  b Experience below-average fluctuations in demand.
  c Sell products that the customer can purchase at a later date if necessary.

Source: 2011 Introduction to Industry and Company Analysis, Reading 59, question 8.

2. An industry that most likely has higher barriers to entry and high barriers to exit is the:
  a. Restaurant industry.
  b. Advertising industry.
  c. Automobile industry.

Source: 2011 Introduction to Industry and Company Analysis, Reading 59, question 13.

Answers to questions from the CFA curriculum are available in the Online Student Companion site to this book in a file folder entitled CFA Curriculum Questions and Solutions.

CASE STUDY 4.1
HP Implements a Transformational Strategy, Again and Again

Key Points

- Failure to develop and implement a coherent business strategy often results in firms reacting to rather than anticipating changes in the marketplace.
- Firms reacting to changing events often adopt strategies that imitate their competitors.
- These "me too" strategies rarely provide any sustainable competitive advantage.

Transformational, when applied to a firm's business strategy, is a term often overused. Nevertheless, Hewlett-Packard (HP), with its share price at a six-year low and substantially underperforming such peers as Apple, IBM, and Dell, announced what was billed as a major strategic redirection for the firm on August 18, 2011. The firm was looking for a way to jumpstart its stock. Since Leo Apotheker took over as CEO in November 2010, HP had lost 44% of its market value through August 2011. A transformational announcement appeared to be in order.

HP, the world's largest technology company by revenue, announced that, after an extensive review of its business portfolio, it had reached an agreement to buy British software maker Autonomy for $11.7 billion. The firm also put a for-sale sign on its personal computer business, with options ranging from divestiture to a spinoff to simply retaining the business. HP said the future of the PC unit, which accounted for more than $40 billion in annual revenue and about $2 billion in operating profit, would be decided over the next 12 months. Apotheker had put this business in jeopardy after he had announced that the WebOS-based TouchPad tablet would be discontinued due to poor sales. The announcement was transformational in that it would move the company away from the consumer electronics market.

Under the terms of the deal, HP will pay 25.50 British pounds, or $42.11, in cash for Autonomy. The price represented a 64% premium. With annual revenue of about $1 billion (only 1% of HP's 2010 revenue), the purchase price represents a multiple of more than ten times Autonomy's annual revenues. HP's then-CEO, Leo Apotheker, indicated that the acquisition would help change HP into a business software giant, along the lines of IBM or Oracle, shedding more of the company's ties to lower-margin consumer products. Autonomy, which makes software that searches and keeps track of corporate and government data, would expedite this change. HP said that the acquisition of Autonomy will complement its existing enterprise offerings and give it valuable intellectual property.

Investors greeted the announcement by trashing HP stock, driving the share price down 20% in a single day, wiping out $16 billion in market value. While some investors may be sympathetic to moving away from the commodity-like

PC business, others were deeply dismayed by the potentially "value-destroying" acquisition of Autonomy, the clumsy handling of the announcement of the wide range of options for the PC business, and HP's disappointing earnings performance. By creating uncertainty among potential customers about the long-term outlook for the business, HP may have succeeded in scaring off potential customers.

With this announcement, HP once again appeared to be lagging well behind its major competitors in implementing a coherent business strategy. It agreed to buy Compaq in 2001 in what turned out to be widely viewed as a failed performance. In contrast, IBM transformed itself by selling its PC business to China's Lenovo in late 2004 and establishing its dominance in the enterprise IT business. HP appears to be trying to replicate IBM's strategy.

Heralded at the time as transformational, the 1997 $25 billion Compaq deal turned out to be hotly contested, marred by stiff opposition from shareholders and a bitter proxy contest led by the son of an HP cofounder. While the deal was eventually passed by shareholder vote, it is still considered controversial, because it increased the firm's presence in the PC industry at a time when the growth rate was slowing and margins were declining, reflecting declining selling prices.

HP planned to move into the lucrative cellphone and tablet computer markets with the its 2010 purchase of Palm, in which it outbid three other companies to acquire the firm for $1.2 billion, ultimately paying a 23% premium. However, sales of webOS

phones and the TouchPad have been disappointing, and the firm decided to discontinue making devices based on webOS, a smartphone operating system it had acquired when it bought Palm in late 2010.

In contrast to the mixed results of the Compaq and Palm acquisitions, HP's purchase of Electronic Data Systems (EDS) for $13.9 billion in 2008 substantially boosted the firm's software services business. IBM's successful exit from the PC business early in 2004 and its ability to derive the bulk of its revenue from the more lucrative services business has been widely acclaimed by investors. Prospects seemed good for this HP acquisition. However, in an admission of the firm's failure to realize EDS's potential, HP in mid-2012 wrote off $8 billion of what it had paid for EDS.

HP has purchased 102 companies since 1989, but with the exceptions of its Compaq and its $1.3 billion purchase of VeriFone, it has not paid more than $500 million in any single deal. These deals were all completed under different management teams. Carly Fiorina was responsible for the Compaq deal, while Mark Hurd pushed for the acquisitions of EDS, Palm, and 3Par. Highly respected for his operational performance, Hurd was terminated in early 2010 on sexual harassment charges.

Under pressure from investors to jettison its current CEO, HP announced on September 22, 2011, that former eBay CEO, Meg Whitman, would replace Leo Apotheker as Chief Executive Officer. In yet another strategic flip-flop, HP announced on October 27, 2011, that it would retain the PC business. The firm's internal analysis indicated that separating the PC business would have cost $1.5 billion in one-time expenses and another $1 billion in increased expenses annually. Citing the deep integration of the PC group in HP's supply chain and procurement efforts, Whitman proclaimed the firm to be stronger with the PC business.[11]

In mid-December 2011, HP announced that it would also reverse its earlier decision to discontinue supporting webOS and stated that it would make webOS available for free under an open-source license for anyone to use. The firm will continue to make enhancements to the webOS system and to build devices dependent on it. By moving to an open-source environment, HP hopes others will adopt the operating system, make improvements, and develop mobile devices using webOS to establish an installed user base. HP could then make additional webOS devices and applications that could be sold to this user base. This strategy is similar to Google's when it made its Android mobile software available for cellphones under an open-source license.

[11] The one-time charges included establishing infrastructure such as new systems for IT, customer support, sales, and distribution for its other operations, which had relied on the PC unit for these services. The ongoing annual expense figure was due to fewer product-bundling opportunities, the need to rebrand PC peripheral products, and the probable reduction in large-purchase discounts on components used by other HP businesses that had been purchased jointly with the PC unit.

HP's share price plunged 11% on November 25, 2012, to $11.73 following its announcement that it had uncovered "accounting irregularities" associated with its earlier acquisition of Autonomy. The revelation required the firm to write down its investment in Autonomy by $8.8 billion, about three-fourths of the purchase price. The charge contributed to a quarterly loss of $6.9 billion for HP. Confidence in both the firm's management and board plummeted, further tarnishing the once-vaunted HP brand.

Discussion Questions

1. Discuss the advantages and disadvantages of fully integrating business units within a parent firm. Be specific.
2. Discuss the possible impact of HP's strategic reversals over the last decade on its various constituencies, such as customers, employees, stockholders, and suppliers. Be specific.
3. Discuss the strategic advantages and disadvantages of diversified versus relatively focused firms. Be specific.
4. To what do you attribute the inconsistent and incoherent strategic flip-flops at Hewlett-Packard during the last decade? Be specific.

Answers to these case discussion questions are available in the Online Instructor's Manual for instructors using this book.

CASE STUDY 4.2
Years in the Making: Kinder Morgan Opportunistically Buys El Paso Corp. for $20.7 Billion

Key Points

- Companies often hold informal merger talks for protracted periods until conditions emerge that are satisfactory to both parties.
- Capital requirements and regulatory hurdles often make buying another firm more attractive than attempting to build the other firm's capabilities independently.

Using a combination of advanced horizontal drilling techniques and hydraulic fracturing, or "fracking" (i.e., shooting water and chemicals deep underground to blast open gas-bearing rocks), U.S. natural gas production has surged in recent years. As a result, proven gas reserves have soared such that the Federal Energy Information Administration estimates that the overall supplies of natural gas would last more than 100 years at current consumption rates. But surging supplies have pushed natural gas prices to $4 per million BTUs down from a peak of $13 in July 2008. Despite the depressed prices, energy companies around the globe have rushed to enter the business of producing shale gas. With energy prices depressed, independent players are struggling to find financing for their projects, prompting larger competitors to engage in buyouts. Exxon acquired XTO Energy in 2009, and Chesapeake Energy sold a partial stake in its shale gas reserves to Chinese companies for billions of dollars. In 2011 alone, oil and gas firms announced $172 billion worth of acquisitions in the continental United States, accounting for about two-thirds of the $261 billion spent on oil and gas acquisitions worldwide.

The increase in energy supplies has strained current pipeline capacity in the United States. Today more than 50 pipeline companies transport oil and gas through networks that do not necessarily transport the fuel where it is needed from where it is being produced. For example, pipeline construction in the Marcellus shale field in Pennsylvania has not kept pace with drilling activity there, limiting the amount of gas that can be sent to the northeast. In the Bakken field in North Dakota, producers are shipping much of their new oil production by train to west coast refineries, and excess gas is being burned off. In the meantime, new oil and gas fields are being developed in Ohio, Kansas, Oklahoma, Texas, and Colorado. According to the Interstate Natural Gas Association of America Foundation, a trade group, pipeline companies are expected to have to build 36,000 miles of large-diameter, high-pressure natural gas pipelines by 2035 to meet market demands, at a cost of $178 billion.

Responding to these developments, on October 17, 2011, Kinder Morgan (Kinder) agreed to buy the El Paso Corporation (El Paso) for $21.1 billion in cash and stock. Including the assumption of debt owed by El Paso and an affiliated business, El Paso

Pipeline Partners, the takeover is valued at about $38 billion. This represents the largest energy deal since Exxon Mobil bought XTO Energy in late 2009.

Kinder Morgan's stock had been declining throughout 2011, and the firm was looking for a way to jump-start earnings growth. The acquisition offers Kinder both the scale and the geographic disposition of pipelines necessary to support the burgeoning supply of shale gas and oil supplies. The acquisition makes Kinder the largest independent transporter of gasoline, diesel, and other petroleum products in the United States. It will also be the largest independent owner and operator of petroleum storage terminals and the largest transporter of carbon dioxide in the United States. The combined firms will operate the only oil sands pipeline to the west coast. To attempt to replicate the El Paso pipeline network would have been time consuming, required large amounts of capital, and faced huge regulatory hurdles.

Kinder will own or operate about 67,000 miles of the more than 500,000 miles of oil and gas pipelines stretching across the United States.[12] Kinder's pipelines in the Rocky Mountains, the Midwest, and Texas will be woven together with El Paso's expansive network that spreads east from the Gulf Coat to New England and to the west through New Mexico, Arizona, Nevada, and California. In buying El Paso, Kinder creates a unified network of interstate pipelines. By increasing its dependence on utilities,

[12]Parfomak, September 26, 2011.

Kinder will reduce its exposure to the more volatile industry end user market. The acquisition also offers significant cost-cutting opportunities resulting from reconfiguring existing pipeline networks.

Kinder paid 14 times El Paso's last 12 months' earnings before interest, taxes, depreciation, and amortization of $2.67 billion. Investors applauded the deal by boosting Kinder's stock by 4.8% to $28.19 on the announcement date. El Paso shares climbed 25% to $24.81. For each share of El Paso, Kinder paid $14.65 in cash, .4187 of a Kinder share, and .640 of a warrant entitling the bearer to buy more Kinder shares at a predetermined price. The purchase price at closing valued the deal at $26.87 per El Paso share and constituted a 47% premium to El Paso 20-day average price prior to the announcement. Kinder's debt will increase to $14.5 billion from $3.2 billion after the acquisition. To help pay for the deal, Kinder is seeking a buyer for El Paso's exploration business. The combined firms will be called Kinder Morgan. Richard D. Kinder, the founder of Kinder Morgan, will be the chairman and CEO.

The proposed takeover was not approved by regulators until May 2, 2012, on the condition that Kinder Morgan agree to sell three U.S. natural gas pipelines. The deal represents the culmination of years of discussion between Kinder Morgan and El Paso. Kinder, which went private in 2006 in a transaction valued at $22 billion, reemerged in an IPO in February 2011, raising nearly $2.9 billion. The

IPO made the deal possible. While Kinder had for years held talks with El Paso's management about a merger, it needed the "currency" of a publicly traded stock to complete such a deal. El Paso shareholders wanted to be able to participate in any future appreciation of the Kinder Morgan shares. Whether the combination of these two firms makes sense depends on the magnitude and timing of the expected resurgence in natural gas prices and the acceptability of shale gas and "fracking" to the regulators.

Discussion Questions

1. Who are Kinder Morgan's customers, and what are their needs?

2. What factors external to Kinder Morgan and El Paso seem to be driving the transaction?

3. What factors internal to Kinder Morgan and El Paso seemed to be driving the transaction?

4. How would the combined firms be able to satisfy these needs better than the competition?

5. Do you believe the transaction can be justified based on your understanding of the strengths and weaknesses of the two firms and perceived opportunities and threats to the two firms in the marketplace?

Answers to these questions are found in the Online Instructor's Manual available for instructors using this book.

Implementation: Search Through Closing
Phases 3 through 10 of the Acquisition Process

A man that is very good at making excuses is probably good at nothing else.—***Ben Franklin***

INSIDE M&A: SONY'S STRATEGIC MISSTEPS

KEY POINTS

- Realizing a complex vision requires highly skilled and consistent execution.
- A clear and concise business strategy is essential for setting investment priorities.
- Corporate financial and human resources most often need to be concentrated in support of a relatively few key initiatives to realize a firm's vision.

As the fifth-largest media conglomerate (measured by revenues), Sony Corporation (Sony) continues to struggle to get it right. Its products and services range from music and movies to financial services, TVs, smartphones, and semi-conductors. The firm's top-three profit contributors include its music, financial services, and movie operations; TV manufacturing has been its greatest profits drag. As the third-largest global manufacturer of TVs, behind Korea's Samsung and LG Electronics, Sony has been unable to offset the slumping demand in the United States and Europe for Bravia TVs, recording nine consecutive yearly losses.

Sony's corporate vision is to provide consumers easy, ubiquitous access to an array of entertainment content. Sony wants to provide both the content and the means to enable consumers to access the content. However, rather than a road-map outlining how the firm intends to achieve this vision, its business strategy lists four broad themes or areas in which it will invest. These themes include networked products and services (LCD TVs, games, mobile phones, and tablet computers), 3-D world (digital imaging), differentiated technologies, and emerging markets. The firm intends to become the leading provider of networked consumer electronics and entertainment, consisting of LCD TVs, games, and mobile phones. Sony intends to enable users of these devices to move seamlessly from one product to another to access content such as movies and television programming. Sony can draw on music from 13 U.S. labels and on movies from Sony Pictures Classics, Columbia, and TriStar Pictures.

As with many companies, Sony's vision seems to exceed its ability to execute. Derailed in recent years by an appreciating yen, a lingering global economic slowdown, an earthquake that crippled its factories, and flooding in Thailand that forced factory closings, Sony recorded its fifth consecutive annual loss for the fiscal year ending March 2012. Cumulative five-year losses totaled more than $6 billion. In 2000, the firm was worth more than $100 billion; however, by late 2012, it was valued at less than $18 billion. This compares to its major competitors, Apple and Samsung, which were valued at $364 billion and $134 billion, respectively, at that time. While whipsawed by a series of largely uncontrollable events, the firm seems to lack the focus to allow it to concentrate its prodigious resources ($17 billion in cash on the balance sheet) behind a relatively few strategic initiatives.

Rather than focus its efforts, Sony's investments have been wide ranging. In 2011 alone, the firm spent $8.5 billion to acquire nine businesses in an effort to shore up its phone and content businesses. Sony teamed with Apple, Microsoft, Research in Motion, Ericsson, and EMC Corp. to purchase patents owned by Nortel Networks Corp used in mobile phones and tablet computers for $4.5 billion in cash. Sony, along with the Blackstone Group and others, also acquired EMI Music Publishing from Citigroup for $2.2 billion. In addition, Sony bought out Ericsson's 50% stake in their mobile phone venture for $1.5 billion in order to integrate the smartphone business with its gaming and tablet offerings. Little progress seems to have been made in shoring up its money-losing TV manufacturing business. The firm's lack of focus or more narrowly defined priorities may be at the center of the firm's poor financial performance.

CHAPTER OVERVIEW

This chapter starts with the presumption that a firm has developed a viable business plan that requires an acquisition to realize its strategic direction. Whereas Chapter 4 addressed the creation of business and acquisition plans (Phases 1 and 2), this chapter focuses on Phases 3 through 10 of the acquisition process, including search, screening, first contact, negotiation, integration planning, closing, integration implementation, and evaluation.[1] A review of this chapter (including practice questions and answers) is contained in the file folder

---

[1]For a detailed illustration of the M&A process outlined in this chapter, see DePamphilis (2011).

entitled Student Study Guide on the companion site to this book (http://booksite. elsevier.com/9780123854872). The companion site also contains a comprehensive due diligence question list.

PHASE 3: THE SEARCH PROCESS

The first step in searching for acquisition candidates is to establish a small number of primary selection criteria, including the industry and the size of the transaction. Deal size is best defined in terms of the maximum purchase price a firm is willing to pay, expressed as a maximum price-to-earnings ratio, book, cash flow, or revenue ratio, or a maximum purchase price stated in terms of dollars. It may also be appropriate to limit the search to a specific geographic area.

Consider a private acute-care hospital holding company that wants to buy a skilled nursing facility within 50 miles of its largest hospital in Allegheny County, Pennsylvania. Management believes it cannot afford to pay more than $45 million for the facility. Its primary selection criteria could include an industry (skilled nursing), a location (Allegheny County), and a maximum price (five times cash flow, not to exceed $45 million). Similarly, a Texas-based manufacturer of patio furniture with manufacturing operations in the southwestern United States seeks to expand its sales in California. The company decides to try to find a patio furniture manufacturer that it can purchase for no more than $100 million. Its primary selection criteria could include an industry (outdoor furniture), a geographic location (California, Arizona, and Nevada), and a maximum purchase price (15 times after-tax earnings, not to exceed $100 million).

The next step is to search available computerized databases using the selection criteria. Common databases and directory services include Disclosure, Dun & Bradstreet, Standard & Poor's *Corporate Register*, and Capital IQ. Firms also may query their law, banking, and accounting firms to identify other candidates. Investment banks, brokers, and leveraged buyout firms are also fertile sources of potential candidates, although they are likely to require an advisory or finder's fee. Such services as Google Finance, Yahoo! Finance, Hoover's, and EDGAR Online enable researchers to obtain data quickly about competitors and customers. These sites provide easy access to a variety of documents filed with the Securities and Exchange Commission. Exhibit 5.1 provides a comprehensive listing of alternative information sources.

If confidentiality is not an issue, a firm may advertise its interest in acquiring a particular type of firm in the *Wall Street Journal* or the trade press. While likely to generate interest, it is less likely to produce high-quality prospects. Rather, it will probably result in a lot of responses from those interested in getting a free valuation of their own company or from brokers claiming that their clients fit the buyer's criteria, as a ruse to convince you that you need the broker's services.[2]

[2] It is important to respond in writing if you receive a solicitation from a broker or finder, particularly if you reject their services. If at a later date you acquire the firm they claim to have represented, the broker or finder may sue your firm for compensation.

EXHIBIT 5.1 INFORMATION SOURCES ON INDIVIDUAL COMPANIES

SEC Filings (Public Companies Only)

10-K. Provides detailed information on a company's annual operations, business conditions, competitors, market conditions, legal proceedings, risk factors in holding the stock, and other, related information.

10-Q. Updates investors about the company's operations each quarter.

S-1. Filed when a company wants to register new stock. Can contain information about the company's operating history and business risks.

S-2. Filed when a company is completing a material transaction, such as a merger or acquisition. Provides substantial detail underlying the terms and conditions of the transaction, the events surrounding the transaction, and justification for the merger or acquisition.

8-K. Filed when a company faces a "material event," such as a merger.

Schedule 14A. A proxy statement. Gives details about the annual meeting and biographies of company officials and directors including stock ownership and pay.

Websites

http://www.aol.com
http://www.bizbuysell.com
http://www.capitaliq.com
http://www.dialog.com
http://www.edgar-online.com
http://edgarscan.pwcglobal.com/serviets.edgarscan
http://www.factset.com
http://finance.yahoo.com
http://www.freeedgar.com
http://www.hooversonline.com
http://www.lexisnexis.com
http://www.mergernetwork.com
http://www.mergers.net
http://www.onesource.com
http://www.quicken.com
http://www.sec.gov
http://www.washingtonresearchers.com
http://www.worldm-anetwork.com

Organizations

Value Line Investment Survey: Information on public companies
Directory of Corporate Affiliations: Corporate affiliations
Lexis/Nexis: Database of general business and legal information
Thomas Register: Organizes firms by products and services
Frost & Sullivan: Industry research
Findex.com: Financial information

Competitive Intelligence Professionals: Information about industries
Dialog Corporation: Industry databases
Wards Business Directory of U.S. and public companies
Predicasts: Provides databases through libraries
Business Periodicals Index: Business and technical article index
Dun & Bradstreet Directories: Information about private and public companies
Experian: Information about private and public companies
Nelson's Directory of Investment Research: Wall Street Research Reports
Standard & Poor's Publications: Industry surveys and corporate records
Harris Infosource: Information about manufacturing companies
Hoover's Handbook of Private Companies: Information on large private firms
Washington Researchers: Information on public and private firms, markets, and industries
The *Wall Street Journal* Transcripts: Wall Street research reports
Directory of Corporate Affiliations (published by Lexis-Nexis Group)

Finding reliable information about privately owned firms is a major problem. Sources such as Dun & Bradstreet and Experian may only provide fragmentary data. Publicly available information may offer additional details. For example, surveys by trade associations or the U.S. Census Bureau often include industry-specific average sales per employee. A private firm's sales can be estimated by multiplying this figure by an estimate of the firm's workforce, which may be obtained by searching the firm's product literature, website, or trade show speeches or even by counting the number of cars in the parking lot during each shift.

Increasingly, companies—even midsize firms—are moving investment banking "in-house." Rather than use brokers or so-called "finders"[3] as part of their acquisition process, they are identifying potential targets, doing valuation, and performing due diligence on their own. This reflects efforts to save on investment banking fees, which can easily be more than $5 million plus expenses on a $500 million transaction.[4]

---

[3] A *broker* has a fiduciary responsibility to either the potential buyer or the seller and is not permitted to represent both parties. Compensation is paid by the client to the broker. A *finder* is someone who introduces both parties but represents neither party. The finder has no fiduciary responsibility to either party and is compensated by either one or both parties.

[4] Actual fee formulas are most often based on the purchase price. The so-called Lehman formula was at one time a commonly used fee structure; in it, broker or finder fees would be equal to 5% of the first $1 million of the purchase price, 4% of the second, 3% of the third, 2% of the fourth, and 1% of the remainder. Today, this formula is often ignored in favor of a negotiated fee structure consisting of a basic fee (or retainer) paid regardless of whether the deal is consummated, an additional closing fee paid on closing, and an "extraordinary" fee paid under unusual circumstances that may delay the eventual closing, such as gaining antitrust approval or achieving a hostile takeover. Fees vary widely, but 1% of the total purchase price plus reimbursement of expenses is often considered reasonable. For small deals, the Lehman formula may apply.

II. THE MERGERS AND ACQUISITIONS PROCESS

PHASE 4: THE SCREENING PROCESS

The screening process is a refinement of the initial search process. It begins by pruning the initial list of potential candidates created using the primary criteria discussed earlier. Because relatively few primary criteria are used, the initial list may be lengthy. It can be shortened using secondary selection criteria, but care should be taken to limit the number of these criteria. An excessively long list of selection criteria will severely limit the number of candidates that pass the screening process. The following selection criteria should be quantified whenever possible.

Market Segment: A lengthy list of candidates can be shortened by identifying a target segment within the industry. For example, a steel fabricated products company may decide to diversify into the aluminum fabricated products industry. Whereas the primary search criterion might have been firms in the aluminum flat-rolled products industry, a secondary criterion could stipulate a segmenting of the market to identify only those companies that make aluminum tubular products.

Product Line: The product line criterion identifies a specific product line within the target market segment. The same steel fabrication firm may decide to focus its search on companies manufacturing aluminum tubular products used for lawn and patio furniture.

Profitability: Profitability should be defined in terms of the percentage return on sales, assets, or total investment. This allows a more accurate comparison among candidates of different sizes. A firm with after-tax earnings of $5 million on sales of $100 million may be less attractive than a firm earning $3 million on sales of $50 million because the latter firm may be more efficient.

Degree of Leverage: Debt-to-equity or debt-to–total capital ratios are used to measure the level of leverage or indebtedness. The acquiring company may not want to purchase a firm whose debt burden may cause the combined company's leverage ratios to jeopardize its credit rating.

Market Share: The acquiring firm may be interested only in firms that are number one or two in market share in the targeted industry or in firms whose market share is some multiple (e.g., two times the next-largest competitor).[5]

Cultural Compatibility: Insights into a firm's corporate culture can be obtained from public statements about the target's vision for the future and its governance practices as well as its reputation as a responsible corporate citizen. Examining employee demographics reveals much about the diversity

---

[5] Firms that have substantially greater market share than their competitors are often able to achieve lower cost positions than their competitors because of economies of scale and experience curve effects.

of a firm's workforce.[6] Finally, an acquirer needs to determine whether it can adapt to the challenges of dealing with foreign firms, such as different languages and customs.

PHASE 5: FIRST CONTACT

Using both the primary and secondary selection criteria makes it possible to bring the search to a close and to begin the next part of the acquisition planning process, first contact. For each target firm, it is necessary to develop an approach strategy in which the potential acquirer develops a profile of each firm to be contacted in order to be able to outline the reasons the target firm should consider an acquisition proposal. Such reasons could include the need for capital, a desire by the owner to "cash out," and succession planning issues.

Research efforts should extend beyond publicly available information and include interviews with customers, suppliers, ex-employees, and trade associations in an effort to understand better the strengths, weaknesses, and objectives of potential target firms. Insights into management, ownership, performance, and business plans help provide a compelling rationale for the proposed acquisition and heighten the prospect of obtaining the target firm's interest.

How initial contact is made depends on the size of the company, whether the target is publicly or privately held, and the acquirer's time frame for completing a transaction. The last can be extremely important. If time permits, there is no substitute for developing a personal relationship with the sellers—especially if theirs is a privately held firm. Developing a rapport often makes it possible to acquire a company that is not thought to be for sale. Personal relationships must be formed only at the highest levels within a privately held target firm. Founders or their heirs often have a strong paternalistic view of their businesses, whether they are large or small. Such firms often have great flexibility in negotiating a deal that "feels right" rather than simply holding out for the highest possible price. In contrast, personal relationships can go only so far when negotiating with a public company that has a fiduciary responsibility to its shareholders to get the best price. If time is a critical factor, acquirers may not have the luxury of developing personal relationships with the seller. Under these circumstances, a more expeditious approach must be taken.

---

[6] America Online's 2001 acquisition of Time Warner highlighted how difficult it can be to integrate a young, heterogeneous employee population with a much older, more homogeneous group. Also, as a much newer firm, AOL had a much less structured management style than was found in Time Warner's more staid environment.

For small companies with which the buyer has no direct contacts, it may only be necessary to initiate contact through a vaguely worded letter expressing interest in a joint venture or marketing alliance. During the follow-up telephone call, be prepared to discuss a range of options with the seller. Preparation before the first telephone contact is essential. If possible, script your comments. Get to the point quickly but indirectly. Identify yourself, your company, and its strengths. Demonstrate your understanding of the contact's business and how an informal partnership could make sense. Be able to explain the benefits of your proposal to the contact—quickly and succinctly. If the opportunity arises, propose a range of options, including an acquisition. Listen carefully to the contact's reaction. If the contact is willing to entertain the notion of an acquisition, request a face-to-face meeting.[7]

Whenever possible, use an intermediary to make contact, generally at the highest level possible in the target firm. In some instances, the appropriate contact is the most senior manager, but it could be a disaffected large shareholder. Intermediaries include members of the acquirer's board of directors or the firm's outside legal counsel, accounting firm, lender, broker/finder, or investment banker. Intermediaries can be less intimidating than if you take a direct approach.

For public companies, contact also should be made through an intermediary at the highest level possible. Discretion is extremely important because of the target's concern about being "put into play"—that is, circumstances suggest that it may be an attractive investment opportunity for other firms. Even rumors of an acquisition can have adverse consequences for the target, as customers and suppliers express concern about a change of ownership and key employees leave; concerned about an uncertain future. Such a change could imply variation in product or service quality, reliability, and the level of service provided under product warranty or maintenance contracts. Suppliers worry about possible disruptions in their production schedules as the transition to the new owner takes place. Employees worry about possible layoffs or changes in compensation.[8] Shareholders may experience a dizzying ride as arbitrageurs, buying on the rumor, bid up the price of the stock, only to bail out if denial of the rumor appears credible.

---

[7]To ensure confidentiality, choose a meeting place that provides sufficient privacy. Create a written agenda for the meeting after soliciting input from all participants. The meeting should start with a review of your company and your perspective on the outlook for the industry. Encourage the potential target firm to provide information on its own operations and its outlook for the industry. Look for areas of consensus. After the meeting, send an e-mail to the other party highlighting what you believe was accomplished, and then await their feedback.

[8]Competitors will do what they can to fan these concerns in an effort to persuade current customers to switch and potential customers to defer buying decisions; key employees will be encouraged to defect to the competition.

Discussing Value

Neither the buyer nor the seller has any incentive to be the first to provide an estimate of value. It is difficult to back away from a number put on the table by either party should new information emerge. Getting a range may be the best you can do. Discussing values for recent acquisitions of similar businesses is one way to get a range. Another is to agree to a formula for calculating the purchase price. The purchase price may be defined in terms of a price to current-year earnings' multiple, enabling both parties to perform due diligence to reach a consensus on the actual current year's earnings for the target firm. The firm's current year's earnings are then multiplied by the previously agreed-on price-to-earnings multiple to estimate the purchase price.

Preliminary Legal of Transaction Documents

Typically, parties to M&A transactions negotiate a confidentiality agreement, a term sheet, and a letter of intent early in the process.

Confidentiality Agreement

All parties to the deal usually want a confidentiality agreement (also called a *nondisclosure agreement*), which is generally mutually binding—that is, it covers all parties to the transaction. In negotiating the agreement, the buyer requests as much audited historical data and supplemental information as the seller is willing to provide. The prudent seller requests similar information about the buyer to assess the buyer's financial credibility. The seller should determine the buyer's credibility as soon as possible so as not to waste time with a potential buyer incapable of raising the financing to complete the transaction. The agreement should cover only information that is not publicly available and should have a reasonable expiration date.[9]

Term Sheet

A term sheet outlines the primary areas of agreement and is often used as the basis for a more detailed letter of intent. A standard term sheet is typically two to four pages long and stipulates the total consideration or purchase price (often as a range), what is being acquired (i.e., assets or stock), limitations on the use of proprietary data, a *no-shop provision* that prevents the seller from sharing the terms of the buyer's proposal with other potential buyers with the hope of instigating an auction environment, and a termination date. Many transactions skip the term sheet and go directly to negotiating a letter of intent.

---

[9] The confidentiality agreement can be negotiated independently or as part of the term sheet or letter of intent.

Letter of Intent

Unlike the confidentiality agreement, not all parties to the deal may want a letter of intent (LOI). While the LOI can be useful in identifying areas of agreement and disagreement early in the process, the rights of all parties to the transaction, and certain protective provisions, it may delay the signing of a definitive purchase agreement and may also result in some legal risk to either the buyer or the seller if the deal is not consummated. Public companies that sign a letter of intent for a transaction that is likely to have a "material" impact on the buyer or seller may need to announce the LOI publicly to comply with securities law.

The LOI formally stipulates the reason for the agreement and major terms and conditions. It also indicates the responsibilities of both parties while the agreement is in force, a reasonable expiration date, and how all fees associated with the transaction will be paid. Major terms and conditions include a brief outline of the deal structure, such as the payment of cash or stock for certain assets and the assumption of certain target company liabilities. The letter may also specify certain conditions, such as an agreement that selected personnel of the target will not compete with the combined companies for some period should they leave. Another condition may indicate that a certain portion of the purchase price will be allocated to the noncompete agreement.[10] The LOI also may place a portion of the purchase price in escrow. The proposed purchase price may be expressed as a specific dollar figure, as a range, or as a multiple of some measure of value, such as operating earnings or cash flow. The LOI also specifies the types of data to be exchanged and the duration and extent of the initial due diligence. The LOI will terminate if the buyer and the seller do not reach agreement by a certain date. Legal, consulting, and asset transfer fees (i.e., payments made to governmental entities when ownership changes hands) may be paid for by the buyer or the seller, or they may be shared.

A well-written LOI usually contains language limiting the extent to which the agreement binds the two parties. Price or other provisions are generally subject to *closing conditions*, such as the buyer's having full access to all of the seller's books and records; having completed due diligence; having obtained financing; and having received approval from boards of directors, stockholders, and regulatory bodies. Other standard conditions include requiring signed employment contracts for key target firm executives and the completion of all necessary M&A documents. Failure to satisfy any of these conditions will invalidate the agreement. The LOI should also describe the due diligence process in some detail, stipulating how the buyer should access the seller's premises, the frequency and duration of such access, and how intrusive such activities should be. The letter of intent is shown by the potential acquirer to prospective financing sources.

---

[10]Such an allocation of the purchase price is in the interests of the buyer because the amount of the allocation can be amortized over the life of the agreement. As such, it can be taken as a tax-deductible expense. However, it may constitute taxable income for the seller.

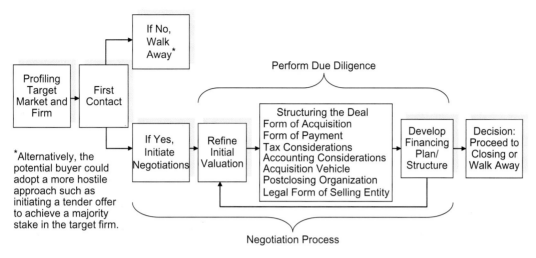

FIGURE 5.1   Viewing negotiation as a process.

PHASE 6: NEGOTIATION

The negotiation phase is often the most complex aspect of the acquisition process. It is during this phase that the actual purchase price paid for the acquired business is determined, and often it will be quite different from the initial valuation of the target company. In this section, the emphasis is on negotiation in the context of problem-solving or interest-based bargaining, in which parties look at their underlying interests rather than simply stating positions and making demands. In most successful negotiations, parties to the transaction search jointly for solutions to problems. All parties must be willing to make concessions that satisfy their own needs as well as the highest-priority needs of the others involved in the negotiations.

The negotiation phase consists of four iterative activities that may begin at different times but tend to overlap (Figure 5.1). *Due diligence* starts as soon as the target is willing to allow it and, if permitted, runs throughout the negotiation process. Another activity is *refining the preliminary valuation* based on new data uncovered as part of due diligence, enabling the buyer to understand the target's value better. A third activity is *deal structuring*, which involves meeting the needs of both parties by addressing issues of risk and reward. The final activity, the *financing plan*, provides a reality check for the buyer by defining the maximum amount the buyer can expect to finance and, in turn, pay for the target company. These activities are detailed next.

Refining Valuation

The starting point for negotiation is to update the preliminary target company valuation based on new information. A buyer requests at least three to five years of historical financial data. While it is desirable to examine data audited in accordance with Generally Accepted Accounting Principles, such data may not be available for small, privately owned companies. The historical data should be *normalized*, or adjusted for nonrecurring gains, losses, or expenses.[11] Such adjustments allow the buyer to smooth out irregularities to understand the dynamics of the business. Each major expense category should be expressed as a percentage of revenue. By observing year-to-year changes in these ratios, trends in the data are more discernible.

Deal Structuring

Deal structuring is the process of identifying and satisfying as many of the highest-priority objectives of the parties involved in the transaction as possible. The process begins with each party determining its own initial negotiating position, potential risks, options for managing risk, risk tolerance, and conditions under which either party will "walk away" from the negotiations. Deal structuring also entails understanding potential sources of disagreement—from simple arguments over basic facts to substantially more complex issues, such as the form of payment and legal, accounting, and tax structures. It also requires identifying conflicts of interest that can influence the outcome of discussions. For example, when a portion of the purchase price depends on the long-term performance of the acquired business, its management—often the former owner—may not behave in a manner that serves the acquirer's best interests.

Decisions made throughout the deal-structuring process influence various attributes of the deal, including how ownership is determined, how assets are transferred, how ownership is protected (i.e., governance), and how risk is apportioned among parties to the transaction. Other attributes include the type, number, and complexity of the documents required for closing; the types of approvals required; and the time needed to complete the transaction. These decisions will influence how the combined companies will be managed, the amount and timing of resources committed, and the magnitude and timing of current and future tax liabilities.

The deal-structuring process can be viewed as comprising a number of interdependent components, including the acquisition vehicle, postclosing organization, legal form of the selling entity, form of payment, form of acquisition, and tax and accounting considerations. The *acquisition vehicle* refers to the legal structure (e.g., corporation or partnership) used to acquire the target company. The *postclosing organization* is the organizational and legal framework (e.g., corporation or partnership) used to manage the combined businesses following the completion of the transaction. The *legal form of the selling entity* refers to whether

---

[11]Nonrecurring gains or losses can result from the sale of land, equipment, product lines, patents, software, or copyrights. Nonrecurring expenses include severance payments, employee signing bonuses, and settlements of litigation.

the seller is a C or Subchapter S Corporation, a limited liability company, or a partnership.

These considerations affect both the tax structure of the deal and the form of payment. The *form of payment* may consist of cash, common stock, debt, or some combination. Some portion of the payment may be deferred or be dependent on the future performance of the acquired entity. The *form of acquisition* reflects both what is being acquired (e.g., stock or assets) and the form of payment. As a general rule, a transaction is taxable if remuneration paid to the target company's shareholders is primarily something other than the acquirer's stock, and it is nontaxable (i.e., tax deferred) if what they receive is largely acquirer stock. Finally, *accounting considerations* refer to the potential impact of financial reporting requirements on the earnings volatility of business combinations, due to the need to revalue acquired assets periodically to their fair market value as new information becomes available. Fair market value is what a willing buyer and seller, having access to the same information, would pay for an asset.[12]

Conducting Due Diligence

Due diligence is an exhaustive review of records and facilities and typically continues throughout the negotiation phase. Although some degree of protection is achieved through a well-written contract, legal documents should never be viewed as a substitute for conducting formal due diligence. Remedies for violating contract representations and warranties often require litigation, with the outcome uncertain. Due diligence may help to avoid the need for costly litigation by enabling the acquirer to identify and value target liabilities and to adjust the purchase price paid at closing accordingly. As such, reliance on contract remedies to recover M&A-related costs may be reduced because the incidence of surprises is likely to be less.[13]

Table 5.1 lists convenient online sources of information that are helpful in conducting due diligence.[14] While due diligence is most often associated with buyers, both sellers and lenders will also conduct due diligence.[15]

An expensive and exhausting process, due diligence is, by its nature, highly intrusive, and it places considerable demands on managers' time and attention. Frequently, the buyer wants as much time as possible, while the seller will want

---

[12] For a more detailed discussion of how to structure M&A transactions, see DePamphilis (2010b).

[13] Even if the acquirer were to win its lawsuit, receiving remuneration for breach of contract may be impossible if the seller declares bankruptcy, disappears, or moves assets to offshore accounts.

[14] A detailed preliminary acquirer due diligence question list is provided on the companion site to this book.

[15] For a detailed discussion of the due diligence process and best practices, see Selim (2003).

TABLE 5.1   Convenient Information Sources for Conducting Due Diligence

Web Address	Content
Securities and Exchange Commission	Financial Information/Security Law Violations
www.sec.gov	Public filings for almost ten years available through the Edgar database
http://www.sec.gov/litigation.shtml	Enforcement actions
U.S. Patent Office	Intellectual Property Rights Information
www.uspto.gov	Search patent database if you have the patent number
www.uspto.gov/patft/index.htmll	
Federal Communications Commission	Regulates Various Commercial Practices
www.fcc.gov	General information
http://www.fcc.gov/searchtools.html	Access to database of individuals sanctioned for illegal marketing practices
U.S. and States Attorneys General Offices	Information on Criminal Activities
http://www.naag.org/ag/full_ag_table.php	Listing of states attorneys general
Better Business Bureau (BBB)	Compiles Consumer Complaints Database
http://search.bbb.org/search.html	
Paid Services	Information on:
U.S. Search (www.ussearch.com)	Criminal Violations
KnowX (www.knowx.com)	Liens/bankruptcies
	Credit history
	Litigation

to limit the length and scope. Due diligence rarely works to the advantage of the seller because a long and detailed due diligence is likely to uncover items the buyer will use as a reason to lower the purchase price. Consequently, sellers may seek to terminate due diligence before the buyer feels it is appropriate.[16] If the target firm succeeds in reducing the amount of information disclosed to the target firm, it can expect to be required to make more representations and

---

[16]One way sellers try to limit due diligence is to sequester the acquirer's team in a data room. Frequently, this is a conference room filled with file cabinets and boxes of documents requested by the buyer's due diligence team. Formal presentations by the seller's key managers are given in the often-cramped conditions of the data room. In other instances, the potential buyer may have limited access to information on a password-protected website, also called a "virtual data room."

warranties as to the accuracy of its claims and promises in the purchase and sale agreement.

The Components of Due Diligence

Three primary reviews comprise due diligence; they often occur concurrently. The *strategic and operational review,* conducted by senior operations and marketing management, asks questions that focus on the seller's management team, operations, and sales and marketing strategies. The *financial review,* directed by financial and accounting personnel, focuses on the accuracy, timeliness, and completeness of the seller's financial statements. A *legal review,* which is conducted by the buyer's legal counsel, deals with corporate records, financial matters, management and employee issues, tangible and intangible assets of the seller, and material contracts and obligations of the seller, such as litigation and claims. Due diligence requires the creation of comprehensive checklists (see website accompanying this book for such a checklist). The interview process provides invaluable sources of information. By asking the same questions of a number of key managers, the acquirer is able to validate the accuracy of its conclusions.

Buyer, Seller, and Lender Due Diligence

Buyers use due diligence to validate assumptions underlying their preliminary valuation and to uncover new sources of value and risk. Key objectives include identifying and confirming sources of value or synergy and mitigating real or potential liability by looking for fatal flaws that reduce value. From the perspective of the buyer's attorney, the due diligence review represents an opportunity to learn about the target firm in order to allocate risk properly among the parties to the negotiation, to unearth issues that reduce the likelihood of closing, and to assist their client in drafting the reps and warranties for the acquisition agreement. Table 5.2 categorizes potential sources of value from synergy that may be uncovered or confirmed during due diligence and the impact these may have on operating performance.

Although the bulk of due diligence is performed by the buyer on the seller, the prudent seller should also perform due diligence on the buyer and on its own personnel and operations. By investigating the buyer, the seller can determine whether the buyer has the financial wherewithal to finance the purchase. As part of its internal due diligence, a seller often requires its managers to sign affidavits attesting (to the "best of their knowledge") to the truthfulness of what is being represented in the contract that pertains to their areas of responsibility. In doing so, the seller hopes to mitigate liability stemming from inaccuracies in the seller's representations and warranties made in the definitive agreement of purchase and sale.

If the acquirer is borrowing to buy a target firm, the lender(s) will want to perform their own due diligence independent of the buyer's effort. Multiple lender investigations, often performed concurrently, can be quite burdensome to the target firm's management and employees. Sellers should agree to these activities only if confident the transaction will be consummated.

TABLE 5.2   Identifying Potential Sources of Value

Potential Source of Value	Examples	Potential Impact
Operating Synergy		
• Eliminating functional overlap	• Reduce duplicate overhead positions	• Improved margins
• Productivity improvement	• Increased output per employee	• Same
• Purchasing discounts	• Volume discounts on material purchases	• Same
• Working capital management	• Reduced days in receivables due to improved collection of accounts receivable	• Improved return on total assets

• Facilities management
  – Economies of scale
  – Economies of scope
• Organizational realignment
	• Fewer days in inventory due to improved inventory turns	• Same

	• Increased production in underutilized facilities	• Same
	• Data centers, R&D functions, call centers, and so on, support multiple product lines/operations	• Same
	• Reducing the number of layers of management	• Reduced bureaucratic inertia
Financial Synergy		
• Increased borrowing capacity	• Target has little debt and many unencumbered assets	• Increased access to financing
• Increased leverage	• Access to lower-cost source of funds	• Lower cost of capital
Marketing/Product Synergy		
• Access to new distribution channels	• Increased sales opportunities	• Increased revenue
• Cross-selling opportunities	• Selling acquirer products to target customers, and vice versa	• Same
• Research and development	• Cross-fertilization of ideas	• More innovation
• Product development	• Increased advertising budget	• Improved market share
Control		
• Opportunity identification	• Acquirer identifies opportunities not seen by target's management	• New growth opportunities
• More proactive management style	• More decisive decision making	• Improved financial returns

Developing the Financing Plan

The last of the four negotiation phase activities is to develop the balance sheet, income, and cash flow statements for the combined firms. Unlike the financial projections of cash flow made to value the target, these statements should include the expected cost of financing the transaction. Developing the financing plan is a key input in determining the purchase price, because it places a limitation on the amount the buyer can offer the seller. The financing plan is appended to the acquirer's business and acquisition plans and is used to obtain financing for the transaction (see Chapter 13). No matter the size of the transaction, lenders and investors will want to see a coherent analysis of why the proposed transaction is a good investment opportunity.

Defining the Purchase Price

The three commonly used definitions of purchase price are *total consideration, total purchase price/enterprise value,* and *net purchase price.* Each serves a different purpose.

Total Consideration

In the purchase agreement, the *total consideration* consists of cash (C), stock (S), new debt issues (D), or some combination of all three. It is a term commonly used in legal documents to reflect the different types of remuneration received by target company shareholders. Note that the remuneration can include both financial and nonfinancial assets, such as real estate. Nonfinancial compensation sometimes is referred to as *payment in kind.* The debt counted in the total consideration is what the target company shareholders receive as payment for their stock, along with any cash or acquiring company stock. Each component should be viewed in present value terms; therefore, the total consideration is itself expressed in present value terms (PV_{TC}). The present value of cash is its face value. The stock component of the total consideration is the present value (PV_S) of future dividends or net cash flows or the acquiring firm's stock price per share times the number of shares to be exchanged for each outstanding share of the seller's stock. New debt issued by the acquiring company as part of the compensation paid to shareholders can be expressed as the present value (PV_{ND}) of the cumulative interest payments plus principal discounted at some appropriate market rate of interest (see Chapter 7).

Total Purchase Price/Enterprise Value

The *total purchase price* (PV_{TPP}) or *enterprise value* of the target firm consists of the total consideration (PV_{TC}) plus the market value of the target firm's debt (PV_{AD}) assumed by the acquiring company. The enterprise value is sometimes expressed as the total purchase price plus net debt. *Net debt* includes the market value of debt assumed by the acquirer less cash and marketable securities on the books of the target firm. The enterprise value of the firm is often quoted in the media as the purchase price because it is most visible to those who are not familiar with the details. It is important to analysts and shareholders alike, because it approximates the total investment[17] made by the acquiring firm. It is

---

[17] Total investment equals what the acquirer pays the shareholders plus assumed liabilities, such as long-term debt.

an approximation because it does not necessarily measure liabilities the acquirer is assuming that are not visible on the target firm's balance sheet. Nor does it reflect the potential for recovering a portion of the total consideration paid to target company shareholders by selling undervalued or redundant assets. These considerations are reflected in the net purchase price, discussed next.

Net Purchase Price

The *net purchase price* (PV_{NPP}) is the total purchase price plus other assumed liabilities (PV_{OAL})[18] less the proceeds from the sale of discretionary or redundant target assets (PV_{DA}) [19] on or off the balance sheet. PV_{OAL} are those assumed liabilities not fully reflected on the target firm's balance sheet or in the estimation of the economic value of the target firm. The net purchase price is the most comprehensive measure of the actual price paid for the target firm. It includes all known cash obligations assumed by the acquirer as well as any portion of the purchase price that is recovered through the sale of assets. The various definitions of price can be summarized as follows:

$$\text{Total consideration} = PV_{TC} = C + PV_S + PV_{ND}$$
$$\text{Total purchase price or enterprise value} = PV_{TPP} = PV_{TC} + PV_{AD}$$
$$\text{Net purchase price} = PV_{NPP} = PV_{TPP} + PV_{OAL} - PV_{DA} = (C + PV_S + PV_{ND} + PV_{AD}) + PV_{OAL} - PV_{DA}$$

Although the total consideration is most important to the target company's shareholders as a measure of what they receive in exchange for their stock, the acquirer's shareholders often focus on the total purchase price/enterprise value

---

[18] If the target firm's balance sheet reserves reflected accurately all known future obligations and there were no potential off-balance-sheet liabilities, there would be no need to adjust the purchase price for assumed liabilities other than for short- and long-term debt assumed by the acquiring company. Earnings would accurately reflect the impact of known liabilities. Operating cash flows, which reflect both earnings and changes in balance-sheet items, would also accurately reflect future liabilities. Therefore, valuations based on a multiple of earnings, book value, or discounted cash flow would accurately reflect the value of the business. In practice, reserves are often inadequate to satisfy pending claims. Common examples include underfunded or underreserved employee pension and healthcare obligations and uncollectable receivables. To the extent that such factors represent a future use of cash, the present value of their future impact should be estimated.

[19] *Discretionary assets* are assets not required to operate the target that can be sold to recover some portion of the purchase price. Such assets include land valued at its historical cost. Other examples include cash balances in excess of normal working capital needs and product lines or operating units considered nonstrategic by the buyer. The sale of discretionary assets is not considered in the calculation of the value of the target because economic value is determined by future operating cash flows before consideration is given to how the transaction will be financed.

as the actual amount paid for the target's equity plus the value of assumed debt. However, the total purchase price tends to ignore other adjustments that should be made to determine actual or pending "out-of-pocket" cash spent by the acquirer. The net purchase price reflects adjustments to the total purchase price and is a much better indicator of whether the acquirer overpaid for the target firm. The application of the various definitions of the purchase price is addressed in more detail in Chapter 9.

PHASE 7: DEVELOPING THE INTEGRATION PLAN

Part of the premerger integration planning process involves the preclosing due diligence activity. One responsibility of the due diligence team is to identify ways in which assets, processes, and other resources can be combined to realize cost savings, productivity improvements, or other perceived synergies. This information is also essential for refining the valuation process by enabling planners to understand better the necessary sequencing of events and the resulting pace at which the expected synergies may be realized.

Contract-Related Issues

Integration planning also involves addressing human resource, customer, and supplier issues that overlap the change of ownership. These are *transitional* issues to resolve as part of the purchase agreement, and it is critical that the seller's responsibilities be negotiated before closing to make the actual transition as smooth as possible. Also, a cooperative effort is most likely made prior to closing. For example, the agreement may stipulate how target company employees will be paid and how their benefit claims will be processed.[20]

A prudent buyer will want to include assurances in the purchase agreement to limit its postclosing risk. Most seller representations and warranties (i.e., claims) made to the buyer refer to the past and present condition of the

---

[20]Systems must be in place to ensure that employees of the acquired company continue to be paid without disruption. If the number of employees is small, this may be accommodated easily by loading the acquirer's payroll computer system with the necessary salary and personal information before closing or by having a third-party payroll processor perform these services. For larger operations or where employees are dispersed geographically, the target's employees may continue to be paid for a specific period using the target's existing payroll system. As for benefits, employee healthcare or disability claims tend to escalate just before a transaction closes as employees, whether they leave or stay with the new firm, file more disability claims for longer periods after downsizing. The sharp increase in such expenses can pose an unexpected financial burden for the acquirer and should be addressed in the merger agreement. For example, all claims incurred within a specific number of days before closing but not submitted by employees until after closing will be reimbursed by the seller. Alternatively, such claims may be paid from an escrow account containing a portion of the purchase price.

seller's business. They pertain to items such as the ownership of securities; real and intellectual property; current levels of receivables, inventory, and debt; and pending lawsuits, worker disability, customer warranty claims; and an assurance that the target's accounting practices are in accordance with Generally Accepted Accounting Principles. Although "reps and warranties" apply primarily to the past and current state of the seller's business, they do have ramifications for the future. If a seller claims there are no lawsuits pending and a lawsuit is filed shortly after closing, the buyer may seek to recover damages from the seller. The buyer also may insist that certain conditions be satisfied before closing can take place. Common closing conditions include employment contracts, agreements not to compete, financing, and regulatory and shareholder approval. Finally, the buyer will want to make the final closing contingent on receiving approval from the appropriate regulatory agencies and shareholders of both companies before any money changes hands.

Earning Trust

Decisions made before closing affect postclosing integration activity.[21] Successfully integrating firms requires getting employees in both firms to work to achieve common objectives. This comes about through building credibility and trust, not through superficial slogans and empty promises. Trust comes from cooperation, keeping commitments, and experiencing success.

Choosing the Integration Manager and Other Critical Decisions

The buyer should designate an integration manager who possesses excellent interpersonal and project management skills. During the integration phase, interpersonal skills are frequently more important than professional and technical skills. The buyer must also determine what is critical to continuing the acquired company's success during the first 12 to 24 months after the closing. Critical activities include identifying key managers, vendors, and customers and determining what is needed to retain them as valued assets. Preclosing integration planning activities should also determine the operating norms or standards required for continued operation of the businesses: executive compensation, labor contracts, billing procedures, product delivery times, and quality metrics. Finally, there must be a communication plan for all stakeholders that can be implemented immediately following closing. See Chapter 6 for more detail.

---

[21] Benefits packages, employment contracts, and retention bonuses to keep key employees typically are negotiated before the closing. Contractual covenants and conditions also affect integration. Earnouts, which are payments made to the seller based on the acquired business's achieving certain profit or revenue targets, can limit the buyer's ability to integrate the target effectively into the acquirer's operations.

PHASE 8: CLOSING

Closing entails obtaining all necessary shareholder, regulatory, and third-party consents (e.g., customer and vendor contracts) and also completing the definitive purchase agreement.

Gaining the Necessary Approvals

The buyer's legal counsel is responsible for ensuring that the transaction is in compliance with securities, antitrust, and state corporation laws. Great care must be exercised to ensure that all filings required by law have been made with the Federal Trade Commission and the Department of Justice. Finally, many deals require approval by the acquirer and target firm shareholders.

Assigning Customer and Vendor Contracts

In a purchase of assets, many customer and vendor contracts cannot be assigned to the buyer without receiving written approval from the other parties. While often a formality, both vendors and customers may attempt to negotiate more favorable terms. Licenses must be approved by the licensor, which can be a major impediment to a timely closing. A major software vendor demanded a substantial increase in royalty payments before agreeing to transfer the software license to the buyer. The vendor knew that the software was critical for the ongoing operation of the target company's data center. From the buyer's perspective, the exorbitant increase in the fee had an adverse impact on the economics of the transaction and nearly caused the deal to collapse.

Completing the Acquisition/Merger Agreement

The acquisition/merger or definitive agreement is the cornerstone of the closing documents. It indicates all of the rights and obligations of the parties both before and after the closing.

Deal Provisions

In an asset or stock purchase, this section of the agreement defines the consideration or form of payment, how it will be paid, and the specific assets or shares to be acquired. In a merger, this section of the agreement defines the number (or fraction) of acquirer shares to be exchanged for each target share.

Price

The purchase price or total consideration may be fixed at the time of closing, subject to future adjustment, or it may be contingent on future performance. In asset transactions, it is common to exclude cash on the target's balance sheet from the transaction; the price paid for noncurrent assets, such as plant and intangible assets, will be fixed, but the price for current assets will depend on their levels at closing following an audit.

Allocation of Price

The buyer often tries to allocate as much of the purchase price as possible to depreciable assets, such as fixed assets, customer lists, and noncompete agreements, enabling them to depreciate or amortize these upwardly revised assets and reduce future taxable income. However, such an allocation may constitute taxable income to the seller. Both parties should agree on how the purchase price should be allocated in an asset transaction before closing, eliminating the chance that conflicting positions will be taken for tax reporting purposes.

Payment Mechanism

Payment may be made at closing by wire transfer or cashier's check, or the buyer may defer the payment of a portion of the purchase price by issuing a promissory note to the seller. The buyer may agree to put the unpaid portion of the purchase price in escrow or through a holdback allowance, thereby facilitating the settlement of claims that might be made in the future.[22]

Assumption of Liabilities

The seller retains those liabilities not assumed by the buyer. In instances such as environmental liabilities, unpaid taxes, and inadequately funded pension obligations, the courts may go after the buyer and the seller. In contrast, the buyer assumes all known and unknown liabilities in a merger or share purchase.

Representations and Warranties

Reps and warranties are claims made as "statements of fact" by buyers and sellers. As currently used, the terms are virtually indistinguishable from one another. They serve three purposes: disclosure, termination rights, and indemnification rights.

> *Disclosure:* Contract reps and warranties should provide for full disclosure of all information germane to the deal, typically covering the areas of greatest concern to both parties. These include financial statements, corporate organization and good standing, capitalization, absence of undisclosed liabilities, current litigation, contracts, title to assets, taxes and tax returns, no violation of laws or regulations, employee benefit plans, labor issues, and insurance coverage.
>
> *Termination rights:* Reps and warranties serve to allocate risk by serving as a closing condition. At closing, representations such as those concerning the state of the business and financial affairs are again reviewed, such that they must still be accurate despite the lapse of time between the signing of the

---

[22] The escrow account involves the buyer's putting a portion of the purchase price in an account held by a third party, while the holdback allowance generally does not.

agreement and the actual closing. If there has been a material change in the target's business or financial affairs between signing and closing, the bidder has the right to terminate the transaction.

Indemnification rights: Often in transactions involving private firms, certain representations will extend beyond closing. As such, they serve as a basis for indemnification, that is, the buyer's being compensated for costs incurred subsequent to closing. For example, a seller may represent that there are no lawsuits pending, which turns out to be untrue after closing when the buyer incurs significant costs to settle a legal dispute initiated before there was a change in control. Indemnification will be discussed in more detail later in this chapter.

Covenants

Covenants are agreements by the parties about actions they agree to take or refrain from taking between signing the definitive agreement and the closing. The seller may be required to continue conducting business in the usual and customary manner and to seek approval for all expenditures that may be considered out of the ordinary, such as one-time dividend payments or sizeable increases in management compensation. In contrast to reps and warranties, covenants do not relate to a point in time (e.g., at signing or closing) but, rather, relate to future behavior between signing and closing. While they usually expire at closing, covenants sometimes survive closing. Typical examples include a buyer's covenant to register stock that it is issuing to the seller and to complete the dissolution of the firm following closing in an asset sale.

Covenants may be either negative (restrictive) or positive (requirement to do something). *Negative* covenants restrict a party from taking certain actions, such as the payment of dividends or the sale of an asset without the permission of the buyer between signing and closing. *Positive* covenants may require the seller to continue to operate its business in a way that is consistent with its past practices. Many purchase agreements include virtually the same language in both representations and covenants. For example, since the target's balance sheet is calculated just prior to signing the agreement, the target represents that the balance sheet that was calculated on a specific date just prior to signing is essentially the same balance sheet on the closing date. Covenants using the same language would require that the target firm not take any action between these two dates that would result in a material change in the balance sheet, such as the payment of a dividend or significant capital expenditure.

Closing Conditions

The satisfaction of negotiated conditions determines whether a party to the agreement must consummate the deal. Among the most important of the closing conditions is the so-called *bring-down provision,* requiring that representations made at the signing are still true as of the closing date. Other examples include obtaining all necessary legal opinions, the execution of other agreements (e.g., promissory notes), and the absence of any "material adverse change" in the condition of the target company. The effects of material adverse change clauses (MACs) in agreements of purchase and sale became very visible during the disruption in the financial markets in 2008. Many firms that had signed M&A contracts looked for a way out. The most common challenge in negotiating such clauses is defining what constitutes materiality—for example, is it a 20% reduction in earnings or sales? Because of the inherent ambiguity, the contract language is usually vague, and it is this very ambiguity that has enabled so many acquirers to withdraw from contracts. Lenders, too, use these clauses to withdraw financing.

Indemnification

In effect, indemnification is the reimbursement of the other party for a loss incurred following closing for which they were not responsible. The definitive agreement requires the seller to indemnify or absolve the buyer of liability in the event of misrepresentations or breaches of warranties or covenants. Similarly, the buyer usually agrees to indemnify the seller. Both parties generally want to limit the period during which the indemnity clauses remain in force.[23]

Other Closing Documents

In addition to resolving the issues just outlined, closing may be complicated by the number and complexity of other documents required to complete the transaction. In addition to the definitive agreement, the more important documents often include patents, licenses, royalty agreements, trade names, and trademarks; labor and employment agreements; leases; mortgages, loan agreements, and lines of credit; stock and bond commitments and details; and supplier and customer contracts. Other documents could include distributor and sales representative agreements; stock option and employee incentive programs; and health and other benefit plans (which must be in place at closing, to eliminate lapsed coverage).

Complete descriptions of all foreign patents, facilities, and investments; insurance policies, coverage, and claims pending; intermediary fee arrangements; litigation pending for and against each party; and environmental compliance issues resolved or on track to be resolved are often part of the closing documents. Furthermore, seller's corporate minutes of the board of directors and any other significant committee information, as well as articles of incorporation, bylaws, stock certificates, and corporate seals, are part of the final documentation.[24]

---

[23] At least one full year of operation and a full audit are necessary to identify claims. Some claims (e.g., environmental) extend beyond the survival period of the indemnity clause. Usually, neither party can submit claims to the other until some minimum threshold, expressed in terms of the number or dollar size of claims, has been exceeded. Firms also may purchase warranty and indemnity insurance, which provides compensation for losses arising from breach of warranties and indemnities given in the merger agreement.

[24] Sherman, 2006

Financing Contingencies

Most well-written agreements of purchase and sale contain a financing contingency. The buyer is not subject to the terms of the contract if the buyer cannot obtain adequate funding to complete the transaction. Breakup fees can be particularly useful to ensure that the buyer will attempt as aggressively as possible to obtain financing. In some instances, the seller may require the buyer to put a nonrefundable deposit in escrow, to be forfeited if the buyer is unable to obtain financing to complete the transaction.[25] Lenders, too, exercise financial contingencies, invoking material adverse change clauses to back out of lending commitments

PHASE 9: IMPLEMENTING POSTCLOSING INTEGRATION

The postclosing integration activity is widely viewed as among the most important phases of the acquisition process. Postclosing integration is discussed in considerable detail in Chapter 6. What follows is a discussion of those activities required immediately following closing. Such activities generally fall into five categories, which are discussed in the next sections.

Communication Plans

Implementing an effective communication plan immediately after the closing is crucial for retaining employees of the acquired firm and maintaining or boosting morale and productivity. The plan should address employee, customer, and vendor concerns. The message always should be honest and consistent. Employees need to understand how their compensation, including benefits, might change under the new ownership. Employees may find a loss of specific benefits palatable if they are perceived as offset by improvements in other benefits or working conditions. Customers want reassurance that there will be no deterioration in product or service quality or delivery time during the transition from old to new ownership. Vendors also are very interested in understanding how the change in ownership will affect their sales to the new firm.

Whenever possible, communication is best done on a face-to-face basis. Senior officers of the acquiring company can be sent to address employee groups (on site, if possible). Senior officers also should contact key customers (preferably in person or at least by telephone) to provide the needed reassurances. Meeting, with complete candor, reasonable requests for information from employees, customers, and vendors immediately following closing will contribute greatly to the

---

[25]Most deals involving privately owned firms do not involve breakup fees, termination fees, or liquidated damages provisions, because such sellers are viewed as highly motivated. In the event the seller refuses to sell the business once having signed an agreement to do so, the buyer has a breach of contract lawsuit that it can bring against the seller.

sense of trust among stakeholders that is necessary for the ultimate success of the acquisition.

Employee Retention

Retaining middle-level managers should be a top priority during this phase of the acquisition process. Frequently, senior managers of the target company that the buyer chooses to retain are asked to sign employment agreements as a condition of closing. Although senior managers provide overall direction for the firm, middle-level managers execute the day-to-day operations of the firm. Plans should be in place to minimize the loss of such people. Bonuses, stock options, and enhanced sales commission schedules are commonly put in place to keep such managers.

Satisfying Cash Flow Requirements

Conversations with middle-level managers following closing often reveal areas in which maintenance expenditures have been deferred. Receivables previously thought to be collectable may have to be written off. Production may be disrupted as employees of the acquired firm find it difficult to adapt to new practices introduced by the acquiring company's management or if inventory levels are inadequate to maintain desired customer delivery times. Finally, more customers than had been anticipated may be lost to competitors that use the change in ownership as an opportunity to woo them away with various types of incentives.

Employing Best Practices

An excellent way for the combined companies to realize potential synergies is to take advantage of the strengths of both companies by using the "best practices" of both. However, in some areas, neither company may be employing what its customers believe to be the best practices in the industry. Management should look beyond its own operations to adopt the practices of other companies in the same or other industries.

Cultural Issues

Corporate cultures reflect the set of beliefs and behaviors of the management and employees of a corporation. Some firms are very paternalistic, and others are very "bottom-line" oriented. Some empower employees, whereas others believe in highly centralized control. Some promote problem solving within a team environment; others encourage individual performance. Inevitably, different corporate cultures impede postacquisition integration efforts. The key to success is taking the time to explain to all of the new firm's employees what behaviors are expected and why and to tell managers that they should "walk the talk."

PHASE 10: CONDUCTING A POSTCLOSING EVALUATION

The primary reasons for conducting a postclosing evaluation of all acquisitions are to determine if the acquisition is meeting expectations, to undertake corrective actions if necessary, and to identify what was done well and what should be done better in future deals.

Do Not Change Performance Benchmarks

Once the acquisition appears to be operating normally, evaluate the actual performance to that projected in the acquisition plan. Success should be defined in terms of actual to planned performance. Too often, management simply ignores the performance targets in the acquisition plan and accepts less than plan performance to justify the acquisition. This may be appropriate if circumstances beyond the firm's control cause a change in the operating environment, such as a recession or a change in the regulatory environment.

Ask the Difficult Questions

The types of questions asked vary, depending on the time elapsed since the closing. After six months, what has the buyer learned about the business? Were the original valuation assumptions reasonable? If not, what did the buyer not understand about the target company, and why? What did the buyer do well? What should have been done differently? What can be done to ensure that the same mistakes are not made in future acquisitions? After 12 months, is the business meeting expectations? If not, what can be done to put the business back on track? Is the cost of fixing the business offset by expected returns? Are the right people in place to manage the business for the long term? After 24 months, does the acquired business still appear attractive? If not, should it be divested? If yes, when and to whom?

Learn from Mistakes

It always pays to identify lessons learned from each transaction. This is often a neglected exercise and results in firms' repeating the same mistakes. This occurs because those involved in the acquisition process may change from one deal to another. Highly acquisitive companies can benefit greatly by dedicating certain legal, human resource, marketing, financial, and business development resources to support acquisitions made throughout the company. Despite evidence that abnormal financial returns to frequent acquirers tend to decline on average,[26] there is evidence that that such firms learn from experience through

---

[26] Fuller et al. (2002) document that acquirers, completing at least five deals within a three-year period, earn an average 1.7% cumulative abnormal return, but from the fifth deal on they earn only 0.52%. While this could reflect overconfidence, Atkas et al. (2009) argue that this is consistent with learning by doing because experienced acquirers are better able to assess expected synergies and are willing to pay more to complete deals.

repetitive deals, especially when the acquirer's CEO remains the same and the successive deals are similar.[27]

SOME THINGS TO REMEMBER

The acquisition process consists of 10 phases. The first phase defines the business plan. If an acquisition is believed necessary to implement the business strategy, an acquisition plan, developed during the second phase, defines the key objectives, available resources, and management preferences for completing an acquisition. The next phase consists of the search for appropriate acquisition candidates. The screening phase is a refinement of the search phase. How the potential acquirer initiates first contact depends on the urgency of completing a deal, target size, and access to highly placed contacts within the target firm. The negotiation phase consists of refining valuation, deal structuring, conducting due diligence, and developing a financing plan. Integration planning must be done before closing. The closing phase includes wading through all the necessary third-party consents and regulatory and shareholder approvals. The postclosing integration phase entails communicating effectively with all stakeholders, retaining key employees, and identifying and resolving immediate cash flow needs. While commonly overlooked, the postclosing evaluation is critical if a firm is to learn from past mistakes.

DISCUSSION QUESTIONS

5.1 Identify at least three criteria that might be used to select a manufacturing firm as a potential acquisition candidate. A financial services firm? A high-technology firm?

5.2 Identify alternative ways to make "first contact" with a potential acquisition target. Why is confidentiality important? Under what circumstances might a potential acquirer make its intentions public?

5.3 What are the differences between total consideration, total purchase price/enterprise value, and net purchase price? How are these different concepts used?

5.4 What is the purpose of the buyer's and the seller's performing due diligence?

5.5 Why is preclosing integration planning important?

5.6 In a rush to complete its purchase of health software producer HBO, McKesson did not perform adequate due diligence but, rather, relied on representations and warranties in the agreement of sale and purchase. Within six months following closing, McKesson announced that it would

---

[27] Atkas et al., 2013

have to reduce revenue by $327 million and net income by $191.5 million for the preceding three fiscal years to correct for accounting irregularities. The company's stock fell by 48%. If HBO's financial statements had been declared to be in accordance with GAAP, would McKesson have been justified in believing that HBO's revenue and profit figures were 100% accurate? Explain your answer.

5.7 Find a transaction currently in the news. Speculate as to what criteria the buyer may have employed to identify the target company as an attractive takeover candidate. Be specific.

5.8 Fresenius, a German manufacturer of dialysis equipment, acquired APP Pharmaceuticals for $4.6 billion. The deal includes an earnout, under which Fresenius would pay as much as $970 million if APP reaches certain future financial targets. What is the purpose of the earnout? How does it affect the buyer and the seller?

5.9 Material adverse change clauses (MACs) are a means for the parties to the contract to determine who will bear the risk of adverse events between the signing of an agreement and the closing. MACs are frequently not stated in dollar terms. How might MACs affect the negotiating strategies of the parties to the agreement during the period between signing and closing?

5.10 Despite disturbing discoveries during due diligence, Mattel acquired The Learning Company (TLC), a leading developer of software for toys, in a stock-for-stock transaction valued at $3.5 billion. Mattel had determined that TLC's receivables were overstated, a $50 million licensing deal had been prematurely put on the balance sheet, and TLC's brands were becoming outdated. TLC had also substantially exaggerated the amount of money put into research and development for new software products. Nevertheless, driven to become a big player in children's software, Mattel closed on the transaction, aware that TLC's cash flows were overstated. After restructuring charges associated with the acquisition, Mattel's consolidated net loss was $82.4 million on sales of $5.5 billion. Mattel's stock fell by more than 35% to end the year at about $14 per share. What could Mattel have done to protect its interests better?

Answers to these Chapter Discussion Questions are available in the Online Instructor's Manual for instructors using this book.

QUESTIONS FROM THE CFA CURRICULUM

5.11 The degree of operating leverage is best described as a measure of the sensitivity of:

a. Net earnings to changes in sales.

b. Fixed operating costs to changes in variable costs.

    c. Operating earnings to changes in the number of units produced and sold.

    d. Source: CFA Institute, 2011, *Measures of Leverage*, Reading 46, question 2.

5.12 The business risk of a particular company is most accurately measured by the company's:

    a. Debt-to-equity ratio.

    b. Efficiency in using assets to generate sales.

    c. Operating leverage and level of uncertainty about demand, output prices, and competition.

Source: CFA Institute, 2011, *Measures of Leverage*, Reading 46, question 4.

Answers to questions from the CFA curriculum are available in the Online Student Companion site to this book in a file folder entitled CFA Curriculum Questions and Solutions.

CASE STUDY 5.1
Exxon Mobil's (Exxon) Unrelenting Pursuit of Natural Gas

Key Points

- Believing the world will be dependent on carbon-based energy for many decades, Exxon continues to pursue aggressively amassing new natural gas and oil reserves.
- This strategy is consistent with its core energy extraction, refining, and distribution skills.
- As the world's largest energy company, Exxon must make big bets on new reserves of unconventional gas and oil to increase future earnings.

Exxon has always had a reputation for taking the long view. By necessity, energy companies cannot respond to short-term gyrations in energy prices, given the long lead time required to discover and develop new energy sources. While energy prices will continue to fluctuate, Exxon is betting that the world will remain dependent on oil and gas for decades to come and that new technology will facilitate accessing so-called unconventional energy sources.

During the last several years, Exxon continued its headlong rush into accumulating shale gas and oil properties that began in earnest in 2009 with the acquisition of natural gas exploration company XTO Energy. While natural gas prices have remained well below their 2008 level, Exxon used the expertise of the former XTO Energy personnel, who are among the most experienced in the industry in extracting oil and gas from shale rock, to identify the most attractive sites globally for future shale development. In 2010, Exxon acquired Ellora Energy Inc., which was active in the Haynesville shale fields in Texas and Louisiana, for $700 million and properties in Arkansas's Fayetteville shale fields from PetroHawk Energy Corp. In 2011, Exxon bought TWP Inc. and Phillips Resources, which were active in the Marcellus shale basin, for a combined $1.7 billion. Exxon is betting that these properties will become valuable when natural gas prices again rise. By mid-2011, Exxon Mobil had added more than 70 trillion cubic feet of unconventional gas and liquid reserves since the XTO deal in late 2009 through acquisitions and new discoveries. Exxon is now the largest natural gas producer in the United States.

The sheer size of the XTO acquisition in 2009 represented a remarkable departure for a firm that had not made a major acquisition during the previous 10 years. Following a series of unsuccessful acquisitions during the late 1970s and early 1980s, the firm seemed to have developed a phobia about acquisitions. Rather than make big acquisitions, Exxon started buying back its stock, purchasing more than $16 billion worth between 1983 and 1990, and spending about $1 billion annually on oil and gas properties and some small acquisitions.

Exxon Mobil Corporation stated publicly in its 2009 annual report that it was committed to being the world's premier petroleum and petrochemical company and that the firm's primary focus in the coming decades would likely remain on its core businesses of oil and gas exploration and production, refining, and chemicals. According to the firm, there appears to be "a pretty bright future" for drilling in previously untapped shale energy properties—as a result of technological advances in horizontal drilling and hydraulic fracturing. No energy source currently solves the challenge of meeting growing energy needs while reducing CO_2 emissions.[28]

Traditionally, energy companies have extracted natural gas by drilling vertical wells into pockets of methane that are often trapped above oil deposits. Energy companies now drill horizontal wells and fracture them with high-pressure water, a practice known as "fracking." That technique has enabled energy firms to release natural gas trapped in the vast shale oil fields in the United States as well as to recover gas and oil from fields previously thought to have been depleted. The natural gas and oil recovered in this manner are often referred to as "unconventional energy resources."

In an effort to bolster its position in the development of unconventional natural gas and oil, Exxon announced on December 14, 2009, that it had reached an agreement to buy XTO Energy in an all-stock deal valued at $31 billion. The deal also included Exxon's assumption of $10 billion in XTO's current debt. This represented a 25% premium to XTO shareholders at the time of the announcement. XTO shares jumped 15% to $47.86, while Exxon's fell by 4.3% to $69.69.

[28] Rex Tillerson, Exxonmobil CEO, 2009 Exxonmobil Annual Report.

The deal values XTO's natural gas reserves at $2.96 per thousand cubic feet of proven reserves, in line with recent deals and about one-half of the NYMEX natural gas futures price at that time.

Known as a wildcat or independent energy producer, the 23-year-old XTO competed aggressively with other independent drillers in the natural gas business, which had boomed with the onset of horizontal drilling and well fracturing to extract energy from older oil fields. However, independent energy producers like XTO typically lack the financial resources required to unlock unconventional gas reserves, unlike the large multinational energy firms like Exxon. The geographic overlap between the proven reserves of the two firms was significant, with both Exxon and XTO having a presence in Colorado, Louisiana, Texas, North Dakota, Pennsylvania, New York, Ohio, and Arkansas. The two firms' combined proven reserves are the equivalent of 45 trillion cubic feet of gas and include shale gas, coal bed methane, and shale oil. These reserves also complement Exxon's U.S. and international holdings.

Exxon is the global leader in oil and gas extraction. Given its size, it is difficult to achieve rapid future earnings growth organically through reinvestment of free cash flow. Consequently, megafirms such as Exxon often turn to large acquisitions to offer their shareholders significant future earnings growth. Given the long lead time required to add to proven reserves and the huge capital requirements to do so, energy companies by necessity must have exceedingly long-term planning and investment horizons. Acquiring XTO is a bet on the future of natural gas. Moreover, XTO has substantial technical expertise in recovering unconventional natural gas resources, which complement Exxon's global resource base, advanced R&D, proven operational capabilities, global scale, and financial capacity.

In the five-year period ending in 2010, the U.S. Energy Information Administration (EIA) estimates that the U.S. total proven natural gas reserves increased by 40% to about 300 trillion cubic feet, or the equivalent of 50 billion barrels of oil. Unconventional natural gas is projected by the EIA to meet most of the nation's domestic natural gas demand by 2030, representing a substantial change in the overall energy consumption pattern in the United States. At current consumption rates, the nation can count on natural gas for at least a century. In addition to its abundance, natural gas is the cleanest burning of the fossil fuels.

A sizeable purchase price premium, the opportunity to share in any upside appreciation in Exxon's share price, and the tax-free nature[29] of the transaction convinced XTO shareholders to approve the deal. Exxon's commitment to manage XTO on a stand-alone basis as a wholly owned subsidiary in which a number of former XTO

---

[29] When target firm shareholders receive primarily acquirer shares for their shares, the transaction is deemed to be tax free, in that no taxes are due until the acquirer shares are sold (see Chapter 12).

managers would be retained garnered senior management support. By keeping XTO largely intact in Fort Worth, Texas, Exxon was able to minimize differences due to Exxon Mobil's and XTO's dissimilar corporate cultures.

Discussion Questions

1. What was the total purchase price/ enterprise value of the transaction?
2. Why did Exxon Mobil's shares decline and XTO Energy's shares rise substantially immediately following the announcement of the takeover?
3. What do you think Exxon Mobil believes are its core skills? Based on your answer to this question, would you characterize this transaction as a related or an unrelated acquisition? Explain your answer.
4. Identify what you believe are the key environmental trends that encouraged Exxon Mobil to acquire XTO Energy.
5. How would you describe Exxon Mobil's long-term objectives, business strategy, and implementation strategy? What alternative implementation strategies could Exxon have pursued? Why do you believe it chose an acquisition strategy? What are the key risks involved in Exxon Mobil's takeover of XTO Energy?

Solutions to these case study discussion questions are found in the Online Instructor's Manual available to instructors using this book.

CASE STUDY 5.2
Microsoft Invests in Barnes & Noble's Nook Technology

Key Points

- Firm size often dictates business strategy.
- Diversifying away from a firm's core skills is often fraught with risk.
- Accumulated corporate cash balances often create potential agency problems.

Microsoft, like Apple, has been in business for three decades. Unlike Apple, Microsoft has failed to achieve and sustain the high growth in earnings and cash flow needed to grow its market value. For years, Microsoft has attempted to reduce its dependence on revenue generated from its Windows operating system software and the Office Products software suite by targeting high-growth segments in the information technology industry. Despite these efforts, the firm continues to generate more than four-fifths of its annual revenue from these two product lines.

The firm's ongoing dependence on its legacy products is not due to a lack of effort to diversify. Since 2009,

Microsoft has spent more than $10 billion in financing strategic alliances and takeovers. A 2009 Internet search partnership with Yahoo Inc. designed to assist Microsoft in overtaking Google by increasing use of its Bing search engine has gained little traction. In 2011, the firm agreed to supply the mobile operating system for smartphones sold by Nokia Corp. Thus far, Windows-powered smartphones have yet to gain a significant market share. That same year the software maker also acquired Skype, the Internet telephony firm, for $8.5 billion in the biggest acquisition in the firm's history. Its contribution to Microsoft's revenue and profit growth is unclear at this time.

Despite a number of acquisitions during the last few years, Microsoft amassed a cash hoard of more than $60 billion by the end of March 2012. The amount of cash creates considerable pressure from shareholders wanting the firm either to return the cash to them through share buybacks and dividends or to reinvest in new high-growth opportunities. In recent years, Microsoft has tried to do both.

Continuing to move aggressively, the software firm announced on April 30, 2012, that it would invest a cumulative $605 million (consisting of $300 million upfront with the balance paid over the next five years to finance ongoing product development and international expansion) in exchange for a 17.6% stake in a new Barnes & Noble (B&N) subsidiary containing B&N's e-titles and the Nook e-reader technology. The new subsidiary also houses B&N's college business,

viewed as a growth area for e-books. Analysts valued the new B&N subsidiary at $1.7 billion, more than twice B&N's consolidated value at the close of business on May 1, 2012. After the announcement, B&N's market value jumped to $1.25 billion.

As a result of the deal, the two firms will settle their patent infringement suits, and B&N will produce a Nook e-reading application for the Windows 8 operating system, which will run on both traditional PCs and tablets. Microsoft, through its Windows 8 product, has been forced to radically redesign its Windows operating system to accommodate a future in which web browsing, movie watching, book reading, and other activities occur on tablets as well as PCs and other mobile devices. While Windows 8 will have an "app store," it is likely to have to be closely aligned with a service for buying books and other forms of entertainment to match better the offerings from its rivals. The partnership is not exclusive to Microsoft, in that B&N can pursue other alliances with the likes of Google. B&N's e-book business is to remain aligned with the brick-and-mortar stores, of which the firm has 691 retail stores and 641 college bookstores.

In making the B&N investment, Microsoft is placing another bet on an industry in which it lags behind its competitors and which puts it in competition with Amazon.com Inc., Apple Inc., and Google Inc. The Nook currently runs on Google's Android software, as does Amazon's Kindle Fire. The two firms will share revenue from sales of e-books. The partnership also has the potential for Microsoft to manufacture e-readers and for future Nook devices to be powered by Microsoft operating systems. In addition to a much-needed cash infusion, B&N will capture additional points of distribution from hundreds of millions of Windows users around the world, potentially reaching consumers who did not do business with B&N.

Previously concerned that B&N would be a marginal competitor in the e-book marketplace, investors boosted B&H shares by 58% to $20.75 on the news. This was the firm's highest closing price in two years. The firm's conventional (physical) book business has declined rapidly. With revenue and profits declining, B&N was looking for a strategic partner to accelerate the growth of its e-book business globally. B&N had been accepting offers from a number of potential partners since it accepted a $204 million investment from Liberty Media in 2011 and had been considering a sale or spin-off of the e-book business.

B&N claims to have 27% of the U.S. e-book title sales, with Amazon capturing 60%. At one time, Amazon had almost a 90% market share of the e-book market, but this has eroded as new players, such as Apple, Google and now Microsoft, have entered. According to market research firm IHS iSuppli, Apple had 62% of the tablet market in 2011, reflecting the success of its iPad, with Amazon's Kindle having a 6% share and B&N's Nook a 5% share. Book publishers appear to have been encouraged by Microsoft's investment in B&N due to their growing concern that Amazon would dominate the e-book market and the

pricing of e-books if B&N were unable to become a viable competitor to Amazon.com.

Unlike rivals such as Apple, Microsoft has relied mainly on partners to create hardware that runs its software, with the exception of the Xbox video game unit and the company's ill-fated Zune media player. Microsoft is constrained by its partnerships, in that if the firm begins to create its own hardware, then it puts itself into direct competition with partners who make hardware such as tablet devices powered by Microsoft operating systems.

Discussion Questions

1. Speculate as to why Microsoft seems to be having trouble diversifying its revenue stream away from Windows and the Office Products suite.
2. What are the key factors external and internal to Microsoft that are driving its investment in Barnes & Noble?
3. Speculate as to how analysts valued B&N's e-book subsidiary at $1.7 billion. In what way might this number understate the value of the subsidiary at the time the Microsoft investment was made?
4. In your opinion, what does Microsoft bring to this partnership? What does Barnes & Noble contribute? What are likely to be the challenges to both parties in making this relationship successful?

Solutions to these questions are found in the Online Instructor's Manual available for instructors using this book.

Postclosing Integration: Mergers, Acquisitions, and Business Alliances

One cannot manage change. One can only be ahead of it …. Unless it is seen as the task of the organization to lead change, the organization will not survive.—**Peter Drucker**

INSIDE M&A: THE CHALLENGES OF INTEGRATING UNITED AND CONTINENTAL AIRLINES

KEY POINTS

- Among the critical early decisions that must be made before implementing integration is the selection of the manager overseeing the process.
- Integration teams commonly consist of managers from both the acquirer firm and the target firm.
- Senior management must remain involved in the postmerger integration process.
- Realizing anticipated synergies is often elusive.

On June 29, 2011, integration executive Lori Gobillot was selected by United Continental Holdings, the parent of both United and Continental airlines, to stitch together United and Continental airlines into the world's largest airline. Having completed the merger in October 2010, United and Continental airlines immediately began the gargantuan task of creating the largest airline in the world. In the area of information technology alone, the two firms had to integrate more than 1400 separate systems, programs, and protocols. Workers from the two airlines were represented by two different unions and were subject to different work rules. Even the airplanes were laid out differently, with United's fleet having first-class cabins and Continental's planes having business and coach only. The combined carriers have routes connecting 373 airports in 63 countries. The combined firms have more than 1300 airplanes.

Jeffry Smisek, CEO of United Continental Holdings, had set expectations high, telling Wall Street analysts that the combined firms expected to generate at least $1.2 billion in cost savings annually within three years. This was to be achieved by rationalizing operations and eliminating redundancies.

Smisek selected Lori Gobillot as the executive in charge of the integration effort because she had coordinated the carrier's due diligence with United during the period prior to the two firms', failed attempt to combine in 2008. Her accumulated knowledge of the two airlines, interpersonal skills, self-discipline, and drive made her a natural choice.

She directed 33 interdisciplinary integration teams that collectively made thousands of decisions, ranging from the fastest way to clean 1260 airplanes and board passengers to which perks to offer in the frequent flyer program. The teams consisted of personnel from both airlines. Members included managers from such functional departments as technology, human resources, fleet management, and network planning and were structured around such activities as operations and a credit card partnership with JPMorgan Chase. In most cases, the teams agreed to retain at least one of the myriad programs already in place for the passengers of one of the airlines so that at least some of the employees would be familiar with the programs.

If she was unable to resolve disagreements within teams, Gobillot invited senior managers to join the deliberations. In order to stay on a tight time schedule, Gobillot emphasized to employees at both firms that the integration effort was not "us versus them" but, rather, that they were all in it together. All had to stay focused on the need to achieve integration on a timely basis while minimizing disruption to daily operations if planned synergies were to be realized.

Nevertheless, despite the hard work and commitment of those involved in the process, history shows that the challenges associated with any postclosing integration are often daunting. The integration of Continental and United was no exception. United pilots have resisted the training they were offered to learn Continental's flight procedures. They even unsuccessfully sued their employer due to the slow pace of negotiations to reach new, unified labor contracts. Customers have been confused by the inability of Continental agents to answer questions about United's flights. Additional confusion was created on March 3, 2012, when the two airlines merged their reservation systems, websites, and frequent flyer programs, a feat that had often been accomplished in stages in prior airline mergers. As a result of alienation of some frequent flyer customers, reservation snafus, and flight delays, revenue has failed thus far to meet expectations. Moreover, by the end of 2012, one-time merger-related expenses totaled almost $1.5 billion.

Many airline mergers in the past have hit rough spots that reduced anticipated ongoing savings and revenue increases. Pilots and flight attendants at

US Airways Group, a combination of US Airways and America West, were still operating under separate contracts with different pay rates, schedules, and work rules six years after the merger. Delta Airlines remains ensnared in a labor dispute that has kept it from equalizing pay and work rules for flight attendants and ramp workers at Delta and Northwest Airlines, which Delta acquired in 2008. The longer these disputes continue, the greater the cultural divide in integrating these businesses.

CHAPTER OVERVIEW

After a transaction closes, integration is on the agenda. The category into which the acquirer falls will influence considerably the extent of integration and the pace at which it takes place. *Financial* buyers—those who buy a business for eventual resale—tend not to integrate the acquired business into another entity. Rather than manage the business, they are inclined to monitor the effectiveness of current management and intervene only if there is a significant and sustained deviation between actual and projected performance. In contrast, *strategic* buyers want to make a profit by managing the acquired business for an extended period, either as a separate subsidiary in a holding company or by merging it into another business. For our purposes here, assume that integration is the goal of the acquirer immediately after the transaction closes. The integration phase is an important contributor to the ultimate success of the merger or acquisition, and ineffective integration is commonly given as one of the primary reasons that M&As sometimes fail to meet expectations.

A practical process makes for effective integration. The critical success factors include careful premerger planning, candid and continuous communication, adopting the right pace for combining the businesses, appointing an integration manager and team with clearly defined goals and lines of authority, and making the difficult decisions early in the process. The chapter concludes with a discussion of how to overcome some of the unique obstacles encountered in integrating business alliances. A chapter review (consisting of practice questions and answers) is available in the file folder entitled "Student Study Guide" on the companion site to this book (http://booksite.elsevier.com/9780123854872).

THE ROLE OF INTEGRATION IN SUCCESSFUL MERGERS AND ACQUISITIONS

Rapid integration is more likely to result in a merger that achieves the acquirer's expectations.[1] For our purposes, the term *rapid* is defined as relative to the pace of normal operations for a firm. Andersen Consulting studied 100 global

[1]Coopers & Lybrand, 1996; Marks, 1996

acquisitions, each valued at more than $500 million, and concluded that most postmerger activities are completed within six months to one year and that integration done quickly generates the financial returns expected by shareholders and minimizes employee turnover and customer attrition.[2]

This does not mean that restructuring ends entirely within this time period. Integration may continue in terms of plant sales or closures for years following the acquisition. Almost one-half of acquirers either sell or close target firms' plants within three years of the acquisition. Acquirers having more experience in managing the target's plants are more likely to retain the target's operations than those whose experience in operating such plants is limited. If we extend the period to five years following closing, plant divestitures and closures increase by an additional nine to ten percent.[3]

Realizing Projected Financial Returns

A simple example demonstrates the importance of rapid integration to realizing projected financial returns. Suppose a firm's current market value of $100 million accurately reflects the firm's future cash flows discounted at its cost of capital (i.e., the financial return the firm must earn or exceed to satisfy the expectations of its shareholders and lenders). Assume an acquirer is willing to pay a $25 million premium for this firm over its current share price, believing it can recover the premium by realizing cost savings resulting from integrating the two firms. The amount of cash the acquirer will have to generate to recover the premium will increase the longer it takes to integrate the target company. If the cost of capital is 10% and integration is completed by the end of the first year, the acquirer will have to earn $27.5 million by the end of the first year to recover the premium plus its cost of capital ($25 + ($25 × 0.10)). If integration is not completed until the end of the second year, the acquirer will have to earn an incremental cash flow of $30.25 million ($27.5 + ($27.5 × 0.10)), and so on.

The Impact of Employee Turnover

Although there is little evidence that firms necessarily experience an actual reduction in their total workforce following an acquisition, there is evidence of increased turnover among management and key employees after a corporate takeover.[4] Some loss of managers is intentional as part of an effort to eliminate redundancies and overlapping positions, but other managers quit during the integration turmoil. In many acquisitions, talent and management skills represent the primary value of the target company to the acquirer—especially in high-technology and service companies, for which assets are largely the embodied

[2] Andersen Consulting, 1999

[3] Maksimovic et al., 2012

[4] Shivdasani, 1993; Walsh and Ellwood, 1991

knowledge of their employees[5]—and it is difficult to measure whether employees that leave represent a significant "brain drain" or loss of key managers. If it does, though, this loss degrades the value of the target company, making the recovery of any premium paid to target shareholders difficult for the buyer.

The cost also may be high simply because the target firm's top, experienced managers are removed as part of the integration process and replaced with new managers—who tend to have a high failure rate in general. When a firm selects an insider (i.e., a person already in the employ of the merged firms) to replace a top manager (e.g., a CEO), the failure rate of the successor (i.e., the successor is no longer with the firm 18 months later) is 34%. When the board selects an outside successor (i.e., one not currently employed by the merged firms) to replace the departing senior manager, the 18-month failure rate is 55%. Therefore, more than half of the time, an outside successor will not succeed, with an insider succeeding about two-thirds of the time.[6]

The cost of employee turnover does not stop with the loss of key employees. The loss of any significant number of employees can be very costly. Current employees have already been recruited and trained; lose them, and you will incur new recruitment and training costs to replace them with equally qualified employees. Moreover, the loss of employees is likely to reduce the morale and productivity of those who remain.

Acquisition-Related Customer Attrition

During normal operations, a business can expect a certain level of churn in its customer list. Depending on the industry, normal churn as a result of competitive conditions can be anywhere from 20 to 40%. A newly merged company will experience a loss of another 5 to 10% of its existing customers as a direct result of a merger,[7] reflecting uncertainty about on-time delivery and product quality and more aggressive postmerger pricing by competitors. Moreover, many companies lose revenue momentum as they concentrate on realizing expected cost synergies. The loss of customers may continue well after closing.[8]

Rapid Integration Does Not Mean Doing Everything at the Same Pace

Rapid integration may result in more immediate realization of synergies, but it also contributes to employee and customer attrition. Therefore, intelligent

---

[5]Lord and Ranft, 2000

[6]Dalton, 2006

[7]Down, 1995

[8]A McKinsey study of 160 acquisitions by 157 publicly traded firms in 11 different industries in 1995 and 1996 found that, on average, these firms grew four percentage points less than their peers during the three years following closing. Moreover, 42% of the sample actually lost ground. Only 12% of the sample showed revenue growth significantly ahead of their peers (Bekier, Bogardus, and Oldham, 2001).

integration involves managing these tradeoffs by quickly identifying and implementing projects that offer the most immediate payoff and deferring those whose disruption would result in the greatest revenue loss. Acquirers often postpone integrating data-processing and customer-service call centers until much later in the integration process if such activities are pivotal to maintaining on-time delivery and high-quality customer service.

INTEGRATION IS A PROCESS, NOT AN EVENT

Integrating a business into the acquirer's operations involves six major activities that fall loosely into the following sequence: premerger planning, resolving communication issues, defining the new organization, developing staffing plans, integrating functions and departments, and building a new corporate culture. Some activities are continuous and, in some respects, unending. For instance, communicating with all major stakeholder groups and developing a new corporate culture are largely continuous activities, running through the integration period and beyond. Table 6.1 outlines the sequence.

Premerger Integration Planning

While some argue that integration planning should begin as soon as the merger is announced,[9] assumptions made before the closing based on information accumulated during due diligence must be re-examined once the transaction is consummated to ensure their validity. The premerger integration planning process enables the acquiring company to refine its original estimate of the value of the target and deal with transition issues in the context of the merger agreement. Furthermore, it gives the buyer an opportunity to insert into the agreement the appropriate representations and warranties as well as conditions of closing that facilitate the postmerger integration process. Finally, the planning process creates a postmerger integration organization to expedite the integration process after the closing.

To minimize potential confusion, it is critical to get the integration manager involved in the process as early as possible—ideally as soon as the target has been identified or at least well before the evaluation and negotiation process begins.[10] Doing so makes it more likely that the strategic rationale for the deal remains well understood by those involved in conducting due diligence and postmerger integration.

[9]Carey and Ogden, 2004

[10]Uhlaner and West, 2008

TABLE 6.1 Viewing Merger Integration as a Process

Integration Planning	Developing Communication Plans	Creating a New Organization	Developing Staffing Plans	Functional Integration	Building a New Corporate Culture
Premerger Planning:	Stakeholders:	Learn from the past	Determine personnel requirements for the new organization	Revalidate due diligence data	Identify cultural issues through corporate profiling
Refine valuation	Employees				
Resolve transition issues	Customers				
Negotiate contractual assurances	Suppliers				
	Investors				
	Lenders				
	Communities (including regulators)				
		Business needs drive organizational structure	Determine resource availability	Conduct performance benchmarking	Integrate through shared:
					Goals
					Standards
					Services
					Space
			Establish staffing plans and timetables	Integrate functions:	
				Operations	
				Information technology	
				Finance	
				Sales	
				Marketing	
				Purchasing	
				R&D	
				Human resources	
			Develop compensation strategy		
			Create needed information systems		

Putting The Postmerger Integration Organization In Place Before Closing

A postmerger integration organization with clearly defined goals and responsibilities should be in place before the closing. For friendly mergers, the organization—including supporting work teams—should consist of individuals from both the acquiring and target companies with a vested interest in the newly formed company. During a hostile takeover, of course, it can be problematic to assemble such a team, given the lack of trust that may exist between the parties to the transaction. The acquiring company will likely find it difficult to access needed information and involve the target company's management in the planning process before the transaction closes.

If the plan is to integrate the target firm into one of the acquirer's business units, it is critical to place responsibility for integration in that business unit. Personnel from the business unit should be well represented on the due diligence team to ensure they understand how best to integrate the target to realize synergies expeditiously.

The Postmerger Integration Organization: Composition and Responsibilities

The postmerger integration organization should consist of a management integration team (MIT) and integration work teams focused on implementing a specific portion of the integration plan. Senior managers from the two merged organizations serve on the MIT, which is charged with realizing synergies identified during the preclosing due diligence. Involving senior managers from both firms captures the best talent from both organizations and sends a comforting signal to all employees that decision makers who understand their particular situations are in agreement.

The MIT's emphasis during the integration period should be on activities that create the greatest value for shareholders. Exhibit 6.1 summarizes the key tasks the MIT must perform to realize anticipated synergies.

In addition to driving the integration effort, the MIT ensures that the managers not involved in the endeavor remain focused on running the business. Dedicated work teams perform the detailed integration work. These teams should also include employees from both the acquiring company and the target company. Other team members might include outside advisors, such as investment bankers, accountants, attorneys, and consultants.

The MIT allocates dedicated resources to the integration effort and clarifies non-team-membership roles and enables day-to-day operations to continue at premerger levels. The MIT should be careful to give the teams not only the responsibility to do certain tasks but also the authority and resources to get the job done. To be effective, the work teams must have access to timely, accurate information, receive candid, timely feedback, and be kept informed of the broader perspective of the overall integration effort to avoid becoming too narrowly focused.

EXHIBIT 6.1 KEY MANAGEMENT INTEGRATION TEAM RESPONSIBILITIES

1. Build a master schedule of what should be done by whom and by what date.
2. Determine the required economic performance for the combined entity.
3. Establish work teams to determine how each function and business unit will be combined (e.g., structure, job design, and staffing levels).
4. Focus the organization on meeting ongoing business commitments and operational performance targets during the integration process.
5. Create an early warning system consisting of performance indicators to ensure that both integration activities and business performance stay on plan.
6. Monitor and expedite key decisions.
7. Establish a rigorous communication campaign to support the integration plan aggressively. Address both internal constituencies (e.g., employees) and external constituencies (e.g., customers, suppliers, and regulatory authorities).

Developing Communication Plans for Key Stakeholders

Before publicly announcing an acquisition, the acquirer should prepare a communication plan targeted at major stakeholder groups.

Employees: Addressing the "Me" Issues Immediately

Employees are interested in any information pertaining to the merger and how it will affect them, often in terms of job security, working conditions, and total compensation. Thus, consistent and candid communication is of paramount importance.

Target firm employees often represent a substantial portion of the acquired company's value, particularly for technology and service-related businesses with few tangible assets. The CEO should lead the effort to communicate to employees at all levels through on-site meetings or via teleconferencing. Communication to employees should be as frequent as possible; it is better to report that there is no change than to remain silent. Direct communication to all employees at both firms is critical. Deteriorating job performance and absences from work are clear signs of workforce anxiety. Many companies find it useful to create a single information source accessible to all employees, be it an individual whose job is to answer questions or a menu-driven automated phone system programmed to respond to commonly asked questions. The best way to communicate in a crisis, however, is through regularly scheduled employee meetings.

All external communication in the form of press releases should be coordinated with the PR department to ensure that the same information is released concurrently to all employees. Internal e-mail systems, voice mail, or intranets may be used to facilitate employee communications. In addition, personal letters, question-and-answer sessions, newsletters, and videotapes are highly effective ways to deliver messages.

Customers: Undercommitting and Overdelivering

Attrition can be minimized if the newly merged firm commits to assuring customers that it will maintain or improve product quality, on-time delivery, and customer service. Commitments should be realistic in terms of what needs to be accomplished during the integration phase. The firm must communicate to customers realistic benefits associated with the merger. From the customer's perspective, the merger can increase the range of products or services offered or provide lower selling prices as a result of economies of scale and new applications of technology.

Suppliers: Developing Long-Term Vendor Relationships

The new company should seek long-term relationships rather than simply ways to reduce costs. Aggressive negotiation may win high-quality products and services at lower prices in the short run, but that may be transitory if the new company is a large customer of the supplier and if the supplier's margins are squeezed continually. The supplier's product or service quality will suffer, and the supplier eventually may exit the business.

Investors: Maintaining Shareholder Loyalty

The new firm must be able to present a compelling vision of the future to investors. In a share exchange, target shareholders become shareholders in the newly formed company. Loyal shareholders tend to provide a more stable ownership base and may contribute to lower share price volatility. All firms attract particular types of investors—some with a preference for high dividends and others for capital gains—and they may clash over their preferences, as America Online's acquisition of Time Warner in January 2000 illustrates. The combined market value of the two firms lost 11% in the four days following the announcement: Investors fretted over what had been created, and there was a selling frenzy that likely involved investors who bought Time Warner for its stable growth and America Online for its meteoric growth rate of 70% per year.

Communities: Building Strong, Credible Relationships

Good working relations with surrounding communities are simply good public relations. Companies should communicate plans to build or keep plants, stores, or office buildings in a community as soon as they can be confident that these actions will be implemented. Such steps often translate into new jobs and increased tax collections for the community.

Creating a New Organization

Despite the requirement to appoint dozens of managers—including heads of key functions, groups, and even divisions—creating a new top management team must be given first priority.

Establishing a Structure

Building new reporting structures for combining companies requires knowledge of the target company's prior organization, some sense as to the effectiveness of this organization, and the future business needs of the new firm. Prior organization charts provide insights into how individuals from both companies will interact within the new company, because they reveal the past experience and future expectations of individuals with regard to reporting relationships.

The next step is to create a structure that meets the business needs of the new firm. Common structures include functional, product or service, and divisional organizations. In a *functional organization*, people are assigned to specific departments, such as accounting, engineering, and marketing. In a *product or service organization*, functional specialists are grouped by product line or service offering, and each has its own accounting, human resources, sales, marketing, customer service, and product development staffs. *Divisional organizations*, in which groups of products are combined into divisions or strategic business units are the most common. Such organizations have their own management teams and tend to be highly decentralized.

The popularity of decentralized versus centralized management structures varies with the state of the economy. During recessions, when top management is under great pressure to cut costs, companies may tend to move toward centralized management structures, only to decentralize when the economy recovers. Highly decentralized authority can retard the pace of integration because there is no single authority to resolve issues or determine policies. A centralized structure may make postmerger integration much easier. Senior management can dictate policies governing all aspects of the combined companies, centralize all types of functions that provide support to operating units, and resolve issues among the operating units. Still, centralized control can be highly detrimental and can destroy value if policies imposed by the central headquarters are inappropriate for the operating units—such as policies that impose too many rigid controls, focus on the wrong issues, hire or promote the wrong managers, or establish the wrong performance measures. Moreover, centralized companies have often multiple layers of management and centralized functions providing services to the operating units. The parent companies pass on the costs of centralized management and support services to the operating units, and these costs often outweigh the benefits.[11]

The benefits of a well-managed, rapid postmerger integration suggest a centralized management structure initially with relatively few management layers. The distance between the CEO and division heads, measured in terms of intermediate positions, has decreased substantially, while the span of a CEO's authority has widened.[12] This does not mean all integration activities should be driven

[11]Campbell, Sadler, and Koch, 1997

[12]Wulf and Rajan (2003) report a 25% decrease in intermediate positions between 1986 and 1999, with about 50% more positions reporting directly to the CEO.

Personnel Requirements	Employee Availability	Staffing Plans and Timetables	Compensation	Personnel Information Systems
Functional requirements	Existing workforce	Needs versus resources	Types	Merge databases
Organizational structure	Local workforce	Management involvement	Integrating plans	Integrate one database into the other
		Contingency plans	Postmerger disparities	Maintain individual databases

FIGURE 6.1 Staffing-strategy sequencing and associated issues.

from the top, but it does mean taking decisive action. Once integration is complete, the new company should move to a more decentralized structure in view of the well-documented costs of centralized corporate organizations.

Developing Staffing Plans

Staffing plans should be formulated early in the integration process. The early development of such plans provides an opportunity to include key personnel from both firms in the integration effort. Other benefits include the increased likelihood of retaining employees with key skills and talents, maintaining corporate continuity, and team building. Figure 6.1 presents the logical sequencing of staffing plans and the major issues are addressed in each segment.

Personnel Requirements

The appropriate organizational structure is one that meets the current functional requirements of the business and is flexible enough to be expanded to satisfy future requirements. Before establishing the organizational structure, the integration team should agree on the specific functions needed to run the combined businesses and project each function's personnel requirements based on a description of the function's ideal structure to achieve its objectives.

Employee Availability

Employee availability refers to the number of each type of employee required by the new organization. The skills of the existing workforce should be documented and compared with the current and future requirements of the new company. The local labor pool can be a source of potential "new hires" for the combined firms to augment the existing workforce. Data should be collected on the educational levels, skills, and demographic composition of the local workforce as well as prevailing wage rates by skill category.

Staffing Plans and Timetable

A detailed staffing plan can be developed once the preceding steps are completed. Gaps in the firm's workforce that need to be filled via outside recruitment can be readily identified. The effort to recruit externally should be tempered by its potentially adverse impact on current-employee morale. Filling needed jobs should be prioritized and phased in over time in recognition of the time required to fill certain types of positions and the impact of major hiring programs on local wage rates in communities with a limited availability of labor.

Compensation

Merging compensation plans must be done in compliance with prevailing regulations and with sensitivity. Total compensation consists of base pay, bonuses or incentive plans, benefits, and special contractual agreements. Bonuses may take the form of a lump sum of cash or stock paid to an employee for meeting or exceeding these targets. Special contractual agreements may consist of noncompete agreements, in which key employees, in exchange for an agreed-on amount of compensation, sign agreements not to compete against the newly formed company if they should leave. Special agreements also may take the form of golden parachutes (i.e., lucrative severance packages) for senior management. Finally, retention bonuses are often given to employees if they agree to stay with the new company for a specific period.[13]

Personnel Information Systems

The acquiring company may choose to merge all personnel data into a new database, merge one corporate database into another, or maintain the separate personnel databases of each business. A single database enables authorized users to access employee data more readily, plan more efficiently for future staffing requirements, and conduct workforce analyses. Maintenance expenses associated with a single database also may be lower. The decision to keep personnel databases separate may reflect plans to divest the unit in the future.

Functional Integration

So far, you have learned about the steps involved in *planning* the integration process. Now let's look at functional integration—the actual *execution* of the plans. The management integration team must first determine the extent to which the two firms' operations and support staffs are to be centralized or decentralized. The main areas of focus should be information technology (IT), manufacturing operations, sales, marketing, finance, purchasing, R&D, and the requirements to staff these functions. However, before any actual integration takes place, it is crucial to revalidate data collected during due diligence, benchmark all operations by comparing them to industry standards, and reset synergy expectations.

---

[13] Following its acquisition of Merrill Lynch in 2008, Bank of America offered Merrill's top financial advisors retention bonuses to minimize potential attrition—believing that the loss of the highest producers among Merrill's 17,000 brokers would have seriously eroded the value of the firm to Bank of America.

Revalidating Due Diligence Data

Data collected during due diligence should be reviewed immediately after closing. The pressure exerted by both buyer and seller to complete the transaction often results in a haphazard preclosing due diligence review. For example, to compress the time devoted to due diligence, sellers often allow buyers access only to senior managers. For similar reasons, site visits by the buyer are often limited to those with the largest number of employees—and so risks and opportunities that might exist at other sites are ignored or remain undiscovered. The buyer's legal and financial reviews are typically conducted only on the largest customer and supplier contracts, promissory notes, and operating and capital leases. Receivables are evaluated, and physical inventory is counted using sampling techniques. The effort to determine whether intellectual property has been properly protected, with key trademarks or service marks registered and copyrights and patents filed, is often spotty.

Benchmarking Performance

Benchmarking important functions such as the acquirer and target manufacturing and IT operations is a useful starting point for determining how to integrate these activities. Standard benchmarks include the International Standards Organization's (ISO) 9000 Quality Systems—Model for Quality Assurance in Design, Development, Production, Installation, and Servicing. Other benchmarks that can be used include the U.S. Food and Drug Administration's Good Manufacturing Practices and the Department of Commerce's Malcolm Baldrige Award.[14]

Reset Synergy Expectations

Companies that re-examine their synergy assumptions after closing seem to achieve higher synergies than those that do not. Companies that are most successful in realizing incremental value resulting from integrating the target firm are often those that use their predeal estimates of synergy as baseline estimates (i.e., the minimum they expect to achieve). Such firms are four times more likely to characterize their deals more highly successful than executives of acquiring firms that do not reset their synergy expectations. Additional value is often realized by making fundamental operational changes or by providing customers with new products or services that were envisioned during the due diligence process.[15] For example, Belgian brewer InBev's 2008 takeover of U.S. brewer Anheuser-Busch initially envisioned eliminating about $1.5 billion in the combined firm's annual operating expenses. Two years later, more than $2 billion in annual expenses had been cut.[16]

---

[14]Sanderson and Uzumeri (1997, p. 135) provide a comprehensive list of standards-setting organizations.

[15]Agrawal, Ferrer, and West (2011)

[16]Berfield (July 10, 2011)

Integrating Manufacturing Operations

The objective should be to re-evaluate overall capacity, the potential for future cost reductions, the age and condition of facilities, the adequacy of maintenance budgets, and compliance with environmental laws and safety laws. The integration should consider carefully whether target facilities that duplicate manufacturing capabilities are potentially more efficient than those of the buyer. As part of the benchmarking process, the operations of both the acquirer and the target company should be compared with industry standards to evaluate their efficiency properly.

Efficiency may be evaluated in terms of following processes: production planning, materials ordering, order entry, and quality control. The production-planning and materials-ordering functions need to coordinate activities because the amount and makeup of the materials ordered depends on the accuracy of sales projections. Inaccurate projections create shortages or costly excess inventory accumulation. Order entry may offer significant opportunities for cost savings. Companies that produce in anticipation of sales, such as automakers, often carry large finished-goods inventories, while others, such as personal computer manufacturers, often build only when an order is received, to minimize working capital requirements. Finally, the efficiency of quality control can be measured in terms of the percentage of products that have to be reworked due to their failure to meet quality standards.

Plant consolidation begins with adopting a set of common systems and standards for all manufacturing activities. Such standards often include the time between production runs, cost per unit of output, and scrap rates. Vertical integration can be achieved by focusing on different stages of production. Different facilities specialize in the production of selected components, which are then shipped to other facilities to assemble the finished product. Finally, a company may close certain facilities whenever there is excess capacity.

Integrating Information Technology

IT spending constitutes an ever-increasing share of most business budgets—and about 80% of software projects fail to meet their performance expectations or deadlines.[17] Nearly one-half are scrapped before completion, and about one-half cost two to three times their original budgets and take three times as long as expected to complete.[18] Managers seem to focus too much on technology and not enough on the people and processes that will use that technology. If the buyer intends to operate the target company independently, the information systems of the two companies may be kept separate as long as communications links between them can be established. If the buyer intends to integrate the target, though, the process can be daunting. Nearly 70% of buyers choose to combine

---

[17] *Financial Times*, 1996

[18] *Wall Street Journal*, November 18, 1996

their information systems immediately after closing, and almost 90% of acquirers eventually combine these operations.[19]

Integrating Finance

Some target companies will be operated as stand-alone operations, while others will be completely merged with the acquirer's existing business. International acquisitions involve companies in geographically remote areas and operate largely independent of the parent. This requires considerable effort to ensure that the buyer can monitor financial results from a distance, even if the parent has its representative on site. The acquirer should also establish a budgeting process and signature approval levels to control spending.

Integrating Sales

Significant cost savings may result from integrating sales forces, which eliminates duplicate sales representatives and related support expenses, such as travel and entertainment expenses, training, and management. A single sales force may also minimize customer confusion by allowing customers to deal with a single salesperson when buying multiple products.

Whether the sales forces of the two firms are wholly integrated or operated independently depends on their relative size, the nature of their products and markets, and their geographic location. A small sales force may be readily combined with a larger sales force if they sell sufficiently similar products and serve similar markets. The sales forces may be kept separate if the products they sell require in-depth understanding of the customers' needs and a detailed knowledge of the product. It is quite common for firms that sell highly complex products such as robotics or enterprise software to employ a particularly well-trained and sophisticated sales force that must employ the "consultative selling" approach. This approach may entail the firm's sales force's working with the customer to develop a solution tailored to their specific needs and may require keeping the sales forces of merged firms separate. Sales forces in globally dispersed businesses are often kept separate to reflect the uniqueness of their markets. However, support activities such as sales training and technical support are often centralized.

Integrating Marketing

Enabling the customer to see a consistent image in advertising and promotional campaigns may be the greatest challenge facing the integration of the marketing function. Steps to ensure consistency, however, should not confuse the customer by radically changing a product's image or how it is sold. The location and degree of integration of the marketing function depend on the global nature of the business, the diversity or uniqueness of product lines, and the pace of change in the marketplace. A business with operations worldwide may be inclined to decentralize marketing to the local countries to increase awareness

---

[19]Cossey, 1991

of local laws and cultural patterns. Companies with a large number of product lines that can be grouped into logical categories or that require extensive product knowledge may decide to disperse the marketing function to the various operating units to keep marketing personnel as close to the customer as possible.

Integrating Purchasing

Managing the merged firm's purchasing function aggressively and efficiently can reduce the total cost of goods and services purchased by merged companies by 10 to 15%.[20] The opportunity to reap such substantial savings from suppliers comes immediately after the closing of the transaction. A merger creates uncertainty among both companies' suppliers, particularly if they might have to compete against each other for business with the combined firms. Many will offer cost savings and new partnership arrangements, given the merged organization's greater bargaining power to renegotiate contracts. The new company may choose to realize savings by reducing the number of suppliers. As part of the premerger due diligence, both the acquirer and the acquired company should identify a short list of their most critical suppliers, with a focus on those accounting for the largest share of purchased materials', expenses.

Integrating Research and Development

Often, the buyer and seller R&D organizations are working on duplicate projects or projects not germane to the buyer's long-term strategy. Senior managers and the integration team must define future areas of R&D collaboration and set priorities for future R&D research. However, barriers to R&D integration abound. Some projects require considerably more time (measured in years) to produce results than others. Another obstacle is that some personnel stand to lose in terms of titles, prestige, and power if they collaborate. Finally, the acquirer's and the target's R&D financial return expectations may differ. The acquirer may wish to give R&D a higher or lower priority in the combined operation of the two companies. A starting point for integrating R&D is to have researchers from both companies share their work with each other and co-locate. Work teams also can follow a balanced scorecard approach for obtaining funding for their projects, scoring R&D projects according to their impact on key stakeholders, such as shareholders and customers. Those projects receiving the highest scores are fully funded.

Integrating Human Resources

Human resources departments have traditionally been highly centralized, responsible for evaluating management, conducting employee surveys, developing staffing plans, and providing training. Human resources departments may be used to evaluate the strengths and weaknesses of potential target company management teams and workforces, integrate the acquirer's and target's

---

[20]Chapman et al. (1998)

management teams, implement pay and benefit plans, and communicate information about acquisitions. Due to expense and a perceived lack of responsiveness, the trend in recent years has been to move the HR function to the operating unit, where hiring and training may be done more effectively. Despite this trend, the administration of benefit plans, management of HR information systems, and organizational development often remains centralized.

Building a New Corporate Culture

Corporate culture is a common set of values, traditions, and beliefs that influence management and employee behavior within a firm. Large, diverse businesses have an overarching culture and a series of subcultures that reflect local conditions. When two companies with different cultures merge, the newly formed company will often take on a new culture that is quite different from either the acquirer's or the target's culture. Cultural differences can instill creativity in the new company or create a contentious environment.

Tangible symbols of culture include statements hung on walls containing the firm's mission and principles as well as status associated with the executive office floor and designated parking spaces. Intangible forms include the behavioral norms communicated through implicit messages about how people are expected to act. Since they represent the extent to which employees and managers actually "walk the talk," these messages are often far more influential in forming and sustaining corporate culture than the tangible trappings of corporate culture.[21] Trust in the corporation is undermined after a merger, in part by the ambiguity of the new organization's identity. Employee acceptance of a common culture can build identification with and trust in the corporation. As ambiguity abates and acceptance of a common culture grows, trust can be restored, especially among those who identified closely with their previous organization.[22]

Identifying Cultural Issues through Cultural Profiling

The first step in building a new corporate culture is to develop a cultural profile of both the acquirer and acquired companies through employee surveys and interviews and by observing management styles and practices. The information is then used to show the similarities and differences between the two cultures as well as their comparative strengths and weaknesses.

The relative size and maturity of the acquirer and target firms can have major implications for cultural integration. Start-up companies typically are highly informal in terms of dress and decision making. Compensation may

---

[21] Kennedy and Moore (2003) argue that the most important source of communication of cultural biases in an organization is the individual behavior of others, especially those with the power to reward appropriate behavior and to punish inappropriate behavior.

[22] Maguire and Phillips, 2008

be largely stock options and other forms of deferred income. Benefits, beyond those required by state and federal law, and "perks" such as company cars are largely nonexistent. Company policies frequently do not exist, are not in writing, or are drawn up only as needed. Internal controls covering employee expense accounts are often minimal. In contrast, larger, mature companies are often more highly structured, with well-defined internal controls, compensation structures, benefits packages, and employment policies all in place because the firms have grown too large and complex to function in an orderly manner without them. Employees usually have clearly defined job descriptions and career paths.

Once senior management reviews the information in the cultural profile, it must decide which characteristics of both cultures to emphasize. The most realistic expectation is that employees in the new company can be encouraged to adopt a shared vision, a set of core values, and behaviors deemed important by senior management. Anything more is probably wishful thinking: A company's culture evolves over a long period, but getting to the point where employees wholly embrace management's desired culture may take years at best or never be achieved.

Overcoming Cultural Differences

Sharing common goals, standards, services, and space can be a highly effective and practical way to integrate disparate cultures.[23] Common goals drive different units to cooperate. At the functional level, setting exact timetables and processes for new-product development can drive different operating units to collaborate as project teams strive to introduce the product by the target date. At the corporate level, incentive plans spanning many years can focus all operating units to pursue the same goals. Although it is helpful in the integration process to have shared or common goals, individuals must still have specific goals to minimize the tendency of some to underperform while benefiting from the collective performance of others.

Shared standards or practices enable one unit or function to adopt the "best practices" found in another. Standards include operating procedures, technological specifications, ethical values, internal controls, employee performance measures, and comparable reward systems throughout the combined companies. Some functional services can be centralized and shared by multiple departments or operating units. Commonly centralized services include: accounting, legal, public relations, internal audit, and information technology. The most common way to share services is to use a common staff. Alternatively, a firm can create a support services unit and allow operating units to purchase services from it or to buy similar services outside the company.

Mixing offices or even locating acquired company employees in space adjacent to the parent's offices is a highly desirable way to improve communication

---

[23]Malekzadeh and Nahavandi, 1990

and idea sharing. Common laboratories, computer rooms, and lunchrooms also facilitate communication and cooperation.[24]

When Time Is Critical

Although every effort should be made to merge corporate cultures by achieving consensus around certain core beliefs and behaviors, the need for nimble decision making may require a more expeditious approach. Japanese corporations have a reputation for taking the time to build consensus before implementing corporate strategies. Historically, this approach has served them well. However, in the increasingly fast pace of the global marketplace, this is a luxury they may not be able to afford. Recent moves by Panasonic in 2012 to consolidate past acquisitions illustrate a growing trend among Japanese conglomerates to buy out minority shareholders in their majority-owned subsidiaries in order to gain full control. Minority investors may impede a firm's ability to implement its business strategy by slowing the decision-making process.

INTEGRATING BUSINESS ALLIANCES

Business alliances also must pay close attention to integration activities. Unlike M&As, alliances usually involve shared control. Successful implementation requires maintaining a good working relationship between venture partners. When this is not possible, the alliance is destined to fail. The breakdown in the working relationship is often a result of inadequate integration.[25]

Integrating Mechanisms

Robert Porter Lynch suggests six integration mechanisms to apply to business alliances: leadership, teamwork and role clarification, control by coordination, policies and values, consensus decision making, and resource commitments.

---

[24] The challenges are enormous in companies with disparate cultures. In early 2006, Jeffrey Bewkes, the president of Time Warner, stopped requiring corporate units to cooperate. It was a complete turnabout from the philosophy espoused following the firm's 2001 merger with AOL. Then, executives promised to create a well-oiled vertically integrated profit generator. Books and magazines and other forms of content would feed the television, movie, and Internet operations. The 2006 change encouraged managers to cooperate only if they could not make more money on the outside. Other media companies, such as Viacom and Liberty Media, have broken themselves up because their efforts to achieve corporate-wide synergies with disparate media businesses proved unsuccessful.

[25] Lynch (1993), pp. 189–205.

Leadership

Although the terms *leadership* and *management* are often used interchangeably, there are critical differences. A leader sets direction and makes things happen, whereas a manager follows through and ensures that things continue to happen. Leadership involves vision, drive, enthusiasm, and selling skills; management involves communication, planning, delegating, coordinating, problem-solving, making choices, and clarifying lines of responsibility. Successful alliances require the proper mix of both sets of skills. The leader must provide direction, values, and behaviors to create a culture that focuses on the alliance's strategic objectives as its top priority. Managers foster teamwork in the shared control environment of the business alliance.

Teamwork and Role Clarification

Teamwork is the underpinning that makes alliances work. Teamwork comes from trust, fairness, and discipline. Teams reach across functional lines and often consist of diverse experts or lower-level managers with critical problem-solving skills. The team provides functional managers with the broader, flexible staffing to augment their own specialized staff. Teams tend to create better coordination and communication at lower levels of the alliance as well as between partners in the venture. Because teams represent individuals with varied backgrounds and possibly conflicting agendas, they may foster rather than resolve conflict.

Coordination

In contrast to an acquisition, no one company is in charge. Alliances do not lend themselves to control through mandate; rather, in the alliance, control is best exerted through coordination. The best alliance managers are those who coordinate activities through effective communication. When problems arise, the manager's role is to manage the decision-making process, not necessarily to make the decision.

Policies and Values

Alliance employees need to understand how decisions are made, what has high priority, who will be held accountable, and how rewards will be determined. When people know where they stand and what to expect, they are better able to deal with ambiguity and uncertainty. This level of clarity can be communicated through a distinct set of policies and procedures that are well understood by joint venture or partnership employees.

Consensus Decision Making

Consensus decision making does not mean that decisions are based on unanimity; rather, decisions are based on the premise that all participants have had an opportunity to express their opinions and are willing to accept the final decision. Operating decisions must be made within a reasonable timeframe. The formal decision-making structure varies with the type of legal structure. Joint ventures often have a board of directors and a management committee that meet quarterly and monthly, respectively. Projects are normally governed by steering committees. Many alliances are started to take advantage of complementary skills or resources available from alliance participants. The alliance can achieve its strategic objective only if all parties to the alliance provide the resources they agreed to commit.

SOME THINGS TO REMEMBER

M&As that are successfully integrated often demonstrate leadership by candidly and continuously communicating a clear vision, a set of values, and clear priorities to all employees. Successful integration efforts are those that are well planned, that appoint an integration manager and a team with clearly defined lines of authority, and that make the tough decisions early in the process, be they about organizational structure, reporting relationships, spans of control, personnel selection, roles and responsibilities, or workforce reduction. The focus must be on those issues with the greatest near-term impact. Because alliances involve shared control, the integration process requires good working relationships with the other participants. Successful integration also requires leadership that is capable of defining a clear sense of direction and well-defined priorities and managers who accomplish their objectives as much by coordinating activities through effective communication as by unilateral decision making.

DISCUSSION QUESTIONS

6.1 Why is the integration phase of the acquisition process considered so important?

6.2 Why should acquired companies be integrated quickly?

6.3 Why is candid and continuous communication so important during the integration phase?

6.4 What messages might be communicated to the various audiences or stakeholders of the new company?

6.5 Cite examples of difficult decisions that should be made early in the integration process.

6.6 When Daimler Benz acquired Chrysler Corporation, it announced that it could take six to eight years to integrate fully the combined firm's global manufacturing operations and certain functions, such as purchasing. Why do you believe it might take that long?

6.7 In your judgment, are acquirers more likely to under- or overestimate anticipated cost savings? Explain your answer.

6.8 Cite examples of expenses you believe are commonly incurred in integrating target companies. Be specific.

6.9 A common justification for mergers of competitors is the potential cross-selling opportunities they would provide. Comment on the challenges that might be involved in making such a marketing strategy work.

6.10 Billed as a merger of equals, Citibank and Travelers resorted to a co-CEO arrangement when they merged. Why do you think they adopted this arrangement? What are the advantages and disadvantages of such an arrangement?

Answers to these Chapter Discussion Questions are available in the Online Instructor's Manual for instructors using this book.

CASE STUDY 6.1
Assessing Procter & Gamble's Acquisition of Gillette: What Worked and What Didn't

Key Points

- Realizing synergies depends on how quickly and seamlessly integration is implemented.
- Cost-related synergies are often more readily realized since the firms involved in the integration tend to have more direct control over cost-reduction activities.
- Realizing revenue-related synergies is more elusive due to the difficulty in assessing customer response to new brands as well as marketing and pricing strategies.

The potential seemed limitless as Procter & Gamble Company (P&G) announced that it had completed its purchase of Gillette Company (Gillette) in late 2005. P&G's chairman and CEO, A.G. Lafley, predicted that the acquisition of Gillette would add one percentage point to the firm's annual revenue growth rate and cost savings would exceed $1 billion annually, while Gillette's chairman and CEO, Jim Kilts, opined that the successful integration of the two best companies in consumer products would be studied in business schools for years to come.

Six years later, things have not turned out as expected. While cost-savings targets were achieved, operating margins faltered. Gillette's businesses, such as its pricey razors, were buffeted by the 2008–2009 recession and have been a drag on P&G's top line. Most of Gillette's top managers have left. P&G's stock price at the end of 2011 stood about 20% above its level on the acquisition announcement date, less than one-half the share price appreciation of such competitors as Unilever and Colgate-Palmolive Company during the same period.

The euphoria was palpable on January 28, 2005, when P&G enthusiastically announced that it had reached an agreement to buy Gillette in a share-for-share exchange valued at $55.6 billion. The combined firms would retain the P&G name and have annual 2005 revenue of more than $60 billion. Half of the new firm's product portfolio would consist of personal care, healthcare, and beauty products, with the remainder consisting of razors and blades and batteries.

P&G had long been viewed as a premier marketing and product innovator of products targeted largely to women. Consequently, P&G assumed that its R&D and marketing skills in developing and promoting women's personal care products could be used to enhance and promote Gillette's women's razors. In contrast, Gillette's marketing strengths centered on developing and promoting products targeted at men. Gillette was best known for its ability to sell an inexpensive product (e.g., razors) and hook customers to a lifetime of refills (e.g., razor blades). Although Gillette was the number 1 and number 2 supplier in the lucrative toothbrush and men's deodorant markets, respectively, it was less successful in improving the profitability of its Duracell battery brand. It had been beset by intense price competition from Energizer and Rayovac Corp., which generally sell for less than Duracell batteries.

Suppliers such as P&G and Gillette had been under considerable pressure from the continuing consolidation in the retail industry due to the ongoing growth of Wal-Mart and industry mergers at that time, such as Sears with Kmart. About 17% of P&G's $51 billion in 2005 revenues and 13% of Gillette's $9 billion annual revenue came from sales to Wal-Mart. The new company, P&G believed, would have more negotiating leverage with retailers for shelf space and in determining selling prices as well as with its own suppliers, such as advertisers and media companies. The broad geographic presence of P&G was expected to facilitate the marketing of such products as razors and batteries in huge developing markets, such as China and India. Cumulative cost cutting was expected to reach $16 billion, including layoffs of about 4% of the new company's workforce of 140,000. Such cost reductions were to be realized by integrating Gillette's deodorant products into P&G's structure as quickly as possible. Other Gillette product lines, such as the razor and battery businesses, were to remain intact.

P&G's corporate culture was often described as conservative, with a "promote-from-within" philosophy. P&G also had a reputation for being resistant to ideas that were not generated within the company. While Gillette's CEO was to become vice chairman of the new company, the role of other senior Gillette managers was less clear in view of the perception that P&G is laden with highly talented top management. Gillette managers were perceived as more disciplined and aggressive cost cutters than their P&G counterparts.

With this as a backdrop, what worked and what didn't? The biggest successes appear to have been the integration of the two firms' enormously complex supply chains and cost reduction; the biggest failures may be the inability to retain most senior Gillette managers and to realize revenue growth projections made at the time the deal was announced. .

Supply chains describe the activities required to get the manufactured product to the store shelf from the time the orders are placed until the firm collects payment. Together the firms had supply chains stretching across 180 countries. Merging the two supply chains was a high priority from the outset because senior management believed that it could contribute, if done properly, $1 billion in cost savings annually and an additional $750 million in annual revenue. Each firm had been analyzing the strengths and weaknesses of each other's supply chain operations for years in an attempt to benchmark industry "best practices." The monumental challenge was to determine how to handle the addition to P&G's supply chain of 100,000 Gillette customers, 50,000 stock-keeping units (SKUs), and $9 billion in revenue. The two firms also needed to develop a single order entry system for both firms' SKUs as well as an integrated distribution system to eliminate redundancies. P&G wanted to complete this process quickly and seamlessly to avoid disrupting its customers' businesses.

The integration process began with the assembly of teams of experienced senior managers from both P&G and Gillette. Reporting directly to the P&G CEO, one senior manager from each firm was appointed as co-leaders of the project. The world was divided into seven regions, and co-leaders from both firms were selected to manage the regional integration. Throughout the process, more than 1,000 full-time employees from the existing staffs of both firms worked from late 2005 to completion in late 2007.

Implementation was done in phases. Latin America was selected first because the integration challenges there were similar to those in other regions and the countries were

small. This presented a relatively low-risk learning opportunity. In just six months after receiving government approval to complete the transaction, the integration of supply chains in five countries in Latin America was completed. In 2006, P&G merged the two supply chains in North America, China, half of Western Europe, and several smaller countries in Eastern Europe. The remaining Western and Eastern European countries were converted in early 2007. Supply chain integration in Japan and the rest of Asia were completed by the end of 2007.

Creating a common information technology (IT) platform for data communication also was critical to integrating the supply chains. As part of the regional projects, Gillette's production and distribution data were transferred to P&G's SAP software system, thereby creating a single IT platform worldwide for all order shipping, billing, and distribution center operations.

While some of the activities were broad in scope, others were very narrow. The addition of 50,000 Gillette SKUs to P&G's IT system required the creation of a common, consistent, and accurate data set such that products made in the United States could be exported successfully to another country. An example of a more specific task involved changing the identification codes printed on the cartons of all Gillette products to reflect the new ownership.

Manufacturing was less of a concern, since the two firms' product lines did not overlap; however, their distribution and warehousing centers did.

As a result of the acquisition, P&G owned more than 500 distribution centers and warehouses worldwide. P&G sought to reduce that number by 50% while retaining the best in the right locations to meet local customer requirements.

While the supply chain integration appears to have reaped significant rewards, revenue growth fell short of expectations. This has been true of most of P&G's acquisitions historically. However, in time, revenue growth in line with earlier expectations may be realized. Sales of Olay and Pantene products did not take off until years after their acquisition as part of P&G's takeover of Richardson-Vicks in 1985. Pantene's revenue did not grow substantially until the early 1990s and Olay's revenues did not grow until the early 2000s.

The Gillette acquisition illustrates the difficulty in evaluating the success or failure of mergers and acquisitions for acquiring company shareholders. Assessing the true impact of the Gillette acquisition remains elusive. Though the acquisition represented a substantial expansion of P&G's product offering and geographic presence, the ability to isolate the specific impact of a single event (i.e., an acquisition) becomes clouded by the introduction of other major and often-uncontrollable events (e.g., the 2008–2009 recession) and their lingering effects. While revenue and margin improvement have been below expectations, Gillette has bolstered P&G's competitive position in the fast-growing Brazilian and Indian markets, thereby boosting the firm's longer-term growth potential, and has strengthened its operations in Europe and the United States. Thus, in this ever-changing world, it will become increasingly difficult with each passing year to identify the portion of revenue growth and margin improvement attributable to the Gillette acquisition and that due to other factors.

Discussion Questions

1. Why is it often considered critical to integrate the target business quickly? Be specific.
2. Given the complexity of these two businesses, do you believe the acquisition of Gillette by P&G made sense? Explain your answer.
3. Why did P&G rely heavily on personnel in both companies to implement postclosing integration?
4. Why do you believe P&G was unable to retain most of Gillette's top managers following the acquisition?

Answers to these questions are found in the Online Instructor's Manual for instructors using this book.

CASE STUDY 6-2
Steel Giants Mittal and Arcelor Adopt a Highly Disciplined Approach to Postclosing Integration

Key Points

- Successful integration requires clearly defined objectives, a clear implementation schedule, ongoing and candid communication, and involvement by senior management.
- Cultural integration is often an ongoing activity.

The merger of Arcelor and Mittal into ArcelorMittal in June 2006 resulted in the creation of the world's largest steel company.[26] With 2007 revenues of $105 billion and its steel production accounting for about 10% of global output, the behemoth has 320,000 employees in 60 countries, and it is a global leader in all its target markets. Arcelor was a product of three European steel companies (Arbed, Aceralia, and Usinor). Similarly, Mittal resulted from a series of international acquisitions. The two firms' downstream (raw material) and upstream (distribution) operations proved to be highly complementary, with Mittal owning much of its iron ore and coal reserves and Arcelor having extensive distribution and service center operations. Like most mergers, ArcelorMittal faced the challenge of integrating management teams; sales, marketing, and product functions; production facilities; and purchasing operations. Unlike many mergers involving direct competitors, a relatively small portion of cost savings would come from eliminating duplicate functions and operations.

ArcelorMittal's top management set three driving objectives before undertaking the postmerger integration effort: achieve rapid integration, manage daily operations effectively, and accelerate revenue and profit growth. The third objective was viewed as the primary motivation for the merger. The goal was to combine what were viewed as entities having highly complementary assets and skills. This goal was quite different from the way Mittal had grown historically, which was a result of acquisitions of turnaround targets focused on cost and productivity improvements.

The formal phase of the integration effort was to be completed in six months. It was crucial to agree on the role of the management integration team (MIT); the key aspects of the integration process, such as how decisions would be made; and the roles and responsibilities of team members. Activities were undertaken in parallel rather than sequentially. Teams consisted of employees from the two firms. People leading task forces came from the business units.

[26] This case relies on information provided in an interview with Jerome Ganboulan (formerly of Arcelor) and William A. Scotting (formerly of Mittal), the two executives charged with directing the postmerger integration effort and is adapted from De Mdedt and Van Hoey (2008).

The teams were then asked to propose a draft organization to the MIT, including the profiles of the people who were to become senior managers. Once the senior managers were selected, they were to build their own teams to identify the synergies and create action plans for realizing thoes synergies. Teams were formed before the organization was announced, and implementation of certain actions began before detailed plans had been developed fully. Progress to plan was monitored on a weekly basis, enabling the MIT to identify obstacles facing the 25 decentralized task forces and, when necessary, resolve issues.

Considerable effort was spent on getting line managers involved in the planning process and selling the merger to their respective operating teams. Initial communication efforts included the launch of a top-management "road show." The new company also established a website and introduced Web TV. Senior executives reported two- to three-minute interviews on various topics, giving everyone with access to a personal computer the ability to watch the interviews onscreen.

Owing to the employee duress resulting from the merger, uncertainty was high, as employees with both firms wondered how the merger would affect them. To address employee concerns, managers were given a well-structured message about the significance of the merger and the direction of the new company. Furthermore, the new brand, ArcelorMittal, was launched in a meeting attended by 500 of the firm's top managers during the spring of 2007.

External communication was conducted in several ways. Immediately following the closing, senior managers traveled to all the major cities and sites of operations, talking to local management and employees in these sites. Typically, media interviews were also conducted around these visits, providing an opportunity to convey the ArcelorMittal message to the communities through the press. In March 2007, the new firm held a media day in Brussels. Journalists were invited to go to the different businesses and review the progress themselves.

Within the first three months following the closing, customers were informed about the advantages of the merger for them, such as enhanced R&D capabilities and wider global coverage. The sales forces of the two organizations were charged with the task of creating a single "face" to the market.

ArcelorMittal's management viewed the merger as an opportunity to conduct interviews and surveys with employees to gain an understanding of their views about the two companies. Employees were asked about the combined firm's strengths and weaknesses and how the new firm should present itself to its various stakeholder groups. This process resulted in a complete rebranding of the combined firms.

ArcelorMittal management set a target for annual cost savings of $1.6 billion, based on experience with earlier acquisitions. The role of the task forces was first to validate this number from the bottom up and then to tell the MIT how the synergies would be achieved. As the merger progressed, it was necessary to get the business units to assume ownership of the process to formulate the initiatives, timetables, and key performance indicators that could be used to track performance against objectives. In some cases, the synergy potential was larger than anticipated while smaller in other situations. The expectation was that the synergy could be realized by mid-2009. The integration objectives were included in the 2007 annual budget plan. As of the end of 2008, the combined firms had realized their goal of annualized cost savings of $1.6 billion, six months earlier than expected.

The integration was deemed complete when the new organization, the brand, the "one face to the customer" requirement, and the synergies were finalized. This occurred within eight months of the closing. However, integration would continue for some time to achieve cultural integration. Cultural differences within the two firms are significant. In effect, neither company was homogeneous from a cultural perspective. ArcelorMittal management viewed this diversity as an advantage in that it provided an opportunity to learn new ideas.

Discussion Questions

1. Why is it important to establish both top-down estimates of synergy (i.e., provided by top management) and bottom-up estimates of synergy (provided by operating units)?
2. How did ArcelorMittal attempt to bridge cultural differences during the integration?
3. Why are communication plans so important? What methods did ArcelorMittal employ to achieve these objectives? Be specific.
4. Comment on ArcelorMittal management's belief that the cultural diversity within the combined firms was an advantage. Be specific.
5. The formal phase of the postmerger integration period was to be completed within six months. Why do you believe that ArcelorMittal's management was eager to integrate the two businesses rapidly? Be specific. What integration activities were to extend beyond the proposed six-month integration period?

Solutions to these questions are found in the Online Instructor's Manual for instructors using this book.

MERGERS AND ACQUISITIONS VALUATION AND MODELING

"Your valuation figures were way off, and it's time to take the fall."

Source: Courtesy of CartoonResource.com BMA124-TS.

Part III covers alternative valuation methods and basic financial modeling techniques as well as how such models may be applied in the merger and acquisition process. The applicability of each valuation methodology varies by situation, with each subject to significant limitations. A valuation approach reflecting a variety of the alternative methodologies is likely to provide a more accurate estimate of firm value than any single approach.

Chapter 7 provides a primer on how to construct valuation cash flows, the discount rates necessary to convert projected cash flows to a present value, and commonly used discounted cash flow (DCF) methods. (How to employ DCF valuation in highly leveraged, distressed, and cross-border transactions is discussed later in Chapters 14, 17, and 18, respectively.) Alternatives to DCF techniques are discussed in Chapter 8, including relative valuation, asset-oriented, and replacement-cost methods. Implicit in the DCF approach to valuation is that management has no flexibility once an investment decision has been made. In practice, management may decide to accelerate, delay, or abandon investments as new information becomes available. The significance of this decision-making flexibility may be reflected in the value of the target firm by adjusting discounted cash flows for the value of so-called *real options*.

Chapter 9 discusses how to build financial models in the context of mergers and acquisitions. Such models are very helpful in answering questions pertaining to valuation, financing, and deal structuring. (Deal-structuring considerations are discussed in detail in Chapters 11 and 12.) Moreover, such models are powerful tools during M&A negotiations, allowing the participants to evaluate rapidly the attractiveness of alternative proposals. Finally, Chapter 10 addresses the unique challenges of valuing privately held firms and how to adjust purchase prices for liquidity and minority discounts as well as for the value of control. This chapter is particularly relevant, since the vast majority of firms involved in mergers and acquisitions are privately held.

Mergers and Acquisitions Cash Flow Valuation Basics

The greater danger for most of us is not that our aim is too high and we might miss it, but that it is too low and we reach it.—Michelangelo

INSIDE M&A: VALUATION METHODOLOGIES AND FAIRNESS OPINION LETTERS

KEY POINTS

- Parties to transactions often employ investment bankers to provide opinions about whether a proposed purchase price is "fair" to their shareholders.
- Alternative valuation methods often result in very different estimates of value, reflecting different assumptions about risk and the amount and timing of future cash flows.

In July 2011, investment bank Goldman Sachs was hired by Immucor Inc., a manufacturer of blood-testing products, to certify that the $27 price per common share offered by well-known buyout firm TPG was fair. These "fairness opinions" represent third-party assertions about the suitability of proposed deals. Goldman assessed Immuncor's fair value by applying discounted cash flow (DCF) analysis to the firm's projected after-tax cash flows between 2012 and 2015 and by comparing it to "similar" publicly traded firms and to recent comparable deals. The analysis involved judgments about differences in financial and operating characteristics affecting the trading values of the firms to which Immucor was compared.

A typical fairness opinion letter provides a range of "fair" prices, with the presumption that the actual deal price should fall within that range. These valuation estimates were presented to Immuncor's board of directors with the usual caveats, that is, the estimates of fair value should reflect an amalgam of the methods used. Goldman also noted that in performing its analyses, it considered industry performance, business conditions, and other matters, many of which are beyond the control of Immucor and that the estimates of fair value are not necessarily indicative of actual values or actual future results.

CHAPTER OVERVIEW

Chapter 7 provides an overview of the basics of valuing mergers and acquisitions using discounted cash flow methods; additional methods are discussed in Chapter 8. A review of this chapter is available in the file folder entitled "Student Study Guide" in the companion website to this book (*http://booksite.elsevier. com/9780123854872*). This site also contains a discussion of how to project cash flows, in a document entitled "Primer on Cash Flow Forecasting."

ESTIMATING REQUIRED FINANCIAL RETURNS

Investors require a minimum rate of return that must be at least equal to what the investor can receive on alternative investments exhibiting a comparable level of perceived risk.

Cost of Equity and the Capital Asset Pricing Model

The cost of equity (k_e) is the rate of return required to induce investors to purchase a firm's equity. It is a return to shareholders after corporate taxes have been paid but before personal taxes. It may be estimated using the capital asset pricing model (CAPM), which measures the relationship between expected risk and return. Presuming investors require higher rates of return for accepting higher levels of risk, the CAPM states that the expected return on an asset is equal to a risk-free rate of return plus a risk premium.

A *risk-free rate of return* is one for which the expected return is certain. That is, it must be free of default risk,[1] and there must be no uncertainty about the reinvestment rate (i.e., the rate of return that can be earned at the end of the investor's holding period). Other types of risk remain, including the potential loss of principal if the security is sold before its maturity date (*market risk*) and

---

[1] *Default risk* refers to the degree of certainty that an investor will receive the nominal value of his investment plus accumulated interest according to the terms of their agreement with the borrower. That is, if $10,000 is invested at some rate of interest for ten years, the investor will receive $10,000 at the end of ten years plus interest paid annually.

the loss of purchasing power due to inflation (*inflation risk*). Despite widespread agreement on the use of U.S. Treasury securities as assets that are free of default risk, analysts differ over whether a short- or long-term Treasury rate should be applied. Which rate should be used depends on how long the investor intends to hold the investment. The investor who anticipates holding an investment for five or ten years should use either a five- or ten-year Treasury bond rate.[2] In this book, a ten-year Treasury bond rate is used to represent the risk-free rate, since it would be most appropriate for a strategic or long-term acquirer.

Estimating Market Risk Premiums

The *market risk*, or *equity premium*, is the additional return in excess of the risk-free rate that investors require to purchase a firm's equity. While the risk premium should therefore be forward looking, obtaining precise estimates of future market returns is exceedingly difficult. Analysts often look to historical data, despite results that vary based on the time periods selected and whether returns are calculated as arithmetic or geometric averages. CAPM relates the cost of equity (k_e) to the risk-free rate of return and market risk premium as follows:

$$\text{CAPM: } k_e = R_f + \beta(R_m - R_f) \tag{7.1}$$

where

R_f = risk-free rate of return
β = beta (See the section of this chapter entitled "Analyzing Risk.")[3]
R_m = expected rate of return on equities
$R_m - R_f$ = 5.5% (i.e., the difference between the return on a diversified portfolio of stocks and the risk-free rate.)[4]

Despite its intuitive appeal, studies show that actual returns on risky assets frequently differ significantly from those returns predicted by CAPM.[5] Since the CAPM measures a stock's risk relative to the overall market and ignores returns

---

[2] A three-month Treasury bill rate is not free of risk for a five- or ten-year period, since interest and principal received at maturity must be reinvested at three-month intervals, resulting in considerable reinvestment risk.

[3] Statistically, a beta measures the variation of an individual stock's return with the overall market as a percent of the variation of the overall market (i.e., the covariance of a stock's return to a broadly defined market index/variance of the broadly defined index).

[4] Fernandez et al. (2012) found the median and average equity risk premium for about four-fifths of the 82 countries surveyed fell within a range of 5.0% to 7.0%. In the United States, the survey documented a median and average equity risk premium used of 5.4% and 5.5%, respectively.

[5] Fama and French (2004, 2006) and Subramanyam (2010); CAPM's reliability is particularly questionable since 2008 due to the suppression of government bond rates (often used as a measure of risk-free rates) due to aggressive purchases of such securities by central banks.

TABLE 7.1   Size Premium Estimates

Market Value ($000,000)	Percentage Points Added to CAPM Estimate	Book Value ($000,000)	Percentage Points Added to CAPM Estimate
>21,589	0	>11,465	0
7150–21,589	1.3	4184–11,465	1.0
2933–7150	2.4	1157–4184	2.1
1556–2933	3.3	923–1157	3.0
687–1556	4.4	382–923	3.7
111–687	5.2	60–382	4.4
<111	7.2	<60	5.6

Source: Size premium estimates were calculated by collapsing the 25 groupings of firms by size in a study conducted by Duff & Phelps LLC into seven categories. Duff & Phelps examined the relationship between firm size and financial returns between 1963 and 2008 and found that small firms displayed a higher premium whether size is measured by market value, book value, or some other performance measure (e.g., operating profit, number of employees). The Duff & Phelps findings were listed in Pratt and Grabowski (2010).

on assets other than stocks, some analysts use *multifactor models*.[6] Studies show that, of those variables improving the CAPM's accuracy, firm size tends to be the most important.[7] The size premium serves as a proxy for factors such as smaller firms being subject to higher default risk and generally being less liquid than large-capitalization firms. Table 7.1 provides estimates of the adjustment to the cost of equity to correct for firm size based on actual data since 1963.[8]

Equation (7.1) can be rewritten to reflect an adjustment for firm size as follows:

$$\text{CAPM: } k_e = R_f + \beta(R_m - R_f) + \text{FSP} \tag{7.2}$$

where FSP = firm size premium.

Assume that a firm has a market value of less than $111 million and a β of 1.75. Also assume that the risk-free rates of return and equity premium are 5% and 5.5%, respectively. The firm's cost of equity using the CAPM method adjusted for firm size can be estimated as follows:

$$k_e = 0.05 + 1.75\,(0.055) + 0.072\ (\text{see Table 7.1}) = 0.218 \times 100 = 21.8\%$$

[6]Such models adjust the CAPM by adding other risk factors that determine asset returns, such as firm size, bond default premiums, the bond term structure, and inflation.

[7]Shapovalova and Alexander (2011)

[8]The magnitude of the size premium should be adjusted to reflect such factors as a comparison of the firm's key financial ratios (e.g., liquidity and leverage) with comparable firms and after interviewing management.

TABLE 7.2   Weighted Average Yield to Maturity of Microsoft's Long-Term Debt

Coupon Rate (%)	Maturity	Book Value (face value in $ millions)	Percentage of Total Debt	Price (% of Par)	Yield to Maturity (%)
0.88	9/27/2013	1250	0.25	99.44	1.09
2.95	6/1/2014	2000	0.40	104.27	1.63
4.20	6/1/2019	1000	0.20	105.00	3.50
5.20	6/1/2039	750	0.15	100.92	5.14
		5000	1.00		2.40

Pretax Cost of Debt

Interest is the cost of borrowing each additional dollar of debt and is tax deductible by the firm; in bankruptcy, bondholders are paid before shareholders as the firm's assets are liquidated. *Default risk*, the likelihood the firm will fail to repay interest and principal on a timely basis, can be measured by the firm's credit rating.[9] Interest paid by the firm on its current debt can be used as an estimate of the current cost of debt if nothing has changed since the firm last borrowed.

When conditions have changed, the analyst must estimate the cost of debt reflecting current market interest rates and default risk. To do so, analysts use the yield to maturity (YTM)[10] of the company's long-term, option-free bonds. This requires knowing the price of the security and its coupon value and face value.[11] In general, the cost of debt is estimated by calculating the YTM on each of the firm's outstanding bond issues. We then compute a weighted average YTM, with the estimated YTM for each issue weighted by its percentage of total debt outstanding. In Table 7.2, Microsoft's weighted average YTM on the bulk of its long-term debt on January 24, 2011, was 2.4%. The source for the YTM

---

[9]Default rates vary from an average of 0.52% for AAA-rated firms over a 15-year period to 54.38% for those rated CCC by Standard & Poor's Corporation. See Burrus and McNamee, 2002.

[10]Yield to maturity is the internal rate of return on a bond held to maturity, assuming scheduled payment of principal and interest, that takes into account the capital gain on a discount bond or capital loss on a premium bond.

[11]YTM is not appropriate for valuing short-term bonds, since their term to maturity is often much less than the duration of the company's cash flows. YTM is affected by the bond's cash flows and not those of the firm's; therefore, it is distorted by corporate bonds, which also have conversion or callable features, since their value will affect the bond's value but not the value of the firm's cash flows.

for each debt issue was found in the Financial Industry Regulatory Authority's (FINRA) Trace database: www.finra.org/marketdata.[12]

YTM represents the most reliable estimate of a firm's cost of debt as long as the firm's debt is investment grade,[13] since the difference between the expected rate of return and the promised rate of return is small. The promised rate of return assumes that the interest and principal are paid on time. The yield to maturity is affected by the cost of debt, the probability of default, and the expected recovery rate on the debt if the firm defaults and is a good proxy for actual future returns on investment-grade debt, since the potential for default is low.

Non-investment-grade debt, rated less than BBB by Standard & Poor's and Baa by Moody's, represents debt whose default risk is significant due to the firm's leverage, deteriorating cash flows, or both. Ideally, the expected yield to maturity would be calculated based on the current market price of the non-investment-grade bond, the probability of default, and the potential recovery rate following default.[14] Since such data are frequently unavailable, an alternative is to use the YTM for a number of similarly rated bonds of other firms. Such bonds include a so-called *default premium,* which reflects the compensation that lenders require over the risk-free rate to buy non-investment-grade debt.

To illustrate, on January 24, 2011, HCA Healthcare Inc.'s 9% fixed rate non-callable bond that would reach maturity on December 15, 2015 (rated CCC by Standard & Poor's and Caa1 by Moody's), had a YTM of 7.41%, according to FINRA's TRACE database. With five-year U.S. Treasury bonds offering a yield to maturity of 1.94%, the implied default risk premium was 5.47% (i.e., 7.41 minus 1.94). This same process could then be repeated for a number of similarly rated bonds in order to calculate an average YTM. For nonrated firms, the analyst may estimate the current pretax cost of debt for a specific firm by comparing debt-to-equity ratios, interest coverage ratios, and operating margins with those of similar rated firms. The analyst would then use the interest rates paid by these comparably rated firms as the pretax cost of debt for the firm being analyzed.[15]

---

[12] FINRA is the largest independent regulator for all securities firms in the Unites States. See http://cxa.marketwatch.com/finra/MarketData/CompanyInfo/default.aspx.

[13] Investment-grade bonds are those whose credit quality is considered to be among the most secure by independent bond-rating agencies: BBB or higher by Standard & Poor's and Baa or higher by Moody's Investors Service.

[14] Titman and Martin (2011), pp. 144–147.

[15] Much of this information can be found in local libraries in such publications as Moody's Company Data; Standard & Poor's Descriptions, the Outlook, and Bond Guide; and Value Line's Investment Survey. In the United States, the FINRA TRACE database also is an excellent source of interest rate information.

Cost of Preferred Stock

Preferred stock is similar to long-term debt, in that its dividend is generally constant and preferred stockholders are paid after debt holders but before common shareholders if the firm is liquidated. Because preferred stock is riskier than debt but less risky than common stock in bankruptcy, the cost to the company to issue preferred stock should be less than the cost of equity but greater than the cost of debt. Viewing preferred dividends as paid in perpetuity, the cost of preferred stock (k_{pr}) can be calculated as dividends per share of preferred stock (d_{pr}) divided by the market value of the preferred stock (PR) (see the section of this chapter entitled "Zero-Growth Valuation Model"). Consequently, if a firm pays a $2 dividend on its preferred stock, whose current market value is $50, the firm's cost of preferred stock is 4% (i.e., $2 ÷ $50). The cost of preferred stock can be generalized as follows:

$$k_{pr} = \frac{d_{pr}}{PR} \tag{7.3}$$

Cost of Capital

The weighted average cost of capital (WACC) is the broadest measure of the firm's cost of funds and represents the return that a firm must earn to induce investors to buy its common stock, preferred stock, and bonds. The WACC[16] is calculated using a weighted average of the firm's cost of equity (k_e), cost of preferred stock (k_{pr}), and pretax cost of debt (i):

$$\text{WACC} = k_e \frac{E}{D + E + PR} + i(1 - t)\frac{D}{D + E + PR} + k_{pr}\frac{PR}{D + E + PR} \tag{7.4}$$

where

E = the market value of common equity
D = the market value of debt
PR = the market value of preferred stock
t = the firm's marginal tax rate

A portion of interest paid on borrowed funds is recoverable by the firm because of the tax deductibility of interest. For every dollar of taxable income, the tax owed is equal to $1 multiplied by t. Since each dollar of interest expense reduces taxable income by an equivalent amount, the actual cost of borrowing is reduced by $(1 - t)$. Therefore, the after-tax cost of borrowed funds to the firm is estimated by multiplying the pretax interest rate, i, by $(1 - t)$.

---

[16]Note that Eq. (7.4) calculates WACC assuming the firm has one type of common equity, long-term debt, and preferred stock. This is for illustrative purposes only, for a firm may not have any preferred stock and may have many different types of common stock and debt of various maturities.

Note that the weights $[E/(D + E + PR)]$, $[D/(D + E + PR)]$, and $[PR/(D + E + PR)]$ associated with the cost of equity, preferred stock, and debt, respectively, reflect the firm's target capital structure or capitalization. These are targets in that they represent the capital structure the firm hopes to achieve and sustain in the future. The actual market value of equity, preferred stock, and debt as a percentage of total capital (i.e., $D + E + PR$) may differ from the target. Market values rather than book values are used because the WACC measures the cost of issuing debt, preferred stock, and equity securities, which are issued at market and not book value. The use of the target capital structure avoids the circular reasoning associated with using the current market value of equity to construct the weighted average cost of capital, which is subsequently used to estimate the firm's current market value. Non-interest-bearing liabilities, such as accounts payable, often are excluded from the estimation of the cost of capital for the firm to simplify the calculation of WACC.[17] Estimates of industry betas, cost of equity, and WACC are provided by firms such as Ibbotson Associates, Value Line, Standard & Poor's, and Bloomberg.

RISK ASSESSMENT

Risk is the degree of uncertainty associated with the outcome of an investment. It consists of two components: *diversifiable,* or *nonsystematic, risk,* such as strikes and lawsuits that are specific to a firm, and a *nondiversifiable,* or *systematic, risk,* such as inflation and war, that affects all firms. *Beta* (β) is a measure of non-diversifiable risk, or the extent to which a firm's financial return changes because of a change in the general stock market's return.

Betas are commonly estimated by regressing the percent change in the total return on a specific stock with that of a broadly defined stock market index. The resulting beta estimated in this manner for an individual security incorporates both the security's volatility and its correlation with the overall stock market.

---

[17] The cost of capital associated with such liabilities (k_{CL}) is included in the price paid to vendors for purchased products and services and affects cash flow through its inclusion in operating expenses (e.g., the price paid for raw materials). However, if a firm uses substantial amounts of current liabilities (CL) such as short-term debt, Eq. (7.4) should be modified as follows:

$$WACC = k_e \frac{E}{D + E + PR + CL} + i(i - t)\frac{D}{D + E + PR + CL}$$
$$+ k_{pr} \frac{PR}{D + E + PR + CL} + k_{CL}(1 - t)\frac{CL}{D + E + PR + CL}$$

Some current liabilities, such as accruals, are interest free, and accounts and notes payable have an associated capital cost approximated by the firm's short-term cost of funds. Since the market and book value of current liabilities are usually similar, book values can be used in calculating capital cost of current liabilities.

Volatility measures the magnitude of a security's fluctuations relative to the over-all stock market, and *correlation* measures the direction. Consequently, when $\beta = 1$, the stock is as risky as the general market. When $\beta < 1$, the stock is less risky; when $\beta > 1$, the stock is riskier than the overall stock market.

The CAPM states that all risk is measured from the perspective of a marginal or incremental investor, who is well diversified. Investors are compensated only for risk that cannot be eliminated through diversification (i.e., nondiversifiable, or systematic, risk).[18] Estimates of public company betas may be obtained by going to finance.yahoo.com, finance.google.com, and reuters.com. Alternatively, a firm's beta may be calculated based on the betas of a sample of similar firms at a moment in time. This process is described in the next section.

Effects of Financial and Operating Leverage on Beta

In the absence of debt, the β is called an *unlevered* β, denoted β_u. β_u is deter-mined by the type of industry in which the firm operates (e.g., cyclical or non-cyclical) and its operating leverage. *Operating leverage*, often measured by the firm's ratio of fixed expenses to total cost of sales, refers to the lift to profitability and financial returns once a firm's revenue exceeds its fixed costs; that is, most of the incremental revenue will contribute to pretax-income growth.[19] If a firm borrows, the unlevered beta must be adjusted to reflect the additional risk asso-ciated with financial leverage, commonly measured by the firm's ratio of debt to equity. By borrowing, the firm is able to invest more in its operation with-out increasing equity, resulting in a proportionately larger (or smaller) return to equity holders. The resulting beta is called a *leveraged* or *levered* β, denoted β_l. Both operating and financial leverage increase the volatility of a firm's financial returns substantially.

Table 7.3 illustrates the effects of operating leverage on financial returns. The three cases reflect the same level of fixed expenses but varying levels of revenue and the resulting impact on financial returns. The illustration assumes in Case 1 that the firm's total cost of sales is 80% of revenue and that fixed expenses com-prise 60% of the total cost of sales. Note the volatility of the firm's return on equity resulting from fluctuations of 25% in the firm's revenue in Cases 2 and 3.

Table 7.4 shows how financial leverage increases the volatility of a firm's financial returns substantially. This is because equity's share of total capi-tal declines faster than the decline in net income as debt's share of total capital

---

[18] Beta in this context applies to the application of CAPM to public firms, where the marginal investor is assumed to be fully diversified. For private firms in which the owner's net worth is disproportionately tied up in the firm, analysts sometimes calculate a total beta, which reflects both systematic and nonsystematic risk. See Chapter 10.

[19] Recall that operating profits equals total revenue less fixed and variable costs. If revenue and fixed and variable costs are $100, $50, and $25 million (variable costs are 25% of revenue), respectively, the firm's operating profits are $25 million. If revenue doubles to $200 million, the firm's profit increases to $100 million (i.e., $200 − $50 − $50).

TABLE 7.3   How Operating Leverage Affects Financial Returns[a]

	Case 1	Case 2: Revenue Increases by 25%	Case 3: Revenue Decreases by 25%
Revenue	100	125	75
Fixed	48	48	48
Variable[b]	32	40	24
Total Cost of Sales	**80**	**88**	**72**
Earnings Before Taxes	20	37	3
Tax Liability @ 40%	8	14.8	1.2
After-Tax Earnings	12	22.2	1.8
Firm Equity	100	100	100
Return on Equity (%)	12	22.2	1.8

[a]All figures are in millions of dollars unless otherwise noted.
[b]In Case 1, variable costs represent 32% of revenue. Assuming this ratio is maintained, variable costs in Cases 2 and 3 are estimated by multiplying total revenue by 0.32.

TABLE 7.4   How Financial Leverage Affects Financial Returns[a]

	Case 1: No Debt	Case 2: 25% Debt to Total Capital	Case 3: 50% Debt to Total Capital
Equity	100	75	50
Debt	0	25	50
Total Capital	100	100	100
Earnings before Interest and Taxes	20	20	20
Interest @ 10%	0	2.5	5
Income before Taxes	20	17.5	15
Less Income Taxes @ 40%	8	7.0	6
After-Tax Earnings	12	10.5	9
After-Tax Returns on Equity (%)	12	14	18

[a]All figures are in millions of dollars unless otherwise noted.

increases. The three cases in the table reflect varying levels of debt but the same earnings before interest and taxes. Between Case 1 and Case 3, net income declines by one-fourth and equity declines by one-half, magnifying the impact on returns.

If a firm's stockholders bear all the risk from operating and financial leverage and interest paid on debt is tax deductible, then leveraged and unleveraged betas can be calculated as follows for a firm whose debt-to-equity ratio is denoted by D/E:

$$\beta_1 = \beta_u[1 + (1 - t)(D/E)] \tag{7.5}$$

and

$$\beta_u = \beta_1/[1 + (1 - t)(D/E)] \tag{7.6}$$

Shareholders view risk as the potential for a firm not to earn sufficient future cash flow to satisfy their minimum required returns. Equation (7.5) implies that increases in a firm's leverage, denoted by D/E, will increase risk, as measured by the firm's levered beta because the firm's interest payments represent fixed expenses that must be paid before payments can be made to shareholders. This increased risk is offset somewhat by the tax deductibility of interest, which increases after-tax cash flow available for shareholders. Thus, the levered beta will, unless offset by other factors, increase with an increase in leverage and decrease with an increase in tax rates.

In summary, β_u is determined by the characteristics of the industry in which the firm competes and the firm's degree of operating leverage. The value of β_l is determined by the same factors and the degree of the firm's financial leverage. Our objective is to estimate a beta that reflects the relationship between risk and return in the future. Estimating beta using historical data assumes the historical relationship will hold in the future, which often is not the case.

An alternative to using historical data is to estimate beta using a sample of similar firms and applying Eqs. (7.5) and (7.6). Referred to as the "bottoms-up" approach (Table 7.5), this three-step process suggests that the target firm's beta reflects the business risk (cyclicality and operating leverage only) of the average firm in the industry better than its own historical risk/return relationship. Step 1 requires selecting firms with similar cyclicality and operating leverage (i.e., firms usually in the same industry). Step 2 involves calculating the average unlevered beta for firms in the sample to eliminate the effects of their current financial leverage on their betas. Finally, in step 3, we relever the average unlevered beta using the debt-to-equity ratio and the marginal tax rate of the target firm to reflect its capital structure and tax rate.

Using Eqs. (7.5) and (7.6), the effects of different amounts of leverage on the cost of equity also can be estimated.[20] The process is as follows:

1. Determine a firm's current equity β^* and $(D/E)^*$;
2. Estimate the unlevered beta to eliminate the effects of the firm's current capital structure:

$$\beta_u = \beta^*/[1 + (1 - t)(D/E)^*]$$

3. Estimate the firm's levered beta: $\beta_1 = \beta_u [1 + (1 - t)(D/E)^{**}]$;
4. Estimate the firm's cost of equity for the new levered beta,

where β^* and $(D/E)^*$ represent the firm's current beta and the market value of the firm's debt-to-equity ratio before additional borrowing takes place. $(D/E)^{**}$

TABLE 7.5　Estimating Abbot Labs' Beta Using the "Bottoms-Up" Approach

Step 1: Select a sample of firms having similar cyclicality and operating leverage			Step 2: Compute the average of the firms' unlevered betas	Step 3: Relever average unlevered beta using the target's debt/equity ratio
Firm	Levered Beta[a]	Debt/Equity[a]	Unlevered Beta[b]	Abbot Labs' Relevered Beta[c]
Abbot Labs	0.2900	0.2662	0.2501	NA
Johnson & Johnson	0.6000	0.0762	0.5738	NA
Merck	0.6600	0.3204	0.5536	NA
Pfizer	0.6800	0.3044	0.5750	NA
			Average = 0.4881	0.4209

[a]Yahoo! Finance (1/29/2011). Beta estimates are based on the historical relationship between the firm's share price and a broadly defined stock index. Abbot Labs is included in the sample because we are comparing direct competitors that are comparable in size whose business risk (operating leverage and cyclicality) is likely to be substantially similar.
[b]$\beta_u = \beta_l / [1 + (1 - t)(D/E)]$, where β_u and β_l are unlevered and levered betas, respectively; the marginal tax rate is 0.4. Abbot Labs (β_u) = 0.2900/[1 + (1 − 0.4)0.2662)] = 0.2501 Johnson & Johnson (β_u) = 0.6000/[1 + (1−0.4)0.0762)] = 0.5738 Merck (β_u) = 0.6600/[1 + (1−0.4)0.3204)] = 0.5536 Pfizer (β_u) = 0.6800/[1 + (1 − 0.4)0.3044)] = 0.5750
[c]$\beta_l = \beta_u [1 + (1 − t)(D/E)]$ using the target firm's (Abbot Labs) debt/equity ratio and marginal tax rate. Abbot Labs' relevered beta = 0.4881[1 + (1 − 0.4)0.2662)] = 0.4209.

is the firm's debt-to-equity ratio after additional borrowing occurs, and t is the firm's marginal tax rate.

In an acquisition, an acquirer may anticipate increasing the target firm's debt level after the closing. To determine the impact on the target's beta of the increased leverage, the target's levered beta, which reflects its preacquisition leverage, must be converted to an unlevered beta, reflecting the target firm's operating leverage and the cyclicality of the industry in which the firm competes. To measure the increasing risk associated with new borrowing, the resulting unlevered beta is then used to estimate the levered beta for the target firm (see Exhibit 7.1).

CALCULATING FREE CASH FLOWS

Common definitions of cash flow used for valuation are cash flow to the firm (FCFF), or enterprise cash flow, and cash flow to equity investors (FCFE), or equity cash flow. Referred to as *valuation cash flows*, they are constructed by adjusting GAAP cash flows for noncash factors.

---

[20]The reestimation of a firm's beta to reflect a change in leverage requires that we first deleverage the firm to remove the effects of the firm's current level of debt on its beta and then releverage the firm using its new level of debt to estimate the new levered beta.

EXHIBIT 7.1 ESTIMATING THE IMPACT OF CHANGING DEBT LEVELS ON THE COST OF EQUITY

Assume that a target's current or preacquisition debt-to-equity ratio is 25%, the current levered beta is 1.05, and the marginal tax rate is 0.4. After the acquisition, the debt-to-equity ratio is expected to rise to 75%. What is the target's postacquisition levered beta?

Answer: Using Eqs. (7.5) and (7.6):

$$\beta_u = \beta_l^*/[1 + (1 - t)(D/E)^*] = 1.05/[1 + (1 - 0.4)(0.25)] = 0.91$$
$$\beta_l = \beta_u[1 + (1 - t)(D/E)^{**}] = 0.91[1 + (1 - 0.4)(0.75)] = 1.32$$

where $(D/E)^*$ and $(D/E)^{**}$ are, respectively, the target's pre- and postacquisition debt-to-equity ratios and β_l^* is the target's preacquisition beta.

Free Cash Flow to the Firm (Enterprise Cash Flow)

Free cash flow to the firm represents cash available to satisfy all investors holding claims against the firm's resources. Claims holders include common stockholders, lenders, and preferred stockholders. Consequently, enterprise cash flow is calculated before the sources of financing are determined and, as such, is not affected by the firm's financial structure.[21]

FCFF can be calculated by adjusting operating earnings before interest and taxes (EBIT) as follows:

$$FCFF = EBIT(1 - \text{Tax Rate}) + \text{Depreciation and Amortization} \qquad (7.7)$$
$$- \text{Gross Capital Expenditures} - \Delta \text{Net Working Capital}$$

Only cash flow from operating and investment activities, but not from financing activities, is included. The tax rate refers to the firm's marginal tax rate. Net working capital is defined as current operating assets (excluding cash balances in excess of the amount required to meet normal operating requirements) less current operating liabilities.[22] Depreciation and amortization expenses are not actual cash outlays and are added to operating income in calculating cash flow.

Selecting the Right Tax Rate

The appropriate tax rate is either the firm's marginal rate (i.e., the rate paid on each additional dollar of earnings) or its effective tax rate (i.e., taxes due divided by taxable income). The marginal tax rate in the United States at this time is usually 40–35% for federal taxes for firms earning more than $10 million and 5% for most state and local taxes. The effective rate is usually less than the marginal rate

---

[21] In practice, the financial structure may affect the firm's cost of capital and, therefore, its value due to the potential for bankruptcy (see Chapter 17).

[22] In some instances, firms may have negative working capital. Since this is unlikely to be sustainable, it is preferable to set net working capital to zero.

due to the use of tax credits to reduce actual taxes paid or accelerated depreciation to defer tax payments. Once tax credits have been used and the ability to further defer taxes has been exhausted, the effective rate can exceed the marginal rate in the future. Effective rates lower than the marginal rate may be used in the early years of cash flow projections, if the current favorable tax treatment is likely to continue into the foreseeable future, and eventually the effective rates may be increased to the firm's marginal tax rate. It is critical to use the marginal rate in calculating after-tax operating income in perpetuity. Otherwise, the implicit assumption is that taxes can be deferred indefinitely.

Dealing with Operating Leases

Operating leases do not require a firm to record an asset or a liability on the balance sheet; instead, the lease charge is recorded as an expense on the income statement, and future lease commitments are recorded in footnotes to the firm's financial statements. Future lease payments should be discounted to the present at the firm's pretax cost of debt (i), since leasing equipment represents an alternative to borrowing, and the present value of the operating lease (PV_{OL}) should be included in the firm's total debt outstanding.[23] Once operating leases are converted to debt, operating lease expense (OLE_{EXP}) must be added to EBIT because it is a financial expense and EBIT represents operating income before such expenses. Lease payments include both an interest expense component (to reflect the cost of borrowing) and a depreciation component (to reflect the anticipated decline in the value of the leased asset).

An estimate of depreciation expense associated with the leased asset (DEP_{OL}) must then be deducted from EBIT, as is depreciation expense associated with other fixed assets owned by the firm, to calculate an "adjusted" EBIT ($EBIT_{ADJ}$). DEP_{OL} may be estimated by dividing the firm's gross plant and equipment by its annual depreciation expense. Studies show that the median asset life for leased equipment is 10.9 years.[24] The $EBIT_{ADJ}$ is then used to calculate free cash flow to the firm. EBIT may be adjusted as follows:

$$EBIT_{ADJ} = EBIT + OLE_{EXP} - DEP_{OL} \qquad (7.8)$$

If EBIT, OLE_{EXP}, PV_{OL}, and the useful life of the leased equipment are $15 million, $2 million, $30 million, and ten years, respectively, then $EBIT_{ADJ}$ equals $14 million [i.e., $15 + $2 − ($30/10)].

Free Cash Flow to Equity Investors (Equity Cash Flow)

Free cash flow to equity investors is the cash flow remaining for returning cash through dividends or share repurchases to current common equity investors or

---

[23]Cornaggia, Franzen, and Simin (2012) have documented a huge shift in the way firms finance their capital assets, with operating lease financing increasing by 745% as a proportion of total debt and capital leases falling by half between 1980 and 2007.

[24]Lim, Mann, and Mihov, 2004

EXHIBIT 7.2 DEFINING VALUATION CASH FLOWS: EQUITY AND ENTERPRISE CASH FLOWS

Free Cash Flow to Common Equity Investors (Equity Cash Flow: FCFE)

$$\text{FCFE} = \{\text{Net Income} + \text{Depreciation and Amortization} - \Delta\text{Working Capital}\}^a$$
$$- \text{Gross Capital Expenditures}^b$$
$$+ \{\text{New Preferred Equity Issues} - \text{Preferred Dividends} + \text{New Debt Issues}$$
$$- \text{Principal Repayments}\}^c$$

⇨   Cash flow (after taxes, debt repayments and new debt issues, preferred dividends, preferred equity issues, and all reinvestment requirements) available for paying dividends and/or repurchasing common equity.

Free Cash Flow to the Firm (Enterprise Cash Flow: FCFF)

$$\text{FCFF} = \{\text{Earnings Before Interest \& Taxes}\,(1 - \text{Tax Rate}) + \text{Depreciation}$$
$$\text{and Amortization} - \Delta\text{Working Capital}\}^a - \text{Gross Capital Expenditures}^b$$

⇨   Cash flow (after taxes and reinvestment requirements) available to repay lenders and/or pay common and preferred dividends and repurchase equity.

[a] Cash from operating activities.
[b] Cash from investing activities.
[c] Cash from financing activities.

for reinvesting in the firm after the firm satisfies all obligations. These obligations include debt payments, capital expenditures, changes in net working capital, and preferred dividend payments. FCFE can be defined as follows:

$$\text{FCFE} = \text{Net Income} + \text{Depreciation and Amortization}$$
$$- \text{Gross Capital Expenditures} - \Delta\text{Net Working Capital}$$
$$+ \text{New Debt and Preferred Equity Issues}$$
$$- \text{Principal Repayments} - \text{Preferred Dividends} \qquad (7.9)$$

Exhibit 7.2 summarizes the key elements of enterprise cash flow, Eq. (7.6), and equity cash flow, Eq. (7.9). Note that equity cash flow reflects operating, investment, and financing activities, whereas enterprise cash flow excludes cash flow from financing activities.

APPLYING DISCOUNTED CASH FLOW METHODS

Widely used in valuation,[25] DCF methods provide estimates of the economic value of a company at a moment in time, which do not need to be adjusted if the

[25] In a survey of more than 300 financial planning professionals, about 80% said they routinely used DCF techniques in evaluating capital projects, including acquisitions (Association for Financial Professionals: March, 2011).

intent is to acquire a small portion of the company. However, if the intention is to obtain a controlling interest in the firm, a control premium must be added to the firm's value to determine the purchase price.[26]

Enterprise Discounted Cash Flow Model (Enterprise or FCFF Method)

The enterprise valuation method, or FCFF, approach discounts the after-tax free cash flow available to the firm from operations at the weighted average cost of capital to obtain the estimated enterprise value. The firm's *enterprise value* (often referred to as *firm value*) reflects the market value of the entire business. It represents the sum of investor claims on the firm's cash flows from all those holding securities, including those holding long-term debt, preferred stock, common shareholders, and minority shareholders. It is commonly calculated as the market value of the firm's common equity plus long-term debt, preferred stock, and minority interest less cash and cash equivalents.[27] Thus measured, the enterprise value represents what an acquirer would have to pay for the target's common and preferred equity and the cost of assuming the responsibility to repay the target's debt while retaining its cash. The firm's common equity value then is determined by subtracting the market value of the firm's debt and other investor claims on cash flow, such as preferred stock and minority (noncontrolling) interest, from the enterprise value.[28] The enterprise method is used when information about the firm's debt repayment schedules or interest expense is limited.

Equity Discounted Cash Flow Model (Equity or FCFE Method)

The equity valuation, or FCFE, approach, discounts the after-tax cash flows available to the firm's shareholders at the cost of equity. This approach is more direct than the enterprise method when the objective is to value the firm's equity. The enterprise, or FCFF, method and the equity, or FCFE, method are illustrated in the following sections of this chapter using three cash flow growth scenarios: zero-growth, constant-growth, and variable-growth rates.

---

[26] A controlling interest generally is considered more valuable to an investor than a minority interest because the investor has the right to approve important decisions affecting the business.

[27] Other long-term liabilities, such as the firm's pension and healthcare obligations, may be ignored if they are fully funded. However, the unfunded portion of such liabilities should be added to enterprise value, while any recoverable surplus should be deducted.

[28] The estimate of equity derived in this manner equals the value of equity determined by discounting the cash flow available to the firm's shareholders at the cost of equity, if assumptions about cash flow and discount rates are consistent.

The Zero-Growth Valuation Model

This model assumes that free cash flow is constant in perpetuity. The value of the firm at time zero (P_0) is the discounted or capitalized value of its annual cash flow.[29] The subscript FCFF or FCFE refers to the definition of cash flow used in the valuation.

$$P_{0,FCFF} = FCFF_0/WACC \qquad (7.10)$$

where $FCFF_0$ is free cash flow to the firm at time 0 and WACC is the cost of capital.

$$P_{0,FCFE} = FCFE_0/k_e \qquad (7.11)$$

where $FCFE_0$ is free cash flow to common equity at time 0 and k_e is the cost of equity.

While simplistic, the zero-growth method has the advantage of being easily understood. There is little evidence that more complex methods provide consistently better valuation estimates, due to their greater requirement for more inputs and assumptions. This method often is used to value commercial real estate transactions and small, privately owned businesses (Exhibit 7.3).

EXHIBIT 7.3   THE ZERO-GROWTH VALUATION MODEL

1. What is the enterprise value of a firm whose annual $FCFF_0$ of $1 million is expected to remain constant in perpetuity and whose cost of capital is 12% [see Eq. (7.10)]?

$$P_{0,FCFF} = \$1/0.12 = \$8.3 \text{ million}$$

2. Calculate the weighted average cost of capital [see Eq. (7.4)] and the enterprise value of a firm whose capital structure consists only of common equity and debt. The firm desires to limit its debt to 30% of total capital.[a] The firm's marginal tax rate is 0.4, and its beta is 1.5. The corporate bond rate is 8%, and the ten-year U.S. Treasury bond rate is 5%. The expected annual return on stocks is 10%. Annual FCFF is expected to remain at $4 million indefinitely.

$$k_e = 0.05 + 1.5 \,(0.10 - 0.05) + 0.125 = 12.5\%$$
$$WACC = 0.125 \times 0.7 + 0.08 \times (1 - 0.4) \times 0.3 = 0.088 + 0.014 = 0.102 = 10.2\%$$
$$P_{0,FCFF} = \$4/0.102 = \$39.2 \text{ million}$$

[a]If the analyst knows a firm's debt-to-equity ratio (D/E), it is possible to calculate the firm's debt-to-total capital ratio [$D/(D + E)$] by dividing (D/E) by ($1 + D/E$), since $D/(D + E) = (D/E)/(1 + D/E) = [(D/E)/(D + E)/E] = (D/E) \times (E/D + E) = D/(D + E)$.

[29]The present value of a constant payment in perpetuity is a diminishing series because it represents the sum of the PVs for each future period. Each PV is smaller than the preceding one; therefore, the perpetuity is a diminishing series that converges to one divided by the discount rate.

The Constant-Growth Valuation Model

The constant-growth model is applicable for firms in mature markets, characterized by a somewhat predictable rate of growth. Examples include beverages, cosmetics, personal care products, prepared foods, and cleaning products. To project growth rates, extrapolate the industry's growth rate over the past five to ten years. The constant-growth model assumes that cash flow grows at a constant rate, g, which is less than the required return, k_e. The assumption that k_e is greater than g is a necessary mathematical condition for deriving the model. In this model, next year's cash flow to the firm ($FCFF_1$), or the first year of the forecast period, is expected to grow at the constant rate of growth, g. Therefore, $FCFF_1 = FCFF_0 (1 + g)$:

$$P_{0,FCFF} = FCFF_1/(WACC - g) \tag{7.12}$$

$$P_{0,FCFE} = FCFE_1/(k_e - g) \tag{7.13}$$

where $FCFE_1 = FCFE_0 (1 + g)$[30]

This simple valuation model also provides a means of estimating the risk premium component of the cost of equity as an alternative to relying on historical information, as is done in the capital asset-pricing model. This model was developed originally to estimate the value of stocks in the current period (P_0) using the level of expected dividends (d_1) in the next period. This model estimates the present value of dividends growing at a constant rate forever. Assuming the stock market values stocks correctly and that we know P_0, d_1, and g, we can estimate k_e. Therefore,

$$P_0 = d_1/(k_e - g) \text{ and } k_e = (d_1/P_0) + g \tag{7.14}$$

For example, if d_1 is $1, g is 10%, and $P_0 = \$10$, then k_e is 20%. See Exhibit 7.4 for an illustration of how to apply the constant-growth model.

The Variable-Growth (Supernormal or Nonconstant) Valuation Model

Many firms experience periods of high growth followed by a period of slower, more stable growth. Examples include cellular phone firms, personal computer firms, and cable TV firms. Such firms experience double-digit growth rates for periods of five to ten years because of low penetration early in the product's life

---

[30]Note that the zero-growth model is a special case of the constant-growth model for which $g = 0$.

EXHIBIT 7.4   THE CONSTANT-GROWTH MODEL

1. Determine the enterprise value of a firm whose projected free cash flow to the firm (enterprise cash flow) *next* year is $1 million, WACC is 12%, and expected annual cash flow growth rate is 6% [see Eq. (7.12)].

$$P_{0,FCFF} = \$1/(0.12 - 0.06) = \$16.7 \text{ million}$$

2. Estimate the equity value of a firm whose cost of equity is 15% and whose free cash flow to equity holders (equity cash flow) in the *prior* year is projected to grow 20% this year and then at a constant 10% annual rate thereafter. The prior year's

$$P_{0,FCFE} = [(\$2.0 \times 1.2)(1.1)]/(0.15 - 0.10) = \$52.8 \text{ million}$$

free cash flow to equity holders is $2 million [see Eq. (7.13)].

cycle. As the market becomes saturated, growth slows to a rate more in line with the overall growth of the economy or the general population. The PV of such firms is equal to the sum of the PV of the discounted cash flows during the high-growth period plus the discounted value of the cash flows generated during the stable-growth period. The discounted value of the cash flows generated during the stable-growth period is often called the *terminal, sustainable, horizon,* or *continuing-growth value.*

The terminal value may be estimated using the constant-growth model.[31] Free cash flow during the first year beyond the nth or final year of the forecast period, $FCFF_{n+1}$, is divided by the difference between the assumed cost of capital and the expected cash flow growth rate beyond the nth-year forecast period. The terminal value is the PV in the nth year of all future cash flows beyond the nth year. To convert the terminal value to its value in the current year, it is necessary to discount it by the discount rate used to convert the nth-year value to a present value. Small changes in assumptions can result in dramatic swings in the terminal value and in the valuation of the firm. Table 7.6 illustrates the sensitivity of a terminal value of $1 million to different spreads between the cost of capital and the stable growth rate. Note that, using the constant-growth model formula, the terminal value declines dramatically as the

---

[31] The use of the constant-growth model provides consistency, since the discounted cash flow methodology is used during both the variable- and stable-growth periods.

TABLE 7.6   Impact of Changes in Assumptions on a Terminal Value of $1 Million

Difference Between Cost of Capital and Cash Flow Growth Rate	Terminal Value ($ Millions)
3%	33.3[a]
4%	25.0
5%	20.0
6%	16.7
7%	14.3

[a]$1.0/0.03.

spread between the cost of capital and expected stable growth for cash flow increases by one percentage point.[32]

Using the definition of free cash flow to the firm, $P_{0,\text{FCFF}}$ can be estimated using the variable-growth model as follows:

$$P_{0,\text{FCFF}} = \sum_{t-1}^{n} \frac{\text{FCFF}_0(1 + g_t)^t}{(1 + \text{WACC})^t} + \frac{P_n}{(1 + \text{WACC})^n} \tag{7.15}$$

where

$$P_n = \frac{\text{FCFF}_n(1 + g_m)}{\text{WACC}_m - g_m}$$

$\text{FCFF}_0 = \text{FCFF}$ in year 0
$\text{WACC} = $ weighted average cost of capital through year n
$\text{WACC}_m = $ cost of capital assumed beyond year n (Note: $\text{WACC} > \text{WACC}_m$)
$P_n = $ value of the firm at the end of year n (terminal value)
$g_t = $ growth rate through year n
$g_m = $ stabilized or long-term growth rate beyond year n (Note: $g_t > g_m$)

Similarly, the value of the firm to equity investors can be estimated using Eq. (7.15). However, projected free cash flows to equity (FCFE) are discounted using the firm's cost of equity.

The cost of capital is assumed to differ between the high-growth and the stable-growth periods when applying the variable-growth model. High-growth rates usually are associated with increased levels of uncertainty. A high-growth firm may have a beta significantly above one. However, when the growth rate becomes stable, it is reasonable to assume that the beta should approximate one. A

[32] Terminal value also may be estimated using price-to-earnings, price-to-cash flow, or price-to-book ratios to value the target as if it were sold at the end of a specific number of years. At the end of the forecast period, the terminal year's earnings, cash flow, or book value is projected and multiplied by a P/E, cash flow, or book value multiple believed to be appropriate for that year.

reasonable approximation of the discount rate to be used during the stable-growth period is to adopt the industry average cost of equity or weighted average cost of capital.

Equation (7.15) can be modified to use the growing-annuity model[33] to approximate the growth during the high-constant-growth period and the constant-growth model for the terminal period. This formulation requires fewer computations if the number of annual cash flow projections is large. As such, $P_{0,FCFF}$ also can be estimated as follows:

$$P_{0,FCFF} = \frac{FCFF_0(1 + g)}{WACC - g}\left[1 - \left(\frac{1 + g}{1 + WACC}\right)^n\right] + \frac{P_n}{(1 + WACC)^n} \qquad (7.16)$$

See Exhibit 7.5 for an illustration of how to apply the variable-growth model and the growing-annuity model.

Determining the Duration of the High-Growth Period

Projected growth rates for sales, profit, and cash flow can be calculated based on the historical experience of the firm or industry.[34] The length of the high-growth period should be longer when the current growth rate of a firm's cash flow is much higher than the stable-growth rate and the firm's market share is small. For example, if the industry is expected to grow at 5% annually and the target firm, which has only a negligible market share, is growing at three times that rate, it may be appropriate to assume a high-growth period of five to ten years. If the terminal value constitutes more than 75% of the total PV, the annual forecast period should be extended beyond the customary five years to at least ten years to reduce its impact on the firm's total market value. Historical evidence shows that sales and profitability tend to revert to normal levels within five to ten years,[35] suggesting that the conventional use of a five- to ten-year annual forecast before calculating a terminal value makes sense.[36]

Determining the Stable or Sustainable Growth Rate

The stable growth rate is generally going to be less than or equal to the overall growth rate of the industry in which the firm competes or the general economy. Stable growth rates in excess of these levels implicitly assume that the firm's cash flow will eventually exceed that of its industry or the general economy.

[33] Ross et al. (2009), pp. 238–240.

[34] See the document entitled "Primer on Cash Flow Forecasting" on the companion site to this text for a discussion on how to apply regression analysis to projecting a firm's cash flow.

[35] Palepu et al. (2004)

[36] More sophisticated forecasts of growth rates involve annual revenue projections for each customer or product, which are summed to provide an estimate of aggregate revenue. A product or service's life cycle (see Chapter 4) is a useful tool for making such projections.

EXHIBIT 7.5　THE VARIABLE-GROWTH VALUATION MODEL

Estimate the enterprise value of a firm (P_0) whose free cash flow is projected to grow at a compound annual average rate of 35% for the next five years. Growth then is expected to slow to a more normal 5% annual rate. The current year's cash flow to the firm is $4 million. The firm's weighted average cost of capital during the high-growth period is 18% and 12% beyond the fifth year, as growth stabilizes. The firm's cash in excess of normal operating balances is assumed to be zero. Therefore, using Eq. (7.15), the present value of cash flows during the high-growth five-year forecast period (PV_{1-5}) is calculated as follows:

$$PV_1 = \frac{\$4.00 \times 1.35}{1.18} + \frac{\$4.00 \times (1.35)^2}{(1.18)^2} + \frac{\$4.00 \times (1.35)^3}{(1.18)^3} + \frac{\$4.00 \times (1.35)^4}{(1.18)^3}$$

$$+ \frac{\$4.00 \times (1.35)^5}{(1.18)^3}$$

$$= \frac{\$5.40}{1.18} + \frac{\$7.29}{(1.18)^2} + \frac{\$9.84}{(1.18)^3} + \frac{\$13.29}{(1.18)^4} + \frac{\$17.93}{(1.18)^5}$$

$$= \$4.58 + \$5.24 + \$5.99 + \$6.85 + \$7.84 = \$30.50$$

Calculation of the terminal value (PV_{TV}) is as follows:

$$PV_{TV} = \frac{[\$4.00 \times (1.35)^5 \times 1.05]/(0.12 - 0.05)}{(1.18)^5} = \frac{\$18.83/0.07}{2.29} = \$117.60$$

$$P_{0,FCFF} = P_{1-5} + PV_{TV} = \$30.50 + \$117.60 = \$148.10$$

Alternatively, using the growing-annuity model to value the high-growth period and the constant-growth model to value the terminal period [see Eq. (7.16)], the present value of free cash flow to the firm could be estimated as follows:

$$PV = \frac{\$4.00 \times 1.35}{0.18 - 0.35} \times \{1 - [(1.35/1.18)^5]\} + \frac{[\$4.00 \times (1.35)^5 \times 1.05]/(0.12 - 0.05)}{(1.18)^5}$$

$$= \$30.50 + \$117.60$$

$$= \$148.10$$

Similarly, for multinational firms, the stable growth rate should not exceed the projected growth rate for the world economy or a particular region of the world.

Determining the Appropriate Discount Rate

The correct discount rate is generally the target's cost of capital if the acquirer is merging with a higher-risk business. However, either the acquirer's or the target's cost of capital may be used if the two firms are equally risky and based in the same country.

USING THE ENTERPRISE METHOD TO ESTIMATE EQUITY VALUE

A firm's common equity value often is calculated by estimating its enterprise value, adding the value of nonoperating assets, and then deducting nonequity claims on future cash flows. Such claims commonly include long-term debt, operating leases, deferred taxes, unfunded pension liabilities, preferred stock, employee options, and minority interests. What follows is a discussion of how to value nonequity claims and nonoperating assets.[37] This approach is especially useful when a firm's capital structure (i.e., debt-to–total capital ratio) is expected to remain stable.

Determining the Market Value of Long-Term Debt

The current value of a firm's debt generally is independent of its enterprise value for financially healthy companies, but this is not true for financially distressed firms and for hybrid securities.

Financially Stable Firms

If the debt repayment schedule is unknown, the market value of debt may be estimated by treating the book value of the firm's debt as a conventional coupon bond, in which interest is paid annually or semiannually and the principal is repaid at maturity. The coupon is the interest on all of the firm's debt, and the principal at maturity is a weighted average of the maturity of all of the debt outstanding. The weighted average principal at maturity is the sum of the amount of debt outstanding for each maturity date multiplied by its share of total debt outstanding. The estimated current market value of the debt then is calculated as the sum of the annuity value of the interest expense per period plus the present value of the principal (see Exhibit 7.6).[38]

Note that the book value of debt may be used unless interest rates have changed significantly since the debt was incurred or the likelihood of default is high. In these situations, value each bond issued by the firm separately by discounting cash flows at yields to maturity for comparably rated debt with similar maturities issued by similar firms. Book value also may be used for floating-rate

---

[37] If these factors already are included in the projections of future cash flows, they should not be deducted from the firm's enterprise value.

[38] The only debt that must be valued is the debt outstanding on the valuation date. Future borrowing is irrelevant if we assume that investments financed with future borrowings earn their cost of capital. As such, net cash flows would be sufficient to satisfy interest and principal payments associated with these borrowings.

EXHIBIT 7.6   ESTIMATING THE MARKET VALUE OF A FIRM'S DEBT AND CAPITALIZED OPERATING LEASES

According to its 10K report, Gromax, Inc., has two debt issues outstanding, with a total book value of $220 million. Annual interest expense on the two issues totals $20 million. The first issue, whose current book value is $120 million, matures at the end of five years; the second issue, whose book value is $100 million, matures in ten years. The weighted average maturity of the two issues is 7.27 years (i.e., $5 \times (120/220) + 10 \times (100/220)$). The current cost of debt maturing in seven to ten years is 8.5%.

The firm's 10K also shows that the firm has annual operating-lease expenses of $2.1, $2.2, $2.3, and $5 million in the fourth year and beyond (the 10K indicated the firm's cumulative value in the fourth year and beyond to be $5 million). (For our purposes, we may assume that the $5 million is paid in the fourth year.) What is the total market value of the firm's total long-term debt, including conventional debt and operating leases?

$$PV_D(\text{Long-Term Debt})^a = \$20 \times \frac{1 - [1/(1.085)^{7.27}]}{0.85} + \frac{\$220}{(1.085)^{7.27}}$$

$$= \$105.27 + \$121.55$$

$$= \$226.82$$

$$PV_{OL}(\text{Operating Leases}) = \frac{\$2.10}{1.085} + \frac{\$2.20}{(1.085)^2} + \frac{\$2.30}{(1.085)^3} + \frac{\$5.00}{(1.085)^4}$$

$$= \$1.94 + \$1.87 + \$1.80 + \$3.61$$

$$= \$9.22$$

$$PV_{TD}(\text{Total Debt}) = \$226.82 + \$9.22 = \$236.04$$

[a]The present value of debt is calculated using the PV of an annuity formula for 7.27 years and an 8.5% interest rate plus the PV of the principal repayment at the end of 7.27 years.

debt, since its market value is unaffected by fluctuations in interest rates. In the United States, the current market value of a company's debt can be determined using the FINRA TRACE database. For example, Home Depot Inc.'s 5.40% fixed coupon bond maturing on March 1, 2016, was priced at $112.25 on September 5, 2010, or 1.1225 times par value. Multiply the book (par) value of debt, which for Home Depot was $3,040,000, by 1.1225 to determine its market value of $3,412,400 on that date.

Financially Distressed Firms

For such firms, the value of debt and equity reflect the riskiness of the firm's cash flows. Therefore, debt and equity are not independent, and the calculation of a firm's equity value cannot be estimated by simply subtracting the market value of the firm's debt from the firm's enterprise value. One solution is to estimate the firm's enterprise value using two scenarios: One in which the firm is able to return to financial health and one in which the firm's position deteriorates. For each scenario, calculate the firm's enterprise value and deduct the book value of the firm's debt and other nonequity claims. Each scenario is weighted by the probability that the analyst attaches to each scenario, such that the resulting equity value estimate represents a probability weighted average of the scenarios.

Hybrid Securities (Convertible Bonds and Preferred Stock)

Convertible bonds and stock represent conventional debt and preferred stock plus a conversion feature, or call option to convert the bonds or stock to shares of common equity at a stipulated price per share. Since the value of the debt reflects the value of common equity, it is not independent of the firm's enterprise value and therefore cannot be deducted from the firm's enterprise value to estimate equity value. One approach to valuing such debt and preferred stock is to assume that all of it will be converted into equity when a target firm is acquired. This makes the most sense when the offer price for the target exceeds the price per share at which the debt can be converted. See Exhibit 9.8 in Chapter 9 for an illustration of this method.

Determining the Market Value of Operating Leases

Both capital and operating leases should also be counted as outstanding debt of the firm. When a lease is classified as a capital lease, the present value of the lease expenses is treated as debt. Interest is imputed on this amount, which corresponds to debt of comparable risk and maturity and is shown on the income statement. Although operating-lease expenses are treated as operating expenses on the income statement, they are not counted as part of debt on the balance sheet for financial reporting purposes. For valuation purposes, operating leases should be included in debt. Future operating-lease expenses are shown in financial statement footnotes. The discount rate may be approximated using the firm's current pretax cost of debt, reflecting the market rate of interest that lessors would charge the firm. The principal amount of the leases also can be estimated by discounting the current year's operating-lease payment as a perpetuity using the firm's cost of debt (see Exhibit 7.6).

Determining the Cash Impact of Deferred Taxes

Deferred tax assets and liabilities arise when the tax treatment of an item is temporarily different from its financial accounting treatment. Such taxes may result from uncollectible accounts receivable, warranties, options expensing, pensions, leases, net operating losses, depreciable assets, and inventories. Deferred taxes have a current and a future or noncurrent impact on cash flow.

The current impact is reflected by adding the change in deferred tax liabilities and subtracting the change in deferred tax assets in the calculation of working capital. The noncurrent impact of deferred assets is generally shown in other long-term assets and deferred tax liabilities in other long-term liabilities on the firm's balance sheet. A deferred tax asset is a future tax benefit, in that deductions not allowed in the current period may be realized in some future period. A deferred tax liability represents the increase in taxes payable in future years. The excess of accelerated depreciation taken for tax purposes over straight-line depreciation often used for financial reporting reduces the firm's current tax liability but increases future tax liabilities when spending on plant and equipment slows. The amount of the deferred tax liability equals the excess of accelerated over straight-line depreciation times the firm's marginal tax rate.

To estimate a firm's equity value, the PV of net deferred tax liabilities (i.e., deferred tax assets less deferred tax liabilities) is deducted from the firm's enterprise value.[39] The use of net deferred tax liabilities is appropriate, since deferred tax liabilities are often larger than deferred tax assets for firms in the absence of significant NOLs. The impact on free cash flow of a change in deferred taxes can be approximated by the difference between a firm's marginal and effective tax rates multiplied by the firm's operating income before interest and taxes. The analyst may assume the effective tax rate is applicable for a specific number of years before reverting to the firm's marginal tax rate. For example, the effective tax rate for five years increases the deferred tax liability to the firm during that period as long as the effective rate is below the marginal rate. The deferred tax liability at the end of the fifth year is estimated by adding to the current cumulated deferred tax liability the additional liability for each of the next five years. This liability is the sum of projected EBIT times the difference between the marginal and effective tax rates. Assuming tax payments on the deferred tax liability at the end of the fifth year will be spread equally over the following 10 years, the PV of the tax payments during that ten-year period is then estimated and discounted back to the current period (see Exhibit 7.7).

Determining the Cash Impact of Unfunded Pension Liabilities

Deduct the PV of such liabilities from the enterprise value to estimate the firm's equity value. Publicly traded firms are required to identify the PV of unfunded pension obligations; if not shown on the firm's balance sheet, such data can be found in the footnotes to the balance sheet.[40]

---

[39] Alternatively, noncurrent deferred taxes may be valued separately, with deferred tax assets added to and deferred tax liabilities subtracted from the firm's enterprise value.

[40] If the unfunded liability is not shown in the footnotes, the footnote should indicate where they have been included.

EXHIBIT 7.7 ESTIMATING COMMON EQUITY VALUE BY DEDUCTING THE MARKET VALUE OF DEBT, PREFERRED STOCK, AND DEFERRED TAXES FROM THE ENTERPRISE VALUE

Operating income, depreciation, working capital, and capital spending are expected to grow 10% annually during the next five years and 5% thereafter. The book value of the firm's debt is $300 million, with annual interest expense of $25 million and term to maturity of four years. The debt is a conventional "interest only" note, with a repayment of principal at maturity. The firm's annual preferred dividend expense is $20 million. The prevailing market yield on preferred stock issued by similar firms is 11%. The firm does not have any operating leases, and pension and healthcare obligations are fully funded. The firm's current cost of debt is 10%. The firm's weighted average cost of capital is 12%. Because it is already approximating the industry average, it is expected to remain at that level beyond the fifth year. Because of tax deferrals, the firm's current effective tax rate of 25% is expected to remain at that level for the next five years. The firm's current net deferred tax liability is $300 million. The projected net deferred tax liability at the end of the fifth year is expected to be paid off in 10 equal amounts during the following decade. The firm's marginal tax rate is 40%, and it will be applied to the calculation of the terminal value. What is the value of the firm to common equity investors?

Financial Data (in $ Million)

	Current Year	Year 1	Year 2	Year 3	Year 4	Year 5
EBIT	$200	$220	$242	$266.2	$292.8	$322.1
EBIT $(1 - t)$	$150	$165	$181.5	$199.7	$219.6	$241.6
Depreciation (Straight line)	$8	$8.8	$9.7	$10.7	$11.7	$12.9
Δ Net Working Capital	$30	$33	$36.	$39.9	$43.9	$48.3
Gross Capital Spending	$40	$44	$48.4	$3.2	$58.6	$64.4
Free Cash Flow to the Firm	$88		$96.8	$106.5	$117.3	$128.8	$141.8

$$P_{0,FCFF}{}^{a} = \frac{\$88.00(1.10)}{0.12 - 0.10} \times \left[1 - \left(\frac{1.10}{1.12}\right)^{5} + \frac{\$93.50^{b} \times 1.05/(0.12 - 0.05)}{(1.12)^{5}}\right]$$

$$= \$416.98 + \$795.81$$
$$= \$1,212.80$$

$$PV_{D}(Debt)^{c} = \$25 \times \frac{1 - 1/(1.04)^{4}}{0.10} + \frac{\$300}{(1.10)^{4}}$$

$$= \$25(3.17) + \$300(0.683)$$
$$= \$79.25 + \$204.90$$
$$= \$284.15$$

$$PV_{PFD}(Preferred\ Stock)^{d} = \frac{\$20.11}{0.11} = \$181.82$$

$$Deferred\ Tax\ Liability\ by\ end\ of\ Year\ 5 = \$300 + (\$220 + \$242 + 266.20$$
$$+ \$292.80$$

$$+\$322.10)(0.40 - 0.25) = \$501.47$$

$$PV_{DEF}(Deferred\ Taxes) = \frac{\$501.47}{10} \times \frac{1 - [1/(1.12)^{10}]/1.12^{5}}{0.12}$$

$$= \frac{\$50.115 \times 5.65}{1.76} = \$160.99$$

$$P_{0,FCFE} = \$1,212.80 - \$284.15 - \$181.82 - \$160.99$$
$$= \$585.84$$

[a]See Eq. (7.16).
[b]The terminal value reflects the recalculation of the fifth-year after-tax operating income using the marginal tax rate of 40% and applying the constant-growth model. Fifth-year free cash flow equals $322.1(1–0.4) + $12.9–$48.3–$64.4 = $93.5.
[c]The present value of debt is calculated using the PV of an annuity for four years and a 10% interest rate plus the PV of the principal repayment at the end of four years. The firm's current cost of debt of 10% is higher than the implied interest rate of 8% ($25/$300) on the loan currently on the firm's books. This suggests that the market rate of interest has increased since the firm borrowed the $300 million "interest only" note.
[d]The market value of preferred stock (PV_{PFD}) is equal to the preferred dividend divided by the cost of preferred stock.

Determining the Cash Impact of Employee Options

Key employees often receive compensation in the form of options to buy a firm's common stock at a stipulated price (i.e., exercise price). Once exercised, these options impact cash flow as firms attempt to repurchase shares to reduce earnings-per-share dilution resulting from the firm's issuance of new shares to those exercising their options. The PV of these future cash outlays to repurchase stock should be deducted from the firm's enterprise value.[41]

[41]Options represent employee compensation and are tax deductible for firms. Accounting rules require firms to report the PV of all stock options outstanding based on estimates provided by option-pricing models (see Chapter 8) in the footnotes to financial statements.

Determining the Cash Impact of Other Provisions and Contingent Liabilities

Provisions (i.e., reserves) for future layoffs due to restructuring are usually recorded on the balance sheet in undiscounted form, since they usually represent cash outlays to be made in the near term. Such provisions should be deducted from the enterprise value because they are equivalent to debt. Contingent liabilities, whose future cash outlays depend on certain events, are shown not on the balance sheet but, rather, in footnotes. Examples include pending litigation and loan guarantees. Since such expenses are tax deductible, estimate the PV of future after-tax cash outlays discounted at the firm's cost of debt, and deduct from the firm's enterprise value.

Determining the Market Value of Minority (or Noncontrolling) Interests

When a firm owns less than 100% of another business, it is shown on the firm's consolidated balance sheet. That portion not owned by the firm is shown as a minority (or noncontrolling) interest. For valuation purposes the minority (or noncontrolling) interest has a claim on the assets of the majority-owned subsidiary and not on the parent firm's assets. If the less than wholly-owned subsidiary is publicly traded, value the minority (or noncontrolling) interest by multiplying the minority's ownership share by the market value of the subsidiary. If the subsidiary is not publicly traded and you as an investor in the subsidiary have access to its financials, value the subsidiary by discounting the subsidiary's cash flows at the cost of capital appropriate for the industry in which it competes. The resulting value of the minority interest also should be deducted from the firm's enterprise value.

VALUING NONOPERATING ASSETS

Assets not used in operating the firm also may contribute to firm value and include excess cash balances, investments in other firms, and unused or underutilized assets. Their value should be added to the firm's enterprise value to determine the total value of the firm.

Cash and Marketable Securities

Excess cash balances are cash and short-term marketable securities held in excess of the target firm's minimum operating cash balance. What constitutes the minimum cash balance depends on the firm's *cash conversion cycle*, which reflects the firm's tendency to build inventory, sell products on credit, and later collect accounts receivable. The length of time cash is committed to working capital can be estimated as the sum of the firm's inventory conversion period plus

EXHIBIT 7.8   ESTIMATING MINIMUM AND EXCESS CASH BALANCES

Prototype Incorporated's current inventory, accounts receivable, and accounts payable are valued at $14 million, $6.5 million, and $6 million, respectively. Projected sales and cost of sales for the coming year total $100 million and $75 million, respectively. Moreover, the value of the firm's current cash and short-term marketable securities is $21,433,000. What minimum cash balance should the firm maintain? What is the firm's current excess cash balance?

$$\frac{\$14,000,000}{\$100,000,000/365} + \frac{\$6,500,000}{\$100,000,000/365} - \frac{\$6,000.00}{75,000,000/365}$$
$$= 51.1 \, \text{days} + 23.7 \, \text{days} + 29.2 \, \text{days} = 45.6 \, \text{days}$$

Minimum Cash Balance $= 45.6 \, \text{days} \times \$100,000,000/365 = \$12,493,151$

Excess Cash Balance $= \$21,433,000 - \$12,493,151 = \$8,939,849$

the receivables collection period less the payables deferral period.[42] To finance this investment in working capital, a firm must maintain a minimum cash balance equal to the average number of days its cash is tied up in working capital times the average dollar value of sales per day. The inventory conversion and receivables collection periods are calculated by dividing the dollar value of the inventory and receivables by average sales per day. The payments deferral period is estimated by dividing the dollar value of payables by the firm's average cost of sales per day. Exhibit 7.8 illustrates how to estimate minimum and excess cash balances.

While excess cash balances should be added to the present value of operating assets, any cash deficiency should be subtracted from the value of operating assets to determine the value of the firm. This reduction in the value reflects the need for the acquirer to invest additional working capital to make up any deficiency.

The method illustrated in Exhibit 7.8 may not work for firms that manage working capital aggressively, so receivables and inventory are very low relative to payables. An alternative is to compare the firm's cash and marketable securities as a percent of revenue with the industry average. If the firm's cash balance exceeds the industry average, the firm has excess cash balances, assuming there are no excess cash balances for the average firm in the industry. For example, if the industry average cash holdings as a percent of annual revenue is 5% and the target firm has 8%, the target holds excess cash equal to 3% of its annual revenue.

---

[42]The inventory conversion period is the average length of time in days required to produce and sell finished goods. The receivables collection period is the average length of time in days required to collect receivables. The payables deferral period is the average length of time in days between the purchase of and payment for materials and labor.

Investments in Other Firms

Such investments, for financial reporting purposes, may be classified as minority passive investments, minority active investments, or majority investments. These investments need to be valued individually and added to the firm's enterprise value to determine the total firm value. See the companion website to this book for an explanation of the valuation methodology in a document entitled "Investments in Other Firms."

Unutilized and Undervalued Assets

Target firm real estate may have a market value in excess of its book value. A firm may have an overfunded pension fund. Intangible assets such as patents and licenses may have substantial value. In the absence of a predictable cash flow stream, their value may be estimated using the Black–Scholes model (see Chapter 8) or the cost of developing comparable technologies.

Patents, Service Marks and Trademarks

A patent without a current application may have value to an external party, which can be determined by a negotiated sale or license to that party. When a patent is linked to a specific product, it is normally valued based on the "cost avoidance" method. This method uses after-tax royalty rates paid on comparable patents multiplied by the projected future stream of revenue from the products whose production depends on the patent discounted to its present value at the cost of capital. Products and services, which depend on a number of patents, are grouped together as a single portfolio and valued as a group using a single royalty rate applied to a declining percentage of the future revenue. Trademarks are the right to use a name, and service marks are the right to use an image associated with a company, product, or concept. Their value is name recognition reflecting the firm's longevity, cumulative advertising expenditures, the effectiveness of its marketing programs, and the consistency of perceived product quality.

Overfunded Pension Plans

Defined benefit pension plans require firms to hold financial assets to meet future obligations. Shareholders have the legal right to assets in excess of what is needed. If such assets are liquidated and paid out to shareholders, the firm has to pay taxes on their value. The after-tax value of such funds may be added to the enterprise value.

PUTTING IT ALL TOGETHER

Table 7.7 shows how Home Depot's equity value is estimated by first determining the firm's total operating value, adding the value of nonoperating assets,

TABLE 7.7 Determining Home Depot's Equity Value Using the Enterprise Method

| | History | | Projections | | | | | | | | | | |
Assumptions	2008	2009	2010	2011	2012	2013	2014	2015	2016	2017	2018	2019
Net Sales Growth Rate %	−0.078	−0.072	−0.040	0.010	0.020	0.040	0.050	0.050	0.040	0.040	0.035	0.030
Operating Profit Margin %	0.061	0.073	0.070	0.065	0.068	0.070	0.072	0.075	0.075	0.078	0.080	0.080
Depreciation Expenditure % of Sales	0.026	0.025	0.025	0.025	0.025	0.025	0.025	0.025	0.025	0.025	0.025	0.025
Effective Tax Rate %	0.356	0.342	0.340	0.340	0.340	0.340	0.340	0.340	0.340	0.340	0.340	0.340
Marginal Tax Rate %			0.400	0.400	0.400	0.400	0.400	0.400	0.400	0.400	0.400	0.400
Working Capital % of Sales	0.048	0.057	0.060	0.060	0.060	0.060	0.060	0.060	0.060	0.060	0.060	0.060
Gross P&E % of Sales	0.049	0.026	0.035	0.035	0.035	0.035	0.035	0.035	0.035	0.035	0.035	0.035
WACC (2010–2019) %[a]			0.073									
WACC Terminal Period %			0.070									
Terminal Period Growth Rate %			0.030									
Valuation ($ Million)												
Net Sales	71288	66176	63529	64164	65448	68065	71469	75042	78044	81166	84006	86,527
Operating Income (EBIT)	4359	4803	4447	4171	4450	4765	5146	5628	5853	6331	6721	6922
Plus: Operating Lease Expense			802	717	640	584	535	535	535	535	535	535
Less: Operating Lease Depreciation[b]			258	258	258	258	258	258	258	258	258	258
Equals: Adjusted EBIT			4991	4630	4832	5091	5423	5905	6130	6608	6998	7199
Adjusted EBIT(1 − t)			3294	3056	3189	3360	3579	3897	4046	4361	4618	4751
Plus: Depreciation and Amortization	1785	1707	1906	1925	1963	2042	2144	2251	2341	2435	2520	2596
Minus: Δ Net Working Capital[c]		1328	275	38	77	157	204	214	180	187	170	151
Minus: Gross P&E Expenditure	1847	966	2224	2246	2291	2382	2501	2626	2732	2841	2940	3028
Equals: Enterprise Cash Flow[d]			2702	2697	2785	2862	3017	3308	3476	3768	4028	4168

PV (2010–2019)	22,048
Terminal Value	47,638
Total Operating Value	69,686
Plus:	
Excess Cash[e]	0
Other Long-Term Assets[f]	256
Equals: Enterprise Value	69,942
Less:	
Market Value of Debt[g]	9469
Capitalized Operating Leases	6450
PV Net Noncurrent DTLs[h]	1102
Stock Options	158
Equals: Equity Value	52,763
Number of Shares (Millions)	1683
Equity Value Per Share	$31.35

<u>Explanatory Notes</u>

[a]**WACC calculation:**

$k_e = 0.0265 + 1.10 (0.055) = 8.43\%$, where 2.65% is the 10-year Treasury bond rate on September 5, 2010, and 1.21 is the firm's beta provided Yahoo! Finance/Capital IQ.

$i = 6.85\%$, pretax cost of debt estimated as the yield to maturity on BBB+ rated debt per Yahoo! Finance on 9/5/2010. Weights for debt and equity of 31% and 69%, respectively, are based on firm's current debt-to-capital ratio held constant throughout the forecast period.

$WACC = 8.70 \times 0.69 + 6.85(1-0.4) \times 0.31 = 7.28$

WACC for terminal period equal to average for comparable retail companies per Yahoo! Finance.

[b]**Operating Leases:**

Capitalized value of operating leases = PV of lease expense provided in financial statement footnotes discounted at firm's cost of debt.
Operating lease equipment estimated useful life = 25 years; estimated annual operating lease depreciation expense = $6450/25 = $258.

[c]Working Capital $3537 $3812 $3850 $3927 $4084 $4503 $4288 $4683 $4870 $5040 $5192

[d]Terminal-period enterprise cash flow recalculated using 40% marginal tax rate.

[e]Excess cash is zero, since minimum balances estimated using Exhibit 7.8 method exceeds actual year-end 2009 cash balances.

[f]Excludes goodwill but includes $33 million in notes receivable.

[g]Market Value of Home Depot Debt:

(Continued)

Coupon	Maturity Date	Face Value (000)		Percent of Par Value (9/5/10)	Market Value
5.20%	March 2011	$1,000,000	×	1.02630	$1,026,300
6.19%	March 2012	$40,000	×	1.03366	$41,346
6.74%	May 2013	$14,285	×	1.03650	$14,806
5.25%	December 2013	$1,258,000	×	1.02630	$1,291,085
5.88%	December 2036	$2,960,000	×	1.10650	$3,275,240
5.40%	March 2016	$3,040,000	×	1.12250	$3,412,400
Capitalized Leases (payments vary from 2010 through 2056)					$408,000
Total Long Term Debt					$9,469,177

[h]*PV of Net Noncurrent DTLs (Net Deferred Tax Assets–Deferred Tax Liabilities) Calculation:*

Future Value as of 2019 = $3570   Adds current net deferred tax liability to the sum of the projected EBIT times the difference between marginal and effective tax rates.

Present Value = $1102   2019 net deferred tax liability paid off in equal amounts during following decade.

and subtracting the value of all nonequity claims. The nonoperating assets in this example include excess cash balances and other long-term assets, while the nonequity claims include the market value of long-term debt, capitalized operating leases, net deferred tax liabilities, and employee stock options. The exhibit is divided into three panels. The top panel displays the primary assumptions underlying the valuation. The second panel shows how the total value of the firm is determined. The bottom panel—"Explanatory Notes"—provides details on how various line items in the exhibit were calculated. Cash flow is projected for ten years, reflecting the anticipated slow recovery of the firm's free cash flow from the 2008–2009 recession. The Excel-based model underlying this exhibit is provided in an Excel file entitled "Determining Home Depot's Equity Value Using the Enterprise Method" on the companion site to this book.

SOME THINGS TO REMEMBER

DCF methods are widely used to estimate the firm value. To do so, GAAP cash flows are adjusted to create enterprise and equity cash flow for valuation purposes. A common way of estimating equity value is to deduct the market value of nonequity claims from its enterprise value and to add the market value of nonoperating assets.

DISCUSSION QUESTIONS

7.1 What is the significance of the weighted average cost of capital? How is it calculated? Do the weights reflect the firm's actual or target debt-to–total capital ratio? Explain your answer.

7.2 What does a firm's β measure? What is the difference between an unlevered and a levered β?

7.3 Under what circumstances is it important to adjust the CAPM model for firm size? Why?

7.4 What are the primary differences between FCFE and FCFF?

7.5 Explain the conditions under which it makes the most sense to use the zero-growth and constant-growth DCF models. Be specific.

7.6 Which DCF valuation methods require the estimation of a terminal value? Why?

7.7 Do small changes in the assumptions pertaining to the estimation of the terminal value have a significant impact on the calculation of the total value of the target firm? If so, why?

7.8 How would you estimate the equity value of a firm if you knew its enterprise value and the present value of all nonoperating assets, nonoperating liabilities, and long-term debt?

7.9 Why is it important to distinguish between operating and nonoperating assets and liabilities when valuing a firm? Be specific.

7.10 Explain how you would value a patent under the following situations: a patent with no current application, a patent linked to an existing product, and a patent portfolio.

Answers to these Chapter Discussion Questions are available in the Online Instructor's Manual for instructors using this book.

QUESTIONS FROM THE CFA CURRICULUM

CFA Institute

7.11 A company's cost of equity is often used as a proxy for investors:
  a. Average required rate of return.
  b. Minimum required rate of return.
  c. Maximum required rate of return.
  Source: 2011 Overview of Equity Securities Reading 58, question 24.

7.12 In the free cash flow to equity model (FCFE), the intrinsic value of a share of stock is calculated as:
  a. The present value of future expected FCFE.
  b. The present value of future expected FCFE plus net borrowing.
  c. The present value of future expected FCFE minus fixed capital investment.
  Source: 2011 Equity Valuation: Concepts and Basic Tools, Reading 60, question 9.

7.13 Enterprise value is most often determined as market capitalization of common equity and preferred stock minus the value of cash equivalents plus the:
  a. Book value of debt.
  b. Market value of debt.
  c. Market value of long-term debt.
  Source: 2011 Equity Valuation: Concepts and Basic Tools, Reading 60, question 31.

7.14 Consider an asset that has a beta of 1.25. If the risk-free rate is 3.25% and the market risk premium is 5.5%, calculate the expected return on the asset.
  Source: 2011 International Asset Pricing, Reading 68, question 1.

Answers to questions from the CFA curriculum are available in the Online Student Companion site to this book in a file folder entitled CFA Curriculum Questions and Solutions.

PRACTICE PROLEMS AND ANSWERS

7.15 ABC Incorporated shares are currently trading for $32 per share. The firm has 1.13 billion shares outstanding. In addition, the market value of the firm's outstanding debt is $2 billion. The ten-year Treasury bond rate is

6.25%. ABC has an outstanding credit record and has earned a AAA rating from the major credit-rating agencies. The current interest rate on AAA corporate bonds is 6.45%. The historical risk premium over the risk-free rate of return is 5.5%. The firm's beta is estimated to be 1.1, and its marginal tax rate, including federal, state, and local taxes, is 40%.

a. What is the cost of equity?

Answer: 12.3%

b. What is the after-tax cost of debt?

Answer: 3.9%

c. What is the weighted average cost of capital?

Answer: 11.9%

7.16 HiFlyer Corporation currently has no debt. Its tax rate is 0.4, and its unlevered beta is estimated by examining comparable companies to be 2.0. The ten-year bond rate is 6.25%, and the historical risk premium over the risk-free rate is 5.5%. Next year, HiFlyer expects to borrow up to 75% of its equity value to fund future growth.

a. Calculate the firm's current cost of equity.

Answer: 17.25%

b. Estimate the firm's cost of equity after the firm increases its leverage to 75% of equity.

Answer: 22.2%

7.17 Abbreviated financial statements for Fletcher Corporation are given in Table 7.8.

TABLE 7.8 Abbreviated Financial Statements for Fletcher Corporation (in $ Million)

	2010	2011
Revenues	$600	$690
Operating expenses	520	600
Depreciation	16	18
Earnings before interest and taxes	64	72
Less interest expense	5	5
Less taxes	23.6	26.8
Equals: net income	35.4	40.2
ADDENDUM:		
Yearend working capital	150	200
Principal repayment	25	25
Capital expenditures	20	10

Yearend working capital in 2009 was $160 million, and the firm's marginal tax rate was 40% in both 2010 and 2011. Estimate the following for 2010 and 2011:

a. Free cash flow to equity.

Answer: $16.4 million in 2010 and –$26.8 million in 2011

b. Free cash flow to the firm.

Answer: $44.4 million in 2010 and $1.2 million in 2011

7.18 In 2011, No Growth Incorporated had operating income before interest and taxes of $220 million. The firm was expected to generate this level of operating income indefinitely. The firm had depreciation expense of $10 million that year. Capital spending totaled $20 million during 2011. At the end of 2010 and 2011, working capital totaled $70 million and $80 million, respectively. The firm's combined marginal state, local, and federal tax rate was 40%, and its outstanding debt had a market value of $1.2 billion. The 10-year Treasury bond rate is 5%, and the borrowing rate for companies exhibiting levels of creditworthiness similar to No Growth is 7%. The historical risk premium for stocks over the risk-free rate of return is 5.5%. No Growth's beta was estimated to be 1.0. The firm had 2.5 million common shares outstanding at the end of 2011. No Growth's target debt-to-total capital ratio is 30%.

a. Estimate free cash flow to the firm in 2011.

Answer: $112 million

b. Estimate the firm's weighted average cost of capital.

Answer: 8.61%

c. Estimate the enterprise value of the firm at the end of 2011, assuming that it will generate the value of free cash flow estimated in (a) indefinitely.

Answer: $1,300.8 million

d. Estimate the value of the equity of the firm at the end of 2011.

Answer: $100.8 million

e. Estimate the value per share at the end of 2011.

Answer: $40.33

7.19 Carlisle Enterprises, a specialty pharmaceutical manufacturer, has been losing market share for three years because several key patents have expired. Free cash flow to the firm is expected to decline rapidly as more competitive generic drugs enter the market. Projected cash flows for the next five years are $8.5 million, $7 million, $5 million, $2 million, and $0.5 million. Cash flow after the fifth year is expected to be negligible. The firm's board has decided to sell the firm to a larger pharmaceutical company that is interested in using Carlisle's product offering to fill gaps in its own product offering until it can develop similar drugs. Carlisle's weighted average cost of capital is 15%. What purchase price must Carlisle obtain to earn its cost of capital?

Answer: $17.4 million

7.20 Ergo Unlimited's current year's free cash flow to equity is $10 million. It is projected to grow at 20% per year for the next five years. It is expected to grow at a more modest 5% beyond the fifth year. The firm estimates that its cost of equity is 12% during the next five years and will drop to 10% beyond the fifth year as the business matures. Estimate the firm's current market value.
Answer: $358.3 million

7.21 In the year in which it intends to go public, a firm has revenues of $20 million and net income after taxes of $2 million. The firm has no debt, and revenue is expected to grow at 20% annually for the next five years and 5% annually thereafter. Net profit margins are expected to remain constant throughout. Annual capital expenditures equal depreciation, and the change in working capital requirements is minimal. The average beta of a publicly traded company in this industry is 1.50, and the average debt-to-equity ratio is 20%. The firm is managed conservatively and will not borrow through the foreseeable future. The Treasury bond rate is 6%, and the marginal tax rate is 40%. The normal spread between the return on stocks and the risk-free rate of return is believed to be 5.5%. Reflecting the slower growth rate in the sixth year and beyond, the discount rate is expected to decline to the industry average cost of capital of 10.4%. Estimate the value of the firm's equity.
Answer: $63.41 million

7.22 The information in Table 7.9 is available for two different common stocks: Company A and Company B.

TABLE 7.9 Common Stocks in Problem 7.22

	Company A	Company B
Free cash flow per share in the current year	$1.00	$5.00
Growth rate in cash flow per share	8%	4%
Beta	1.3	0.8
Risk-free return	7%	7%
Expected return on all stocks	13.5%	13.5%

a. Estimate the cost of equity for each firm.
Answer: Company A = 15.45%; Company B = 12.2%
b. Assume that the companies' growth will continue at the same rates indefinitely. Estimate the per-share value of each company's common stock.
Answer: Company A = $13.42; Company B = $61.00

7.23 You have been asked to estimate the beta of a high-technology firm that has three divisions with the characteristics shown in Table 7.10.
a. What is the beta of the equity of the firm?
Answer: 1.52

TABLE 7.10 High-Technology Company in Problem 7.23

Division	Beta	Market Value ($ Million)
Personal computers	1.60	100
Software	2.00	150
Computer mainframes	1.20	250

b. If the risk-free return is 5% and the spread between the return on all stocks is 5.5%, estimate the cost of equity for the software division.
Answer: 16%

c. What is the cost of equity for the entire firm?
Answer: 13.4%

d. Free cash flow to equity investors in the current year (FCFE) for the entire firm is $7.4 million and for the software division is $3.1 million. If the total firm and the software division are expected to grow at the same 8% rate into the foreseeable future, estimate the market value of the firm and of the software division.
Answer: PV (total firm) = $147.96; PV (software division) = $41.88

7.24 Financial Corporation wants to acquire Great Western Inc. Financial has estimated the enterprise value of Great Western at $104 million. The market value of Great Western's long-term debt is $15 million, and cash balances in excess of the firm's normal working capital requirements are $3 million. Financial estimates the present value of certain licenses that Great Western is not currently using to be $4 million. Great Western is the defendant in several outstanding lawsuits. Financial Corporation's legal department estimates the potential future cost of this litigation to be $3 million, with an estimated present value of $2.5 million. Great Western has 2 million common shares outstanding. What is the adjusted equity value of Great Western per common share?
Answer: $46.75/share

Solutions to these Practice Problems are available in the Online Instructor's Manual for instructors using this book.

CASE STUDY 7.1
Hewlett-Packard Outbids Dell Computer to Acquire 3PAR

On September 2, 2010, a little more than two weeks after Dell's initial bid for 3PAR, Dell Computer withdrew from a bidding war with Hewlett-Packard when HP announced that it had raised its previous offer by 10% to $33 a share. Dell's last bid had been $32 per share, which had trumped HP's previous bid the day before of $30 per share. The final HP bid valued 3PAR at $2.1 billion versus Dell's original offer of $1.1 billion.

3PAR was sought after due to the growing acceptance of its storage product technology in the emerging "cloud computing" market. 3PAR's storage products enable firms to store and manage their data more efficiently at geographically remote data centers accessible through the Internet. While 3PAR has been a consistent money loser, its revenues had been growing at more than 50% annually since it went public in 2007. The deal valued 3PAR at 12.5 times 2009 sales in an industry that has rarely spent more than five times sales to acquire companies. HP's motivation for its rich bid seems to have been a bet on a fast-growing technology that could help energize the firm's growth. While impressive at $115 billion in annual revenues and $7.7 billion in net income in 2009, the firm's revenue and earnings have slowed due to the 2008–2009 global recession and the maturing market.

Table 7.11 provides selected financial data on 3PAR and a set of valuation assumptions. Note that HP's marginal tax rate is used rather than 3PAR's much lower effective tax rate, to reflect potential tax savings to HP from 3PAR's cumulative operating losses. Given HP's $10 billion–plus pretax profit, HP is expected to utilize 3PARs deferred tax assets fully in the current tax year. The continued 3PAR high sales-growth rate reflects

the HP expectation that its extensive global sales force can expand the sale of 3PAR products. To support further development of the 3PAR products, the valuation assumptions reflect an increase in plant and equipment spending in excess of depreciation and amortization through 2015; however, beyond 2015, capital spending is expected to grow at the same rate as depreciation as the business moves from a growth mode to a maintenance mode. 3PAR's operating margin is expected to show a slow recovery, reflecting the impact of escalating marketing expenses and the cost of training the HP sales force in the promotion of the 3PAR technology.

Discussion Questions

1. Estimate 3PAR's equity value per share based on the assumptions and selected 3PAR data provided in Table 7.11.
2. Why is it appropriate to utilize at least a ten-year annual time horizon before estimating a terminal value in valuing firms such as 3PAR?
3. What portion of the purchase price can be financed by 3PAR's nonoperating assets?
4. Does the deal still make sense for HP if the terminal-period growth rate is 3% rather than 5%? Explain your answer.

Solutions to these questions are found in the Online Instructor's Manual available to instructors using this book.

TABLE 7.11 3PAR Valuation Assumptions and Selected Historical Data

	History	Projections									
	2009	2010	2011	2012	2013	2014	2015	2016	2017	2018	2019
ASSUMPTIONS											
Sales Growth Rate %	0.508	0.450	0.400	0.400	.400	0.350	0.300	0.250	0.200	0.100	0.100
Operating Margin % of Sales	−0.020	−0.010	−0.010	0.020	0.040	0.080	0.100	0.120	0.150	0.150	0.150
Depreciation Expense % of Sales	0.036	0.034	0.060	0.060	0.060	0.060	0.060	0.070	0.070	0.070	0.060
Marginal Tax Rate %		0.400	0.400	0.400	0.400	0.400	0.400	0.400	0.400	0.400	0.400
Working Capital % of Sale	0.104	0.114	0.100	0.100	0.100	0.100	0.100	0.100	0.100	0.100	0.100
Gross P&E % of Sales	0.087	0.050	0.080	0.080	0.080	0.080	0.080	0.070	0.070	0.060	0.060
WACC (2010–2019) %		0.093									
WACC (Terminal Period) %		0.085									
Terminal Period Growth Rate %	0.050										
Working Capital ($ Million)	112.8	126.4									
Total Cash ($ Million)	103.7	111.2									
Minimum Cash (5% of Sales)	8.4	12.65									
W Cap Excluding Excess Cash	17.5	27.85									
SELECTED FINANCIAL DATA ($ MILLION)											
Sales	168										
Depreciation Expense & Amortization	6.1										
Gross Plant & Equipment	14.6										
Excess Cash	98.55										
Deferred Tax Assets	73.1										
PV of Operating Leases	22.0										
Number of Shares Outstanding	61.8										

Relative, Asset-Oriented, and Real-Option Valuation Basics

Happiness is a personal choice. We can be angry about the things we do not have or happy about the things we do. —**Nick Vujicic**

INSIDE M&A: BRISTOL-MYERS SQUIBB PLACES A BIG BET ON INHIBITEX

KEY POINTS

- DCF valuation assumes implicitly that management has little decision-making flexibility once an investment decision is made.
- In practice, management may accelerate, delay, or abandon the original investment as new information is obtained.

Pharmaceutical firms in the United States are facing major revenue declines during the next several years because of patent expirations for many drugs that account for a substantial portion of their annual revenue. The loss of patent protection will enable generic drug makers to sell similar drugs at much lower prices, thereby depressing selling prices for such drugs across the industry. In response, major pharmaceutical firms are inclined to buy smaller drug development companies whose research and developments efforts show promise in order to offset the expected decline in their future revenues as some "blockbuster" drugs lose patent protection.

Aware that its top-selling blood thinner, Plavix, would lose patent protection in May 2012, Bristol-Myers Squibb (Bristol-Myers) moved aggressively to shed its infant formula and other noncore businesses to focus on pharmaceuticals. Such restructuring has reduced employment from 40,000 in 2008 to 26,000 in 2011. Bristol-Myers' strategy has been either to acquire firms with promising drugs under development or to develop them internally. However, the firm faced an uphill struggle to offset the potential loss of $6.7 billion in annual Plavix revenue, which represented about one-third of the firm's total annual revenue.

In early January 2012, Bristol-Myers announced that it had reached an agreement to purchase hepatitis C drug developer Inhibitex Inc. for $2.5 billion. Inhibitex focuses on treatments for bacterial and viral infections. It had annual revenue of only $1.9 million and an operating loss of $22.7 million in 2011. The lofty purchase price reflected Bristol-Myers' growth expectations for the firm's hepatitis C treatment INX-189, based on very early phase one clinical testing trials, with larger trials scheduled for 2013. The all-cash deal for $26 per share represented a 164% premium to Inhibitex's closing price on January 10, 2012.

Bristol-Myers valued Inhibitex in terms of the expected cash flows resulting from the commercialization of hepatitis C treatment INX-189. Standard discounted cash flow analysis assumes implicitly that once Bristol-Myers makes an investment decision, it cannot change its mind. In reality, management has a series of so-called real options enabling them to make changes to their original investment decision contingent on certain future developments.

These options include the decision to expand (i.e., accelerate investment at a later date), delay the initial investment, or abandon an investment. With respect to Bristol-Myers' acquisition of Inhibitex, the major uncertainties deal with the actual timing and amount of the projected cash flows. In practice, Bristol-Myers' management could expand or accelerate investment in the new Inhibitex drug, contingent on the results of subsequent trials. The firm could also delay additional investment until more promising results are obtained. Finally, if the test results suggest that the firm is not likely to realize the originally anticipated developments, it could abandon or exit the business by spinning-off or divesting Inhibitex or by shutting it down. The bottom line is that management has considerably greater decision-making flexibility than is implicit in traditional discounted cash flow analysis.

CHAPTER OVERVIEW

Chapter 7 discussed in detail how DCF analysis is applied to M&A valuation. This chapter addresses alternative methods of valuation, including relative-valuation (i.e., market-based) methods, asset-oriented methods, real-options analysis, and replacement cost. The chapter concludes with a summary of the strengths and weaknesses of the alternative valuation methods (including discounted cash flow) and when it is appropriate to apply each methodology. A review of this chapter is available in the file folder entitled "Student Study Guide" on the companion site to this book (*http://booksite.elsevier.com/9780123854872*).

RELATIVE-VALUATION METHODS

Relative valuation involves valuing assets based on how similar assets are valued in the marketplace. Such methods assume a firm's market value can be approximated by a value indicator for comparable companies, comparable transactions, or comparable industry averages. Value indicators could include the firm's earnings, operating cash flow, EBITDA (i.e., earnings before interest and taxes, depreciation, and amortization), sales, and book value. This approach often is described as market based, since it reflects the amounts investors are willing to pay for each dollar of earnings, cash flow, sales, or book value at a moment in time. As such, it reflects theoretically the collective wisdom of investors in the marketplace. Because of the requirement for positive current or near-term earnings or cash flow, this approach is meaningful only for companies with a positive, stable earnings or cash flow stream.

If comparable companies are available, the market value of a target firm, $T(MV_T)$, can be estimated by solving the following equation:

$$MV_T = (MV_C / VI_C) \times VI_T \tag{8.1}$$

where

MV_C = market value of comparable company C
VI_C = value indicator for comparable company C
VI_T = value indicator for firm T
(MV_C/VI_C) = market value multiple for the comparable company

For example, if the price-to-earnings (P/E) ratio for the comparable firm is 10 (MV_C/VI_C) and after-tax earnings of the target firm are $2 million (VI_T), the market value of the target firm at that moment in time is $20 million (MV_T). Relative-value methods are used for three reasons. First, they are simple to calculate and require far fewer assumptions than discounted cash flow techniques. Second, relative valuation is easier to explain than DCF methods. Finally, the use of market-based techniques is more likely to reflect current market demand and supply conditions. The relationship expressed in Eq. (8.1) can be used to estimate the value of the target firm in all the relative-valuation and asset-oriented methods discussed in this chapter.

The analyst must follow certain guidelines in applying relative-valuation methods. First, when using multiples (e.g., MV_C/VI_C), it is critical to ensure that the multiple is defined in the same way for all comparable firms. For example, when using a price-to-earnings ratio, earnings may be defined as trailing (i.e., prior), current, or projected. The definition must be applied consistently to all firms in the sample. Also, the numerator and the denominator of the multiple must be defined in the same way. If the numerator in the price-to-earnings ratio is defined as price per share, the denominator must be calculated as earnings per share. Second, the analyst must examine the distribution of the multiples of the firms being compared and eliminate outliers, those whose values are substantially different from others in the sample.

The Comparable-Companies Method

Applying this approach requires that the analyst identify companies that are substantially similar to the target firm. Generally speaking, a comparable firm is one whose profitability, potential growth rate in earnings or cash flows, and perceived risk are similar to those of the firm to be valued. By defining comparable companies broadly, it is possible to utilize firms in other industries. As such, a computer hardware manufacturer can be compared to a telecom firm as long as they are comparable in terms of profitability, growth, and risk. Consequently, if the firm to be valued has a 15% return on equity (i.e., profitability), expected earnings or cash flow growth rates of 10% annually (i.e., growth), and a beta of 1.3 or debt-to-equity ratio of 1 (i.e., risk), the analyst must find a firm with similar characteristics in either the same industry or another industry. In practice, analysts often look for comparable firms in the same industry and that are similar in terms of such things as markets served, product offering, degree of leverage, and size.[1]

To determine if the firms you have selected are truly comparable, estimate the correlation between the operating income or revenue of the target firm and those of the comparable firms. If the correlation is positive and high, the firms are comparable.[2] Even when companies appear to be substantially similar, there are likely to be significant differences in valuation at any moment in time. For example, the announcement of a pending acquisition may boost the share prices of competitors as investors anticipate takeover bids for these firms. The impact of such events abates with the passage of time. Consequently, comparisons made at different times can provide distinctly different results. By taking an average of multiples over six months or one year, these differences may be minimized. Note that valuations derived using the comparable companies method do not include a purchase price premium.

Table 8.1 illustrates how to apply the comparable companies' method to value Spanish oil company Repsol YPF. Repsol is a geographically diversified integrated oil and gas company; as such, it has economic and political risks and growth characteristics similar to other globally diversified integrated oil and gas companies. The estimated value of Repsol based on the comparable companies' method is $51.81 billion, versus its actual June 25, 2008, market capitalization of $49.83 billion.

The analyst needs to be mindful of changes in fundamentals that can affect multiples. These fundamentals include a firm's ability to generate and grow earnings and cash flow through reinvestment in the firm's operations as well as the risk associated with the firm's earnings and cash flows. Since multiples are affected by each of these variables, changes in the variables affect multiples. Firms with lower earnings and cash flow generation potential, lower growth

---

[1]Smaller firms, other things equal, are more prone to default than larger firms, which generally have a larger asset base and a larger and more diversified revenue stream than smaller firms. Consequently, the analyst should take care not to compare firms that are substantially different in size.

[2]Similarly, if the firm has multiple product lines, collect comparable firms for each product line and estimate the correlation coefficient.

TABLE 8.1   Valuing Repsol YPF Using Comparable Integrated Oil Companies

	Target Valuation Based on Following Multiples (MV$_C$/VI$_C$)				
	Trailing P/E[a]	Forward P/E[b]	Price/Sales	Price/Book	Average
Comparable Company	Col. 1	Col. 2	Col. 3	Col. 4	Cols. 1–4
Exxon Mobil Corp. (XOM)	11.25	8.73	1.17	3.71	
British Petroleum (BP)	9.18	7.68	0.69	2.17	
Chevron Corp. (CVX)	10.79	8.05	0.91	2.54	
Royal Dutch Shell (RDS-B)	7.36	8.35	0.61	1.86	
ConocoPhillips (COP)	11.92	6.89	0.77	1.59	
Total SA (TOT)	8.75	8.73	0.80	2.53	
Eni SpA (E)	3.17	7.91	0.36	0.81	
PetroChina Co. (PTR)	11.96	10.75	1.75	2.10	
Average Multiple (MV$_C$/VI$_C$) Times	9.30	8.39	0.88	2.16	
Repsol YPF Projections (VI$_T$)[c]	$4.38	$3.27	$92.66	$26.49	
Equals Estimated Market Value of Target[c]	$40.72	$27.42	$81.77	$57.32	$51.81

[a]Trailing 52-week averages.
[b]Projected 52-week averages.
[c]Billions of dollars.

prospects, and higher risk should trade at multiples less than firms with higher earnings and cash flow generation capability, higher growth prospects, and less risk. Therefore, the analyst needs to understand why one firm's multiple is less than a comparable firm's before concluding that it is under- or overvalued. For example, a firm with a P/E of ten may not be more expensive than a comparable firm with a P/E of eight if the former's growth prospects, profitability, and the rate at which profits are reinvested in the firm are higher than the latter firm's.

Recent Comparable Transactions Method

Also referred to as the *precedent-transactions method*, the multiples used to estimate the value of the target are based on purchase prices of comparable companies that were recently acquired. Price-to-earnings, sales, cash flow, EBITDA, and book-value ratios are calculated using the purchase price for the recent comparable transaction. Earnings, sales, cash flow, EBITDA, and book value for the target are subsequently multiplied by these ratios to obtain an estimate of the market value of the target company. The estimated value of the target firm obtained using recent comparable transactions already reflects a purchase price premium, unlike the comparable-companies approach to valuation. The obvious limitation to the comparable-transactions method is the difficulty in finding truly comparable, recent transactions. Recent transactions can be found in other industries as long as they are similar to the target firm in terms of profitability, expected earnings and cash flow growth, and perceived risk. Table 8.1 could be used to illustrate how the recent-transaction valuation method may be applied simply by replacing the data in the column headed "Comparable Company" with data for "Recent Comparable Transactions."

Same- or Comparable-Industries Method

Using this approach, the target company's net income, revenue, cash flow, EBITDA, and book value are multiplied by the ratio of the market value of shareholders' equity to net income, revenue, cash flow, EBITDA, or book value for the average company in the target firm's industry or a comparable industry (see Exhibit 8.1). Such information can be obtained from Standard & Poor's, Value Line, Moody's, Dun & Bradstreet, and Wall Street analysts. The primary advantage of this technique is the ease of use. Disadvantages include the presumption that industry multiples are actually comparable. The use of the industry average may overlook the fact that companies, even in the same industry, can have drastically different expected growth rates, returns on invested capital, and debt-to–total capital ratios.

Valuations Based on Analysts' Projections superior to those Using Historical Data

An analyst using industry or comparable company multiples must decide whether to use multiples based on current or projected earnings or cash flows or some other measure of value. While projections based on Wall Street analysts' forecasts may not be unbiased, empirical evidence suggests that forecasts of

---

EXHIBIT 8.1   **VALUING A TARGET COMPANY USING THE SAME- OR COMPARABLE-INDUSTRIES METHOD**

As of June 25, 2008, Repsol YPF, a Spanish integrated oil and gas producer, had projected earnings per share for the coming year of $3.27 (see Table 8.1). The industry average price-to-earnings ratio at that time for integrated oil and gas companies was 12.4. Estimate the firm's price per share [see Eq. (8.1)].

$$MV_T = (MV_{IND} / VI_{IND}) \times VI_T$$
$$= 12.4 \times \$3.27 = \$40.54/\text{share}(6/25/08 \text{ actual price} = \$39.18)$$

where

MV_T = market value per share of the target company

MV_{IND}/VI_{IND} = market value per share of the average firm in the industry divided by a value indicator for that average firm in the industry (e.g., industry average price-to-earnings ratio)

VI_T = value indicator for the target firm (e.g., projected earnings per share)

---

earnings and other value indicators are better predictors of firm value than value indicators based on historical data.[3]

Earnings Show Better Short-Run Correlation With Stock Returns than Does Cash Flow

Considerable attention has been paid to whether cash flow, earnings, or dividends are better predictors of a firm's value.[4] Studies suggest that cash flows and earnings are highly positively correlated with stock returns over long periods, such as five-year intervals, such that either may be used in firm valuation. However, for shorter time periods, earnings show a stronger correlation with stock returns than do cash flows.[5] Cash flow is more often used for valuation than earnings or dividends simply because firms often do not pay dividends or generate profits for a significant period.

Enterprise Value to EBITDA Method

In recent years, analysts have increasingly valued firms by multiplying the enterprise value (EV) to EBITDA multiple based on comparable companies or recent transactions by the target firm's EBITDA. That is, if the EV/EBITDA multiple for a sample of comparable firms or recent transactions is eight and the target's EBITDA is $10 million, the value of the target is $80 million.

In this chapter, enterprise value is viewed from the perspective of the liability, or "right-hand," side of the balance sheet.[6] As such, the enterprise value consists of the sum of the market values of long-term debt (MV_D), preferred equity (MV_{PF}), common equity (MV_{FCFE}), and minority interest excluding cash. Other long-term liabilities often are ignored, and cash is assumed to be equal to cash and short-term marketable securities on the balance sheet.[7] Cash and short-term marketable securities are deducted from the firm's enterprise value, since interest income from such cash is not counted in the calculation of EBITDA. The inclusion of cash would overstate the enterprise-value-to-EBITDA multiple. The EV-to-EBITDA multiple is commonly expressed as follows:

$$EV/EBITDA = [MV_{FCFE} + MV_{PF} + (MV_D - Cash)]/EBITDA \qquad (8.2)$$

[3]Moonchul and Ritter, 1999; Liu, Nissim, and Thomas, 2002
[4]Differences in earnings, cash flows, and dividends are often attributable to timing differences (i.e., differences between when a cash outlay is recorded and when it is actually incurred). If based on consistent assumptions, the PV of future earnings, cash flows, and dividends will be equal. See Liu et al. (2002).
[5]Cheng et al., 1996; Dechow, 1994; Sloan, 1996; Liu et al., 2007
[6]In Chapter 7, enterprise value was discussed from the perspective of the asset, or "left-hand," side of the balance sheet as the PV of cash flows from operating assets and liabilities available for lenders and common and preferred shareholders (i.e., free cash flow to the firm). Thus defined, enterprise value was adjusted for the value of nonoperating assets and liabilities to estimate the value of common equity.
[7]Ignoring the firm's pension and healthcare obligations makes sense only if they are fully funded.

where $(MV_D - Cash)$ is often referred to as net debt.

Many consider the enterprise value a more accurate representation of firm value than equity value because it reflects the obligation of the acquirer to pay off assumed liabilities, such as long-term debt.

The enterprise value to EBITDA valuation method is useful because more firms are likely to have negative earnings rather than negative EBITDA. Consequently, relative-valuation methods are more often applicable when EBITDA is used as the value indicator. Furthermore, net or operating income can be significantly affected by the way the firm chooses to calculate depreciation (e.g., straight line versus accelerated). Such problems do not arise with EBITDA, which is estimated before deducting depreciation and amortization expense. Finally, the multiple can be compared more readily among firms exhibiting different levels of leverage than for other measures of earnings, since the numerator represents the total value of the firm irrespective of its distribution between debt and equity and the denominator measures earnings before interest.

A major shortcoming of EBITDA as a value indicator is that it provides a good estimate of the firm's assets already in place but ignores the impact of new investment on future cash flows. This is not a problem as long as the firm is not growing. Despite this limitation, EBITDA is more often used than a multiple based on free cash flow to the firm (FCFF), since FCFF is frequently negative due to increases in working capital and capital spending in excess of depreciation. EBIDA multiples are most often used for mature businesses, for which most of the value comes from the firm's existing assets. Exhibit 8.2 illustrates how to construct EV/EBITDA multiples.

EXHIBIT 8.2   CALCULATING ENTERPRISE VALUE TO EBITDA MULTIPLES

Repsol and Eni are geographically diversified integrated oil and gas companies. As of December 31, 2006, the market value of Repsol's common equity was $40.36 billion, and Eni's was $54.30 billion. Neither firm had preferred stock outstanding. Repsol's and Eni's outstanding debt consists primarily of interest-only notes with a balloon payment at maturity. The average maturity date is 12 years for Repsol's debt and 10 years for Eni's. Market rates of interest for firms like Repsol and Eni at that time for debt maturing within 10 to 12 years were 7.5% and 7%, respectively. Repsol's and Eni's current income, balance sheet, and cash flow statements as of December 31, 2006, are shown in the following table.

Financial Statements		
Income Statement (12/31/06)	Repsol YPF	Eni SpA ($ Billion)
Revenue	72.70	114.70
Cost of Sales	48.60	75.90
Other Expenses	16.10	11.20

Earnings before Interest and Taxes	8.00	27.60
Interest Expense	0.70	0.30
Earnings before Taxes	7.30	27.30
Taxes	3.10	14.10
Net Income	4.20	13.20
Balance Sheet (12/31/06)		
Cash	3.80	6.20
Other Current Assets	14.60	29.80
Long-Term Assets	42.70	77.20
Total Assets	**61.10**	**113.20**
Current Liabilities	13.30	28.30
Long-Term Debt	14.60	8.80
Other Long-Term Liabilities	8.80	26.40
Total Liabilities	**36.70**	**63.50**
Shareholders' Equity	24.40	49.70
Equity + Total Liabilities	**61.10**	**113.20**
Cash Flow (12/31/06)		
Net Income	4.20	13.20
Depreciation	4.10	8.10
Change in Working Capital	−0.40	1.10
Investments	−6.90	−9.30
Financing	−1.20	−9.40
Change in Cash Balances	−0.20	3.70

Source: *Edgar Online.*
Which firm has the higher enterprise-value-to-EBITDA ratio? [Hint: Use Eq. (8.2).]
Answer: *Repsol Market Value of Existing Debt*

$$PV_D(\text{PV of Repsol Long-Term Delay}^a = \$0.70 \times \frac{1 - 1/(1.075)^{12}}{0.075} + \frac{\$14.60}{(1.075)^{12}}$$
$$= \$0.7 \times 7.74 + \$6.13 = \$11.55 \text{ billion}$$

$$PV_D(\text{PV of Eni Long-Term Debt})^b = \$0.30 \times \frac{1 - 1/(1.070)^{10}}{0.07} + \frac{\$8.80}{(1.07)^{10}}$$
$$= \$0.3 \times 7.02 + \$4.47 = \$6.58 \text{ billion}$$

Enterprise-to-EBITDA Ratio

(Market value of equity + Market Value of Debt − Cash)/(EBIT + Depreciation):[c]
Repsol: ($40.36 + $11.55 − $3.80)/($8.00 + $4.10) = $3.98
Eni: ($54.30 + $6.58 − $6.20)/($27.60 + $8.10) = $1.53

[a]The present value of debt is calculated using the PV of an annuity formula for 12 years and a 7.5% interest rate plus the PV of the principal repayment of $14.6 billion at the end of 12 years. Note that only annual interest expense of $.7 million is used in the calculation of the PV of the annuity payment because the debt is treated as a balloon note.
[b]The present value of debt is calculated using the PV of an annuity formula for ten years and a 7% interest rate plus the PV of the principal repayment of $8.8 billion at the end of ten years.
[c]A firm's financial statements frequently include depreciation in the cost of sales. Therefore, EBITDA may be calculated by adding EBIT from the income statement and depreciation shown on the cash flow statement.

Adjusting Relative-Valuation Methods for Firm Growth Rates

Assume that Firm A and Firm B are direct competitors and have price-to-earnings ratios of 20 and 15, respectively. Which is the cheaper firm? It is not possible to answer this question without knowing how fast the earnings of the two firms are growing. For this reason, relative-valuation methods may be adjusted for differences in growth rates among firms. Due to its simplicity, the most common adjustment is the PEG ratio, calculated by dividing the firm's P/E ratio by the expected growth rate in earnings. The comparison of a firm's P/E ratio to its projected earnings is helpful in identifying stocks of firms that are under- or overvalued. Firms with P/E ratios less than their projected growth rates may be considered undervalued, while those with P/E ratios greater than their projected growth rates may be viewed as overvalued. Note that growth rates do not increase multiples unless financial returns improve. Investors are willing to pay more for each dollar of future earnings only if they expect to earn a higher future rate of return.[8]

The PEG ratio can be helpful in in selecting the most attractive acquisition target from among a number of potential targets. Attractiveness is defined as that target which is most undervalued. Undervaluation is the extent to which a firm's current share price less than share price estimated using the PEG ratio. While the PEG ratio uses P/E ratios, other ratios may be employed, such as price to cash flow, EBITDA, revenue, and the like.

Eq. (8.3) gives an estimate of the implied market value per share for a target firm (MV_T) based on the PEG ratio for comparable companies.

$$\frac{MV_C / VI_C}{VI_{TGR}} = A$$

[8]Investors may be willing to pay considerably more for a stock whose PEG ratio is greater than one if they believe the future increase in earnings will result in future financial returns that significantly exceed the firm's cost of equity.

and

$$MV_T = A \times VI_{TGR} \times VI_T \tag{8.3}$$

where

A = PEG ratio—that is, market price–to–value indicator ratio (MV_C/VI_C) for comparable firms relative to the growth rate of the value indicator (VI_{CGR}) for comparable firms

VI_T = value indicator for the target firm

VI_{TGR} = projected growth rate of the value indicator for the target firm.

Because this method uses an equity multiple (e.g., price per share/net income per share), consistency suggests that the growth rate in the value indicator should be expressed on a per-share basis. Therefore, if the value indicator is net income per share, then the growth in the value indicator should be the growth rate for net income per share and not net income.

PEG ratios are useful for comparing firms whose expected growth rates are positive and different. This method implies a zero value for firms that are not growing and a negative value for those whose projected growth rates are negative. The practical implications are that firms that are not growing are not likely to increase in market value, while those exhibiting negative growth are apt to experience declining firm values.[9] Exhibit 8.3 illustrates how to apply the PEG ratio.

EXHIBIT 8.3   APPLYING THE PEG RATIO

An analyst is asked to determine whether Basic Energy Service (BES) or Composite Production Services (CPS) is more attractive as an acquisition target. Both firms provide engineering, construction, and specialty services to the oil, gas, refinery, and petrochemical industries. BES and CPS have projected annual earnings-per-share growth rates of 15% and 9%, respectively. BES's and CPS's current earnings per share are $2.05 and $3.15, respectively. The current share prices as of June 25, 2008, for BES is $31.48 and for CPX is $26.00. The industry average price-to-earnings ratio and growth rate are 12.4 and 11%, respectively. Based on this information, which firm is a more attractive takeover target as of the point in time the firms are being compared? [*Hint*: Use Eq. (8.3).] The PEG ratio focuses on P/E ratios and earnings growth rates. What other factors if known might change your answer to the previous question?

Industry average PEG ratio: $12.4/11 = 1.1273$[a]

BES: Implied share price $= 1.1273 \times 15 \times \$2.05 = \$34.66$

CPX: Implied share price $= 1.1273 \times 9 \times \$3.15 = \$31.96$

---

[9] As a means of selecting attractive takeover targets, the PEG ratio can be calculated for each firm and the firms ranked from lowest (most undervalued) to highest (most overvalued) in terms of their PEG ratios. While helpful in determining the most attractive acquisition targets (i.e., most undervalued), this ranking does not indicate the extent to which a firm is under- or overvalued as compared to its current share price.

Answer: The percentage difference between the implied and actual share prices for BES and CPX is 10.1% [i.e., ($34.66 − $31.48)/$31.48] and 22.9% [i.e., ($31.96 − $26.00)/$26.00], respectively. CPX is much more undervalued than BES at that moment in time according to this methodology. However, BES could be a more attractive target than CPX if it generates increasing future financial returns and its projected earnings stream is viewed as less risky. Therefore, BES could exhibit greater potential and less uncertain future profitability than CPX.

a Solving $MV_T = A \times VI_{TGR} \times VI_T$ using the target's PEG ratio, where MV_T is the market value of the target firm, VI_T is the target's value indicator, and VI_{TGR} is VI_T's growth rate, provides the firm's share price in period T, since this formula is an identity. An industry average PEG ratio may be used to estimate the firm's intrinsic value, assuming that the target firm and the average firm in the industry exhibit the same relationship between price-to-earnings ratios and earnings growth rates.

Data Source: Yahoo! Finance.

Value-Driver-Based Valuation

In the absence of earnings, factors that drive firm value may be used for valuation purposes and commonly are used to value start-up companies and IPOs, which often have little or no earnings history. Measures of profitability and cash flow are manifestations of these value drivers. Value drivers exist for each major function within the firm, including sales, marketing, and distribution; customer service; operations and manufacturing; and purchasing.

There are both micro value drivers and macro value drivers. *Micro value drivers* are those that influence specific functions within the firm directly. Micro value drivers for sales, marketing, and distribution could include: product quality measures, such as part defects per 100,000 units sold, on-time delivery, the number of multiyear subscribers, and the ratio of product price to some measure of perceived quality. Customer service drivers could include average waiting time on the telephone, the number of billing errors as a percent of total invoices, and the time required to correct such errors. Operational value drivers include the average collection period, inventory turnover, and the number of units produced per manufacturing employee hour. Purchasing value drivers include average payment period, on-time vendor delivery, and the quality of purchased materials and services. *Macro value drivers* are more encompassing than micro value drivers by affecting all aspects of the firm. Examples of macro value drivers include: market share, overall customer satisfaction as measured by survey results, total asset turns (i.e., sales to total assets), revenue per employee, and "same-store sales" in retailing.

Using value drivers to value businesses is straightforward. First, the analyst identifies the key drivers of firm value. Second, the market value for comparable companies is divided by the value driver selected for the target to calculate the dollars of market value per unit of value driver. Third, this figure is multiplied by the same value driver for the target company. Assume that the key macro value driver in an industry is market share. How investors value market share can be estimated by dividing the market leader's market value by its market share. If the market leader has a market value and market share of $300 million and 30%, respectively, the market is valuing each percentage point of market share at $10 million (i.e., $300 million ÷ 30). If the target company in the same industry has a 20% market share, an estimate of the market value of the target company is $200 million (20 points of market share times $10 million).

Similarly, the market value of comparable companies could be divided by other known value drivers. Examples include the number of visitors or page views per month for an Internet content provider, the number of subscribers to a magazine, cost per hotel room for a hotel chain, and the number of households with TVs in a specific geographic area for a cable TV company. AT&T's acquisitions of the cable companies TCI and Media One in the late 1990s would appear to have been a "bargain," since it spent an average of $5000 per household (the price paid for each company divided by the number of customer households acquired) in purchasing these companies' customers. In contrast, Deutsche Telekom and Mannesmann spent $6000 and $7000 per customer, respectively, in buying mobile phone companies One 2 One and Orange PLC.

The major advantage of this approach is its simplicity. Its major disadvantage is the implied assumption that a single value driver or factor is representative of the total value of the business. The bankruptcy of many dot-com firms between 2000 and 2002 illustrates how this valuation technique can be misused. Many of these firms had never shown any earnings, yet they exhibited huge market valuations as investors justified these lofty values by using page views and registered users of supposedly comparable firms to value any firm associated with the Internet.

ASSET-ORIENTED METHODS

Such methods typically value firms based on tangible book, breakup, and liquidation values.

Tangible Book Value (Shareholders' Equity Less Goodwill) Method

Book value is a much-maligned value indicator because book asset values rarely reflect actual market values (see Exhibit 8.4). The value of land frequently is understated on the balance sheet, whereas inventory often is overstated if it is old or obsolete. The applicability of this approach varies by industry. Although book values generally do not mirror actual market values for manufacturing companies, they may be more accurate for distribution companies, whose assets are largely composed of inventory exhibiting high inventory turnover rates. Examples of such companies include pharmaceutical distributor Bergen Brunswick and personal computer distributor Ingram Micro. Book value is also widely used for valuing financial services companies, where tangible book value consists mostly of liquid assets.

EXHIBIT 8.4   VALUING COMPANIES USING BOOK VALUE

Ingram Micro Inc. and its subsidiaries distribute information technology products worldwide. The firm's market price per share on August 21, 2008, was $19.30. Ingram's projected five-year average annual net income growth rate is 9.5%, and its beta is 0.89. The firm's shareholders' equity is $3.4 billion and goodwill is $0.7 billion. Ingram has 172 million (0.172 billion) shares outstanding. The following firms represent Ingram's primary competitors.

	Market Value/Tangible Book Value	Beta	Projected Five-Year Net Income Growth Rate (%)
Tech Data	0.91	0.90	11.6
Synnex Corporation	0.70	0.40	6.9
Avnet	1.01	1.09	12.1
Arrow	0.93	0.97	13.2

Ingram's tangible book value per share (VI_T) = ($3.4 – $0.7)/0.172 = $15.70.

Based on risk as measured by the firm's beta and the five-year projected earnings growth rate, Synnex is believed to exhibit significantly different risk and growth characteristics from Ingram and is excluded from the calculation of the ratio of industry average market value to tangible book value. Therefore, the appropriate industry average ratio (MV_{IND}/VI_{IND}) = 0.95 [i.e., (0.91 + 1.01 + 0.93)/3].

Ingram's implied value per share = MV_T = (MV_{IND}/VI_{IND}) × VI_T = 0.95 × $15.70 = $14.92.

Based on the implied value per share, Ingram was overvalued on August 21, 2008, when its share price was $19.30.

Data Source: Yahoo! Finance.

Breakup Value

Breakup value is the price of the firm's assets sold separately less its liabilities and expenses incurred in dividing up the firm. Diversified companies often are valued by investors as if broken up and sold as discrete units, as well as their going concern or synergistic value as a consolidated operation. If the breakup value exceeds the going concern value, shareholder value may be maximized by splitting up the firm. In mid-2012, News Corporation, a media conglomerate, announced its decision to divide the firm into two independent units: entertainment and publishing. Estimated after-tax earnings for the entertainment unit and publishing unit for the fiscal year ending June 2012 were $3.1 and $.5 billion, respectively. If valued at Disney Corporation's price-to-earnings ratio of 17, the entertainment businesses were worth $52.7 billion at that time; if valued at newspaper conglomerate Gannett Inc.'s 7.3 P/E, the publishing businesses were worth $3.7 billion. The resulting estimated breakup value of $56.4 billion versus its market value on July 7, 2012, of $50.4 billion suggested the firm was undervalued by about 12%.

Exhibit 8.5 illustrates the estimation of the breakup value of JPMorgan Chase. Value is determined for each of the firm's lines of business by multiplying its

EXHIBIT 8.5   CALCULATING THE BREAKUP VALUE OF JPMORGAN CHASE

Line of Business	Services Provided by Line of Business	Industry Market Multiple	After-Tax Earnings ($Billions)	Fair Market Value of Equity ($Billions)	Average June 2012 Price-to-Earnings Ratio for Large:
Investment Bank	Advisory, underwriting, and market making	13.3 ×	6.8	90.4	Investment banks (e.g., Goldman Sachs)
Retail Financial Services	Consumer & residential mortgage lending	13.2 ×	1.7	22.4	Diversified financial services firms (e.g., American Express)
Card Services & Auto	Credit card, auto, & student Loans	13.2 ×	4.5	59.4	Diversified financial services firms (e.g., American Express)
Commercial Banking	Middle-market lending, term lending, & corporate client Banking	11.1 ×	2.4	26.6	Money-center banks, excluding JPMorgan Chase (e.g., Citigroup Inc.)
Treasury & Securities Services	Global corporate cash management services	11.1 ×	1.2	13.3	Money center banks, excluding JPMorgan Chase (e.g. Citigroup Inc.)
Asset Management	Private banking, retail & institutional investment management	17.2 ×	1.6	27.5	Mutual funds (e.g., T. Rowe Price)
Private Equity	Corporate overhead & private equity activities	13.2 ×	.6	7.9	Private equity firms (e.g., KKR)
Total Fair Market Value				247.5	

Sources: JPMorgan Chase 2011 10K and Yahoo Finance.

2011 reported net income by the average June 2012 price-to-earnings multiple for the industry in which the business competes and then summing each operation's value to determine the firm's total equity value. The implicit assumption is that the interdependencies among the firm's business units are limited, such that they can be sold separately without a significant degradation of the value of any individual unit. Reflecting the impact of highly publicized trading losses, global turmoil, and an increasingly restrictive regulatory environment, the firm's July 6, 2012, market capitalization of $129.4 billion suggested that it was undervalued by as much as 48%.

Generally speaking, banks may value their current loan portfolio and subtract outstanding debt. Bank loan portfolios often are categorized by type (e.g., residential mortgage, auto loans), maturity, and the likelihood of default (i.e., risk). PV can then be determined by estimating the average maturity, interest earnings, and the rate of return on loan portfolios of similar risk. Suppose a bank holds a $100 million loan portfolio, whose average maturity is 10 years, on which it earns 6% ($6 million) annually. Because of the bank's excellent underwriting practices, its loan portfolio exhibits a lower average default rate than portfolios of similar maturities and rates of interest. Reflecting their higher default rate, these similar portfolios yield a 5% market rate of return. The fair market value of the bank's loan portfolio is $110 million,[10] which exceeds its book value because the 6% return on the loan portfolio exceeds the market interest rate used to discount the future cash flows. The equity associated with this loan portfolio could then be determined by deducting all deposits, debt, and nonequity claims from its fair market value.

Liquidation Value

The terms *liquidation* and *breakup value* often are used interchangeably. However, there are subtle distinctions. Liquidation may be involuntary, as a result of bankruptcy, or voluntary, if a firm is viewed by its owners as worth more in liquidation than as a going concern. Liquidation and breakup strategies are explored further in Chapters 16 and 17.

Analysts may estimate the liquidation value of a target company to determine the minimum value of the company in the worst-case scenario of liquidation. It is particularly appropriate for financially distressed firms. Analysts often assume the assets can be sold in an orderly fashion, often defined as nine to 12 months. Under these circumstances, high-quality receivables typically can be sold for 80 to 90% of their book value. Inventories might realize 80 to 90% of their book value, depending on the condition and the degree of obsolescence. The value of inventory may also vary, depending on whether it consists of finished,

---

[10]PV($100 million) = Annuity Value of $6 million annually for 10 years discounted at 5% + $100 million/$(1.05)^{10}$ = $48.6 million + $61.4 million = $110 million.

intermediate, or raw materials. More rapid liquidation might reduce the value of inventories to 60 to 65% of their book value. The liquidation value of equipment varies widely, depending on the age and condition.

Inventories need to be reviewed in terms of obsolescence, receivables in terms of the ease with which they may be collected, equipment in terms of age and effectiveness, and real estate in terms of current market value. Equipment, such as lathes and computers, with a zero book value may have a significant economic value (i.e., useful life). Land can be a hidden source of value because it frequently is undervalued on GAAP balance sheets. Prepaid assets, such as insurance premiums, can sometimes be liquidated, with a portion of the premium recovered. The liquidation value is reduced dramatically if the assets have to be liquidated in "fire sale" conditions, under which assets are sold to the first bidder rather than the highest bidder (see Exhibit 8.6).

The Replacement-Cost Method

Replacement cost is the cost to replace a firm's assets at current market prices. Equity value is determined by deducting the PV of the firm's liabilities. Valuing the assets separately in terms of what it would cost to replace them may seriously understate the firm's true value, since synergies created when the assets are used in combination are not considered. This approach should not be used

EXHIBIT 8.6   CALCULATING LIQUIDATION VALUE

Limited Options Corporation has declared bankruptcy, and the firm's creditors have asked the trustee to estimate its liquidation value assuming orderly sale conditions. Note that this example does not take into account legal fees, taxes, management fees, and contractually required employee severance expenses. These expenses can comprise a substantial percentage of the proceeds from liquidation.

Balance Sheet Item	Book Value ($ Million)	Orderly Sale Value ($ Million)
Cash	100	100
Receivables	500	450
Inventory	800	720
Equipment (after Depreciation)	200	60
Land	200	300
Total Assets	1800	1630
Total Liabilities	1600	1600
Shareholders' Equity	200	30

if the firm has significant intangible assets due to the difficulty in valuing such assets.

THE WEIGHTED-AVERAGE VALUATION METHOD

No valuation method is universally accepted as the best measure of a firm's value. Consequently, the weighted-average method of valuation represents a compromise position.[11] This approach involves calculating the expected value (EXPV) or weighted average of a range of potential outcomes. The weights, which must sum to one, reflect the analyst's relative confidence in the various methodologies employed to value a business. Assuming that an analyst is equally confident in the accuracy of both methods, the expected value of a target firm valued at $12 million using discounted cash flow and $15 million using the comparable-companies method can be written as follows:

$$EXPV = 0.5 \times \$12 + 0.5 \times \$15 = \$13.5 \text{ million}$$

Neither valuation method includes a purchase price premium. Thus, a premium will have to be added to the expected value to obtain a reasonable purchase price for the target firm.

ADJUSTING VALUATION ESTIMATES FOR PURCHASE PRICE PREMIUMS

With the exception of the recent-transactions method, the individual valuation estimates comprising the weighted average estimate do not reflect a purchase premium. The premium generally reflects those paid on recent acquisitions of similar firms, the percentage of synergy provided by the target firm, and the relative leverage of the two parties.[12] Exhibit 8.7 illustrates a practical way of calculating the expected value of the target firm, including a purchase premium, using estimates from multiple valuation methods. In the example, the purchase price premium associated with the estimate provided by the recent-comparable-transactions method is applied to estimates provided by the other valuation methodologies.

[11] Liu et al. (2002) provide empirical support for using multiple valuation methods to estimate firm value.

[12] An analyst should be careful not to add an acquisition premium mechanically to the target's estimated value based on the comparable-companies method if there is evidence that the market values of "comparable firms" already reflects acquisition activity elsewhere in the industry. Rival firms' share prices will rise in response to the announced acquisition of a competitor (Song et al., 2000). Akhigbe et al. (2000) find that the increase in rivals' share prices may be even greater if the acquisition attempt is unsuccessful because investors believe that the bidder will attempt to acquire other firms in the same industry.

EXHIBIT 8.7 WEIGHTED-AVERAGE VALUATION OF ALTERNATIVE METHODOLOGIES

An analyst has estimated the value of a company using multiple valuation methodologies. The discounted cash flow value is $220 million, the comparable-transactions value is $234 million, the P/E-based value is $224 million, and the firm's breakup value is $200 million. The breakup value was estimated using DCF methodology. The analyst has greater confidence in certain methodologies than others. The purchase price paid for the recent comparable transaction represented a 20% premium over the value of the firm at the time of the takeover announcement. Estimate the weighted average value of the firm using all valuation methodologies and the weights or relative importance the analyst assigns to each methodology.

Estimated Value ($ Million) Col. 1	Estimated Value Including 20% Premium ($ Million) Col. 2	Relative Weight (as Determined by Analyst) Col. 3	Weighted Average ($ Million) Col. 2× Col. 3
220	264.0	30	79.2
234	234.0[a]	40	93.6
224	268.8	20	53.8
200	240.0	10	24.0
		1.00	250.6

[a]Note that the comparable-recent-transactions estimate already contains a 20% purchase price premium.

REAL-OPTIONS ANALYSIS

An *option* is the right, but not the obligation, to buy, sell, or use property for a period of time in exchange for a specific amount of money. Those traded on financial exchanges, such as puts and calls, are called *financial options*. Options that involve real assets, such as licenses, copyrights, trademarks, and patents, are called *real options*. Other examples of real options include the right to buy land, commercial property, and equipment. Such assets can be valued as call options if their current value exceeds the difference between the asset's current value and some preset level. For example, if a business has an option to lease office space at a predetermined price, the value of that option increases as lease rates for this type of office space increase. The asset can be valued as a put option if its value increases as the value of the underlying asset falls below a predetermined level. To illustrate, if a business has an option to sell an office building at a preset price, its value increases as the value of the office building declines.

Real options reflect management's ability to adopt and later revise corporate investment decisions.[13] Real options can impact substantially the value

[13]Real options should not be confused with a firm's strategic options, such as adopting a cost leadership, differentiation, or a focus business strategy (see Chapter 4).

of an investment in a single project and should be considered when valuing such investments. However, real options can be costly to obtain (e.g., the right to extend a lease or purchase property), complex to value, and dependent on problematic assumptions. As such, they should not be pursued unless the firm has the resources to exploit the option and they add significantly to the value of the firm.

Identifying Real Options Embedded or Implied in M&A Decisions

Investment decisions, including M&As, often contain certain "embedded or implied options," such as the ability to accelerate growth by adding to the initial investment (i.e., expand), delay the timing of the initial investment (i.e., delay), or walk away from the project (i.e., abandon). Microsoft was confronted with a series of real options in its 2008 effort to acquire Yahoo!. If Yahoo! had accepted its bid, Microsoft could have chosen to accelerate investment contingent on the successful integration of Yahoo! and MSN (i.e., option to expand) or spin off or divest the combined MSN/Yahoo! business if the integration effort failed (option to abandon). Unable to achieve a negotiated agreement with Yahoo!, Microsoft chose to walk away, keeping open the possibility of returning to acquire or partner with Yahoo! at a later date (i.e., option to delay). In 2009, Microsoft entered into search partnership with Yahoo!.

Swiss mining company Xstrata PLC executed an option to delay when it dropped its $10 billion bid for platinum producer Lonmin PLC because of its inability to get financing. However, Xstrata signaled that it would resume efforts to acquire Lonmin at a later date by buying 24.9% of the firm's depressed shares in the open market. Already owning 10.7% of the target's shares, the additional purchase gave Xstrata a 35.6% stake in Lonmin at a low average cost, effectively blocking potential competing bids. As a bet on the future acceptance of ImClone's new colon cancer-fighting drug Erbitux, Eli Lilly's purchase of ImClone for $6.5 billion at a 51% premium reflected an implied option to expand. That is, Eli Lily could determine the rate of new investment in manufacturing, distribution, and marketing to support this drug's potential growth.

Valuing Real Options for Mergers and Acquisitions

Three ways to value real options are discussed in this book. The first is to use discounted cash flow, relative-valuation, or asset-oriented methods and ignore alternative real options by assuming that their value is essentially zero. The second is to value the real options in the context of a decision tree, an expanded timeline that branches into alternative paths whenever an event can have multiple outcomes. The decision tree branches at points called *nodes* and is most useful whenever the investment is subject to a relatively small number of probable outcomes and can be made in stages. The third method involves the valuation of the real option as a put or call, assuming that the underlying asset has the characteristics of a financial option. A widely used method for valuing a financial option is the Black-Scholes model, which is typically applied to "European options," those that can be exercised only at the expiration date of the option.[14]

Valuing Real Options Using a Decision Tree Framework

Table 8.3 (later in the chapter) shows how real options may affect the NPV of an acquisition in which management has identified two cash flow scenarios (i.e., a successful and an unsuccessful acquisition). Each pair of cash flow scenarios is associated with different options: The option to immediately acquire, delay, or abandon the acquisition. Each outcome is shown as a "branch" on a tree. Each branch shows the cash flows and probabilities of each scenario displayed as a timeline. The probability of realizing the "successful" cash flow projections is assumed to be 60% and that of realizing the "unsuccessful" one is 40%. The expected enterprise cash flow of the target firm is the sum of the future cash flows of the "successful" and "unsuccessful" scenarios multiplied by the estimated probability associated with each scenario. The target firm is assumed to have been acquired for $300 million, and the NPV is estimated using a 15% discount rate. The terminal value assumes a 5% growth rate. With an NPV of –$7 million, the immediate-investment option suggests that the acquisition should not be undertaken.

Recognizing that the target could be sold or liquidated, the expected NPV is $92 million, implying the acquisition should be undertaken. This assumes the target is sold or liquidated at the end of the third year following its acquisition for $152 million. Note that the cash flow in year 3 is $150 million, reflecting the difference between $152 million and the –$2 million in operating cash flow during the third year. The expected NPV with the option to delay is estimated at $34 million. Note that the investment is made after a one-year delay only if the potential acquirer feels confident that competitive market conditions will support the projected "successful" scenario cash flows. Consequently, the "unsuccessful" scenario's cash flows are zero. Figure 8.1 summarizes the results provided in Table 8.2 in a decision tree framework. Of the three options considered, valuing the target, including the value of the cash flows, with the option to abandon appears to be the most attractive investment strategy based on NPV. The values of the abandon and delay options are estimated as the difference between each of their NPVs and the NPV for the "immediate investment or acquisition" case.

Valuing Real Options Using the Black-Scholes Model

Options to assets whose cash flows have large variances and a long time before they expire are typically more valuable than those with smaller variances

---

[14] A more flexible method is the binomial valuation model used to value so-called American options, which may be exercised at any time before expiration. While the binomial model allows for changing key assumptions over time, it requires many inputs, making it far more complex and problematic than the Black-Sholes approach.

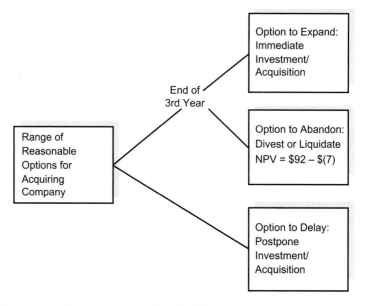

FIGURE 8.1   Real-options decision tree. *Note:* See Table 8.3 (later in the chapter) for data.

and less time remaining. The greater variance and time to expiration increases the chance that the factors affecting cash flows will change a project from one with a negative NPV to one with a positive NPV. If the values of certain variables are known, we can use the Black-Scholes model to establish a theoretical price for an option. The limitations of the Black-Scholes model are the difficulty in estimating key assumptions (particularly risk), its assumptions that interest rates and risk are constant, that it can be exercised only on the expiration date, and that taxes and transactions costs are minimal. The basic Black-Scholes formula for valuing a call option is as follows:

$$C = SN(d_1) - Ee^{-Rt}N(d_2) \tag{8.4}$$

where

$$C = \text{theoretical call option value}$$
$$d_1 = \frac{\ln(S/E) + [R + (1/2)\sigma^2]t}{\sigma\sqrt{t}}$$
$$d_2 = d_1 - \sigma\sqrt{t}$$

S = stock price or underlying asset price
E = exercise or strike price
R = risk free interest rate corresponding to the life of the option
σ^2 = variance (a measure of risk) of the stock's or underlying asset's return
t = time to expiration of the option
$N(d_1)$ and $N(d_2)$ = cumulative normal probability values of d_1 and d_2

TABLE 8.2 The Impact of Real Options on Valuing Mergers and Acquisitions

	Year 0	Year 1	Year 2	Year 3	Year 4	Year 5	Year 6	Year 7	Year 8	Year 9
First Branch: Option for Immediate Investment/Acquisition										
Enterprise Cash Flows		Projected Target Firm Cash Flows								
Successful Case	−300	30	35	40	45	50	55	60	65	
Unsuccessful Case	−300	−5	−5	−5	−5	−5	−5	−5	−5	
Weighted Cash Flows										
Successful Case (60%)	0	18	21	24	27	30	33	36	39	
Unsuccessful Case (40%)	0	−2	−2	−2	−2	−2	−2	−2	−2	
Expected Enterprise Cash Flow	−300	16	19	22	25	28	31	34	37	
Expected NPV Years 1–8 @ 15%										−166
Expected Terminal Value @ 13%, sustainable growth rate = 5%										159
Expected Total NPV										−7
Second Branch: Option to Abandon (Divest or Liquidate)										
Enterprise Cash Flows		Projected Target Firm Cash Flows								
Successful Case	−300	30	35	40	45	50	55	60	65	
Unsuccessful Case	−300	−5	−5	−5	−5	−5	−5	−5	−5	
Weighted Cash Flows										
Successful Case (60%)	0	18	21	24	27	30	33	36	39	
Unsuccessful Case (40%)	0	−2	−2	150	0	0	0	0	0	
Expected Enterprise Cash Flow	−300	16	19	174	27	30	33	36	39	

(Continued)

TABLE 8.2 (Continued)

	Year 0	Year 1	Year 2	Year 3	Year 4	Year 5	Year 6	Year 7	Year 8	Year 9
Expected NPV Years 1–6 @15%										–75
Expected Terminal Value @ 13%, sustainable growth rate = 5%										167
Expected Total NPV										92

Third Branch: Option to Delay Investment/Acquisition

	Year 0	Year 1	Year 2	Year 3	Year 4	Year 5	Year 6	Year 7	Year 8	Year 9
Enterprise Cash Flows	Projected Target Firm Cash Flows									
Successful Case	0	–300	35	40	45	50	55	60	65	70
Unsuccessful Case	0	–300	0	0	0	0	0	0	0	0
Weighted Cash Flows										
Successful Case (60%)	0	0	21	24	27	30	33	36	39	42
Unsuccessful Case (40%)	0	0	0	0	0	0	0	0	0	0
Expected Enterprise Cash Flow	0	–300	21	24	27	30	33	36	39	42
Expected NPV @ 15%										–146
Expected Terminal Value @ 13%, sustainable growth rate = 5%										180
Expected Total NPV										34

Note: The NPV for the delay option is discounted at the end of year 1, while the other options are discounted from year 0 (i.e., the present).

The term Ee^{-Rt} is the present value of the exercise price when continuous discounting is used. The terms $N(d_1)$ and $N(d_2)$, which involve the cumulative probability function, are the terms that take risk into account. $N(d_1)$ and $N(d_2)$ measure the probability that the value of the call option will pay off and the probability that the option will be exercised, respectively. These two values are Z-scores from the normal probability function, and they can be found in cumulative normal distribution function tables for the standard normal random variable in many statistics books.

The variance (i.e., risk) to be used in the Black-Scholes model can be estimated in a number of ways. First, risk could be estimated as the variance in the stock prices of similar firms or the associated cash flows. The average variance in the share prices of U.S. oil services companies could be used as the variance in valuing a real option associated with the potential purchase of an oil services firm.[15] Second, the variance of cash flows from similar prior investments can be used. A pharmaceutical company may use the variance associated with the cash flows of previously developed comparable drugs in valuing an option to invest in a new drug. A third method is to use commonly available software to conduct Monte Carlo simulation analyses.[16]

Assuming that the necessary inputs (e.g., risk) can be estimated, a real option can be valued as a put or call option. The net present value (NPV) of an investment can be adjusted for the value of the real option as follows:

$$\text{Total NPV} = \text{Present Value} - \text{Investment} + \text{Option Value} \qquad (8.5)$$

Option to Expand

To value a firm with an option to expand, the analyst must define the potential value of the option. For example, suppose a firm has an opportunity to enter a new market. The analyst must project cash flows that accrue to the firm if it enters the market. The cost of entering the market becomes the option's exercise price, and the present value of the expected cash flows resulting from entering the market becomes the value of the firm or underlying asset. The present value is likely to be less than the initial entry costs, or the firm would already have entered the market. The variance of the firm's value can be estimated by using the variances of the market values of publicly traded firms that currently participate in that market. The option's life is the length of time during which the firm expects to achieve a competitive advantage by entering the market now. Exhibit 8.8 illustrates how to value an option to expand.

---

[15] In another example, if an acquirer of an oil company recognizes that, in buying the target, it would have a call option (real option to expand) to develop the firm's oil reserves at a later date, it could choose to value separately the target as a stand-alone entity and the option to develop the firm's reserves at some time in the future. The variance in world oil prices may be used as a proxy for the risk associated with an option to develop the reserves.

[16] A Monte Carlo simulation is a mathematical method for accounting for risk in decision making.

EXHIBIT 8.8   VALUING AN OPTION TO EXPAND USING THE BLACK-SCHOLES MODEL

AJAX Inc. is negotiating to acquire Comet Inc. to broaden its product offering. Based on its projections of Comet's cash flows as a stand-alone business, AJAX cannot justify paying more than $150 million for Comet. However, Comet is insisting on a price of $160 million. Following additional due diligence, AJAX believes that if it applies its technology, Comet's product growth rate could be accelerated significantly. By buying Comet, AJAX is buying an option to expand in a market in which it is not participating currently by retooling Comet's manufacturing operations. The cost of retooling to utilize AJAX's technology fully requires an initial investment of $100 million. The present value of the expected cash flows from making this investment today is $80 million. Consequently, based on this information, paying the higher purchase price cannot be justified by making the investment in retooling now.

However, if Comet (employing AJAX's new technology) could be first to market with the new product offering, it could achieve a dominant market share. While the new product would be expensive to produce in small quantities, the cost of production is expected to fall as larger volumes are sold, making Comet the low-cost manufacturer. Moreover, because of patent protection, AJAX believes that it is unlikely that competitors will be able to develop a superior technology for at least ten years. An analysis of similar investments in the past suggests that the variance of the projected cash flows is 20%. The option is expected to expire in ten years, reflecting the time remaining on AJAX's patent. The current ten-year Treasury bond rate (corresponding to the expected term of the option) is 6%. Is the value of the option to expand, expressed as a call option, sufficient to justify paying Comet's asking price of $160 million [see Eq. (8.4)]?

Solution

Value of the asset (PV of cash flows from retooling Comet's operations)	= $80 million
Exercise price (PV of the cost of retooling Comet's operations)	= $100 million
Variance of the cash flows	= 0.20
Time to expiration	= 10 years
Risk-free interest rate	= .06

$$d_1 = \frac{\ln(\$80/\$100) + [0.06 + (1/2)0.2]10}{\sqrt{0.2}\sqrt{10}} = \frac{-0.2231 + 1.600}{0.4472 \times 3.1623} = \frac{1.3769}{1.4142} = 0.9736$$

$$d_2 = 0.9736 - 1.4142 = -0.4406$$

$$C = \$80(0.8340) - \$100(2.7183)^{-0.06\times10}(0.3300) = \$66.72 - \$18.11 =$$
$$\$48.61 \text{(value of the call option)}$$

The net present value of the investment in retooling Comet's operations, including the value of the call option, is $28.61 million [i.e., $80 – ($100 + $48.61)]. Including the value of the option, AJAX could pay Comet up to $178.61 million (i.e., $150 million + $28.61 million). Therefore, it does make sense for AJAX to exercise its option to retool Comet's operations, and AJAX can justify paying Comet its $160 million asking price.

Note: Z-values for d_1 and d_2 were obtained from a cumulative standardized normal distribution $N(d)$ table in Levine, Berenson, and Stephan (1999), pp. E6–E7.

Option to Delay

The underlying asset is the project to which the firm has exclusive rights. The current value is the present value of expected cash flows from undertaking the project now. The variance of cash flows from similar past projects or acquisitions can be used to estimate the variance for the project under consideration. A firm exercises an option to delay when it decides to postpone investing in a project. The option's exercise price is the cost of making the initial investment.

The option to delay expires whenever the exclusive rights to the project end. Since the option eventually expires, excess profits associated with having the option disappear as other competitors emerge to exploit the opportunity. This opportunity cost associated with delaying implementation of an investment is similar to an adjustment made to the Black-Scholes model for stocks that pay dividends. The payment of a dividend is equivalent to reducing the value of the stock, since such funds are not reinvested in the firm to support future growth. Consequently, for a project whose expected cash flows are spread evenly throughout the option period, each year the project is delayed, the firm will lose one year of profits that it could have earned. Therefore, the annual cost of delay is $1/n$, where n is the time period for which the option is valid. If cash flows are not spread evenly, the cost of delay may be estimated as the projected cash flow for the next period as a percent of the current present value (see Exhibit 8.9). Eq. (8.4) may be modified to reflect these considerations.

$$C = SN(d_1)e^{-DYt} - Ee^{-Rt}N(d_2)$$

(8.6)

where

$$d_1 = \frac{\ln(S/E) + [R - DY + (1/2)\sigma^2]t}{\sigma\sqrt{t}}$$

$$d_2 = d_1 - \sigma\sqrt{t}$$

$$DY = \text{dividend yield or opportunity cost}$$

Option to Abandon

For a project with a remaining life of n years, the value of continuing the project should be compared to its value in liquidation or sale (i.e., abandonment). The project should be continued if its value exceeds the liquidation value or

EXHIBIT 8.9   VALUING AN OPTION TO DELAY USING THE BLACK-SCHOLES MODEL

Aztec Corp. has an opportunity to acquire Pharmaceuticals Unlimited, which has a new cancer-fighting drug recently approved by the Food and Drug Administration. While current market studies indicate that the new drug's market acceptance will be slow due to competing drugs, it is believed that the drug will have meteoric growth potential in the long term as new applications are identified. The R&D and commercialization costs associated with exploiting new applications are expected to require an upfront investment of $60 million. However, Aztec can delay making this investment until it is more confident of the new drug's actual growth potential.

It is believed that Pharmaceuticals Unlimited's research and development efforts give it a five-year time period before competitors will have similar drugs on the market to exploit these new applications. However, if the higher growth for the new drug and its related applications does not materialize, Aztec estimates that the NPV for Pharmaceuticals Unlimited to be $(30). That is, if the new cancer-fighting drug does not realize its potential, it makes no sense for Aztec to acquire Pharmaceuticals Unlimited. Cash flows from previous drug introductions have exhibited a variance equal to 50% of the present value of the cash flows. Simulating alternative growth scenarios for this new drug provides an expected value of $40 million. The five-year Treasury bond rate (corresponding to the expected term of the option) is 6%. Despite the negative NPV associated with the acquisition, does the existence of the option to delay, valued as a call option, justify Aztec's acquiring Pharmaceuticals Unlimited [see Eq. (8.6)]?

Solution

Value of the asset (PV of projected cash flows for the new drug)	= $40 million
Exercise price (investment required to develop the new drug fully)	= $60 million
Variance of the cash flows	= 0.5
Time to expiration (t)	= 5 years
Risk-free interest rate	= 0.06
Dividend yield or opportunity cost (cost of delay = 1/5)	= 0.2

$$d_1 = \frac{ln(\$40/\$60) + [0.06 - 0.2 + (1/2)0.5]5}{\sqrt{0.5}\sqrt{5}} = \frac{-0.4055 + 0.5500}{0.7071 \times 2.2361} = \frac{0.1445}{1.5811} = 0.0914$$

$d_2 = 0.0914 - 10914 - 1.5811 = -1.4897$

$C = \$40(0.5359)2.7183^{-0.2 \times 5} - \$60(0.0681)(2.7183)^{-0.06 \times 5}$

$\quad = \$40(0.5359)0.3679 - \$60(0.0681)0.7408$

$\quad = 7.89 - 389 - 3.03 = \$4.86$ million (value of the call option)

The modest $4.86 million value of the call option is insufficient to offset the negative NPV of $30 million associated with the acquisition. Consequently, Aztec should not acquire Pharmaceuticals Unlimited.

Note: Z-values for d_1 and d_2 were obtained from a cumulative standardized normal distribution $N(d)$ table in Levine, Berenson, and Stephan (1999), pp. E6–E7.

sale value. Otherwise, the project should be abandoned. The option to abandon is equivalent to a put option (i.e., the right to sell an asset for a predetermined price at or before a stipulated time). The Black-Scholes formula for valuing a call option can be rewritten to value a put option (P) as follows [see Eq. (8.4)]:

$$P = S\{1 - N(d_2)\}e^{-Rt} - E\{1 - N(d_1)\}e^{-DYt}$$

(8.7)

where

$$P = \text{theoretical put option value}$$
$$d_1 = \frac{\ln(S/E) + [R - DY + (1/2)\sigma^2]t}{\sigma\sqrt{t}}$$
$$d_2 = d_1 - \sigma\sqrt{t}$$

Exhibit 8.10 illustrates how the abandonment or put option can be applied.

EXHIBIT 8.10   VALUING AN OPTION TO ABANDON USING THE BLACK-SCHOLES MODEL

BETA Inc. has agreed to acquire a 30% ownership stake in Bernard Mining for $225 million to finance the development of new mining operations. The mines are expected to have an economically useful life of 35 years. BETA estimates that the PV of its share of the cash flows would be $210 million, resulting in a negative NPV of $15 million (i.e., $210 million – $225 million). To induce BETA to make the investment, Bernard Mining has given BETA a put option enabling it to sell its share (i.e., abandon its investment) to Bernard at any point during the next five years for $175 million. The put option limits the downside risk to BETA.

In evaluating the terms of the deal, BETA needs to value the put option, whose present value will vary depending on when it is exercised. BETA estimates the average variance in the present values of future cash flows to be 20%, based on the variance of the share prices of publicly traded similar mining companies. Since the value of the mines will diminish over time as the reserves are depleted, the present value of the investment will diminish over time because there will be fewer years of cash flows remaining. The dividend yield or opportunity cost is estimated to be one divided by the number of years of profitable reserves remaining. The risk-free rate of return is 4%. Is the value of the put option sufficient to justify making the investment despite the negative net present value of the investment without the inclusion of the option value [see Eq. (8.7)]?

Solution

Present or expected value of BETA's 30% share of Bernard SA	= $210 million
Exercise price of put option	= $175 million
Time to expiration of put option	= 5
Variance	= 20%
Dividend yield (1/35)	= 0.029

$$d_1 = \frac{\ln(\$210/\$175) + [0.04 - 0.029 + (1/2)0.2]5}{\sqrt{0.2}\sqrt{5}} = \frac{0.1823 + 0.5550}{0.4472 \times 2.2361} = \frac{0.7373}{1.0} = 0.7373$$

$$d_2 = 0.7373 - 17373 - 1.000 = -0.2627$$

$$P = \$210 \times (1 - 01 - 0.6026) \times 2.7183^{-0.04 \times 5} - \$175 \times (1 - 01 - 0.7673) \times 2.7183^{-0.029 \times 5}$$
$$= \$210 \times 0.3974 \times 0.8187 - \$175 \times 0.2327 \times 0.8650 = \$33.10$$

The value of the put option represents the additional value created by reducing risk associated with the investment. This additional value justifies the investment, because the sum of the NPV of $(15) million and the put option of $33.10 million gives a total NPV of $18.10 million.

Note: Z-scores for d_1 and d_2 were obtained from a cumulative standardized normal distribution $N(d)$ table in Levine, Berenson, and Stephan (1999), pp. E6–E7.

DETERMINING WHEN TO USE THE DIFFERENT APPROACHES TO VALUATION

Table 8.3 summarizes when it is most appropriate to use each valuation method, including discounted cash flow discussed in detail in Chapter 7, as well as the relative-valuation, asset-oriented, replacement-cost, and real-options methods discussed in this chapter. If a controlling interest is desired, a control premium must be added to the estimated firm value to determine the purchase price. Recall that the comparable-recent-transactions method already contains a premium.

SOME THINGS TO REMEMBER

Relative-valuation and asset-oriented techniques offer alternatives to DCF estimates. Since no single valuation approach ensures accuracy, analysts often

TABLE 8.3   When to Use Various Valuation Methodologies

Methodology	Use This Methodology When:
Discounted Cash Flow	• The firm is publicly traded or private with identifiable cash flows • A start-up has some history to facilitate cash flow forecasts • An analyst has a long time horizon • An analyst has confidence in forecasting the firm's cash flows • Current or near-term earnings or cash flows are negative but are expected to turn positive in the future • A firm's competitive advantage is expected to be sustainable • The magnitude and timing of cash flows vary significantly
Comparable Companies	• There are many firms exhibiting similar growth, return, and risk characteristics • An analyst has a short-term time horizon • Prior, current, or near-term earnings or cash flows are positive • An analyst has confidence that the markets are, on average, right • Sufficient information to predict cash flows is lacking • Firms are cyclical. For P/E ratios, use normalized earnings (i.e., earnings averaged throughout the business cycle) • Growth rate differences among firms are large. Use the PEG ratio
Comparable Transactions	• Recent transactions of similar firms exist • An analyst has a short-term time horizon • An analyst has confidence the markets are, on average, right • Sufficient information to predict cash flows is lacking
Same or Comparable Industry	• Firms within an industry or a comparable industry are substantially similar in terms of profitability, growth, and risk • An analyst has confidence the markets are, on average, right • Sufficient information to predict cash flows is lacking
Replacement-Cost Approach	• An analyst wants to know the current cost of replicating a firm's assets • The firm's assets are easily identifiable, tangible, and separable • The firm's earnings or cash flows are negative
Tangible Book Value	• The firms' assets are highly liquid • The firm is a financial services or product distribution business • The firm's earnings and cash flows are negative
Breakup Value	• The sum of the value of the businesses or product lines comprising a firm are believed to exceed its value as a going concern
Liquidation Value	• An analyst wants to know asset values if they were liquidated today • Assets are separable, tangible, and marketable • Firms are bankrupt or subject to substantial financial distress • An orderly liquidation is possible
Real Options (Contingent Claims)	• Additional value can be created if management has a viable option to expand, delay, or abandon an investment • Assets not currently generating cash flows have the potential to do so • The markets have not valued the management decision-making flexibility associated with the option • Assets have characteristics most resembling financial options • The asset owner has some degree of exclusivity (e.g., a patent)

choose to use a weighted average of several valuation methods to increase their level of confidence in the final estimate. Real options refer to management's ability to revise corporate investment decisions after they have been made.

DISCUSSION QUESTIONS

8.1 Does the application of the comparable companies' valuation method require the addition of an acquisition premium? Why or why not?

8.2 Which is generally considered more accurate: the comparable-companies method or the recent-transactions method? Explain your answer.

8.3 What key assumptions are implicit in using the comparable-companies valuation method? Also the recent-comparable-transactions method?

8.4 Explain the primary differences between the income (discounted cash flow), market-based, and asset-oriented valuation methods.

8.5 Under what circumstances might it be more appropriate to use relative-valuation methods rather than the DCF approach? Be specific.

8.6 PEG ratios allow for the adjustment of relative-valuation methods for the expected growth of the firm. How might this be helpful in selecting potential acquisition targets? Be specific.

8.7 How is the liquidation value of a firm calculated? Why is the assumption of orderly liquidation important?

8.8 What are real options, and how are they applied in valuing acquisitions?

8.9 Give examples of pre- and postclosing real options. Be specific.

8.10 Conventional DCF analysis does not incorporate the effects of real options into the valuation of an asset. How might an analyst incorporate the potential impact of real options into conventional DCF valuation methods?

Answers to these Chapter Discussion Questions are available in the Online Instructor's Manual for instructors using this book.

QUESTIONS FROM THE CFA CURRICULUM

8.11 In asset-based valuation models, the intrinsic value of a common share of stock is based on the:
  a. Estimated market value of the company's asset.
  b. Estimated market value of the company's assets plus liabilities.
  c. Estimated market value of the company's assets minus liabilities.
  Source: 2011 Equity Valuation: Concepts and Basic Tools, Reading 60, question 3.

8.12 An analyst makes the following statement: "Use of P/E and other multiples for analysis is not effective because the multiples are based on

CFA Institute

historical data and because not all companies have positive accounting earnings." The analyst's statement is most likely:

   a. Inaccurate with respect to both historical data and earnings.

   b. Accurate with respect to historical data and inaccurate with respect to earnings.

   c. Inaccurate with respect to historical data and accurate with respect to earnings.

   Source: 2011 Equity Valuation: Concept and Basic Tools, Reading 60, question 23.

8.13 An analyst prepared a table of the average trailing 12-month price to earnings (P/E), price to cash flow (P/CF), and price to sales (P/S) for the Tanaka Corporation for the years 2005 to 2008.

Year	P/E	P/CF	P/S
2005	4.9	5.4	1.2
2006	6.1	8.6	1.5
2007	8.3	7.3	1.9
2008	9.2	7.9	2.3

As of the date of the valuation in 2009, the trailing 12-month P/E, P/CF, and P/S were 9.2, 8.0, and 2.5, respectively. Based on the information provided, the analyst reasonably concludes Tanaka shares are most likely:

   a. Overvalued.

   b. Undervalued.

   c. Fairly valued.

   Source: Equity Valuation: Concepts and Basic Tools, Reading 60, question 24.

8.14 Which of the following is most likely considered a weakness of present-value models?

   a. Present-value models cannot be used for companies that do not pay dividends.

   b. Small changes in model assumptions and inputs can result in large changes in the computed intrinsic value of the security.

   c. The value of the security depends on the investor's holding period; thus, comparing valuations of different companies for different investors is difficult.

   Source: 2011 Equity Valuation: Concepts and Basic Tools, Reading 60, question 36.

Answers to questions from the CFA curriculum are available in the Online Student Companion site to this book in a file folder entitled CFA Curriculum Questions and Solutions.

PRACTICE PROBLEMS AND ANSWERS

8.15 BigCo's chief financial officer is trying to determine a fair value for PrivCo, a nonpublicly traded firm that BigCo is considering acquiring. Several of

PrivCo's competitors, Ion International and Zenon, are publicly traded. Ion and Zenon have P/E ratios of 20 and 15, respectively. Moreover, Ion and Zenon's shares trade at a multiple of earnings before interest, taxes, depreciation, and amortization (EBITDA) of ten and eight, respectively. BigCo estimates that next year PrivCo will achieve net income and EBITDA of $4 million and $8 million, respectively. To gain a controlling interest in the firm, BigCo expects to have to pay at least a 30% premium to the firm's market value. What should BigCo expect to pay for PrivCo?

a. Based on P/E ratios?

Answer: $91 million

b. Based on EBITDA?

Answer: $93.6 million

8.16 LAFCO Industries believes that its two primary product lines, automotive and commercial aircraft valves, are becoming obsolete rapidly. Its free cash flow is diminishing quickly as it loses market share to new firms entering its industry. LAFCO has $200 million in debt outstanding. Senior management expects the automotive and commercial aircraft valve product lines to generate $25 million and $15 million, respectively, in earnings before interest, taxes, depreciation, and amortization next year. The operating liabilities associated with these two product lines are minimal. Senior management also believes that it will not be able to upgrade these product lines because of declining cash flow and excessive current leverage. A competitor to its automotive valve business last year sold for ten times EBITDA. Moreover, a company similar to its commercial aircraft valve product line sold last month for 12 times EBITDA. Estimate LAFCO's breakup value before taxes.

Answer: $230 million

8.17 Siebel Incorporated, a nonpublicly traded company, has 2009 after-tax earnings of $20 million, which are expected to grow at 5% annually into the foreseeable future. The firm is debt free, capital spending equals the firm's rate of depreciation, and the annual change in working capital is expected to be minimal. The firm's beta is estimated to be 2.0, the ten-year Treasury bond is 5%, and the historical risk premium of stocks over the risk-free rate is 5.5%. Publicly traded Rand Technology, a direct competitor of Siebel's, was sold recently at a purchase price of 11 times its 2009 after-tax earnings, which included a 20% premium over its current market price. Aware of the premium paid for the purchase of Rand, Siebel's equity owners would like to determine what it might be worth if they were to attempt to sell the firm in the near future. They chose to value the firm using the discounted-cash-flow and comparable-recent-transactions methods. They believe that either method provides an equally valid estimate of the firm's value.

a. What is the value of Siebel using the DCF method?

Answer: $229.1 million

b. What is the value using the comparable-recent-transactions method?

Answer: $220 million

c. What would be the value of the firm if we combine the results of both methods?
   Answer: $224.5 million

8.18 Titanic Corporation reached an agreement with its creditors to voluntarily liquidate its assets and use the proceeds to pay off as much of its liabilities as possible. The firm anticipates that it will be able to sell off its assets in an orderly fashion, realizing as much as 70% of the book value of its receivables, 40% of its inventory, and 25% of its net fixed assets (excluding land). However, the firm believes that the land on which it is located can be sold for 120% of book value. The firm has legal and professional expenses associated with the liquidation process of $2.9 million. The firm has only common stock outstanding. Using Table 8.4, estimate the amount of cash that would remain for the firm's common shareholders once all assets have been liquidated.
   Answer: **$1.3 million**

TABLE 8.4   Titanic Corporation Balance Sheet

Balance Sheet Item	Book Value of Assets	Liquidation Value
Cash	$10	
Accounts receivable	$20	
Inventory	$15	
Net fixed assets excluding land	$8	
Land	$6	
Total assets	$59	
Total liabilities	$35	
Shareholders' equity	$24	

8.19 Best's Foods is seeking to acquire the Heinz Baking Company, whose shareholders' equity and goodwill are $41 million and $7 million, respectively. A comparable bakery was recently acquired for $400 million, 30% more than its tangible book value (TBV). What was the tangible book value of the recently acquired bakery? How much should Best's Foods expect to have to pay for the Heinz Baking Company? Show your work.
   Answer: The TBV of the recently acquired bakery = $307.7 million, and the likely purchase price of Heinz = $44.2 million.

8.20 Delhi Automotive Inc. is the leading supplier of specialty fasteners for passenger cars in the U.S. market, with an estimated 25% share of this $5 billion market. Delhi's rapid growth in recent years has been fueled by high levels of reinvestment in the firm. While this has resulted in the firm's having "state-of-the-art" plants, it has also resulted in the firm's showing limited profitability and positive cash flow. Delhi is privately owned and has announced that it is going to undertake an initial public offering in the near future. Investors know that economies of scale are important in this high-fixed-cost industry and understand that market share is an important determinant of future profitability. Thornton Auto Inc., a publicly traded firm and the leader in this market, has an estimated market share of 38% and an $800 million market value. How should investors value the Delhi IPO? Show your work.

Answer: $526.3 million

8.21 Photon Inc. is considering acquiring one of its competitors. Photon's management wants to buy a firm it believes is most undervalued. The firm's three major competitors, AJAX, BABO, and COMET, have current market values of $375 million, $310 million, and $265 million, respectively. AJAX's FCFE is expected to grow at 10% annually, while BABO's and COMET's FCFEs are projected to grow by 12% and 14% per year, respectively. AJAX, BABO, and COMET's current year FCFE are $24 million, $22 million, and $17 million, respectively. The industry average price-to-FCFE ratio and growth rate are 10% and 8%, respectively. Estimate the market value of each of the three potential acquisition targets based on the information provided. Which firm is the most undervalued? Which firm is most overvalued? Show your work.

Answer: AJAX is most overvalued, and Comet is most undervalued.

8.22 Acquirer Incorporated's management believes that the most reliable way to value a potential target firm is by averaging multiple valuation methods, since all methods have their shortcomings. Consequently, Acquirer's chief financial officer estimates that the value of Target Inc. could range, before an acquisition premium is added, from a high of $650 million using discounted cash flow analysis to a low of $500 million using the comparable-companies relative-valuation method. A valuation based on a recent comparable transaction is $672 million. The CFO anticipates that Target Inc.'s management and shareholders would be willing to sell for a 20% acquisition premium, based on the premium paid for the recent comparable transaction. The CEO asks the CFO to provide a single estimate of the value of Target Inc. based on the three estimates. In calculating a weighted average of the three estimates, she gives a value of 0.5 to the recent transactions method, 0.3 to the DCF estimate, and 0.2 to the comparable-companies estimate. What is the weighted average estimate she gives to the CEO? Show your work.

Answer: $690 million

8.23 An investor group has the opportunity to purchase a firm whose primary asset is ownership of the exclusive rights to develop a parcel of undeveloped land sometime during the next five years. Without considering the value of the option to develop the property, the investor group believes the net present value of the firm is $(10) million. However, to convert the property to commercial use (i.e., exercise the option), the investors have to invest $60 million immediately in infrastructure improvements. The primary uncertainty associated with the property is how rapidly the surrounding area will grow. Based on their experience with similar properties, the investors estimate that the variance of the projected cash flows is 5% of NPV, which is $55 million. Assume the risk-free rate of return is 4%. What is the value of the call option the investor group would obtain by buying the firm? Is it sufficient to justify the acquisition of the firm? Show your work.

Answer: The value of the option is $13.47 million. The investor group should buy the firm, since the value of the option more than offsets the $(10) million NPV of the firm if the call option were not exercised.

8.24 Acquirer Company's management believes that there is a 60% chance that Target Company's free cash flow to the firm will grow at 20% per year during the next five years from this year's level of $5 million. Sustainable growth beyond the fifth year is estimated at 4% per year. However, they also believe that there is a 40% chance that cash flow will grow at half that annual rate during the next five years and then at a 4% rate thereafter. The discount rate is estimated to be 15% during the high-growth period and 12% during the sustainable-growth period. What is the expected value of Target Company?

Answer: $94.93 million

Solutions to these Practice Problems are available in the Online Instructor's Manual for instructors using this book.

CASE STUDY 8.1
Is Texas Instruments Overpaying for National Semiconductor? as Always, it Depends

Key Points

- Valuation is far more an art than a science, and understanding the limitations of individual valuation methods is critical.
- Averaging multiple valuation methods is often the most reliable means of valuing a firm.
- Evaluating success of an individual acquisition is best viewed in the context of an acquirer's overall business strategy.

Value is in the eye of the beholder. Various indicators often provide a wide range of estimates. No single method seems to provide consistently accurate valuation estimates. Which method the analyst ultimately selects often depends on the availability of data and on the analyst's own biases. Whether a specific acquisition should be viewed as successful depends on the extent to which it helps the acquirer realize a successful business strategy.

At $25 per share in cash, Texas Instruments (TI) announced on March 5, 2011, that it had reached an agreement to acquire National

Semiconductor (NS). The resulting 78% premium over NS's closing share price the day prior to the announcement raised eyebrows. After showing little activity in the days immediately prior to the announcement, NS's share price soared by 71% and TI's share price rose by 2.25% immediately following the announcement. While it is normal for the target's share price to rise sharply to reflect the magnitude of the premium, the acquirer's share price sometimes remains unchanged or even declines. The increase in TI's share price seems to suggest agreement among investors that the acquisition made sense. However, within days, analysts began to ask the question that bedevils so many takeovers. Did Texas Instruments overpay for National Semiconductor?

Whether TI overpaid depends on how you measure value and how you interpret the results. Looking at recent semiconductor industry transactions, the magnitude of the premium is almost twice the average paid on 196 acquisitions in the semiconductor industry during the last several years. Based on price-to-earnings ratio analysis, TI paid 19.1 times NS's 2012 estimated earnings, as compared to 14.3 times industry average earnings for the same year. This implied that TI was willing to pay $19.10 per share for each dollar of the next year's earnings per NS share. In contrast, investors were generally willing to pay on average on $14.30 for each dollar of 2012 earnings for the average firm in the semiconductor industry. Using a ratio of market capitalization (market price) to sales, it also appears that

TI's premium is excessive. TI paid four times NS's current annual sales, well above other key competitors. such as Maxim Integrated Products and Intersil, which traded at 3.2 and 1.8 times sales, respectively.

The enterprise-value-to-sales ratio compares the value of a firm to its revenue and gives investors an idea of how much it costs to buy the company's sales. Some analysts believe that it is a more useful indicator than a market-capitalization-to-sales ratio, which considers only how equity investors value each dollar of sales, since the market-cap-to-sales ratio ignores that the firm's current debt must be repaid. By this measure, TI is willing to pay $4.40 for each dollar of revenue, as compared to $3.80 per dollar of sales for the average semiconductor firm. Another useful valuation ratio, the price-to-earnings ratio divided by the earnings growth rate (PEG ratio), also suggested that TI might have overpaid. The PEG ratio relates what investors are willing to pay for a firm per dollar of earnings to the growth rate of earnings. At 1.28 prior to the TI takeover, NS was trading at a premium to its growth rate according to this measure. After the acquisition, the PEG ratio jumped to 2.09.

While suggesting strongly that TI overpaid, these measures may be seriously biased. A large percentage of TI's and NS's revenue comes from the production and sale of analog chips, a rapidly growing segment of the semiconductor industry. Part of the growth in analog chips is expected to come from the explosive growth of smartphones and tablets, where their use in regulating electricity consumption is crucial to longer battery life. Consequently, many of the previous acquisitions in the semiconductor industry are of firms that do not compete in the analog chip market; as such, they are not entirely comparable. Moreover, many of these acquisitions came amidst a sluggish economic recovery and were made at "fire-sale" prices.

With the exception of comparisons with recent comparable transactions, all of these valuation measures do not consider directly the value of synergy. There was little overlap between TI's and NS's product offering. TI believes that they can increase substantially NS's sales by selling their products through TI's much larger sales force. Furthermore, TI added 12,000 new analog chip products, bringing its combined offering to more than 30,000 products. TI also gets access to a number of analog engineers, who are highly specialized and relatively rare. Finally, in the highly fragmented semiconductor industry, consolidation among competitors may lead to higher average selling prices than would have been realized otherwise.

The acquisition of NS by TI should be viewed in the context of a longer-term strategy in which TI is seeking an ever-increasing share of the $42 billion analog chip market, which many analysts expect to outgrow the overall semiconductor market during the next three to five years. Following the financial crisis in 2008, TI acquired analog chip manufacturing facilities at "fire-sale" prices to boost the firm's capacity. The NS acquisition will give TI a 17% share of this rapidly growing market segment.

Discussion Questions

1. Most studies purporting to measure the success or failure of acquisitions base their findings of the performance of acquirer share prices on the announcement date of the acquisition or on accounting performance measures during the three to five years following the acquisition. This requires that acquisitions be evaluated on a "stand-alone" basis. Do you agree or disagree with this methodology? Why or why not?

2. Despite their limitations, why is the judicious application of the various valuation methods critical to the acquirer in determining an appropriate purchase price?

3. Scenario analysis involves valuing businesses based on different sets assumptions about the future. What are the advantages and disadvantages of applying this methodology in determining an appropriate purchase price?

4. Do you agree or disagree with the following statement? Valuation is more an art than a science. Explain your answer.

Solutions to these questions are provided in the Online Instructor's Guide accompanying this manual.

Applying Financial Models
To Value, Structure, and Negotiate
Mergers and Acquisitions

There are two kinds of forecasters: the ones who don't know and the ones who don't know they don't know. —**John Kenneth Galbraith**

INSIDE M&A: HP BUYS EDS—THE ROLE OF FINANCIAL MODELS IN DECISION MAKING

KEY POINTS

- Financial models address valuation, deal structuring, and financing issues.
- Financial models enable the rapid consideration of alternative scenarios by changing key assumptions underlying valuation, deal structuring, and financing decisions.
- As such, models also help define the range of risks associated with an investment.

Personal computer printer behemoth Hewlett-Packard (HP) had just announced its agreement to buy Electronic Data Systems (EDS) for $13.9 billion in an all-cash deal. The purchase price represented a 33% premium for EDS, a systems integration, consulting, and services firm. Expressing their dismay, investors drove HP's share price down by 11% in a single day following the announcement. In a meeting arranged to respond to questions about the deal, HP's chief executive, Mark Hurd, found himself barraged by concerns about how the firm intended to recover the sizeable premium it had paid for EDS. The CEO had been a Wall Street darling since he had assumed his position three years earlier. Under his direction, the firm's profits rose sharply as it successfully cut costs while growing revenue and integrating several acquisitions. Asked

299

how HP expected to generate substantial synergies by combining two very different organizations, Mr. Hurd indicated that the firm and its advisors had done "double-digit thousands of hours" in due diligence and financial modeling and that they were satisfied that the cost synergies were there. In an effort to demonstrate how conservative they had been, the CEO indicated that potential revenue synergies had not even been included in their financial models. However, he was convinced that there were significant upside revenue opportunities.

CHAPTER OVERVIEW

Financial models assess the implications of alternative valuation scenarios, deal structures, and financing arrangements related to M&As. This chapter illustrates a process for building such models and how they may be used in the deal-negotiating process. The spreadsheets and formulas for the models described in this chapter are available in the file folder entitled "Mergers and Acquisitions Valuation and Structuring Model" on the companion website to this book (http://booksite.elsevier.com/9780123854872). A review of this chapter is available in the file folder entitled "Student Study Guide" on the companion website, which also contains a discussion of how to interpret the financial ratios commonly generated by financial models. Appendix A provides more detail on how to use the companion site M&A model, and Appendix B discusses common methods of "balancing" such models.

LIMITATIONS OF FINANCIAL DATA

The quality of a model's output is dependent on the reliability of data used to build the model. Consequently, analysts must understand on what basis numbers are collected and reported.

Generally Accepted Accounting Principles and International Standards

U.S. public companies prepare their financial statements in accordance with *Generally Accepted Accounting Principles* (GAAP). GAAP financial statements are those prepared in agreement with guidelines established by the Financial Accounting Standards Board (FASB). GAAP is a rules-based system, giving explicit instructions for every situation that the FASB has anticipated. In contrast, *international accounting standards* (IAS) are a principles-based system, with more generalized standards. GAAP and IAS currently exhibit significant differences.

When, and the extent to which GAAP and IAS systems converge are open questions. While it may be possible to establish consistent accounting standards across countries, it is unclear if adherence to such standards can be enforced without a global regulatory authority, and it is even less clear if individual countries would submit to such an authority. In the absence of strict enforcement of consistent standards, do the benefits of converging accounting systems outweigh the cost of implementing a new system? By some estimates, the cost of converting to international accounting standards for S&P 500 companies could range from $40 billion to $60 billion over three years. While increased consistency and transparency could lower the cost of capital, the lack of an enforcement mechanism may limit the extent to which this occurs.[1] As will be discussed in Chapter 12, after a two-year study, the U.S. Securities and Exchange Commission decided in mid-2012 to postpone any decision to push for convergence.

Pro Forma Accounting

Pro forma financial statements present financial data in a way that may describe more accurately a firm's current or projected performance. Because there are no accepted standards for pro forma accounting, pro forma statements may deviate substantially from GAAP statements. Pro forma statements show what an acquirer's and target's combined financial performance would look like if they were merged. Although public firms still are required to file their financial statements with the Securities and Exchange Commission in accordance with GAAP, companies often argue that pro forma statements provide investors with a more realistic view of a company's core performance than does GAAP reporting. Although pro forma statements provide useful insight into how a proposed combination of businesses might look, such liberal accounting techniques can easily hide a company's poor performance. Exhibit 9.1 suggests some ways in which an analyst can tell if a firm is engaging in inappropriate accounting practices.

EXHIBIT 9.1 ACCOUNTING DISCREPANCY RED FLAGS

1. **The source of the revenue is questionable.** Examples include revenue from selling to an affiliated party or selling something to a customer in exchange for something other than cash.
2. **Income is inflated by nonrecurring gains.** Gains on the sale of assets may be inflated by an artificially low book value of the assets sold.
3. **Deferred revenue shows a large increase.** Deferred revenue increases as a firm collects money from customers in advance of delivering its products and is reduced as the products are delivered. A jump in this item could mean the firm is having trouble delivering its products.
4. **Reserves for bad debt are declining as a percentage of revenue.** This implies the firm may be boosting revenue by not reserving enough to cover losses from uncollectable accounts.

---

[1] Reilly, David, "Convergence Flaws," Presentation to the American Accounting Association, Tampa, Florida, January 29, 2011.

5. **Growth in accounts receivable exceeds substantially the increase in revenue or inventory.** This may mean that a firm is having difficulty in selling its products (i.e., inventories are accumulating) or that it is having difficulty collecting what it is owed.

6. **The growth in net income is much different from the growth in cash from operations.** Because it is more difficult to "manage" cash flow than to "manage" net income (often distorted due to improper revenue recognition), this could indicate that net income is being misstated.

7. **An increasing gap between a firm's income reported on its financial statements and its tax income.** In general, the relationship between book and tax accounting is likely to remain constant over time, unless there are changes in tax rules or accounting standards.

8. **Unexpected large asset write-offs.** This may reflect management inertia in incorporating changing business circumstances into its accounting estimates.

9. **Extensive use of related-party transactions.** Such transactions may not be subject to the same discipline and high standards of integrity as unrelated-party transactions.

10. **Changes in auditing firms that are not well justified.** The firm may be seeking a firm that will accept its aggressive accounting positions.

THE MODEL-BUILDING PROCESS

The logic underlying the Excel-based M&A model found on the companion website follows the process discussed in this chapter (Table 9.1). First, value the acquirer and target as *stand-alone businesses*, those whose financial statements reflect all the costs incurred and revenues realized by the business. Second, value the consolidated acquirer and target firms, including the effects of synergy.[2] Third, determine the initial offer price for the target firm. Fourth, determine the acquirer's ability to finance the purchase using an appropriate financial structure.

Step 1. Value Acquirer (PV_A) and Target (PV_T) Firms as Stand-Alone Businesses

A merger or acquisition makes sense to the acquirer's shareholders only if the combined value of the target and acquiring firms exceeds the sum of their stand-alone values. Therefore, the first step of the model-building process outlined in Table 9.1 requires the valuation of each firm on a stand-alone basis, which necessitates understanding the basis of industry competition.

[2]The appropriate discount rate for the combined firms is generally the target's cost of capital; if the two firms have similar risk profiles and are based in the same country, either firm's cost of capital could be used. It is particularly important to use the target's cost of capital if the acquirer is merging with a higher-risk business, resulting in an increase in the acquirer's cost of capital.

TABLE 9.1   The Mergers and Acquisitions Model-Building Process

Step 1. Value Acquirer and Target as Stand-Alone Firms	Step 2. Value Acquirer and Target Firms, Including Synergy	Step 3. Determine Initial Offer Price for Target Firm Transaction	Step 4. Determine Combined Firms' Ability to Finance
1. Understand specific firm and industry competitive dynamics (see Chapter 4: Figure 4.2)	1. Estimate: a. Sources and destroyers of value and b. Implementation costs incurred to realize synergy	1. Estimate minimum and maximum purchase price range	1. Estimate impact of alternative financing structures
2. Normalize 3–5 years of historical financial data (i.e., add or subtract nonrecurring losses/ expenses or gains to smooth data)	2. Consolidate the acquirer and target stand-alone values, including the effects of synergy	2. Determine the amount of synergy the acquirer is willing to share with target shareholders	2. Select a financing structure that: a. Meets the acquirer's required financial returns b. Meets the target's primary needs c. Does not raise the cost of debt or violate loan covenants d. d. Minimizes EPS dilution and short-term reduction in financial returns
3. Project normalized cash flow based on expected market growth and industry competition; calculate stand-alone value of the acquirer and the target	3. Estimate the value of net synergy (i.e., consolidated firms, including synergy less stand-alone values of acquirer and target)	3. Determine the appropriate composition of the offer price (i.e., cash, stock, or some combination)	

Note: Key assumptions made for each step should be clearly stated.

Understand Specific Firm and Industry Competitive Dynamics

A valuation's accuracy depends on understanding the historical competitive dynamics of the industry and of the company within the industry as well as the reliability of the data used in the valuation. *Competitive dynamics* simply refers to the factors within the industry that determine industry profitability and cash flow. A careful examination of historical information can provide insights into key relationships among various operating variables. Examples of relevant historical relationships include seasonal or cyclical movements in the data, the relationship between fixed and variable expenses, and the impact on revenue of changes in product prices and unit sales.

If the factors affecting sales, profit, and cash flow historically are expected to exert the same influence in the future, a firm's financial statements may be projected by extrapolating historical growth rates in key variables, such as revenue. If the factors affecting sales growth are expected to change due to the introduction of new products, total revenue growth may accelerate from its historical trend. In contrast, the emergence of additional competitors may limit revenue growth by eroding the firm's market share and selling prices. Answers to the questions posed in Figure 9.1 are generally supplied by management and provide helpful insights into how financial performance can be projected.

Normalize Historical Data

To ensure that these historical relationships can be accurately defined, it is necessary to *normalize* the data by removing nonrecurring changes and questionable accounting practices. Cash flow may be adjusted by adding back unusually large increases in reserves or deducting large decreases in reserves from free cash flow to the firm. Similar adjustments can be made for significant nonrecurring gains or losses on the sale of assets or nonrecurring expenses, such as those associated with the settlement of a lawsuit or warranty claim. Monthly revenue

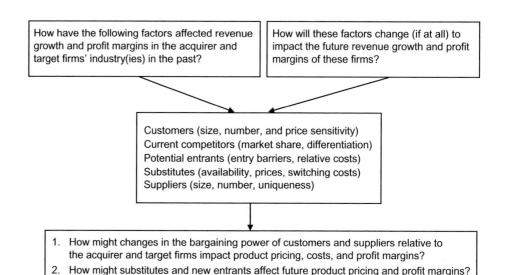

FIGURE 9.1 Using the Porter Five Forces Model[a] to project acquirer and target financial performance.

[a] See Chapter 4 and Exhibit 4-2 for a more detailed discussion of the Porter Five Forces Model.

may be aggregated into quarterly or even annual data to minimize period-to-period distortions in earnings or cash flow resulting from inappropriate accounting practices.[3]

Common-size financial statements are frequently used to uncover data irregularities. These statements may be constructed by calculating the percentage each line item of the income statement, balance sheet, and cash flow statement is of annual sales for each quarter or year for which historical data are available. Common-size financial statements are useful for comparing businesses of different sizes in the same industry at a specific moment in time. Called *cross-sectional comparisons*, such analyses may indicate that the ratio of capital spending to sales for the target firm is much less than for other firms in the industry. This discrepancy may simply reflect "catch-up" spending at the target's competitors, or it may suggest that the target is deferring necessary plant and equipment spending. To determine which is true, it is necessary to calculate common-size financial statements for the target firm and its primary competitors over a number of consecutive periods. Called a *multiperiod comparison*, these analyses help confirm whether the target simply has completed a large portion of capital spending that others in the industry are undertaking currently or is behind in making necessary expenditures.[4]

Financial ratio analysis is the calculation of performance ratios from data in a firm's financial statements to identify the firm's financial strengths and weaknesses. Such analysis helps identify potential problems requiring further examination during due diligence. Because ratios adjust for firm size, they enable the analyst to compare a firm's ratios with industry averages to discover if the company is out of line with competitors. A successful competitor's performance ratios may be used if industry average data[5] are not available. A file entitled "A Primer on Applying and Interpreting Financial Ratios" on the companion website discusses how to use such ratios.

Project Normalized Cash Flow

Normalized cash flows should be projected for at least five years, and possibly more, until they turn positive or the growth rate slows to what is believed to be a sustainable pace. Projections should reflect the best information about

---

[3]While public companies are required to provide financial data for only the current year and the two prior years, it is highly desirable to use data spanning at least one business cycle (i.e., about five to seven years) to identify trends.

[4]Even if it is not possible to collect sufficient data to undertake cross-sectional and multiperiod comparisons of both the target firm and its direct competitors, constructing common-size statements for the target firm only can provide useful insights. Abnormally large increases or decreases in these ratios from one period to the next highlight the need for further examination to explain why these fluctuations occurred.

[5]Industry data are found in such publications as *The Almanac of Business and Industrial Financial Ratios* (Prentice Hall), *Annual Statement Studies* (Robert Morris Associates), *Dun's Review* (Dun and Bradstreet), *Industry Norms and Key Business Ratios* (Dun and Bradstreet), and Value Line Investment Survey for Company and Industry Ratios.

product demand growth, future pricing, technological changes, new competitors, new product and service offerings from current competitors, potential supply disruptions, increases in raw material and labor costs, and possible new product or service substitutes. Projections also should include the revenue and costs associated with known new product introductions and capital expenditures, as well as additional expenses, required to maintain or expand operations by the acquiring and target firms during the forecast period.

A simple model to project cash flow involves the projection of revenue and the various components of cash flow as a percent of projected revenue. For example, cost of sales, depreciation, gross capital spending, and the change in working capital are projected as a percent of projected revenue. What percentage is applied to projected revenue for these components of free cash flow to the firm may be determined by calculating their historical ratio to revenue. In this simple model, revenue drives cash flow growth. Thus, attention must be given to projecting revenue by forecasting unit growth and selling prices, the product of which provides estimated revenue. Common projection methods include *trend extrapolation* and *scenario analysis*.[6]

To illustrate this process, consider the income, balance sheet, and cash flow statements for Alanco Technologies Inc., a provider of wireless systems for tracking the movement of freight and people. In 2010, Alanco acquired StarTrak Systems, a provider of global positioning satellite tracking and wireless subscription data services to the transportation industry. Alanco believed that the acquisition would help it develop new markets for its products and services for wireless tracking and management of people and assets. With StarTrak less than 10% of Alanco's size, Alanco believed that most of the synergy would come from cross-selling its products to StarTrak's customers rather than from cost savings. Alanco's management understood that a successful acquisition would create more shareholder value at an acceptable level of risk than if the firm continued its current "go it alone" strategy. Consequently, Alanco valued its own business on a stand-alone basis (Table 9.2), StarTrak's business as a stand-alone unit (financials not shown), estimated potential synergy (Table 9.3), and combined firms, including the effects of potential synergy (Table 9.4). The difference between the combined valuation with synergy and the sum of the two businesses valued as stand-alone operations provided an estimate of the potential incremental value that could be created from the acquisition of StarTrak.

Note that the layout in Table 9.2 is identical to those worksheets provided for the M&A Valuation and Structuring Model on the companion website. The assumptions provided in the top panel drive the forecast of the various line items for the income, balance sheet, and cash flow statements. The historical financial

---

[6]Trend extrapolation entails extending present trends into the future using historical growth rates or multiple-regression techniques. Scenario analysis projects multiple outlooks, with each differing in terms of key variables (e.g., growth in gross domestic product, industry sales growth, fluctuations in exchange rates) or issues (e.g., competitive new product introductions, new technologies, and new regulations).

TABLE 9.2 Step 1: Acquirer (Alanco) 5-Year Forecast and Stand-Alone Valuation

Forecast Assumptions		2011	2012	2013	2014	2015
Net Sales Growth Rate (%)		4.0	4.0	4.0	4.0	4.0
Cost of Sales (Variable)/Sales %		52.5	51.5	51.0	50.5	50.5
Depreciation & Amortization/Gross Fixed Assets (%)		8.3	8.3	8.3	8.3	8.3
Selling Expenses/Sales (%)		14.5	14.5	14.5	14.5	14.5
General & Administration Expenses/Sales		19.0	18.5	18.0	17.2	16.4
Interest on Cash and Marketable Securities		5.0	5.0	5.0	5.0	5.0
Interest on New Debt (%)		8.3	8.3	8.3	8.3	8.3
Effective Tax Rate		18.0	22.0	25.0	30.0	37.0
Other Current Operations Assets/Sales (%)		35.0	35.0	35.0	35.0	35.0
Other Assets/Sales (%)		35.0	30.0	25.0	20.0	20.0
Gross Fixed Assets/Sales (%)		25.0	25.0	25.0	25.0	25.0
Minimum Cash Balance/Sales (%)		4.5	4.5	4.5	4.5	4.5
Current Liabilities/Sales (%)		30.0	30.0	28.0	26.0	25.0
Common Shares Outstanding*		426	426	426	426	426
Cost of Capital: 2011–2015 (%)	11.81					
Cost of Capital: Terminal Period (%)	10.31					
Sustainable Cash Flow Growth Rate (%)	4.00					
Market Value of Long-Term Debt**	$1,171					

TABLE 9.2 (Continued)

Income Statement**	Historical Financials				Projected Financials				
	2007	2008	2009	2010	2011	2012	2013	2014	2015
Net Sales	4,779	4,698	4,596	4,670	4,857	5,051	5,253	5,463	5,682
Less: Variable Cost of Sales	2,315	2,286	2,333	2,415	2,449	2,496	2,570	2,646	2,751
- Depreciation	100	103	81	75	101	105	109	113	118
Total Cost of Sales	2,415	2,389	2,414	2,490	2,550	2,601	2,679	2,759	2,869
Gross Profit	2,364	2,310	2,182	2,180	2,307	2,450	2,574	2,704	2,812
Less: Sales Expense	761	786	685	681	704	732	762	792	824
- General and Administrative Expenses	780	863	868	908	923	934	946	940	942
- Amortization of Intangibles	32	41	52	52	52	52	52	52	52
- Other Expense (Income), Net	1	5	(5)	(19)	(16)	(16)	(16)	(16)	(16)
Total Sales and G&A Expenses	1,574	1,695	1,599	1,622	1,663	1,703	1,743	1,768	1,792
Operating Income (EBIT)	790	615	583	558	644	747	831	936	1,021
Plus: Interest Income					23	40	47	74	96
Less: Interest Expense	90	111	132	153	127	128	121	96	96
Net Profits before Taxes	700	504	451	405	540	659	757	915	1,021
Less: Taxes	201	131	62	55	97	145	189	274	376
Net Profits after Taxes	500	373	390	350	443	514	567	640	643

Balance Sheet†	2007	2008	2009	2010	2011	2012	2013	2014	2015
Cash	695	213	247	232	219	227	236	246	255
Other Operating Assets	1,767	1,845	1,605	1,519	1,700	1,768	1,839	1,912	1,989
Total Current Assets	2,462	2,058	1,852	1,752	1,918	1,995	2,075	2,158	2,244
Investments					245	582	711	1,235	1,674
Gross Fixed Assets	939	1,159	1,147	1,121	1,214	1,263	1,313	1,366	1,420
Less: Accumulated Depreciation & Amortization	337	422	422	473	574	679	788	901	1,019

	2007	2008	2009	2010	2011	2012	2013	2014	2015
Net Fixed Assets	602	737	725	648	640	584	526	465	402
Other Assets	852	1,819	2,097	1,914	1,914	1,913	1,913	1,913	1,913
Total Assets	3,915	4,613	4,674	4,313	4,718	5,075	5,224	5,771	6,233
Current Liabilities	1,173	1,317	1,565	1,502	1,457	1,515	1,471	1,420	1,420
Long-Term Debt	664	984	983	1,242	1,242	1,021	640	589	400
Other Liabilities	144	141	163	166	172	179	186	194	201
Total Liabilities	1,962	2,442	2,711	2,910	2,872	2,715	2,297	2,203	2,022
Common Stock	728	2,041	1,923	1,836	1,836	1,836	1,836	1,836	1,836
Retained Earnings	1,205	130	40	(433)	10	524	1,091	1,731	2,375
Shareholders' Equity	1,933	2,171	1,963	1,403	1,846	2,360	2,927	3,668	4,211
Total Liabilities & Shareholders' Equity	3,915	4,613	4,674	4,314	4,718	5,075	6,224	5,771	6,233
Shares Outstanding*	291.6	390.8	421.6	426	426	426	426	426	426
Earnings Per Share ($)	1.71	.95	.92	.82	1.04	1.21	1.33	1.50	1.51
Long-Term Debt/Equity (%)	37	48	53	93	70	46	24	18	9.5
Addendum: Working Capital*	1,288	741	287	249	461	480	604	78	624
Cash Flow Statement	**2007**	**2008**	**2009**	**2010**	**2011**	**2012**	**2013**	**2014**	**2015**
EBIT (1 − t)	584	455	503	482	528	583	623	655	643
Plus: Depreciation and Amortization	132	144	133	127	153	157	161	165	170
Less: Gross Capital Expenditures	201	221	(12)	(26)	93	49	51	53	55
Less: Change in Working Capital	(200)	(548)	(454)	(37)	212	18	124	133	88
− Free Cash Flow	695	926	1,102	672	375	67	609	635	672
PV: 2011–2015	$2,100								
PV: Terminal Value	$6,342								
Total PV (Market Value of the Firm)	$8,442								
Less: Market Value of Long-Term Debt	$1,171								
Plus: Excess Cash (Investments)	$245								
Equity Value	$7,517								
Equity Value per Share	$17.64								

*Millions of shares
**Millions of dollars
†As of December 31, 2010

TABLE 9.3   Step 2: Synergy Estimation[a]

	2011[*]	2012	2013	2014	2015
Incremental Sales Synergy – Sales of Alanco services to StarTrak customers		100	150	200	250
Cost of Sales Synergy – Elimination of third-party manufacturing and service contracts by bringing outside manufacturing in-house	4	11	14	14	14

Selling Expense Synergy
– Shutdown of Houston sales office (elimination of 20 sales
  employees by the end of 2011 at $100,000 per employee,
  including benefits)
	2	3	3	3	3

General & Administrative Expense Synergy
– Elimination of 38 finance and accounting personnel in Los
  Angeles headquarters by the end of 2011 at $80,000 per
  employee, including benefits
	2	3	3	3	3

Implementation/Integration Expenses – Severance – Lease buyouts – Retention bonuses **Total**	0.7 0.1 <u>0.2</u> 1.0				

[a]Note that incremental sales and cost savings are realized gradually due to the time required to implement such plans.
[*]In millions of dollars.

data provide recent trends. As is typical, the terminal value comprises about three-fourths of the total present value (i.e., $8,442 million) of Alanco's projected operating cash flows. Nonoperating assets, such as the $245 million in excess cash balances, are added to the total present value of the firm's operating cash flows.

Step 2. Value Acquirer and Target Firms, Including Synergy

Synergy consists of sources of value that *add* to the economic value (i.e., ability to generate future cash flows) of the combined firms. However, factors that destroy value also should be considered in the estimation of the economic value of the combined firms. That is, since synergy is measured in terms of cash flows, it can be positive or negative. To determine if certain cash flows result from synergy, ask if they can be generated only if the businesses are combined. If the answer to this question is yes, then the cash flow in question is due to synergy.

Net synergy (NS) is the difference between sources and destroyers of value. The common approach to estimating the present value of net synergy is to subtract the sum of the PVs of the acquirer and target firms on a stand-alone basis from the PV of the consolidated acquirer and target firms, including the effects of synergy.[7] This approach has the advantage of creating an interactive model to

[7] Alternatively, the present value of net synergy can be estimated by calculating the PV of the difference between the cash flows from sources and destroyers of value.

TABLE 9.4 Step 2: Consolidated Alanco and StarTrak 5-Year Forecast and Valuation

Forecast Assumptions		2011	2012	2013	2014	2015
Cost of Sales Synergy		4	11	14	14	14
Selling Expenses Synergy		2	3	3	3	3
G&A Expenses Synergy		2	3	3	3	3
Incremental Sales Synergy			100	0.150	200	250
Integration Expenses		(1)				
Cost of Capital: 2011–2015 (%)	11.81					
Cost of Capital: Terminal Period (%)	10.31					
Sustainable Cash Flow Growth Rate (%)	4.0					
Market Value of Long-Term Debt*	$1,172					

Income Statement*	2007	2008	2009	2010	2011	2012	2013	2014	2015
Net Sales of Combined Firms	4,821	4,764	4,779	4,922	5,147	5,285	5,470	5,659	5,848
Incremental Sales Due to Synergy						100	150	200	250
Total Sales	4,821	4,784	4,779	4,922	5,147	5,385	5,620	5,859	6,098
Less: Variable Costs of Sales	2,339	2,335	2,436	2,556	2,620	2,692	2,784	2,877	2,994
Depreciation & Amortization	101	106	86	84	104	109	113	118	123
Cost of Sales Synergy					(4)	(11)	(14)	(14)	(14)
Total Cost of Sales	2,440	2,441	2,521	2,640	2,721	2,790	2,884	2,981	3,103
Gross Profit	2,380	2,343	2,258	,282	2,426	2,595	2,736	2,879	2,995
Less: Sales Expense	767	799	712	719	748	782	817	852	886
Sales Expense Synergy					(2)	(3)	(3)	(3)	(3)

TABLE 9.4 (Continued)

	2007	2008	2009	2010	2011	2012	2013	2014	2015
General & Administrative Expenses	785	874	891	951	965	983	997	996	990
General & Administrative Expenses Synergy					(2)	(3)	(3)	(3)	(3)
Total Sales, General & Administrative Expenses	1,552	1,673	1,603	1,670	1,709	1.59	1,808	1,842	1,870
Integration Expense					1				
Amortization of Intangibles	32	41	52	52	52	52	52	52	52
Other Expense (Income), net	2	6	(9)	(34)	(32)	(32)	(32)	(32)	(32)
Total Cost of Sales and G&A Expense	1,586	1,720	1,646	1,688	1,731	1,779	1,828	1,861	1,890
Operating Profits (EBIT)	794	623	612	594	696	816	909	1,018	1,105
Plus: Interest Income			2	4	29	48	58	87	113
Less: Interest Expense	91	111	132	153	127	129	122	96	96
Net Profits before Taxes	704	512	482	445	597	736	845	1,009	1,122
Less: Taxes	201	133	70	67	112	163	10	297	402
Net Profits after Taxes	502	379	411	378	485	573	635	712	719
Balance Sheet	**2007**	**2008**	**2009**	**2010**	**2011**	**2012**	**2013**	**2014**	**2015**
Cash	698	225	344	275	236	247	258	270	281
Other Operating Assets	1,779	1,861	1,665	1,605	1,787	1,868	1,949	2,031	2,113
Total Current Assets	2,477	2,086	2,009	1,880	2,023	2,115	2,207	2,301	2,394
Investments					347	742	940	1,539	2,056
Gross Fixed Assets	942	1,165	1,164	1,150	1,249	1,303	1,357	1,413	1,470
Less: Accumulated Depreciation & Amortization	338	424	427	484	588	697	810	926	1,051
Net Fixed Assets	604	741	737	667	661	606	547	485	419
Other Assets	877	1,844	2,161	2,015	2,010	2,005	1,999	1,994	1,989
Total Assets	3,958	4,672	4,907	4,562	5,040	5,468	5,693	6,319	6,861
Current Liabilities	1,185	1,332	1,610	1,544	1,530	1,599	1,563	1,520	1,524

	2007	2008	2009	2010	2011	2012	2013	2014	2015
Long-Term Debt	670	989	983	1,243	1,244	1,022	641	589	400
Other Liabilities	144	141	164	167	174	181	188	196	204
Total Liabilities	1,999	2,463	2,757	2,954	2,947	2,802	2,392	2,305	2,128
Common Stock	750	2,068	2,078	1,980	1,980	1,980	1,980	1,980	1,980
Retained Earnings	1,210	141	72	(372)	113	687	1,322	2,034	2,752
Shareholders' Equity	1,960	2,209	2,150	1,608	2,093	2,666	3,302	4,014	4,733
Total Liabilities & Shareholders' Equity	3,959	4,672	4,907	4,562	5,040	5,468	5,693	6,319	6,861
Addendum: Working Capital	1,292	754	400	336	493	517	644	781	870
Shares Outstanding*	299	399	435	445	445	445	445	445	445
Cash Flow Statement	**2007**	**2008**	**2009**	**2010**	**2011**	**2012**	**2013**	**2014**	**2015**
EBIT(1 – t)	567	462	523	505	565	636	683	718	708
Plus: Depreciation and Amortization	133	147	138	136	156	161	165	170	175
Less: Gross Capital Expenditures	204	223	(2)	(13)	99	54	55	56	57
Less: Change in Working Capital	(204)	(537)	(355)	(64)	157	23	128	137	88
PV: 2011–2015	$2,336								
PV: Terminal Value	$6,964								
Total PV (Market Value of the Firm)	$9,300								
Less: Market Value of Long-Term Debt	$1,171								
Plus: Excess Cash Investment	$347								
Equity Value	$8,475								

*Millions of shares

simulate alternative scenarios, including different financing and deal-structuring assumptions.

Sources of Value

The most common include potential cost savings resulting from shared overhead, duplicate facilities, and overlapping distribution channels (e.g., direct sales forces, websites). Synergy related to cost savings is more easily realized than synergy due to other sources.[8] Potential sources of value also include assets not recorded on the balance sheet at fair value and off-balance-sheet items. Common examples include land and "obsolete" inventory and equipment. Underutilized borrowing capacity also can make an acquisition target more attractive. The addition of the target's assets, low level of indebtedness, and strong cash flow from operations could enable the buyer to increase substantially the borrowing levels of the combined companies.[9] Other sources of value include access to intellectual property (e.g., patents, trade names, and rights to royalty streams), new technologies and processes, and new customer groups. Likewise, income tax losses and tax credits also may represent an important source of value by reducing the combined firms' current and future tax burden.

Destroyers of Value

Factors destroying value include poor product quality, excessive wage and benefit levels, low productivity, and high employee turnover. A lack of or badly written contracts often results in customer disputes about terms, conditions, and amounts owed. Verbal agreements made with customers by the seller's sales representatives may become obligations for the buyer. Environmental issues, product liabilities, and unresolved lawsuits are also major potential destroyers of value for the buyer.

Implementation Costs

In calculating net synergy, it is important to include the costs associated with recruiting and training, realizing cost savings, achieving productivity improvements, layoffs, and exploiting revenue opportunities. Employee attrition following closing will add to recruitment and training costs. Cost savings due to layoffs frequently are offset in the early years by severance expenses.[10] Realizing

---

[8]Christofferson, McNish, and Sias, 2004. In addition to cost savings from eliminating duplicate functions, Fee et. al. (2012) document that acquirers frequently cut advertising and marketing budgets substantially following closing.

[9]The incremental borrowing capacity can be approximated by comparing the combined firms' current debt-to-total capital ratio with the industry average. For example, assume Firm A's acquisition of Firm B results in a reduction in the combined firms' debt-to–total capital ratio to 0.25 (e.g., debt represents $250 million of the new firm's total capital of $1 billion). If the same ratio for the industry is 0.5, the new firm may be able to increase its borrowing by $250 million to raise its debt-to–total capital ratio to the industry average. Such incremental borrowing often is used to finance a portion of the purchase price paid for the target firm.

[10]How a company treats its employees during layoffs has a significant impact on the morale of those that remain and on the firm's ability to hire future employees.

productivity gains requires more spending in new structures and equipment or redesigning workflow. Exploiting revenue-raising opportunities may require training the sales force of the combined firms in selling each firm's products or services and additional advertising expenditures to inform current or potential customers of what has taken place.

See Table 9.4 for estimated sources of synergy resulting from the combination of Alanco and StarTrak, which presents the consolidated financial statements (including the effects of synergy) for the two firms. The impact of synergy is illustrated on the income statement in terms of incremental revenue as well as savings from cost of sales and selling, general, and administrative expense reductions. Note how synergy-related revenue is added to total revenue, and synergy-related reductions in cost of sales, selling expenses, and general and administrative expenses are deducted from their respective line items on the income statement.

Step 3. Determine the Magnitude and Composition of the Offer Price for the Target Firm

Many factors affect the amount and form of payment of the initial offer price. Which are most important depends largely on the circumstances surrounding the transaction. In some cases, these factors can be quantified (e.g., synergy), while others are largely subjective (e.g., the degree of acquirer shareholder and management risk aversion). The amount of the initial offer price may also reflect a premium for control. While the actual value of control is difficult to quantify, a bidder may be willing to pay more to gain control if it is believed that this would provide for better decision making and the implementation of a more effective strategy. Table 9.5 identifies factors affecting the magnitude and composition of the offer price. The remainder of this section of the chapter addresses how some of these factors can be incorporated into financial models.

Estimating the Minimum and Maximum Offer Price Range

The initial offer price lies between the minimum[11] and maximum offer prices. In a stock purchase deal, the minimum price is the target's stand-alone present value (PV_T) or its current market value (MV_T) (i.e., the target's current stock price times its shares outstanding). The maximum price is the sum of the minimum price plus

---

[11] The notion of a minimum price should be viewed as a starting point for determining an offer price and does not preclude circumstances in which the buyer may be able to buy a target at a significant discount to its intrinsic value. For small, privately owned firms, either the buyer or seller may not have access to all relevant information about the economic value of the target. Markets for private firms may also be illiquid; sellers seeking to "cash out" quickly may be willing to sell at a significant discount from the firm's intrinsic value. The cost of performing due diligence and the risks associated with buying nonpublic firms often are significant and encourage the buyer to offer less than what the buyer may believe is the target's true worth.

TABLE 9.5   Determinants of Magnitude and Composition of Initial Offer Price

Factors Affecting:	Magnitude	Composition
Acquirer's Perspective	• Estimated net synergy • Perceived contribution of target to net synergy • Willingness to share net synergy with target shareholders • Relative attractiveness of alternative investment opportunities • Number of potential bidders • Effectiveness of target's defenses • Public disclosure requirements (may result in preemptive bid) • Degree of management's risk aversion • Perceived value of control	• Current borrowing capacity • After-tax cost of debt versus cost of equity • Size and duration of potential EPS dilution (impacts attractiveness of share exchange) • Size of transaction (may make borrowing impractical) • Desire for risk sharing (may result in contingent or deferred payments) • Extent to which acquirer shares are overvalued (makes an all-equity transaction more attractive)
Target's Perspective	• Number of potential bidders • Perceived contribution of target to net synergy • Perception of bidder as friendly or hostile • Effectiveness of defenses • Size of potential tax liability (may require increase in purchase price) • Stand-alone valuation • Availability of recent comparable transactions • Relative attractiveness of investment opportunities	• Perceived attractiveness of acquirer stock • Shareholder preference for cash versus stock • Size of potential tax liability (may make share exchange the most attractive option) • Perceived upside potential of target (may result in contingent payout)

the present value of net synergy (PV_{NS}).[12] The initial offer price (PV_{IOP}) is the sum of the minimum purchase price and a percentage, α between 0 and 1, of PV_{NS} (see Exhibit 9.2). Note, α represents that portion of net synergy shared with target shareholders and not the purchase price premium. Once the offer price has been determined, the purchase price premium may be estimated by comparing the offer price to the target's preannouncement share price. The offer price should also be compared to similar recent deals to determine if it is excessive.[13]

[12] Note that the maximum price may be overstated if the current market value of the target firm reflects investor expectations of an impending takeover. As such, the current market value may reflect a portion of future synergies.

[13] The percent difference between purchase price multiples of the target's earnings, cash flow, sales, book value, and so on can be compared to similar multiples of recent comparable transactions to determine the relative magnitude of the price paid for the target versus those of comparable deals. For example, if the price-to-earnings ratio paid for the target firm is 12 versus 10 paid for comparable recent deals, the implicit relative purchase premium paid for the target is 20%.

EXHIBIT 9.2   DETERMINING THE OFFER PRICE (PV$_{OP}$)—PURCHASE OF STOCK[a]

a. $PV_{MIN} = PV_T$ or MV_T, whichever is greater. MV_T is the target firm's current share price times the number of shares outstanding.

b. $PV_{MAX} = PV_{MIN} + PV_{NS}$, where $PV_{NS} = PV$ (sources of value) – PV (destroyers of value).

c. $PV_{OP} = PV_{MIN} + \alpha\, PV_{NS}$, where $0 \leq \alpha \leq 1$.

d. Offer price range for the target firm = $(PV_T$ or $MV_T) < PV_{OP} < (PV_T$ or $MV_T) + PV_{NS}$.

[a]In an asset purchase, the assets acquired by and liabilities assumed by the buyer are referred to as *net acquired assets* (i.e., acquired assets less assumed liabilities). The minimum purchase price is the liquidation value of net acquired assets; the maximum purchase price equals the minimum price plus the PV of net synergy, and the initial offer price equals the PV of net acquired assets plus some portion of the PV of net synergy.

To determine α the acquirer may estimate the portion of net synergy supplied by the target firm.[14] If it is determined that the target would contribute 30% of net synergy, the acquirer may share up to that amount with the target's shareholders. To discourage potential bidders, acquirers might make preemptive bids that are so attractive that the target's board could not reject the offer for fear of possible shareholder lawsuits, resulting in more than 30% of net synergy being shared with the target. In other instances, the acquirer may share less than 30% if it is concerned that realizing synergy on a timely basis is problematic. Ultimately, the distribution of net synergy between the buyer and the seller reflects their relative negotiating leverage.

The offer price should fall between the minimum and maximum prices for three reasons. First, it is unlikely that the target company can be purchased at the minimum price, because the acquirer normally has to pay a premium to induce target shareholders to sell their shares. In an asset purchase, the rational seller would not sell at a price below the after-tax liquidation value of the net acquired assets, since this represents what the seller could obtain by liquidating rather than selling the assets. Second, at the maximum end of the range, the acquiring company would be ceding all of the net synergy value created by combining the two firms to the target's shareholders. Finally, it often is prudent to pay significantly less than the maximum price, because of the uncertainty of realizing estimated synergy.

[14]The percentage of net synergy contributed by the target can be estimated by calculating the contribution to incremental cash flow attributable to cross-selling acquirer products to the target's customers or to cost savings resulting from a reduction in the number of target employees. These represent incremental cash flows that are possible as a result of the deal.

Determining the Appropriate Composition of the Offer Price

The offer price could consist of acquirer stock, debt, cash, or some combination. The actual composition depends on what is acceptable to the target and the acquirer and what the financial structure of the combined firms can support.[15] These factors are discussed next.

Share-Exchange Ratios

The exchange of an acquirer's shares for the target firm's shares requires the calculation of the appropriate exchange ratio. The share-exchange ratio (SER) can be negotiated as a fixed number of shares of the acquirer's stock to be exchanged for each share of the target's stock. Alternatively, SER can be defined in terms of the dollar value of the negotiated offer price per share of target stock (P_{OP}) to the dollar value of the acquirer's share price (P_A). The SER is calculated via the following equation:

$$SER = P_{OP} / P_A$$

The SER can be less than, equal to, or greater than 1, depending on the value of the acquirer's shares relative to the offer price on the date set during the negotiation for valuing the transaction. Exhibit 9.3 illustrates how share-exchange ratios can be used to estimate the number of acquirer shares that must be issued in a share-for-share exchange and the resulting distribution of ownership in the combined firms between the acquirer and former target shareholders.

Fully Diluted Shares Outstanding

When the target firm has outstanding management stock options and convertible securities, it is necessary to adjust the offer price to reflect the extent to which options and convertible securities will be exchanged for new common shares. If the acquirer is intent on buying all the target's outstanding shares, these new shares also have to be purchased. Convertible securities commonly include preferred stock and debentures.[16] Information on the number of options outstanding,

[15]In this chapter, the initial offer price is the market value or economic value (i.e., present value of the target firm defined as a stand-alone business) plus some portion of net synergy. In Chapter 5, the offer or purchase price was defined in a different context, as total consideration, total purchase price or enterprise value, and net purchase price. These definitions were provided with the implicit assumption that the acquiring company had determined the economic value of the firm on a stand-alone basis and the value of net synergy. Economic value is determined before any consideration is given to how the transaction will be financed.

[16]Convertible preferred stock can be exchanged for common stock at a specific price at the discretion of the shareholder. The value of the common stock for which the preferred stock is exchanged is called the *conversion price*. If the par value of the preferred stock is $150 and the conversion price is $30, the conversion ratio is 5 to 1. That is, the preferred shareholder would receive five shares of common stock upon conversion. Convertible debentures are debt backed by the general creditworthiness of the firm rather than by specific assets that can be converted into a specific number of common shares after a stipulated time period.

EXHIBIT 9.3   APPLYING SHARE-EXCHANGE RATIOS

Assume that Acquirer Corp. agrees to buy all the shares of Target Corp. in a share-for-share exchange, the offer price per Target share and Acquirer's share prices are $25.50 and $37.25, respectively, and the number of Acquirer and Target shares outstanding are 10 million and 2 million, respectively. The number of Acquirer shares exchanged for each Target share, the number of new Acquirer shares issued, total shares outstanding of the combined firms, and the percentage of total shares owned by Acquirer and Target shareholders are estimated as follows:

Share-exchange ratio: Target shareholders would receive 0.6846 shares ($25.50/$37.25) of Acquirer's stock for each share they exchange.

Acquirer shares issued: Acquirer would have to issue 1,369,200 new shares [0.6846(SER) × 2,000,000 (Target's outstanding shares)] to purchase all of Target's shares.

Total shares outstanding: Since Target's shares are cancelled, the total number of shares outstanding for the combined firms is 11,369,200 [10,000,000 (preacquisition Acquirer shares outstanding) + 1,369,200 (newly issued Acquirer shares)].

Ownership distribution: Acquirer shareholders would own 88% [i.e., 10,000,000 (preacquisition acquirer shares)/11,369,200 (preacquisition Acquirer shares + newly issued Acquirer shares)] of the combined firms, and Target shareholders would own the remaining 12%.

vesting periods[17] and their associated exercise prices, as well as convertible securities generally are available in the footnotes to the financial statements of the target firm.[18] With respect to convertible securities, it is reasonable to assume that such securities will be converted to common equity if the conversion price is less than the offer price for each common share. Such securities are said to be "in the money." Table 9.6 illustrates the calculation of the target firm's fully diluted shares outstanding and the impact on the equity value of the target firm. Table 9.7 summarizes the steps involved in determining the offer price.

Step 4. Determine the Combined Firms' Ability to Finance the Transaction

Consolidated target and acquirer financial statements, including synergy, are run through a series of scenarios to determine the impact on such variables as earnings, leverage, covenants, and borrowing costs. For example, each scenario

---

[17] A *vesting period* is the time elapsed before an option holder has the right to exercise a stock option.

[18] Options not currently vested may become fully vested upon a change in control, thereby increasing the number of "options that could be converted to common shares. Such options should be added to the number of "in the money" options in calculating the number of fully diluted shares outstanding.

TABLE 9.6　Calculating the Target's Fully Diluted Shares Outstanding and Equity Value (Using If-Converted Method)

Assumptions about Target		Comment
Basic Shares Outstanding	2,000,000 shares	
In-the-Money Options[a]	150,000 shares	Exercise price = $15/share
Convertible Securities:		
Convertible Debentures [Par value = $1,000; convertible into 50 shares of common stock; implied conversion price = $20 (i.e., $1,000/50)]	$10,000,000	Debentures outstanding = $10,000,000/$1,000 = 10,000 If fully converted = 10,000 × 50 = 500,000 common shares
Preferred Stock (Par value = $60; convertible into 3 common shares; implied conversion price = $20 [i.e., $60/3)]	$5,000,000	Preferred shares outstanding = $5,000,000/$60 = 83,333 If fully converted = 83,333 × 3 = 250,000 common shares
Offer Price per Share	$30	Purchase price offered for each target share outstanding

Total Shares Outstanding[b] = 2,000,000 + 150,000 + 500,000 + 250,000
$$= 2,900,000$$

Target Equity Value[c] = (2,900,000 × $30) − (150,000 × $15)
$$= \$87,000,000 - \$2,250,000$$
$$= \$84,750,000$$

[a] An option whose exercise price is below the market value of the firm's share price.
[b] Total shares outstanding = Issued shares + Shares from "in-the-money" options and convertible securities.
[c] Purchase price adjusted for new acquirer shares issued for convertible shares or debt less cash received from "in-the-money" option holders. Option holders are not required to pay cash for such shares if the firm allows them to exercise their options to buy common shares and simultaneously to sell such shares.

TABLE 9.7　Step 3: Offer Price Determination

Deal Terms and Conditions	
Cash Portion of Offer Price	0
Equity Portion of Offer Price	100%
% of Synergy Shared with Target	30%
Specific Firm Data	
Acquirer Share Price	$16.03
Target Share Price	$14.25
Target Shares Outstanding	
Basic Shares Outstanding	18.1

TABLE 9.7   Step 3: Offer Price Determination

	"In-the-Money" Options Converted to Common	0.2			

"In-the-Money" Options Converted to Common	0.2		
Convertible Preferred Converted to Common	0.8		
Total Target Shares Outstanding[*]	19.1		
Acquirer Shares Outstanding[*]	426		

Model Output	Stand-Alone Value		Consolidated Acquirer + Target		Value of Synergy
	Acquirer	Target	Without Synergy (1)	With Synergy (2)	PV$_{NS}$ (1) – (2)
Discounted Cash Flow Valuations[**]	$7,517	$591	$8,107	$8,475	$368
Minimum Offer Price (PV$_{MIN}$)[**]	$272				
Maximum Offer Price (PV$_{MAX}$)[**]	$640				
Offer Price Per Share ($)	$20.02				
Purchase Price Premium per Share (%)	41%				
Cash Per Share ($)	0				
New Shares Issued by Acquirer[*]	23.867				
Total Shares Outstanding for the Combined Firms[*]	450				

Ownership Distribution in New Firm

Acquirer Shareholders	95%
Target Shareholders	5%

Addendum:

Discounted cash flow valuations provided by Steps 1 and 2 of the M&A model.

Minimum offer price = target share price × total target shares outstanding = $14.25 × 19.1 = $272.18

Maximum offer price = minimum price + net synergy = $272 + $368 = $640

Offer price per share = (minimum offer price + 0.3 × net synergy)/total target shares outstanding = ($272 + 0.3 × $368)/19.1 = $20.02

Purchase price premium = (Offer price per share/target share price) – 1 = ($20.02/$14.25) – 1 = 40.5%

New shares issued by acquirer = share-exchange ratio × total target shares outstanding = ($20.02/$16.03) × 19.1 = 23.9 million

Total shares outstanding for the combined firms = Acquirer shares outstanding + New shares issued by the acquirer = 426 + 23.9 = 450 million

Ownership Distribution:

Acquirer shareholders = acquirer shares outstanding/total shares outstanding for the combined firms = 426/450 = 0.947 × 100 = 94.7%

Target shareholders = 1–0.947 = 0.053 × 100 = 5.3%

[*]*Millions of shares*

[**]*Millions of dollars*

could represent different amounts of leverage as measured by the firm's debt-to-equity ratio. In theory, the optimal capital structure is the one maximizing the firm's share price. Since many factors affect share price, it is difficult to determine the exact capital structure that maximizes the firm's share price. In practice, financial managers forecast how changes in debt will affect those ratios that impact a firm's creditworthiness, including the interest-coverage ratio, debt-to-equity ratio, times interest-earned ratio, and the like. They subsequently discuss their projected pro forma statements with lenders and bond-rating agencies, which in turn compare the firm's credit ratios with those of other firms in the same industry to assess the borrower's ability to repay their debt. Ultimately, interaction among the borrower, lenders, and rating agencies is what determines the amount and composition of combined firms' capital structure.

For purposes of model building, the appropriate financing structure can be estimated by selecting the structure that satisfies certain predetermined selection criteria. These selection criteria should be determined as part of the process of developing the acquisition plan. For a public company, the appropriate capital structure could be that scenario whose debt-to-equity ratio results in the highest net present value for cash flows generated by the combined firms, the least near-term EPS dilution, no violation of loan covenants, and no significant increase in borrowing costs. Excluding EPS considerations, private companies could determine the appropriate capital structure in the same manner. Table 9.8 displays the consolidated financial statements for Alanco and StarTrak, including the effects

TABLE 9.8   Combined Firms' Financing Capacity

	Projected Financials				
Income Statement ($ Million)	**2011**	**2012**	**2013**	**2014**	**2015**
Net Sales	5,147	5,385	5,620	5,859	6,098
Less Cost of Sales	2,721	2,790	2,884	2,981	3,103
Gross Profit	2,426	2,595	2,736	2,879	2,995
Less: Sales, General & Administrative Expenses	1,730	1,779	1,828	1,861	1,890
Integration Expenses	**(1)**				
Operating Profits (EBIT)	696	816	909	1,018	1,105
Plus: Interest Income	29	48	58	87	113
Less: Interest Expense	127	129	122	96	96
Net Profits before Taxes	597	736	845	1,009	1,122
Less: Taxes	112	163	210	297	402
Net Profits after Taxes	485	573	635	712	719

TABLE 9.8   Continued

Income Statement ($ Million)	Projected Financials				
	2011	2012	2013	2014	2015
Balance Sheet (December 31)					
Cash & Marketable Securities	582	989	1,198	1,809	2,340
Other Current Assets	1,787	1,868	1,949	2,301	2,113
Total Current Assets	2,369	2,857	3,147	3,840	4,453
Gross Fixed Assets	1,249	1,303	1,357	1,413	1,470
Less: Accumulated Depreciation	588	697	810	928	1,051
Net Fixed Assets	661	606	547	485	419
Other Assets	2,010	2,005	1,999	1,994	1,989
Total Assets	5,040	5,468	5,693	6,319	6,861
Current Liabilities	1,530	1,599	1,563	1,520	1,524
Long-Term Debt	1,244	1,022	641	589	400
Other Liabilities	174	181	188	196	204
Common Stock	1,980	1,980	1,980	1,980	1,980
Retained Earnings	113	687	1,322	2,034	2,753
Shareholders' Equity	2,093	2,666	3,302	4,014	4,733
Total Liabilities + Shareholders' Equity	5,040	5,468	5,693	6,319	6,861
Key Performance Indicators					
Long-Term Debt/Equity	59%	38%	19%	15%	8%
Interest Coverage Ratio (EBIT/Interest Expense)	5.48	6.33	7.45	10.60	11.57
Current Ratio (Current Assets/Current Liabilities)	1.55	1.79	2.01	2.53	2.92
Earnings Per Share (*Note*: Total shares = 450,000,000)	1.08	1.27	1.41	1.58	1.60

Addendum:
Selected Loan Covenants:
    Long-Term Debt/Equity ≤ 0.75
    Interest Coverage Ratio (EBIT/Interest Expense) ≥ 2.5
    Current Ratio (Current Assets/Current Liabilities) ≥ 1.25

of synergy and financing. The addendum provides selected loan covenants and the projected performance of the combined firms with respect to these covenants and in terms of earnings per share. The pro formas suggest that the acquisition can be financed without any deterioration in earnings per share, violation of existing loan covenants, deterioration in liquidity, or increase in interest expense.

ASSESSING IMPACT OF M&A'S ON POSTACQUISITION EARNINGS PER SHARE

The acquirer's initial offer generally is the lowest point between the minimum and maximum prices consistent with what the acquirer believes is acceptable to the target firm. If the target's financial performance is remarkable, the target may receive a higher premium, pushing the offer price closer to the maximum price. The acquirer may make a bid close to the maximum price to preempt other potential acquirers. Acquirer hubris or an auction environment may push the final purchase price to or even above the maximum price. Under any circumstance, increasing the offer price involves tradeoffs. Offer price simulation models enable the acquirer to see tradeoffs between changes in the offer price and postacquisition EPS. Even a short-term reduction in EPS may dissuade some CEOs from pursuing a target firm. Acquirer management may establish a baseline below which postacquisition EPS cannot fall: a "go/no go"-decision rule.

An acquisition may add to the acquirer's postacquisition EPS (accretion) or reduce EPS (dilution). An acquirer may accept near-term dilution in EPS if the longer-term contribution of the acquisition to EPS is highly attractive. While dilution may be acceptable in the year (possibly even two years) following closing, actual dilution should not be worse than what the acquirer projects at closing; otherwise, management is likely to lose investor confidence. The acquirer may vary the offer price by changing the amount of net synergy shared with the target firm's shareholders. Increases in the offer price affect the postacquisition EPS for a given set of assumptions about the deal's terms and conditions and firm-specific data. Terms and conditions include the cash and stock portion of the purchase price. Firm-specific data include the preacquisition share prices, the number of common shares outstanding for each firm, the PV of net synergy, and postacquisition projected net income available for common equity.

Table 9.9 illustrates different scenarios for postacquisition EPS generated by varying the amount of synergy shared with the target based on a 75% equity/25% cash offer price. The relatively small reduction in EPS in each year as the offer price increases reflects the small number of new shares the acquirer has to issue to acquire the target's shares. The table reflects the resulting minimum, maximum, and initial offer price, assuming that the acquirer is willing to give up 30% of projected synergy. At that level of synergy sharing, the equity of the new firm will be 95% owned by the acquirer's shareholders, with the remainder owned by the target's shareholders. An Excel-based offer price simulation model is available on the companion website to this textbook.

TABLE 9.9 Offer Price Simulation Model

Deal Terms and Conditions

Cash Portion of Offer Price (%)	0.25
Equity Portion of Offer Price (%)	0.75
Percent of Anticipated Synergy Shared with Target (%)	0.3

Specific Firm Data

Acquirer Share Price ($/Share)	16.03
Target Share Price ($/Share)	14.25
Target Shares Outstanding (Millions)	19.10
Acquirer Shares Outstanding, Preclosing (Millions)	426.00
PV of Anticipated Net Synergy ($M)	368.00

Alternative Scenarios Based on Different Amounts of Synergy Shared With Target

Calculated Data		% Shared Synergy	Offer Price ($M)	Offer Price Per Share	Post-Acq. Total Shares	Postacquisition EPS				
						2008	**2009**	**2010**	**2011**	**2012**
Calculated Data		**0.1**	**309**	**16.18**	**445**	**1.09**	**1.29**	**1.43**	**1.60**	**1.61**
Minimum Offer Price ($M)	272	0.2	346	18.10	448	1.08	1.28	1.42	1.59	1.61
Maximum Offer Price ($M)	640	0.3	383	20.03	450	1.08	1.27	1.41	1.58	1.60
Initial Offer Price ($M)	383	0.4	419	21.96	452	1.07	1.27	1.40	1.57	1.59
Initial Offer Price Per Share ($)	20.03	0.5	456	23.88	454	1.07	1.26	1.40	1.57	1.58
Purchase Price Premium Per Share (%)	0.41	0.6	493	25.81	457	1.06	1.25	1.39	1.56	1.57
Composition of Purchase Price Per Target Share		0.7	530	27.74	459	1.06	1.25	1.38	1.55	1.57

TABLE 9.9 Continued

Acquirer Equity Per Target Share	15.02	567	29.66	461	1.05	1.24	1.38	1.54	1.56
Cash Per Target Share ($)	5.01	603	31.59	464	1.05	1.24	1.37	1.54	1.55
Share Exchange Ratio	1.25	640	33.52	466	1.04	1.23	1.36	1.53	1.54
New Shares Issued by Acquirer	23.87								
Acquirer Shares Outstanding, Post-Closing (Millions)	449.87								

Ownership Distribution in New Firm

Acquirer Shareholders (%)	0.95
Target Shareholders (%)	0.05

Consolidated Acquirer & Target Net Income

	2008	2009	2010	2011	2012
Postacquisition Consolidated Net Income ($M)	485	573	635	712	719

Note: This model is available on the companion website to this textbook in an Excel worksheet entitled "Offer Price Simulation Model."

SOME THINGS TO REMEMBER

Financial modeling in the context of M&As facilitates deal valuation, structuring, and financing. The process outlined in this chapter entails four steps: valuing the acquirer and target firms as stand-alone businesses; valuing the consolidated financials of the acquirer and target firms, including synergy; estimating the initial offer price; and determining the appropriate capital structure of the combined firms.

DISCUSSION QUESTIONS

9.1 Why should a target company be valued as a stand-alone business? Give examples of the types of adjustments that might have to be made if the target is part of a larger company.

9.2 Define the minimum and maximum purchase price range for a target company.

9.3 What are the differences between the final negotiated price, total consideration, total purchase price, and net purchase price?

9.4 Can the offer price ever exceed the maximum purchase price? If yes, why? If no, why not?

9.5 Why is it important to state clearly the assumptions underlying a valuation?

9.6 Assume two firms have little geographic overlap in terms of sales and facilities. If they were to merge, how might this affect the potential for synergy?

9.7 Dow Chemical, a leading manufacturer of chemicals, in announcing that it had an agreement to acquire competitor Rohm and Haas, said it expected to broaden its current product offering by offering the higher-margin Rohm and Haas products. What would you identify as possible synergies between these two businesses? In what ways could the combination of these two firms erode combined cash flows?

9.8 Dow Chemical's acquisition of Rohm and Haas included a 74% premium over the firm's preannouncement share price. What is the probable process Dow employed in determining the stunning magnitude of this premium?

9.9 For most transactions, the full impact of net synergy will not be realized for many months. Why? What factors could account for the delay?

9.10 How does the presence of management options and convertible securities affect the calculation of the offer price for the target firm?

Answers to these Chapter Discussion Questions are available in the Online Instructor's Manual for instructors using this book.

QUESTIONS FROM THE CFA CURRICULUM

9.11 Which of the following statements about company analysis is most accurate?
  a. The complexity of spreadsheet modeling ensures precise forecasts of financial statements.
  b. The interpretation of financial ratios should focus on comparing the company's results over time but not with competitors.
  c. The corporate profile would include a description of the company's business, investment activities, governance, and strengths and weaknesses.
  Source: CFA Institute 2011 Introduction to Industry and Company Analysis, Reading 59, question 31.
9.12 Discuss how understanding a company's business might be useful in performing a sensitivity analysis related to a valuation of the company.
  Source: CFA Institute 2011 Equity Valuation: Applications and Processes, Reading 35, question 6.

Answers to questions from the CFA Curriculum are available in the Online Student Companion site to this book in a file folder entitled CFA Curriculum Questions and Solutions.

PRACTICE PROBLEMS AND ANSWERS

9.13 Acquiring Company is considering the acquisition of Target Company in a share-for-share transaction in which Target Company would receive $50.00 for each share of its common stock. Acquiring Company does not expect any change in its P/E multiple after the merger.

	Acquiring Co.	Target Co.
Earnings available for common stock	$150,000	$30,000
Number of shares of common stock outstanding	60,000	20,000
Market price per share	$60.00	$40.00

Using the preceding information about these two firms and showing your work, calculate the following:
  a. Purchase price premium. *Answer:* 25%
  b. Share-exchange ratio. *Answer:* 0.8333
  c. New shares issued by Acquiring Company. *Answer:* 16,666
  d. Total shares outstanding of the combined companies. *Answer:* 76,666
  e. Postmerger EPS of the combined companies. *Answer:* $2.35
  f. Premerger EPS of Acquiring Company. *Answer:* $2.50
  g. Postmerger share price. *Answer:* $56.40, compared with $60.00 premerger
9.14 Acquiring Company is considering buying Target Company. Target Company is a small biotechnology firm that develops products licensed to the major

pharmaceutical firms. Development costs are expected to generate negative cash flows during the first two years of the forecast period of $(10) million and $(5) million, respectively. Licensing fees are expected to generate positive cash flows during years 3 through 5 of the forecast period of $5 million, $10 million, and $15 million, respectively. Because of the emergence of competitive products, cash flow is expected to grow at a modest 5% annually after the fifth year. The discount rate for the first five years is estimated to be 20% and then drop to the industry average rate of 10% beyond the fifth year. Also, the present value of the estimated net synergy by combining Acquiring and Target companies is $30 million. Calculate the minimum and maximum purchase prices for Target Company. Show your work.

Answer: **Minimum price: $128.5 million; Maximum price: $158.5 million.**

9.15 Using the Excel-Based Offer Price Simulation Model (Table 9.9) on the companion website, what would the initial offer price be if the amount of synergy shared with the target firm's shareholders was 50%? What is the offer price, and what would the ownership distribution be if the percentage of synergy shared increased to 80% and the composition of the purchase price were all acquirer stock?

Solutions to these Practice Problems are available in the Online Instructor's Manual for instructors using this book.

CASE STUDY 9.1
Microsoft Buys Skype in an All-Cash Deal

Key Points

- Skype represents both a defensive acquisition and a significant enhancement to Microsoft's current product offering.
- To realize its cost of capital, Microsoft must realize synergies on a timely basis.
- Simulation of alternative scenarios using financial models helps the analyst assess a range of outcomes and associated risks.

Internet IPO valuations during the first half of 2011 smacked of another dotcom bubble. Talk of Facebook's commanding a $100 billion valuation reverberated around Wall Street. Against this backdrop, Microsoft paid an eye-popping premium for Skype, the leading provider of voice and video calling over the Internet. In hindsight, it looks like Microsoft made a "preemptive" bid, despite the absence of serious alternative bidders, when Internet valuations were inflated.

Founded in 2003, Skype became an overnight sensation by offering for free its Internet-based voice and video calling service. While the firm experienced sustained increases in usage, its major challenge has been and continues to be converting users of its free PC-to-PC phone services into paying customers. While the Luxembourg-based firm claims to have 663 million total users, most are not active callers. In early 2005, eBay, the online auction behemoth, offered $2.6 billion for the firm, with a potential payout of additional $1.5 billion in performance-based incentives. The value eBay saw in acquiring Skype was the potential for integrating Skype technology with its online auctions, enabling those participating in the auction to converse using both video and voice communication. However, this application of the technology was not readily accepted, and Skype could not produce sustained profitability for eBay. By early 2009, an investor group consisting of Silver Lake Partners, the Canadian Pension Plan Investment Board, and venture capital firm Index Ventures acquired a 70% interest in Skype for $1.92 billion, valuing the firm at $2.74 billion; eBay retained the remaining 30%.

Shortly after eBay's divestiture of Skype, the Skype founders, who had retained the patent rights to key technologies, sued the investor group for patent infringement. The settlement of the lawsuit in late 2009 resulted in the founders' receiving a 14% stake in the firm. Index Ventures sold its interest in the firm. During the next two years, the remaining investors pushed the firm to focus on development, shortened product cycles, and forging new partnerships. Skype moved to build out its services in the mobile space and the enterprise space. Skype's staff was increased to about 1,000 in early 2011, 40% above its 2009 yearend level. Between 2009 and 2010, operating performance improved dramatically, with revenue almost tripling to $860 million and operating profits moving from a loss to a $424 million profit. In early 2011, the firm announced that it would undertake an IPO in August to raise $100 million.

Seeking to jumpstart growth, Microsoft had been negotiating a partnership with the investor group that owned Skype in late 2010. When Google showed interest in acquiring Skype, Steve Ballmer, Microsoft's CEO, initiated an unsolicited bid for the firm. Skype investors refused to consider offers less than $7 billion, because the investor group believed that the IPO would place a value on the entire business of at least that amount. On May 11, 2011, Microsoft announced that it had reached an agreement to acquire Skype for $8.5 billion in an all-cash deal, the biggest in Microsoft's 36-year history.

Microsoft is betting it can use Internet calling to catch up in mobile and web advertising. The firm was willing to pay what some consider an extravagant price to cover Skype's outstanding debt and to prevent competitors such as Google from acquiring the firm.

In this regard, the acquisition was defensive in nature as well as an attempt to extend the capability to a range of other Microsoft products. Specifically, Microsoft intends to add Skype, which boasts 170 million active users per month who use an average 100 minutes per month, to Microsoft's Outlook e-mail, Xbox game console, Windows mobile phones, and corporate phone software. Microsoft also made it clear that it did not intend to reduce free offerings. Microsoft also justified the high premium paid in part by noting that it expected the stock to appreciate after the IPO and that it would cost more to acquire the firm later. Microsoft is hoping that by integrating Skype into Microsoft products, the firm can hasten the mainstream adoption of video communications. Skype could give Microsoft its first leading consumer Internet service and help promote its other businesses, such as smartphone software, Office productivity programs and Xbox.

Buying Skype gives Microsoft access to popular mobile applications, videoconferencing, and video chatting, which are already included in both Google and Apple devices. Since Skype lets cellphone users make free or cheap calls over the telecommunications carriers' data networks, people could become less reliant on expensive, unlimited voice plans, which in turn could cut into the amount of revenue that wireless carriers are able to bring in from their customers. Of course,

Skype has been available for some time on a number of smartphones, including the iPhone and smartphones powered by the Android operating system. The deal could cool relations between Microsoft and wireless carriers, which would not bode well as the firm works with Nokia in an attempt to gain a foothold in the smartphone industry. Carriers have the final decision in terms of what they choose to sell and market in their stores.

Microsoft is paying 10 times 2010 revenue; Google, with its established track record, trades at about 5 times last year's revenue. If Microsoft is able to realize anticipated synergies with other products, the investment may pay off handsomely. However, the challenges are considerable. Microsoft expects the deal to integrate Skype's voice, video, and messaging tools with Office e-mail and its mobile operating system. The recent deal with Nokia to utilize Microsoft smartphone software on Nokia handsets could support efforts to promote Microsoft's smartphone platform, which currently is well behind Apple's iPhone and Google's Android operating systems. Widespread recognition of Skype's brand name could also help Microsoft to compete with Apple's FaceTime video calling. Moreover, Microsoft could expand its revenues from increasing video conferencing by its business customers.

Table 9.10 provides the assumptions underlying a stand-alone valuation of Skype. The $6.3 billion

TABLE 9.10 Skype Stand-Alone Valuation

	Actual	Forecast Period									
	2010	2011	2012	2013	2014	2015	2016	2017	2018	2019	2020
ASSUMPTIONS											
Net Revenue Growth Rate (%)	0.35	0.35	0.35	0.35	0.35	0.35	0.3	0.25	0.2	0.15	0.1
EBIT as % of Net Revenue	0.49	0.45	0.45	0.42	0.4	0.38	0.36	0.34	0.32	0.3	0.3
Marginal Tax Rate (%)	0	0	0	0.15	0.2	0.2	0.25	0.25	0.25	0.25	0.25
Working Capital as % of Net Revenue	−12.8	0	0.15	0.2	0.2	0.25	0.3	0.35	0.35	0.35	0.35
Amort./Deprec. as % of Net Revenue	13.2	0.13	0.1	0.09	0.08	0.07	0.06	0.05	0.04	0.04	0.04
Capital Spending as % Net Revenue	0.036	0.036	0.04	0.045	0.05	0.05	0.05	0.05	0.05	0.05	0.05
Software Industry Avg. Levered Beta[a]	1.06										
Software Industry Avg. Debt/Equity[a]	0.05										
Software Industry Avg. Debt/Total Capital[a]	0.05										
Software Industry Avg. Unlevered Beta[a]	1.03										
Skype Debt-to-Equity Ratio[b]	0.22										
Skype Levered Beta	1.35										
Skype Cost of Equity	0.12										
Skype Cost of Borrowing	0.03										
Skype Cost of Capital (2011–2020)	0.11										
Skype Cost of Capital (Terminal Period)	0.09										
Terminal-Period Growth Rate (%)	0.05										
Terminal-Period Marginal Tax Rate (%)	0.4										

Selected Financial Data: ($ Millions)

Net Revenue	860	1,161	1,567	2,115	2,856	3,855	5,012	6,265	7,518	8,646	9,510
EBIT	424	522	705	888	1,142	1,465	1,804	2,130	2,406	2,594	2,853
EBIT(1-T)	424	522	705	755	914	1,172	1,353	1,598	1,804	1,945	2,140
Depreciations & Amortization	114	151	157	190	228	270	301	313	301	346	380
Working Capital	−110	0	235	423	571	964	1,504	2,193	2,631	3,026	3,329
ΔWorking Capital		110	235	188	148	393	540	689	439	395	303
Capital Spending	31	42	63	95	143	193	251	313	376	432	476
Free Cash Flow to the Firm		521	564	662	851	856	864	908	1,291	1,464	1,742

Present Value (2011–2010)	5,078
Terminal-Period Cash Flow	1,314
Terminal Value	1,266
Total NPV (Enterprise Value)	6,344
Equity Value	5,543

Debt Maturity: (12/21/2010)	Book Value	Weights	Weighted Maturity
2011	38,512	0.05	0.05
2012	38,512	0.05	0.10
2013	67,397	0.09	0.27
2014	452,521	0.61	2.44
2015	144,422	0.19	0.97
Total Debt Outstanding	741,364		
Weighted Avg. Maturity			3.84
Market Value of Debt			801.41

[a] http://pages.stern.nyu.edu/~adamodar/New_Home_Page/data.html.
[b] All Skype historical data from Skype SA Form S-1 Registration Statement, United States Securities and Exchange Commission, March 4, 2011.

TABLE 9.11　Skype Valuation Range

	Base Case	Optimistic Case	Col. 2/Col. 1	Pessimistic Case	Col. 4/Col. 1
	Col. 1	Col. 2	Col. 3	Col. 4	Col. 5
Enterprise Value	$6.3	$9.3	47.6%	$4.1	(34.9)%
Equity Value	$5.5	$8.5	54.6%	$3.3	(40)%

enterprise (equity plus debt) and $5.5 billion equity valuations are driven primarily by sustained high revenue-growth rates and continued robust operating margins. By using a 10-year annual forecast period, the terminal value represents a modest one-fifth of the firm's enterprise value. At the end of 2010, Skype, with debt comprising about 22% of total capital, was four times more leveraged than the industry average of 5%. Reflecting this higher volatility, Skype's levered beta of 1.35 compared to 1.06 for the industry average. The firm's weighted average cost of capital assumes Skype has a target debt-to-equity ratio equal to the current industry average and that revenue growth rates and operating profit margins will in time mirror those more typical of maturing software firms. Existing tax loss carryforwards would likely shelter the firm's income from taxes for at least the next several years. While the firm's marginal tax rate is expected to remain in line with that of other large software firms, after-tax operating profits are recalculated using a marginal tax rate of 40%

to estimate cash flows during the terminal period to avoid suggesting that the firm could defer the potential tax liability indefinitely.

If we assume the annual growth rate in net revenue is 10 percentage points higher than assumed in Table 9.10, Skype's enterprise and equity values surge to $9.3 billion and $8.5 billion, respectively. In contrast, if we pessimistically assume that revenue grows by 10 percentage points less per year, the enterprise and equity values plummet to $4.1 billion and $3.3 billion, respectively. In the more optimistic case, Microsoft would appear to have purchased Skype at a bargain price; however, if revenue grows much more slowly than anticipated, Microsoft would be exceedingly hard-pressed to generate sufficient synergy to earn its cost of capital. Hence, a range of reasonable-growth assumptions suggests that the valuation could vary widely (see Table 9.11).

Entitled "Skype Valuation Model," the Excel model on which Table 9.10 is based is available on the companion website to this book (http://booksite.elsevier.com/9780123854872). The reader is invited to create alternative scenarios by changing key assumptions, including the revenue growth rate, operating margin, and discount rates during the 10-year annual forecast period and the terminal period. The usefulness of such models often is more in identifying the range of potential outcomes than in providing highly accurate estimates.

Discussion Questions

1. What factors might cause Skype's stand-alone valuation net revenue growth to slow and operating profit margin to shrink? Be specific.
2. What challenges would you expect Microsoft to face in realizing the anticipated synergies? As the manager in charge of integration, what would you do to overcome these challenges?
3. Assuming the stand-alone valuation in Table 9.10 is accurate, what is the implied present value of Microsoft's anticipated synergies required for the firm to earn its cost of capital?
4. The acquisition of Skype could also be viewed as defensive. How would you put a value on the defensive nature of this acquisition?

Answers to these questions are found in the Online Instructor's Manual available to instructors using this book

CASE STUDY 9.2
Cleveland Cliffs Fails to Complete Its Attempted Takeover of Alpha Natural Resources in a Commodity Play

Key Points

- Financial models enable the assessment of the impact of different offer prices on postacquisition net present value and earnings per share.
- Such assessments enable negotiators to develop offers and counteroffers quickly during the negotiation process.

In an effort to exploit the long-term upward trend in commodity prices, Cleveland Cliffs, an iron ore mining company, failed in its attempt to acquire Alpha Natural Resource, a metallurgical coal mining firm, in late 2008 for a combination of cash and stock. In a joint press release on November 19, 2008, the firms announced that their merger agreement had been terminated due to adverse "macroeconomic conditions" at that time. Nevertheless, the transaction illustrates how a simple simulation model can be used to investigate the impact of alternative offer prices on postacquisition earnings per share.

When first announced in mid-2008, the deal was valued at about $10 billion. Alpha shareholders would receive total consideration of $131.42 per share, an approximate 46% premium over the firm's preannouncement share price. The new firm was to be renamed Cliffs Natural Resources and would have become one of the largest U.S. diversified mining and natural resources firms. The additional scale of operations, purchasing economies, and eliminating redundant overhead were expected to generate about $290 million in cost savings annually. The cash and equity portions of the offer price were 17.4% and 82.6%, respectively. See Table 9.12. The present value of anticipated synergy discounted in perpetuity at Cliffs' estimated cost of capital of 11% was about $2.65 billion. Posttransaction net income projections were derived from Wall Street estimates.

Discussion Questions

1. Purchase price premiums contain a synergy premium and a control premium. The control premium represents the amount an acquirer is willing to pay for the right to direct the operations of the target firm. Assume that Cliffs would not have been justified in paying a control premium for acquiring Alpha. Consequently, the Cliffs' offer price should have reflected only a premium for synergy. According to Table 9.12, did Cliffs overpay for Alpha? Explain your answer.

2. Based on the information in Table 9.12 and the initial offer price of $10 billion, did this transaction implicitly include a control premium? How much? In what way could the implied control premium have simply reflected Cliffs' potentially overpaying for the business? Explain your answer.

3. The difference in postacquisition EPS between an offer price in which Cliffs shared 100% of synergy and one in which it would share only 10% of synergy is about 22 percent (i.e., $3.72 \div $3.04 in 2008). To what do you attribute this substantial difference?

Answers to these questions are found in the Online Instructor's Manual available to instructors using this book.

TABLE 9.12 Cleveland Cliffs' Attempted Acquisition of Alpha Natural Resources: Offer Price Simulation Model

Deal Terms and Conditions

Cash Portion of Offer Price (%)	0.174
Equity Portion of Offer Price (%)	0.826
Percent of Anticipated Synergy Shared with Target (%)	1.00

Specific Firm Data

Acquirer Share Price ($/Share)	102.50
Target Share Price ($/Share)	90.27
Target Shares Outstanding (Millions)	64.40
Acquirer Shares Outstanding, Preclosing (Millions)	44.60
PV of Anticipated Net Synergy ($M) @ 11% WACC)	2,650

Alternative Scenarios Based on Different Amounts of Synergy Shared with Target

					Postacquisition EPS				
Calculated Data	% Shared Synergy	Offer Price ($M)	Offer Price per Share	Postacquisition Total Shares	2008	2009	2010	2011	2012
	0.1	6,078	94.38	104	3.72	4.09	4.42	4.73	4.96
Minimum Offer Price ($M)	5,813	0.2	6,343	98.50	106	3.63	3.99	4.31	4.61	4.84
Maximum Offer Price ($M)	8,463	0.3	6,608	102.61	109	3.55	3.90	4.21	4.50	4.72
Initial Offer Price ($M)	8,463	0.4	6,873	106.73	112	3.47	3.81	4.11	4.40	4.61
Initial Offer Price Per Share ($)	131.42	0.5	7,138	110.84	114	3.39	3.72	4.02	4.30	4.51

TABLE 9.12 Continued

Deal Terms and Conditions

Purchase Price Premium per Share (%)	0.46				
Composition of Purchase Price per Target Share:	0.6	0.7	0.8	0.9	1.0
Acquirer Equity per Target Share	108.55				
Cash per Target Share ($)	22.87				
Share-Exchange Ratio	1.28				
New Shares Issued by Acquirer	82.57				
Acquirer Shares Outstanding, Postclosing (Millions)	127.17				

	117	119	122	125	127
	114.96	119.07	123.19	127.30	131.42
	7,403	7,668	7,933	8,198	8,463
	3.31	3.64	3.93	4.20	4.41
	3.24	3.56	3.84	4.11	4.31
	3.17	3.48	3.76	4.02	4.22
	3.11	3.41	3.68	3.94	4.13
	3.04	3.34	3.61	3.86	4.05

Ownership Distribution in New Firm

Acquirer Shareholders (%)	0.35
Target Shareholders (%)	0.65

Consolidated Acquirer & Target Net Income

	2009	2010	2011	2012	2013
Postacquisition Consolidated Net Income ($M)	387	425	459	491	515

APPENDIX A

Utilizing the M&A Model on the Companion Website to This Book

The spreadsheet model on the companion website follows the four-step model-building process discussed in this chapter. Each worksheet is identified by a self-explanatory title and an acronym or "short name" used in developing the worksheet linkages. Appendices A and B at the end of the Excel spreadsheets include the projected timeline, milestones, and individual(s) responsible for each activity required to complete the transaction. See Table 9.13 for a brief description of the purpose of each worksheet.

Each worksheet follows the same layout: The assumptions are listed in the top panel, historical data in the lower-left panel, and forecast period data in the lower-right panel. In place of existing historical data, fill in the data for the firm you wish to analyze in cells not containing formulas. Do not delete existing formulas in the sections marked "historical period" or "forecast period" unless you wish to customize the model. To replace existing data in the forecast-period panel, change the forecast assumptions at the

top of the spreadsheet. A number of the worksheets use Excel's "iteration" calculation option. This option may have to be turned on for the worksheets to operate correctly, particularly due to the inherent circularity in these models. For example, the change in cash and investments affects interest income, which in turn affects net income and the change in cash and investments. If the program gives you a "circular reference" warning, please go to Tools, Options, and Calculation and turn on the iteration feature. One hundred iterations usually are enough to solve any "circular reference," but the number may vary with different versions of Excel. Individual simulations may be made most efficiently by making relatively small incremental changes to a few key assumptions underlying the model. Key variables include sales growth rates, the cost of sales as a percent of sales, cash flow growth rates during the terminal period, and the discount rate applied during the annual forecast period and the terminal period. Changes should be made to only one variable at a time.

TABLE 9.13   Model Structure

Step	Worksheet Title	Objective (Tab Short Name)
1	Determine Acquirer and Target Stand-Alone Valuation	Identify assumptions and estimate preacquisition value of stand-alone strategies
1	Acquirer 5-Year Forecast and Stand-Alone Valuation	Provides stand-alone valuation (BP_App_B1)
1	Acquirer Historical Data and Financial Ratios	Provides consistency check between projected and historical data (BP_App_B2)
1	Acquirer Debt Repayment Schedules	Estimate firm's preacquisition debt (BP_App_B3)

TABLE 9.13   Model Structure

Step	Worksheet Title	Objective (Tab Short Name)
1	Acquirer Cost of Equity and Capital Calculation	Displays assumptions (BP_App_B4)
1	Target 5-Year Forecast and Stand-Alone Valuation	See above (AP_App_B1)
1	Target Historical Data and Financial Ratios	See above (AP_App_B2)
1	Target Debt Repayment Schedules	See above (AP_App_B3)
1	Target Cost of Equity and Capital Calculation	See above (AP_App_B4)
2	Value Combined Acquirer and Target, Including Synergy	Identify assumptions and estimate postacquisition value
2	Combined Firm's 5-Year Forecast and Valuation	Provides valuation (AP_App_C)
2	Synergy Estimation	Displays assumptions underlying estimates (AP_App_D)
3	Determine Initial Offer Price for Target Firm	Estimate negotiating price range
3	Offer Price Determination	Estimate minimum and maximum offer prices AP_App_E)
3	Alternative Valuation Summaries	Displays alternative valuation methodologies employed (AP_App_F)
4	Determine Combined Firm's Ability to Finance Transaction	Reality check (AP_App_G)
Appendix A: Acquisition Timeline		Provides key activities schedule (AP_App_A1)
Appendix B: Summary Milestones and Responsible Individuals		Benchmarks performance to timeline (AP_App_A2)

APPENDIX B

M&A Model Balance-Sheet Adjustment Mechanism

Projecting each line item of the balance sheet as a percent of sales does not ensure that the projected balance sheet will balance. Financial analysts commonly "plug" into financial models an adjustment equal to the difference between assets and liabilities plus shareholders' equity. While this may make sense for one-year budget forecasting, it becomes very cumbersome in multiyear projections. Moreover, it becomes very time consuming to run multiple scenarios based on different sets of assumptions. By forcing the model to balance automatically, these problems can be eliminated. While practical, this automatic adjustment mechanism rests on the simplistic notion that a firm will borrow if cash flow is negative and add to cash balances if cash flow is positive. This assumption ignores other options available to the firm, such as using excess cash flow to reduce outstanding debt, repurchase stock, or pay dividends.

The balance-sheet adjustment methodology illustrated in Table 9.14 requires that the analyst separate current assets into operating and nonoperating assets. Operating assets include minimum operating cash balances and other operating assets (e.g., receivables, inventories, and assets such as prepaid items). Current nonoperating assets are investments (i.e., cash generated in excess of minimum operating balances invested in short-term marketable securities). The firm issues new debt whenever cash outflows exceed cash inflows. Investments increase whenever cash outflows are less than cash inflows. For example, if net fixed assets (NFA) were the only balance-sheet item that grew from one period to the next, new debt issued (ND) would increase by an amount equal to the increase in net fixed assets. In contrast, if current liabilities were the only balance-sheet entry to rise from one period to the next, nonoperating investments (I) would increase by an amount equal to the increase in current liabilities. In either example, the balance sheet will balance automatically.

The Microsoft Excel formulae that underlie the model's adjustment mechanism correspond to conditional ("if, then") instructions. If in a given year the firm is borrowing (i.e., new debt is positive), the investment row in the model's Step 1 worksheet is zero for that year. The amount of new debt would equal the difference between total assets less short-term nonoperating investments and total liabilities less new debt plus shareholders' equity. If in a given year the firm is not borrowing (i.e., new debt is zero), the investment row in the model's Step 1 worksheet is positive. The amount of short-term nonoperating investment would be equal to the difference between total liabilities less new debt plus shareholders' equity and total assets less short-term nonoperating investment. The same logic applies to the balancing mechanism for the Step 2 and Step 4 worksheets.

TABLE 9.14   Model Balance-Sheet Adjustment Mechanism

Assets	Liabilities
Current Operating Assets	Current Liabilities (CL)
Cash Needed for Operations (C)	
Other Current Assets (OCA)	Other Liabilities (OL)
Total Current Operating Assets (TCOA)	
Short-Term (Nonoperating) Investments (I)	Long-Term Debt (LTD)
	Existing Debt (ED)
	New Debt (ND)
Net Fixed Assets (NFA)	
Other Assets (OA)	
Total Assets (TA)	Total Liabilities (TL)
	Shareholders' Equity (SE)

Cash Outflows Exceed Cash Inflows:
- If $(TA - I) > (TL - ND) + SE$, the firm must borrow.

Cash Outflows Are Less Than Cash Inflows:
- If $(TA - I) < (TL - ND) + SE$, the firm's nonoperating investments increase.

Cash Outflows Equal Cash Inflows:
- If $(TA - I) = (TL - ND) + SE$, there is no change in borrowing or nonoperating investments.

Analysis and Valuation of Privately Held Firms

Maier's Law: If the facts do not conform to the theory, they must be disposed of.

INSIDE M&A: TAKING ADVANTAGE OF A "CUPCAKE BUBBLE"

KEY POINTS

- Financing growth represents a common challenge for most small businesses.
- Selling a portion of the business either to private investors or in a public offering represents a common way for small businesses to finance major expansion plans.

When Crumbs first opened in 2003 on the Upper West Side of Manhattan, the bakery offered three varieties of cupcakes among 150 other items. When the cupcakes became increasingly popular, the bakery began introducing cupcakes with different toppings and decorations. The firm's founders, Jason and Mia Bauer, followed a straightforward business model: Hold costs down, and minimize investment in equipment. Although all of Crumbs' cupcake recipes are Mia Bauer's, there are no kitchens or ovens on the premises. Instead, Crumbs outsources all of the baking activities to commercial facilities. The firm avoids advertising, preferring to give away free cupcakes when it opens a new store and to rely on word of mouth. By keeping costs low, the firm has expanded without adding debt. The firm targets locations with high daytime foot traffic, such as urban markets. In 2010, the firm sold 13 million cupcakes through 34 locations, accounting for $31 million in revenue and $2.5 million in earnings before interest, taxes, and depreciation. Crumbs' success spawned a desire to accelerate growth by opening up as many as 200 new locations by 2014. The challenge was how to finance such a rapid expansion.

The Bauers were no strangers to raising capital to finance the ongoing growth of their business, having sold one-half of the firm to Edwin Lewis, former CEO of Tommy Hilfiger, for $10 million in 2008. This enabled them to reinvest a portion in the business to sustain growth as well as to draw cash out of the business for their personal use. However, this time the magnitude of their financing requirements proved daunting. The couple was reluctant to burden the business with excessive debt, well aware that this had contributed to the demise of so many other rapidly growing businesses. Equity could be sold directly in the private placement market or to the public. Private placements could be expensive and may not provide the amount of financing needed; tapping the public markets directly through an IPO required dealing with underwriters and a level of financial expertise they lacked. Selling to another firm seemed to satisfy best their primary objectives: Get access to capital, retain their top management positions, and utilize the financial expertise of others to tap the public capital markets and to share in any future value creation.

The 57th Street General Acquisition Corporation (57th Street), a special-purpose acquisition company, or SPAC, appeared to meet their needs. In May 2010, 57th Street raised $54.5 million through an IPO, with the proceeds placed in a trust pending the completion of planned acquisitions.[1] One year later, 57th Street announced it had acquired Crumbs for $27 million in cash and $39 million in 57th Street stock. On June 30, 2011, 57th Street announced that NASDAQ had approved the listing of its common stock, giving Crumbs a market value of nearly $60 million.

CHAPTER OVERVIEW

Approximately three-fourths of all acquisitions in the United States involve privately owned corporations.[2] Such firms are those whose securities are not registered with state or federal authorities. As such, they are prohibited from being traded in the public securities markets. The lack of such markets makes valuing private businesses particularly challenging. Nevertheless, the need to value such businesses may arise for a variety of reasons. Investors and small business owners may need a valuation as part of a merger or acquisition, for settling an estate, or because employees wish to exercise their stock options. Employee stock ownership plans (ESOPs) also may require periodic valuations. In other instances,

---

[1] SPACs are shell, or blank-check, companies that have no operations but go public with the intention of merging with or acquiring a company with the proceeds of the SPAC's initial public offering.

[2] Capron and Shen, 2007

shareholder disputes, court cases, divorce, or the payment of gift or estate taxes may necessitate a valuation.

This chapter discusses how the analyst deals with problems not normally found in public firms. Since issues concerning making initial contact and negotiating with the owners of private businesses were addressed in Chapter 5, this chapter focuses on the challenges of valuing such firms and adjusting firm value for control premiums, minority discounts, and liquidity discounts. This chapter also includes a discussion of how corporate shells, created through reverse mergers, and leveraged ESOPs are used to acquire privately owned companies and how PIPE financing may be used to fund their ongoing operations. A review of this chapter is available in the file folder entitled "Student Study Guide" on the companion site to this book (http://booksite.elsevier.com/9780123854872).

WHAT ARE PRIVATELY HELD COMPANIES?

Small privately owned firms often are referred to as *closely held*, since usually only a few shareholders control the operating and managerial policies of the firm. Most closely held firms are family-owned businesses,[3] accounting for about 90% of the approximately 33 million businesses in the United States.[4] Family-owned firms often are beset by severe challenges, including management succession, limited access to financing, poor governance, informal management structure, poorly trained management, and a preference for ownership over growth. Such firms tend to be less acquisitive than public firms, especially when they result in diluting current ownership.[5]

Firms that are family owned but not managed by family members are often well managed, since family shareholders with large equity stakes monitor carefully those charged with managing the business.[6] However, management by the founders' children typically affects firm value adversely.[7] This may result from the limited pool of family members available for taking control of the business. Succession is one of the most difficult challenges to resolve, with family-owned firms viewing succession as the transfer of ownership more than as a transfer of management. Problems arise from inadequate preparation of the younger

[3] All closely held firms are not small, since families control the operating policies at many large, publicly traded companies. In such firms, family influence is exercised by family members holding senior management positions or board seats and through holding supervoting stock. Examples of large publicly traded family businesses include Wal-Mart, Ford Motor, Loew's, and Bechtel Group, each of which has annual revenues of more than $20 billion.

[4] Astrachan and Shanker, 2003

[5] Bouzgarrou et al., 2013; Frank et al., 2012; Caprio et al., 2011

[6] Bennedsen et al., 2006; Perez-Gonzalez, 2006; Villalonga and Amit, 2006

[7] Claessens et al., 2002; Morck and Yeung, 2000

generation of family members and the limited pool of potential successors, who might not even have the talent or the interest to take over. Many firms look to overcome these challenges by selling the business.

GOVERNANCE ISSUES

The market model of corporate governance explained in Chapter 3 relies on a large dispersed class of investors in which ownership and corporate control are separate. This model overlooks the fact that family-owned firms often have different interests, time horizons, and strategies from investors in publicly owned firms. In many countries, family-owned firms have been successful because of their shared interests and because investors place a higher value on the long-term health of the business rather than on short-term performance.[8] There is empirical evidence that the control model (in which ownership and control are concentrated in a single investor group) is more applicable to family-owned firms than is the market model.[9] Director independence, an important attribute of the market model, appears to be less important for family-owned firms. A board consisting of owners focused on the long-term growth of the business for future generations of the family may be far more committed to the firm than are outsiders.

CHALLENGES OF VALUING PRIVATELY HELD COMPANIES

The anonymity of many privately held firms, the potential for data manipulation, problems specific to small firms, and the tendency of owners of private firms to manage in a way to minimize tax liabilities create a number of significant valuation issues.

Lack of Externally Generated Information

There is generally a lack of analyses of private firms generated by sources outside of the company. Private firms provide little incentive for outside analysts to cover them because of the absence of a public market for their securities. Consequently, there are few forecasts of their performance other than those provided by the firm's management. Press coverage is usually quite limited, and what is available is often based on information provided by the firm's management. Even companies (e.g., Dun & Bradstreet) purporting to offer demographic and financial information on small privately held firms use largely superficial and infrequent telephone interviews with the management of such firms as their primary source of such information.

[8] Habbershon and Williams, 1999; De Visscher, Aronoff, and Ward, 1995

[9] Astrachan and Shanker, 2003

Lack of Internal Controls and Inadequate Reporting Systems

Private firms generally do not have the same level of controls and reporting systems as public firms, which are required to prepare audited financial statements and are subject to Sarbanes-Oxley.[10] The lack of formal controls, such as systems to approve and monitor how money is spent, invites fraud and misuse of private-firm resources. With intellectual property being a substantial portion of the value of many private firms, the lack of documentation also constitutes a key valuation issue. Often only one or two individuals within the firm know how to reproduce valuable intangible assets such as software, chemical formulas, and recipes, and the loss of such individuals can destroy a firm. Moreover, customer lists and the terms and conditions associated with key customer relationships also may be undocumented, creating the basis for customer disputes when a change in ownership occurs.

Firm-Specific Problems

Private firms may lack product, industry, and geographic diversification. There may be insufficient management talent to allow the firm to develop new products for its current markets or expand into new markets. Firm profits may be highly sensitive to fluctuations in demand because of significant fixed expenses. Its small size may restrict its influence with regulators and unions and limit its ability to gain access to distribution channels and leverage with suppliers and customers. Finally, the company may have an excellent product but very little brand recognition.

Common Forms of Manipulating Reported Income

Revenue and operating expenses may be misstated. How this may occur is explained next.

Misstating Revenue

Revenue may be over- or understated, depending on the owner's objectives. If the intent is tax minimization, businesses operating on a cash basis may opt to report less revenue because of the difficulty outside parties have in tracking transactions. Private business owners intending to sell a business may be inclined to inflate revenue if the firm is to be sold. Common examples include manufacturers, which rely on others to distribute their products. These manufacturers can inflate revenue in the current accounting period by booking as revenue, products shipped to resellers without adequately adjusting for probable returns. Membership or subscription businesses, such as health clubs and magazine publishers, may inflate revenue by booking the full value of multiyear

---

[10] Foley and Lardner, 2007

contracts in the current period rather than prorating the payment received at the beginning of the contract period over the life of the contract.[11]

Manipulation of Operating Expenses

Owners of private businesses attempting to minimize taxes may give themselves and family members higher-than-normal salaries, benefits, and bonuses. Other examples of cost manipulation include extraordinary expenses that are really other forms of compensation for the owner, his or her family, and key employees, which may include the rent on the owner's summer home or hunting lodge and salaries for the pilot and captain of the owner's airplane and yacht. Current or potential customers sometimes are allowed to use these assets. Owners frequently argue that these expenses are necessary to maintain customer relationships or close large contracts and are therefore legitimate business expenses. Other areas commonly abused include travel and entertainment, insurance, and excessive payments to vendors supplying services to the firm. Due diligence frequently uncovers situations in which the owner or a family member is either an investor in or an owner of the vendor supplying the products or services.

Alternatively, if the business owner's objective is to maximize the firm's selling price, salaries, benefits, and other operating costs may be understated significantly. An examination of the historical trend in the firm's profitability may reveal that profits are being manipulated. A sudden improvement in operating profits in the year in which the business is being offered for sale may suggest that expenses have historically been overstated, revenues understated, or both.

PROCESS FOR VALUING PRIVATELY HELD BUSINESSES

To address the challenges presented by privately owned firms, an analyst should adopt a four-step procedure. Step 1 requires adjustment of the target firm's financial data to reflect true profitability and cash flow in the current period. Step 2 entails determining the appropriate valuation methodology. Step 3 requires estimating the proper discount rate. Finally, in the fourth step, firm value is adjusted for a control premium (if appropriate), a liquidity discount, and a minority discount (if an investor takes a less-than-controlling ownership stake in a firm).

STEP 1: ADJUSTING FINANCIAL STATEMENTS

The purpose of adjusting the income statement is to provide an accurate estimate of the current year's net or pretax income, earnings before interest

---

[11] Such booking activity boosts current profitability because not all the costs associated with multiyear contracts, such as customer service, are incurred in the period in which the full amount of revenue is booked.

and taxes (EBIT), or earnings before interest, taxes, depreciation, and amortization (EBITDA). The various measures of income should reflect accurately all costs actually incurred in generating the level of revenue, adjusted for doubtful accounts the firm booked in the current period. They also should reflect other expenditures (e.g., training and advertising) that must be incurred in the current period to sustain the anticipated growth in revenue. The importance of establishing accurate current or base-year data is evident when we consider how businesses—particularly small, closely held businesses—are often valued. If the current year's profit data are incorrect, future projections of the dollar value would be inaccurate, even if the projected growth rate is accurate. Furthermore, valuations based on relative valuation methods such as price-to–current year earnings ratios would be biased to the extent that estimates of the target's current income are inaccurate.

EBITDA has become an increasingly popular measure of value for privately held firms. The use of this measure facilitates the comparison of firms because it eliminates the potential distortion in earnings performance due to differences in depreciation methods and financial leverage among firms. Furthermore, this indicator is often more readily applicable in relative valuation methods than other measures of profitability, since firms are more likely to display positive EBITDA than EBIT or net income figures. Despite its convenience, the analyst needs to be mindful that EBITDA is only one component of cash flow and ignores the impact on cash flow of changes in net working capital, investing, and financing activities.

Making Informed Adjustments

While finding reliable current information on privately held firms is challenging, information is available. The first step for the analyst is to search the Internet for references to the target firm. This search should unearth a number of sources of information on the target firm. Table 10.1 provides a partial list of websites containing information on private firms.

Salaries and Benefits

Before drawing any conclusions, the analyst should determine the actual work performed by all key employees and the compensation received for performing a similar job in the same industry. Comparative salary data can be obtained by employing the services of a compensation consultant familiar with the industry or simply by scanning "employee wanted" advertisements in the industry trade press and magazines and the "help wanted" pages of the local newspaper. Depending on the industry, benefits can range from 14% to 50% of an employee's base salary. Certain employee benefits, such as Social Security and Medicare taxes, are mandated by law and, therefore, an uncontrollable cost of doing business. Other types of benefits may be more controllable and include items such as pension contributions and life insurance coverage, which are calculated as a percentage of base salary. Efforts by the buyer to trim salaries

TABLE 10.1   Sources of Information on Private Firms.

Source/Web Address	Content
Research Firms	
Washington Researchers: www.washingtonresearchers.com	Provide listing of sources such as local government officials, local chambers of commerce, state government regulatory bodies, credit-reporting agencies, and local citizen groups
Fuld & Company: www.fuld.com	
Databases	
Dun & Bradstreet: www.smallbusiness.dnb.com	Information on firms' payments histories and limited financial data
Hoover's: www.hoovers.com	Data on 40,000 international and domestic firms, IPOs, not-for-profits, trade associations, and small businesses; and limited data on 18 million other companies
Integra: www.integrainfo.com	Provides industry benchmarking data
Standard & Poor's NetAdvantage: www.netadvantage.standardandpoors.com	Financial data and management and directors' bibliographies on 125,000 firms
InfoUSA www.infousa.com	Industry benchmarking and company specific data
Forbes: www.forbes.com/list	Provides list of top privately held firms annually
Inc: www.inc.com/inc5000	Provides list of 500 of the fastest-growing firms annually

that appear to be excessive also reduce these types of benefits. However, benefit reductions often contribute to higher operating costs in the short run due to higher employee turnover, the need to retrain replacements, and the potential negative impact on the productivity of those that remain. In many situations, the owner's spouse or other family members may be on the payroll without providing significant service to the company. A rational buyer would not continue these unnecessary or unnecessarily high salaries; thus, adjustments should be made accordingly.

Travel, Meals, and Entertainment

Travel and entertainment (T&E) expenditures tend to be one of the first cost categories cut when a potential buyer attempts to value a target company. What may look excessive to one who is relatively unfamiliar with the industry may in fact be necessary for retaining current customers and acquiring new customers. Establishing, building, and maintaining relationships is particularly important for personal and business services companies, such as consulting and law firms. Account management may require consultative selling at the customer's site.

A complex product like software may require on-site training. Indiscriminant reduction in the T&E budget could lead to a loss of customers following a change in ownership.[12]

Auto Expenses and Personal Life Insurance

Ask if such expenses represent a key component of the overall compensation required to attract and retain key employees. This can be determined by comparing total compensation paid to employees of the target firm with compensation packages offered to employees in similar positions in the same industry in the same region. A similar review should be undertaken with respect to the composition of benefits packages.

Family Members

Similar questions need to be asked about family members on the payroll. Frequently, they perform real services and tend to be highly motivated because of their close affinity with the business. If the business has been in existence for many years, the loss of key family members who built relationships with customers over the years may result in a subsequent loss of key accounts. Moreover, family members may be those who possess proprietary knowledge.

Rent or Lease Payments in Excess of Fair Market Value

Check who owns the buildings housing the business or the equipment used by the business. This is a common method of transferring company funds to the business owner, who also owns the building, in excess of their stated salary and benefits.

Professional Services Fees

Professional services could include legal, accounting, personnel, and actuarial services. Once again, check for any nonbusiness relationship between the business owner and the firm providing the service. Always consider any special circumstances that may justify unusually high fees. An industry that is subject to continuing regulation and review may incur what appear to be abnormally high legal and accounting expenses.

Depreciation Expense

Accelerated depreciation methodologies may make sense for tax purposes, but they may seriously understate current earnings. For financial reporting purposes, it may be appropriate to convert depreciation schedules from accelerated to straight-line depreciation if this results in a better matching of when expenses actually are incurred and revenue actually is received.

---

[12]Recent changes in tax laws have made the impact of inflated meals and entertainment expenses more burdensome. For tax purposes, only one-half of entertainment and meals, in certain circumstances, are deductible expenses.

Reserves

Current reserves may be inadequate to reflect future events. An increase in reserves lowers taxable income, whereas a decrease in reserves raises taxable income. Collection problems may be uncovered following an analysis of accounts receivable. It may be necessary to add to reserves for doubtful accounts. Similarly, the target firm may not have adequately reserved for future obligations to employees under existing pension and healthcare plans. Reserves also may have to be increased to reflect known environmental and litigation exposures.

Accounting for Inventory

During periods of inflation, businesses frequently use the last-in, first-out (LIFO) method to account for inventories. This approach results in an increase in the cost of sales that reflects the most recent and presumably highest-cost inventory; therefore, it reduces gross profit and taxable income. The use of LIFO during inflationary periods also tends to lower the value of inventory on the balance sheet because the items in inventory are valued at the lower cost of production associated with earlier time periods. In contrast, the use of first-in, first-out (FIFO) accounting for inventory assumes that inventory is sold in the chronological order in which it was purchased. When prices are increasing, the FIFO method produces a higher ending inventory, a lower cost of goods sold, and higher gross profit. Although it may make sense for tax purposes to use LIFO, the buyer's objective for valuation purposes should be to obtain a realistic estimate of actual earnings in the current period. FIFO accounting appears to be most logical for products that are perishable or subject to rapid obsolescence and, therefore, are most likely to be sold in chronological order. LIFO makes sense when inflation is expected to remain high.

Areas that are Commonly Understated

Projected sales increases normally require more aggressive marketing efforts, more effective customer service support, and better employee training. Nonetheless, it is common to see the ratio of annual advertising and training expenses to annual sales decline during the period of highest projected growth in forecasts developed by either the seller or the buyer. The seller wants to boost the purchase price. The buyer simply may be overly optimistic about how much more effectively they can manage the business or because they want a lender to finance the deal. Other areas that are commonly understated in projections but that can never really be escaped include the expense associated with environmental cleanup, employee safety, and pending litigation.

Areas that are Commonly Overlooked

The value in a business often is more in its intangible than tangible assets. The best examples include the high valuations placed on many Internet-related and biotechnology companies. Intangible assets may include customer lists, patents, licenses, distributorship agreements, leases, regulatory approvals, noncompete agreements, and employment contracts. For these items to represent incremental value, they must represent sources of revenue or cost reduction not already reflected in the target's operating cash flows.

Explaining Adjustments to Financial Statements

Table 10.2 illustrates how historical and projected financial statements received from the target as part of the due diligence process could be restated to reflect what the buyer believes to be a more accurate description of revenue and costs. Adjusting the historical financials provides insight into what the firm could have done had it been managed differently. Adjusting the projected financials also enables the analyst to use what he or she considers more realistic assumptions. Note that the cost of sales is divided into direct and indirect expenses. Direct cost of sales relates to costs incurred directly in the production process. Indirect costs are those incurred as a result of the various functions (e.g., senior management) supporting the production process. The actual historical costs are displayed above the "explanation of adjustments" line. Some adjustments represent "add backs" to profit, while others reduce profit. The adjusted EBITDA numbers at the bottom of the table represent what the buyer believes to be the most realistic estimate of the profitability of the business. Finally, by displaying the data historically, the buyer can see trends that may be useful in projecting the firm's profitability.

In this illustration, the buyer believes that because of the nature of the business, inventories are more accurately valued on a FIFO rather than LIFO basis. This change in inventory cost accounting results in a sizeable boost to the firm's profitability. Due diligence also revealed that the firm was overstaffed and that it could be operated by eliminating the full-time position held by the former owner (including fees received as a member of the firm's board of directors) and a number of part-time positions held by the owner's family members. Although some cost items are reduced, others are increased. Office space is reduced, thereby lowering rental expense as a result of the elimination of regional sales offices. However, the sales- and marketing-related portion of the travel and entertainment budget is increased to accommodate the increased travel necessary to service out-of-state customers. Likewise, advertising expenses will have to be increased to promote the firm's products in those regions. The new buyer also believes the firm's historical training budget to be inadequate to sustain the growth of the business and more than doubles spending in this category.

STEP 2: APPLYING VALUATION METHODOLOGIES TO PRIVATELY HELD COMPANIES

Methods employed to value private firms are similar to those discussed elsewhere in this book. However, in the absence of public markets, alternative

TABLE 10.2   Adjusting the Target Firm's Financial Statements[a]

	Year 1	Year 2	Year 3	Year 4	Year 5
Revenue ($ thousands)	8,000.0	8,400.0	8,820.0	9,261.0	9,724.1
Less: Direct Cost of Sales (COS), excluding Depreciation & Amortization	5,440.0	5,712.0	5,997.6	6,297.5	6,612.4
Equals: Gross Profit	2,560.0	2,688.0	2,822.4	2,963.5	3,111.7
Less: Indirect Cost of Sales					
Salaries & Benefits	1,200.0	1,260.0	1,323.0	1,389.2	1,458.6
Rent	320.0	336.0	352.8	370.4	389.0
Insurance	160.0	168.0	176.4	185.2	194.5
Advertising	80.0	84.0	88.2	92.6	97.2
Travel & Entertainment	240.0	252.0	264.6	277.8	291.7
Director Fees	50.0	50.0	50.0	50.0	50.0
Training	10.0	10.0	10.0	10.0	10.0
All Other Indirect Expenses	240.0	252.0	264.6	277.8	291.7
Equals: EBITDA	260.0	276.0	292.8	310.4	329.0
Explanation of Adjustments	**Add Backs/(Deductions)**				
LIFO direct COS is higher than FIFO cost; adjustment converts to FIFO costs	200.0	210.0	220.5	231.5	243.1
Eliminate part-time family members' salaries and benefits	150.0	157.5	165.4	173.6	182.3
Eliminate owner's salary, benefits, and director fees	125.0	131.3	137.8	144.7	151.9
Increase targeted advertising to sustain regional brand recognition	(50.0)	(52.5)	(55.1)	(57.9)	(60.8)
Increase T&E expense to support out-of-state customer accounts	(75.0)	(78.8)	(82.7)	(86.8)	(91.2)
Reduce office space (rent) by closing regional sales offices	120.0	126.0	132.3	138.9	145.9
Increase training budget	(25.0)	(26.3)	(27.6)	(28.9)	(30.4)
Adjusted EBITDA	705.0	743.3	783.4	825.6	869.9

[a]The reader may simulate alternative assumptions by accessing a file entitled "Excel Spreadsheet for Adjusting Target Firm Financials" available on the companion website.

definitions of value often are employed, and the valuation methods are subject to adjustments not commonly applied to public firms.

Defining Value

Fair market value is the cash or cash-equivalent price that a willing buyer would propose and a willing seller would accept for a business if both parties have access to all relevant information. Fair market value assumes that neither party is under any obligation to buy or sell. It is easier to obtain the fair market value for a public company because of the existence of public markets in which stock in the company is actively traded. The concept may be applied to privately held firms if similar publicly traded companies exist. Because finding substantially similar companies is difficult, valuation professionals have developed a related concept called fair value. *Fair value* is applied when no strong market exists for a business or it is not possible to identify the value of similar firms. Fair value is, by necessity, more subjective because it represents the dollar value of a business based on an appraisal of its tangible and intangible assets.[13]

Selecting the Appropriate Valuation Methodology

Appraisers, brokers, and investment bankers generally classify valuation methodologies into four approaches: income (discounted cash flow), relative or market based, replacement cost, and asset oriented. These are discussed next as they apply to private businesses.

The Income or Discounted Cash Flow (DCF) Approach

Factors affecting this method include the definition of income or cash flow, the timing of those cash flows, and the selection of an appropriate discount or capitalization rate. The terms *discount rate* and *capitalization rate* often are used interchangeably. Whenever the growth rate of a firm's cash flows is projected to vary over time, *discount rate* generally refers to the factor used to convert the projected cash flows to present values. If the cash flows of the firm are not expected to grow or are expected to grow at a constant rate indefinitely, the discount rate used by practitioners often is referred to as the *capitalization rate*. Capitalization rates may be converted to multiples for valuation purposes (see Exhibit 10.1).

---

[13]Fair value is the statutory standard applicable in cases of dissenting stockholders' appraisal rights. Following a merger or corporate dissolution, shareholders in many states have the right to have their shares appraised and to receive fair value in cash. In states adopting the Uniform Business Corporation Act, fair value refers to the value of the shares immediately before the corporate decision to which the shareholder objects, excluding any appreciation or depreciation in anticipation of the corporate decision. In contrast, according to the Financial Accounting Standards Board Statement 157, effective November 15, 2007, fair value is the price determined in an orderly transaction between market participants (Pratt and Niculita, 2008).

EXHIBIT 10.1   APPLYING CAPITALIZATION MULTIPLES

Assume Firm A and Firm B's current year cash flows are $1.5 million and the discount rate is 8%. Firm A's cash flows are not expected to grow, while Firm B's cash flows are expected to grow at 4% in perpetuity. What is the current market value of each firm?

Answer: Firm A is valued using the zero-growth method and Firm B the constant-growth DCF method.

Firm A: $1.5 million × (1/.08) = $1.5 million × 12.5 = $18.75 million
Firm B: $1.5 million × (1.04)/(0.08 − 0.04) = $1.5 million × 26 = $39 million

The perpetuity and constant-growth capitalization multiples are 12.5 and 26, respectively, and imply that investors are willing to pay $12.5 and $26 for each dollar of cash flow.

While more complex DCF methods are commonly used to value private firms, capitalization multiples may be used when owners lack sophistication in financial matters. Such multiples are easy to calculate and communicate to the parties involved and may facilitate completion of the deal. Also, there is little empirical evidence that more complex valuation methods necessarily result in more accurate valuation estimates. Although the DCF method is widely used, it is not used exclusively. Other valuation methodologies are used, depending on the facts and circumstances of the particular case.

The Relative-Value (or Market-Based) Approach

This approach also may be used in valuing private firms by business brokers or appraisers to establish a purchase price. The Internal Revenue Service and the U.S. tax courts have encouraged the use of market-based valuation techniques. Therefore, in valuing private companies, it is always important to keep in mind what factors the IRS thinks are relevant to the process, because the IRS may contest any sale requiring the payment of estate, capital gains, or unearned-income taxes. The IRS's positions on specific tax issues can be determined by reviewing revenue rulings. A *revenue ruling* is an official interpretation by the IRS of the Internal Revenue Code, related statutes, tax treaties, and regulations. Revenue Ruling 59–60 describes the general factors that the IRS and tax courts consider relevant in valuing private businesses. These factors include general economic conditions, the specific conditions in the industry, the type of business, historical trends in the industry, the firm's performance, and the firm's book value. In addition, the IRS and tax courts consider the ability of the company to generate earnings and pay dividends; the amount of intangibles such as goodwill; recent sales of stock; and the stock prices of companies engaged in the same or similar line of business.

The Replacement-Cost Approach

This approach states that the assets of a business are worth what it costs to replace them and is most applicable to businesses that have substantial amounts of tangible assets for which the actual cost to replace them can be determined. This method is often not useful in valuing a business whose assets are primarily intangible. Moreover, the replacement-cost approach ignores the value created by operating the assets as a going concern.[14]

The Asset-Oriented Approach

Book value is an accounting concept and often is not considered a good measure of market value because book values usually reflect historical rather than current market values. However, as noted in Chapter 8, tangible book value (i.e., book value less intangible assets) may be a good proxy for the current market value for both financial services and product distribution companies. Breakup value is an estimate of what the value of a business would be if each of its primary assets were sold independently. Liquidation value is a reflection of the firm under duress. For a listing of when to use the various valuation methodologies, see Table 8.4 in Chapter 8.

STEP 3: DEVELOPING DISCOUNT RATES

While the discount or capitalization rate can be derived using a variety of methods, the focus in this chapter is on the weighted-average cost of capital or the cost of equity. The capital asset pricing model (CAPM) provides an estimate of the acquiring firm's cost of equity, which may be used as the discount or capitalization rate when the firm is debt free. However, there is empirical evidence that CAPM tends to understate financial rates of return on small companies.[15] What follows is a discussion of ways to adjust CAPM to improve its accuracy in estimating the cost of equity for small privately owned, firms.

Estimating a Private Firm's Beta and Cost of Equity

CAPM assumes the cost of equity is determined by the marginal or incremental investor. Although both public and private firms are subject to systematic risk, nonsystematic risk associated with publicly traded firms can be eliminated by such investors holding a properly diversified portfolio of securities. This

---

[14] The replacement-cost approach sometimes is used to value intangible assets by examining the amount of historical investment associated with the asset. For example, the cumulative historical advertising spending targeted at developing a particular product, brand or image may be a reasonable proxy for the intangible value of the brand name or image. However, changing consumer tastes may make this method misleading.

[15] Ibbotson et al., 1997; Kaplan et al., 1998

often is not true for closely held firms. For firms in which the owner is most often the only (or primary) investor, the marginal investor is the current owner because of the frequent difficulty in attracting new investors.[16] Since the owner's net worth is primarily his or her ownership stake in the business, the owner is not likely to be well diversified. Betas for these firms understate the true exposure of these firms to risk, which would include both systematic and nonsystematic risk. Thus, unlike investors in publicly traded firms, owners of private firms are concerned about total risk and not just systematic risk.

To approximate total risk for owners of closely held firms, the analyst may estimate the *total beta*. The total beta is calculated by dividing the CAPM market beta (β) for a security by the correlation coefficient for comparable public firms with the overall stock market.[17] Because the correlation with the overall market has been removed, the total beta captures the security's risk as a stand-alone asset rather than as part of a well-diversified portfolio. The correlation coefficient may be estimated by taking the square root of the average coefficient of determination (R^2) for comparable public companies, obtained from linear regressions of their share prices against the overall stock market. The total beta (β_{tot}) may be expressed as follows:

$$\beta_{tot} = \beta / \sqrt{R^2} \qquad\qquad (10.1)$$

The total beta will provide a cost of equity for an investor who is completely invested in a single business.[18] When there is insufficient historical information to use regression analysis, the total beta may be estimated using the bottom-up process discussed in Chapter 7 (see Table 7.5).

Critics of total betas argue that betas estimated using historical regression analysis or the comparable company betas are inherently unstable, with

---

[16] The business owner may not want new investors because of a desire to retain control.

[17] Unlike the CAPM beta, which measures a security's volatility relative to the market and its correlation with the overall market, the total beta measures only the volatility of the security compared to market volatility. In a linear regression, $\beta = Cov(i, m)/\sigma_m^2$ and may be rewritten as $(\sigma_i/\sigma_m)R$, since $(\sigma_i/\sigma_m) \times [Cov(i, m)/(\sigma_i \times \sigma_m)] = Cov(i, m)/\sigma_m^2$, where σ_i is the standard deviation (volatility) of an ith security, σ_m is the standard deviation of the overall stock market, and R is the correlation coefficient $[Cov(i, m)/(\sigma_i \times \sigma_m)]$ between the ith security and the overall stock market. By multiplying (σ_i/σ_m), a measure of systematic and nonsystematic risk, by R, which lies between zero and 1, the CAPM beta provides an estimate of the systematic portion of total risk. Note that the total beta will generally be larger than the CAPM beta because the estimated correlation coefficient is between zero and 1; the total beta and the CAPM market beta are equal only if $R=1$.

[18] It is incorrect to use the total beta if a private company is being acquired by a public company or is going public, since the public firm's shareholders or investors in the IPO are assumed to be able to diversify away company-specific risk. If a private company investor is partially diversified (such as a hedge fund having investments in multiple industries), the investor's beta would be higher than the market beta but lower than the total beta.

estimates varying depending on methodology employed and time period selected. An alternative to the total beta to estimate the cost of equity is the *buildup method*, which represents the sum of the risks associated with a particular class of assets. This methodology assumes the firm's market beta is equal to 1 and adds to the CAPM's estimate of a firm's cost of equity an estimate of firm size, industry risk, and company-specific risk. These factors are an attempt to measure nonsystematic risk.

Firm-size adjustments reflect the assumption that on average, larger firms are less likely to default than smaller firms; the industry adjustment reflects the observation that certain industries are more cyclical (and therefore riskier) than others. Examples of company-specific risks for small privately owned firms include a lack of professional management, excessive dependence on a single customer or supplier, lack of access to capital, and a narrow product focus. Reflecting these factors, the buildup method could be displayed as follows:

$$k_e = R_f + ERP + FSP + IND + CSR \qquad (10.2)$$

where

k_e = cost of equity
R_f = risk-free return
ERP = equity risk premium (market return on stocks less the risk-free rate)
FSP = firm-size premium
IND = industry-risk premium
CSR = company-specific-risk premium

Data for firm-size and industry-risk premiums are available from Morningstar's Ibbotson *Stocks, Bonds, Bills & Inflation* from 1926 to the present; and Duff & Phelps *Risk Premium Report* from 1963 to the present.[19] Estimating company-specific-risk premiums requires qualitative analysis, usually consisting of management interviews and site visits. The magnitude of the company-specific-risk premium could be adjusted up or down to reflect such factors as leverage, size, and earnings/cash flow volatility. Other subjective factors could include management depth and acumen, customer concentration, product substitutes, potential new entrants, and product diversification.[20]

---

[19] Morningstar's Ibbotson provides equity-risk premiums for 10 size deciles based on companies' market capitalizations. The 10th decile is further subdivided for firms with market caps from as low as $1.2 million. The firm also provides 500 industry-level-risk premiums. Duff & Phelps provides equity-risk premiums by grouping companies into 25 size categories based on eight different definitions of size. The definitions include market cap, book value, 5-year average net income, market value of invested capital, 5-year average EBITDA, sales, number of employees, and total assets. Analysts can use these data to benchmark the subject company without having to estimate the market value of equity because they would use the Ibbotson data.

[20] For an excellent discussion of how business appraisers use the buildup method, see W. Miller (2010).

While commonly used by practitioners, the buildup method also is problematic, because it assumes that the size, industry and company-specific-risk premiums are additive. If so, they would have to be independent or uncorrelated. It is likely that the factors captured by the size premium also are reflected in the industry- and company-specific-risk premiums, potentially resulting in "double-counting" their impact in estimating the magnitude of the firm's cost of equity. Furthermore, subjective adjustments made to the company-specific-risk premium based on the experience and intuition of the appraiser could also result in significant bias.

Estimating the Cost of Private-Firm Debt

Private firms can seldom access public debt markets and are usually not rated by the credit-rating agencies. Most debt is bank debt, and the interest expense on loans on the firm's books that are more than a year old may not reflect what it actually would cost the firm to borrow currently. The common solution is to assume that private firms can borrow at the same rate as comparable publicly listed firms or to estimate an appropriate bond rating for the company based on financial ratios and to use the interest rate that public firms with similar ratings pay. An analyst can identify publicly traded company bond ratings using the various Internet bond-screening services (e.g., finance.yahoo.com/bonds) to search for bonds with various credit ratings. Royal Caribbean Cruise Lines LTD had a BBB rating and a 2.7 interest coverage ratio in 2009 and would have to pay 7.0% to 7.5% for bonds maturing in 7–10 years. Consequently, firms with similar interest-coverage ratios could have similar credit ratings. If the private firm to be valued had a similar interest-coverage ratio and wanted to borrow for a similar time period, it is likely that it would have had to pay a comparable rate of interest.[21] Other sources of information about the interest rates that firms of a certain credit rating pay often are available in major financial newspapers, such as *The Wall Street Journal, Investors' Business Daily*, and *Barron's*.[22]

Determining the Appropriate Tax Rate

Throughout this book, a corporate marginal tax rate of 40% has been used in calculating the after-tax cost of debt in valuing public firms. When the acquirer of a private firm is a public firm, using the 40% corporate marginal tax rate is generally correct. However, for acquirers that are private firms or individuals, the choice of the tax rate to use depends on the nature of the buyer. The right

[21] If the maturity date, coupon rate, how frequently interest is paid, and the face value of a private firm's outstanding debt are known, the market value of such debt can be estimated using the yield to maturity on comparable debt that is currently traded for firms of similar risk.

[22] Unlike the estimation of the cost of equity for small privately held firms, it is unnecessary to adjust the cost of debt for specific business risk, since it should already be reflected in the interest rate charged to firms of similar risk.

marginal tax rate could be as high as 40% if a public company is the acquirer or as low as zero if the buyer is a nonprofit entity. The marginal tax rate should reflect the highest marginal personal income tax rate if the buyer(s) are individuals.

If the acquirer is organized as a sole proprietorship, where the business's income is recorded on the owner's tax return, the right tax rate would be the highest marginal personal income tax rate. For partnerships, limited liability companies, and sub-chapter S corporations, where all income is distributed to partners, members, and owners, respectively, the correct tax rate would be a weighted average of the owners' marginal tax rates. The weights should reflect the owners' respective ownership percentages. If the buyers are wealthy individuals, it is necessary to adjust estimates of the cost of equity obtained by examining comparable public firms for the impact of personal taxes. If the cost of equity for public firms is 10% and the personal tax rate on dividends and capital gains is 15%, the cost of equity would be 8.5% (i.e., $10\% \times (1 - 0.15)$).[23]

Estimating the Cost of Capital

In the presence of debt, the cost-of-capital method should be used to estimate the discount or capitalization rate. This method involves the calculation of a weighted average of the cost of equity and the after-tax cost of debt. The weights should reflect market values rather than book values. Private firms represent a greater challenge than public firms, in that the market value of their equity and debt is not readily available. Calculating the cost of capital requires the use of the market value rather than the book value of debt-to–total capital ratios. Private firms provide such ratios only in book terms. A common solution is to use what the firm's management has set as its target debt-to-equity ratio in determining the weights to be used or to assume that the private firms will eventually adopt the industry average debt-to-equity ratio.[24] When the growth period for the firm's cash flow is expected to vary, the cost of capital estimated for the high-growth period can be expected to decline when the firm begins to grow at a more sustainable rate, often the industry average growth rate. At that point, the firm presumably begins to take on the risk and growth characteristics of the typical firm in the industry. Thus, the discount rate may be assumed to be the industry average cost of capital during the sustainable-growth period. Exhibit 10.2 illustrates how to calculate a private firm's beta, cost of equity, and cost of capital.

[23] The cost of equity for public firms is after corporate taxes are paid but before personal taxes. When all profits are distributed to investors, it is necessary to adjust the cost of equity for the investor's personal tax rates.

[24] The firm's target D/E ratio should be consistent with the debt-to-total capital and equity-to-total capital weights used in the weighted-average cost of capital. This consistency can be achieved simply by dividing the target D/E (or the industry D/E if that is what is used) by $(1 + D/E)$ to estimate the implied debt-to-total capital ratio. Subtracting this ratio from 1 provides the implied equity-to-total capital ratio.

EXHIBIT 10.2   VALUING PRIVATE FIRMS

Acuity Lighting, a regional manufacturer and distributor of custom lighting fixtures, has revenues of $10 million and an EBIT of $2 million in the current year (i.e., year 0). The book value of the firm's debt is $5 million. The firm's debt matures at the end of five years and has annual interest expense of $400,000. The firm's marginal tax rate is 40%, the same as the industry average. Capital spending equals depreciation in year 0, and both are expected to grow at the same rate. As a result of excellent working capital management, the future change in working capital is expected to be essentially zero. The firm's revenue is expected to grow 15% annually for the next five years and 5% per year thereafter. The firm's current operating profit margin is expected to remain constant throughout the forecast period. As a result of the deceleration of its growth rate to a more sustainable rate, Acuity Lighting is expected to assume the risk and growth characteristics of the average firm in the industry during the sustainable-growth period. Consequently, its discount rate during this period is expected to decline to the industry average cost of capital of 11%. The industry average beta and debt-to-equity ratio are 2 and 0.4, respectively. The R^2 associated with a linear regression of the share prices of comparable publicly traded companies with the overall stock market is 25. The 10-year U.S. Treasury bond rate is 4.5%, and the historical equity premium on all stocks is 5.5%. Acuity Lighting's interest coverage ratio is 2.89, equivalent to a BBB credit rating. BBB-rated firms are currently paying a pretax cost of debt of 7.5%. Acuity Lighting's management has established the firm's target debt-to-equity ratio at 0.5 based on the firm's profitability and growth characteristics. Estimate the equity value of the firm.

Calculate Acuity's cost of equity using the methodology discussed in Chapter 7 (Table 7.5) and the weighted average cost of capital. This requires computing the average of comparable firms' unlevered betas and relevering the average unlevered beta using the target's debt-to-equity ratio:

1. Unlevered beta for publicly traded firms in the same industry = $2/(1 + 0.6 \times 0.4)$ = 1.61, where 2 is the industry's average levered beta, 0.6 is (1–tax rate), and 0.4 is the average debt-to-equity ratio for firms in this industry.
2. The total beta (see Eq. (10.1)) is $1.61/\sqrt{.25} = 3.22$ (Note: The total beta reflects only operating and industry risk.)
3. Acuity's levered beta = $3.22 \times (1 + 0.6 \times 0.5) = 4.19$, where 0.5 is the target debt-to-equity ratio established by Acuity's management.
4. Acuity's cost of equity = $4.5 + 4.19 \times 5.5 = 27.6$.
5. Acuity's after-tax cost of debt = $7.5 \times (1 - 0.4) = 4.5$, where 7.5 is the pretax cost of debt.
6. Acuity's WACC = $(27.6 \times 0.67) + (4.5 \times 0.33) = 19.98$, where the firm's debt–to–total capital ratio (D/TC) is determined by dividing Acuity's debt-to-equity target (D/E) by 1 + D/E. Therefore,

$$D/TC = 0.5/(1 + 0.5) = 0.33 \text{ and equity to total capital} = 1 - 0.33 = 0.67$$

Value Acuity by means of the FCFF DCF model using the data provided in Table 10.3.

$$\text{Present Value of FCFF} = \frac{\$1,380,000}{1.1998} + \frac{\$1,587,000}{(1.1998)^2} + \frac{\$1,825,050}{(1.1998)^3} + \frac{\$2,098,807}{(1.1998)^4}$$

$$+ \frac{\$2,413,628}{(1.1998)^5}$$

$$= \$1,150,192 + \$1,102,451 + \$1,056,692 + \$1,012,831$$

$$+ \$970,792$$

$$= \$5,292,958$$

$$\text{PPV of Terminal value} = [\$2,534,310/(0.11 - 0.05)]/(1.1824)^5 = \$18,276,220$$

$$\text{Total Present Value} = \$5,292,958 + \$18,276,220 = \$23,569,178$$

$$\text{Market Value of Acuity's Debt} = \$400,000 \times \frac{[(1 - (1/(1.075)^5)]}{.075} + \frac{\$5,000,000}{(1.075)^5}$$

$$= \$1,618,354 + \$3,482,793$$

$$= \$5,101,147$$

$$\text{Value of Equity} = \$23,569,178 - \$5,101,147 = \$18,468,031$$

STEP 4: APPLYING CONTROL PREMIUMS, LIQUIDITY, AND MINORITY DISCOUNTS

In Exhibit 9.2 in Chapter 9, the maximum purchase price of a target firm (PV_{MAX}) is defined as its current market or stand-alone value (i.e., the minimum price, or PV_{MIN}) plus the value of anticipated net synergies (i.e., PV_{NS}):

$$PV_{MAX} = PV_{MIN} + PV_{NS} \tag{10.3}$$

This is a reasonable representation of the maximum offer price for firms whose shares are traded in liquid markets and where no single shareholder (i.e., block shareholder) can direct the activities of the business. Examples of such firms could include Microsoft, IBM, and General Electric. However, when markets are illiquid and there are block shareholders with the ability to influence strategic decisions

TABLE 10.3   FCFF Model

	Year					
	1	2	3	4	5	6
EBIT[a]	$2,300,000	$2,645,000	$3,041,750	$3,498,012	$4,022,714	$4,223,850
EBIT (1–Tax Rate)[b]	$1,380,000	$1,587,000	$1,825,050	$2,098,807	$2,413,628	$2,534,310

[a]EBIT grows at 15% annually for the first five years and 5% thereafter.
[b]Capital spending equals depreciation in year 0, and both are expected to grow at the same rate. Moreover, the change in working capital is zero. Therefore, free cash flow equals after-tax EBIT.

made by the firm, the maximum offer price for the firm needs to be adjusted for liquidity risk and the value of control. These concepts are explored next.

Liquidity Discounts

Liquidity is the ease with which investors can sell assets without a serious loss in the value of their investment. An investor in a private company may find it difficult to sell his or her shares quickly because of limited interest in the company. It may be necessary to sell at a significant discount from what was paid for the shares. Liquidity or marketability risk may be expressed as a *liquidity* or *marketability discount*, which equals the reduction in the offer price for the target firm by an amount equal to the potential loss of value when sold.

Empirical studies of liquidity discounts demonstrate that they exist, but there is substantial disagreement over their magnitude. While pre-1992 studies found discounts as high as 50%,[25] studies since 1999 indicate more modest discounts, ranging from 5% to 35%, with an average discount of about 20%.[26] The decline in the discount since 1990 reflects a reduction in the Rule 144 holding period for restricted shares[27] and improved market liquidity. The latter is due to better business governance practices, lower transaction costs, greater access to information via the Internet, and the emergence of markets for trading nonpublic stocks.[28]

Purchase Price Premiums, Control Premiums, and Minority Discounts

For many transactions, the purchase price premium includes both a premium for anticipated synergy and a premium for control. The value of control is different from the value of synergy, which represents revenue increases and cost savings that result from combining two firms. In contrast, the value of control provides the right to direct the activities of the target firm on an ongoing basis. While control is often assumed to require a greater-than-50% ownership stake, effective control can be achieved at less than 50% ownership if other shareholders own relatively smaller stakes and do not vote as a block. Consequently, an investor may be willing to pay a significant premium to purchase a less-than-50% stake if the investor believes that effective control over key decisions can be achieved.

Control includes the ability to select management; determine compensation; set policy; acquire and liquidate assets; award contracts; make acquisitions; sell

---

[25] Pratt, 2008

[26] Johnson,1999; Aschwald, 2000; Finnerty, 2002; Loughran and Ritter, 2002; Officer, 2007; Comment, 2012

[27] Restricted shares are those issued by public firms, with the caveat that they not be traded for a specific time period; as such, such shares can be sold only through a private placement under the provisions of the SEC's Rule 144, usually at a discount because of their lack of marketability. In 1997, the SEC reduced the holding period for restricted stock from two years to one, making such shares more liquid.

[28] Examples of markets for nonpublic companies include secondmarket.com, sharespost.com and peqx.com.

or recapitalize the company; and register the company's stock for a public offering. The more control a block investor has, the less influence a minority investor has and the less valuable is the minority investor's stock. Therefore, a *control premium* is the amount an investor is willing to pay to direct the activities of the firm. A *minority discount* is the reduction in the value of the investment because the minority owners have little control over the firm's operations.

Purchase price premiums may reflect only control premiums when a buyer acquires a target firm and manages it as an independent operating subsidiary. The *pure control premium* is the value the acquirer believes can be created by replacing incompetent management, changing the strategic direction of the firm, gaining a foothold in a market not currently served, or achieving unrelated diversification.[29] The empirical evidence available to measure the control premium is limited, resulting in considerable disagreement about its size. Country comparison studies indicate a huge variation in median control premiums from as little as 2–5% in countries where corporate ownership often is widely dispersed and investor protections are effective to as much as 60–65% in countries where ownership tends to be concentrated and governance practices are poor.[30] Median estimates across countries are 10–12%.

The Relationship between Liquidity Discounts and Control Premiums

Market liquidity and the value of control tend to move in opposite directions—that is, whenever it is easy for shareholders to sell their shares, the benefits of control diminish. Why? Because shareholders who are dissatisfied with the decisions made by controlling shareholders may choose to sell their shares, thereby driving down the value of the controlling shareholder's interest. When it is difficult for shareholders to sell without incurring significant losses (i.e., the market is illiquid), investors place a greater value on control. Minority shareholders have no easy way to dispose of their investment, since they cannot force the sale of the firm and the controlling shareholder has little incentive to acquire their shares, except at a steep discount. The controlling shareholder can continue to make decisions that may not be in the best interests of the minority shareholders, with minimal consequences. Therefore, the sizes of control premiums and liquidity discounts tend to be positively correlated, since the value of control increases as market liquidity decreases (i.e., liquidity discounts increase).

---

[29] Another example of a pure control premium is that paid for a firm going private through a leveraged buyout, in that the target firm generally is merged into a shell corporation, with no synergy being created, and managed for cash after having been recapitalized. While the firm's management team may remain intact, the board of directors usually consists of representatives of the financial sponsor (i.e., equity or block investor).

[30] Weifeng, Zhaoguo, and Shasha, 2008; Massari, Monge, and Zanetti, 2006; Dyck and Zingales, 2004; Nenova, 2003; Hanouna, Sarin, and Shapiro, 2001

Equation (10.3) can be rewritten to reflect the interdependent relationship between the control premium (CP) and the liquidity discount (LD) as follows:

$$\begin{aligned}
PV_{MAX} &= (PV_{MIN} + PV_{NS})(1 + CP\%)(1 - LD\%) \\
PV_{MAX} &= (PV_{MIN} + PV_{NS})(1 - LD\% + CP\% - LD\% \times CP\%) \\
PV_{MAX} &= (PV_{MIN} + PV_{NS})[1 - LD\% + CP\%(1 - LD\%)]
\end{aligned} \qquad (10.4)$$

where

CP% = control premium expressed as a percentage of the maximum purchase price
LD% = liquidity discount expressed as a percentage of the maximum purchase price

The multiplicative form of Eq. (10.3) shown in Eq. (10.4) results in a term (i.e., LD% × CP%) that serves as an estimate of the interaction between the control premium and the liquidity discount.[31] This interaction term reflects the potential reduction in the value of control [i.e., CP%(1–LD%)] resulting from disaffected minority shareholders' taking a more active role in monitoring the firm's performance. This could result in proxy contests to change decisions made by the board and management or the composition of the board, as well as litigation.[32]

Estimating Liquidity Discounts, Control Premiums, and Minority Discounts

There is no such thing as a standard liquidity discount or control premium because the size of the discount or premium should reflect firm-specific factors.

Factors Affecting the Liquidity Discount

The median liquidity discount for empirical studies since the early 1990s is about 20%. Table 10.4 suggests a methodology for adjusting a private firm for liquidity risk, where an analyst starts with the median liquidity discount of 20% and adjusts for factors specific to the target firm. Such factors include firm size, liquid assets as a percent of total assets, financial returns, and cash flow growth and leverage as compared to the industry. While not intended to be an exhaustive list, these factors were selected based on the findings of empirical studies of restricted stocks.

---

[31] If control premiums and minority discounts; and control premiums and liquidity discounts are positively correlated, minority discounts and liquidity discounts must be positively correlated.

[32] PV_{MAX} may also be adjusted for illiquidity and value of control by adjusting the cost of equity (k_e). Assume $k_e = k(1 + CP\%)(1 - LD\%)$, where k is the cost of equity, including the effects of illiquidity and the value of control, then $k = k_e/(1 + CP\%)(1 - LD\%)$. That is, k decreases with an increasing value of control (PV_{MAX} increases) and increases with increasing illiquidity (PV_{MAX} decreases).

TABLE 10.4   Estimating the Size of the Liquidity Discount

Factor	Guideline	Adjust 20% Median Discount as Follows
Firm size	• Large • Small	• Reduce discount • Increase discount
Liquid assets as % of total assets	• >50% • <50%	• Reduce discount • Increase discount
Financial returns	• 2 × industry median[a] • ½ × industry median	• Reduce discount • Increase discount
Cash-flow growth rate	• 2 × industry median • ½ × industry median	• Reduce discount • Increase discount
Leverage	• ½ × industry median • 2 × industry median	• Reduce discount • Increase discount
Estimated firm-specific liquidity discount		= 20% ± adjustments

[a]*Industry median financial information often is available from industry trade associations, conference presentations, Wall Street analysts' reports, Yahoo! Finance, Barron's, Investor's Business Daily, The Wall Street Journal, and similar publications and websites.*

The liquidity discount should be smaller for more highly liquid firms, since liquid assets generally can be converted quickly to cash with minimal loss of value. Furthermore, firms whose financial returns exceed significantly the industry average have an easier time attracting investors and should be subject to a smaller liquidity discount than firms that are underperforming the industry. Likewise, firms with relatively low leverage and high cash flow growth should be subject to a smaller liquidity discount than more leveraged firms with slower cash flow growth because they have a lower breakeven point and are less likely to default or become insolvent.

Factors Affecting the Control Premium

Factors affecting the size of the control premium include the perceived ability of the target's current management, the extent to which operating expenses are discretionary, the value of nonoperating assets, and the net present value of currently unexploited business opportunities. The value of replacing incompetent management is difficult to quantify, since it reflects the potential for better future decision making. The value of nonoperating assets and discretionary expenses are quantified by estimating the after-tax sale value of redundant assets and the pretax profit improvement from eliminating redundant personnel. While relatively easy to measure, such actions may be impossible to implement without having control of the business.[33]

---

[33] This is true because such decisions could involve eliminating the positions of members of the family owning the business, or selling an asset owned by the business but used primarily by the family owning the business.

TABLE 10.5   Estimating the Size of the Control Premium to Reflect the Value of Changing the Target's Business Strategy and Operating Practices

Factor	Guideline	Adjust 10% Median Control Premium as Follows[a]
Target management	• Retain • Replace	• No change in premium • Increase premium
Discretionary expenses	• Cut if potential savings >5% of total expenses • Do not cut if potential savings <5% of total expenses	• Increase premium • No change in premium
Nonoperating assets	• Sell if potential after-tax gain >10% of purchase price[b] • Defer decision if potential after-tax gain <10% of purchase price	• Increase premium • No change in premium
Alternative business opportunities	• Pursue if NPV >20% of target's stand-alone value • Do not pursue if NPV <20% of target's stand-alone value	• Increase premium • No change in premium
Estimated firm-specific control premium		= 10% + adjustments

[a]The 10% premium represents the median estimate from the Nenova (2003) and Dyck and Zingales (2004) studies for countries perceived to have relatively stronger investor protection and law enforcement.
[b]The purchase price refers to the price paid for the controlling interest in the target.

If the target business is to be run as currently managed, no control premium should be added to the purchase price. If the acquirer intends to take actions possible only if the acquirer has control, the purchase price should include a control premium sufficient to gain a controlling interest. Table 10.5 provides a methodology for adjusting a control premium to be applied to a specific business. The 10% premium in the table is for illustrative purposes only and is intended to provide a starting point. The actual premium selected should reflect the analyst's perception of what is appropriate given the country's legal system and propensity to enforce laws and the extent to which the firm's ownership tends to be concentrated or widely dispersed.

The percentages applied to the discretionary expenses' share of total expenses, nonoperating assets as a percent of total assets, and the NPV of alternative strategies reflect risks inherent in cutting costs, selling assets, and pursuing other investment opportunities. These risks include a decline in morale and productivity following layoffs; the management time involved in selling assets and the possible disruption of the business; and the potential for overestimating the NPV of other investments. In other words, the perceived benefits of these decisions should be large enough to offset the associated risks. Additional adjustments not shown in Table 10.5 may be necessary to reflect state statutes affecting the rights of controlling and minority shareholders.[34]

As a practical matter, business appraisers frequently rely on the *Control Premium Study*, published annually by FactSet Mergerstat. Another source is Duff and Phelps. The use of these data is problematic, since the control-premium estimates provided by these firms include the estimated value of synergy as well as the amount paid to gain control.[35]

Factors Affecting the Minority Discount

Minority discounts reflect the loss of influence due to the power of a controlling-block investor. Intuitively, the magnitude of the discount should relate to the size of the control premium. The larger the control premium, the greater the perceived value of being able to direct the activities of the business and the value of special privileges that come at the expense of the minority investor. Reflecting the relationship between control premium and minority discounts, FactSet Mergerstat estimates minority discounts by using the following formula:

Implied Median Minority Discount = $1 - [1/(1 + \text{median premium paid})]$ (10.5)

Equation (10.5) implies that an investor would pay a higher price for control of a company and a lesser amount for a minority stake (i.e., larger control premiums are associated with larger minority discounts). While Eq. (10.5) is used routinely by practitioners to estimate minority discounts, there is little empirical support for this largely intuitive relationship.[36]

Exhibit 10.3 shows what an investor should pay for a controlling interest and for a minority interest. The example assumes that 50.1% ownership is required for a controlling interest. In practice, control may be achieved with less than a majority ownership position if there are numerous other minority investors or the investor is buying supervoting shares. The reader should note how the 20% median liquidity discount rate (based on recent empirical studies) is adjusted for the specific risk and return characteristics of the target firm. Furthermore, the

---

[34] In more than one-half of the states, major corporate actions, such as a merger, a sale, a liquidation, or a recapitalization of a firm, may be approved by a simple majority vote of the firm's shareholders. Other states require at least a two-thirds majority to approve such decisions. A majority of the states have dissolution statutes that make it possible for minority shareholders to force dissolution of a corporation if they can show there is a deadlock in their negotiations with the controlling shareholders or that their rights are being violated.

[35] Damodaran (2002) suggests that the way to estimate a control premium is to view it as equal to the difference between the PV of a firm if it were being operated optimally, and its PV the way it is currently being managed. This presumes the analyst can determine accurately the value-optimizing strategy for the target firm.

[36] Minority rights are protected in some states by requiring two-thirds voting approval of certain major corporate decisions, implying that minority ownership interests may be subject to a smaller discount in such states.

EXHIBIT 10.3 INCORPORATING LIQUIDITY RISK, CONTROL PREMIUMS, AND MINORITY DISCOUNTS IN VALUING A PRIVATE BUSINESS

Lighting Group Incorporated (LGI), a holding company, wants to acquire a controlling interest in Acuity Lighting, whose estimated stand-alone equity value equals $18,468,031 (see Exhibit 10.2). LGI believes that the present value of synergies due to cost savings is $2,250,000 ($PV_{SYN}$) related to the potential for bulk purchase discounts and cost savings related to eliminating duplicate overhead and combining warehousing operations. LGI believes that the value of Acuity, including synergy, can be increased by at least 10% by applying professional management methods (and implicitly by making better management decisions). To achieve these efficiencies, LGI must gain control of Acuity. LGI is willing to pay a control premium of as much as 10%. The minority discount is derived from Eq. (10.5). The factors used to adjust the 20% median liquidity discount are taken from Table 10.4. The magnitudes of the adjustments are the opinion of the analyst. LGI's analysts have used Yahoo! Finance to obtain the industry data in Table 10.6 for the home furniture and fixtures industry.

What is the maximum purchase price LGI should pay for a 50.1% controlling interest in the business?; for a minority 20% interest in the business?

To adjust for presumed liquidity risk of the target due to lack of a liquid market, LGI discounts its offer to purchase 50.1% of the firm's equity by 16%.

Using Eq. (10.4), we get:

$$
\begin{aligned}
PV_{MAX} &= (PV_{MIN} + PV_{NS})(1 - LD\%)(1 + CP\%) \\
&= [(\$18,468,031 + \$2,250,000)(1 - 0.16)(1 + 0.10)] \times 0.501 \\
&= \$20,718,031 \times 0.924 \times 0.501 \\
&= \$9,590,873 \text{ (maximum purchase price for 50.1\%)}
\end{aligned}
$$

If LGI were to acquire only a 20% stake in Acuity, it is unlikely that there would be any synergy, because LGL would lack the authority to implement potential cost-saving measures without the approval of the controlling shareholders. Because it is a minority investment, there is no control premium, but a minority discount for lack of control should be estimated. This is accomplished by using Eq. (10.5)—that is, $1 - [1/(1 + 0.10)] = 9.1$.

$$
\begin{aligned}
PV_{MAX} &= [\$18,468,873 \times (1 - 0.16)(1 - 0.091)] \times 0.2 \\
&= \$2,820,419 \text{(maximum purchase price for 20\%)}
\end{aligned}
$$

control premium is equal to what the acquirer believes is the minimum increase in value created by achieving a controlling interest. Also, observe how the direct relationship between control premiums and minority discounts is used to estimate the size of the minority discount. Finally, see how median estimates of liquidity discounts and control premiums can serve as guidelines in valuation analyses.

TABLE 10.6   Industry Data

Factor	Acuity Lighting	Home Furniture and Fixtures Industry	Adjustments to 20% Median Liquidity Discount
Median liquidity discount[a]	NA	NA	20.0%
Firm size	Small	NA	+2.0
Liquid assets as % of total assets	>50%	NA	−2.0
Return on equity	19.7%	9.7%	−2.0
Cash flow growth rate	15%	12.6%	0.0
Leverage (debt to equity)	0.22[b]	1.02	−2.0
Estimated liquidity discount for Acuity Lighting			16.0%

NA = Not available or not applicable
[a]Median estimate of the liquidity discount of empirical studies (excluding pre-IPO studies) since 1992.
[b]From Exhibit 10.2: $5,101,147/$23,569,178 = .27

REVERSE MERGERS

In a *reverse merger*, a private firm merges with a publicly traded target (often a corporate shell) in a statutory merger in which the public firm survives. Even though the public shell company survives, with the private firm becoming its wholly owned subsidiary, the former shareholders of the private firm have a majority ownership stake in the public company. This is the reverse of most mergers, in that shareholders of the surviving firm usually end up with a majority interest in the combined firms.

The Value of Corporate Shells

Merging with an existing corporate shell of a publicly traded company may be a reasonable alternative for a firm wanting to go public that either is unable to provide the two years of audited financial statements required by the SEC or is unwilling to incur the costs of an IPO. After the private company acquires a majority of the shell's stock and completes the reverse merger, it appoints new management and elects a new board of directors. The owners of the private firm receive most of the shares of the shell corporation, often more than 90%, and control the shell's board of directors. The new firm must have a minimum of 300 shareholders to be listed on the NASDAQ Small Cap Market. Shell corporations usually are of two types. The first type is a failed public company whose shareholders want to sell what remains to recover some of their losses. The second type is a shell that has been created for the sole purpose of being sold as a shell in a reverse merger. The latter type typically carries less risk of having unknown liabilities.

Are Reverse Mergers Cheaper Than IPOs?

Reverse mergers typically cost between $50,000 and $100,000, about one-quarter of the expense of an IPO, and can be completed in about 60 days, or one-third of the time to complete a typical IPO.[37] Despite these advantages, reverse mergers may take as long as IPOs and are sometimes more complex. The acquiring company must still perform due diligence on the target and communicate information on the shell corporation to the exchange on which its stock will be traded and prepare a prospectus. It can often take months to settle outstanding claims against the shell corporation. Public exchanges often require the same level of information for companies going through reverse mergers as those undertaking IPOs. The principal concern is that the shell company may contain unseen liabilities, such as unpaid bills or pending litigation, which in some instances can make the reverse merger far more costly than an IPO. Indeed, private firms that have gone public through a reverse merger have been delisted from public exchanges because they could not meet the exchange's listing requirements at a faster rate than those using an IPO.[38]

In recent years, reverse mergers have been subject to increasing abuse. See Case Study 10.1 for an example of a company taken public via a reverse merger and the potential for fraud. In late 2011, the SEC moved to increase shareholder protections by prohibiting reverse-merger firms from applying to list on the NASDAQ, the New York Stock Exchange, and NYSE Amex until they had completed a one-year "seasoning period" by trading on the OTC Bulletin Board or on another regulated U.S. or foreign exchange. The firm also must file all required reports with the SEC and maintain a minimum share price for at least 30 of the 60 trading days before its listing application can be submitted to an exchange and the exchange can approve the listing.

Financing Reverse Mergers

Private investment in public equities (PIPEs) is a commonly used method of financing reverse mergers. In a PIPE offering, a firm with publicly traded shares sells, usually at a discount, newly issued but unregistered securities, typically stock or debt convertible into stock, directly to investors in a private transaction. Hedge funds are common buyers of such issues. The issuing firm is required to file a shelf registration statement, Form S-3, with the SEC as quickly as possible (usually between 10 and 45 days after issuance) and to use its "best efforts" to complete registration within 30 days after filing. PIPEs often are used in conjunction with a reverse merger to provide companies with not just an alternative way to go public but also financing once they are listed on the public exchange. For example, assume a private company is merged into a publicly traded firm through a reverse merger. As the surviving entity, the public company raises

[37] Sweeney, 2005

[38] Cyree and Walker, 2008

funds through a privately placed equity issue (i.e., PIPE financing). The private firm is now a publicly traded company with the funds to finance future capital requirements.[39]

USING LEVERAGED EMPLOYEE STOCK OWNERSHIP PLANS (ESOPS) TO BUY PRIVATE COMPANIES

An ESOP is a trust established by an employer on behalf of its employees; its assets are allocated to employees and are not taxed until withdrawn by employees. ESOPs generally must invest at least 50% of their assets in employer stock. Employees frequently use leveraged ESOPs to buy out owners of private companies who have most of their net worth in the firm. For firms with ESOPs, the business owner sells at least 30% of their stock to the ESOP, which pays for the stock with borrowed funds. The owner may invest the proceeds and defer taxes if the investment is made within 12 months of the sale of the stock to the ESOP, the ESOP owns at least 30% of the firm, and neither the owner nor his or her family participates in the ESOP. The firm makes tax-deductible contributions to the ESOP in an amount sufficient to repay interest and principal. Shares held by the ESOP, which serve as collateral for the loan, are distributed to employees as the loan is repaid. As the outstanding loan balance is reduced, the shares are allocated to employees, who eventually own the firm.[40]

EMPIRICAL STUDIES OF SHAREHOLDER RETURNS

As noted in Chapter 1, target shareholders of both public and private firms routinely experience abnormal positive returns when a bid is announced for the firm. In contrast, acquirer shareholders may experience abnormal negative returns on the announcement date, particularly when using stock to purchase large publicly traded firms. However, substantial empirical evidence shows that public acquirers using their stock to buy privately held firms experience significant abnormal positive returns around the transaction announcement date. Other studies suggest that acquirers of private firms often experience abnormal positive returns regardless of the form of payment. These studies are discussed next.

---

[39]To issuers, PIPEs offer the advantage of being able to be completed more quickly, cheaply, and confidentially than a public stock offering, which requires registration upfront and a more elaborate investor "road show" to sell the securities to public investors. Frequently sold as private placements, PIPEs are most suitable for raising small amounts of financing, typically in the range of $5 million to $10 million.

[40]Only C and S corporations generating pretax incomes of at least $100,000 annually are eligible to form ESOPs.

Public-company shareholders earn an average positive 2.6% abnormal return when using stock rather than cash to acquire privately held firms.[41] Ownership of privately held companies tends to be highly concentrated, so an exchange of stock tends to create a few very large block stockholders. Close monitoring of management may contribute to these returns. These findings are consistent with studies conducted in Canada, the United Kingdom, and Western Europe.[42]

Firms acquiring private firms often earn excess returns regardless of the form of payment.[43] Acquirers can also earn excess returns of as much as 2.1% when buying private firms or 2.6% for subsidiaries of public companies.[44] The abnormal returns may reflect the tendency of acquirers to pay less for nonpublicly traded companies, due to the relative difficulty in buying private firms or subsidiaries of public companies.[45] In both cases, shares are not publicly traded and access to information is limited. Moreover, there may be fewer bidders for nonpublicly traded companies. Thus, these targets may be acquired at a discount from their true economic value, allowing the acquirer to realize a larger share of the anticipated synergies.

Other factors that may contribute to these positive abnormal returns for acquirers of private companies include the introduction of more professional management into the privately held firms and tax considerations. Public companies may introduce more professional management systems into the target firms, thereby enhancing the target's value. The acquirer's use of stock rather than cash may also induce the seller to accept a lower price, since it allows sellers to defer taxes on any gains until they decide to sell their shares.[46]

SOME THINGS TO REMEMBER

Valuing private firms is more challenging than valuing public firms, due to the absence of published share price data and the unique problems associated with private companies. When markets are illiquid and block shareholders exert control over the firm, the offer price for the target must be adjusted for liquidity

---

[41] Chang, 1998

[42] Draper and Paudyal, 2006; Ben-Amar and André, 2006; Bigelli and Mengoli, 2004; Boehmer, 2000; Dumontier and Pecherot, 2001. These results are consistent with studies of returns to companies that issue stock and convertible debt in private placements (Fields and Mais, 1991; Hertzel and Smith, 1993). In private placements, large shareholders are effective monitors of managerial performance, thereby enhancing the prospects of the issuing firm (Demsetz and Lehn, 1996). Wruck and Wu (2009) argue that relationships such as board representation developed between investors and issuers contribute to improved firm performance due to increased monitoring of performance and improved corporate governance.

[43] Ang and Kohers, 2001

[44] Fuller, Netter, and Stegemoller, 2002

[45] Capron and Shen, 2007; Madura, 2012

[46] Poulsen and Stegemoller, 2002

risk and the value of control. In contrast to studies involving
public firms, buyers of private firms in the United States an
ize significant abnormal positive returns, particularly in shar

DISCUSSION QUESTIONS

10.1 What is the capitalization rate, and how does it relate
discount rate?

10.2 What are the common ways of estimating the capitali:

10.3 What is the liquidity discount, and what are common
this discount?

10.4 Give examples of private company costs that might b
explain why.

10.5 How can an analyst determine if the target's costs and revenues are
under- or- overstated?

10.6 Why might shell corporations have value?

10.7 Why might succession planning be more challenging for a family firm?

10.8 What are some of the reasons a family-owned or privately owned
business may want to go public? What are some of the reasons that
discourage such firms from going public?

10.9 Why are family-owned firms often attractive to private equity investors?

10.10 Rank from the highest to lowest the liquidity discount you would apply
if you, as a business appraiser, had been asked to value the following
businesses: (a) a local, profitable hardware store; (b) a money-losing
laundry; (c) a large privately owned firm with significant excess cash
balances and other liquid short-term investments; and (d) a pool cleaning
service whose primary tangible assets consist of a two-year-old truck and
miscellaneous equipment. Explain your ranking.

*Answers to these Chapter Discussion Questions are available in the Online
Instructor's Manual for instructors using this book.*

QUESTIONS FROM THE CFA CURRICULUM

10.11 Using the buildup method and assuming that no adjustment for industry
risk is required, calculate an equity discount rate for a small company
given the following information:
a. Equity-risk premium = 5.0%
b. Midcap equity-risk premium = 3.5%
c. Small stock-risk premium = 4.2%
d. Total return on intermediate-term bonds = 5.3%
e. Company-specific-risk premium = 3.0%
f. 20-year Treasury bond yield as of the valuation date = 4.5%
Source: CFA Institute 2011 Private Company Valuation, Reading 46, question 2

An appraiser has been asked to determine the combined level of valuation discounts for a small equity interest in a private company. The appraiser concluded that an appropriate control premium is 15%. A discount for lack of marketability was estimated at 25%. Given these factors, what is the combined discount?

Source CFA Institute 2011 Private Company Valuation, Reading 46, question 5

Answers to questions from the CFA curriculum are available in the Online Student Companion site to this book in a file folder entitled CFA Curriculum Questions and Solutions.

PRACTICE PROBLEMS AND ANSWERS

10.13 It usually is appropriate to adjust the financials received from the target firm to reflect any changes that you, as the new owner, would make to create an adjusted EBITDA. Using the "Excel-Based Spreadsheet" on "How to Adjust Target Firm's Financial Statements" on the companion website, make at least three adjustments to the target's financials to determine the impact on the adjusted EBITDA. (*Note*: The adjustments should be made in the section on the spreadsheet entitled "Adjustments to Target Firm's Financials.") Explain your rationale for each adjustment.

10.14 Based on its growth prospects, a private investor values a local bakery at $750,000. She believes that cost savings having a PV of $50,000 can be achieved by changing staffing levels and store hours. She believes the appropriate liquidity discount is 20%. A recent transaction in the same city required the buyer to pay a 5% premium to the average price for similar businesses to gain a controlling interest in a bakery. What is the most she should be willing to pay for a 50.1% stake in the bakery? *Answer:* $336,672

10.15 You have been asked by an investor to value a restaurant. Last year, the restaurant earned pretax operating income of $300,000. Income has grown 4% annually during the last five years, and it is expected to continue growing at that rate into the foreseeable future. The annual change in working capital is $20,000, and capital spending for maintenance exceeded depreciation in the prior year by $15,000. Both working capital and the excess of capital spending over depreciation are projected to grow at the same rate as operating income. By introducing modern management methods, you believe the pretax operating-income growth rate can be increased to 6% beyond the second year and sustained at that rate into the foreseeable future.

The 10-year Treasury bond rate is 5%, the equity-risk premium is 5.5%, and the marginal federal, state, and local tax rate is 40%. The beta and debt-to-equity ratio for publicly traded firms in the restaurant industry are 2 and 1.5, respectively. The business's target debt-to-equity ratio is 1, and its pretax cost of borrowing, based on its recent borrowing activities, is 7%. The business-specific-risk premium for firms of this size is estimated to be 6%. The liquidity-risk premium is believed to be 15%, relatively low for firms of this type due to the excellent reputation of the restaurant. Since the current chef and the staff are expected to remain when the business is sold, the quality of the restaurant is expected to be maintained. The investor is willing to pay a 10% premium to reflect the value of control.

a. What is free cash flow to the firm in year 1? *Answer*: $150,800
b. What is free cash flow to the firm in year 2? *Answer*: $156,832
c. What is the firm's cost of equity? *Answer*: 20.2%
d. What is the firm's after-tax cost of debt? *Answer*: 4.2%
e. What is the firm's target debt-to–total capital ratio? *Answer*: 0.5
f. What is the weighted average cost of capital? *Answer*: 12.2%
g. What is the business worth? *Answer*: $2,226,448

Solutions to these practice exercises and problems are available in the Online Instructor's Manual for instructors using this book.

CASE STUDY 10.1
Shell Game: Going Public Through Reverse Mergers

Key Points

- Reverse mergers represent an alternative to an initial public offering (IPO) for a private company wanting to go public.
- The challenge with reverse mergers often is gaining access to accurate financial statements and quantifying current or potential liabilities.
- Performing adequate due diligence may be difficult, but it is the key to reducing risk.

The highly liquid U.S. equity markets have proven to be an attractive way of gaining access to capital for both privately owned domestic and foreign firms. Common ways of doing so have involved IPOs and reverse mergers. While both methods allow the private firm's shares to be publicly traded, only the IPO necessarily results in raising capital, which affects the length of time and complexity of the process of going public.

To undertake a reverse merger, a firm finds a shell corporation with relatively few shareholders who are interested in selling their stock. The shell corporation's shareholders often are interested in either selling their shares for cash, owning even a relatively small portion of a financially viable company to recover their initial investments, or transferring the shell's liabilities to new investors. Alternatively, the private firm may merge with an existing special-purpose acquisition company (SPAC) already registered for public stock trading. SPACs are shell, or "blank-check," companies that have no operations but go public with the intention of merging with or acquiring a company with the proceeds of the SPAC's IPO.

In a merger, it is common for the surviving firm to be viewed as the acquirer, since its shareholders usually end up with a majority ownership stake in the merged firms; the other party to the merger is viewed as the target firm because its former shareholders often hold only a minority interest in the combined companies. In a reverse merger, the opposite happens. Even though the publicly traded shell company survives the merger, with the private firm becoming its wholly owned subsidiary, the former shareholders of the private firm end up with a majority ownership stake in the combined firms. While conventional IPOs can take months to complete, reverse mergers can take only a few weeks. Moreover, as the reverse merger is solely a mechanism to convert a private company into a public entity, the process is less dependent on financial market conditions because the company often is not proposing to raise capital.

The speed with which a firm can go public as compared to an IPO often is attractive to foreign firms desirous of entering U.S. capital markets quickly. In recent years, private equity investors have found the comparative ease of the reverse merger process convenient, because it has enabled them to take public their investments in both domestic and foreign firms. Recently, the story of the rapid growth of Chinese firms has held considerable allure for investors, prompting a flurry of reverse mergers involving Chinese-based firms. With speed

comes additional risk. Shell company shareholders may simply be looking for investors to take over their liabilities, such as pending litigation, safety hazards, environmental problems, and unpaid tax liabilities. To prevent the public shell's shareholders from dumping their shares immediately following the merger, investors are required to hold their shares for a specific period of time. The recent entry of Chinese firms into the U.S. public equity markets illustrates the potential for fraud. Of the 159 Chinese-based firms that have been listed since 2006 via a reverse merger, 36 have been suspended or have halted trading in the United States after auditors found significant accounting issues. Eleven more firms have been delisted from major U.S. stock exchanges.

Huiheng Medical (Huiheng) is one such firm that came under SEC scrutiny, having first listed its shares on the over-the-counter (OTC) market in early 2008. The firm claimed it was China's leading provider of gamma-ray technology, a cancer-fighting technology, and boasted of having a strong order backlog and access to Western management expertise through a joint venture. What follows is a discussion of how the firm went public and the participants in that process. The firms involved in the reverse merger process included Mill Basin Technologies (Mill), a Nevada incorporated and publicly listed shell corporation; and Allied Moral Holdings (Allied), a privately owned Virgin Islands company with subsidiaries, including Huiheng Medical, primarily in China. Mill was the successor firm to Pinewood Imports (Pinewood), a Nevada-based corporation, formed in November 2002 to import pine molding. Ceasing operations in September 2006 to become a shell corporation, Pinewood changed its name to Mill Basin Technologies. The firm began to search for a merger partner and registered shares for public trading in 2006 in anticipation of raising funds.

The reverse merger process employed by Allied, the privately owned operating company and owner of Huiheng, to merge with Mill, the public shell corporation, early in 2008 to become a publicly listed firm is described in the following steps. Allied is the target firm, and Mill is the acquiring firm.

Step 1. Negotiate terms and conditions: Premerger, Mill and Allied had 10,150,000 and 13,000,000 common shares outstanding, respectively. Mill also had 266,666 preferred shares outstanding. Mill and Allied agreed to a merger in which each Allied shareholder would receive one share of Mill stock for each Allied share they held. With Mill as the surviving entity, former Allied shareholders would own 96.65% of Mill's shares, and Mill's former shareholders would own the rest.

Step 2. Recapitalize the acquiring firm: Prior to the share exchange, shareholders in Mill, the shell corporation, recapitalized the firm by contributing 9,700,000 of the shares they owned prior to the merger to Treasury stock,

effectively reducing the number of Mill common shares outstanding to 450,000 (10,150,000 − 9,700,000). The objective of the recapitalization was to limit the total number of common shares outstanding postmerger in order to support the price of the new firm's shares. Such recapitalizations often are undertaken to reduce the number of shares outstanding following closing in order to support the combined firms' share price once it begins to trade on a public exchange.[47] The firm's earnings per share are increased for a given level of earnings by reducing the number of common shares outstanding.

Step 3. Close the deal: The terms of the merger called for Mill (the acquirer) to purchase 100% of the outstanding Allied (the target) common and preferred shares, which required Mill to issue 13,000,000 new common shares and 266,666 new preferred shares. All premerger Allied shares were cancelled. Mill Basin Technologies was renamed Huiheng Medical, reflecting potential investor interest at that time in both Chinese firms and in the healthcare industry. See Exhibit 10.4 for an illustration of the premerger recapitalization of Mill, the postmerger equity structure

---

[47] Without the reduction in Mill's premerger shares outstanding, total shares outstanding postmerger would have been 23,150,000 [10,150,000 (Mill shares premerger) + 13,000,000 (Allied shares premerger)] rather than the 13,450,000 after the recapitalization.

of the combined firms, and the resulting ownership distribution.

While Huiheng traded as high as $13 in late 2008, it plummeted to $1.60 in early 2012, reflecting the failure of the firm to achieve any significant revenue and income in the cancer market, an inability to get an auditing firm to approve their financial statements, and the absence of any significant order backlog. Having reported net income as high as $9 million in 2007, just prior to completing the reverse merger, the firm was losing money and burning through its remaining cash. The firm was left looking at alternative applications for its technology, such as preserving food with radiation.

Huiheng's SEC filings state that the firm designs, develops, and markets radiation therapy systems used to treat cancer and acknowledge that the firm had experienced delays selling its technology in China and had no international sales in 2009 or 2010. The filings also show the reverse merger was directed by Richard Propper, a venture capitalist and CEO of Chardan Capital, a San Diego merchant bank with expertise in helping Chinese firms enter the U.S. equity markets. Chardan Capital invested $10 million in Huiheng in exchange for more than 52,000 shares of the firm's preferred stock. Chardan and Roth Capital Partners, a California investment bank, were co-underwriters for a planned 2008 Huiheng stock offering that was later withdrawn. Chardan had been fined $40,000 for three violations of short-selling rules from 2005 to 2009. Roth is a defendant in alleged securities' fraud lawsuits involving other Chinese reverse merger firms.[48]

[48] McCoy and Chu, December 26, 2011

EXHIBIT 10.4 MILL BASIN TECHNOLOGIES (MILL)

Premerger Equity Structure:
    Common 10,150,000
    Series A Preferred 266,666
Recapitalized Equity Structure:
    Common 450,000[a]
    Series A Preferred 266,666
New Mill Shares Issued to Acquire 100% of Allied Shares:
    Common 13,000,000
    Series A Preferred 266,666
Postmerger Equity Structure:
    Common 13,450,000[b]
    Series A Preferred 266,666
Postmerger Ownership Distribution of Common Shares:
    Former Allied Shareholders: 96.65%[c]
    Former Mill Shareholders: 3.35%

[a]Mill shareholders contributed 9,700,000 shares of their premerger holdings to Treasury stock, cutting the number of Mill shares outstanding to 450,000 in order to reduce the total number of shares outstanding postmerger, which would equal Mill's premerger shares outstanding plus the newly issued shares. This also could have been achieved by the Mill shareholders' agreeing to a reverse stock split. The 10,150,000 premerger Mill shares outstanding could be reduced to 450,000 through a reverse split in which Mill shareholders receive 1 new Mill share for each 22.555 outstanding prior to the merger.

[b]Postmerger Mill Basin Technologies' capital structure equals the 450,000 premerger Mill common shares resulting from the recapitalization plus the 13,000,000 newly issued common shares plus 266,666 Series A preferred shares.

[c](13,000,000/13,450,000)

Huiheng ran into legal problems soon after its reverse merger. Harborview Master Fund, Diverse Trading Ltd., and Monarch Capital Fund, institutional investors having a controlling interest in Huiheng, approved the reverse merger and invested $1.25 million in exchange for stock. However, they sued Huiheng and Chardan Capital in 2009 as Huiheng's promise of orders failed to materialize. The lawsuit charged that Huiheng bribed Chinese hospital officials to win purchasing deals. The firm's initial investors forced the firm to buy back their shares as a result of a legal settlement of their lawsuit in which they argued that the firm had committed fraud when it went public. The lawsuit alleged that the firm's public statements about the efficacy of its technology and order backlog were highly inflated. Huiheng and its codefendants settled out of court in 2010 with no admission of liability by buying back some of its stock. In 2011, the firm had difficulty in collecting receivables and generating cash. That same year, Huiheng's operations in China were struggling and were on the verge of ceasing production.

Discussion Questions

1. What are common reasons for a private firm to go public?
2. What are corporate shells, and how can they create value? Be specific.
3. Who are the participants in the case study, and what are their roles in the reverse merger?
4. Discuss the pros and cons of a reverse merger versus an IPO.
5. What are the auditing challenges associated with reverse mergers? How can investors protect themselves from the liabilities that may be contained in corporate shells?
6. Mill was recapitalized just prior to completing its merger with Allied. What was the purpose of the recapitalization? Did it affect the ability of the combined firms to generate future earnings? Explain your answers.

Solutions to this case are provided in the Online Instructor's Manual available for instructors using this book.

CASE STUDY 10.2

Determining Liquidity Discounts: The Taylor Devices and Tayco Development Merger

Key Points

- Privately held shares or shares for which there is not a readily available resale market often can only be sold at a discount from what is believed to be their intrinsic value.
- However, estimating the magnitude of the discount often is highly problematic.

This discussion[49] is a highly summarized version of how a business valuation firm evaluated the liquidity risk associated with Taylor Devices' unregistered common stock, registered common shares, and a minority investment in a business that it was planning to sell following its merger with Tayco Development. The estimated liquidity discounts were used in a joint proxy statement submitted to the SEC by the two firms to justify the value of the offer the boards of Taylor Devices and Tayco Development had negotiated.

Taylor Devices and Tayco Development agreed to merge in early 2008. Tayco would be merged into Taylor, with Taylor as the surviving entity. The merger would enable Tayco's patents and intellectual property to be fully integrated into Taylor's manufacturing operations, since intellectual property rights transfer with the Tayco stock. Each share of Tayco

[49]Source: SEC Form S4 filing of a proxy statement for Taylor Devices and Tayco Development dated 1/15/08.

common stock would be converted into one share of Taylor common stock, according to the terms of the deal. Taylor's common stock is traded on the NASDAQ Small Cap Market under the symbol TAYD, and on January 8, 2009 (the last trading day before the date of the filing of the joint proxy statement with the SEC), the stock closed at $6.29 per share. Tayco common stock is traded over the counter on Pink Sheets (i.e., an informal trading network) under the trading symbol TYCO.PK, and it closed on January 8, 2009, at $5.11 per share.

An appraisal firm was hired to value Taylor's unregistered shares, which were treated as if they were restricted shares because there was no established market for trading in these shares. The appraiser believed that the risk of Taylor's unregistered shares is greater than for letter stocks, which have a stipulated period during which the shares cannot be sold, because the Taylor shares lacked a date indicating when they could be sold. Using this line of reasoning, the appraisal firm estimated a liquidity discount of 20%, which it believed approximated the potential loss that holders of these shares might incur in attempting to sell their shares. The block of registered Taylor stock differs from the unregistered shares, in that they are not subject to Rule 144. Based on the trading volume of Taylor common stock over the preceding 12 months, the appraiser believed that it would likely take less than one year to convert the block of registered stock into cash and estimated the discount at 13%, consistent with the Aschwald (2000) studies.

The appraisal firm also was asked to estimate the liquidity discount for the sale of Taylor's minority investment in a real estate development business. Due to the increase in liquidity of restricted stocks since 1990, the business appraiser argued that restricted-stock studies conducted before that date may provide a better proxy for liquidity discounts for this type of investment. Interests in closely held firms are more like letter-stock transactions occurring before the changes in SEC Rule 144 beginning in 1990, when the holding period was reduced from three years to two, and later (after 1997) to one. Such firms have little ability to raise capital in public markets due to their small size, and they face high transaction costs. Based on the SEC and other prior 1990 studies, the liquidity discount for this investment was expected to be between 30% and 35%. Pre-IPO studies could push it higher to a range of 40–45%. The appraisal firm argued that the discount for most minority-interest investments tended to fall in the range of 25–45%. Because of the small size of the real estate development business, the liquidity discount is believed by the appraisal firm to be at the higher end of the range.

Discussion Questions

1. Explain how the appraiser estimated the liquidity discount for the unregistered shares.
2. What other factors could the appraiser have used to estimate the liquidity discount?
3. In view of your answer to question 2, how might these factors have changed the appraiser's conclusions? Be specific.
4. Based on the 13% liquidity discount estimated by the business appraiser, what was the actual purchase price premium paid to Tayco shareholders for each of their common shares?

Solutions to these questions are available on the Online Instructor's Manual for instructors using this book.

DEAL-STRUCTURING AND FINANCING STRATEGIES

"Well, it looks like the merger is off."

Cartoonstock.com jmo1977

Part IV illustrates how deal structuring and financing are inextricably linked. The structure of the deal determines what needs to be financed: the amount to be paid for the target's stock or assets plus assumed liabilities less cash proceeds from the sale of nonstrategic target assets. Whether what needs to be financed can in fact be funded determines whether the deal gets done.

This section describes how consensus is reached during the deal-structuring or bargaining process by satisfying the primary demands of the parties involved in the transaction, subject to acceptable levels of risk. The output of this process is an agreement or deal structure between two parties (the acquirer and the target firms) defining the rights and obligations of the parties involved. The chapters in this section also discuss the implications of various aspects of deal structuring in managing risk, the effects of risk on how deals are done, and the challenges of financing transactions, particularly those that are highly leveraged.

Chapter 11 outlines the major facets of the deal-structuring process, including the acquisition vehicle and post-closing organization; the form of acquisition; the form of payment; and the legal form of selling entity and how changes in one area of the deal often impact significantly other parts of the agreement. Specific ways to bridge major differences on price also are discussed. Chapter 12 addresses tax considerations, including alternative forms of taxable and non-taxable structures, and how they impact reaching agreement. This chapter also discusses such accounting issues as how business combinations are recorded for financial-reporting purposes and the impact of purchase accounting on financial statements and reported earnings.

Chapter 13 focuses on the ways in which M&A transactions are financed and the critical role played by private equity firms and hedge funds in financing highly leveraged deals. This chapter also discusses how leveraged buyouts (LBOs), the deal structure commonly used in takeovers by private equity investors and hedge funds, are structured, and the factors critical to their success. Finally, Chapter 14 addresses alternative ways of valuing highly leveraged transactions and the strengths and weaknesses of such methods. Which methodology is employed ultimately depends on the availability of data and the willingness of the analyst to accept the assumptions underlying each methodology. Basic concepts used in building LBO financial models and estimating a firm's borrowing capacity also are discussed.

Structuring the Deal
Payment and Legal Considerations

*If you can't convince them, confuse them. —**Harry S. Truman***

INSIDE M&A: ILLUSTRATING HOW DEAL STRUCTURE AFFECTS VALUE—THE FACEBOOK/INSTAGRAM DEAL

KEY POINTS

- Deal structures affect value by limiting risk to the parties involved or exposing them to risk.
- The value of cash received at closing is certain, whereas the value of stock is not.
- Mechanisms exist to limit such risk; however, they often come with a cost to the party seeking risk mitigation.

While we always look smarter after the fact, social networking giant Facebook's acquisition of Instagram, a popular photo-sharing service, highlights risks common to such deals. Instagram's user base was exploding; Facebook viewed it as a potential competitor and as a means of extending its own product offering to photo-sharing on smartphones and tablet computers. However, the two-year-old Instagram had no revenue and consisted of a technology platform, a growing and active user base, and 24 employees. Facebook announced on April 12, 2012, that it had reached an agreement, reportedly hammered out in less than 48 hours, to buy Instagram for $1 billion, an outsized valuation by most measures.

The purchase price consisted of $300 million in cash and 23 million shares of common stock for all of the outstanding Instagram shares. The combination of cash and stock is usually offered to give selling-firm shareholders the favorable tax advantages of acquirer stock, the certainty of cash, and the opportunity to participate in any potential appreciation of the acquiring firm's shares. The deal value was predicated on a Facebook share price of $31 per share, giving Facebook a market value at the time of $75 billion. What is perhaps most remarkable about this transaction is the price paid, the speed with which it was negotiated, and the absence of protections for the Instagram shareholders. These issues are discussed next.

Called an important milestone by Facebook founder and CEO Mark Zuckerberg, the deal reflected the dangers of valuing a firm primarily on its potential. This is an issue that Facebook tackled following its IPO on May 18, 2012. Originally offered at $38 per share, the stock soon plummeted to less than half that value as investors doubted the firm's long-term profitability.

Facebook's dual class shareholder structure gives Mr. Zuckerberg effective control of the firm, despite owning only 28.4% of outstanding class B shares. This control made it possible for the lofty valuation to be placed on Instagram and for the deal to be negotiated so rapidly. Indeed, the Instagram offer price may have reflected the euphoria preceding the Facebook IPO. The heady environment immediately prior to the Facebook IPO also may have convinced the Instagram shareholders that they had little to lose and much to gain by accepting a mostly stock deal involving a fixed share-exchange ratio. That is, the number of Facebook shares exchanged for each Instagram share would remain unchanged, despite any appreciation (depreciation) in Facebook shares between the signing of the agreement and the closing of the deal.

The downside risk to Instagram shareholders was evident by the September 6, 2012, closing date, for the value of the deal had plummeted to about $715 million, with Facebook shares having closed at $18.05 a share. Instagram shareholders experienced a substantial loss in value, which could have been averted by adjusting the purchase price within a range if Facebook's share price fluctuated significantly between signing and closing. Alternatively, Instagram could have negotiated the right to cancel the deal due a material change in the value of the transaction.

CHAPTER OVERVIEW

Once management has determined that an acquisition is the best way to implement the firm's business strategy, a target has been selected, and the preliminary financial analysis is satisfactory, it is time to consider how to structure the deal properly. A *deal structure* is an agreement between two parties (the acquirer and the target firms) defining their rights and obligations. The way in which this agreement is reached is called the *deal-structuring process*. In this chapter, this process is described in terms of seven interdependent components: acquisition vehicle, the postclosing organization, the form of payment, the legal form of the selling entity, the form of acquisition, accounting considerations, and tax considerations.

The focus in this chapter is on the form of payment, the form of acquisition, and alternative forms of legal structures in which ownership is conveyed and how they interact to impact the overall deal. The implications of alternative tax structures, how deals are recorded for financial-reporting purposes, and how they might affect the deal-structuring process are discussed in detail in Chapter 12. A review of this chapter is available in the file folder entitled "Student Study Guide" on the companion website to this book (http://booksite. elsevier.com/9780123854872).

THE DEAL-STRUCTURING PROCESS

The *deal-structuring process* involves satisfying as many of the primary acquirer and target objectives and determining how risk will be shared. *Risk sharing* refers to the extent to which the acquirer assumes the target's liabilities. The appropriate deal structure is that which satisfies, subject to an acceptable level of risk, the primary objectives of the parties involved and clearly states their rights and obligations. The process may be highly complex, involving multiple parties, approvals, forms of payment, and sources of financing. Decisions made in one area often affect other areas of the deal. Containing risk associated with a complex deal is analogous to squeezing one end of a water balloon, which simply forces the contents to shift elsewhere.

Key Components of the Deal-Structuring Process

The process begins with addressing a set of key questions, shown on the left-hand side of Figure. 11.1. Answers to these questions help define initial negotiating positions, potential risks, options for managing risk, levels of tolerance for risk, and conditions under which either party will walk away from the negotiations. The key components of the process are discussed next.

The *acquisition vehicle* refers to the legal structure created to acquire the target company. The *postclosing organization*, or structure, is the organizational and legal framework used to manage the combined businesses following the consummation of the transaction. Commonly used structures for both the acquisition vehicle and the postclosing organization include the corporate, division, holding company, joint venture (JV), partnership, limited liability company (LLC), and employee stock ownership plan (ESOP) structures. Although the two structures are often the same before and after completion of the transaction, the postclosing organization may differ from the acquisition vehicle, depending on the acquirer's strategic objectives for the combined firms.

The *form of payment*, or total consideration, may consist of cash, common stock, debt, or a combination of all three types. The payment may be fixed at a moment in time, contingent on the target's future performance, or payable over time. The *form of acquisition* reflects what is being acquired (stock or assets) and how ownership is conveyed. *Accounting considerations* address the impact of

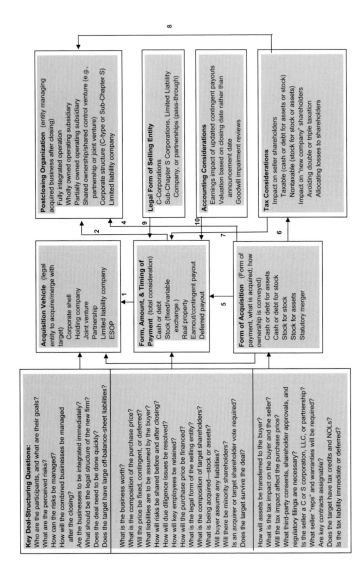

FIGURE. 11.1 **Mergers and acquisitions deal-structuring process.**

financial reporting requirements on the future earnings of the combined businesses. *Tax considerations* entail tax structures that determine whether a deal is taxable or nontaxable to the seller's shareholders. The *legal form of the selling entity* also has tax implications.

Common Linkages

Figure 11.1 explains through examples common interactions among various components of the deal structure. These are discussed in more detail later in this chapter, and in Chapter 12.

Form of Payment (Figure 11.1, Arrows 1 and 2) Affects Choice of Acquisition Vehicle and Postclosing Organization

The buyer may offer a purchase price contingent on the future performance of the target and choose to acquire and operate the target as a wholly owned subsidiary within a holding company during the term of the earnout (deferred payout). This facilitates monitoring the operation's performance and minimizes possible post-earnout litigation initiated by earnout participants.

Effects of Form of Acquisition (Figure 11.1, Arrows 3–6)

Choice of acquisition vehicle and postclosing organization: If the form of acquisition is a statutory merger, all liabilities transfer to the buyer, who may acquire and operate the target within a holding company to provide some protection from the target's liabilities.

Form, timing, and amount of payment: The assumption of all seller liabilities in a merger or stock purchase may cause the buyer to alter the terms of the deal to include more debt or installment payments, to reduce the present value of the purchase price, or both.

Tax considerations: The transaction may be tax free to the seller if the acquirer uses its stock to acquire substantially all of the seller's assets or stock.

Effects of Tax Considerations (Figure 11.1, Arrows 7 and 8)

Amount, timing, and composition of the purchase price: If the deal is taxable to the target shareholders, the purchase price often is increased to offset the target shareholders' tax liability. The higher purchase price could alter the composition of the purchase price as the buyer defers a portion of the price or includes more debt to lower its present value.

Selection of postclosing organization: The desire to minimize taxes encourages the use of S corporations, LLCs and partnerships to eliminate double taxation; tax benefits also pass through to LLC members and partners in partnerships.

Legal Form of Selling Entity (Figure 11.1, Arrow 9) Affects Form of Payment

Because of the potential for deferring shareholder tax liabilities, target firms qualifying as C corporations often prefer to exchange their stock or assets for acquirer shares. Owners of S corporations, LLCs, and partnerships are largely indifferent to a deal's tax status because the proceeds of the sale are taxed at the owners' ordinary tax rate.

Accounting Considerations (Figure 11.1, Arrow 10) Affect Form, Amount, and Timing of Payment

The requirement to adjust more frequently the fair value of contingent payments makes earnouts less attractive as a form of payment due to the potential increase in earnings volatility. Equity as a form of payment may be less attractive due to the potential for changes in its value between deal announcement date and closing date. The potential for future write-downs may discourage overpayment by acquirers due to the required periodic review of fair market versus book values. Table. 11.1 provides a summary of these common linkages.

FORM OF ACQUISITION VEHICLE AND POSTCLOSING ORGANIZATION

Choosing an acquisition vehicle or postclosing organization requires consideration of the cost and formality of organization, ease of transferring ownership, continuity of existence, management control, ease of financing, ease of integration, method of distribution of profits, extent of personal liability, and taxation. Each form of legal entity has different risk, financing, tax, and control

TABLE 11.1   Summary of Common Linkages within the Deal-Structuring Process

Component of Deal-Structuring Process:	Influences choice of:
Form, Amount, and Timing of Payment	Acquisition vehicle
	Postclosing organization
	Accounting considerations
	Tax structure (taxable or nontaxable)
Form of Acquisition	Acquisition vehicle
	Postclosing organization
	Form, amount, and timing of payment
	Tax structure (taxable or nontaxable)
Tax Considerations	Form, amount, and timing of payment
	Postclosing organization
Legal Form of Selling Entity	Tax structure (taxable or nontaxable)

implications for the acquirer.[1] The selection of the appropriate entity can help to mitigate risk, maximize financing flexibility, and minimize the net cost of the acquisition.

Choosing the Appropriate Acquisition Vehicle

The corporate structure is the most commonly used acquisition vehicle, since it offers most of the features acquirers desire, including limited liability, financing flexibility, continuity of ownership, and deal flexibility (e.g., option to engage in a tax-free deal). A partnership may be appropriate if it is important to share risk, to involve partners with special attributes, to avoid double taxation, or in special situations.[2] For small privately owned firms, an employee stock ownership plan structure may be a convenient vehicle for transferring the owner's interest in the business to the employees while offering significant tax advantages. Non-U.S. buyers intending to make additional acquisitions may prefer a holding company structure, enabling the buyer to control other companies by owning only a small portion of the company's voting stock.

Choosing the Appropriate Postclosing Organization

The postclosing organization can be the same as that chosen for the acquisition vehicle. Common postclosing structures include divisional[3] and holding company arrangements. While holding companies are often corporations, they also represent a distinct way of organizing and operating the firm. The choice of postclosing organization depends on the objectives of the acquirer. The acquiring firm may choose a structure that facilitates postclosing integration, minimizes risk from the target's known and unknown liabilities, minimizes taxes, passes through losses to shelter the owners' tax liabilities, preserves unique target attributes, maintains target independence during the duration of an earnout, or preserves the tax-free status of the deal.

---

[1] The various forms of potential acquisition vehicles and their specific advantages and disadvantages are discussed in considerable detail in Chapter 15.

[2] Certain situations often require specific types of partnership arrangements. For example, a *master limited partnership* (MLP) is used in industries where cash flow is relatively predictable, such as oil and gas extraction; and distribution and real estate. As with other limited partnerships, it is not subject to double taxation, and its investors are subject to limited liability; unlike other partnerships, its units can be more easily bought and sold than those of private partnerships and privately owned corporations, and often trade in the same manner as shares of common stock. MLPs are considered in default if all profits are not distributed.

[3] A division is not a separate legal entity but, rather, an organizational unit, and it is distinguished from a legal subsidiary in that it typically will not have its own stock or board of directors that meets regularly. Divisions may have managers with the same titles normally associated with separate legal entities, such as a president or chief operating officer. Because a division is not a separate legal entity, its liabilities are the responsibility of the parent.

If the acquirer intends to integrate the target immediately after closing, the corporate or divisional structure often is preferred because it offers the greatest control. In JVs and partnerships, the dispersed ownership may render decision making slower or more contentious. Implementation is more likely to depend on close cooperation and consensus building, which may slow efforts at rapid integration of the acquired company. Realizing synergies may be more protracted than if management control is more centralized within the parent.

A holding company structure may be preferable when the target has significant liabilities, an earnout is involved, the target is a foreign firm, or the acquirer is a financial investor. The parent may be able to isolate target liabilities within the subsidiary, and the subsidiary could be forced into bankruptcy without jeopardizing the parent. When the target is a foreign firm, operating it separately from the rest of the acquirer's operations may minimize disruption from cultural differences. Finally, a financial buyer may use a holding company structure because the buyer has no interest in operating the target firm for any length of time. A partnership or JV structure may be appropriate if the risk and the value of tax benefits are high. The total investment in the target is shared. The acquired firm may benefit because of the expertise that the different partners or owners might provide. A partnership or LLC eliminates double taxation and passes current operating losses, tax credits, and loss carryforwards and carrybacks to the owners.

LEGAL FORM OF THE SELLING ENTITY

Seller concerns about the form of the transaction may depend on whether it is an S corporation, a limited liability company, a partnership, or a C corporation. C corporations are subject to double taxation, whereas S corporations, partnerships, and LLCs are not (see Exhibit. 11.1).

FORM OF PAYMENT

The purchase price is mostly stock about one-fourth of the time, with the remaining deals involving mostly cash. When the target firm is large and publicly traded, the purchase price consists primarily of stock about 60% of the time.[4] This section addresses the different forms of payment used and why one form may be preferred over another.

Cash

Acquirers may use cash if the firm has significant borrowing capacity, substantial excess cash reserves, and undervalued shares and wishes to maintain

[4]Netter et al., 2011

EXHIBIT 11.1 HOW THE SELLER'S LEGAL FORM AFFECTS THE FORM OF PAYMENT

Assume that a business owner starting with an initial investment of $100,000 sells her business for $1 million. Different legal structures have different tax impacts:

1. After-tax proceeds of a stock sale are ($1,000,000 − $100,000) × (1−0.15) = $765,000. The S corporation shareholder or limited liability company member holding shares for more than one year pays a maximum capital gains tax equal to 15% of the gain on the sale.[a]

2. After-tax proceeds from an asset sale are ($1,000,000 − $100,000) × (1−0.4) × (1−0.15) = $900,000 × 0.51 = $459,000. A C corporation typically pays tax equal to 40% (i.e., 35% federal and 5% state and local), and the shareholder pays a maximum capital gains tax equal to 15%, resulting in double taxation of the gain on sale.

Implications

1. C corporation shareholders generally prefer acquirer stock for their stock or assets to avoid double taxation.

2. S corporation and LLC owners often are indifferent to an asset sale or stock sale because 100% of the corporation's income passes through the corporation untaxed to the owners, who are subject to their own personal tax rates. The S corporation shareholders or LLC members still may prefer a share-for-share exchange if they are interested in deferring their tax liability or are attracted by the long-term growth potential of the acquirer's stock.

[a] This is the capital gains tax rate as of the time of this writing.

control. A cash purchase could be financed from additional borrowing, excess cash balances, or some combination. Undervalued shares could result in substantial dilution of the acquirer's current shareholders' ownership position. A bidder may use cash rather than shares if the voting control of its dominant shareholder is threatened as a result of the issuance of voting stock to acquire the target.[5] The preference for using cash appears to be much higher in Western European countries, where ownership tends to be more heavily concentrated in publicly traded firms, than in the United States. In Europe, 63% of publicly traded firms have a single shareholder directly or indirectly controlling 20% or more of the voting shares; the U.S. figure is 28%.[6] The seller's shareholders may prefer cash if they believe the acquirer's shares have limited appreciation potential and have a high tax basis in their stock.[7] The high basis implies lower capital gains and less need to defer the payment of taxes.

[5] Faccio and Masulis, 2005
[6] Faccio and Lang, 2002
[7] Burch et al., 2012

Noncash

The use of stock is more complicated than cash because of the need to comply with prevailing securities laws. The acquirer may choose to use stock if it is believed to be overvalued and has limited borrowing capacity and excess cash balances. Acquirer stock also may be used as the primary form of payment when the integration of the target firm is expected to be lengthy in order to minimize the amount of indebtedness required to complete the takeover. By maintaining the ability to borrow, the acquirer is able to finance unanticipated cash outlays during the integration period and to pursue investment opportunities that might arise.[8] Firms whose actual leverage exceeds their desired leverage are more likely to use some form of payment other than cash in making acquisitions.[9] Furthermore, acquirer stock may be a useful form of payment when valuing the target firm is difficult, such as when the target has hard-to-value intangible assets, new product entries, or large R&D outlays. In accepting acquirer stock, a seller may have less incentive to negotiate an overvalued purchase price if it wishes to participate in any appreciation of the stock it receives.[10] Other forms of noncash payment include real property, rights to intellectual property, royalties, earnouts, and contingent payments.

Sellers often demand acquirer shares as the primary form of payment due to the ability to defer the payment of taxes. Acquirer shares might be especially attractive if their growth prospects are strong.[11] Seller shareholders may find debt unattractive because of the acquirer's perceived high risk of default. Debt or equity securities issued by nonpublic firms may also be illiquid because of the small size of the resale market for such securities.

Cash and Stock in Combination

Offering target shareholders multiple payment options may encourage more participation in tender offers. Some target shareholders may want a combination of acquirer stock and cash if they are unsure of the appreciation potential of the acquirer's stock. Others may prefer a combination of cash and stock if they need the cash to pay taxes due on the sale of their shares. Also, acquirers, unable to borrow to finance an all-cash offer or unwilling to absorb the dilution in an all-stock offer, may choose to offer the target firm a combination of stock and cash.

The multiple-option bidding strategy creates uncertainty, since the amount of cash the acquirer ultimately will have to pay to target shareholders is unclear, because the number of shareholders choosing the all-cash or cash-and-stock option is not known prior to completion of the tender offer. Acquirers resolve

[8] Huang et al., 2011

[9] Uysal, 2011

[10] Officer et al. (2007). Note that simply accepting acquirer stock does not guarantee the seller will not attempt to negotiate an overvalued purchase price if the seller intends to sell the acquirer shares immediately following closing.

[11] Ismail and Krause, 2010

this issue by including a *proration clause* in tender offers and merger agreements that allows them to fix—at the time the tender offer is initiated—the amount of cash they will ultimately have to pay out.[12]

Convertible Securities

An acquirer and a target often have inadequate information about the other, even after completing due diligence. The acquirer is anxious about overpaying, and the target is concerned about the fairness of the offer. The use of acquirer stock as the primary form of payment may mitigate some of this concern because target shareholders hoping to participate in any future appreciation are less likely to withhold important information. However, this does not address the issue of the fairness of the purchase price to target shareholders.

Convertible securities[13] offer the potential of resolving the concerns of the acquirer and the target when both are lacking in critical information about the other. Bidders believing their shares are undervalued are reluctant to use stock, to avoid diluting their current shareholders. To communicate their belief, such bidders may offer convertible debt as a form of payment. Target shareholders may find such offers attractive, because they provide a floor equal to the value of the debt at maturity plus accumulated interest payments as well as the potential for participating in future share appreciation. In contrast, bidders believing their shares are overvalued are more inclined to offer stock rather than cash or convertible securities. If the convertible securities are unlikely to be converted due to the limited share price appreciation of the bidder's stock, the securities will remain as debt and burden the firm with substantial leverage. There is empirical evidence that the use of convertible securities when both parties are lacking in needed information can benefit both the bidder and the seller. Bidder and target abnormal announcement date returns for such deals are 1.86% and 6.89%, respectively.[14]

MANAGING RISK AND REACHING CONSENSUS ON PURCHASE PRICE

Balance-sheet adjustments and escrow accounts; earnouts; contingent value rights; rights to intellectual property and licensing fees; and consulting

---

[12] Assume the acquisition cost is $100 million, the acquirer wishes to limit cash paid to target firm shareholders to one-half of that amount, and the acquirer offers the target firm's shareholders a choice of stock or cash. If the amount of money given to target shareholders who choose to receive cash exceeds $50 million, the proration clause enables the acquirer to pay all target firm shareholders tendering their shares one-half of the purchase price in cash and the remainder in stock.

[13] Convertible bonds and preferred stock can be converted into a predetermined number of a firm's common shares if the shares exceed the price per share at which a convertible security can be converted into common stock.

[14] Finnerty et al., 2012

agreements may be used to close the deal when the buyer and seller cannot reach agreement on price.

Postclosing Balance-Sheet Price Adjustments and Escrow Accounts

About four-fifths of M&As require some purchase price adjustment, resulting most often from a restatement of operating earnings or cash flow or working capital.[15] Escrow or holdback accounts and adjustments to the target's balance sheet are most often used in cash rather than stock-for-stock purchases (particularly when the number of target shareholders is large). They rely on an audit of the target firm to determine its true value and are applicable only when what is being acquired is clearly identifiable, such as in a purchase of tangible assets. The buyer and seller typically share the cost of the audit. With *escrow accounts*, the buyer retains a portion of the purchase price until completion of a postclosing audit of the target's financial statements. Escrow accounts may also be used to cover continuing claims beyond closing.

Balance-sheet adjustments are used when the elapsed time between the agreement on price and the actual closing date is lengthy. The balance sheet may change significantly, so the purchase price is adjusted up or down. Such adjustments can be used to guarantee the value of the target firm's shareholder equity or, more narrowly, to ensure the value of working capital. With a shareholder equity guarantee, both parties agree at signing to an estimate of the target's equity value on the closing date. The purchase price is then increased or decreased to reflect any change in the book value of the target's equity between the signing and closing dates due net profit earned (or lost) during this period. Agreement may be reached more easily between the buyer and the seller with a working capital guarantee, which ensures against changes in the firm's net current operating assets.[16] As Table 11.2 indicates, the buyer reduces the total

TABLE 11.2　Working Capital Guarantee

Balance-Sheet Adjustments ($ Million)

	Purchase Price		Purchase Price Reduction	Purchase Price Increase
	At Time of Negotiation	At Closing		
If Working Capital Equals	110	100	10	
If Working Capital Equals	110	125		15

[15] RSM McGladrey, Inc., survey of 75 middle-market private equity investors (2011).

[16] It is critical to define clearly what constitutes working capital and equity in the agreement of purchase and sale, since—similar to equity—what constitutes working capital may be ambiguous.

purchase price by an amount equal to the decrease in net working capital or shareholders' equity of the target and increases the purchase price by any increase in these measures during this period.

Earnouts and Other Contingent Payments

Earnouts and warrants frequently are used whenever the buyer and the seller cannot agree on price or when the parties involved wish to participate in the upside potential of the business. Earnout agreements may also be used to retain and motivate key target firm managers. An *earnout agreement* is a financial contract whereby a portion of the purchase price of a company is to be paid in the future, contingent on realizing the future earnings level or some other performance measure agreed on earlier. A subscription warrant, or simply *warrant*, is a type of security—often issued with a bond or preferred stock—that entitles the holder to purchase an amount of common stock at a stipulated price. The exercise price is usually higher than the price at the time the warrant is issued. Warrants may be converted over a period of many months to many years.

The earnout typically requires that the acquired business be operated as a wholly owned subsidiary of the acquiring company under the management of the former owners or key executives.[17] Some earnouts are payable only if a certain performance threshold is achieved; others depend on average performance over several periods; and still others may involve periodic payments, depending on the achievement of interim performance measures rather than a single, lump-sum payment at the end of the earnout period. The value of the earnout is often capped. In some cases, the seller may have the option to repurchase the company at some predetermined percentage of the original purchase price if the buyer is unable to pay the earnout at maturity.

Exhibit. 11.2 illustrates how an earnout formula could be constructed reflecting these considerations. The purchase price has two components. At closing, the seller receives a lump-sum payment of $100 million. The seller and the buyer agree to a baseline projection for a three-year period and that the seller will receive a fixed multiple of the average annual performance of the acquired business in excess of the baseline projection. Thus, the earnout provides an incentive for the seller to operate the business as efficiently as possible.[18] By multiplying the anticipated multiple investors will pay for operating cash flow at the end of

---

[17] The calculation of such goals and the resulting payments should be kept simple to avoid disputes.

[18] The baseline projection often is what the buyer used to value the seller's business. Shareholder value for the buyer is created whenever the acquired business's actual performance exceeds the baseline projection and the multiple applied by investors at the end of the three-year period exceeds the multiple used to calculate the earnout payment, assuming that the baseline projection values the business accurately and that the buyer does not overpay.

EXHIBIT 11.2 HYPOTHETICAL EARNOUT AS PART OF THE PURCHASE PRICE

1. Lump-sum payment at closing: The seller receives $100 million.
2. Earnout payment: The seller receives four times the excess of the actual average annual net operating cash flow over the baseline projection after three years, not to exceed $35 million.

	Base Year (First Full Year of Ownership)		
	Year 1	Year 2	Year 3
Baseline Projection (Net Cash Flow)	$10	$12	$15
Actual Performance (Net Cash Flow)	$15	$20	$25

Earn-out at the end of three years:[a]

$$\frac{(\$15 - \$10) + (\$20 - \$12) + (\$25 - \$15)}{3} \times 4 = \$30.67$$

Potential Increase in Shareholder Value:[b]

$$\left\{ \frac{(\$15 - \$10) + (\$20 - \$12) + (\$25 - \$15)}{3} \times 10 \right\} - \$30.67 = \$46$$

[a] The cash flow multiple of 4 applied to the earnout is a result of negotiation before closing.

[b] The cash flow multiple of 10 applied to the potential increase in shareholder value for the buyer is the multiple the buyer anticipates that investors would apply to a three-year average of actual operating cash flow at the end of the three-year period.

the three-year period by projected cash flow, it is possible to estimate the potential increase in shareholder value.[19]

Used in 3% of deals, earnouts are more common when the targets are small private firms or subsidiaries of larger firms rather than large publicly traded firms. Such contracts are more easily written and enforced when there are relatively few shareholders.[20] Earnouts are most common in high-tech and service industries, when the acquirer and target firms are in different industries, when

---

[19] Earn-outs may demotivate management if the acquired firm does not perform well enough to achieve any payout under the earn-out formula or if the acquired firm exceeds the performance targets substantially, effectively guaranteeing the maximum payout under the plan. The management of the acquired firm may cut back on training expenses or make only those investments that improve short-term profits. To avoid such pitfalls, it may be appropriate to set multiple targets including revenue, income, and investment.

[20] Srikant, Frankel, and Wolfson, 2001

the target firm has a significant number of assets not recorded on the balance sheet, when buyer access to information is limited, and when little integration will be attempted.

Earnouts on average account for 45% of the price paid for private firms and 33% for subsidiary acquisitions, and target firm shareholders tend to realize about 62% of the potential earnout amount. In deals involving earnouts, acquirers earn abnormal returns, ranging from 1.5%[21] to 5.4%,[22] around the announcement date, much more than deals not involving earnouts. Positive abnormal returns to acquiring company shareholders may be a result of investor perception that with an earnout, the buyer is less likely to overpay and more likely to retain key target firm talent.

Contingent Value Rights (CVRs)

CVR securities issued by the acquirer commit it to pay additional cash or securities to the holder of the CVR (i.e., the seller) if the acquirer's share price falls below a specified level at some future date. They can be traded on public exchanges. Their use suggests that the acquirer believes that its shares are unlikely to fall below their current level. CVRs are sometimes granted when the buyer and the seller are far apart on the purchase price. A CVR is more suitable for a public company or a private firm with many shareholders than is an earnout, because it can be transferred to many investors. Earnouts are more often used with sales of private firms rather than for sales of public firms, since they are designed to motivate a firm's managers who have a significant degree of control over the firm's future performance.[23]

Drug companies frequently use CVRs as a portion of the payment made to acquire other drug companies whose products do not have a proven track record, to reduce the risk of overpaying. In 2011, Forest Labs agreed to buy Clinical Data, whose antidepressant Viibryd had received regulatory approval, for $1.2 billion, or $30 a share. The purchase price was about $3 less than the level at which it had been trading. Clinical Data agreed to the deal because Forest Labs issued CVRs that could result in payment of an additional $6 per share if revenue related to this drug achieves certain future targets.

Rights, Royalties, and Fees

Intellectual property, royalties from licenses, and fee-based consulting or employment contracts are other forms of payment used to resolve price differences between the buyer and the seller. The right to use a proprietary process or

[21] Barbopoulos and Sudarsanam, 2012

[22] Kohers and Ang, 2000

[23] Chatterjee and Yan (2008) document that acquirers issuing CVRs realize abnormal announcement date returns of 5.4% because investors view their use as confirmation that the acquirer believes their shares are undervalued.

technology for free or at a below-market rate may interest former owners considering other business opportunities.[24] Such arrangements should be coupled with agreements not to compete in the same industry as their former firm. Table 11.3 summarizes the advantages and disadvantages of these various forms of payment.

CONSTRUCTING COLLAR ARRANGEMENTS

Unlike all-cash deals, large fluctuations in the acquirer's share price can threaten to change the terms of the deal or lead to its termination in share-for-share exchanges. *Fixed share-exchange agreements*, which preclude any change in the number of acquirer shares exchanged for each target share, are commonly used in share exchanges because they involve both firms' share prices, allowing each party to share in the risk or benefit from fluctuating share prices. The acquirer's risk is that its shares will appreciate between signing and closing, raising the cost of the deal. The seller's risk is a potential drop in the value of the acquirer's share price, resulting in a lower-than-expected purchase price. While the buyer will know exactly how many shares will have to be issued to complete the deal, the acquirer and the target will be subject to significant uncertainty about the final value of the deal. Alternatively, a *fixed-value agreement* fixes the value of the offer price per share by allowing the share-exchange ratio to vary or float. An increase in the value of the acquirer's share price results in fewer acquirer shares being issued, to keep the value of the deal unchanged, while a decrease would require that additional shares be issued.

Both fixed-value and fixed-share-exchange agreements sometimes include a collar arrangement. For fixed-value agreements, the share-exchange ratio is allowed to vary within a narrow range; for fixed-share-exchange agreements, the offer price per share (deal value) is allowed to fluctuate within narrow limits.[25] Collar arrangements can be constructed as follows:

Offer Price per Share = Share Exchange Ratio (SER) × Acquirer's Share Price (ASP)

$$= \left\{ \frac{\text{Offer Price per Share}}{\text{Acquirer's Share Price}} \right\} \times \text{Acquirer's Share Price}$$

Collar Range: $\text{SER}_L \times \text{ASP}_L$ (lower limit) $\leq$ Offer Price per Share $\leq \text{SER}_U \times \text{ASP}_U$ (upper limit)

where $\text{ASP}_U > \text{ASP}_L$, $\text{SER}_U < \text{SER}_L$, and subscripts L and U refer to lower and upper limits.

[24] Note that such an arrangement, if priced at below-market rates or free to the seller, would represent taxable income to the seller.

[25] According to Factset MergerMetrics, about 15% of deals include some form of a collar. Merger contracts often contain "material adverse-effects clauses" allowing parties to the contract to withdraw from or renegotiate the deal. Officer (2004) argues that collars reduce the likelihood of renegotiation due to unanticipated changes in share prices.

TABLE 11.3   Evaluating Alternative Forms of Payment

Form of Payment	Advantages	Disadvantages
Cash (Including highly marketable securities)	*Buyer*: Simplicity. *Seller:* Ensures payment if acquirer's creditworthiness is questionable.	*Buyer:* Must rely solely on protections afforded in the contract to recover claims. *Seller:* Creates immediate tax liability.
Stock –Common –Preferred –Convertible Preferred	*Buyer:* High P/E relative to seller's P/E may increase the value of the combined firms. *Seller:* Defers taxes and provides potential price increase. Retains interest in the business.	*Buyer:* Adds complexity; potential EPS dilution. *Seller:* Potential decrease in purchase price if the value of equity received declines. May delay closing because of SEC registration requirements.
Debt —Secured —Unsecured —Convertible	*Buyer:* Interest expense is tax deductible. *Seller:* Defers tax liability on the principal.	*Buyer:* Adds complexity and increases leverage. *Seller:* Risk of default.
Performance-Related Earnouts	*Buyer:* Shifts some portion of the risk to the seller. *Seller:* Potential for a higher purchase price.	*Buyer:* May limit the integration of the businesses. *Seller:* Increases the uncertainty of the sales price.
Purchase Price Adjustments	*Buyer:* Protection from eroding values of working capital before closing. *Seller:* Protection from increasing values of working capital before closing.	*Buyer:* Audit expense. *Seller:* Audit expense. (Note that buyers and sellers often split the audit expense.)
Real Property —Real Estate —Plant and Equipment —Business or Product Line	*Buyer:* Minimizes use of cash. *Seller:* May minimize tax liability.	*Buyer:* Opportunity cost. *Seller:* Real property may be illiquid.
Rights to Intellectual Property —License —Franchise	*Buyer:* Minimizes cash use. *Seller:* Gains access to valuable rights, and spreads taxable income over time.	*Buyer:* Potential for setting up a new competitor. *Seller:* Illiquid; income taxed at ordinary rates.
Royalties from —License —Franchise	*Buyer:* Minimizes cash use. *Seller:* Spreads taxable income over time.	*Buyer:* Opportunity cost. *Seller:* Income taxed at ordinary rates.
Fee-based —Consulting Contract —Employment Agreement	*Buyer:* Uses seller's expertise and removes seller as a potential competitor. *Seller:* Augments the purchase price and allows the seller to stay with the business.	*Buyer:* May involve demotivated employees. *Seller:* Limits ability to compete in the same business. Income taxed at ordinary rates.

TABLE 11.3 (Continued)

Form of Payment	Advantages	Disadvantages
Contingent Value Rights	*Buyer:* Minimizes upfront payment. *Seller:* Provides for minimum payout guarantee.	*Buyer:* Commits buyer to minimum payout. *Seller:* Buyer may ask for purchase price reduction.
Staged or Distributed Payouts	*Buyer:* Reduces amount of upfront investment. *Seller:* Reduces buyer angst about certain future events.	*Buyer:* May result in underfunding of needed investments. *Seller:* Lower present value of purchase price.

Case Study 11.1 illustrates the use of both fixed value and fixed share exchange agreements. Within the first collar (fixed value), the purchase price is fixed by allowing the share exchange ratio to vary, giving the seller some degree of certainty inside a narrow range within which the acquirer share price floats; the second collar (fixed share exchange) allows the acquirer's share price (and therefore deal value) to vary within a specific range with both the buyer and seller sharing the risk. Finally, if the acquirer's share price rises above a certain level, the purchase price is capped; if it falls below a floor price, the seller can walk away. Table 11.4 illustrates the effect of a 1% increase or decrease in the acquirer's $11.73 share price under various collar arrangements.

FORM OF ACQUISITION

What acquirers purchase (target stock or assets) and how ownership is transferred from the target to the acquirer is called the *form of acquisition*. Each form affects the deal structure differently.[26]

An *asset purchase* involves the sale of all or a portion of the assets of the target to the buyer or its subsidiary in exchange for buyer stock, cash, debt, or some combination. The buyer may assume all, some, or none of the target's liabilities. The purchase price is paid directly to the target firm. A *stock purchase* involves the sale of the outstanding stock of the target to the buyer or its subsidiary by the target's shareholders. Unlike an asset purchase, the purchase price is paid to the target firm's shareholders. This is the biggest difference between the two methods, and it has significant tax implications for the seller's shareholders (see Chapter 12).

A *statutory or direct merger* involves the combination of the target with the buyer or a subsidiary formed to complete the merger. One corporation survives the merger and the other disappears. The surviving corporation can be the buyer, the target, or the buyer's subsidiary. Merger terminology usually refers

[26]For more information on this topic, see DePamphilis (2010b), Chapter 11.

CASE STUDY 11.1
Flextronics Acquires International DisplayWorks Using Multiple Collar Arrangements

Key Points

- Collar arrangements may involve fixed-share-exchange and/or fixed-value agreements.
- Both buyers and sellers may benefit from such arrangements.

Flextronics, a camera modules producer, acquired International DisplayWorks (IDW), an LCD maker, in a share exchange valued at $300 million. The share-exchange ratio was calculated using the Flextronics average daily closing share price for the 20 trading days ending on the fifth trading day preceding the closing.[a] Transaction terms included these three collars:

1. *Fixed-Value Agreement:* The offer price involved an exchange ratio floating inside a 10% collar above and below a Flextronics share price of $11.73 and a fixed purchase price of $6.55 for each share of IDW common stock. The range in which the exchange ratio floats can be expressed as follows:[b]

$$(\$6.55/\$10.55) \times \$10.55 \leq (\$6.55/\$11.73)$$
$$\times \$11.73 \leq (\$6.55/\$12.90) \times \$12.90$$

$$0.6209 \times \$10.55 \leq 0.5584 \times \$11.73 \leq 0.5078$$
$$\times \$12.90$$

If Flextronics' stock price declines by as much as 10% to $10.55, 0.6209 shares of Flextronics stock (i.e., $6.55/ $10.55) is issued for each IDW share.

If Flextronics' stock price increases by as much as 10% to $12.90, 0.5078 shares of Flextronics' stock (i.e., $6.55/$12.90) is issued for each IDW share.

2. *Fixed-Share-Exchange Agreement:* The offer price involved a fixed exchange ratio inside a collar 11% and 15% above and below $11.73, resulting in a floating purchase price if the Flextronics's stock increases or decreases between 11% and 15% from $11.73 per share.

3. IDW has the right to terminate the agreement if Flextronics's share price falls by more than 15% below $11.73. If Flextronics' share price increases by more than 15% above $11.73, the exchange ratio floats based on a fixed purchase price of $6.85 per share.[c]

---

[a] Calculating the acquirer share price as a 20-day average ending five days prior to closing reduces the chance of using an aberrant price per share and provides time to update the purchase agreement.

[b] The share-exchange ratio varies within ± 10% of the Flextronics' $11.73 share price.

[c] IDW is protected against a "free fall" in the Flextronics share price, while the purchase price is capped at $6.85.

TABLE 11.4   Flextronics-IDW Fixed-Value and Fixed-Share-Exchange Agreements
(All Changes in Offer Price Based on a 1% Change from $11.73)

	% Change	Offer Price	% Change	Offer Price
		($6.55/$11.73) × $11.73 = $6.55		($6.55/$11.73) × $11.73 = $6.55
Fixed Value	1	($6.55/$11.85) × $11.85 = $6.55	(1)	($6.55/$11.61) × $11.61 = $6.55
	2	($6.55/$11.96) × $11.96 = $6.55	(2)	($6.55/$11.50) × $11.50 = $6.55
	3	($6.55/$12.08) × $12.08 = $6.55	(3)	($6.55/$11.38) × $11.38 = $6.55
	4	($6.55/$12.20) × $12.20 = $6.55	(4)	($6.55/$11.26) × $11.26 = $6.55
	5	($6.55/$12.32) × $12.32 = $6.55	(5)	($6.55/$11.14) × $11.14 = $6.55
	6	($6.55/$12.43) × $12.43 = $6.55	(6)	($6.55/$11.03) × $11.03 = $6.55
	7	($6.55/$12.55) × $12.55 = $6.55	(7)	($6.55/$10.91) × $10.91 = $6.55
	8	($6.55/$12.67) × 12.67 = $6.55	(8)	($6.55/$10.79) × $10.79 = $6.55
	9	($6.55/$12.79) × $12.79 = $6.55	(9)	($6.55/$10.67) × $10.67 = $6.55
Fixed SER	10	($6.55/$12.90) × $12.90 = $6.55	(10)	($6.55/$10.56) × $10.56 = $6.55
	11	($6.55/$12.90) × $13.02 = $6.61	(11)	($6.55/$10.56) × $10.44 = $6.48
	12	($6.55/$12.90) × $13.14 = $6.67	(12)	($6.55/$10.56) × $10.32 = $6.40
	13	($6.55/$12.90) × $13.25 = $6.73	(13)	($6.55/$10.56) × $10.21 = $6.33
	14	($6.55/$12.90) × $13.37 = $6.79	(14)	($6.55/$10.56) × $10.09 = $6.26
	15	($6.55/$12.90) × $13.49 = $6.85	(15)	($6.55/$10.56) × $9.97 = $6.18
	>15	SER floats based on fixed $6.85	>(15)	IDW may terminate agreement

to the bidder as the *surviving corporation* and to the target as the *disappearing corporation*. Knowing which company is to survive is critical under merger law because of *successor liability*, which states that the surviving corporation receives by operation of law, all rights and liabilities of both the bidder company and the target company in accordance with the statutes of the state in which the combined businesses will be incorporated.[27] Dissenting or minority shareholders are required to sell their shares, although some state statutes grant them the right to be paid the appraised value of their shares. *Stock-for-stock* or *stock-for-assets* deals represent alternatives to a merger.

State statutes usually require shareholder approval by both the bidder and target firms in a merger. However, no acquirer shareholder vote is required if the form of payment is cash, the number of new acquirer shares issued is less than 20% of the firm's outstanding shares, or if the number of shares previously authorized is sufficient to complete the deal. These exceptions are discussed in more detail later in this chapter. The most important difference between a merger and a stock-for-stock purchase is that the latter does not require a target shareholder vote, since target shareholders are giving their assent by willingly selling their shares. By purchasing all of the target's stock for acquirer stock or at least a controlling interest, the target firm is left intact as a wholly-owned (or at least controlled) subsidiary of the bidder. Table 11.5 highlights the advantages and disadvantages of these alternative forms of acquisition.

Purchase of Assets

In an asset purchase, a buyer acquires all rights a seller has to an asset for cash, stock, or some combination. An asset purchase may be the most practical way to complete the transaction when the acquirer is interested only in a product line or division of the parent firm with multiple product lines or divisions that are not organized as separate legal subsidiaries. The seller retains ownership of the shares of stock of the business. Only assets and liabilities identified in the agreement of purchase and sale are transferred to the buyer.

In a *cash-for-assets* acquisition, the acquirer pays cash for the seller's assets and may choose to accept some or all of the seller's liabilities.[28] Seller shareholders must approve the transaction whenever the seller's board votes to sell all or "substantially all" of the firm's assets and the firm is liquidated. After paying for any liabilities not assumed by the buyer, the assets remaining with the seller and the cash received from the acquiring firm are transferred to the seller's

---

[27] Because of successor liability, the bidder can realize significant cost savings by not having to transfer individual target assets and liabilities separately that would have otherwise required the payment of transfer taxes. For the creditor, all of the assets of the surviving corporation are available to satisfy its liabilities due to successor liability.

[28] In cases where the buyer purchases most of the assets of a target firm, courts have ruled that the buyer is also responsible for the target's liabilities.

TABLE 11.5 Advantages and Disadvantages of Alternative Forms of Acquisition

Alternative Forms	Advantages	Disadvantages
Cash Purchase of Assets	**Buyer**	**Buyer**
	• Allows targeted purchase of assets	• Loses NOLs[b] and tax credits
	• Asset write-up	• Loses rights to intellectual property
	• May renegotiate union and benefits agreements in the absence of a successor clause[a] in the labor agreement	• May require consents to assignment of contracts
	• May avoid the need for shareholder approval	• Exposed to liabilities transferring with assets (e.g., warranty claims)
	• No minority shareholders	• Subject to taxes on any gains resulting in asset write-up
		• Subject to lengthy documentation of assets in the contract
	Seller	**Seller**
	• Maintains corporate existence and ownership of assets not acquired	• Potential double taxation if shell is liquidated
	• Retains NOLs and tax credits	• Subject to state transfer taxes
		• Necessity of disposing of unwanted residual assets
		• Requires shareholder approval if substantially all of the firm's assets are sold
Cash Purchase of Stock	**Buyer**	**Buyer**
	• Assets/liabilities transfer automatically	• Responsible for known and unknown liabilities
	• May avoid the need to get consents to assignment for contracts	• No asset write-up unless 338 election is adopted by buyer and seller[c]
	• Less documentation	• Union and employee benefit agreements do not terminate
	• NOLs and tax credits pass to buyer	• Potential for minority shareholders[d]
	• No state transfer taxes	
	• May insulate from target liabilities if kept as a subsidiary	
	• No shareholder approval if funded by cash or debt	
	• Enables circumvention of target's board in hostile tender offer	
	Seller	**Seller**
	• Liabilities generally pass to the buyer	• Loss of NOLs and tax credits
	• May receive favorable tax treatment if acquirer stock received in payment	• Favorable tax treatment is lost if buyer and seller adopt 338 election[c]

TABLE 11.5 (Continued)

Alternative Forms	Advantages	Disadvantages
Statutory Merger	**Buyer** • Flexible form of payment (stock, cash, or debt) • Assets and liabilities transfer automatically, without lengthy documentation • No state transfer taxes • No minority shareholders because shareholders are required to tender shares (minority freeze-out) • May avoid shareholder approval	**Buyer** • May have to pay dissenting shareholders' appraised value of stock • May be time consuming because of the need for target shareholder and board approvals, which may delay closing
	Seller • Favorable tax treatment if the purchase price is primarily in acquirer stock • Allows for continuing interest in combined companies • Flexible form of payment	**Seller** • May be time consuming • Target firm often does not survive • May not qualify for favorable tax status
Stock-for-Stock Transaction	**Buyer** • May operate target company as a subsidiary • See purchase of stock above	**Buyer** • May postpone realization of synergies • See purchase of stock above
	Seller See purchase of stock above	**Seller** See purchase of stock above
Stock-for-Assets Transaction	**Buyer** • See purchase of assets above	**Buyer** • May dilute buyer's ownership position • See purchase of assets above
	Seller See purchase of assets above	**Seller** See purchase of assets above
Staged Transactions	• Provides greater strategic flexibility	• May postpone realization of synergies

[a]*If the employer and union negotiated a "successor clause" into their collective bargaining agreement covering the workforce in the target firm, the terms of the agreement may still apply to the workforce of the new business.*
[b]*Net operating loss carryforwards or carrybacks.*
[c]*In Section 338 of the U.S. tax code, the acquirer in a purchase of 80% or more of the stock of the target may elect to treat the acquisition as if it were an acquisition of the target's assets. The seller must agree with the election.*
[d]*Minority shareholders in a subsidiary may be eliminated by a so-called back-end merger following the initial purchase of target stock. As a result of the merger, minority shareholders are required to abide by the majority vote of all shareholders and to sell their shares to the acquirer. If the acquirer owns more than 90% of the target's shares, it may be able to use a short-form merger, which does not require any shareholder vote.*

shareholders in a liquidating distribution.[29] In a *stock-for-assets* transaction, once approved by the seller's board and shareholders, the seller's shareholders receive buyer stock in exchange for the seller's assets and assumed liabilities. In a second stage, the seller dissolves the corporation following shareholder ratification of such a move, leaving its shareholders with buyer stock.

Advantages and Disadvantages from the Buyer's Perspective

The *advantages* from the buyer's standpoint include being selective as to which assets of the target to purchase. The buyer is not responsible for the seller's liabilities unless assumed under the contract. However, the buyer can be held responsible for certain liabilities, such as environmental claims, property taxes, and, in some states, substantial pension liabilities and product liability claims. To protect against such risks, buyers usually insist on *indemnification* that holds the seller responsible for payment of damages resulting from such claims.[30] Another advantage is that asset purchases enable buyers to revalue acquired assets to market value under the purchase method of accounting (see Chapter 12). This increase in the tax basis of the acquired assets to fair market value provides for higher depreciation and amortization expense deductions for tax purposes. Absent successor clauses in the contract, the asset purchase results in the termination of union agreements if less than 50% of the workforce in the new firm is unionized, thereby providing an opportunity to renegotiate agreements viewed as too restrictive.

Among the *disadvantages* to a purchase of assets is that the buyer loses the seller's net operating losses and tax credits, and rights to assets such as licenses, franchises, and patents cannot be transferred, which are viewed as owned by the target shareholders. The buyer often must seek the consent of customers and vendors to transfer existing contracts to the buyer. The transaction often is more complex and costly, because acquired assets must be listed in appendices to the definitive agreement, the sale of and titles to each asset transferred must be recorded, and state title *transfer taxes* must be paid. Moreover, a lender's consent may be required if the assets to be sold are being used as collateral for loans.

Advantages and Disadvantages from the Seller's Perspective

Among the *advantages*, sellers are able to maintain their corporate existence and thus ownership of tangible assets not acquired by the buyer and of

---

[29] Selling "substantially all" assets does not necessarily mean that most of the firm's assets have been sold; rather, it could refer to a small percentage of the firm's total assets that are critical to the ongoing operation of the business. Hence, the firm may be forced to liquidate if a sale of assets does not leave the firm with "significant continuing business activity"—that is, at least 25% of total pretransaction operating assets and 25% of pretransaction income or revenue. Unless required by the firm's bylaws, the buyer's shareholders do not vote to approve the transaction.

[30] Note that in most purchase agreements, buyers and sellers agree to indemnify each other from claims for which they are directly responsible. Liability under such arrangements usually is subject to specific dollar limits and is in force only for a specific period.

intangible assets such as licenses, franchises, and patents. The seller retains the right to use all tax credits and accumulated net operating losses to shelter future income from taxes. The *disadvantages* include the potential double taxation of the seller. If the tax basis in the assets is low, the seller may experience a sizeable gain on the sale; if the corporation subsequently is liquidated, the seller may be responsible for the recapture of taxes deferred as a result of the use of accelerated rather than straight-line depreciation. If the number of assets transferred is large, the amount of state transfer taxes may become onerous. Whether the seller or the buyer actually pays the transfer taxes or they are shared is negotiable.

Purchase of Stock

In *cash-for-stock* or *stock-for-stock* transactions, the buyer purchases the seller's stock directly from the seller's shareholders. For a public company, the acquirer would make a tender offer, because public-company shareholders are likely to be too numerous to deal with individually. A purchase of stock is the approach most often taken in hostile takeovers. If the buyer is unable to convince all of the seller's shareholders to tender their shares, then a minority of seller shareholders remains outstanding. The target firm would then be viewed as a partially owned subsidiary of the acquiring company. No seller shareholder approval is required in such transactions because the seller's shareholders are expressing approval by tendering their shares.

Advantages and Disadvantages from the Buyer's Perspective

Advantages include the automatic transfer of all assets with the target's stock, the avoidance of state asset transfer taxes, and the transfer of net operating losses and tax credits to the buyer. The purchase of the seller's stock provides for the continuity of contracts and corporate identity. However, the consent of some customers and vendors may be required before a contract is transferred if it is stipulated in the contract. While the acquirer's board normally approves any major acquisition, approval by shareholders is not required if the purchase is financed with cash or debt. If stock that has not yet been authorized is used, shareholder approval is required.

Among the *disadvantages*, the buyer is liable for all unknown, undisclosed, or contingent liabilities. The seller's tax basis is carried over to the buyer at historical cost;[31] therefore, there is no step-up in the cost basis of assets, and no tax shelter is created. Dissenting shareholders in many states have the right to have their shares appraised, with the option of being paid the appraised value of their shares or remaining minority shareholders. The purchase of stock does not terminate existing union agreements or employee benefit plans. The existence

---

[31] This is true unless the seller consents to take a 338 tax code election, which can create a tax liability for the seller.

of minority shareholders creates significant administrative costs and practical concerns.[32]

Advantages and Disadvantages from the Seller's Perspective

Sellers often prefer a stock purchase to an asset purchase because the seller is free of future obligations, because all liabilities transfer to the buyer, and the seller is able to defer paying taxes if the form of payment is mostly buyer stock. *Disadvantages* for the seller include the inability to retain certain assets and the loss of net operating losses, tax credits, and intellectual property rights.

Mergers

In a merger, two or more firms combine, with only one surviving. Unlike purchases of target stock, mergers require approval of both the target's and acquirer's boards and are subsequently submitted to both firms' shareholders for approval. However, there are some exceptions, which are addressed later in this chapter. Usually a simple majority of all the outstanding voting shares must ratify the proposal, which is then registered with the appropriate state authority.

Statutory and Subsidiary Mergers

In a *statutory merger*, the acquiring company assumes the assets and liabilities of the target in accordance with the statutes of the state in which the combined firms will be incorporated. A *subsidiary merger* involves the target's becoming a subsidiary of the parent. To the public, the target firm may be operated under its brand name but will be owned and controlled by the acquirer. Most mergers are structured as subsidiary mergers in which the acquiring firm creates a new corporate subsidiary that merges with the target.

Statutory Consolidations

Technically not a merger, a *statutory consolidation* requires all legal entities to be consolidated into a new company, usually with a new name, whereas in a merger either the acquirer or the target survives. The new corporate entity created as a result of consolidation assumes ownership of the assets and liabilities of the consolidated organizations. Stockholders in merged companies typically exchange their shares for shares in the new company. This form of acquisition is not widely used among for-profit entities, but it has proven to be a successful form of acquisition for nonprofit organizations.

Mergers of Equals

A *merger of equals* is a structure usually applied whenever the participants are comparable in size, competitive position, profitability, and market

[32]The parent incurs significant additional expenses to submit annual reports, hold annual shareholder meetings, and conduct a formal board election process. Furthermore, implementing strategic business decisions may be inhibited by lawsuits initiated by disaffected minority shareholders.

capitalization—which can make it unclear whether one party is ceding control to the other and which party provides the greater synergy. Consequently, target firm shareholders rarely receive any significant premium for their shares. It is common for the new firm to be managed by the former CEOs of the merged firms as coequals and for the new firm's board to have equal representation from the boards of the merged firms.[33] However, it is relatively uncommon for the ownership split to be equally divided.[34]

Tender Offers

An alternative to a traditional merger, which accomplishes the same objective, is the *two-step acquisition*. In the first step, the acquirer buys through a stock purchase the majority of the target's outstanding stock from its shareholders in a tender offer; in the second step, a *squeeze-out/freeze-out merger* or *back-end merger* is approved by the acquirer as majority shareholder. Minority shareholders are required to sell their shares.

Shareholder Approvals

Target shareholders usually must give consent if all or "substantially all" of the firm's assets are being acquired.[35] While no acquirer shareholder vote is mandatory when the form of payment is cash because there is no dilution of current shareholders, there are certain instances in which no vote is required by the acquirer's shareholders in share-for-share exchanges. The first, the so-called *small-scale merger exception*, involves a transaction not considered material.[36] The second, a *short-form merger* or the *parent-submerger exception*, occurs when a subsidiary is being merged into the parent and the parent owns a substantial majority (over 90% in some states) of the subsidiary's stock before the transaction. The third exception involves use of a *triangular merger*, in which the acquirer establishes a merger subsidiary in which it is the sole shareholder. The only approval required is that of the board of directors of the subsidiary, which

---

[33] Research by Wulf (2004) suggests that target firm CEOs often negotiate to retain a significant degree of control in the merged firm for both their board and their management in exchange for a lower premium for their shareholders.

[34] According to Mallea (2008), only 14% have a 50/50 split.

[35] "Substantially all" refers to the sale of assets critical to the ongoing operation of the business. Target shareholders do not get approval rights in short-form mergers in which the parent owns over 90% of a subsidiary's stock.

[36] Acquiring-firm shareholders cannot vote unless their ownership in the acquiring firm is diluted by more than one-sixth, or 16.67% (i.e., acquirer owns at least 83.33% of the firm's voting shares following closing). This effectively limits the acquirer to issuing no more than 20% of its total shares outstanding. For example, if the acquirer has 80 million shares outstanding and issues 16 million new shares (i.e., 0.2×80 million), its current shareholders are not diluted by more than one-sixth (i.e., 16/(16 million + 80 million) equals one-sixth, or 16.67%). Issuing more than 16 million new shares would violate the small-scale merger exception.

may be the same as that of the parent or acquiring company.[37] Finally, no share-holder approval is needed if the number of shares previously authorized under the firm's articles of incorporation is sufficient to complete the deal.

Top-Up Options

Such options are granted by the target to the bidding firm, whose tender offer is short of the 90% threshold to qualify as a short-form merger, to buy up newly issued target shares to reach the threshold. Since the option ensures that the merger will be approved, the bidder benefits by avoiding the delay associated with back-end mergers requiring a shareholder vote if the acquirer is unable to get enough target shares to implement a short-form merger. The target firm benefits by eliminating potential changes in the value of the bidder's shares that are offered in exchange for target shares that could occur between signing and closing.

Special Applications of Basic Structures

In a *leveraged buyout (LBO)*, a financial sponsor or equity investor creates a shell corporation funded by equity provided by the sponsor. In the first stage, the shell corporation raises cash by borrowing from banks and selling debt to institutional investors. In the second stage, the shell corporation buys 50.1% of the target's stock, squeezing out minority shareholders with a back-end merger in which the remaining shareholders receive debt or preferred stock. *Single-firm recapitalizations* are undertaken to squeeze out minority shareholders. To do so, a firm creates a wholly owned shell corporation and merges itself into the shell in a statutory merger. Stock in the original firm is cancelled, with the majority shareholders in the original firm receiving stock in the surviving firm and minority shareholders receiving cash or debt. *Staged transactions* involve an acquirer completing a takeover in stages spread over an extended period of time. They may be used to structure an earnout, enable the target to complete the development of a technology or process, or await regulatory approval of a license or patent.

SOME THINGS TO REMEMBER

Deal structuring entails satisfying the key objectives of the parties involved and how risk will be shared. The process defines initial negotiating positions, risks, options for managing risk, levels of risk tolerance, and conditions under which the buyer or seller will walk away from the deal.

---

[37] The listing requirements of all major U.S. stock exchanges may still force acquirer shareholder approval if the number of new shares issued to finance the transaction is greater than or equal to 20% of the acquirer's common shares outstanding prior to the deal. Such deals are deemed to be material.

DISCUSSION QUESTIONS

11.1 What are the advantages and disadvantages of a purchase of assets from the perspectives of the buyer and the seller?

11.2 What are the advantages and disadvantages of a purchase of stock from the perspectives of the buyer and the seller?

11.3 What are the advantages and disadvantages of a statutory merger?

11.4 What are the reasons some acquirers choose to undertake a staged or multistep takeover?

11.5 What forms of acquisition represent common alternatives to a merger? Under what circumstances might these alternative structures be employed?

11.6 Comment on the following statement: A premium offered by a bidder over a target's share price is not necessarily a fair price; a fair price is not necessarily an adequate price.

11.7 In a year marked by turmoil in the global credit markets, Mars Corporation was able to negotiate a reverse breakup fee structure in its acquisition of Wrigley Corporation. This structure allowed Mars to walk away from the transaction at any time by paying a $1 billion fee to Wrigley. Speculate as to the motivation behind Mars and Wrigley negotiating such a fee.

11.8 Despite disturbing discoveries during due diligence, Mattel acquired The Learning Company, a leading developer of software for toys, in a stock exchange valued at $3.5 billion. Mattel had determined that TLC's receivables were overstated because product returns from distributors were not deducted from receivables and its allowance for bad debt was inadequate. Also, a $50 million licensing deal also had been prematurely put on the balance sheet. Nevertheless, driven by the appeal of rapidly becoming a big player in the children's software market, Mattel closed on the transaction, aware that TLC's cash flows were overstated. Despite being aware of extensive problems, Mattel proceeded to acquire The Learning Company. Why? What could Mattel have done to protect its interests better? Be specific.

11.9 Describe the conditions under which an earnout may be most appropriate.

11.10 Deutsche Bank announced that it would buy the commercial banking assets (including a number of branches) of the Netherlands' ABN Amro for $1.13 billion. What liabilities, if any, would Deutsche Bank have to (or want to) assume? Explain your answer.

Solutions to these Chapter Discussion Questions are found in the Online Instructor's Manual for instructors using this book.

CASE STUDY 11.2
Sanofi Acquires Genzyme in a Test of Wills

Key Points

- Contingent value rights help bridge price differences between buyers and sellers when the target's future earnings performance is dependent on the realization of a specific event.
- They are most appropriate when the target firm is a large publicly traded firm with numerous shareholders.

Facing a patent expiration precipice in 2015, big pharmaceutical companies have been scrambling to find new sources of revenue to offset probable revenue losses as many of their most popular drugs lose patent protection. Generic drug companies are expected to make replacement drugs and sell them at a much lower price.

Focusing on the biotechnology market, French-based drug company Sanofi-Aventis SA (Sanofi) announced on February 17, 2011, the takeover of U.S.-based Genzyme Corp. (Genzyme) for $74 per share, or $20.1 billion in cash, plus a contingent value right (CVR). The CVR could add as much as $14 a share or another $3.8 billion, to the purchase price if Genzyme is able to achieve certain performance targets. According to the terms of the agreement, Genzyme will retain its name and operate as a separate unit focusing on rare diseases, an area in which it had excelled. The purchase price represented a 48% premium over Genzyme's share price of $50

per share immediately preceding the announcement.

The acquisition represented the end of a nine-month effort that began on May 23, 2010, when Sanofi CEO Chris Viehbacher first approached Genzyme's Henri Termeer, the firm's founder and CEO. Sanofi expressed interest in Genzyme at a time when debt was cheap and when Genzyme's share price was depressed, having fallen from a 2008 peak of $83.25 to $47.16 in June 2010. Genzyme's depressed share price reflected manufacturing problems that had lowered sales of its best-selling products. Genzyme continued to recover from the manufacturing challenges that had temporarily shut down operations at its main site in 2009. The plant is the sole source of Genzyme's top-selling products, Gaucher's disease treatment Cerezyme and Fabry disease drug Fabrazyme. Both were in short supply throughout 2010 due to the plant's shutdown. By year-end, the supply shortages were less acute. Sanofi was convinced that other potential bidders were too occupied with integrating recent deals to enter into a bidding war.

In an effort to get Genzyme to engage in discussions and to permit Sanofi to perform due diligence, Sanofi submitted a formal bid of $69 per share on July 29, 2010. However, Sanofi continued to ignore the unsolicited offer. The offer was 38% above Genzyme's price on July 1, 2010, when investors began to speculate that

Genzyme was "in play." Sanofi was betting that the Genzyme shareholders would accept the offer rather than risk seeing their shares fall to $50. The shares, however, traded sharply higher at $70.49 per share, signaling that investors were expecting Sanofi to have to increase its bid. Viehbacher said he might increase the bid if Genzyme would be willing to disclose more information about the firm's ongoing manufacturing problems and the promising new market potential for its multiple sclerosis drug.

In a letter made public on August 29, 2010, Sanofi indicated that it had been trying to engage Genzyme in acquisition talks for months and that its formal bid had been rejected by Genzyme without any further discussion on August 11, 2010. The letter concludes with a thinly disguised threat that "all alternatives to complete the transaction" would be considered and that "Sanofi is confident that Genzyme shareholders will support the proposal." In responding to the public disclosure of the letter, the Genzyme board said it was not prepared to engage in merger negotiations with Sanofi based on an opportunistic proposal with an unrealistic starting price that dramatically undervalued the company. Termeer said publicly that the firm was worth at least $80 per share. He based this value on the improvement in the firm's manufacturing operations and the revenue potential of Lemtrada, Genzyme's experimental treatment for multiple sclerosis, which once approved for sale by the FDA was projected by Genzyme to generate

billions of dollars annually. Despite Genzyme's refusal to participate in takeover discussions, Sanofi declined to raise its initial offer in view of the absence of other bidders.

Sanofi finally initiated an all-cash hostile tender offer for all of the outstanding Genzyme shares at $69 per share on October 4, 2010. Set to expire initially on December 16, 2010, the tender offer was later extended to January 21, 2011, when the two parties started to discuss a contingent value right (CVR) as a means of bridging their disparate views on the value of Genzyme. Initially, Genzyme projected peak annual sales of $3.5 billion for Lemtrada and $700 million for Sanofi. At the end of January, the parties announced that they had signed a nondisclosure agreement to give Sanofi access to Genzyme's financial statements.

The CVR helped to allay fears that Sanofi would overpay and that the drug Lemtrada would not be approved by the FDA. Under the terms of the CVR, Genzyme shareholders would receive $1 per share if Genzyme were able to meet certain production targets in 2011 for Cerezyme and Fabrazyme, whose output had been sharply curtailed by viral contamination at its plant in 2009. Each right would yield an additional $1 if Lemtrada wins FDA approval. Additional payments will be made if Lemtrada hits certain other annual revenue targets. The CVR, which runs until the end of 2020, entitles holders to a series of payments that could cumulatively be worth up to $14 per share if Lemtrada reaches $2.8 billion in annual sales.

The Genzyme transaction was structured as a tender offer to be followed immediately with a back-end short-form merger. The short-form merger enables an acquirer, without a shareholder vote, to squeeze out any minority shareholders not tendering their shares during the tender offer period. To execute the short-form merger, the purchase agreement included a top-up option granted by the Genzyme board to Sanofi. The "top-up" option would be triggered when Sanofi acquired 75% of Genzyme's outstanding shares through its tender offer. The 75% threshold could have been lower had Genzyme had more authorized but unissued shares to make up the difference between the 90% requirement for the short-form merger and the number of shares accumulated as a result of the tender offer. The deal also involved the so-called dual-track model of simultaneously filing a proxy statement for a shareholders' meeting and vote on the merger while the tender offer is occurring to ensure that the deal closes as soon as possible.

Discussion Questions

1. The deal was structured as a tender offer coupled with a top-up option to be followed by a back-end short-form merger. Why might this structure be preferable to a more common statutory merger deal or a tender offer followed by a back-end merger requiring a shareholder vote?
2. Speculate as to the purpose of the dual-track model in which the bidder initiates a tender offer and simultaneously files a prospectus to hold a shareholders meeting and vote on a merger.
3. Describe the takeover tactics employed by Sanofi. Discuss why each one might have been used.
4. Describe the anti-takeover strategy employed by Genzyme. Discuss why each may have been employed. In your opinion, did the Genzyme strategy work?
5. What alternatives could Sanofi have used instead of the CVR to bridge the gap in how the parties valued Genzyme? Discuss the advantages and disadvantages of each.
6. How might both the target firm and the bidding firm benefit from the top-up option?
7. How might the existence of a CVR limit Sanofi's ability to realize certain types of synergies? Be specific.

Solutions to these questions are provided in the Online Instructor's Manual for instructors using this book.

CASE STUDY 11.3
Swiss Pharmaceutical Giant Novartis Takes Control of Alcon

Key Points

- Parent firms frequently find it appropriate to buy out minority shareholders to reduce costs and to simplify future decision making.
- Acquirers may negotiate call options with the target firm after securing a minority position to implement so-called creeping takeovers.

In December 2010, Swiss pharmaceutical company Novartis AG completed its effort to acquire, for $12.9 billion, the remaining 23% of U.S.-listed eye care group Alcon Incorporated (Alcon) that it did not already own. This brought the total purchase price for 100% of Alcon to $52.2 billion. Novartis had been trying to purchase Alcon's remaining publicly traded shares since January 2010, but its original offer of 2.8 Novartis shares, valued at $153 per Alcon share, met stiff resistance from Alcon's independent board of directors, which had repeatedly dismissed the Novartis bid as "grossly inadequate." Novartis finally relented, agreeing to pay $168 per share, the average price it had paid for the Alcon shares it already owned, and to guarantee that price by paying cash equal to the difference between $168 and the value of 2.8 Novartis shares immediately prior to closing. If the value of Novartis shares were to appreciate before closing such that the value of 2.8 shares exceeded $168, the number of Novartis shares

would be reduced. By acquiring all outstanding Alcon shares, Novartis avoided interference by minority shareholders in making key business decisions, achieved certain operating synergies, and eliminated the expense of having public shareholders.

In 2008, with global financial markets in turmoil, Novartis acquired, for cash, a minority position in food giant Nestlé's wholly owned subsidiary Alcon. Nestlé had acquired 100% of Alcon in 1978 and retained that position until 2002, when it undertook an IPO of 23% of its shares. In April 2008, Novartis acquired 25% of Alcon for $143 per share from Nestlé. As part of this transaction, Novartis and Nestlé received a call and a put option, respectively, which could be exercised at $181 per Alcon share from January 2010 to July 2011. On January 4, 2010, Novartis exercised its call option to buy Nestlé's remaining 52% ownership stake in Alcon that it did not already own. By doing so, Novartis increased its total ownership position in Alcon to about 77%. The total price paid by Novartis for this position amounted to $39.3 billion ($11.2 billion in 2008 plus $28.1 billion in 2010). On the same day, Novartis also offered to acquire the remaining publicly held shares that it did not already own in a share exchange valued at $153 per share in which 2.8 shares of its stock would be exchanged for each Alcon share.

While the Nestlé deal seemed likely to receive regulatory approval, the offer to the minority shareholders was assailed immediately as too low. At $153 per share, the offer was well below the Alcon closing price on January 4, 2010, of $164.35. The Alcon publicly traded share price may have been elevated by investors' anticipating a higher bid. Novartis argued that without this speculation, the publicly traded Alcon share price would have been $137, and the $153 per share price Novartis offered the minority shareholders would have represented an approximate 12% premium to that price. The minority shareholders, who included several large hedge funds, argued that they were entitled to $181 per share, the amount paid to Nestlé. Alcon's publicly traded shares dropped 5% to $156.97 on the news of the Novartis takeover. Novartis' shares also lost 3%, falling to $52.81. On August 9, 2010, Novartis received approval from European Union regulators to buy the stake in Alcon, making it easier for it to take full control of Alcon.

With the buyout of Nestlé's stake in Alcon completed, Novartis was now faced with acquiring the remaining 23% of the outstanding shares of Alcon stock held by the public. Under Swiss takeover law, Novartis needed a majority of Alcon board members and two-thirds of shareholders to approve the terms for the merger to take effect and for Alcon shares to convert automatically into Novartis shares. Once it owned 77% of Alcon's stock, Novartis only needed to place five of its own nominated directors on the Alcon board to replace the five directors previously named by Nestlé to the board. Alcon's independent directors set up an independent director committee (IDC), arguing that the price offered to minority shareholders was too low and that the new directors, having been nominated by Novartis, should abstain from voting on the Novartis takeover because of their conflict of interest. The IDC preferred a negotiated merger to a "cram down" or forced merger in which the minority shares convert to Novartis shares at the 2.8 share-exchange offer.

Provisions in the Swiss takeover code require a mandatory offer whenever a bidder purchases more than 33.3% of another firm's stock. In a mandatory offer, Novartis would also be subject to the Swiss code's minimum-bid rule, which would require Novartis to pay $181 per share in cash to Alcon's minority shareholders, the same bid offered to Nestlé. By replacing the Nestlé-appointed directors with their own slate of candidates and owning more than two-thirds of the Alcon shares, Novartis argued that they were not subject to mandatory-bid requirements. Novartis was betting on the continued appreciation of its shares, valued in Swiss francs, due to an ongoing appreciation of the Swiss currency and its improving operating performance, to eventually win over holders of the publicly traded Alcon shares. However, by late 2010, Novartis's patience appears to have worn thin. While not always the case, the resistance of the independent directors paid off for those investors holding publicly traded shares.

Discussion Questions

1. Speculate as to why Novartis acquired only a 25% ownership stake in Alcon in 2008.

2. Why was the price ($181 per share) at which Novartis exercised its call option in 2010 to increase its stake in Alcon to 77% so much higher than what it paid ($143 per share) for an approximate 25% stake in Alcon in early 2008?

3. Alcon and Novartis shares dropped by 5% and 3%, respectively, immediately following the announcement that Novartis would exercise its option to buy Nestlé's majority holdings of Alcon shares. Explain why this may have happened.

4. How do Swiss takeover laws compare to comparable U.S. laws? Which do you find more appropriate, and why?

5. Discuss how Novartis may have arrived at the estimate of $137 per share as the intrinsic value of Alcon shares. What are the key underlying assumptions? Do you believe the minority shareholders should receive the same price as Nestlé? Explain your answer.

Solutions to these case study discussion questions are available in the Online Instructor's Manual for instructors using this book.

Structuring the Deal

Tax and Accounting Considerations

When people find they can vote themselves money, that will herald the end of the republic.—**Benjamin Franklin**

INSIDE M&A: JOHNSON & JOHNSON USES FINANCIAL ENGINEERING TO ACQUIRE SYNTHES CORPORATION

KEY POINTS

- While tax considerations rarely are the primary motivation for takeovers, they make transactions more attractive.
- Tax considerations may impact where and when investments such as M&As are made.
- Foreign cash balances give multinational corporations flexibility in financing M&As.

United States–based Johnson & Johnson (J&J), the world's largest health-care products company, employed creative tax strategies in undertaking the biggest takeover in its history. When J&J first announced that it would acquire Swiss medical device maker Synthes for $19.7 million in stock and cash, the firm indicated that the deal would dilute the value of the shares held by its current shareholders due to the issuance of 204 million new shares. Investors expressed their dismay by pushing the firm's share price down immediately following the announcement. J&J looked for a way to make the deal more attractive to investors while preserving the composition of the purchase price paid to Synthes' shareholders (two-thirds stock and the remainder in cash). They could defer the payment of taxes on that portion of the purchase price received in J&J shares until such shares were sold; however, they would incur an immediate tax liability on any cash received.

Having found a loophole in the IRS's guidelines for utilizing funds held in foreign subsidiaries, J&J was able to make the deal's financing structure accretive to earnings following closing. In 2011, the IRS had ruled that cash held in foreign operations repatriated to the United States would be considered a dividend paid by the subsidiary to the parent, subject to the appropriate tax rate. Because the United States has the highest corporate tax rate among developed countries, U.S. multinational firms have an incentive to reinvest earnings of their foreign subsidiaries abroad.

With this in mind, J&J used the foreign earnings held by its Irish subsidiary to buy 204 million of its own shares, valued at $12.9 billion, held by Goldman Sachs and JPMorgan, which had previously acquired J&J shares in the open market. The buyback of J&J shares held by these investment banks increased the consolidated firm's earnings per share. These shares, along with cash, were exchanged for outstanding Synthes' shares to fund the transaction. J&J also avoided a hefty tax payment by not repatriating these earnings to the United States, where they would have been taxed at a 35% corporate rate rather than the 12% rate in Ireland. Investors reacted favorably, boosting J&J's share price by more than 2% in mid-2012, when the firm announced the deal would be accretive rather than dilutive. Presumably, the IRS will move to prevent future deals from being financed in a similar manner.

CHAPTER OVERVIEW

While Chapter 11 discusses in detail the first five components of the deal-structuring process, this chapter focuses on the implications of tax and accounting considerations within the deal-structuring process. While taxes are important, the fundamental economics of the deal should always be the deciding factor, and any tax benefits reinforce a purchase decision. The impact of accounting considerations on deal structuring can be more subtle and could imperil the acquirer's current and future earnings performance. A review of this chapter (including practice questions and answers) is available in the file folder entitled "Student Study Guide" on the companion website to this book (http://booksite.elsevier.com/9780123854872).

ALTERNATIVE TAX STRUCTURES

Tax considerations generally are less important for buyers than for sellers. Buyers are concerned primarily with determining the basis of the acquired assets and avoiding any liability for tax problems the target may have. The tax basis determines future taxable gains for the buyer in the event such assets are sold and also the level from which they may be depreciated. In contrast, the seller

TABLE 12.1   Alternative Taxable and Nontaxable Structures

Taxable Transactions: Immediately Taxable to Target Shareholders	Nontaxable Transactions: Tax Deferred to Target Shareholders

1. Purchase of assets with cash[a]
 2. Purchase of stock with cash
 3. Statutory cash mergers and consolidations
    a. Direct merger (cash for stock)
    b. Forward triangular merger (cash for assets)
    c. Reverse triangular merger (cash for stock)
	1. Type "A" reorganization
	    a. Statutory stock merger or consolidation (mostly acquirer stock for stock)[b]
	    b. Forward triangular merger (asset purchase)
	    c. Reverse triangular merger (stock purchase)
	 2. Type "B" reorganization (stock for stock)
	 3. Type "C" reorganization (stock for assets)
	 4. Type "D" divisive merger

[a]*The form of payment consists mostly of consideration other than acquirer stock. Such consideration is called boot and could consist of cash, debt, or other nonequity compensation.*
[b]*Acquirer stock usually comprises 50% or more of the total consideration. The exception for Type "A" reorganizations is for reverse triangular mergers.*

usually is concerned about how to structure the deal to defer the payment of any taxes owed. Table 12.1 summarizes the most commonly used taxable and tax-free structures, including both statutory mergers (two-party transactions) and triangular mergers (three-party transactions). The implications of these alternative structures are explored in detail in the following sections.

TAXABLE TRANSACTIONS

A deal is taxable to target shareholders if it involves purchasing the target's stock or assets using mostly cash, debt, or nonequity consideration.[1] Taxable deals include a cash purchase of target assets, a cash purchase of target stock, or a statutory cash merger or consolidation, which commonly includes direct cash mergers and triangular forward and reverse cash mergers.

Taxable Mergers

In a direct statutory cash merger (i.e., the form of payment is cash), the acquirer and target boards reach a negotiated settlement, and both firms, with certain exceptions, must receive approval from their respective shareholders. The target is then merged into the acquirer or the acquirer into the target, with only one surviving. Assets and liabilities on and off the balance sheet automatically transfer to the surviving firm. To protect themselves from target liabilities, acquirers often employ so-called triangular mergers. In such deals, the target is merged into an acquirer's operating or shell acquisition subsidiary, with the

---

[1]*Nonequity, cash*, and *boot* are terms used to describe forms of payment other than acquirer equity.

subsidiary surviving (called a *forward triangular cash merger*), or the subsidiary is merged into the target, with the target surviving (called a *reverse triangular cash merger*). Direct cash mergers and forward triangular mergers are treated as a taxable purchase of assets, with cash and reverse triangular mergers treated as a taxable purchase of stock with cash. The tax consequences of these deals are discussed next.

Taxable Purchase of Target Assets with Cash

If a transaction involves a cash purchase of target assets, with the buyer assuming none, some, or all of the target's liabilities, the target's tax cost or basis in the acquired assets is increased, or stepped up, to its fair market value (FMV), equal to the purchase price (less any assumed liabilities) paid by the acquirer. The additional depreciation in future years reduces the present value of the tax liability of the combined firms. The target firm realizes an immediate gain or loss on assets sold equal to the difference between the FMV of the asset and the asset's book value less accumulated depreciation. The target's shareholders could be taxed twice—once when the firm pays taxes on any gains and again when the proceeds from the sale are paid to the shareholders as either a dividend or a distribution following liquidation of the corporation. A liquidation of the target firm may occur if a buyer acquires enough of the assets of the target to cause it to cease operations.[2] To compensate the target company shareholders for any tax liability they may incur, the buyer usually will have to increase the purchase price.[3] Taxable transactions have become somewhat more attractive to acquiring firms since 1993, when a change in legislation allowed acquirers to amortize certain intangible assets for tax purposes.[4]

---

[2] The IRS views transactions resulting in the liquidation of the target as actual sales rather than reorganizations, in which the target shareholders have an ongoing interest in the combined firms. Thus, the target's tax attributes may not be used by the acquirer following closing because they cease to exist along with the target. However, they may be used to offset any gain realized by the target resulting from the sale of its assets.

[3] Ayers, Lefanowicz, and Robinson, 2003

[4] Intangible assets are addressed under Section 197 of the IRS Code. Such assets include goodwill; going concern value; books and records; customer lists; licenses; permits; franchises; and trademarks, and must be amortized over 15 years for tax purposes. While no immediate loss on goodwill can be recognized for tax purposes, the basis of other intangible assets purchased in the same transaction giving rise to the goodwill must be increased by the amount of the goodwill write-down. The resulting write-up of these intangible assets is then amortized over their remaining amortizable lives. Moreover, the current tax code allows operating losses to be used to recover taxes paid in the preceding two years and to reduce future tax liabilities up to 20 years.

Taxable Purchase of Target Stock with Cash

Taxable transactions often involve the purchase of the target's voting stock to avoid potential double taxation of gains to the target's shareholders. An asset purchase automatically triggers a tax on any gain on the sale by the target firm and another tax on any payment of the after-tax proceeds to shareholders. Taxable stock purchases avoid double taxation because the transaction takes place between the acquirer and the target firm's shareholders. However, target shareholders may realize a gain or loss on the sale of their stock. Assets may not be stepped up to their FMV in these types of transactions. Since from the IRS's viewpoint, the target firm continues to exist, the target's tax attributes (e.g., investment tax credits and net operating losses) may be used by the acquirer following the transaction, but their use may be limited by Sections 382 and 383 of the Internal Revenue Code. Table 12.2 summarizes the key characteristics of the various forms of taxable deals.

Section 338 Election

Section 338 elections are an option with a taxable purchase of target stock. The acquirer and target firms can jointly elect Section 338 of the Internal Revenue Code and record assets and liabilities at their FMV for tax purposes. This allows a purchaser of 80% or more of the voting stock and market value of the target to treat the acquisition of stock as an asset purchase. The target's net acquired assets are increased to their FMV, triggering a taxable gain when the deal is completed.[5] For legal purposes, the sale of target stock under a 338 election still is treated as a purchase of stock by the buyer. Section 338 elections are rare because the tax liability triggered by the transaction often exceeds the present value of the tax savings from the step-up in the tax basis of the net acquired assets. A 338 election is most useful when the target has substantial net operating losses (NOLs) or tax credit carryovers that the acquirer can use to offset any taxable gain triggered by the transaction.

TAX-FREE TRANSACTIONS

A deal is tax-free if the form of payment is mostly acquirer stock. Deals may be partially taxable if the target shareholders receive something other than the acquirer's stock. This nonequity consideration, or *boot*, generally is taxable as

---

[5]Benefits to the acquirer of a 338 election include the avoidance of having to transfer assets and obtain consents to assignment of all contracts (as would be required in a direct purchase of assets) while still benefiting from the write-up of assets. Asset transfer, sales, and use taxes may also be avoided. Either the acquirer or the target must pay the taxes on any gain on the sale.

TABLE 12.2 Key Characteristics of Alternative Transaction Structures that are Taxable (to Target Shareholders)

Transaction Structure	Form of Payment	Acquirer Retains Tax Attributes of Target	Target Survives?	Parent Exposure to Target Liabilities	Shareholder Vote Required?		Minority Freeze Out?	Automatic Transfer of Contracts?[b]
					Acquirer	Target		
Cash Purchase of Stock	Mostly cash, debt, or other nonequity payment	Yes, assuming no asset step-up due to 338 election[a]	Yes	High	No[d]	No, but shareholders may not sell shares	No	Yes
Cash Purchase of Assets	Mostly cash, debt, other nonequity payment	No, but can step-up assets	Perhaps[c]	Low, except for assumed liabilities	No[d]	Yes, if sale of assets is substantial	No minority created	No
Statutory Cash Merger or Consolidation	Mostly cash, debt, or other nonequity payment	Yes, but no step-up in assets	No, if target merged into acquirer	High, if target merged into acquirer	Yes	Yes	Yes[e]	Yes
Forward Triangular Cash Merger (IRS views as asset purchase)	Mostly cash, debt, or other nonequity payment	No, but can step-up assets	No	Low—limited by subsidiary relationship	No[d]	Yes	Yes	No
Reverse Triangular Cash Merger (IRS views as stock purchase)	Mostly cash, debt, or other nonequity payment	Yes	Yes	Low—limited by subsidiary	No[d]	Yes	Yes	Yes

[a]An acquirer may treat a stock purchase as an asset purchase if it and the target agree to invoke a Section 338 election. Such an election would allow a step-up in net acquired assets and result in the loss of the target's tax attributes.

[b]Contracts, leases, licenses, and rights to intellectual property automatically transfer unless contracts stipulate that consent to assignment is required.

[c]The target may choose to liquidate if the sale of assets is substantial and to distribute the proceeds to its shareholders or to continue as a shell.

[d]May be required by public stock exchanges or by legal counsel if deemed material to the acquiring firm or if the parent needs to authorize new stock. In practice, most big mergers require shareholder approval.

[e]Target shareholders must accept terms due to a merger, although in some states dissident shareholders have appraisal rights for their shares.

ordinary income. If the transaction is tax-free, there is no step-up of net acquired assets to their FMV.

Qualifying a Transaction for Tax-Free Treatment

To qualify as tax-free, a deal must provide for continuity of ownership interests, continuity of business enterprise, have a valid business purpose, and satisfy the step-transaction doctrine. To demonstrate *continuity of ownership interests*, target shareholders must own a substantial part of the value of the combined firms. This requires the purchase price to consist mostly of acquirer stock. *Continuity of business enterprise* requires the acquirer to use a significant portion of the target's "historic business assets" in a business[6] to demonstrate a long-term commitment on the part of the acquirer to the target. This usually means an acquirer must buy "substantially all" of the target's assets. Further, the transaction must have a valid business purpose, such as maximizing the profits of the acquiring corporation, rather than only for tax avoidance. Finally, under the *step-transaction doctrine*, the deal cannot be part of a larger plan that would have constituted a taxable deal.[7] Tax-free deals are also called *tax-free reorganizations.* The continuity of interests, business enterprise, and step-doctrine requirements are intended to prevent transactions that more closely resemble a sale from qualifying as a tax-free reorganization.

Alternative Tax-Free Reorganizations

The most common is the type "A" reorganization used in direct statutory mergers or consolidations (mostly acquirer stock for stock), forward triangular mergers (asset purchases), and reverse triangular mergers (stock purchases). Type "B" reorganizations are stock-for-stock acquisitions, and type "C" reorganizations are stock-for-assets acquisitions. Type "D" reorganizations may be applied to acquisitions or restructuring.[8]

For a *type "A" statutory merger* (Figure 12.1) or *consolidation* (Figure 12.2), payment can include cash, voting or nonvoting common or preferred stock, notes, or

---

[6] The acquirer must purchase assets critical to continuing the target's business. Acquirers often purchase at least 80% of the target's assets to ensure that they are in compliance with IRS guidelines.

[7] The step-transaction doctrine might be applied by the IRS as follows: Firm A buys the stock or assets of Firm B with its stock and characterizes it as a tax-free deal. A year later, it sells B. The IRS may disallow the original deal as tax-free, arguing that the merger and subsequent sale were part of a larger plan to postpone the payment of taxes.

[8] An acquisitive type "D" reorganization requires that the acquiring firm receive at least 80% of the stock in the target firm in exchange for the acquirer's voting stock. Divisive type "D" reorganizations are used in spin-offs, split-offs, and split-ups and involve a firm's transferring all or some of its assets to a subsidiary it controls in exchange for subsidiary stock or securities.

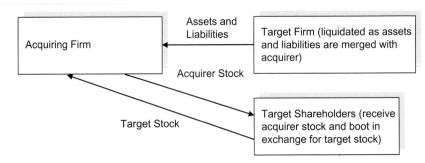

FIGURE 12.1   **Direct statutory stock merger ("A" reorganization).** Note that this figure depicts the acquirer surviving. In practice, either the acquirer or the target could survive the merger.

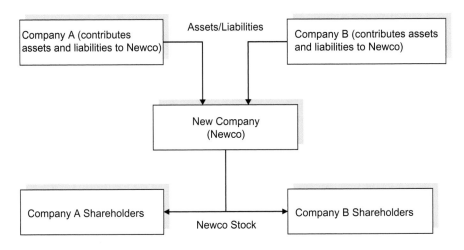

FIGURE 12.2   **Statutory stock consolidation ("A" reorganization).**

some combination. At least 50% of the purchase price must be acquirer stock to satisfy the IRS requirement of continuity of interests. Type "A" reorganizations are widely used because there is no requirement to use voting stock and acquirers can avoid dilution by issuing nonvoting shares. The buyer also may acquire less than 100% of the target's net assets. Finally, there is no limit on the amount of cash that can be used in the purchase price, as is true of type "B" and "C" reorganizations. Since some target shareholders will want cash, some stock, and some both, the acquirer is better able to satisfy the different needs of the target shareholders than in other types of reorganizations.

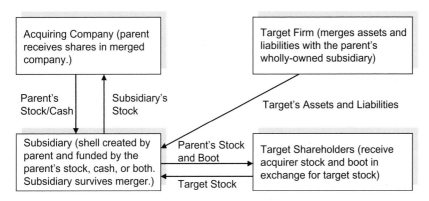

FIGURE 12.3   **A forward triangular stock merger ("A" reorganization).**

With a *type "A" forward triangular stock merger*, the parent funds the shell corporation by buying stock issued by the shell with its own stock (Figure 12.3). All of the target's stock is acquired by the subsidiary with the parent's stock, the target's stock is cancelled, the acquirer subsidiary survives, and the target's assets and liabilities are merged into the subsidiary. The IRS views such deals as an asset purchase since the target does not survive. The parent's stock may be voting or nonvoting, and the acquirer must purchase "substantially all" of the target's assets and liabilities (defined as at least 70% and 90% of the FMV of the target's gross and net assets, respectively).[9] At least 50% of the purchase price must consist of acquirer stock.

The advantages of the forward triangular merger include the flexible form of payment and the avoidance of approval by the parent firm's shareholders. Public exchanges still may require shareholder approval if the amount of the parent stock used to acquire the target exceeds 20% of the parent's voting shares outstanding. Other advantages include the possible insulation of the parent from the target's liabilities, which remain in the subsidiary, and the avoidance of asset transfer taxes, because the target's assets go directly to the parent's wholly owned subsidiary. The target's tax attributes that transfer to the buyer are subject to limitation. Since the target disappears, contract rights do not automatically transfer to the acquirer, which must obtain the consent of the other parties to the contracts to reassign them to the buyer.

With a *type A reverse triangular stock merger*, the acquirer forms a shell subsidiary, which is merged into the target (Figure 12.4). As the survivor, the target becomes the acquirer's wholly owned subsidiary. The target's shares are cancelled, and target shareholders receive the parent's shares. The parent, which owned all of the subsidiary stock, now owns all of the new target stock and,

[9] Asset sales by the target prior to the deal may threaten the tax-free status of the deal if it is viewed as a violation of the step doctrine. Tax-free deals such as spin-offs are disallowed within two years before or after the merger.

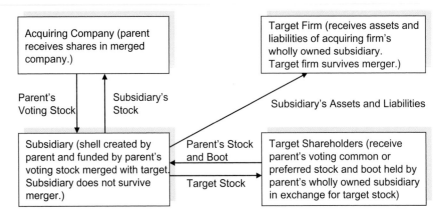

FIGURE 12.4   A reverse triangular stock merger ("A" reorganization).

indirectly, all of the target's assets and liabilities. At least 80% of the total consideration paid to the target must be in acquirer voting common or preferred stock. The IRS views reverse triangular mergers as a purchase of stock, since the target survives the transaction.

The reverse triangular merger may eliminate the need for parent firm shareholder approval, because the parent is the sole shareholder in the sub. Because the target firm survives, the target can retain any nonassignable franchise, lease, or other valuable contract rights. By not dissolving the target, the acquirer avoids accelerating[10] the repayment of loans outstanding. Insurance, banking, and public utility regulators may require the target to remain in existence. The major drawback is the need to use acquirer voting shares to buy at least 80% of the target's outstanding shares.

In a *type "B" stock-for-stock reorganization*, the acquirer must use voting common or preferred stock to buy at least 80% of the target's outstanding voting and nonvoting stock in a tender offer (Figure 12.5). Any cash or debt disqualifies the deal as a type "B" structure.[11] Type "B" deals are used as an alternative to a merger or consolidation. The target's stock does not have to be purchased all at once, which allows for a creeping merger because the target's stock may be purchased over 12 months or less as part of a formal acquisition plan. Type "B" reorganizations are useful if the acquirer wishes to conserve cash or its borrowing capacity. Since shares are being acquired directly from shareholders, there is no need for a target shareholder vote. Finally, contracts and licenses transfer with the stock, which obviates the need to receive consent to assignment, unless

[10]Loan agreements often require the repayment of loans if a change of control of the borrower takes place.

[11]Cash may be used to purchase fractional shares.

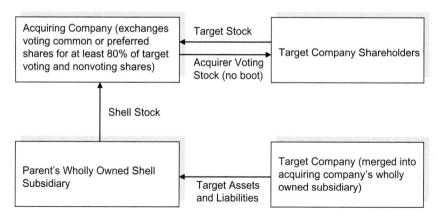

FIGURE 12.5 **Type "B" stock-for-stock reorganization.**

specified in contracts. The target firm is either retained as a subsidiary or merged into the parent.[12]

The *type "C" stock-for-assets reorganization* is used when the acquirer does not want to assume any undisclosed liabilities (Figure 12.6). It requires that at least 70% and 90% of the FMV of the target's gross and net assets, respectively, be acquired in exchange for acquirer voting stock. Consideration paid in cash cannot exceed 20% of the FMV of the target's assets; any liabilities assumed by the acquirer must be deducted from the 20%. Since assumed liabilities frequently exceed 20% of the FMV of the acquired assets, the form of payment generally is all stock. The target dissolves and distributes the acquirer's stock to the target's shareholders. The requirement to use only voting stock discourages the use of type "C" reorganizations. Table 12.3 summarizes the key characteristics of alternative tax-free deal structures.

Treatment of Target Tax Attributes in M&A Deals

Tax attributes, such as net operating loss carryforwards and carrybacks; capital loss carryovers; excess credit carryovers; tax basis in company assets; and tax basis in subsidiary companies, can represent considerable value to acquiring firms in terms of tax savings. The IRS allows acquirers to realize tax savings from additional depreciation resulting from the revaluation of net acquired target

---

[12] A type "B" stock-for-stock deal is equivalent to a reverse triangular merger, since the target firm becomes the acquirer's subsidiary. The primary difference between a reverse triangular merger and a type "B" stock-for-stock deal is the requirement to use at least 80% acquirer voting or preferred stock to buy target shares, in contrast to the need to use 100% acquirer voting common or preferred stock in a type "B" share-for-share reorganization.

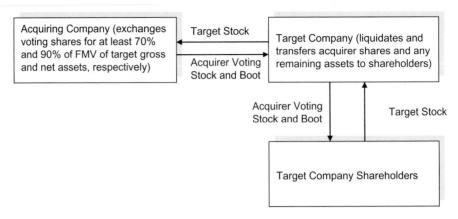

FIGURE 12.6   **Type "C" stock-for-assets reorganization.**

assets to their fair FMV[13] *or* from the target's other tax attributes, but not both. Thus, acquirers *can* use a target's tax attributes in tax-free reorganizations and in taxable purchases of stock, since net acquired assets *are not revalued* to their FMV. Acquirers *cannot* use the target's tax attributes in taxable purchases of assets and taxable purchases of stock undertaken as a 338 election, since net acquired assets *are revalued* to their FMV.[14]

Tax-Free Transactions Arising from 1031 "Like-Kind" Exchanges

The prospect of being able to defer taxable gains is often associated with 1031 exchanges of real estate property or other income-producing properties. By postponing tax payments, investors have more money to reinvest in new assets. Assume a property was purchased 10 years ago for $5 million and is now worth $15 million. If the property were sold with no subsequent purchase of a similar property within the required period, the federal capital gains tax bill would be $1.5 million [i.e., ($15 − $5) × 0.15], where 0.15 is the capital gains tax rate, as of this writing. This ignores the potential for state taxes or depreciation recapture taxes owed if the owner took deductions for depreciation. However, by entering into a 1031 exchange, the owner could use the entire $15 million from the sale of the property as a down payment on a more expensive property. If the investor acquires a property of a lesser value, taxes are owed on the difference.

---

[13] Acquirers realize additional tax savings by depreciating net acquired target assets whose value has been increased to their FMV, which is generally higher than their book value listed on the target's balance sheet.

[14] When tax attributes do survive and carry over (transfer) to the acquirer, their use is limited by Sections 382 (net operating losses) and 383 (tax credit and capital loss carryforwards). When tax attributes do not survive, they may still be used to offset gains on the sale of target assets.

TABLE 12.3 Key Characteristics of Alternative Transaction Structures that are Tax-Free (to Target Shareholders)[a]

Transaction Structure (Type of Reorganization)	Form of Payment	Limitation[b]	Acquirer Retains Target Tax Attributes	Target Survives?	Parent Exposure to Target Liabilities	Shareholder Vote Required?		Minority Freeze Out?	Automatic Transfer of Contracts?[c]
						Acquirer	Target		
Statutory Merger or Consolidation (Type "A" Reorganization)	At least 50% parent voting or nonvoting stock	Assets and liabilities pass automatically to buyer	Yes, but no asset step-up	No	High	Yes	Yes	Yes	No, since target is liquidated
Forward Triangular Merger (Type "A" Reorganization)	At least 50% parent voting or nonvoting stock	Must purchase at least 70% and 90% of FMV of gross and net assets unless LLC acquiring sub	Yes, but no asset step-up	No	Low, limited by subsidiary[d]	No[f,g]	Yes	Yes	No, since target is liquidated
Reverse Triangular Merger (Type "A" Reorganization)	At least 80% parent voting stock (common/ preferred)	Must purchase at least 80% of voting and of nonvoting shares	Yes, but no asset step-up	Yes	Low, limited by subsidiary[d]	No[f,g]	Yes	Yes	Yes, target retains nonassignable contracts, etc.
Purchase of Stock— without a Merger (Type "B" Reorganization)	100% parent voting stock (common/ preferred)	Must purchase at least 80% of voting and of nonvoting shares	Yes, but no asset step-up	Yes	Low, limited by subsidiary[d]	No[f]	No, because shares bought directly from shareholders	No	Yes

(Continued)

TABLE 12.3 Key Characteristics of Alternative Transaction Structures that are Tax-Free (to Target Shareholders)[a] (Continued)

Transaction Structure (Type of Reorganization)	Form of Payment[b]	Limitation[b]	Acquirer Retains Target Tax Attributes?	Target Survives?	Parent Exposure to Target Liabilities	Shareholder Vote Required? Acquirer	Shareholder Vote Required? Target	Minority Freeze Out?	Automatic Transfer of Contracts?[c]
Purchase of Assets (Type "C" Reorganization)	100% voting stock[h]	Must purchase at least 70% and 90% of FMV of gross and net assets	Yes, but no asset step-up	No	Low,[e] except for assumed liabilities	No[f]	Yes, if sale of assets substantial	No minority created	No

[a]Target shareholders are taxed at ordinary rates on any "boot" received (i.e., anything other than acquiring company stock).

[b]Asset sales or spin-offs two years prior (may reflect effort to reduce size of purchase) or subsequent to (violates continuity requirement) closing may invalidate tax-free status. Forward triangular mergers do not require any limitations on purchase of target net assets if a so-called "disregarded unit," such as an LLC, is used as the acquiring entity and the target is a C corporation that ceases to exist as a result of the transaction. Disregarded units are businesses that are pass-through entities (i.e., not subject to the double taxation of C corporations) and include limited liability companies or Subchapter S corporations.

[c]Contracts, leases, licenses, and rights to intellectual property automatically transfer with the stock unless contracts stipulate that consent to assignment is required. Moreover, target retains any nonassignable franchise, lease, or other contract rights as long as the target is the surviving entity as in a reverse triangular merger.

[d]Acquirer may be insulated from a target's liabilities as long as it is held in a subsidiary, except for liabilities such as unpaid taxes, unfunded pension obligations, and environmental liabilities.

[e]The parent is responsible for those liabilities conveying with the assets, such as warranty claims.

[f]May be required by public stock exchanges or by legal counsel if deemed material to the acquiring firm or if the parent needs to authorize new stock.

[g]Mergers are generally ill-suited for hostile transactions because they require approval of both the target's board and target's shareholders.

[h]While cash may be used to pay for up to 20% of the FMV of net assets, it must be offset by assumed liabilities, making the purchase price usually 100% stock.

OTHER TAX CONSIDERATIONS AFFECTING CORPORATE RESTRUCTURING

The treatment of net operating losses, corporate capital gains taxes, the alternative corporate minimum tax, and Morris Trust transactions are discussed next.

Net Operating Losses (NOLs)

NOLs are created when firms generate negative taxable income or losses and can be carried back 2 years to recover past tax payments and forward 20 years to reduce future taxable income. When acquired net assets are stepped up for tax purposes, the target's NOLs may be used immediately by the acquirer to offset the gain on an asset sale. For deals not resulting in an asset write-up for tax-reporting purposes, the target's NOLs may be used by the acquirer in future years, subject to the limitation specified in Section 382 of the IRC code.[15] Despite annual limits to carryforwards and carrybacks, NOLs may represent a significant source of value to acquirers that should be considered in valuing a target. Google's 2011 acquisition of Motorola Mobility enabled it to reap an expected annual $700 million in tax savings on future earnings and to reduce its immediate tax bill by $1 billion due to Motorola's accumulated net operating losses.[16] Because the acquirer can never be sure that future income will be sufficient to realize the value of the NOLs before they expire, loss carryforwards alone rarely justify an acquisition.

Corporate Capital Gains Taxes

Since both short- and long-term corporate capital gains are taxed as ordinary income subject to a maximum federal corporate tax rate of 35%, acquirers often use legal structures in which participants are taxed at their personal tax rates for the profits distributed to them directly. These include master limited partnerships, Subchapter S corporations, and limited liability companies.

Alternative Corporate Minimum Tax

Under certain circumstances in which corporate taxes have been significantly reduced, corporations may be subject to an alternative minimum tax with a flat rate of 20%. The introduction of the alternative minimum tax has reduced

---

[15] Section 382 of the IRS code was created to prevent acquisitions of companies with substantial NOLs solely to reduce the acquirer's taxable income, without having a valid business purpose other than tax avoidance. Section 382 imposes an *annual* limit on the use of the target firm's NOLs that do survive the transaction and transfer to the acquirer equal to the minimum of the market value of the target's stock multiplied by the long-term tax-exempt interest rate, taxable income of the combined company, or the amount of unused NOLs remaining.

[16] Browning and Byrnes, 2011

returns significantly to investors in leveraged buyouts, which—by intent—are highly leveraged and have little (if any) taxable income because of their high annual interest expense.

Morris Trust Transactions

Tax code rules for Morris Trust transactions restrict how certain types of corporate deals can be structured to avoid taxes. Assume that if Firm A sells an operating unit to Firm B, it makes a profit on the deal on which it would owe taxes. To avoid paying those taxes, Firm A spins off the operating unit as a dividend to its shareholders in a tax-free transaction. The operating unit, still owned by Firm A's shareholders, is subsequently merged with Firm B, and shareholders in Firm A thus become shareholders in Firm B. By spinning off the operating unit, Firm A avoided paying corporate taxes on taxable gains, and Firm A's shareholders defer paying personal taxes on any gains until they sell their stock in Firm B. To make such deals less attractive, the tax code was amended in 1997 to require that taxes be paid unless no cash changed hands and Firm A's shareholders end up as majority owners in Firm B. Merger partners such as Firm B in these types of transactions must be significantly smaller than Firm A to ensure that Firm A's shareholders end up the majority shareholders in Firm B, reducing the number of potential deal candidates.

Master Limited Partnerships (MLPs)

MLPs are a type of limited partnership whose shares or units are publicly traded; its investors are subject to limited liability; and its units can be more easily bought and sold than those of private partnerships and privately owned corporations. The partnership interests are divided into units that trade in the same manner as shares of common stock. Not subject to double taxation, the MLP is treated like any other partnership for which income is allocated pro rata to the partners. Unit holders receive their proportionate share of tax-deductible expenses such as depletion and depreciation expenses as well as investment tax credits attributable to the partnership's operations. By passing on tax-deductible expenses to investors, MLP distributions may be tax-free; where tax-deductible expenses exceed the amount of the MLP's cash distribution, the excess may be applied to shelter the investor's other pretax income. Unlike common stock dividends paid by corporations, quarterly payouts to investors in MLPs are mandatory. In MLPs, a missed mandatory quarterly payment constitutes an event of default. Because of these mandatory payments, MLPs are commonly found in industries that have predictable cash flows, such as natural resources and real estate.

FINANCIAL REPORTING OF BUSINESS COMBINATIONS

A company maintaining its financial statements under International Financial Reporting Standards (IFRS) or Generally Accepted Accounting Principles

(GAAP) needs to account for business combinations using the purchase method (also called the *acquisition method*).[17] According to the *purchase method of accounting*, the purchase price or acquisition cost is determined and then, using a cost-allocation approach, assigned first to tangible and then to intangible net assets and recorded on the books of the acquiring company. *Net assets* refers to acquired assets less assumed liabilities. Any excess of the purchase price over the fair value[18] of the acquired net assets is recorded as goodwill. Goodwill is an asset representing future economic benefits arising from acquired assets that were not identified individually. Current accounting standards stipulated in SFAS 141R require an acquirer to recognize the assets acquired, the liabilities assumed, and any noncontrolling interest in the target to be measured at their fair value as of the acquisition date. The acquisition date generally corresponds to the closing date rather than to the announcement or signing date.

Recognizing Acquired Net Assets and Goodwill at Fair Value

To make comparison of different transactions easier, current accounting rules require recognizing 100% of the assets acquired and liabilities assumed, even if the acquirer buys less than 100% of the target. This results in the recognition of the target's business in its entirety, regardless of whether 51%, 100%, or any percentage of the target in between is acquired. Thus, the portion of the target that was not acquired (i.e., the noncontrolling or minority interest) is also recognized, causing the buyer to account for the goodwill attributable to both it as well as to the noncontrolling interest. Noncontrolling/minority interest is reported in the consolidated balance sheet within the equity account, separately from the parent's equity. Moreover, the revenues, expenses, gains, losses, net income or loss, and other income associated with the noncontrolling interest should be reported on the consolidated income statement.

For example, if Firm A were to buy 50.1% of Firm B, reflecting its effective control, Firm A must add 100% of Firm B's acquired assets and assumed liabilities to its assets and liabilities and record the value of the 49.9% noncontrolling, or minority interest in shareholders' equity. This treats the noncontrolling interest as simply another form of equity and recognizes that Firm A is responsible for managing all of the acquired assets and assumed liabilities. Similarly, 100% of Firm B's earnings are included in Firm A's income statement less that portion attributable to the 49.9% minority owner and added to the retained earnings of the consolidated firms.[19]

[17] See IFRS 3 and SFAS (Statements of Financial Accounting Standards) 141, respectively.

[18] According to SFAS 157, fair value is the price that would be received in selling an asset or paid to transfer a liability between willing participants on the date an asset or liability is estimated.

[19] On a nonconsolidated basis, Firm B will be operated within Firm A as a majority-owned subsidiary, with Firm A's investment in Firm B shown at cost, according to the equity method of accounting. The value of this investment will increase with Firm B's net income and decrease with dividends paid to Firm A.

Recognizing and Measuring Net Acquired Assets in Step (or Stage) Transactions

Staged transactions are required to recognize the acquired net assets as well as the noncontrolling interest in the target firm at the full amounts of their fair values. Net acquired assets at each step must be revalued to the current FMV. The acquirer must disclose gains or losses due to the reestimation of the formerly noncontrolling interests on the income statement.

Recognizing Contingent Considerations

Contingencies are uncertainties—such as potential legal, environmental, and warranty claims about which the future may not be fully known at the time a transaction is consummated—that may result in future assets or liabilities. The acquirer must report an asset or liability arising from a contingency to be recognized at its acquisition-date fair value. As new information becomes available, the acquirer must revalue the asset or liability and record the impact of changes in their fair values on earnings, thereby contributing to potential earnings volatility.

In-Process Research and Development Assets

An acquirer must recognize separately from goodwill the acquisition-date fair values of R&D assets acquired in the business combination. Such assets will remain on the books as an asset with an indefinite life until the project's outcome is known. If the project is a success, the firm will amortize the asset over the estimated useful life; if the research project is abandoned, the R&D asset will be expensed. Furthermore, various intangibles, including customer lists and assembled workforce, may be valued separately from goodwill and reported as assets on the consolidated balance sheet.

Expensing Deal Costs

Transaction-related costs such as legal, accounting, and investment banking fees are recorded as an expense on the closing date and charged against current earnings. Firms may need to explain the nature of the costs incurred in closing a deal and the impact of such costs on the earnings of the combined firms. Financing costs, such as expenses incurred as a result of new debt and equity issues, will continue to be capitalized and amortized over time.

IMPACT OF PURCHASE ACCOUNTING ON BUSINESS COMBINATIONS

A long-term asset is *impaired* if its fair value falls below its book or carrying value. Impairment could occur due to loss of customers, loss of contracts, loss of key personnel, obsolescence of technology, litigation, patent expiration, failure to achieve anticipated cost savings, overall market slowdown, and so on. When assets are impaired, the firm must report a loss equal to the difference between the asset's fair value and its carrying (or book) value. The write-down of assets associated with an acquisition constitutes a public admission by the firm's management of having overpaid for the acquired assets.[20] Acquirers using overvalued shares as the form of payment often tend to overpay for the target and experience subsequent write-offs of goodwill.[21]

Balance-Sheet Considerations

For financial-reporting purposes, the purchase price (PP) paid (including the fair value of any noncontrolling interest in the target at the acquisition date) for the target company consists of the FMV of total identifiable acquired tangible and intangible assets (FMV_{TA}) less total assumed liabilities (FMV_{TL}) plus goodwill (FMV_{GW}). The difference between FMV_{TA} and FMV_{TL} is called *net asset value*. These relationships can be summarized as follows:

Purchase price (total consideration):
$$PP = FMV_{TA} - FMV_{TL} + FMV_{GW} \tag{12.1}$$

Calculation of goodwill:
$$FMV_{GW} = PP - FMV_{TA} + FMV_{TL}$$
$$= PP - (FMV_{TA} - FMV_{TL}) \tag{12.2}$$

From Eq. (12.2), it should be noted that as net asset value increases, FMV_{GW} decreases. Also note that the calculation of goodwill can result in either a positive (i.e., PP > net asset value) or a negative (i.e., PP < net asset value). Negative goodwill arises if the acquired assets are purchased at a discount to their FMV and is referred to under SFAS 141R as a "bargain purchase."[22]

Table 12.4 illustrates how the purchase method of accounting can be applied in business combinations. Assume acquirer buys 100% of target's equity for $1 billion in cash on December 31, 2012. Columns 1 and 2 present the preacquisition

---

[20] In an effort to minimize goodwill, auditors often require that factors underlying goodwill be tied to specific intangible assets for which fair value can be estimated, such as customer lists and brand names. These intangible assets must be capitalized and shown on the balance sheet. If the anticipated cash flows associated with such assets have not materialized, the carrying value of the assets must be written down to reflect its current value.

[21] Gu et al., 2011

[22] A bargain purchase is a business combination in which the total acquisition-date fair value of the acquired net assets exceeds the fair value of the purchase price plus the fair value of any noncontrolling interest in the target. Such a purchase may arise due to forced liquidation or distressed sales. SFAS 141R requires the acquirer to recognize that excess on the consolidated income statement as a gain attributable to the acquisition.

TABLE 12.4   Example of Purchase Method of Accounting

	Acquirer Preacquisition Book Value[*]	Target Preacquisition Book Value[*]	Target Fair Market Value[*]	Acquirer Postacquisition Value[*]
	Column 1	Column 2	Column 3	Column 4
Current Assets	12,000	1,200	1,200	13,200
Long-Term Assets	7,000	1,000	1,400	8,400
Goodwill				100[c]
Total Assets	19,000	2,200	2,600	21,700
Current Liabilities	10,000	1,000	1,000	11,000
Long-Term Debt	3,000	600	700	3,700
Common Equity	2,000	300	1,000[a]	3,000
Retained Earnings	4,000	300		4,000
Equity + Liabilities	19,000	2,200	2,700[b]	21,700

[*]Millions of dollars.
[a]The FMV of the target's equity is equal to the purchase price. Note that the value of the target's retained earnings is implicitly included in the purchase price paid for the target's equity.
[b]The difference of $100 million between the FMV of the target's equity plus liabilities less total assets represents the unallocated portion of the purchase price.
[c]Goodwill = Purchase Price − FMV of Net Acquired Assets = $1,000 − ($2,600 − $1,000 − $700).

book values of the two firms' balance sheets. Column 3 reflects the restatement of the book value of the target's balance sheet in column 2 to their FMV. As the sum of columns 1 and 3, column 4 presents the acquirer's postacquisition balance sheet. This includes the acquirer's book value of the preacquisition balance sheet plus the FMV of the target's balance sheet. As shown in column 3, total assets are less than shareholders' equity plus total liabilities by $100 million, reflecting the unallocated portion of the purchase price, or goodwill. This $100 million is shown in column 4 as goodwill on the postacquisition acquirer balance sheet to equate total assets with equity plus total liabilities. Note that the difference between the acquirer's preacquisition and postacquisition equity is equal to the $1 billion purchase price.

Exhibit 12.1 shows the calculation of goodwill in a transaction in which the acquirer purchases less than 100% of the target's outstanding shares but is still required to account for all of the target's net acquired assets, including 100% of goodwill. Exhibit 12.2 lists valuation guidelines for each major balance-sheet category.

Table 12.5 illustrates the balance-sheet impacts of purchase accounting on the acquirer's balance sheet and the effects of impairment subsequent to closing. Assume that Acquirer Inc. purchases Target Inc. on December 31, 2012 (the acquisition/closing date), for $500 million. Identifiable acquired assets and

EXHIBIT 12.1   ESTIMATING GOODWILL

On January 1, 2012, the closing date, Acquirer Inc. purchased 80% of Target Inc.'s 1 million shares outstanding at $50 per share, for a total value of $40 million (i.e., $0.8 \times 1,000,000$ shares outstanding $\times$ $50/share). On that date, the fair value of the net assets acquired from Target was estimated to be $42 million. Acquirer paid a 20% control premium, which was already included in the $50-per-share purchase price. The implied minority discount of the minority shares is 16.7% [i.e., $1 - (1/(1 + 0.2))$].[a] What is the value of the goodwill shown on Acquirer's consolidated balance sheet? What portion of that goodwill is attributable to the minority interest retained by Target's shareholders? What is the FMV of the 20% minority interest, measured on the basis of fair value per share?

Goodwill shown on Acquirer's balance sheet: From Eq. (12.2), goodwill (FMV_{GW}) can be estimated as follows:

$$FMV_{GW} = PP - (FMV_{TA} - FMV_{TL}) = \$50,000,000 - \$42,000,000 = \$8,000,000$$

where $50,000,000 = $50/share \times 1,000,000$ shares outstanding.

Goodwill attributable to the minority interest: Note that 20% of the total shares outstanding equals 200,000 shares, with a market value of $10 million ($50/share \times 200,000$). Therefore, the amount of goodwill attributable to the minority interest is calculated as follows:

Fair Value of Minority Interest:	$10,000,000
Less: 20% fair value of net acquired assets ($0.2 \times $42,000,000$):	$8,400,000
Equal: Goodwill attributable to minority interest:	$ 1,600,000

Fair value of the minority interest per share: Since the fair value of Acquirer's interest in Target and Target's retained interest are proportional to their respective ownership interest, the value of the ownership distribution of the majority and minority owners is as follows:

Acquirer Interest ($0.8 \times 1,000,000 \times $50/share$):	$40,000,000
Target Minority Interest ($0.2 \times 1,000,000 \times $50/share$):	$10,000,000
Total Market Value:	$50,000,000

The FMV per share of the minority interest is $41.65 [i.e., ($10,000,000/200,000) \times (1 - 0.167)$]. The minority share value is less than the share price of the controlling shareholders (i.e., $50/share) because it must be discounted for the relative lack of influence of minority shareholders on the firm's decision-making process.

[a] See Chapter 10 for a discussion of how to calculate control premiums and minority discounts.

EXHIBIT 12.2 GUIDELINES FOR VALUING ACQUIRED ASSETS AND LIABILITIES

1. Cash and accounts receivable, reduced for bad debt and returns, are valued at their values on the books of the target on the acquisition/closing date.
2. Marketable securities are valued at their realizable value after transaction costs.
3. Inventories are broken down into finished goods and raw materials. Finished goods are valued at their liquidation value; raw material inventories are valued at their current replacement cost. Target last-in, first-out inventory reserves are eliminated.
4. Property, plant, and equipment are valued at the FMV on the acquisition/closing date.
5. Accounts payable and accrued expenses are valued at the levels stated on the target's books on the acquisition/closing date.
6. Notes payable and long-term debt are valued at their net present value of the future cash payments discounted at the current market rate of interest for similar securities.
7. Pension fund obligations are booked at the excess or deficiency of the present value of the projected benefit obligations over the present value of pension fund assets. This may result in an asset's or liability's being recorded by the consolidated firms.
8. All other liabilities are recorded at their net present value of future cash payments.
9. Intangible assets are booked at their appraised values on the acquisition/closing date.
10. Goodwill is the difference between the purchase price and the FMV of the target's net asset value. Positive goodwill is recorded as an asset, whereas negative goodwill (i.e., a bargain purchase) is shown as a gain on the acquirer's consolidated income statement.

assumed liabilities are shown at their fair value on the acquisition date. The excess of the purchase price over the fair value of net acquired assets is shown as goodwill. The fair value of the "reporting unit" (i.e., Target Inc.) is determined annually to ensure that its fair value exceeds its carrying (book) value. As of December 31, 2013, it is determined that the fair value of Target Inc. has fallen below its carrying value, due largely to the loss of a number of key customers.

Income Statement and Cash Flow Considerations

For reporting purposes, an upward valuation of tangible and intangible assets, other than goodwill, raises depreciation and amortization expenses, which lowers operating and net income. For tax purposes, goodwill created

TABLE 12.5   Balance-Sheet Impacts of Purchase Accounting

Target Inc. December 31, 2012, Purchase Price (Total Consideration)		**$500,000,000**
Fair Values of Target Inc.'s Net Assets on December 31, 2012		
Current Assets	$40,000,000	
Plant and Equipment	$200,000,000	
Customer List	$180,000,000	
Copyrights	$120,000,000	
Current Liabilities	$(35,000,000)	
Long-Term Debt	$(100,000,000)	
Value Assigned to Identifiable Net Assets		$405,000,000
Value Assigned to Goodwill		$ 95,000,000
Carrying Value as of December 31, 2012		$500,000,000
Fair Values of Target Inc.'s Net Assets on December 31, 2013		$400,000,000[a]
Current Assets	$ 30,000,000	
Plant and Equipment	$175,000,000	
Customer List	$100,000,000	
Copyrights	$120,000,000	
Current Liabilities	$(25,000,000)	
Long-Term Debt	$(90,000,000)	
Fair Value of Identifiable Net Assets		$310,000,000
Value of Goodwill		$ 90,000,000
Carrying Value after Impairment on December 31, 2013		$400,000,000
Impairment Loss (Difference between December 31, 2013, and December 31, 2012, carrying values)		$(100,000,000)

[a]Note that the December 31, 2013, carrying value is estimated based on the discounted value of projected cash flows of the reporting unit and therefore represents the FMV of the unit on that date. The fair value is composed of the sum of the fair values of identifiable net assets plus goodwill.

after July 1993 may be amortized up to 15 years and is tax deductible. Goodwill booked before July 1993 is not tax deductible. Cash flow benefits from the tax deductibility of additional depreciation and amortization expenses that are written off over the useful lives of the assets. If the purchase price paid is less than the target's net asset value, the acquirer records a one-time gain equal to the difference on its income statement. If the carrying value of the net asset value subsequently falls below its FMV, the acquirer records a one-time loss equal to the difference.

International Accounting Standards

The objective of the International Accounting Standards Board (IASB) is the convergence of accounting standards worldwide and the establishment of global standards, sometimes referred to as "global GAAP." The IASB issues International Financial Reporting Standards (IFRS), and, since 2005, firms in the European Union have had to conform to IFRS directives. Concerns in the United States about moving to international standards from GAAP include higher taxes (if the conversion results in increases in reported earnings), increased implementation costs, and litigation. In a report issued in mid-2012, the U.S. Securities and Exchange Commission indicated that if the United States ultimately decides to shift to international rules, it will use a hybrid structure incorporating certain IFRS rules into the U.S. system of accounting standards.[23]

RECAPITALIZATION ("RECAP") ACCOUNTING

Business combinations qualifying for recapitalization accounting do not have to be recorded using purchase accounting. "Recap" accounting is designed to record restructuring actions reflecting changes in a firm's capital structure without having any impact on the firm's assets and liabilities and triggering any tax liabilities. It applies to firms engaging in internal reorganizations, repurchasing their own stock, undertaking LBOs, or executing reverse mergers. The SEC views such activities as not having a material impact on the assets and liabilities of the firm and in which participants have a continuing interest in the surviving entity. Each of these scenarios is discussed next.

When two entities have the same parent, transfers of assets between these entities are viewed as reorganizations internal to the firm, that do not result in a change in control impacting the value of the operating assets and liabilities of the firm. Such transfers do not require any revaluation of the firm's assets and liabilities. Recap accounting also applies when a firm buys its own stock; the repurchased shares, valued at the price paid for the stock, are included in treasury stock, which is deducted from the firm's shareholders' equity. Treasury stock is made up of reacquired shares that the company had previously issued to the public. This activity reduces the shares outstanding. The transaction does not have any impact on the value of the firm's assets or liabilities, and it does not require any change in the book value of the corporation's assets or liabilities. The full impact of the transaction is centered in the firm's shareholders' equity.

Recap accounting also may be used for the financial reporting of LBOs. In LBOs, the buyout firm often creates a shell subsidiary and merges it into the target, with the target surviving. Target firm assets and liabilities are shown at their pretransaction book values. Since there is no write-up (or write-down) to FMV, there is no additional depreciation and amortization that would reduce

[23]United States Securities and Exchange Commission, July 13, 2012

the firm's net income. The LBO buyout firm may use recap accounting rather than purchase accounting if it anticipates exiting the firm through an IPO, since reported earnings are higher than they would have been under purchase accounting and no goodwill is created. The target's shareholders' equity usually is negative, since the repurchased stock is shown as treasury stock, which is deducted from shareholders' equity. To qualify for recap accounting, the shareholders of the firm undergoing the leveraged buyout (the target) must retain an interest in the recapitalized firm of 5% to 20%. The SEC views that merger of the LBO buyout firm's sub into the target, with the target surviving, as a recapitalization of the target rather than as a business combination in which the survivor gained valuable assets due to the deal.

Finally, recap accounting is employed to record reverse mergers. Reverse mergers involve a private firm merging into a public shell corporation with nominal net assets, with the public company surviving. The owners of the private firm typically have effective or actual control of the surviving company at closing, with the former public shell shareholders having an ongoing minority interest in the recapitalized firm. The SEC views reverse mergers as changes in the acquiring firm's capital structure rather than as a business combination in which the shell corporation had significant pretransaction assets whose value was impacted by the transaction; as such, recap accounting is employed for reporting purposes.

SOME THINGS TO REMEMBER

While important, taxes are rarely the deciding factor in most M&A deals, which happen because they make good business sense. A deal is tax-free if mostly acquirer stock is used to buy the target's stock or assets; otherwise, it is taxable. For financial-reporting purposes, M&As (except those qualifying for recapitalization accounting) must be recorded using the purchase method.

DISCUSSION QUESTIONS

12.1 When does the IRS consider a transaction to be nontaxable to the target firm's shareholders? What is the justification for the IRS position?

12.2 What are the advantages and disadvantages of a tax-free transaction for the buyer?

12.3 Under what circumstances can the assets of the acquired firm be increased to FMV when the transaction is deemed a taxable purchase of stock?

12.4 What is goodwill and how is it created?

12.5 Under what circumstances might an asset become impaired? How might this event affect the way in which acquirers bid for target firms?

12.6 Why do boards of directors of both acquiring and target companies often obtain so-called fairness opinions from outside investment advisors or accounting firms? What valuation methodologies might be employed in constructing these opinions? Should stockholders have confidence in such opinions? Why or why not?

12.7 Archer Daniel Midland (ADM) wants to acquire AgriCorp to augment its ethanol manufacturing capability. AgriCorp wants the deal to be tax-free. ADM wants to preserve AgriCorp's investment tax credits and tax loss carryforwards so that they transfer in the transaction. Also, ADM plans on selling certain unwanted AgriCorp assets to help finance the transaction. How would you structure the deal so that both parties' objectives could be achieved?

12.8 Tangible assets are often increased to FMV following a transaction and depreciated faster than their economic lives. What is the potential impact on post-transaction EPS, cash flow, and balance sheet?

12.9 Discuss how the form of acquisition (i.e., asset purchase or stock deal) could affect the net present value or internal rate of return of the deal calculated postclosing.

12.10 What are some of the important tax-related issues the boards of the acquirer and target companies may need to address prior to entering negotiations? How might the resolution of these issues affect the form of payment and form of acquisition?

Solutions to these Chapter Discussion Questions are found in the Online Instructor's Manual for instructors using this book.

QUESTIONS FROM THE CFA CURRICULUM

12.11 You are researching XMI Corporation (XMI). XMI has shown steady earnings-per-share growth (18% annually for the last seven years) and trades at a very high multiple to earnings (its P/E is currently 40% above the average P/E for a group of the most comparable stocks). XMI has generally grown through acquisition, by using XMI stock to purchase other companies whose stock traded at lower P/Es. In investigating the financial disclosures of these acquired companies and talking to industry contacts, you conclude that XMI has been forcing the companies it acquires to accelerate the payment of expenses before the acquisition deals are closed. As one example, XMI asks acquired companies to pay immediately all pending accounts payable, whether or not they are due. Subsequent to the acquisition, XMI reinstitutes normal expense payment patterns.

　a. What are the effects of XMI's preacquisition expensing policies?

　b. The statement is made that XMI's "P/E is currently 40% above the average P/E for a group of the most comparable stocks." What type of valuation model is implicit in that statement?

 **CFA Institute**

Source: CFA Institute 2011 Equity Valuation: Applications and Processes, Reading 35, question 8.

12.12 The initial measurement of goodwill is:
  a. Not subject to management discretion
  b. Based on an acquisition's purchase price
  c. Based on the acquired company's book value

Source: CFA Institute , 2011 Understanding the Balance Sheet, Reading 33, question 10.

Answers to questions from the CFA curriculum are available in the Online Student Companion website to this book in a file folder entitled CFA Cuirriculum Questions and Solutions.

PRACTICE PROBLEMS AND ANSWERS

12.13 Target Company has incurred $5 million in losses during the past three years. Acquiring Company anticipates pretax earnings of $3 million in each of the next three years. What is the difference between the taxes that Acquiring Company would have paid before the merger as compared to actual taxes paid after the merger, assuming a marginal tax rate of 40%? *Answer*: $2 million.

12.14 Acquiring Company buys 100% of Target Company's equity for $5 million in cash. As an analyst, you are given the premerger balance sheets for the two companies (Table 12.6). Assuming plant and equipment are revalued upward by $500,000, what will be the combined companies' shareholders' equity plus total liabilities? What is the difference between Acquiring Company's shareholders' equity and the shareholders' equity of the combined companies?

TABLE 12.6 Premerger Balance Sheets for Companies in Problem 12.14 ($ Million)

	Acquiring Company	Target Company
Current Assets	600,000	800,000
Plant and Equipment	1,200,000	1,500,000
Total Assets	1,800,000	2,300,000
Long-Term Debt	500,000	300,000
Shareholders' Equity	1,300,000	2,000,000
Shareholders' Equity + Total Liabilities	1,800,000	2.300,000

Answer: The combined companies' shareholders' equity plus total liabilities is $7.1 million, and the change between the combined companies' and Acquiring Company's shareholders' equity is $5 million. Note that the change in the acquirer's equity equals the purchase price.

Solutions to these problems are found in the Online Instructor's Manual available to instructors using this text.

CASE STUDY 12.1
Energy Transfer Outbids Williams Companies for Southern Union—Alternative Bidding Strategies

Key Points

- Higher bids involving stock and cash may be less attractive than a lower all-cash bid due to the uncertain nature of the value of the acquirer's stock.
- Master limited partnerships represent an alternative means for financing a transaction in industries in which cash flows are relatively predictable.

Energy pipeline company Southern Union (Southern) offered significant synergistic opportunities for competitors Energy Transfer Equity (ETE) and The Williams Companies (Williams). Increasing interest in natural gas as a less polluting but still affordable alternative to coal and oil motivated both ETE and Williams to pursue Southern in mid-2011. Williams, already the nation's largest pipeline company, accounting for about 12% of the nation's natural gas distribution by volume, viewed the acquisition as a means of solidifying its premier position in the energy distribution industry. ETE saw Southern as a way of doubling its pipeline capacity and catapulting itself into the number-one position in the industry.

ETE is a publicly traded partnership and is the general partner and owns 100% of the incentive distribution rights of Energy Transfer Partners, L.P. (ETP), consisting of approximately 50.2 million ETP limited partnership units. The firm also is the general partner and owns 100% of the distribution rights of Regency Energy Partners (REP), consisting of approximately 26.3 million REP limited partnership units. Williams manages most of its pipeline assets through its primary publicly traded master limited partnership known as Williams Partners. Southern owns and operates more than 20,000 miles of pipelines in the United States (Southeast, Midwest, and Great Lakes regions as well as Texas and New Mexico). It also owns local gas distribution companies that serve more than half a million end users in Missouri and Massachusetts.

While both ETE and Williams were attracted to Southern because the firm's shares were believed to be undervalued, the potential synergies also are significant. ETE would transform the firm by expanding its business into the Midwest and Florida and offers a very good complement to ETE's existing Texas-focused operations. For Williams, it would create the dominant natural gas pipeline system for the Midwest and Northeast and give it ownership interests in two pipelines running into Florida.

Despite the transition of exploration and production companies to liquids for distribution, Southern continued to trade, largely as an annuity offering a steady, predictable financial return. During the six-month period prior to the start of the bidding war,

Southern's stock was caught in a trading range between $27 and $30 per share. That changed in mid-June, when a $33-per-share bid from ETE, consisting of both cash and stock valued by Southern at $4.2 billion, put Southern in "play." The initial ETE offer was immediately followed by a series of four offers and counteroffers, resulting in an all-cash counteroffer of $44 per share from The Williams Companies, valuing Southern at $5.5 billion. This bid was later topped with an ETE offer of $44.25 per Southern share, boosting Southern's valuation to approximately $5.6 billion.

Williams's $44 all-cash offer did not include a financing contingency, but it did include a "hell or high water" clause that would commit the company to taking all necessary steps to obtain regulatory approval; later ETE added a similar provision to their proposal. The clause is meant to assuage Southern shareholder concerns that a deal with Williams or ETE could lead to antitrust lawsuits in states like Florida. The bidding boosted Southern's shares from a prebid share price of $28 to a final purchase price of $44.25 per share.

Williams argued, to no avail, that its bid was superior to ETE's, in that its value was certain, in contrast to ETE's, which gave Southern's shareholders a choice to receive $40 per share or 0.903 ETE common units whose value was subject to fluctuations in the demand for energy. ETE pointed out not only that their bid was higher than Williams' but also that shareholders could choose to make

their payout tax-free if they were paid in stock. The final ETE bid quickly received the backing of Southern's two biggest shareholders, the firm's founder and chairman, George Lindemann, and its president, Eric D. Herschmann.

ETE removed any concerns about the firm's ability to finance the cash portion of the transaction when it announced on August 5, 2011, that it had received financing commitments for $3.7 billion from a syndicate consisting of 11 U.S. and foreign banks. The firm also announced that it had received regulatory approval from the Federal Trade Commission to complete the transaction.

As part of the agreement with ETE, Southern contributed its 50% interest in Citrus Corporation to Energy Transfer Partners for $2 billion. The cash proceeds from the transfer will be used to repay a portion of the acquisition financing and to repay existing Southern Union debt in order for Southern to maintain its investment-grade credit rating. Following completion of the deal, ETE moved Southern's pipeline assets into Energy Transfer Partners and Regency Energy Partners, eliminating their being subject to double taxation. These actions helped to offset a portion of the purchase price paid to acquire Southern Union.

In retrospect, ETE may have invited the Williams bid because of the confusing nature of its initial bid. According to the firm's first bid, Southern shareholders would receive Series B units that would yield at least 8.25%. However, depending on the outcome of a series of subsequent events, they could end up getting a combination of cash, ETE common, and Energy Transfer Partners' common or continuing to hold those Series B units. Some of the possible outcomes would be tax-free to Southern shareholders and some taxable. In contrast, the Williams bid is a straightforward all-cash bid whose value is unambiguous and represented an 18% premium for Southern shareholders. The disadvantage of the Williams bid is that it would be taxable; furthermore, it was contingent on Williams' completing full due diligence.

Discussion Questions

1. If you were a Southern shareholder, would you have found the Williams or the Energy Transfer Equity bid more attractive? Explain your answer.

2. The all-cash Williams bid was contingent on the firm's completing full due diligence on Southern Union. How might this represent a potential risk to Southern's shareholders?

3. Energy Transfer Equity transferred Southern Union's pipeline assets into its primary master limited partnerships in order to finance a portion of the purchase price. In what way could this action be viewed as a means of financing a portion of the purchase price? In what way might this action have created a tax liability for Energy Transfer Equity?

4. What do you believe are the key assumptions underlying the Energy Transfer Equity and the Williams valuations of Southern Union?

CASE STUDY 12.2
Teva Pharmaceuticals Buys Barr Pharmaceuticals to Create a Global Powerhouse

Key Points

- Foreign acquirers often choose to own U.S. firms in limited liability corporations.
- American Depository Shares (ADSs) often are used by foreign buyers, since their shares do not trade directly on U.S. stock exchanges.
- Despite a significant regulatory review, the firms employed a fixed share-exchange ratio in calculating the purchase price, leaving each at risk of Teva share price changes.

On December 23, 2008, Teva Pharmaceuticals Ltd. completed its acquisition of U.S.-based Barr Pharmaceuticals Inc. The merged businesses created a firm with a significant presence in 60 countries and about $14 billion in annual sales. Teva Pharmaceutical Industries Ltd. is headquartered in Israel and is the world's leading generic-pharmaceuticals company. The firm develops, manufactures, and markets generic and human pharmaceutical ingredients called *biologics* as well as animal health pharmaceutical products. Over 80% of Teva's revenue is generated in North America and Europe.

Barr is a U.S.-headquartered global specialty pharmaceuticals company that operates in more than 30 countries. Barr's operations are based primarily in North America and Europe, with its key markets being the United States, Croatia, Germany, Poland, and Russia. With annual sales of about $2.5 billion, Barr is engaged primarily in the development, manufacture, and marketing of generic and proprietary pharmaceuticals and is one of the world's leading generic-drug companies. Barr also is involved actively in the development of generic biologic products, an area that Barr believes provides significant prospects for long-term earnings and profitability.

Based on the average closing price of Teva American Depository Shares (ADSs) on NASDAQ on July 16, 2008, the last trading day in the United States before the merger's announcement, the total purchase price was approximately $7.4 billion, consisting of a combination of Teva shares and cash. Each ADS represents one ordinary share of Teva deposited with a custodian bank.[24] As a result of the transaction, Barr shareholders owned approximately 7.3% of Teva after the merger. The merger agreement provides that each share of Barr common stock issued and outstanding immediately prior to the effective time of the merger was to be converted into the right to receive 0.6272 ordinary

---

[24] ADSs may be issued in uncertificated form or certified as an American Depositary Receipt, or ADR. ADRs provide evidence that a specified number of ADSs have been deposited by Teva commensurate with the number of new ADSs issued to Barr shareholders.

shares of Teva, which trade in the United States as American Depository Shares, and $39.90 in cash. The 0.6272 represents the share-exchange ratio stipulated in the merger agreement. The value of the portion of the merger consideration comprising Teva ADSs could have changed between signing and closing, because the share-exchange ratio was fixed, per the merger agreement.

By most measures, the offer price for Barr shares constituted an attractive premium over the value of Barr shares prior to the merger announcement. Based on the closing price of a Teva ADS on the NASDAQ Stock Exchange on July 16, 2008, the consideration for each outstanding share of Barr common stock for Barr shareholders represented a premium of approximately 42% over the closing price of Barr common stock on July 16, 2008, the last trading day in the United States before the merger announcement. Since the merger qualified as a tax-free reorganization under U.S. federal income tax laws, a U.S. holder of Barr common stock generally did not recognize any gain or loss under U.S. federal income tax laws on the exchange of Barr common stock for Teva ADSs. A U.S. holder generally would recognize a gain on cash received in exchange for the holder's Barr common stock.

Teva was motivated to acquire Barr because of the desire to achieve increased economies of scale and scope as well as greater geographic coverage, with significant growth potential in emerging markets. Barr's U.S. generics drug offering in the United States is highly complementary with Teva's and extends Teva's product offering and product development pipeline into new and attractive product categories, such as a substantial women's healthcare business. The merger also is a response to the ongoing global trend of consolidation among the purchasers of pharmaceutical products as governments are increasingly becoming the primary purchaser of generic drugs.

Under the merger agreement, a wholly owned Teva corporate subsidiary, the Boron Acquisition Corp. (i.e., acquisition vehicle), merged with Barr, with Barr surviving the merger as a wholly owned subsidiary of Teva. Immediately following the closing of the merger, Barr was merged into a newly formed limited liability company (i.e., postclosing organization), also wholly owned by Teva, which is the surviving company in the second step of the merger. As such, Barr became a wholly owned subsidiary of Teva and ceased to be traded on the New York Stock Exchange.

The merger agreement contained standard preclosing covenants, in which Barr agreed to conduct its business only in the ordinary course (i.e., as it has historically, in a manner consistent with common business practices) and not to alter any supplier, customer, or employee agreements or declare any dividends or buy back any outstanding stock. Barr also agreed not to engage in one or more transactions or investments or assume any debt exceeding $25 million. The firm also promised not to change any accounting practices in any material way or in a manner inconsistent with generally accepted accounting principles. Barr also committed not to solicit alternative bids from any other possible investors between the signing of the merger agreement and the closing.

Teva agreed that from the period immediately following closing and ending on the first anniversary of closing it would require Barr or its subsidiaries to maintain each compensation and benefit plan in existence prior to closing. All annual base salary and wage rates of each Barr employee would be maintained at no less than the levels in effect before closing. Bonus plans also would be maintained at levels no less favorable than those in existence before the closing of the merger.

The key closing conditions that applied to both Teva and Barr included satisfaction of required regulatory and shareholder approvals, compliance with all prevailing laws, and that no representations and warranties were found to have been breached. Moreover, both parties had to provide a certificate signed by the chief executive officer and the chief financial officer that their firms had performed in all material respects all obligations required to be performed in accordance with the merger agreement prior to the closing date and that neither business had suffered any material damage between the signing and the closing.

The merger agreement had to be approved by a majority of the outstanding voting shares of Barr common stock. Shareholders failing to vote or abstaining were counted as votes against the merger agreement. Shareholders were entitled to vote on the merger agreement if they held Barr common stock at the close of business on the record date, which was October 10, 2008. Since the shares issued by Teva in exchange for Barr's stock had already been authorized and did not exceed 20% of Teva's shares outstanding (i.e., the threshold on some public stock exchanges at which firms are required to obtain shareholder approval), the merger was not subject to a vote of Teva's shareholders.

Teva and Barr each notified the U.S. Federal Trade Commission and the Antitrust Division of the U.S. Department of Justice of the proposed deal in order to comply with prevailing antitrust regulations. Each party subsequently received a "second request for information" from the FTC, whose effect was to extend the HSR waiting period another 30 days. Teva and Barr received FTC and Justice Department approval once potential antitrust concerns had been dispelled. Given the global nature of the merger, the two firms also had to file with the European Union Antitrust Commission as well as with other country regulatory authorities.

Discussion Questions

1. Why do you believe that Teva chose to acquire the outstanding stock

of Barr rather than selected assets? Explain your answer.

2. Mergers of businesses with operations in many countries must seek approval from a number of regulatory agencies. How might this affect the time between the signing of the agreement and the actual closing? How might the ability to realize synergy following the merger of the two businesses be affected by actions required by the regulatory authorities before granting their approval? Be specific.

3. What is the importance of the preclosing covenants signed by both Teva and Barr?

4. What is the importance of the closing conditions in the merger agreement? What could happen if any of the closing conditions are breached (i.e., violated)?

5. Speculate as to why Teva offered Barr shareholders a combination of Teva stock and cash for each Barr share outstanding and why Barr was willing to accept a fixed share-exchange ratio rather than some type of collar arrangement.

Solutions to these questions are provided in the Online Instructor's Manual for instructors using this book.

Financing the Deal
Private Equity, Hedge Funds, and Other Sources of Financing

A billion dollars isn't what it used to be. —**Nelson Bunker Hunt**

INSIDE M&A: LESSONS FROM PEP BOYS' ABORTED ATTEMPT TO GO PRIVATE

KEY POINTS

- LBOs in recent years have involved financial sponsors' providing a larger portion of the purchase price in cash than in the past.
- Financial sponsors focus increasingly on targets in which they have previous or related experience.
- Deals that would have been completed in the early 2000s are more likely to be terminated or subject to renegotiation than in the past.

"It ain't over till it's over," quipped former New York Yankees' catcher Yogi Berra, famous for his malapropisms. The oft-quoted comment was once again proven true in Pep Boys' unsuccessful attempt to go private in 2012. On May 30, 2012, after nearly two years of discussions between Pep Boys and several interested parties, the firm announced that a buyout agreement with the Gores Group (Gores), valued at approximately $1 billion (including assumed debt), had collapsed, a victim of Pep Boys' declining operating performance. The firm's shares fell 20% on the news to $8.89 per share, well below its level following the all-cash $15-a-share deal with Gores announced in January 2012. The terms of the transaction also included a termination fee if either party failed to complete the deal by July 27, 2012. The failed transaction illustrates the characteristics and potential pitfalls common to contemporary LBOs.

Pep Boys, a U.S. auto parts and repair business, operates more than 7,000 service bays in over 700 locations in 35 states and Puerto Rico. With its share price lagging the overall stock market in recent years, the firm's board of directors explored a range of options for boosting the firm's value and ultimately decided to put the firm up for sale. Gores was attracted initially by what appeared to be a low purchase price, stable cash flow, and the firm's real estate holdings (many of the firm's store sites are owned by the firm). Such assets could be used as collateral underlying loans to finance a portion of the purchase price. Furthermore, Gores has experience in retailing, having several retailers among their portfolio of companies, including J. Mendel and Mexx.

The transaction reflected a structure common for deals of this type. Pep Boys had entered into a merger agreement with Auto Acquisitions Group (the parent), a shell corporation funded by cash provided by Gores as the financial sponsor, and the parent's wholly owned subsidiary (Merger Sub). The parent would contribute cash to Merger Sub, with Merger Sub borrowing the remainder from several lenders. Merger Sub would subsequently buy Pep Boys' outstanding shares and merge with the firm. Pep Boys would survive as a wholly owned subsidiary of the parent. The purpose of this reverse triangular merger was to preserve the Pep Boys' brand name and facilitate the transfer of supplier and customer contracts. The parent also was to have been organized as a holding company to afford investors some degree of protection from Pep Boys' liabilities. The purchase price was to have been financed by an equity contribution of $489 million from limited partnerships managed by Gores and the balance by loans provided by Barclays Bank PLC, Credit Suisse AG, and Wells Fargo Bank.

Upon learning that the Pep Boys' reported earnings for the first quarter of 2012 would be well below expectations, Gores attempted to renegotiate the terms of the deal, arguing that Pep Boys had breached the deal's agreements. With Pep Boys unwilling to accept a lower valuation, Gores exercised its right to terminate the deal by paying the $50 million breakup fee and agreed to reimburse Pep Boys for other costs it had incurred related to the deal. Pep Boys said the firm will use the proceeds of the breakup fee to refinance a portion of its outstanding debt.

CHAPTER OVERVIEW

This chapter begins with a discussion of common sources of M&A financing. The role of private equity firms in financing highly leveraged transactions is discussed in detail. Highly leveraged transactions, typically referred to as *leveraged buyouts (LBOs)*, are discussed in the context of a financing strategy. The terms *buyout firm* and *financial sponsor* are used interchangeably (because they are in the literature on the subject) throughout the chapter, to include a variety of investor groups. The companion website to this book (http://booksite.elsevier.com/9780123854872) contains a review of this chapter in the file folder entitled "Student Study Guide."

HOW ARE M&A TRANSACTIONS COMMONLY FINANCED?

M&A transactions typically are financed by using cash, equity, debt, or some combination thereof. Which source of financing is chosen depends on a variety of factors, including current capital market conditions, the liquidity and creditworthiness of the acquiring and target firms, and the incremental borrowing capacity of the combined acquiring and target firms. The range of financing sources and the context in which they are used are discussed next.

Financing Options: Borrowing

An acquirer or financial sponsor may tap into an array of alternative sources of borrowing, including asset- and cash flow–based lending, long-term financing, and leveraged bank loans.

Asset-Based (Secured) Lending

Under asset-based lending, the borrower pledges certain assets as collateral. These loans are often short-term (i.e., less than one year in maturity) and secured by assets that can be liquidated easily, such as accounts receivable and inventory. Borrowers often seek *revolving lines of credit* on which they draw on a daily basis. Under a revolving credit arrangement, the bank agrees to make loans up to a maximum for a specified period, usually a year or more. As the borrower repays a portion of the loan, an amount equal to the repayment can be borrowed again under the terms of the agreement. In addition to interest on the notes, the bank charges a fee for the commitment to hold the funds available. For a fee, the borrower may choose to convert the revolving credit line into a term loan. A *term loan* usually has a maturity of two to ten years and typically is secured by the asset that is being financed, such as new capital equipment.[1]

Loan documents define the rights and obligations of the parties to the loan. The *loan agreement* stipulates the terms and conditions under which the lender will loan the firm funds; the *security agreement* specifies which of the borrower's assets will be pledged to secure the loan; and the *promissory note* commits the borrower to repay the loan, even if the assets, when liquidated, do not fully cover the unpaid balance.[2] If the borrower defaults on the loan, the lender can

---

[1] Acquiring firms often prefer to borrow funds on an unsecured basis because the added administrative costs involved in pledging assets as security raise the total cost of borrowing significantly. Secured borrowing also can be onerous because the security agreements can severely limit a company's future borrowing, ability to pay dividends, make investments, and manage working capital aggressively.

[2] The security agreement is filed at a state regulatory office in the state where the collateral is located. Future lenders can check with this office to see which assets a firm has pledged and which are free to be used as future collateral. The filing of this security agreement legally establishes the lender's security interest in the collateral.

seize and sell the collateral to recover the value of the loan.[3] Loan agreements often have *cross-default provisions* that allow a lender to collect its loan immediately if the borrower is in default on a loan to another lender.

These documents contain certain security provisions and protective positive and negative covenants limiting what the borrower may do as long as the loan is outstanding. Typical *security provisions* include the assignment of payments due to the lender, an assignment of a portion of the receivables or inventories, and a pledge of marketable securities held by the borrower. An *affirmative covenant* in a loan agreement specifies the actions the borrower agrees to take during the term of the loan. These typically include furnishing periodic financial statements to the lender, carrying sufficient insurance to cover insurable business risks, maintaining a minimum amount of net working capital, and retaining key management personnel. A *negative covenant* restricts the actions of the borrower. They include limiting the amount of dividends that can be paid; the level of compensation that may be given to the borrower's employees; the total amount of borrower indebtedness; capital investments; and the sale of certain assets.

Cash Flow (Unsecured) Lenders

Cash flow lenders view the borrower's future capability to generate cash flow as the primary means of recovering a loan and the borrower's assets as a secondary source of funds in the event of default. In the mid-1980s, LBO capital structures assumed increasing amounts of unsecured debt. Unsecured debt that lies between senior debt and the equity, called *mezzanine financing*, includes senior subordinated debt, subordinated debt, and bridge financing. It frequently consists of high-yield junk bonds, which may also include zero-coupon deferred-interest debentures (i.e., bonds whose interest is not paid until maturity) used to increase the postacquisition cash flow of the acquired entity. Unsecured financing often consists of several layers of debt, each subordinate in liquidation to the next-most-senior issue. Those with the lowest level of security typically offer the highest yields, to compensate for their higher level of risk in the event of default. *Bridge financing* consists of unsecured loans, often provided by investment banks or hedge funds, to supply short-term financing pending the sale of subordinated debt (i.e., long-term or "permanent" financing). Bridge financing usually is replaced six to nine months after the closing date of the LBO transaction.

Types of Long-Term Financing

The attractiveness of long-term debt is its relatively low after-tax cost and the potential for leverage to improve earnings per share and returns on equity. Too much debt can increase the risk of default. Long-term debt issues are classified

---

[3] The process of determining which of a firm's assets are free from liens is made easier today by commercial credit-reporting repositories, such as Dun & Bradstreet, Experian, Equifax, and Transunion.

as *senior* or *junior* in liquidation. Senior debt has a higher-priority claim to a firm's earnings and assets than junior debt. Unsecured debt also may be classified according to whether it is subordinated to other types of debt. In general, *subordinated debentures* are junior to other types of debt, including bank loans, because they are unsecured and backed only by the overall creditworthiness of the borrower.

Convertible bonds are types of debt that are convertible, at some predetermined ratio (i.e., a specific number of shares per bond), into shares of stock of the issuing company. It normally has a relatively low coupon rate. The bond buyer is compensated primarily by the ability to convert the bond to common stock at a substantial discount from the stock's market value. Current shareholders will experience earnings or ownership dilution when the bondholders convert their bonds into new shares.

The extent to which a debt issue is junior to other debt depends on the restrictions placed on the company in an agreement called an *indenture*, a contract between the firm that issues the long-term debt securities and the lenders. The indenture details the nature of the issue, specifies the way in which the principal must be repaid, and specifies affirmative and negative covenants applicable to the long-term debt issue. Debt issues often are rated by various *credit-rating agencies* according to their relative degree of risk. The agencies consider such factors as a firm's earnings stability, interest coverage ratios, debt as a percent of total capital, the degree of subordination, and the firm's past performance in meeting its debt service requirements.[4]

Junk Bonds

Junk bonds are high-yield bonds that credit-rating agencies have deemed either to be below investment grade or to have no rating.[5] When originally issued, junk bonds frequently yield more than 4 percentage points above the yields on U.S. Treasury debt of comparable maturity. Junk bond prices tend to be positively correlated with equity prices. As a firm's cash flow improves, its share price generally rises due to improving future cash flow expectations, and the firm's junk bond prices increase, reflecting the lower likelihood of default. Junk bond financing exploded in the early 1980s but has become less important due to the popularity of leveraged bank loans.

Leveraged Bank Loans

Leveraged loans are defined as unrated or noninvestment-grade bank loans and include second mortgages, which typically have a floating rate and give lenders

---

[4]Rating agencies include Moody's Investors Services and Standard & Poor's Corporation. Each has its own scale for identifying the risk of an issue. For Moody's, the ratings are Aaa (the lowest risk category), Aa, A, Baa, Ba, B, Caa, Ca, and C (the highest risk). For S&P, AAA denotes the lowest risk category, and risk rises progressively through ratings AA, A, BBB, BB, B, CCC, CC, C, and D.

[5]Moody's usually rates noninvestment-grade bonds Ba or lower; for S&P, it is BB or lower.

a lower level of security than first mortgages. Some analysts include mezzanine or senior unsecured debt and *payment-in-kind notes*, for which interest is paid in the form of more debt. Leveraged loans are often less costly than junk bonds for borrowers because they are senior to high-yield bonds in a firm's capital structure. Globally, the syndicated loan market, including leveraged loans, senior unsecured debt, and payment-in-kind notes, is growing more rapidly than public markets for debt and equity. Syndicated loans are those typically issued through a consortium of institutions, including hedge funds, pension funds, and insurance companies to individual borrowers.

Financing Options: Common and Preferred Equity

There are many varieties of common stock, and some pay dividends and provide voting rights. Other common shares have multiple voting rights. In addition to voting rights, common shareholders sometimes receive rights offerings that allow them to maintain their proportional ownership in the company in the event that the company issues another stock offering. Common shareholders with rights may, but are not obligated to, acquire as many shares of the new stock as needed to maintain their proportional ownership in the company. Although preferred stockholders receive dividends rather than interest, their shares often are considered a fixed-income security. Dividends on preferred stock are generally constant over time, like interest payments on debt, but the firm is generally not obligated to pay them at a specific time.[6] In liquidation, bondholders are paid first, then preferred stockholders, and lastly common stockholders. To conserve cash, LBOs frequently issue *paid-in-kind* (PIK) *preferred stock*, where dividends are paid in the form of more preferred stock.[7]

Seller Financing

Seller financing is one way to "close the gap" between what sellers want and what a buyer is willing to pay on the purchase price. It involves the seller's deferring the receipt of a portion of the purchase price until some future date—in effect, providing a loan to the buyer. A buyer may be willing to pay the seller's asking price if a portion is deferred because the buyer recognizes that the loan will reduce the present value of the purchase price. The advantages to the buyer

---

[6] Unpaid dividends cumulate for eventual payment by the issuer if the preferred stock is a special cumulative issue.

[7] To attract investors to start-ups, preferred stock may have additional benefits or preferences; for example, if a company is sold or goes public, investors get a multiple of their initial investment before common shareholders get anything; other preferences could include board seats and veto rights over important decisions.

TABLE 13.1   Alternative Financing by Type of Security and Lending Source

Type of Security		Debt	
	Backed By	**Lenders Loan Up to**	**Lending Source**
Secured Debt			
Short-Term (< 1 Year) Debt	Liens generally on receivables and inventories	50–80%, depending on quality	Banks and finance companies
Intermediate-Term (1–10 Years) Debt	Liens on land and equipment	Up to 80% of appraised value of equipment and 50% of real estate	Life insurance companies, private equity investors, pension and hedge funds
Unsecured or Mezzanine Debt (Subordinated and Junior Subordinated Debt, Including Seller Financing)	Cash-generating capabilities of the borrower	Face value of securities	Life insurance companies, pension funds, private equity, and hedge funds
First Layer			
Second Layer			
Etc.			
Bridge Financing			
Payment-in-Kind			

Type of Security		Equity
Preferred Stock – Cash Dividends – Convertible – Payment-in-Kind	Cash-generating capabilities of the firm	Life insurance companies, pension funds, hedge funds, private equity, and angel investors
Common Stock	Cash-generating capabilities of the firm	Same

include a lower overall risk of the transaction (because of the need to provide less capital at the time of closing) and the shifting of operational risk to the seller if the buyer ultimately defaults on the loan to the seller.[8] Table 13.1 summarizes the alternative forms of financing.

[8]Many businesses do not want to use seller financing, since it requires that they accept the risk that the note will not be repaid. Such financing is necessary, though, when bank financing is not an option. The drying up of bank lending in 2008 and 2009 due to the slumping economy and the crisis of confidence in the credit markets resulted in increased reliance on seller financing to complete the sale of small-to-intermediate-size businesses.

WHAT IS THE ROLE OF PRIVATE EQUITY, HEDGE, AND VENTURE CAPITAL FUNDS IN DEAL FINANCING?

Private equity, hedge, and venture capital funds take money from large institutions such as pension funds, borrow additional cash, and buy private and public companies. Private equity funds invest for the long-term and often take an active role in managing the firms they acquire. Hedge funds are viewed more as traders than as investors, investing in a wide variety of assets (be it stocks, commodities or foreign currency), holding them for a short time, and then selling. Finally, venture capital funds take money from institutional investors and make numerous small investments in start-ups. At the end of 2012, global assets under management by hedge funds, private equity firms, and venture capital funds totalled about $2 trillion, $1 trillion, and $240 billion, respectively.[9] The amount of new financing raised by these investor groups may be leveraged by as much as $4 dollars for every $1 dollar of equity capital. In the global buyout boom of 2007 and 2008, new monies flowing into these funds exceeded $1 trillion, suggesting that these investor groups controlled as much as $4 trillion dollars in potential buyout financing.

In deal financing, these investor groups play the role of financial intermediaries and "lenders of last resort" for firms having limited access to capital. Moreover, private equity investors provide financial engineering and operating expertise and monitor management activities such that private equity–owned firms often show superior operational performance and are less likely to go bankrupt than comparably leveraged firms. These roles are discussed next.

Financial Intermediaries

Private equity, hedge, and venture capital funds represent conduits between investors/lenders and borrowers, pooling these resources and investing in firms with attractive growth prospects. All three typically exit their investments via sales to strategic buyers, IPOs, or another buyout fund. However, their roles in financing M&A activity differ in significant ways. Private equity firms use substantial leverage to acquire firms, remain invested for up to 10 years, and often take an active operational role in firms in which they have an ownership stake. While hedge funds also use leverage to acquire firms outright, they are more likely to provide financing for takeovers through short-term loans or minority equity stakes. Finally, venture capital funds' primary role is to finance nascent businesses.

Private equity, hedge, and venture capital funds usually are limited partnerships (for U.S. investors) or offshore investment corporations (for non-U.S. or tax-exempt investors) in which the general partner (GP) has made a substantial

---

[9]Estimates of assets under management are obtained from the Hedge Fund Research Institute, the Private Equity Growth Capital Council, and the National Venture Capital Association.

personal investment, allowing the GP to wield substantial control. Partnerships offer favorable tax benefits, a finite life, and investor liability limited to the amount of their investment. Institutional investors, such as pension funds, endowments, insurance companies, and private banks, as well as high-net-worth individuals, typically invest in these types of funds as limited partners. Once a partnership has reached its target size, the partnership closes to further investment, whether from new or existing investors.

While partners may invest their own funds, the bulk of the equity funds are raised from institutional investors. Public and private pension funds in the United States provide 42% of the capital for all private equity investments according to the Private Equity Growth Capital Council. At the end of 2011, public pension funds had about $250 billion invested in private equity funds according to Wilshire Trust Universe Comparison Service. Such investments now account for about 11% of all pension fund assets.[10]

Why would pension fund managers pour money into private equity if their performance were not viewed as superior? Possibly a herd mentality, the way in which performance data are presented by private equity funds,[11] or superior performance. Presumably, superior performance is the key. Successful private equity funds raise new funds every three to five years to remain in business. Consequently, they must be able to demonstrate an ability to outperform other investment types to remain in business and grow.

Private equity, hedge, and venture capital funds' revenue has both a fixed and a variable component. General partners (GPs) earn most of the private equity firm's revenue through management fees, often as much as 70%.[12] Management fees commonly equal 2% of assets under management annually. General partners can also earn variable revenue from so-called *carried interest*, or the percentage of profits, often 20%, accruing to the GP. The carried interest percentage may be applied without the fund's having achieved any minimum financial return for investors or may be triggered only if a certain preset return is achieved, often 8%. Private equity funds also receive fees from their portfolio companies for completing transactions, arranging financing, performing due diligence, and monitoring business performance.

Lenders and Investors of Last Resort

Since 1995, hedge funds and private equity funds have participated in more than half of the private equity placements (i.e., sales to a select number of investors rather than the general public) in the United States. Contributing more than one-fourth of the total capital raised, hedge funds have consistently been the largest single investor group in these types of transactions.[13] Such investments

[10] Corkery, February 12, 2012, pp. C1–C2

[11] Gottschalg, *The Economist*, January 28, 2012, pp. 73–74

[12] Metrick et al., 2010

[13] Brophy et al., 2009

have frequently allowed firms in which hedge and private equity firms invest to improve profitability, increase capital expenditures, and grow revenue faster than their peers. The increase in capital outlays is greatest for firms in industries reliant more on external financing (e.g., manufacturing) than on internal financing (e.g., software).[14]

Publicly traded firms using private placements tend to be small, young, and poorly performing. With reliable data often lacking, these firms have difficulty obtaining financing.[15] Since security issues by such firms often tend to be relatively small, their limited trading volume and subsequent lack of liquidity make them unsuitable for the public stock exchanges. Consequently, such firms often undertake transactions called *private investments in public equity* (PIPE).[16] With few options, firms issuing private placements of equities often have little leverage in negotiating with investors. Therefore, many of the private placements grant investors "repricing rights," which protect investors from a decline in the price of their holdings by requiring firms to issue more shares if the price of the privately placed shares decreases.

Hedge funds are often willing to purchase a PIPE because they insulate their portfolios from price declines. Hedge funds can purchase PIPE securities that cannot be sold in public markets until they are registered with the SEC at discounts from the issuing firms and simultaneously sell short the securities of the issuing firms that are already trading on public markets. Although firms obtaining funding from hedge funds perform relatively poorly, hedge funds investing in PIPE securities perform relatively well, because they buy such securities at substantial discounts (affording some protection from price declines), protect their investment through repricing rights and short-selling, and sell their investments after a relatively short period. By being able to protect their investments in this manner, hedge funds are able to serve "as investors of last resort" for firms having difficulty borrowing.

Providers of Financial Engineering and Operational Expertise for Target Firms

In this context, *financial engineering* describes the creation of a viable capital structure that magnifies financial returns to equity investors. The additional leverage drives the need to improve operating performance to meet debt service requirements; in turn, the anticipated improvement in operating performance enables the firm to assume greater leverage. In this manner, leverage and operating performance are inextricably linked. Successful private equity investors manage the relationship between leverage and operating performance, realizing superior financial returns and operating performance on average relative to their peers. Furthermore, private equity firms seem better able to survive financial

[14] Boucly, 2011

[15] Wu, 2004

[16] See Chapter 10 for a more detailed discussion of PIPE transactions.

distress than other, comparably leveraged firms. These conclusions are supported by an examination of financial returns to both pre-buyout shareholders, who benefit from the premium paid for their shares as a result of the leveraged buyout, and post-buyout shareholders.

Pre-buyout Returns to LBO Target Firm Shareholders

Numerous studies document that pre-buyout shareholder returns often exceed 40% on the announcement date for nondivisional buyouts. The commonly cited sources of these sizeable returns to pre-buyout target shareholders are the anticipated improvement in the target's operating performance (i.e., cost reduction, productivity improvement, and revenue enhancement) due to management incentives, the discipline imposed on management to repay debt, and future tax savings.[17] Because tax benefits are highly predictable, their value is largely reflected in premiums offered to shareholders of firms subject to LBOs.[18]

Post-buyout Returns to LBO Shareholders

Public-to-private LBOs on average improve a firm's operating profits and cash flow, irrespective of methodology, benchmarks, and time period. However, there is evidence that more recent public-to-private LBOs may have a more modest impact on operating performance than those of the 1980s.[19] Post-buyout empirical studies imply that the effect of increased operating efficiency following a leveraged buyout is not fully reflected in the pre-LBO premium.

Large-sample studies in the United States, the United Kingdom, and France consistently show that companies in private equity portfolios improve their operations more than their competitors on average, as measured by their profit margins and cash flows. Private equity funds accelerate the process of creative destruction that invigorates the economy by replacing mature, often moribund, firms with more innovative, dynamic ones, tending to increase productivity by more than 2%.[20] Some studies document that average private equity fund returns in the United States have exceeded those of public markets in both the short-term and the long-term. On average, private equity funds have earned at least 18–20% more over the life of their investments than the S&P500 during the same period; private equity firms also have outperformed public equities in both

---

[17] Guo et al., 2011; Renneboog et al., 2007; Weir et al., 2005; Ofek, 1994; Kaplan, 1989; Lehn and Poulsen, 1988

[18] Kaplan, 1989b; Newbould et al., 1992

[19] Cumming et al. (2007), in a summary of much of the literature on post-LBO performance, conclude that LBOs and especially MBOs enhance firm operating performance. However, Guo et al. (2011) find that the improvement in operating performance following public-to-private LBOs has been more modest during the period from 1990 to 2006 than during the 1980s. Weir et al (2007) found similar results over roughly the same period.

[20] Harford and Kolasinski, 2012; Davis et al., 2011; Stromberg et al., 2011; Guo et al., 2011; Lerner et al., 2011; Kaplan and Stromberg, 2009; Wright et al., 2008

good and bad markets.[21] These higher returns compensate private equity investors for the relative illiquidity of their investments as compared to more conventional investments, such as equities.[22]

Contrary viewpoints note that the financial returns for private equity funds are self-reported and therefore problematic and may be distorted by measurement errors, choice of methodology, and failure to include all management fees. A widely quoted study for the period between 1980 and 2001 found that financial returns to private equity limited partners once all fees were considered were equivalent to what they could have earned if they had invested in the S&P500.[23]

Private Equity–Owned Firms and Financial Distress

Firms acquired by private equity investors do not display a higher default rate than other, similarly leveraged firms. Furthermore, firms financed with private equity funds are less likely to be liquidated and exit Chapter 11 sooner than comparably leveraged firms.[24] Private equity–backed firms exhibited a default rate between 1980 and 2002 of 1.2% versus Moody's Investors Services reported default rate of 1.6% for all U.S. corporate bond issuers during the same period.[25] Bankruptcy rates among private equity buyouts of European firms showed that experienced private equity investors were better able to manage financial distress and avoid bankruptcy than their peer companies. The success of private equity investors in avoiding bankruptcy reflects their selection of undervalued but less financially distressed firms as buyout targets[26] and their ability to manage the additional leverage once the buyout is completed.[27]

LEVERAGED BUYOUTS AS FINANCING STRATEGIES

Leveraged buyouts refer to a commonly used financing strategy often employed by private equity firms to acquire companies using a substantial amount of debt to pay for the cost of the acquisition. Such leverage magnifies financial returns to equity (see Table 13.2).

In a typical LBO transaction, the tangible assets of the firm to be acquired are used as collateral for the loans. The most highly liquid assets often are used as collateral for obtaining bank financing. Such assets commonly include receivables and inventory. The firm's fixed assets usually are used to secure a portion of

---

[21] Harris et al., 2011; Robinson, 2011; Kaplan, 2012

[22] Frazoni et al., 2012

[23] Kaplan and Schoar, 2005

[24] Stromberg et al., 2011

[25] Kaplan and Stromberg, 2009

[26] Dittmar et al. (2012) document that private equity firms excel at identifying targets with high potential for operational improvement.

[27] Tykova and Borell, November 2, 2011

TABLE 13.2 Impact of Leverage on Return to Shareholders[a]

	All-Cash Purchase	50% Cash/50% Debt	20% Cash/80% Debt
Purchase Price	$100	$100	$100
Equity (Cash Investment)	100	50	20
Borrowings	0	50	80
Earnings before Interest, Taxes, Depreciation, and Amortization	20	20	20
Interest @ 10%	0	5	8
Depreciation and Amortization	2	2	2
Income before Taxes	18	13	10
Less Income Taxes @ 40%	7.2	5.2	4
Net Income	$10.8	$7.8	$6
After-Tax Return on Equity	10.8%	15.6%	30%

[a]Unless otherwise noted, all numbers are in millions of dollars.

long-term senior financing. Subordinated debt, either unrated or low-rated debt, is used to raise the balance of the purchase price. When a public company is subject to a leveraged buyout, it is said to be *going private* because the equity of the firm has been purchased by a small group of investors and is no longer publicly traded.

LBOs are characterized by a substantial increase in a firm's post-LBO debt-to-equity ratio, usually as a result of the substantial increase in borrowing to purchase shares held by its prebuyout private or public shareholders. However, in some instances, a firm's leverage increases even though there is no significant increase in borrowing. This may result from the way in which the target firm's assets are used to finance the buyout. The investor group initiating the takeover may use the target's excess cash balances or sell certain target assets using the proceeds to buy out current shareholders. If the amount of the target's debt outstanding remains unchanged, the target firm's debt-to-equity ratio will rise due to the decline in the firm's equity (i.e., assets decline relative to liabilities, shrinking the firm's equity).

Historically, empirical studies of LBOs have been subject to small samples due to limited data availability, survival bias,[28] and a focus on public-to-private

[28]Failed firms were excluded from the performance studies because they no longer existed.

LBO deals. Insights provided by more recent studies, often based on much larger samples over longer time periods,[29] are discussed in the following sections.[30]

The Private Equity Market is a Global Phenomenon

While U.S. private equity investors have been more active for a longer time period, the number of non-U.S. private equity deals has grown to be larger than those in the United States. Undertaking public-to-private LBO deals in different countries is influenced by the ability to squeeze out minority shareholders. The United States, the United Kingdom, and Ireland tend to be the less restrictive, while Italy, Denmark, Finland, and Spain tend to be far more restrictive.[31]

Pure Management Buyouts are Rare

Only one in five LBOs between 1970 and 2007 involved pure management buyouts (MBOs), in which individual investors (typically the target firm's management) acquired the firm in a leveraged transaction. The majority were undertaken by a traditional private equity financial sponsor providing most of the equity financing. MBOs can create potential conflicts of interest. In its effort to take the firm private in 2007, the top management of oil and gas pipeline company Kinder Morgan waited more than two months before informing the firm's board of its desire to take the firm private. It is customary for boards under such circumstances to create a committee within the board consisting of independent members to solicit other bids. While the board did eventually create such as committee, the board's lack of awareness of the pending management proposal gave management an important lead over potential bidders in structuring a proposal.

LBO Transactions Span Many Different Industries

While private equity deals occur in a variety of industries, including chemicals, machinery, and retailing, buyout activity has shifted increasingly to the high-tech market segments. The shift may reflect a change in the composition of U.S. industry or simply a shortage of targets deemed appropriate by private equity investors in the more traditional industries.

[29] The data for the large sample studies come from Standard & Poor's Capital IQ and the U.S. Census Bureau databases. The studies compare a sample of LBO target firms with a control sample. Selected for comparative purposes, firms in control samples are known to be similar to the private equity transaction sample in all respects except for not having undergone an LBO.

[30] Observations in this section pertaining to changes having taken place between 1970 and 2007 are based on the findings of Kaplan and Stromberg (2009), who analyzed 21,397 private equity deals during this time period in the largest and most exhaustive study of its type.

[31] Wright et al., 2008

Sales to Strategic Buyers Represent the Most Common Exit Strategy

LBO financial sponsors and management are able to realize their expected financial returns on exiting the business. Constituting about 13% of total transactions since the 1970s, initial public offerings (i.e., IPOs) declined in importance as an exit strategy. At 39% of all exits, the most common ways of exiting buyouts is through a sale to a strategic buyer;[32] the second most common method, at 24%, is a sale to another buyout firm in so-called secondary buyouts.

Selling to a strategic buyer often results in the best price because the buyer may be able to generate significant synergies by combining the firm with its existing business. If the original buyout firm's investment fund is coming to an end, the firm may sell the LBO to another buyout firm that is looking for new investment opportunities. An IPO is often less attractive due to the massive amount of public disclosure required, the substantial commitment of management time, the difficulty in timing the market, and the potential for valuing the IPO incorrectly. The original investors also can cash out while management remains in charge of the business through a *leveraged recapitalization*: borrowing additional funds to repurchase stock from other shareholders. This strategy may be employed once the firm has paid off its original debt.

Empirical studies show that strategic buyers tend to benefit from acquisitions of private equity–backed firms experiencing announcement-date abnormal returns of 1% to 3%. Strategic acquirers of venture capital–backed firms, private equity investors who invest in firms at their earliest stage of development, display positive announcement-date returns of about 3%.[33]

Most LBOs Involve Acquisitions of Private Firms

Public-to-private transactions, although the focus of most prior research, accounted for only 6.7% of all transactions between 1970 and 2007, whereas they did comprise 28% of the dollar value of such deals, since public firms usually are larger than private ones. Private-firm takeovers constituted 47% of all deals between 1970 and 2007. During the same period, buyouts of divisions of firms accounted for 31% of the transactions and 31% of total deal value.

The Effects of LBOs on Innovation

It has long been recognized that economic growth is influenced significantly by the rate of innovation, which is in turn affected by the level of R&D spending.[34] Although early studies found a correlation between more debt and lower R&D spending,[35] more recent studies demonstrate that increased leverage tends

[32] Harford and Kolasinski, 2012

[33] Harford and Kolasinski, 2012; Masulis and Nahata, 2011

[34] Jaffe and Trajtenberg, 2002

[35] Hall, 1992; Himmelberg and Petersen, 1994

to reduce R&D only for the smallest firms.[36] Studies show that LBOs increase R&D spending on an absolute basis and relative to their peers.[37] Moreover, private equity–financed LBOs may tend to improve the rate of innovation.[38]

Private equity firms' expertise with respect to strategy development; operational, financial, and human resource management; marketing and sales; and M&As may create an innovative environment. Private equity sponsors' relationships with customers, suppliers, lenders, and other investors assist in leveraging the innovation process. They also play an important role in assessing incumbent management skills and those of their potential replacements.[39] Finally, LBO targets are more likely to implement innovative marketing programs (e.g., design, packaging, and promotion) to increase sales and market share.[40]

The Effects of LBOs on Employment Growth

After a buyout, employment in existing operations tends to decline relative to other companies in the same industry by about 3%. However, employment in new operations tends to increase relative to other companies in the same industry by more than 2%. Therefore, the overall impact on employment of private equity transactions is a modest 1% decline. However, the picture varies by industry, with net job losses (gains less losses) concentrated in buyouts of retailers. Excluding retailers, the overall net employment change appears to be neutral or positive. In France, private equity transactions lead to employment increases.[41] These findings are consistent with the notion that private equity groups act as catalysts to shrink inefficient segments of underperforming firms. Furthermore, new ventures undertaken by firms show substantially higher job creation rates than those in current businesses, creating the potential for higher long-term employment gains than at firms not having undergone buyouts.

A recent U.S. government study found that in private equity–financed transactions between 2004 and 2008, employment growth typically grew following the takeover by the private equity investors as compared to the growth in employment at these firms prior to the takeover. The same report also concluded that private equity LBOs generally had a positive impact on the financial performance of the acquired companies.[42]

---

[36] Hao and Jaffe, 1993

[37] Lichtenberg and Siegel, 1990

[38] Lerner, Sorensen, and Strömberg (2011) found the rate of innovation, as measured by the quantity and generality of patents, does not change following private equity investments. In fact, the patents of private equity–backed firms applied for in the years following the investment by the private equity firm are more frequently cited, suggesting some improvement in the rate of innovation.

[39] Meuleman et al., 2009

[40] Le Nadant and Perdreau,, 2012

[41] Davis et al., October 1, 2011

[42] U.S. General Accountability Office, 2008

Private Equity Firm Collaboration

To finance the increased average size of targets taken private in the early to mid-2000s, buyout firms started to bid for target firms as groups of investors, often called *clubbing*.[43] Banding together to buy large LBO targets could result in lower takeover premiums for target firms by reducing the number of bidders or increase premiums by mitigating risk and allowing for a pooling of resources. The evidence concerning how club deals impact target firm shareholders is mixed. For deals involving large private equity firms and relatively few bidders, club bidding may depress purchase premiums.[44] However, when the number of independent bidders is high, there is little evidence of anticompetitive activity,[45] and purchase premiums may be increased.[46] Still other researchers find no correlation between purchase premiums and club deals.[47]

WHAT FACTORS ARE CRITICAL TO SUCCESSFUL LBOs?

While many factors contribute to the success of LBOs, studies suggest that target selection, not overpaying, and improving operating performance are among the most important.

Target Selection

Traditionally, firms that represent good candidates for an LBO are those that have substantial unused borrowing capacity, tangible assets, predictable positive operating cash flow, and assets that are not critical to the continuing operation of the business.[48] Competent and highly motivated management is always crucial to the eventual success of the LBO. Finally, firms in certain types of industries or that are part of larger firms often represent attractive opportunities.

Firms with Unused Borrowing Capacity and Redundant Assets

Factors enhancing borrowing capacity include target firm cash in excess of working capital needs, relatively low leverage, and a strong performance track record. Firms with undervalued assets may use such assets as collateral for loans from asset-based lenders. Undervalued assets also provide a significant

---

[43] Boone and Mulherin (2011) found that nearly half of all acquisitions by private equity firms between 2003 and 2007 involved clubbing. Officer et al. (2010) found similar results between 2002 and 2006.

[44] Officer et al., 2010

[45] Boone and Mulherin, 2011

[46] Meuleman and Wright (2007), Guo et al. (2008), and Marquez et al. (2013) found some evidence that "clubbing" is associated with higher target transaction prices when the number of independent bidders is large.

[47] U.S. General Accountability Office, 2008

[48] Carow and Roden, 1998

tax shelter because they may be revalued following closing of the deal to their fair market value and depreciated or amortized over their allowable tax lives. In addition, operating assets, such as subsidiaries that are not germane to the target's core business and that can be sold quickly for cash, can be divested to accelerate the payoff of debt.

Firms with Significant Agency Problems

LBOs may alleviate conflicts between managers intent on empire building and shareholders seeking competitive financial returns. The imposition of the discipline of repaying debt forces managers to focus on operational improvements. Public firms having undertaken LBOs often are those that have exhibited high free cash flows and limited investment opportunities.

Firms Whose Management is Competent and Motivated

While management competence is necessary for success, it does not ensure exceptional firm performance. Management must be highly motivated by the prospect of substantial financial gains in a relatively short time. Consequently, management of the firm to be taken private is normally given an opportunity to own a significant portion of the firm's equity.

Firms in Attractive Industries

Typical targets are in mature industries, such as manufacturing, retailing, textiles, food processing, apparel, and soft drinks. Such industries usually are characterized by large tangible book values, modest growth prospects, stable cash flow, and limited R&D, new product, or technology spending. Such industries are not dependent on technologies and production processes that are subject to rapid change. Empirical studies have shown that industries that have high free cash flows and limited growth opportunities are good candidates for LBOs.[49]

Firms That Are Large-Company Operating Divisions

The best candidates for management buyouts often are underperforming divisions of larger companies, in which the division is no longer considered critical to the parent firm's overarching strategy. Frequently, such divisions have excessive overhead, often required by the parent, and expenses are allocated to the division by the parent for services, such as legal, auditing, and treasury functions, that could be purchased less expensively from sources outside the parent firm.

Firms Without Change-of-Control Covenants

Such covenants in bond indentures either limit the amount of debt a firm can add or require the company to buy back outstanding debt, sometimes at a premium, whenever a change of control occurs. Firms with bonds lacking such covenants are twice as likely to be the target of an LBO.[50]

[49] Opler and Titman, 1993; Phan, 1995
[50] Billett, Jiang, and Lie, 2010

Not Overpaying

Overpaying for LBOs can be disastrous. Failure to meet debt service obligations in a timely fashion often requires that the LBO firm renegotiate the terms of the loan agreements with the lenders. If the parties to the transaction cannot reach a compromise, the firm may be forced to file for bankruptcy, often wiping out the initial investors. Highly leveraged firms also are subject to aggressive tactics from major competitors, who understand that taking on large amounts of debt raises the breakeven point for the firm. If the amount borrowed is made even more excessive as a result of having paid more than the economic value of the target firm, competitors may opt to gain market share by cutting product prices. The ability of the LBO firm to match such price cuts is limited because of the need to meet required interest and principal repayments.

Improving Operating Performance

Ways to improve performance include negotiating employee wage and benefit concessions in exchange for a profit-sharing or stock ownership plan and outsourcing services once provided by the parent. Other options include moving the corporate headquarters to a less expensive location, pruning unprofitable customer accounts, and eliminating such perks as corporate aircraft. As board members, buyout specialists, such as LBO funds, tend to take a much more active role in monitoring management performance. Research shows that new owners choosing to retain their investment longer, such as private equity investors, have more time to put controls and reporting–monitoring systems in place, enhancing the firm's competitive performance.[51] Other factors contributing to post-buyout returns include professional management, willingness to make the difficult decisions, and often the private equity firm's reputation.[52]

HOW DO LBOs CREATE VALUE?

A number of factors combine to create value in a leveraged buyout. Public firms create value through LBOs by reducing underperformance related to

---

[51] Cao and Lerner, 2006

[52] Katz (2008) reports that private equity–sponsored firms display superior performance after they go public, due to professional ownership, tighter monitoring, and the reputations of the private equity firms. Gurung and Lerner (2008) find that private equity groups have a greater capacity to squeeze more productivity out of companies during times of financial stress than do other types of acquirers. Acharya and Kehoe (2010) conclude that private equity firms contribute the most to firms when their representatives on the boards of these firms have relevant industry experience. Guo et al. (2011) find that post-buyout performance improves due to the discipline debt imposes on management and better alignment between management shareholders due to managements typically owning a large part of the firm's equity. Cornelli et al. (2013) show that, as private equity investors learn more about a CEO's competence, their willingness to take corrective action adds to improved firm performance.

agency conflicts between management and shareholders; for private firms, LBOs improve access to capital. For both public and private firms, LBOs create value by temporarily shielding the firm from taxes, reducing debt, improving operating performance, and timing properly the sale of the business. See Figure 13.1.

Alleviating Public Firm Agency Problems

While access to liquid public capital markets enables a firm to lower its cost of capital, participating in public markets may create disagreements between the board and management on one hand and shareholders on the other so-called agency problems.[53] Public firms may be subject to conflicts between managers engaging in empire building and shareholders seeking competitive financial returns. The discipline imposed by leverage forces management to focus on improving performance. Public-to-private LBOs often engage in asset sales and reduced capital spending to improve performance rather than build empires.[54]

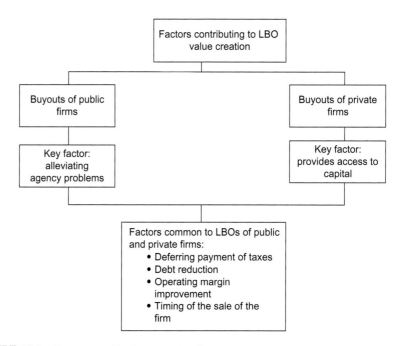

FIGURE 13.1   **Factors contributing to LBO value creation.**

[53] Boot, Gopalan, and Thakor, 2008

[54] There is evidence that the Sarbanes-Oxley Act of 2002 also encouraged LBOs by adding to the cost of governance for firms as a result of the onerous reporting requirements of the bill. This has been a particular burden to smaller firms (Engel et al., 2004; Hartman, 2005; Kamar et al., 2006). Leuz et al. (2008) document a spike in delistings of public firms attributable to the passage of the Sarbanes-Oxley Act of 2002.

Providing Access to Capital for Private Firms

For private firms, agency problems are less significant than in public firms, due to the concentration of ownership and control. Private firms often undertake LBOs to gain access to capital and to enable owners and managers to take cash out of the business partially or totally.[55] Private equity firms, through LBOs, can alleviate investment constraints in private firms by providing the owners with a complete or partial exit. Given access to additional capital, buyouts led by private equity firms result in target firms, unlike public firms when taken private, increasing asset and revenue growth, employment, and capital expenditures. Private firms having undergone LBOs also tend to be more profitable and experience faster growth than their peers.[56]

Creating a Tax Shield

LBOs often do not pay taxes for five to seven years or longer following the buyout, due to the tax deductibility of interest and the additional depreciation resulting from the write-up of net acquired assets to fair market value.[57] Profits are shielded from taxes until a substantial portion of the outstanding debt is repaid and the assets depreciated. LBO investors utilize cumulative free cash flow to increase firm value by repaying debt and improving operating performance.

Debt Reduction

When debt is repaid, the equity value of the firm increases in direct proportion to the reduction in outstanding debt—equity increases by $1 for each $1 of debt repaid—assuming the financial sponsor can sell the firm for at least what it paid for the company. Debt reduction also contributes to cash flow by eliminating future interest and principal payments.[58]

Improvement in Operating Margin

When a firm reinvests cumulative free cash flow, the firm's profit margins can increase by improving efficiency, introducing new products, and making

[55] Asker et al., 2010; Gao et al., 2010; Brav, 2009

[56] Chung, 2011; Boucly et al., 2011

[57] This assumes that the LBO is recorded using purchase accounting rather than recapitalization accounting, which does not permit asset revaluation. Recap accounting may be used if the LBO is expected to be taken public through an IPO and the financial sponsor wishes to maximize reporting earnings. For more details, see Chapter 12.

[58] Not all LBOs reduce their post-takeover leverage. Cohn et al. (2011) find that some firms do not reduce their leverage even if they generate cash flow in excess of their investment needs. Such LBOs may add to leverage to pay dividends and to acquire other businesses. Private equity firms can pay dividends only when banks are willing to lend more money, which happens only when the banks expect to be paid back.

acquisitions. The margin increase augments operating cash flow, which in turn raises the firm's equity value, if the level of risk is unchanged.

Timing the Sale of the Firm

LBOs may benefit from rising industry multiples while the firm is private. The amount of the increase in firm value depends on the valuation multiple investors place on each dollar of earnings, cash flow, or EBITDA when the firm is sold. LBO investors create value by timing the sale of the firm to coincide with the decline of the firm's leverage to the industry average leverage and with favorable industry conditions. This occurs when the firm assumes the risks of the average firm in the industry and when the industry in which the business competes is most attractive to investors, a point at which valuation multiples are likely to be the highest.[59]

Table 13.3 provides a numerical example of how LBOs create value by "paying down" debt, in part using cash generated by tax savings, by improving the firm's operating margins, and by increasing the market multiple applied to the firm's EBITDA in the year in which the firm is sold.[60] Each case assumes that the sponsor group pays $500 million for the target firm and finances the transaction by borrowing $400 million and contributing $100 million in equity. The sponsor group is assumed to exit the LBO at the end of seven years. In Case 1, all cumulative free cash flow is used to reduce outstanding debt. Case 2 assumes the same exit multiple as Case 1 but that cumulative free cash flow is higher due to margin improvement and lower interest and principal repayments as a result of debt reduction. Case 3 assumes the same cumulative free cash flow available for debt repayment and EBITDA as in Case 2 but a higher exit multiple.

COMMON LBO DEAL AND CAPITAL STRUCTURES

Deal structures refer to the mechanism for transferring ownership; *capital structures* describe the way in which these deals are financed. These considerations are discussed next.

---

[59]The annual return on equity (ROE) of the firm will decline, as the impact of leverage declines, to the industry average ROE, which usually occurs when the firm's debt–to–total capital ratio approximates the industry average ratio. At this point, the financial sponsor is unable to earn excess returns by continuing to operate the business. Table 13.2 illustrates this point. ROE is highest when leverage is highest and lowest when leverage is zero, subject to the caveat that ROE could decline due to escalating borrowing costs if debt were to be viewed by lenders as excessive.

[60]Guo et al. (2011) find that operating performance, tax benefits, and market multiples applied when the investor group exits the business each explain about one-fourth of the financial returns to buyout investors.

TABLE 13.3 LBOs Create Value by Reducing Debt, Improving Margins, and Increasing Exit Multiples

	Case 1: Debt Reduction	Case 2: Debt Reduction + Margin Improvement	Case 3: Debt Reduction + Margin Improvement + Higher Exit Multiples
LBO FORMATION YEAR			
Total Debt	$400,000,000	$400,000,000	$400,000,000
Equity	$100,000,000	$100,000,000	$100,000,000
Transaction Value	$500,000,000	$500,000,000	$500,000,000
EXIT-YEAR (YEAR 7) ASSUMPTIONS			
Cumulative Cash Available for Debt Repayment[a]	$150,000,000	$185,000,000	$185,000,000
Net Debt[b]	$250,000,000	$215,000,000	$215,000,000
EBITDA	$100,000,000	$130,000,000	$130,000,000
EBITDA Multiple	7.0 ×	7.0 ×	8.0 ×
Enterprise Value[c]	$700,000,000	$910,000,000	$1,040,000,000
Equity Value[d]	$450,000,000	$695,000,000	$825,000,000
Internal Rate of Return	24%	31.9%	35.2%
Cash on Cash Return[e]	4.5 ×	6.95 ×	8.25 ×

[a]Cumulative cash available for debt repayment and EBITDA increase between Case 1 and Case 2 due to improving margins and lower interest and principal repayments, reflecting the reduction in net debt.
[b]Net Debt = Total Debt − Cumulative Cash Available for Debt Repayment = $400 million − $185 million = $215 million.
[c]Enterprise Value = EBITDA in the 7th Year × EBITDA multiple in the 7th Year.
[d]Equity Value = Enterprise Value in the 7th Year − Net Debt.
[e]The equity value when the firm is sold divided by the initial equity contribution. The internal rate of return (IRR) represents a more accurate financial return because it accounts for the time value of money.

Common Deal Structures

Due to the epidemic of bankruptcies of cash flow–based LBOs in the late 1980s, the most common form of LBO today is the asset-based LBO. This type of LBO can be accomplished in one of two ways: the sale of assets by the target to the acquiring company, with the seller using the cash received to pay off outstanding liabilities, or a merger of the target into the acquiring company (direct merger) or a wholly owned subsidiary of the acquiring company (subsidiary merger). For small companies, a reverse stock split may be used to take the firm private. An important objective of "going private" transactions is to reduce the number of shareholders to below 300 to enable the public firm to delist from many public stock exchanges.

In a *direct merger*, the firm to be taken private merges with a firm controlled by the financial sponsor, with the seller receiving cash for stock. The lender will make the loan to the buyer once the security agreements are in place and the target's stock has been pledged against the loan. The target then is merged into the acquiring company, which is the surviving corporation. In a *subsidiary merger* (see Case Study 13.1), the company (i.e., the parent) controlled by the financial sponsor creates a new shell subsidiary (merger sub) and contributes cash or stock in exchange for the subsidiary's stock.[61] The subsidiary raises additional funds by borrowing from lenders whose loans are collateralized by the stock of the target firm at closing. The subsidiary then makes a tender offer for the outstanding public shares and merges with the target, often with the target surviving as a wholly owned subsidiary of the parent. This may be done to avoid any negative impact that the new company might have on existing customer or creditor relationships.

A *reverse stock split* enables a corporation to reduce the number of shares outstanding. The total number of shares will have the same market value after the reverse split as before, but each share will be worth more. Reverse splits may be used to take a firm private where a firm is short of cash. The majority shareholders retain their stock after the split, while the minority shareholders receive a cash payment. MagStar Technologies, a Minnesota-based manufacturer intending to go private, announced a reverse split in which each 2,000 shares of the firm's common stock would be converted into 1 share of common stock, and holders of fewer than 2,000 shares would receive cash of $0.425 per pre-split share. The split reduced the number of shareholders to less than 300, the minimum required to list on many public exchanges. Under Minnesota law, the board of directors of a company may amend the firm's articles of incorporation to conduct the reverse split without shareholder approval.

Common Capital Structures

LBOs tend to have complicated capital structures consisting of bank debt, high-yield debt, mezzanine debt, and private equity provided primarily by the financial sponsor (Figure 13.2). As secured debt, the bank debt generally is the most senior in the capital structure in the event of liquidation. Given that such loans usually mature within five to seven years, interest rates on them often vary at a fixed spread or difference over the London Interbank Offered Rate. Bank loans usually must be paid off before other types of debt. Bank credit facilities consist of revolving-credit and term loans.[62] A revolving-credit facility is used to satisfy daily liquidity requirements, secured by the firm's most liquid assets such as receivables and inventory. Term loans are usually secured by the firm's longer-lived assets and are granted in tranches (or slices), denoted as A, B, C, and D, with A the most senior and D the least of all bank financing. While bank

---

[61]The parent makes an equity contribution rather than a loan, usually in the form of cash so as not to leverage excessively the merger sub.

[62]Credit or loan facilities may represent a single loan or a collection of loans to a borrower. Such facilities vary in terms of what is being financed, the type of collateral, terms, and duration.

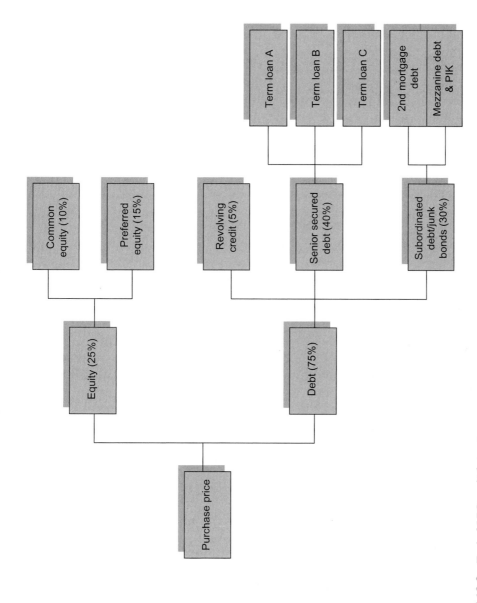

FIGURE 13.2   **Typical LBO capital structure.**

debt in the A tranche usually must be amortized or paid off before other forms of debt can be paid, the remaining tranches generally involve little or no amortization. While lenders in the A tranche often sell such loans to other commercial banks, loans in the B, C, and D tranches often are sold to hedge funds and mutual funds. Loans in B, C, and D tranches commonly are referred to as *leveraged loans*, reflecting their risk relative to loans in the A tranche.

The next layer of LBO capital structure consists of unsecured subordinated debt, also referred to as *junk bonds*. Interest is fixed and represents a constant percentage or spread over the U.S. Treasury bond rate. The amount of the spread depends on the credit quality of the debt. Often callable at a premium, this debt usually has a 7- to 10-year maturity range, with the debt often paid off in a single payment. Such loans often are referred to as *bullet loans*. As an alternative to high-yield publicly traded junk bonds, second mortgage or lien loans became popular between 2003 and mid-2007. Often called *mezzanine debt*, such loans are privately placed with hedge funds and collateralized loan obligation (CLO) investors. They are secured by the firm's assets but are subordinated to the bank debt in liquidation. By pooling large numbers of first and second mortgage loans (so-called noninvestment-grade or leveraged loans) and subdividing the pool into tranches, CLO investors sell tranches to institutional investors such as pension funds. Such debt may be issued with warrants to buy equity in the firm. The final layer of the capital structure consists of equity (common and preferred) contributed by the financial sponsor (usually a single private equity or hedge fund or a number of them) and management.

Legal Pitfalls of Improperly Structured LBOs

Fraudulent conveyance laws are intended to protect creditors from unjustified transfers of property by a firm in financial distress. Such statutes apply when a firm goes bankrupt following events such as a leveraged buyout. Under the law, the firm created by the LBO must be strong enough financially to meet its obligations to current and future creditors. If the court finds the new firm to have been inadequately capitalized, the lender could be stripped of its secured position in the company's assets, or its claims on the assets could be made subordinate to those of the general or unsecured creditors. Consequently, lenders, sellers, directors, or their agents, including auditors and investment bankers, may be required to compensate the general creditors.

SOME THINGS TO REMEMBER

M&A transactions typically are financed by using cash, equity, debt, or some combination thereof, with funding sources ranging from cash on hand to commercial banks to seller financing. Highly leveraged transactions, typically referred to as leveraged buyouts (LBOs), often are structured by financial sponsors such as hedge funds, private equity firms, and venture capitalists.

DISCUSSION QUESTIONS

13.1 What are the primary ways in which an LBO is financed?

13.2 How do loan and security covenants affect the way in which an LBO is managed? Note the differences between positive and negative covenants.

13.3 Describe common strategies LBO firms use to exit their investment. Discuss the circumstances under which some methods of "cashing out" are preferred to others.

13.4 Hospital chain HCA relied heavily on revenue growth in its effort to take the firm private. On July 24, 2006, management again announced that it would "go private" in a deal valued at $33 billion, including the assumption of $11.7 billion in existing debt. Would you consider a hospital chain a good or bad candidate for an LBO? Explain your answer.

13.5 Seven private investment firms acquired 100% of the outstanding stock of SunGard Data Systems Inc. (SunGard) in late 2005. SunGard is a financial-software firm known for providing application and transaction software services and creating backup data systems in the event of disaster. The company's software manages 70% of the transactions made on the NASDAQ stock exchange, but its biggest business is creating backup data systems in case a client's main systems are disabled by a natural disaster, blackout, or terrorist attack. Its large client base for disaster recovery and backup systems provides a substantial and predictable cash flow. Furthermore, the firm had substantial amounts of largely unencumbered current assets. The deal left SunGard with a nearly 5-to-1 debt-to-equity ratio. Why do you believe lenders might have been willing to finance such a highly leveraged transaction?

13.6 Cox Enterprises announced on August 3, 2004, a proposal to buy the remaining 38% of Cox Communications' shares that it did not already own. Cox Enterprises stated that the increasingly competitive cable industry environment makes investment in the cable industry best done through a private company structure. Why would the firm believe that increasing future levels of investment would be best done as a private company?

13.7 Following Cox Enterprises' announcement on August 3, 2004, of its intent to buy the remaining 38% of Cox Communications' shares that it did not already own, the Cox Communications board of directors formed a special committee of independent directors to consider the proposal. Why?

13.8 Qwest Communications agreed to sell its slow but steadily growing yellow pages business, QwestDex, to a consortium led by the Carlyle Group, and Welsh, Carson, Anderson, and Stowe for $7.1 billion. Why do you believe the private equity groups found the yellow pages business attractive? Explain the following statement: "A business with high growth potential may not be a good candidate for an LBO."

13.9 Describe the potential benefits and costs of LBOs to stakeholders, including shareholders, employers, lenders, customers, and communities, in which the firm undergoing the buyout may have operations. Do you believe that, on average, LBOs provide a net benefit or a cost to society? Explain your answer.

13.10 Sony's long-term vision has been to create synergy between its consumer electronics products business and its music, movies, and games. On September 14, 2004, a consortium consisting of Sony Corp. of America, Providence Equity Partners, Texas Pacific Group, and DLJ Merchant Banking Partners agreed to acquire MGM for $4.8 billion. In what way do you believe that Sony's objectives might differ from those of the private equity investors making up the remainder of the consortium? How might such differences affect the management of MGM? Identify possible short-term and long-term effects.

Answers to these Chapter Discussion Questions are available in the Online Instructor's Manual for instructors using this book.

QUESTIONS FROM THE CFA CURRICULUM

13.11 Venture capital investments:
   a. Can be publicly traded.
   b. Do not require a long-term commitment of funds.
   c. Provide mezzanine financing to institutional investors.

Source: CFA Institute 2011 Overview of Equity Securities Reading 58, question 6.

13.12 Which of the following statements most accurately describe one difference between private and public equity firms?
   a. Private equity firms are focused more on short-term results than are public firms.
   b. Private equity firms' regulatory and investor relations operations are less costly than those of public firms.
   c. Private equity firms are incentivized to be more open with investors about governance and compensation than are public firms.

Source: CFA Institute 2011 Overview of Equity Securities Reading 58, question 7.

Answers to questions from the CFA curriculum are available in the Online Student Companion website to this book in a file folder entitled CFA Curriculum Questions and Solutions.

CASE STUDY 13.1

Hollywood's Biggest Independent Studios Combine in a Leveraged Buyout

Key Points

- LBOs allow buyouts using relatively little cash and often rely heavily on the target firm's assets to finance the transaction.
- Private equity investors often "cash out" of their investments by selling to a strategic buyer.

The Lionsgate-Summit tie-up represented the culmination of more than four years of intermittent discussions between the two firms. The number of studios making and releasing movies has been shrinking amid falling DVD sales and continued efforts to transition to digital distribution. As the largest independent studios in Hollywood, both firms saw their cash flow whipsawed as one blockbuster hit would be followed by a series of failures. Film and TV program libraries offered the only source of cash flow stability due to the recurring fees paid by those licensing the rights to use this proprietary content.

Lionsgate first approached Summit about a buyout in 2008 in an effort to bolster its film and TV library. However, it was not until early 2012 that the two sides could reach agreement. The time was ripe because Summit's investors were looking for a way to cash in on the success of the firm's *Twilight* movies series. Consisting of four films, this series had grossed $2.5 billion worldwide. On February 2, 2012, Lionsgate announced that it had reached an agreement to acquire Summit Entertainment by paying Summit shareholders $412.5 million in cash and stock for all of their outstanding shares and assumed debt of $506.3 million. According to the merger agreement, Lionsgate would provide administrative, production, and distribution services to Summit for a 10% servicing fee. Layoffs are expected at both firms as they merge redundant departments in their film operations, such as marketing, production, and distribution. The acquisition provides a windfall to Summit's investors, including eBay cofounder Jeff Skoll's film company Media and private equity fund Traverse Management. These investors had previously received a $200 million dividend as part of a recapitalization in early 2011 and gained handsomely from the sale to Lionsgate.

Lionsgate is a diversified film and television production and distribution company, with a film library of 13,000 titles. The firm's major distribution channels include home entertainment and prepackaged media (DVDs); digital distribution (on-demand TV) and pay TV (premium network programming). Summit, also a producer and distributor of film and TV content, has a less consistent track record in realizing successful releases, with the *Twilight* "franchise" its primary success. However, Summit does have strong international licensing operations, with arrangements in the United

States, Canada, Germany, France, Scandinavia, Spain, and Australia. The acquisition also strengthens Lionsgate's position as a leading content supplier and, controlling the *Twilight* and *Hunger Games* franchises, positions Lionsgate as a market leader for young adult audiences. The combination also results in cost and revenue synergies, more diversified cash flow streams, and greater access to international distribution channels.

Figure 13.3 illustrates the subsidiary structure for completing the buyout of Summit Entertainment LLC. As is typical of such transactions, Lionsgate created a merger subsidiary (Merger Sub) and funded the subsidiary with its equity contribution of $100 million in cash and $69 million in Lionsgate stock, receiving 100% of the subsidiary's stock in exchange. Merger Sub was further capitalized by a bank term loan of $500 million. Following a tender offer to Summit's shareholders by Merger Sub, Merger Sub was merged into Summit Entertainment, with Summit surviving as a wholly owned subsidiary of Lionsgate in a reverse triangular merger. At closing, $284.4 million of Summit's excess cash was used to finance the total cost of the deal.

Table 13.4 summarizes the sources of financing for the buyout and shows how these funds were used to pay for the deal. Lionsgate financed the total cost of the deal of $953.4 million (consisting of $412.5 million for Summit stock + the pretransaction term loan of $506.3 million + $34.6 million in transaction-related fees and expenses)

as follows: $100 million in cash from Lionsgate and $69 million in Lionsgate stock + $284.4 million of the $310 million in cash on Summit's balance sheet at closing + a new $500 million term loan. Summit's $506.3 million term loan B was refinanced with the new term loan for $500 million as part of the transaction. The new term loan is an obligation of and is secured by the assets of Summit and its subsidiaries. It also is secured by a loan guarantee provided by Merger Sub, created by Lionsgate to consummate the transaction. The guarantee is secured by the equity in Summit held by Merger Sub. Lionsgate anticipates paying off the term loan well in advance of its 2016 maturity date out of future cash flows from new movie releases. Summit's pretransaction net debt was $196.3 million (pretransaction term loan of $506.3 less total cash on the balance sheet of $310 million). Postclosing net debt increased to $474.4 million (postclosing term loan of $500 million less $25.6 million in total cash of the balance sheet).

Table 13.5 presents the key features of the new term loan B facility. Note how Summit's assets are used as collateral to secure the loan. In addition, the lender has first priority on the proceeds from certain types of transactions, giving them priority access to such funds. Cash distributions are not possible until the loan is almost paid off, and even then the size of such distributions is limited. Finally, loan covenants require Summit to maintain a comparatively liquid position during the term of the loan.

Discussion Questions

1. What about Lionsgate's acquisition of Summit indicates that this transaction should be characterized as a leveraged buyout? How does Lionsgate use Summit's assets to help finance the deal? Be specific.
2. How are the $34.6 million in fees and expenses associated with the transaction paid for (see Table 13.4)? Be specific.
3. Speculate as to why Lionsgate refinanced as part of the transaction the existing Summit Term Loan B due in 2016 that had been borrowed in the early 2000s.
4. Do you believe that Summit is a good candidate for a leveraged buyout? Explain your answer.
5. Why is Summit Entertainment organized as a limited liability company?
6. Why did Lionsgate make an equity contribution in the form of cash and stock to the Merger Sub rather than making the cash portion of the contributed capital in the form of a loan?

A solution to this case study is provided in the Online Instructors Manual for instructors using this book.

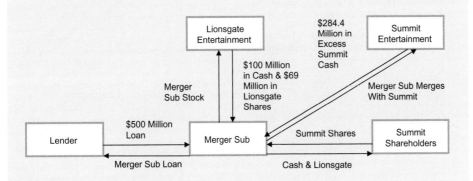

FIGURE 13.3   **Lionsgate-Summit legal and financing structure.**

TABLE 13.4   Lionsgate-Summit Transaction Overview

Sources of Funds ($ Millions)		Uses of Funds ($ Millions)	
Lionsgate Cash Consideration[a]	100.0	Seller Consideration	412.5
Lionsgate Stock Consideration[b]	69.0	Repay Term Loan	506.3
Summit Cash on Balance Sheet	284.4	Fees and expenses	34.6
New Term Loan	500.0		
Total	953.4		953.4

Summit Pro Forma Capitalization

As of 12/30/11	$ Millions	Pro Forma Adjustment ($ Millions)	$ Millions
Cash[c]	310	(284.4)	25.6
Revolver ($200 million)	—	—	NA[d]
Prior Term Loan B Due 9/2016	506.3	(506.3)	0.0
New Term Loan B Due 9/2016	0.0	500.0	500.0
Total Debt	506.3	(6.3)	500.0
Contributed Equity[e]			169.0

Source: Lionsgate 8K filing with the Securities and Exchange Commission on 2/1/2012.
[a]*Includes $55 million of Lionsgate cash and $45 million of convertible bond proceeds.*
[b]*Includes $20 million of stock consideration to be issued to Summit sellers 60 days after closing.*
[c]*Total cash balance prior to the transaction announcement. $284 million is excess Summit cash used by Lionsgate to finance a portion of the deal. The remaining $25.6 million is cash needed to meet working capital requirements.*
[d]*Revolver commitments terminated for the acquisition.*
[e]*Consists of $100 million in cash from Lionsgate and $69 million in Lionsgate stock.*

TABLE 13.5   Initial Terms and Conditions of the New Term Loan B Facility

Item	Comment
Borrower	Summit Entertainment LLC (Lionsgate subsidiary)
Guarantor	Merger Sub
Security	First priority security interest in tangible and intangible assets
	Pledge of equity interests of Summit and guarantor
	Assignments of all trademarks and copyrights
	Direct assignment of all proceeds payable to borrowers or any guarantor under all existing license and distribution agreements
Facilities	$500 million senior secured term loan B
Ratings	B1/B +
Maturity	September 2016
Mandatory Amortization	$13.75 million, paid quarterly
Pricing	To be determined
Incremental Facility	None
Optional Prepayments	Up to one year at the discretion of the borrower

TABLE 13.5   (Continued)

Mandatory Prepayments	100% of proceeds from asset sales
	100% of insurance proceeds
	50% of excess cash flow as defined in purchase agreement
	Excess over mandatory maximum cash balance allowance
Permitted Distributions	No distributions before loan facility is 75% amortized
	Only distributions of up to $25 million allowed once loan is 75% amortized
Financial Maintenance Covenants	Fixed charge coverage ratio of 1.25 to 1
	Minimum liquidity ratio of at least 1.1 to 1

CASE STUDY 13.2
TXU Goes Private in the Largest Private Equity Transaction in History—The Dark Side of Leverage

Key Points

- The 2007/2008 financial crisis left many LBOs excessively leveraged.
- As structured, the TXU buyout (now Energy Future Holdings) left no margin for error.
- Excessive leverage severely limits the firm's future financial options.

Before the buyout, TXU, a Dallas-based energy giant, was a highly profitable utility. Historically low interest rates and an overly optimistic outlook for natural gas prices set the stage for the largest private equity deal in history. The 2007 buyout of TXU was valued at $48 billion and, at the time, appeared to offer such promise that several of Wall Street's largest lenders—including the likes of Lehman Brothers and Citigroup—invested, along with such storied names in

private equity as KKR, TPG, and Goldman Sachs (Goldman). However, the price of gas plummeted, eroding TXU's cash flow. Since the deal closed in October 2007, investors who bought $40 billion of TXU's debt have experienced losses as high as 70% to 80% of their value. The other $8 billion used to finance the deal came from the private equity investors, banks, and large institutional investors. They, too, have suffered huge losses. Having met its obligations to date, the firm faces a $20 billion debt repayment coming due in 2014.

Wall Street banks were competing in 2007 to make loans to buyout firms on easier terms, with the banks also investing their own funds in the deal. The allure to the banks was the prospect of dividing up as much as $1.1 billion in fees for originating the loans, repackaging such loans into pools called *collateralized loan obligations*, and reselling them to long-term investors such as pension funds and insurance companies. In doing so, the loans would be removed from the banks' balance sheets, eliminating potential losses that could arise if the deal soured at a later date. Furthermore, the deal appeared to be attractive as an investment opportunity because some banks put up $500 million of their own cash for a stake in TXU.

The financial sponsor group, consisting of KKR Texas Pacific Group, and Goldman, created a shell corporation, referred to as Merger Sub Parent, and its wholly owned subsidiary Merger Sub. TXU was merged into Merger Sub, with Merger Sub surviving. Each outstanding share of TXU common stock was converted into the right to receive $69.25 in cash. Total cash required for the purchase was provided by the financial sponsor group and lenders (Creditor Group) to Merger Sub. Regulatory authorities required that the debt associated with the transaction be held at the level of the Merger Sub Parent holding company so as not to leverage the utility further.

Subsequent to closing, the new company was reorganized into independent businesses under a new holding company, controlled by the Sponsor Group, called Texas Holdings (TH). Merger Sub (which owns TXU) was renamed Energy Future Holdings. TH's direct subsidiaries are EFH and Oncor (an energy distribution business formerly held by TXU). EFH's primary direct subsidiary is Texas Competitive Electric Holdings, which holds TXU's public utility operating assets and liabilities. All TXU non-sponsor group–related debt incurred to finance the transaction is held by EFH, while any debt incurred by the sponsor group is shown on the TH balance sheet. This legal structure allows for the concentration of debt in TH and EFH, separate from the cash-generating assets held by Oncor and Texas Competitive Electric Holdings.

Loan covenants limit EFH's and its subsidiaries' ability to issue new debt or preferred stock; pay dividends on, repurchase, or make distributions of capital stock or make other restricted payments; make investments; sell or transfer assets; consolidate, merge, sell, or dispose of all or substantially all its assets; and repay, repurchase, or modify debt. A breach of any of these covenants could result in default. Table 13.6 illustrates selected covenants in which certain ratios must be maintained either above or below stipulated thresholds. Note that EFH was in violation of certain covenants when you compare actual December 31, 2009 (the last year for which public information is available), ratios with required threshold levels.

Things clearly have not turned out as expected. The firm faces an almost-untenable capital structure. The firm's debt traded at between 20 and 30 cents on the dollar throughout most of 2012. The $8 billion equity invested in the deal has been virtually wiped out on paper. Absent a turnaround in natural gas prices, EFH is left with seeking a way to reduce substantially the burden of the pending 2014 $20 billion loan payment with its lenders through a debt-for-equity swap or more favorable terms on existing debt or by pursuing Chapter 11 bankruptcy. EFH has posted eight consecutive quarterly losses. In December 2012, in an effort to extend debt maturities to buy time for a turnaround and to reduce interest expense, EFH exchanged $1.15 billion of new payment-in-kind notes (interest is paid with more debt) for existing notes with a face value of $1.6 billion. By any measure, this transaction illustrates the dark side of leverage.

Discussion Questions

1. How does the postclosing holding company structure protect the interests of the financial sponsor group and the utility's customers but potentially jeopardize creditor interests in the event of bankruptcy?
2. What was the purpose of the preclosing covenants and closing conditions as described in the merger agreement?

3. Loan covenants exist to protect the lender. How might such covenants inhibit EFH from meeting its 2014 $20 billion obligations?
4. As CEO of EFH, what would you recommend to the board of directors as an appropriate strategy for paying the $20 billion in debt that is maturing in 2014?
5. In the fourth quarter of 2008 and the first quarter of 2009, EFC Holdings recorded goodwill-impairment charges of about $8 billion. The substantial write-down of the net acquired suggests that the purchase price paid for TXU was too high. How might this impact KKR's, TPG's, and Goldman's abilities to earn financial returns expected by their investors on the TXU acquisition? How might this write-down impact EFH's ability to meet the $20 billion debt maturing in 2014?

Solutions to these case study discussion questions are available in the Online Instructor's Manual for instructors using this book.

TABLE 13.6   EFH Holdings Debt Covenants

	December 31, 2009	Threshold Level as of December 31, 2009
MAINTENANCE COVENANT		
TCEH Secured Facilities: Ratio of Secured debt to adjusted EBITDA	4.76 – 1.00	Must not exceed 7.25 – 1.00
DEBT INCURRENCE COVENANTS		
EFH Corp Senior Notes:		
EFH Corp fixed charge coverage ratio	1.2 – 1.0	At least 2.0 – 1.0
TCEH fixed charge coverage ratio	1.5 – 1.0	At least 2.0 – 1.0

TABLE 13.6   (Continued)

	December 31, 2009	Threshold Level as of December 31, 2009
EFH Corp 9.75% Notes:		
EFH Corp fixed charge coverage ratio	1.2 – 1.0	At least 2.0 – 1.0
TCEH fixed charge coverage ratio	1.5 – 1.0	At least 2.0 – 1.0
TCEH Senior Notes:		
TCEH fixed charge coverage ratio	1.5 – 1.0	At least 2.0 – 1.0
TCEH Senior Secured Facilities:		
TCEH fixed charge coverage ratio	1.5 – 1.0	At least 2.0 – 1.0
RESTRICTED PAYMENTS/LIMITATIONS ON INVESTMENTS COVENANTS		
EFH Corp Senior Notes:		
General restrictions		
EFH Corp fixed charge coverage ratio	1.4 – 1.0	At least 2.0 – 1.0
General restrictions		
EFH Fixed Charge coverage ratio	1.2 – 1.0	At least 2.0 – 1.0
EFH Corp leverage ratio	9.4 – 1.0	≤7.0 – 1.0
EFH Corp 9.75% Notes:		
General restrictions		
EFH Corp fixed charge coverage ratio	1.4 – 1.0	At least 2.0 – 1.0
General restrictions		
EFH Corp fixed charge coverage ratio	1.2 – 1.0	At least 2.0 – 1.0
EFH Corp leverage ratio	9.4 – 1.0	≤7.0 – 1.0
TCEH Senior Notes:		
TCEH fixed charge coverage ratio	1.5 – 1.0	At least 2.0 – 1.0

Highly Leveraged Transactions
LBO Valuation and Modeling Basics

No one spends other people's money as carefully as they spend their own.—**Milton Friedman**

INSIDE M&A: KINDER MORGAN'S TAKEOVER OF EL PASO RAISES ETHICAL QUESTIONS

KEY POINTS

- Investor perceptions of CEO, board, and advisor behavior in transactions matters.
- Real or perceived conflicts of interest may trigger litigation.
- However, proving alleged conflicts of interest can be daunting, especially if the takeover premium is substantial and shareholders approve the deal.

Kinder Morgan's acquisition of El Paso Corporation closed in mid-2012 in a deal valued at $21.1 billion, making the combined firms the largest independent energy pipeline company in the United States (see Case Study 4.2). Investors greeted the announcement of the deal on October 17, 2011, by bidding up Kinder Morgan's and El Paso's shares by 4.8% and 25%, respectively. However, within weeks, the deal was embroiled in controversy over the alleged conflicts of interest of El Paso's CEO, Douglas Foshee, and the firm's investment advisor, Goldman Sachs.

Some El Paso shareholders sued to block the deal, arguing that Goldman's position on both sides of the deal likely led to an artificially low purchase price for the firm. That is, Goldman served as an advisor to El Paso on the deal while also owning, through its private equity arm, a 19% stake in Kinder Morgan valued at more than $4 billion and had two appointees on the Kinder Morgan board. Despite Goldman's having disclosed this information to management, El Paso continued to use the firm in an advisory capacity. Furthermore, the lead Goldman investment banker on the transaction owned $340,000 worth of Kinder Morgan. It was later determined that Mr. Foshee had disclosed to Richard Kinder, Kinder Morgan's CEO, on two separate occasions during the negotiations that he was interested in buying El Paso's oil and gas exploration business from Kinder Morgan once the deal was completed.

Investor concerns ranged from the parties involved showing very poor judgment to highly inappropriate behavior. Apparently, Leo Strine, the Chancellor of the Delaware Court of Chancery, where the case was adjudicated, concurred with the plaintiffs. While refusing to halt the takeover, Chancellor Strine faulted Mr. Foshee for negotiating the deal largely on his own and not disclosing to the El Paso board his intention to buy El Paso's oil and gas exploration business following closing. Strine noted that he did not halt the deal, because that would have deprived the El Paso shareholders of the purchase price premium; however, the tone of his summary comments certainly left open the option for disaffected shareholders to seek monetary damages.

Goldman's potential conflicts are equally intriguing. Goldman stood to benefit on both sides of the transaction, collecting a $20 million advisory fee from El Paso and seeing its $4 billion stake in Kinder Morgan appreciate. To attenuate this conflict, Morgan Stanley was brought in to write a fairness opinion letter. However, Morgan would be paid only if El Paso was sold and not if it were spun off. If the later strategy were undertaken, Goldman's investment in Kinder Morgan would not have benefitted from the appreciation of Kinder Morgan's shares resulting from the anticipated synergy in combining the two firms. Consequently, it could be argued that Goldman used its advisory role to direct El Paso's restructuring decisions toward that option that would benefit them the most.

While the potential conflicts of interest are apparent, the deal proved attractive to El Paso investors, with shareholders owning more than three-fourths of the outstanding shares voting in favor of the deal. In a letter to employees, Douglas Foshee noted that "I have a substantial stake in the company (El Paso) and I've never sold a share of stock or exercised a stock option. As such, I've always viewed my interests as fully aligned with those of El Paso's shareholders."

CHAPTER OVERVIEW

Chapter 13 addressed common sources of deal financing and the role of private equity investors and hedge funds in financing transactions. The focus in Chapter 14 is on how to value highly leveraged transactions via commonly used methods. This chapter concludes with a discussion of how investors evaluate LBO investment opportunities and typical formats used in building LBO financial models. Such models serve to determine the maximum amount of leverage that can be supported by the target firm consistent with the investor's desired financial returns.

Transactions involving large amounts of debt to finance the purchase price generally are described as leveraged buyouts. In a leveraged buyout (LBO), borrowed funds, often secured by assets of the target firm, are used to pay for most of the purchase price, with the remainder provided by a financial sponsor, such as a private equity investor group or hedge fund. LBOs can be of an entire company or divisions of a company. LBO targets can be private or public firms. As in prior chapters, the terms *buyout firm* and *financial sponsor* are used interchangeably throughout this chapter to include the variety of investor groups, such as private equity investors and hedge funds, which commonly engage in LBO transactions. A detailed "Microsoft Excel-Based Leveraged Buyout Valuation and Structuring Model" is available on the companion website to this book (*http:// booksite.elsevier.com/9780123854872*). The companion website also contains a review of this chapter in the file folder entitled "Student Study Guide."

HOW ARE LBOs VALUED?

An LBO can be valued from the perspective of common equity investors only, or of all those who supply funds, including common and preferred investors and lenders. Conventional capital budgeting procedures may be used to evaluate the LBO. The transaction makes sense from the standpoint of all investors if the present value of the cash flows to the firm (PV_{FCFF}) or enterprise value, discounted at the weighted-average cost of capital, equals or exceeds the total investment, consisting of debt, common equity, and preferred equity ($I_{D + E + PFD}$) required to buy the outstanding shares of the target company:

$$PV_{FCFF} - I_{D+E+PFD} \geq 0 \tag{14.1}$$

Equation (14.1) implies that the target firm can earn its cost of capital and can return sufficient cash flow to all investors and lenders, enabling them to meet or exceed their required returns. However, it is possible for a leveraged buyout to make sense to common equity investors but not to other investors, such as pre-LBO debt holders and preferred stockholders.[1]

What follows is a discussion of two methods for valuing leveraged buyouts. The cost of capital method adjusts future cash flows for changes in the cost of

---

[1] Once the LBO has been consummated, the firm's ability to meet its obligations to current debt and preferred stockholders may deteriorate. The firm's pre-LBO debt and preferred stock may be revalued in the market by investors to reflect this higher perceived risk, resulting in a significant reduction in the market value of both debt and preferred equity owned by pre-LBO investors. Although there is little evidence to show that this is typical of LBOs, this revaluation may characterize large LBOs, such as RJR Nabisco in 1989, HCA in 2006, and TXU Corp in 2007.

capital as the firm reduces its outstanding debt. The second method, adjusted present value, sums the value of the firm without debt plus the value of future tax savings resulting from the tax deductibility of interest.

Valuing LBOs: The Cost of Capital (CC) Method

If the debt-to-equity ratio is expected to be constant, discounting future cash flows with a constant weighted average cost of capital (CC) is appropriate. However, assuming a constant debt-to-equity ratio for highly leveraged transactions is inconsistent with actual practice. Many firms reduce their outstanding debt relative to equity, and such changes in the capital structure distort valuation estimates based on traditional DCF methods.[2]

The high leverage associated with leveraged buyouts increases the riskiness of the cash flows available to equity investors as a result of the increase in fixed obligations to lenders. The cost of equity should be adjusted for the increased leverage of the firm. However, since the debt is to be paid off over time, the cost of equity will decrease. Therefore, in valuing a leveraged buyout, the analyst must project free cash flows and adjust the discount rate to reflect changes in the capital structure. Instead of discounting the cash flows at a constant discount rate, the discount rate must decline with the firm's declining debt-to-equity ratio. A four-step methodology for adjusting the discount rate to reflect a firm's declining leverage is discussed next.

Step 1: Project Annual Cash Flows Until the Target Debt/Equity Ratio is Achieved

Step 1 involves projecting free cash flow to equity (FCFE)—that is, the cash flow available for common equity holders, annually until the LBO reaches its target debt-to-equity (D/E) ratio. The target D/E ratio often is the industry average ratio or one that would appear acceptable to strategic buyers or IPO investors or the point at which the firm resumes paying taxes.

Step 2: Project Debt-to-Equity Ratios

The decline in debt-to-equity ratios depends on known debt repayment schedules and the projected growth in the market value of shareholders' equity. The latter can be assumed to grow in line with the anticipated growth in net income.

Step 3: Adjust the Discount Rate to Reflect Changing Risk

The high leverage associated with an LBO increases the risk of the cash flows available for equity investors. As the LBO's high debt level is reduced, the cost of equity needs to be adjusted to reflect the decline in risk, as measured by the

[2]Oded et al., 2011

firm's levered beta (β_{FL}). This adjustment may be estimated, starting with the firm's levered beta in period 1 (β_{FL1}), as follows:

$$\beta_{FL1} = \beta_{IUL1}[1 + (D/E)_{F1}(1 - t_F)] \tag{14.2}$$

β_{IUL1} is the comparable firm unlevered β in period 1; $(D/E)_{F1}$ and t_F are the firm's debt-to-equity ratio and marginal tax rate, respectively, and $\beta_{IUL1} = \beta_{IL1}/[1 + (D/E)_{I1}(1 - t_I)]$, where β_{IL1},$(D/E)_{I1}$,and t_I are the comparable firm's levered β, debt-to-equity ratio, and tax rate, respectively. The firm's β in each successive period should be recalculated using the target firm's projected debt-to-equity ratio for that period. The target firm's cost of equity (k_e) must be recalculated each period using that period's estimated β determined by Eq. (14.2).

Because the firm's cost of equity changes over time, the firm's cumulative cost of equity is used to discount projected cash flows.[3] This reflects the fact that each period's cash flows generate a different rate of return. The cumulative cost of equity is represented as follows:

$$
\begin{aligned}
PV_1 &= FCFE_1/(1 + k_{e1}) \\
PV_2 &= FCFE_2/[(1 + k_{e1})(1 + k_{e2})] \\
&\ \vdots \\
PV_n &= FCFE_n/[(1 + k_{e1})(1 + k_{e2})\cdots(1 + k_{e(n-1)})(1 + k_{en})]
\end{aligned}
\tag{14.3}
$$

Step 4: Determine if the Deal Makes Sense

Making sense of the deal requires calculating the PV of FCFE discounted by the cumulative cost of equity generalized by Eq. (14.3), including the terminal value. Calculate the terminal value of equity (TVE) and of the firm in year t:

$$\text{Terminal value of equity (TVE)} = FCFE_{t+1}/(k_e - g) \tag{14.4}$$

k_e, and g represent, respectively, the cost of equity and the cash flow growth rate that can be sustained during the terminal period. TVE represents the PV of the dollar proceeds available to the firm at time t, generated by selling equity to the public, to a strategic buyer, or to another LBO firm. A similar calculation would be made for the terminal value of the firm, using the appropriate weighted average cost of capital for the terminal period, which would then be converted to a present value and added to the PV of free cash flows to the firm. Table 14.1 shows how to calculate the value of an LBO using the cost of capital method. The deal makes sense to common equity investors if the total PV exceeds the value of the equity investment in the deal and to lenders and preferred equity investors if the total PV of FCFF is greater than the total cost of the

---

[3] Recall that the future value of \$1 (FV\$1) in two years invested at a 5% return in the first year and 8% in the second year is \$1 × [(1 + 0.05)(1 + 0.08)] = \$1.13; the present value of \$1 received in two years earning the same rates of return (PV\$1) is \$1/[(1 + 0.05)(1 + 0.08)] = \$0.88.

TABLE 14.1 Present Value of Equity Cash Flow Using the Cost of Capital (CC) Method

Process Steps	Forecast Period						
	2013	2014	2015	2016	2017	2018	2019
Step 1: Project Annual Cash Flows ($Mil)[a]	0.30	0.20	1.80	7.40	7.70	8.10	8.50
Step 2: Project Debt-to-Equity Ratios (D/E)[a]	1.46	1.02	0.68	0.48	0.32	0.18	0.05
Step 3: Adjust Discount Rate to Reflect Changing Risk							

ASSUMPTIONS

Comparable Firm

Leveraged Beta (β_l)	2.40
Debt/Equity Ratio	0.30
Unlevered Beta (β_u)[b]	2.03
Marginal Tax Rate (%)	0.40
10-Year U.S. Treasury Bond Rate (%)	0.05
Risk Premium on Stocks (%)	0.055

Year	D/E	Leveraged Beta[c]	Cost of Equity (k_e)[d]	Cumulative Cost of Equity
2013	1.46	3.81	25.96	$1/(1 + .2596) = .7939$
2014	1.02	3.27	22.99	$1/(1 + .2596)(1 + .2299) = .6455$
2015	0.68	2.86	20.73	$1/(1 + .2596)(1 + .2299)(1 + .2073) = .5347$
2016	0.48	2.61	19.36	$1/(1 + .2596)(1 + .2299)(1 + .2073)(1 + .1936) = .4479$
2017	0.32	2.42	18.31	$1/(1 + .2596)(1 + .2299)(1 + .2073)(1 + .1936)(1 + .1831) = .3786$
2018	0.18	2.25	17.38	$1/(1 + .2596)(1 + .2299)(1 + .2073)(1 + .1936)(1 + .1831)(1 + .1738) = .3226$
2019	0.05	2.09	16.50	$1/(1 + .2596)(1 + .2299)(1 + .2073)(1 + .1936)(1 + .1831)(1 + .1738)(1 + .1650) = 2769$

Step 4: Determine If Deal Makes Sense

ASSUMPTIONS

Terminal-Period Growth Rate (%)	0.05					
Terminal-Period Cost of Equity (%)[e]	0.10					
PV of Annual Cash Flows (2013–2019, $Mil)[f]	0.24	0.13	0.96	3.31	2.92	2.61	2.35
Sum of Annual Cash Flows (2013–2019)	12.53					
Terminal Value ($Mil)	44.72					
Total PV ($Mil)	57.25					

The deal makes sense for equity investors if NPV $\geq$ 0.

[a] Projections come from the Excel-Based LBO Valuation and Structuring Model available on the website accompanying this book. Assumes the firm's target D/E is zero. When achieved, the financial sponsor will exit the business.

[b] $\beta_u = \beta_l/[1 + (D/E)(1 − t)] = 2.4/(1 + 0.3 \times 0.6) = 2.03$

[c] For 2013, $\beta_l = \beta_u[1 + (D/E)(1 − t)] = 2.03 \times [1 + (1.46)(1 − 0.4)] = 3.81$, where 2.03 is the unlevered comparable firm beta
For 2014, $\beta_l = 2.03 \times [1 + (1.02)(1 − 0.4)] = 3.27$
For 2015, $\beta_l = 2.03 \times ([1 + (0.68)(1 − 0.4)] = 2.86$, and so on[d]

[d] For 2013, $k_e = 0.05 + 3.81(0.055) = 0.2596 \times 100 = 25.96$
For 2014, $k_e = 0.05 + 3.27(0.055) = 0.2299 \times 100 = 22.99$ For 2015, $k_e = 0.05 + 2.86(0.055) = 0.20.73 \times 100 = 20.73$ and so on

[e] Industry average cost of equity

[f] PV calculated by multiplying each year's cash flow by the cumulative cost of equity for that year, e.g., for 2013, $0.7939 \times \$.30 = \$.24$.

deal. The Excel-based spreadsheet for this table is available on the companion website to this textbook.

Valuing LBOs: Adjusted Present Value (APV) Method

Some analysts suggest that the bias from a variable discount rate is avoidable by separating the value of a firm's operations into two components: the firm's value as if it were debt free and the value of interest tax savings, or tax shield. The total value of the firm is the PV of the firm's free cash flows to equity investors (i.e., unlevered cash flows) plus the PV of future tax savings discounted at the firm's unlevered cost of equity.[4] The unlevered cost of equity is the appropriate discount rate rather than the cost of debt or a risk-free rate because tax savings are subject to risk, since the firm may default on its debt or be unable to utilize the tax savings due to continuing operating losses.[5]

The justification for the adjusted present value (APV) method reflects the theoretical notion that firm value is unaffected by the way in which it is financed.[6] However, studies suggest that for LBOs, the availability and cost of financing do indeed impact financing and investment decisions.[7] In the presence of taxes, firms may be less leveraged than they should be, given the potentially large tax benefits associated with debt.[8] Firms can increase market value by increasing leverage to the point at which the additional contribution of the tax shield to the firm's market value begins to decline.[9] However, management's decision to increase leverage, affects, and is affected by, the firm's credit rating.

---

[4] Additional tax savings could be realized resulting from the write-up of the target's assets to their fair market value, yielding additional depreciation expense. Some analysts also add the present value of these future tax savings to the unlevered value of the firm.

[5] Brigham and Ehrhardt (2005), p. 597

[6] Brealey and Myers, 1996. This concept assumes that investors have access to perfect information, that the firm is not growing and no new borrowing is required, and that there are no taxes and transaction costs and implicitly that the firm is free of default risk. Under these assumptions, the decision to invest is affected by the earning power and risk associated with the firm's assets and not by the way the investment is financed.

[7] Axelson et al. (2009) argue that the capital structure in buyouts requires a different explanation than in public firms, where investment decisions are believed to be made independent of the way in which they are financed. With respect to LBOs, the availability of financing appears to impact the decision to invest in LBOs, unlike public firms, which is consistent with the widely held view among buyout practitioners that the size and frequency of LBOs are driven by the availability and cost of financing.

[8] Elkamhi et al., 2012. Many firms, such as Intel and Exxon, would appear to have far less leverage than could be justified based on potential tax savings. However, such firms often choose to limit leverage to retain the flexibility to pursue unanticipated opportunities when they arise.

[9] Graham (2000) argues that many firms would benefit by adding additional debt; however, this notion is disputed by Blouin et al. (2012), who document that the tax savings associated with increased leverage often are substantially overstated.

Consequently, the tax benefits of higher leverage may be partially or entirely off-set by the higher probability of default due to an increase in leverage.[10]

For the APV method to be applicable in highly leveraged transactions, the analyst needs to introduce the costs of financial distress. The direct cost of financial distress includes the costs associated with reorganization in bankruptcy and, ultimately, liquidation (see Chapter 17). Such costs include legal and accounting fees. However, financial distress can have a material indirect cost, even on firms that are able to avoid bankruptcy or liquidation.[11] Consequently, in applying the APV method, the present value of a highly leveraged transaction (PV_{HL}) would reflect the present value of the firm without leverage (PV_{UL}) plus the present value of tax savings (i.e., interest expense, i, times the firm's marginal tax rate, t, or tax shield PV_{ti} resulting from leverage) less the present value of expected financial distress PV_{FD}):

$$PV_{HL} = PV_{UL} + PV_{ti} - PV_{FD} \qquad (14.5)$$

where $PV_{FD} = \mu FD$.

FD is the expected cost of financial distress, and μ is the probability of financial distress. Unfortunately, FD and μ cannot be easily or reliably estimated and often are ignored by analysts using the APV method. Failure to include an estimate of the cost and probability of financial distress is likely to result in an overestimate of the value of the firm using the APV method. Despite these concerns, many analysts continue to apply the APV method because of its relative simplicity, as illustrated in the following four-step process.

Step 1: Estimate the Present Value of the Target Firm's Unlevered Cash Flows

For the period during which the debt–to–total capital ratio is changing, the analyst should project free cash flows to equity (i.e., unlevered cash flows). During the firm's terminal period, the debt–to–total capital structure is assumed to be stable and the free cash flows are projected to grow at a constant rate. Estimate the unlevered cost of equity (COE) for discounting cash flows during the period in which the capital structure is changing and the weighted average cost of capital (WACC) for discounting during the terminal period. The WACC is estimated using the proportions of debt and equity that make up the firm's capital structure in the final year of the period during which the capital structure is changing.

---

[10] Molina (2006), and Almeida and Philippon (2007) show that the risk-adjusted costs of distress can be so large as to totally offset the tax benefits derived from debt. This is particularly true during periods of economic downturn.

[11] Indirect costs include the loss of customers, employee turnover, less favorable terms from suppliers, higher borrowing costs, management distraction costs, higher operating expenses, and reduced overall competitiveness.

Step 2: Estimate the Present Value of Anticipated Tax Savings

Project the annual tax savings resulting from the tax deductibility of interest. Discount projected tax savings at the firm's unlevered cost of equity, since it reflects a higher level of risk than either the WACC or the after-tax cost of debt. Tax savings are subject to risk comparable to the firm's cash flows, in that a highly leveraged firm may default or the tax savings may go unused.

Step 3: Estimate the Potential Cost of Financial Distress

The magnitude of the cost of financial distress can range from 10% to 30% of a firm's predistressed market value.[12] The probability of financial distress can be estimated by analyzing bond ratings[13] and the cumulative probabilities of default for bonds in different ratings classes over 5- and 10-year periods (see Table 14.2).[14]

TABLE 14.2   Bond Rating and Probability of Default

Rating	Cumulative Probability of Distress(%)	
	5 Years	10 Years
AAA	0.04	0.07
AA	0.44	0.51
A +	0.47	0.57
A	0.20	0.66
A –	3.00	5.00
BBB	6.44	7.54
BB	11.90	19.63
B +	19.20	28.25
B	27.50	36.80
B –	31.10	42.12
CCC	46.26	59.02
CC	54.15	66.60
C +	65.15	75.16
C	72.15	81.03
C –	80.00	87.16

Source: Altman, 2007.

[12] Andrade and Kaplan, 1998. Branch (2002) concludes that the impact of bankruptcy on a firm's predistressed value falls within a range of 12% to 20%. More recently, Korteweg (2010) estimates that the impact falls within a range of 15% to 30% of predistressed firm value.
[13] While the failure of the credit-rating agencies to anticipate the extreme financial distress in the credit markets experienced in 2008 and 2009 casts doubt on the use of credit ratings to assess financial distress, there are few reliable alternatives at this time.

Step 4: Determine if the Deal Makes Sense

The total value of the firm is the sum of the PV of the firm's cash flows to equity, interest tax savings, and terminal value discounted at the firm's unlevered cost of equity less the anticipated cost of financial distress [see Eq. (14.5)]. Note that the terminal value is calculated using WACC but that it is discounted to the present using the unlevered cost of equity, because it represents the present value of cash flows in the final year of the period in which the firm's capital structure is changing and beyond. For the deal to make sense, the present value of Eq. (14.5) less the value of equity invested in the transaction (i.e., NPV) must be greater than or equal to 0.

Table 14.3 illustrates the APV method with assumptions consistent with the valuation of the target firm using the cost of capital method in Table 14.1. Assuming that the firm has a C– credit rating, the PV of the expected cost of bankruptcy is $21.59 million and is calculated as the cumulative probability of default over 10 years for a company rated C– [i.e., 0.8716 per Table 14.2 times the expected cost of bankruptcy (i.e., 0.30 × $82.56 million)]. Note that the estimate provided by the APV method is $87.43 million (i.e., $82.56 + $4.87 million) before the adjustment for financial distress. This is 44.2% [i.e., ($82.56/$57.25) – 1] more than the estimate provided using the CC method shown in Table 14.1. After adjusting for financial distress, the estimate declines to $65.85 million, versus the $57.25 million estimated using the CC method, a difference of about 15%.

Comparing Cost of Capital and Adjusted Present Value Methods

The cost of capital method adjusts future cash flows for changes in the cost of capital as the firm reduces its outstanding debt. The second method, adjusted present value, sums the value of the firm without debt plus the value of future tax savings resulting from the tax deductibility of interest. The cost of capital approach has the advantage of specifically attempting to adjust the discount rate for changes in risk; however, it is more cumbersome to calculate than the APV scheme. While the APV method is relatively simple to calculate, it relies on highly problematic assumptions.[15] It ignores the impact of leverage on the discount rate as debt is repaid, which implies that adding debt will always increase firm value by increasing the tax shield. Incorporating the effects of leverage into

---

[14] Altman and Kishore, 2001; Altman, 2007. Cumulative probability estimates reflect the likelihood of a particular outcome based on previous outcomes or events. They are used when reductions in cash flows due to financial distress in earlier years impact cash flows in subsequent years, because the firm may be forced to underinvest. Assume that the probability of a firm experiencing financial distress in year 1 is 20%. If the firm ceases to exist at the end of the first year due to financial distress, there will be no cash flows in year 2. If we assume that the likelihood of distress in year 2 is again 20%, the likelihood of the firm producing cash flows in the third year is only 64% [i.e., (1 – 0.2)(1 – 0.2)] and so on.

[15] For an excellent discussion of alternative valuation methods for highly leveraged firms, see Ruback (2002).

TABLE 14.3 Present Value of Equity Cash Flows Using the Adjusted Present Value Method

Process Steps	2013	2014	2015	2016	2017	2018	2019
STEP 1: ESTIMATE PV OF TARGET FIRM'S UNLEVERED CASH FLOWS							
ASSUMPTIONS:							
Annual Equity Cash Flows	0.30	0.20	1.80	7.40	7.70	8.10	8.50
Marginal Tax Rate	0.40						
Comparable-Firm Unlevered Beta	2.03						
10-Year U.S. Treasury Bond Rate (%)	0.05						
Risk Premium on Stocks (%)	0.055						
Terminal-Period Growth Rate (%)	0.045						
2013–2019 Unlevered Cost of Equity (%)[a]	0.162						
Terminal-Period WACC (%)[b]	0.159						
PV of 2013–2019 Annual Cash Flows							15.51
Plus: PV of Terminal Value							67.05
Equals: Total PV Excluding Tax & Cost of Financial Distress							82.56
STEP 2: ESTIMATE PV OF ANTICIPATED TAX SAVINGS							
ASSUMPTIONS:							
Annual interest Expense	3.00	2.66	2.17	1.67	1.33	1.00	0.67
Interest Tax Savings (Tax Shield)[c]	1.80	1.60	1.30	1.00	0.80	0.60	0.40
PV of Tax Shield @ 16.2%							4.87

STEP 3: ESTIMATE THE POTENTIAL COST OF FINANCIAL DISTRESS

ASSUMPTIONS:

Target Firm Credit Rating	C –	
Cumulative Default Probability for a Firm Rated C– over 10 Years (see Table 14.2)	0.8716	
Expected Cost of Financial Distress per Andrade and Kaplan (1998) and Korteweg (2010) as a % of Firm Value	0.30	
Potential Cost of Financial Distress		21.59

STEP 4: DETERMINE IF DEAL MAKES SENSE

Total PV Excluding Tax Shield and Cost of Financial Distress	82.56
Plus: PV of Tax Shield	4.87
Less: Expected Cost of Financial Distress	21.59
Equals: Total PV Including Tax Shield and Financial Distress	65.85

[a]$k_e = 0.05 + 2.03(.055) = 0.162 \times 100 = 16.2\%$
[b]The discount rate in the terminal period reflects the presence of debt. The target D/E ratio is taken from Table 14.1, which shows D/E in 2019 at 5%. Recall the proportion debt is of total capital can be determined by dividing the target D/E ratio by (1 + D/E), or 0.05/1.05. Therefore, debt is 5% of total capital and equity is 95% during the terminal period. If the borrowing rate for this firm is 10%, WACC = $0.05 \times 0.10 + 0.95 \times 0.162 = 15.9\%$.
[c]Tax shield = $0.4 \times$ annual interest expense

the APV method requires the estimation of the cost and probability of financial distress for highly leveraged firms, a challenging and often highly subjective undertaking. Finally, it is unclear whether the true discount rate that should be used for the APV approach is the cost of debt, unlevered k_e, or somewhere between the two.

LBO VALUATION AND STRUCTURING MODEL BASICS

An LBO model determines what a firm is worth in a highly leveraged deal and is applied when there is the potential for a financial buyer or sponsor to acquire the business. The model helps define the amount of debt a firm can support given its assets and cash flows. Investment bankers employ such analyses in addition to DCF and relative valuation methods to value firms they wish to sell. The intent is to provide financial buyers with an LBO opportunity that offers a financial return in excess of their desired rate of return while allowing the target to retain financial flexibility to meet future operating challenges. The following sections discuss a useful template for evaluating LBO opportunities and for building LBO models. The Excel-based spreadsheets underlying these sections, found on the companion website to this book, are entitled "Excel-Based LBO Valuation and Structuring Model" and "Excel-Based Model to Estimate Borrowing Capacity." The reader is encouraged to examine the formulas that support these spreadsheets.

Evaluating LBO Opportunities

LBO models are similar to DCF valuations in that they require projected cash flows, terminal values, present values, and discount rates. However, the DCF analysis solves for the present value of the firm, while the LBO model solves for the internal rate of return (IRR). While the DCF approach often is more theoretically sound than the IRR approach (which can have multiple solutions), IRR is more widely used in LBO analyses, since investors find it more intuitively appealing. The IRR is the discount rate that equates the projected cash flows and terminal value with the initial equity investment[16] and enables investors to compare easily their expected return to their desired return (often 20% to 30%). The LBO model also requires the determination of whether there is sufficient future cash flow to operate the target firm while meeting interest and principal repayments and potentially paying dividends to the private equity investors. Financial buyers often attempt to determine the highest amount of debt possible (i.e., the borrowing capacity[17] of the target firm) to minimize their equity investment in order to maximize the IRR.

---

[16] $\text{NPV} = -\text{CF}_0 + \text{CF}_1/(1 + \text{IRR}) + \text{CF}_2/(1 + \text{IRR})^2 + \cdots + \text{CF}_N/(1 + \text{IRR})^N = 0.$

[17] *Borrowing capacity* is defined as the amount of debt a firm can borrow without materially increasing its cost of borrowing or violating loan covenants on existing debt while maintaining the ability to engage in future borrowing to satisfy unexpected liquidity requirements.

While analysts differ on the measure of cash flow to use in evaluating LBO opportunities, EBITDA is the common choice despite its shortcomings.[18] The target's enterprise value or purchase price commonly is estimated by multiplying an enterprise value multiple for comparable recent transactions by the target's EBITDA.[19] This equation can be expressed as follows:

$$EV_{TF} = (EV/EBITDA) \times EBITDA_{TF} \tag{14.6}$$

where

EV_{TF} = enterprise value (purchase price) of the target firm
$EBITDA_{TF}$ = target firm's earnings before interest, taxes, depreciation, and amortization
$EV/EBITDA$ = recent comparable LBO transaction enterprise value to EBITDA multiple

Once estimated, how the enterprise value (EV_{TF}) is financed in terms of debt and equity contributed by the financial sponsor can be shown as follows:

$$EV_{TF} = (D_{TF} + E_{TF}) \tag{14.7}$$

where

D_{TF} = net debt (i.e., total debt less cash and marketable securities held by the target firm)
E_{TF} = financial sponsor's equity contribution to the target firm's enterprise value

For a given enterprise value and level of net debt, we estimate the financial sponsor's initial equity contribution by solving Eq. (14.7) for E_{TF}. Net debt includes both the target firm's preacquisition debt (often refinanced after the buyout) and debt borrowed by the financial sponsor to finance the purchase price. Note how the target's cash and marketable securities can be used to pay for a portion of the deal. In summary, Eq. (14.6) estimates the enterprise value (purchase price) and Eq. (14.7) shows how it will be financed.

---

[18] Some analysts use EBITDA as a proxy for cash flow. EBITDA supporters argue that it represents a convenient proxy for the cash available to meet the cost (i.e., interest, depreciation, and amortization) of long-term assets. In essence, EBITDA provides a simple way of determining how long the firm can continue to service its debt without additional financing. EBITDA is not affected by the method the firm employs in depreciating its assets. EBITDA can be misleading because it ignores changes in working capital and implicitly assumes that capital expenditures needed to maintain the business are equal to depreciation. Free cash flow to the firm may be a better measure of how much cash a company is generating, since it includes changes in working capital and capital expenditures.

[19] By using the comparable recent transactions method to value the target firm, the analyst is implicitly including a purchase price premium in estimating the purchase price.

What follows is a simple five-step process employed to assess the attractiveness of a firm as a potential LBO target. Step 1 entails projecting a firm's future cash flows. Step 2 involves estimating the maximum borrowing capacity of the firm. Step 3 entails determining the firm's enterprise value or purchase price. Step 4 requires estimating the initial equity contribution to be made by the financial sponsor, which equals the difference between the enterprise value and the amount of the firm's maximum borrowing capacity.[20] Step 5 entails calculating the IRR on the financial sponsor's initial equity investment. The deal would make sense to the financial sponsor if the resulting IRR is equal to or greater than their target IRR.

Step 1: Project Cash Flows

To determine cash available for financing a target's future debt obligations, the analyst projects the firm's income statement, balance sheet, and cash flow statement. Projected cash flow in excess of the firm's operating requirements is used to satisfy principal and interest repayments.

Step 2: Determine the Firm's Borrowing Capacity

The firm's maximum borrowing capacity reflects both projected cash flows and assets that may be used for collateral and confirmed in discussions with potential lenders. Table 14.4 illustrates a simple model to estimate a firm's borrowing capacity using the information developed in Step 1. The estimate of borrowing capacity is expressed as a multiple of EBITDA. The model is divided into three panels: assumptions, estimating cash available for debt reduction, and estimating borrowing capacity. Year 0 represents the year immediately prior to the closing date (i.e., the beginning of year 1). The beginning debt figures are shown as of December 31 in year 0. Assume that, based on similar transactions, the analyst believes that a buyout firm will be able to borrow about 5.5 times EBITDA of $200 million (i.e., about $1.1 billion) and that the buyout firm has a target debt mix consisting of 75% senior debt and 25% subordinated debt. Assume investors in the buyout firm wish to exit the business within eight years once the senior debt has been repaid. The investors intend to use 100% of cash available for debt reduction to pay off senior debt, and the subordinated debt is payable as a balloon note beyond year 8.

Using a trial-and-error method, insert a starting value for senior debt of $800 million in year 0. This $800 million starting number is in line with the firm's assumed target debt mix (i.e., 0.75 × total potential borrowing of $1.1 billion is equal to about $800 million). Senior debt outstanding at the end of the eighth year is $75.7 million. If we now try $700 million in senior debt in year 0, the amount of senior debt outstanding at the end of the eighth year is $(63.3). Using the midpoint between $700 and $800 million, we insert $750 million for senior

[20] For example, if the buyer were planning on paying $50 million for a company using $25 million of senior debt and $15 million of mezzanine debt, the equity contribution would be $10 million (i.e., $50 − $25 − $15).

TABLE 14.4 Determining Borrowing Capacity

					Year				
ASSUMPTIONS	0	1	2	3	4	5	6	7	8
Sales Growth %	0	1.05	1.05	1.05	1.05	1.05	1.05	1.05	1.05
Cost of Sales (COS) as % of Sales	0.50	0.50	0.50	0.50	0.50	0.50	0.50	0.50	0.50
Sales, General and Admin. Exp. as % of Sales	0.10	0.10	0.10	0.10	0.10	0.10	0.10	0.10	0.10
Depreciation as % of Sales	0.03	0.03	0.03	0.03	0.03	0.03	0.03	0.03	0.03
Amortization as % of Sales	0.01	0.01	0.01	0.01	0.01	0.01	0.01	0.01	0.01
Interest on Cash and Marketable Securities %	0.03	0.03	0.03	0.03	0.03	0.03	0.03	0.03	0.03
Interest on Senior Debt %	0.07	0.07	0.07	0.07	0.07	0.07	0.07	0.07	0.07
Interest on Subordinated Debt %	0.09	0.09	0.09	0.09	0.09	0.09	0.09	0.09	0.09
Tax Rate	0.40	0.40	0.40	0.40	0.40	0.40	0.40	0.40	0.40
Cash & Marketable Securities as % Sales	0.01	0.01	0.01	0.01	0.01	0.01	0.01	0.01	0.01
Change in Working Capital as % of Sales	0.02	0.02	0.02	0.02	0.02	0.02	0.02	0.02	0.02
Capital Expenditures as % of Sales	0.03	0.03	0.03	0.03	0.03	0.03	0.03	0.03	0.03
CASH AVAILABLE FOR DEBT REDUCTION ($ MILLION)									
Sales	500.0	525.0	551.3	578.8	607.8	638.1	670.0	703.6	738.7
Less: Cost of Sales	250.0	262.5	275.6	289.4	303.9	319.1	335.0	351.8	369.4
Less: Sales, General Admin. Exp.	50.0	52.5	55.1	57.9	60.8	63.8	67.0	70.4	73.9
Equals: EBITDA	200.0	210.0	220.5	231.5	243.1	255.3	268.0	281.4	295.5
Less: Depreciation	15.0	15.8	16.5	17.4	18.2	19.1	20.1	21.1	22.2
Less: Amortization	5.0	5.3	5.5	5.8	6.1	6.4	6.7	7.0	7.4
Plus: Interest Income	0.2	0.2	0.2	0.2	0.2	0.2	0.2	0.2	0.2

TABLE 14.4 (Continued)

	Year								
CASH AVAILABLE FOR DEBT REDUCTION ($ MILLION)									
Less: Interest Expense									
Senior Debt		52.2	47.9	43.1	37.7	31.7	24.9	17.4	9.1
Subordinated Debt		27.0	27.0	27.0	27.0	27.0	27.0	27.0	27.0
Total Interest Expense		79.2	74.9	70.1	64.7	58.7	51.9	44.4	36.1
Equals: Income Before Tax		110.0	123.7	138.4	154.3	171.3	189.5	209.1	230.0
Less: Taxes Paid		44.0	49.5	55.4	61.7	68.5	75.8	83.6	92.0
Equals: Net Income After Tax		66.0	74.2	83.1	92.6	102.8	113.7	125.4	138.0
Plus: Depreciation and Amortization Expense		21.0	22.1	23.2	24.3	25.5	26.8	28.1	29.5
Less Change in Working Capital		10.5	11.0	11.6	12.2	12.8	13.4	14.1	14.8
Less Capital Expenditures		15.8	16.5	17.4	18.2	19.1	20.1	21.1	22.2
Equals: Cash Available for Debt Reduction		60.7	68.7	77.3	86.5	96.4	107.0	118.4	130.6
BORROWING CAPACITY									
Cash Balance	5.0	5.3	5.5	5.8	6.1	6.4	6.7	7.0	7.4
Senior Debt Outstanding at Year-End[a]	745.6	684.8	616.1	538.9	452.4	356.0	249.0	130.6	0.0
Subordinated Debt Outstanding at Year-End[b]	300.0	300.0	300.0	300.0	300.0	300.0	300.0	300.0	300.0
Total Debt	1,045.6	984.8	916.1	838.9	752.4	656.0	549.0	430.6	300.0
Net Debt to EBITDA Ratio	5.20	4.66	4.13	3.60	3.07	2.55	2.02	1.51	0.99
Interest Coverage (EBITDA/Net Interest Exp.)	0.00	2.66	2.95	3.31	3.77	4.37	5.18	6.36	8.23

[a] Assumes 100% of cash available for debt reduction is used to pay off senior debt.
[b] Subordinated debt payable as a balloon note in year 10.

debt in year 0, resulting in $6.2 million in remaining debt at the end of the eighth year. Additional fine-tuning results in a zero balance at the end of year 8 if we use a starting value of $745.6 million for senior debt. Consequently, the firm's maximum total debt (i.e., borrowing capacity) based on the assumptions underlying Table 14.4 is estimated at $1,045.6 million.

Step 3: Estimate the Target's Enterprise Value (Purchase Price)

Equation (14.6) provides an estimate of the target firm's enterprise value. Multiples may be adjusted up or down, depending on the perceived riskiness of future cash flows. Assume the financial sponsor believes that the appropriate enterprise-to-EBITDA multiple for the target firm's EBITDA following a review of recent comparable LBO deals is 7. From Eq. (14.6), the enterprise value for the target firm (EVTF) can be estimated as 7 × $210 (Year 1 EBITDA in Table 14.4), or $1,470 million.

Step 4: Estimate the Financial Sponsor's Initial Equity Contribution

Using the target firm's maximum borrowing capacity of $1,045.6 million determined in Step 2, and the $1,470 million enterprise value estimated in Step 3, we can solve Eq. (14.7) to estimate the financial sponsor's initial equity contribution as $424.4 million (i.e., $1,470 − $1,045.6).

Step 5: Analyze Financial Returns

The IRR calculation considers the initial equity investment in the firm and additional capital contributions as cash outflows and any dividends as cash inflows plus the exit or residual value of the business when sold. The financial multiple applied to the equity value on the exit date is usually the same as used by the financial sponsor when determining the target firm's preliminary valuation. The firm's equity value is the sale value on the exit date less the value of debt repaid and any transaction fees. Due to their high sensitivity to the multiple applied to exit-year cash flows and the number of years the investment is to be held, financial returns are usually displayed as a range reflecting different assumptions about exit multiples. If the calculated IRR is less than the target IRR, the financial sponsor can substitute lower enterprise values (purchase prices) into Eq. (14.7), as described in Step 3, resulting in lower initial capital contributions, and recalculate the IRR until it exceeds the target IRR or walk away from the target firm.

Standard LBO Formats Used in Building LBO Models

Once the financial sponsor finds an attractive LBO candidate, the target's financial statements are restated to reflect the firm's new capital structure. Table 14.5 summarizes the key elements of the analysis. The "Sources and Uses of Funds" section in the table shows how the transaction is to be financed. Representing total funds required, the "Uses" section shows where the cash will go and comprises payments to the target firm's owners, including cash, any

TABLE 14.5 Leveraged Buyout Model Output Summary

Sources (Cash Inflows) and Uses (Cash Outflows) of Funds:

Sources of Funds	Amount($)	Interest Rate (%)	Uses of Funds	Amt. ($)
Cash From Balance Sheet	$0.0	0.0%	Cash to Owners	$70.0
New Revolving Loan	$12.0	9.0%	Seller's Equity	$0.0
New Senior Debt	$20.0	9.0%	Seller's Note	$0.0
New Subordinated Debt	$15.0	12.0%	Excess Cash	$0.0
New Preferred Stock (PIK)	$22.0	12.0%	Paid to Owners	$70.0
New Common Stock	$3.0	0.0%	Debt Repayment	$0.0
			Buyer Expenses	$2.0
Total Sources	$72.0		Total Uses	$72.0

Pro Forma Capital Structure

Form of Debt and Equity	Market Value	% of Total Capital
Revolving Loan	$12.0	16.7%
Senior Debt	$20.0	27.8%
Subordinated Debt	$15.0	20.8%
Total Debt	$47.0	65.3%
Preferred Equity	$22.0	30.6%
Common Equity	$3.0	4.2%
Total Equity	$25.0	34.7%
Total Capital	$72.0	

Fully Diluted Ownership Distribution

Equity Investment	Ownership Distribution ($)			% Distribution			Fully Diluted Ownership Distribution				
	Common	Preferred	Total	Common	Preferred	Preoption Ownership	Common	Warrants	Preoption Ownership	Perform. Options	Fully Dil. Ownership
Equity Investor	1.5	22.0	23.5	50.0%	100.0%	50.0%	50.0%	0.0%	50.0%	0.0%	50.0%
Management	1.5	0.0	1.5	50.0%	0.0%	50.0%	50.0%	0.0%	50.0%	0.0%	50.0%
Total Equity Investment	$3.0	$22.0	$25.0	100.0%	100.0%	100.0%	100.0%	0.0%	100.0%	0.0%	100.0%

Internal Rates of Return

Internal Rates of Return	Total Investor Return (%)			Equity Investor Investment Gain ($)			Management Investment Gain ($)		
	2017	2018	2019	2017	2018	2019	2017	2018	2019
	5 Years	6 Years	7 Years	5 Years	6 Years	7 Years	5 Years	6 Years	7 Years
Multiple of Adjusted Equity Cash Flow for 5-, 6-, and 7-Yr. Holding Periods									
8 × Terminal-Yr. CF	0.42	0.35	0.33	$66.6	$78.9	$96.0	$4.3	$5.0	$6.1
9 × Terminal-Yr. CF	0.46	0.39	0.35	$73.8	$86.6	$104.5	$4.7	$5.5	$6.7
10 × Terminal-Yr. CF	0.51	0.42	0.37	$81.0	$94.2	$113.0	$5.2	$6.0	$7.2

Financial Projections and Analysis	Historical Period			Forecast Period						
	2010	2011	2012	2013	2014	2015	2016	2017	2018	2019
NetSales	$177.6	$183.5	$190.4	$197.1	$205.0	$214.2	$223.8	$233.9	$244.4	$255.4
Annual Growth Rate	4.2%	3.3%	3.8%	3.5%	4.0%	4.5%	4.5%	4.5%	4.5%	4.5%
EBIT as % of Net Revenue	5.5%	1.3%	5.1%	8.5%	9.5%	10.2%	11.2%	11.4%	11.4%	11.4%
Adjusted Enterprise Cash Flow[a]	$4.2	$0.2	$0.1	$9.5	$9.6	$10.8	$13.0	$13.4	$14.2	$14.9
Adjusted Equity Cash Flow[b]	$4.2	$0.2	$0.1	$0.3	$0.2	$1.8	$7.4	$7.7	$8.1	$8.5
Total Debt Outstanding	0	0	$47.0	$39.5	$31.5	$23.8	$19.2	$14.3	$8.8	$2.7
Total Debt/Adjusted Enterprise Cash Flow	0.0	0.0	NA	4.1	3.3	2.2	1.5	1.1	0.6	0.2
EBIT/Interest Expense	0	0	0	3.6	4.9	6.6	10.1	13.3	18.6	30.9
PV of Adjusted Equity Cash Flow @ 26%	$57.2									
PV of 2004-2010 Adj. Equity CF/Terminal Value	28.1%									

[a]EBIT(1 − t) + Depreciation and Amortization − Gross Capital Spending − Change in Working Capital − Change in Investments Available for Sale
[b]Net Income + Depreciation and Amortization − Gross Capital Spending − Change in Working Capital − Principal Repayments − Change in Investments Available for Sale (i.e., increases in such investments are a negative cash flow entry but represent cash in excess of normal operating needs.)

equity retained by the seller, any seller's notes, and any excess cash retained by the sellers. The "Uses" section also contains the refinancing of any existing debt on the balance sheet of the target firm and any transaction fees. The "Sources" section describes various sources of financing, including new debt, any existing cash that is being used to finance the transaction, and the common and preferred equity being contributed by the financial sponsor. The equity contribution represents the difference between uses and all other sources of financing. It is a "plug" adjustment and represents the amount the financial sponsor must contribute in addition to the borrowed funds to finance the purchase price fully. The "Pro Forma Capital Structure" section provides the percent distribution of the firm's capital structure among the various types of debt and equity. The "Equity Ownership" section illustrates the distribution of ownership between the financial sponsor and management. The "Internal Rates of Return" section provides the projected financial returns in both percentages and dollar amounts for three potential exit years as well as the multiple applied to the exit-year's cash flow. The final segment, entitled "Financial Projections and Analysis," provides summarized income, cash flow, and balance-sheet data.

The pro forma Excel-based balance sheet contained on the LBO model on the companion website reflects changes to the existing balance sheet of the target firm altered to reflect the new capital structure of the firm. Shareholders' equity is dramatically reduced immediately following closing due to the large reduction in paid-in capital.[21] The new balance sheet also reflects the goodwill resulting from the excess of the purchase price over the fair market value of the net acquired assets and any interest expense that can be capitalized under current accounting rules. The balance-sheet projections are based on the pro forma balance sheet, with the debt outstanding and interest expense reflecting the repayment schedules associated with each type of debt. The model also reflects a projected sale value on the assumed exit date. The internal rates of return represent the average annual compounded rate at which the financial sponsor's equity investment grows, assuming no dividend payments or additional equity contributions.

SOME THINGS TO REMEMBER

Common ways of valuing highly leveraged deals include the cost of capital (CC) method and the adjusted present value (APV) method. While the first method is more complicated, APV requires the estimation of the cost and probability of financial distress for highly leveraged firms. LBO models are employed when there is the potential for a financial buyer to acquire a business.

---

[21] The target firm's shareholders' equity often becomes negative following an LBO because the buyout of the firm's shareholders increases treasury stock, which is deducted from shareholders' equity for financial-reporting purposes.

DISCUSSION QUESTIONS

14.1 The adjusted present value model is based on the notion that the value of a firm can be divided into the present value of the firm's cash flows to equity investors plus the present value of the tax shield. What is the critical assumption underlying this premise? In your view, under what circumstances might this assumption not be practical?

14.2 How should the adjusted present value method be modified when it is applied to highly leveraged transactions?

14.3 What is the cost of financial distress? Be specific.

14.4 What does the APV valuation implicitly assume that makes its results highly problematic in valuing highly leveraged businesses?

14.5 What is a firm's tax shield, and how can it be estimated?

14.6 What are the primary advantages and disadvantages of using the cost of capital and adjusted present value methods to value highly leveraged transactions?

14.7 Investment bankers sometimes value firms using LBO analyses in addition to conventional DCF and relative-valuation methods. Under what circumstances does it make sense to employ a leveraged buyout analysis as one means of valuing a firm?

14.8 In what way is a conventional DCF analysis similar to a leveraged buyout analysis of a target and in what ways are they different?

14.9 How may a firm's borrowing capacity be defined?

14.10 The internal rate of return is a crucial decision variable for LBO investors. What are the critical assumptions that must be made in its calculation?

Answers to these Chapter Discussion Questions are available in the Online Instructor's Manual for instructors using this book.

QUESTIONS FROM THE CFA CURRICULUM

14.11 The market value of equity can be calculated as enterprise value:
  a. Minus market value of debt, preferred stock, and short-term investments
  b. Plus market value of debt, preferred stock, and short-term investments
  c. Minus market value of debt and preferred stock plus short-term investments
  Source: CFA Institute 2011 Equity Valuation: Concepts and Basic Tools, Reading 60, question 28.

14.12 Westcott-Smith is a privately held investment management company. Two other investment counseling companies, which want to be acquired, have contacted Westcott-Smith about purchasing their business. Company A's price is $2 million. Company B's price is $3 million. After analysis, Westcott-Smith estimates that Company A's profitability is consistent with a perpetuity of $300,000 a year and Company B's prospects are consistent with a perpetuity of $435,000 per year. Westcott-Smith has a budget that limits acquisitions to a maximum purchase cost of $4 million. Its opportunity cost of capital relative to undertaking either project is 12%.

    a. Determine which company or companies (if any) Westcott-Smith should purchase according to the NPV rule.

    b. Determine which company or companies (if any) Westcott-Smith should purchase according to the IRR rule.

    c. State which company or companies (if any) Westcott-Smith should purchase. Justify your answer.

Source: CFA Institute, 2011, Discounting Cash Flow Applications, Reading 6, question 5.

Answers to questions from the CFA curriculum are available in the Online Student Companion site to this book in a file folder entitled CFA Curriculum Questions and Solutions.

PRACTICE PROBLEMS

14.13 Assume that, based on similar transactions, an analyst believes that a buyout firm will be able to borrow about 5.5 times first-year EBITDA of $200 million (i.e., about $1.1 billion) and that the buyout firm has a target senior-to-subordinated debt split of 75% to 25%. Further assume that investors in the buyout firm wish to exit the business within eight years after having repaid all of the senior debt. To accomplish this objective, the investors intend to use 100% of cash available for debt reduction to pay off senior debt, and the subordinated debt is payable as a balloon note beyond year 8. Using the scenario in the template "Excel-Based Model to Estimate Firm Borrowing Capacity" on the companion website as the base case, answer the following questions.

    a. Will the buyout firm be able to exit its investment by the eighth year if sales grow at 3%, rather than the 5% assumed in the base case, and still satisfy the assumptions in the base-case scenario? After rerunning the model using the lower sales growth rate, what does this tell you about the model's sensitivity to relatively small changes in assumptions?

    b. How does this slower sales growth scenario affect the amount the buyout firm could borrow initially if the investors still want to exit the business by the eighth year after paying off 100% of the senior debt and maintain the same senior-to-subordinated debt split?

14.14 By some estimates, as many as one-fourth of the LBOs between 1987 and 1990 (the first mega-LBO boom) went bankrupt. The data in Table 14.6 illustrate the extent of the leverage associated with the largest completed LBOs of 2006 and 2007 (the most recent mega-LBO boom). Equity Office Properties and Alltel have been sold. Use the data given in Table 14.6 to calculate the equity contribution made by the buyout

TABLE 14.6   Top-Ten Completed Buyouts of 2006 and 2007 Ranked by Deal Enterprise Value

Target	Bidder(s)	Enterprise Value (EV) ($ Billion)	Net Debt % of EV	Equity % of EV	Value of Equity ($ Billion)	Interest Coverage[a] Ratio
TXU	KKR, TPG, Goldman Sachs	43.8	89.5	?	?	1
Equity Office Properties	Blackstone	38.9	Sold	NA	NA	Sold
HCA	Bain, KKR, Merrill Lynch	32.7	82.4	?	?	1.6
Alltel	TPG, Goldman Sachs	27.9	Sold	NA	NA	Sold
First Data	KKR	27.7	79.2	?	?	1
Harrah's Entertainment	TPG, Apollo	27.4	83.7	?	?	0.8
Hilton Hotels	Blackstone	25.8	75.9	?	?	1.1
Alliance Boots	KKR	20.8	83.5	?	?	1.1
Freescale Semiconductor	Blackstone, Permira, Carlyle, TPG	17.6	49.6	?	?	1.6
Intelsat	BC Partners	16.4	88.9	?	?	1
Average		27.9	81	?	?	1

Source: The Economist, *July 2008, p. 85.*
[a]*EBITDA less capital expenditures divided by estimated interest expense.*

firms as a percent of enterprise value and the dollar value of their equity contribution. What other factors would you want to know in evaluating the likelihood that these LBOs will end up in bankruptcy?

A solution to these problems is available in the Online Instructor's Manual for instructors using this book.

CASE STUDY 14.1
Immucor is Acquired by TPG Capital

Key Points

- Two-stage tender offers coupled with a top-up option increase both

the speed and the certainty of closing.

- Holding company structures commonly are used in leveraged

buyouts because of the potential risk associated with such transactions.

- It is especially critical to assess the credibility of assumptions underlying projected financial performance in highly leveraged transactions.

Investment bank Goldman Sachs had been hired to conduct an auction for the sale of Immucor, Inc., after the firm's board had analyzed strategic alternatives for the firm, ranging from maintaining the firm as a stand-alone business to strategic alliances to the outright sale of the firm. What follows is a description of how the firm was taken private by a well-known private equity company, ending years as a publicly traded firm.

Immucor, Inc., a Georgia corporation, develops, manufactures, and sells reagents and automated systems used by blood banks, hospitals, and reference laboratories for testing blood to determine its suitability for blood transfusions. As the leading supplier of such products, the firm has a 55% market share, a 39% operating profit margin (the highest in the industry), and a sustainable and predictable cash flow. Nevertheless, there were signs in 2010 that something had to change. While an aging population would increase the number of transfusions, intensifying customer price resistance could moderate drastically the firm's future sales growth. Developing new, more cost-effective products would require significant future spending in research and development. Annual revenue in the fiscal year ending in May 2011 topped out at $330 million,

only $1 million more than the prior year, after several years of sluggish growth. The firm's share price had underperformed the overall stock market since 2008.

Following a nine-month auction process in which a dozen firms and investment groups expressed interest in bidding on Immucor, the firm reduced the number of bids it would consider to two finalists. On May 17, 2011, TPG, a well-known private equity buyout fund, submitted a nonbinding, preliminary indication of interest reflecting a purchase price in cash of $25.00 to $27.00 per share, subject to more detailed due diligence. While the price was attractive to Immucor's board, other deal issues remained.

These issues included Immucor's desire for a dual, or two-tiered, tender offer and one-step merger coupled with a top-up option to provide greater speed and assurance of closing. Subject to the merger agreement, Immucor would grant to TPG an irrevocable top-up option to purchase at the offer price the number of shares it needed to own at least 90% of Immucor's outstanding shares on a fully diluted basis. Immucor also wanted a "go shop" provision of up to six weeks to determine if other firms might be willing to make an offer and for TPG to agree to a reverse breakup fee of $85 million if it could not complete the deal, regardless of the reason. Moreover, Immucor wanted TPG to withdraw its demand for Immucor to reimburse TPG's merger-related expenses up to $25 million. Other issues related to closing conditions, termination rights, and the definition of what constituted a "material adverse change." In addition, Immucor insisted on TPG's agreeing to a "hell or high water" standard on all antitrust regulatory approvals in an effort to minimize regulator risk. Such a standard effectively forces the buyer to pay the reverse termination fee if for any reason antitrust approval cannot be obtained.

On July 1, 2011, Immucor and TPG announced that they had reached agreement, in which TPG would offer $27 per share in an all-cash deal valued at $1.97 billion. The firm's stock jumped $6.26, or 30%, on the news. The merger agreement also included a $90 million breakup fee for either firm if either one could not or chose not to close. The $1.97 billion is the amount necessary to purchase all of the issued and outstanding Immucor shares, to repay the Immucor's outstanding debt, to pay all transaction-related fees, and to finance the firm's working capital. Lenders JPMorgan Chase and Citibank agreed to supply $1.28 billion in debt financing, consisting of a $650 million senior secured loan facility, $500 million in a senior unsecured bridge loan facility, and a $130 million senior secured revolving loan facility. TPG would supply $690 million as an equity contribution. The debt and equity financing would be provided at closing. Enterprise value multiples for transactions of comparable businesses had been averaging about 11.5 times EBITDA during the preceding two years.

Parties to the merger agreement included Immucor, IVD Holdings Inc., and IVD Acquisitions Corp. (Figure 14.1). IVD Holdings Inc., a Delaware corporation, is a shell corporation formed solely for the purpose of acquiring Immucor, completing the transaction outlined in the merger agreement, and arranging financing. IVD Holdings Inc.,'s parent is an affiliate of TPG Partners VI, a limited liability partnership managed by TPG. TPG Partners VI provides the funds that will be used by IVD holdings to make its equity contribution. IVD Acquisition Corporation, a Georgia corporation, was formed by IVD Holdings Inc., for the sole purpose of entering into the merger agreement and completing the merger. Following a tender offer to acquire Immucor's outstanding shares, IVD Acquisitions Corp was merged into Immucor, with Immucor surviving as a wholly owned subsidiary of IVD Holdings Inc.

Table 14.7 provides abbreviated income and cash flow statements. Operating profit margins are essentially held constant at about 38% throughout the five-year forecast period. The projected cash available for debt repayment is a critical projection because it provides an implicit margin of safety in terms of Immucor's ability to repay its debt incurred as a result of going private.

Discussion Questions

1. Do you believe Immucor was an attractive candidate for a leveraged buyout? Explain your answer.
2. What is the purpose of the top-up option?

3. Why does TPG contribute cash rather than lend the money to IVD Acquisitions Corporation?

4. Why is Immucor merged with an acquisition subsidiary, IVD Acquisitions Corporation, and not with IVD Holdings?

5. Do you believe that TPG may have overpaid for Immucor? Explain your answer.

6. Accelerating revenue growth is the primary driver of cash available for debt repayment. Explain why cash available for debt repayment may be overstated in the projected cash flow statement.

7. What is the purpose of the bridge and revolving loan facilities?

8. What type of a merger is described in Figure 14.1? In this type of merger, which is the surviving entity, Immucor or IVD Acquisitions Corporation? Why is it structured this way?

9. Is this transaction likely to be taxable or nontaxable to pre-buyout Immucor shareholders? Is Immucor post-buyout likely to be paying much in the way of taxes during the several years following closing? Explain your answer.

A solution to this case study is provided in the Online Instructors Manual for instructors using this book.

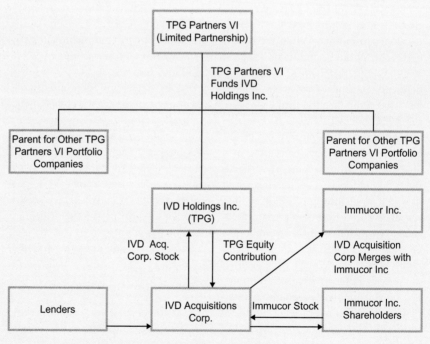

FIGURE 14.1   **Immucor merger and financing structure.**

TABLE 14.7   Immucor Pro Forma Financial Projections

	FY2012 Est.	FY2013 Est.	FY2014 Est.	FY2015 Est.	FY2016 Est.
ABBREVIATED INCOME STATEMENT ($ MILLIONS)					
Revenue	344.7	368.2	395.6	421.9	450.9
EBIT	128	138.1	151.6	163.2	175.9
EBITDA	147.1	159.1	174.6	188.2	203.0
ABBREVIATED CASH FLOW STATEMENT ($ MILLIONS)					
Cash from Operations	87.6	94.7	106.9	121.7	132.7
Cash from Investing	(12.1)	(12.9)	(13.8)	(14.8)	(15.8)
Cash Available for Debt Repayment	75.5	81.8	93.1	106.9	116.9

Source: Securities and Exchange Commission Form PRER14A Preliminary Proxy Statement

CASE STUDY 14.2
HCA Goes Public…Again!

Key Points

- LBOs create value for equity investors through a combination of leverage, tax savings, improving operating performance, and properly timing when investors "cash out."
- LBO leverage and valuation multiples are often measured relative to EBITDA.
- When financial sponsors exit LBOs, the firm's shareholders' equity often is negative.
- HCA's successful IPO in 2011 seems more a result of the ebullient equity market than its improved operating performance.

Hospital Corporation of America (HCA), the biggest for-profit hospital chain in the United States, has a history of going private through leveraged buyouts (Table 14.8). The firm initially went private in 1989. When it went public in 1992, its backers were well rewarded. While HCA's share price doubled (not including stock splits) between the 1992 IPO and 2006, HCA executives, frustrated as the rate of share price appreciation failed to keep pace with gains in cash flow, share buybacks, and increasing dividends, decided to go private again in 2006. The recovery in the equity markets in 2011 encouraged the firm and its financial backers to undertake an IPO again.

Despite an enthusiastic investor response to the March 11, 2011, initial public offering, HCA faces significant future risks. While the expansion of healthcare coverage to 32 million Americans beginning in 2014 will increase potential revenue, the growing reliance on government

TABLE 14.8   HCA Transaction TimeLine

1989	HCA goes private in an LBO valued at $5.1 billion.
1992	HCA goes public, with investors increasing the value of their initial investment eightfold.
2006	HCA goes private in a highly leveraged transaction valued at $33 billion. Private equity investors contribute 23% of the purchase price for HCA and borrowed the remainder.
2007–2010	HCA cuts costs and improves annual EBITDA cash flow growth from 5% in 2006 to 7% in 2010.
2010	HCA uses improving cash flows to issue $4.3 billion of dividends to owners, recovering nearly all of their initial $4.9 billion investment in 2006 and making any future gains nearly all profit.
2011	HCA goes public, selling 18% of its shares to new shareholders and raising $3.9 billion. Of this total, $2.7 billion is retained by HCA; the remaining $1.2 billion is paid to private equity investors.

reimbursement (currently 41% of total revenue) is likely to pressure profit margins. Reimbursement rates to providers will be squeezed due to pressures to restrain growth in Medicare and Medicaid expenditures.

The private equity investors in this deal appear to have timed the market perfectly. When HCA filed in May 2010 to go public, U.S. IPOs were faltering. During the first four months of 2010, IPO deals raised on average 13% less than expected. Rather than proceed in such an uncertain climate with an IPO, the owners paid themselves $4.3 billion in dividends through a so-called dividend recapitalization, in which a firm borrows to pay a dividend to shareholders. By delaying the IPO until early 2011, the LBO investors and the founding Frist family more than tripled their initial investment.

Table 14.9 illustrates the extent to which this delay in implementing the IPO affected valuation. Enterprise value can be estimated by multiplying EBITDA by the enterprise-to-EBITDA multiple for similar firms. By using HCA's 2010 EBITDA to estimate the firm's enterprise value in both early 2010 and early 2011, we can estimate the increase in enterprise value due to an increase in the multiple only. The approximate 12-month delay resulted in a $15.2 billion (51%) increase in the firm's valuation.

See Table 14.10 for an illustration of the firm's complex capital structure shortly before the March 8, 2011, IPO. The capital structure is tiered to reflect the priority of creditor claims on the firm's assets in liquidation and consists of senior secured first lien (claim) debt, senior secured second lien (claim) debt, and unsecured debt. The wide variation in effective interest rates reflects the variation in the maturity of the loans and whether they have a first or a second claim on assets in the event of liquidation.

Credit facilities refer to lending arrangements such as revolving credit and term loans. The senior credit facilities contain a number of covenants designed to protect lenders restricting HCA's ability to incur additional indebtedness, repay subordinated indebtedness, create liens on assets, sell assets, make investments or loans, pay dividends, and enter into sale and leaseback transactions. In addition, HCA must maintain a maximum total-leverage ratio covenant under the cash flow credit facility and a minimum interest-coverage ratio. Senior second lien debt consists of both cash-pay and payment in kind (PIK) toggle loans. *Cash-pay notes* are loans whose interest is paid in cash, in contrast to *toggle PIK loans*, whose interest may be paid either in cash or in kind (i.e., distributions consist of more debt). So-called "toggle" notes are those that allow the borrower to switch from paying cash to making "in-kind" payments. This feature allows the issuers to reduce cash interest payments if necessary.

HCA and its financial backers have a history of undertaking highly leveraged transactions with complex capital structures. HCA had been taken private on July 24, 2006, amid a frenzy of LBOs in a deal valued at $33 billion, including $11.7 billion in assumed debt. The approximate $21.3 billion purchase price for HCA's stock (i.e., $33 billion less $11.7 billion) was financed by a $4.9 billion capital contribution and $16.4 billion in debt of varying maturities. HCA also took out a $4 billion revolving credit line to satisfy immediate working capital requirements. Of the $4.9 billion equity contribution, Bain and KKR

(Kohlberg, Kravis, and Roberts) each invested $1.2 billion. Merrill Lynch (now owned by Bank of America), Citigroup, and Bank of America contributed $1.5 billion. The company cofounder, Thomas Frist Jr., provided $950 million (consisting mostly of his holdings of HCA shares), with the remainder coming from 1,400 other HCA executives. Merrill Lynch, Citigroup, and Bank of America also were lenders in the transaction to take HCA private. Under the Dodd-Frank Act of 2010, lenders are now prohibited from also investing in such transactions.

While most LBOs are predicated on improving operating performance (i.e., profit margins) through a combination of aggressive cost cutting and revenue growth, HCA laid out an unconventional approach in its effort to take the firm private. The firm's publicly announced strategy was to improve performance through growth rather than through cost cutting. With the highest operating profit margins in the industry, it appeared that HCA's cash flows could not be improved significantly by cost cutting. Revenue growth at the firm's network of 182 hospitals and 94 surgery centers was expected to benefit from an aging U.S. population and the resulting increase in healthcare spending.

As of December 31, 2006, immediately after the LBO, the firm's leverage, as measured by the ratio of total debt to EBITDA, was 6.7. By year-end 2010, the debt to EBITDA had dropped to 5.1. Most of the reduction in leverage during that four-year period was accomplished through growth in EBITDA, which grew by about $1.7 billion, or 33%, to $5.6 billion in 2010, versus $4.2 billion in 2006. This improvement in operating performance was accomplished through an expansion of profitable hospital service lines, divestiture of some underperforming hospitals, and more aggressive collection of receivables, which reduced bad debt expense. HCA announced that it would use a portion of the $2.6 billion proceeds from the IPO to lower the debt-to-EBITDA ratio to 4.4, which is consistent with its publicly traded peers.

Discussion Questions

1. The private equity investors in HCA decided in 2010 to declare dividends totaling $4.3 billion financed with HCA borrowings. Presumably, if the additional borrowing had not taken place, the firms' leverage would have been lower prior to the IPO in March 2011 and the potential IPO share price could have been higher. If you were a private equity fund manager, would you have decided to pay a dividend or to have allowed HCA's leverage to decline further in anticipation of the IPO?

2. Based on what you know about HCA and the outlook for the U.S. healthcare industry, in what sense do you believe HCA was an attractive LBO candidate and in what sense was it not? Be specific.

3. Critics of LBOs often argue that such transactions contribute little to society and serve only to enrich the financial sponsor. Do you agree or disagree with this statement? Support your conclusion.

4. HCA had a negative shareholders' equity at the end of 2010 of $(11.93) billion, just prior to the IPO, making the firm technically insolvent. Nonetheless, the investor response to the IPO was highly enthusiastic. Why do you believe this was the case?

5. Assume you are a private equity investor responsible for designing the optimal capital structure for a firm you intend to acquire through a leveraged buyout. What factors would you take into consideration in constructing the optimal capital structure? Be specific.

A solution to this case study is provided in the Online Instructors Manual for instructors using this book.

TABLE 14.9   Increase in HCA Enterprise Value Due to Timing of the IPO

YEAR-END 2009	
EBITDA[a]	$ 5.63 billon
Enterprise/EBITDA Multiple[b]	5.29 ×
Enterprise Value	$ 29.78 billion

TABLE 14.9 Increase in HCA Enterprise Value Due to Timing of the IPO

YEAR-END 2010

EBITDA[a]	$ 5.63 billion
Enterprise/EBITDA Multiple[c]	7.99 ×
Enterprise Value	$44.98
Increase in Enterprise Value by Undertaking IPO in 2011 Rather Than 2010	$15.2 billion

[a]EBITDA for 2010. Source: Yahoo Finance.
[b]Average enterprise/EBITDA multiples for Community Health Systems, Trust Health Corporation, Universal Health Services, Health Management Associates, Life Point Hospitals, Rehabcare Group, Medcath Corp., and Sunlink Health Systems.
[c]Source: Yahoo Finance.

TABLE 14.10 Consolidated HCA Long-Term Debt as of 12/31/2010 ($ Millions)

Senior Secured Asset–Based Revolving Credit Facility (Effective Interest Rate = 1.5%)	$1.88
Senior Secured Revolving Credit Facility (Effective Interest Rate = 1.8%)	729
Senior Secured Term Loan Facilities (Effective Interest Rate = 6.9%)	7,530
Senior Secured First Lien Notes (Effective Interest Rate = 8.4%)	4,075
Other Senior Secured Debt (Effective Interest Rate = 7.1%)	322
Total First Lien Debt	**14,531**
Senior Secured Cash-Pay Notes (Effective Interest Rate of 9.7%)	4,501
Senior Secured Toggle Notes (Effective Interest Rate of 10%)	1,578
Second Lien Debt	**6,079**
Senior Unsecured Notes (Effective Interest Rate = 7.1%)	7,615
Total Debt (Average Life of 6.1 years, rates averaging 7.3%)	**28,225**
Less Amounts Due Within One Year	592
Total Long-Term Debt	**$27,633**

ALTERNATIVE BUSINESS AND RESTRUCTURING STRATEGIES

"Ms. Collins, have someone find out if I made my fortune taking companies public or taking them private."

Courtesy of www.Cartoonstock.com. BMA 235-SH

The preceding sections of this book dealt primarily with mergers and acquisitions as a means of fueling corporate growth within a specific country. Part V addresses alternative strategic options for growth, including cross-border M&A transactions and business alliances. This section also discusses what can be done if corporations believe that more value can be created by exiting certain businesses or product lines or by reorganizing or liquidating either outside of or under the protection of the bankruptcy court.

Chapter 15 outlines the common motives for entering business alliances, ranging from minority investments to joint ventures as alternatives to mergers and acquisitions, as well as the critical success factors for establishing alliances, alternative legal forms, and ways of resolving common deal-structuring issues. Common exit strategies or restructuring strategies are discussed in Chapters 16 and 17. Chapter 16 describes how corporations choose from among a range of restructuring options, including divestitures, spin-offs, split-ups, equity carve-outs, and split-offs to improve shareholder value.

Chapter 17 focuses on failing firms that may attempt to preserve shareholder value by negotiating voluntarily with creditors to restructure their outstanding debt outside of bankruptcy court; alternatively, such firms may choose or be compelled to seek the protection of the court system. Chapter 17 also describes methodologies for predicting corporate default or bankruptcy and how to value failing businesses. Finally, Chapter 18 outlines common motives for international expansion, describes widely used international market–entry strategies, and how to value, structure, and finance cross-border transactions.

Business Alliances
Joint Ventures, Partnerships, Strategic Alliances, and Licensing

Humility is not thinking less of you. It is thinking less about you.—**Rick Warren**

INSIDE M&A: EXXON-MOBIL AND RUSSIA'S ROSNEFT CREATE ARCTIC OIL AND GAS EXPLORATION JOINT VENTURE

KEY POINTS

- Contractual commitments in cross-border alliances are effective only to the extent they are enforced by each country's legal system.
- The success of most alliances ultimately depends on the extent to which each partner needs the capabilities and resources of the other.

Exxon-Mobil (Exxon) finalized an agreement with the government-owned Russian oil and gas giant Rosneft on April 16, 2012, to create a joint venture to explore for oil and gas in three designated areas in the Russian portion of the Arctic Ocean known as the Kara Sea. The agreement superseded a similar but failed agreement with British Petroleum (BP) earlier in the year. Rosneft's attempt to strike a similar pact with BP in 2011 fell apart because the British company had a joint venture with a separate group of private Russian investors, which blocked the Rosneft deal in an international court. While BP had planned to swap stock, Exxon agreed to give Rosneft assets elsewhere in the world, including some that Exxon owns in the deep waters of the Gulf of Mexico and in Texas. Future investments could total tens of billions of dollars. The final agreement was contingent on Russia's reducing taxes imposed on oil and gas companies.

The U.S. Geological Survey estimates that the Arctic holds one-fifth of the world's undiscovered, recoverable oil and natural gas. The Kara Sea has an estimated 36 billion barrels of recoverable oil reserves. Total oil and gas reserves are estimated to be 110 billion barrels of oil equivalent, four times Exxon's proven worldwide reserves. Drilling is expected to start in 2015, with Exxon shouldering most of the costs. In exchange for access to these Rosneft properties, the agreement gives Rosneft an option to invest in certain U.S. properties. Rosneft will own two-thirds and Exxon the remainder of the joint venture. The initial commitment by the two companies is to invest $3.2 billion in exploration in the Kara Sea.

As a world leader in Arctic exploration, Exxon is willing to share its expertise with Rosneft, as well as to transfer technology, in exchange for access to Russia's Arctic region. The Russians are particularly interested in learning the latest techniques employed in hydraulic fracturing (so-called fracking) of underground oil and gas deposits trapped in shale rock. This deal also allows the Russian petroleum industry to diversify internationally. While Russia currently pumps more oil than Saudi Arabia, its onshore oil fields are in decline, threatening a major source of Russian export revenue. Furthermore, Rosneft receives an option to acquire an equity interest in certain Exxon projects in North America, including deep-water drilling in the Gulf of Mexico and fields in Texas. In addition, Rosneft will have an opportunity to invest in Exxon properties and projects outside of the United States. Granting Rosneft options to invest in certain Exxon assets was an important precondition for getting agreement on the joint venture.

The Russian government had long demanded reciprocity as part of any deal. This required that in exchange for any ownership in Russian assets, the Russian partner should have the opportunity to invest in assets owned by the other partner. The value of the assets Rosneft would own in the United States would be in proportion to those Exxon would own in Russia. The agreement is risky, in view of Russia's history of reneging on deals with Western oil companies. For example, in 2006, it compelled Royal Dutch Shell to sell 50% of a Sakhalin offshore property to state-owned Gazprom after Shell had spent more than $20 billion of its own money and that of other investors to build the project's infrastructure.

CHAPTER OVERVIEW

What all business alliances have in common is that they generally involve sharing the risk, reward, and control among all participants. The term *business alliance* is used throughout this chapter to describe the various forms of cooperative relationships common in business today, including joint ventures, partnerships, strategic alliances, equity partnerships, licensing agreements, and franchise alliances. The primary theme of this chapter is that well-constructed business alliances often represent viable alternatives to mergers and acquisitions, and they always should be considered one of the many options for achieving strategic business objectives.

The principal differences in the various types of business alliances were discussed in some detail in Chapter 1 and are therefore only summarized in Table 15.1. This chapter discusses the wide variety of motives for business alliances and the factors common to most successful alliances. Also addressed are the advantages and disadvantages of alternative legal structures, important deal-structuring issues, and empirical studies that purport to measure the contribution of business alliances to creating shareholder wealth. A review of this chapter (including practice questions and answers) is available in the file folder entitled "Student Study Guide" on the companion website (*http://booksite.elsevier.com/9780123854872*) to this book.

MOTIVATIONS FOR BUSINESS ALLIANCES

Money alone rarely provides for a successful long-term business alliance. A partner often can obtain funding from a variety of sources but may be able to obtain access to a set of skills or nonfinancial resources only from another party. The motivations for an alliance vary widely and are discussed next.

Risk Sharing

Risk often is perceived to be greater, the more money, management time, or other resources a company has committed to an endeavor and the less certain the outcome. To mitigate perceived risk, companies often enter into alliances to gain access to know-how and scarce resources or to reduce the amount of resources they would have to commit if they were to do it on their own. For example, in late 2004, General Motors and DaimlerChrysler, the largest and fifth-largest auto manufacturers in the world, respectively, agreed to jointly develop hybrid gasoline–electric engines for cars and light trucks. Neither corporation felt comfortable in assuming the full cost and risk associated with developing this new automotive technology. Moreover, each company was willing to contribute the results of its own internal R&D efforts to the joint development of a technology to be shared by the two companies.[1]

Sharing Proprietary Knowledge

Given the pace at which technology changes, the risk is high that a competitor will be able to develop a superior technology before a firm can bring its own new technology to market. Consequently, high-technology companies with expertise in a specific technology often combine their efforts with those of another company or companies with complementary know-how, to reduce the risk of failing to develop the "right" technology. Such alliances often do result in knowledge sharing between alliance partners. For example, Chinese battery maker BYD Ltd. and German automaker Daimler AG, a leader in electric car

---

[1] Gomes-Casseres et al., 2006

TABLE 15.1   Key Differences Among Business Alliances

Type	Key Characteristics
Joint Ventures	• Independent legal entity involving two or more parties • May be organized as a corporation, partnership, or other legal/business organization selected by the parties • Ownership, responsibilities, risks, and rewards allocated to parties • Each party retains corporate identity and autonomy • Created by parties contributing assets for a specific purpose and for a limited duration
Strategic Alliances (e.g., technology transfer, R&D sharing, and cross-marketing)	• Do not involve the formation of separate legal entities • May be precursor to a joint venture, partnership, or acquisition • Generally not passive, but involve cross-training, coordinated product development, and long-term contracts based on performance metrics such as product quality rather than price
Equity Partnerships	• Have all the characteristics of an alliance • Involve making minority investment in the other party (e.g., 5% to 10%) • Minority investor may have an option to buy a larger stake in the other party
Licensing – Product – Process – Merchandise and Trademark	• Patent, trademark, or copyright licensed in exchange for a royalty or fee • Generally no sharing of risk or reward • Generally stipulates what is being sold, how and where it can be used, and for how long • Payments usually consist of an initial fee and royalties based on a percentage of future license sales
Franchising Alliances	• Network of alliances in which partners are linked by licensing agreements (e.g., fast-food chains, hardware stores) • Often grant exclusive rights to sell or distribute goods or services in specific geographic areas or markets • Licensees may be required to purchase goods and services from other firms in the alliance
Network Alliances	• Interconnecting alliances among companies crossing international and industrial boundaries (e.g., airlines) • May involve companies collaborating in one market while competing in others (e.g., computers, airlines, cellular telephones) • Most often formed to access skills from different but increasingly interconnected industries
Exclusive Agreements	• Usually involve rights for manufacturing or marketing specific products or services • Each party benefits from the specific skills or assets the other party brings to the relationship

technology, announced a 50/50 joint venture in mid-2010 targeted at the Chinese electric car market. More recently, automakers Ford, Daimler, and Renault-Nissan announced in early 2013 that each firm would invest equally in an alliance to accelerate the development of a common hydrogen fuel cell technology to power their own cars.

Sharing Management Skills and Resources

Firms often lack the management skills and resources to solve complex tasks and projects. These deficiencies can be remedied by aligning with other firms that possess the requisite skills and proprietary knowledge. Building contractors and real estate developers have collaborated for years by pooling their resources to construct, market, and manage, large, complex commercial projects. The contribution of Dow Chemical management personnel to a JV with Cordis, a small pacemaker manufacturer, enabled the JV to keep pace with accelerating production. Reflecting the bureaucratic inertia often found in megacorporations, large pharmaceutical firms actively seek partnerships with smaller, more nimble, and innovative firms as a way of revitalizing their new-drug pipelines. Such relationships are also commonplace among biotechnology firms. Small biotechnology firms are in fact likely to fund their R&D through JVs with large corporations, with the larger partner receiving the controlling interest.[2]

In early 2009, Walt Disney Studios announced that it had entered a long-term distribution agreement with DreamWorks Studios to utilize Disney's marketing skills to distribute six DreamWorks' films annually. Also in 2009, Italy's Fiat acquired a 35% stake in U.S. carmaker Chrysler and an option to take a controlling interest in the firm in exchange for sharing products and platforms for small cars with Chrysler. The deal was designed to help Fiat boost its sales volumes to compete in the global auto market and to enable Chrysler to enter more foreign markets, gain access to fuel-efficient technology, and expand its small-car offering. In mid-2011, Fiat acquired 51% of Chrysler for $1.27 billion.

Sharing Substantial Capital Outlays

Regional and foreign cellular phone carriers were encouraged to join forces to achieve the scale necessary to support the creation of national networks. Vodafone and Verizon Communications joined forces in 1999 to form Verizon Wireless. SBC and Bell Atlantic formed the Cingular Wireless partnership, which acquired AT&T Wireless in early 2004. More recently, Microsoft agreed in early 2012 to invest almost $600 million over five years in Barnes & Noble's e-book business to assist in the development and marketing of the firm's Nook e-book reader.

Securing Sources of Supply

The chemical industry is highly vulnerable to swings in energy costs and other raw materials. Chemical companies such as Dow, Hercules, and Olin have used JVs to build new plants throughout the world. When shortages of raw materials threaten future production, these firms commonly form JVs to secure future sources of supply. Similarly, CNOOC, the large Chinese oil concern, has been busily investing in oil and natural gas assets in highly diverse geographic areas to obtain reliable sources of supply. CNOOC's efforts in recent years have

[2] Lerner, Shane, and Tsai, 2003

ranged from outright acquisition (e.g., the attempted takeover of Unocal in the United States) to long-term contracts (e.g., Canadian tar sands) to joint ventures in various locations in Africa (e.g., Sudan and Kenya).

Cost Reduction

In the 1980s and 1990s, retailers and financial services firms outsourced such back-office activities as information and application processing to such firms as IBM and EDS. Others outsourced payroll processing and benefits management to such firms as ADP. More recently, firms entered so-called logistics alliances covering both transportation and warehousing services and utilizing a single provider for these services.[3] Companies also may choose to combine their manufacturing operations in a single facility with the capacity to meet the production requirements of all parties involved. By building a large facility, the firms jointly can benefit from economies of scale. Examples include Hitachi and Mitsubishi's forming an $8 billion-a-year semiconductor JV and Canon and Toshiba's spending a combined $1.8 billion to create a joint manufacturing operation to satisfy their requirements for surface-conduction electron-emitter displays (SEDs) for TVs.

Gaining Access to New Markets

Accessing new customers is often a highly expensive effort involving substantial initial marketing costs, such as advertising, promotion, warehousing, and distribution expenses. The cost may be prohibitive unless alternative distribution channels providing access to the targeted markets can be found. For example, in late 2006, eBay granted Google the exclusive right to display text advertisements on eBay's auction websites outside the United States, with eBay sharing in the revenue generated by the advertisements. Earlier that same year, Yahoo! signed a similar agreement with eBay for sites within the United States. Both Google and Yahoo! were able to expand their advertising reach without having to make substantial additional investments. A company may enter into an alliance to sell its products through another firm's direct sales force, telemarketing operation, retail outlets, or Internet site. The alliance may involve the payment of a percentage of revenue generated in this manner to the firm whose distribution channel is being used. Alternatively, firms may enter into a cross-marketing relationship, in which they agree to sell the other firm's products through their own distribution channels.

Globalization

The dizzying pace of international competition increased the demand for alliances and JVs to enable companies to enter markets in which they lack

[3]Schmid, 2001

production or distribution channels or in which laws prohibit 100% foreign ownership of a business. Many companies, such as General Motors and Ford, take minority equity positions in other companies within the industry to gain access to foreign markets. By aligning with Lenovo Group as a strategic partner in 2007, IBM hoped to enlarge dramatically its market share in China. More recently, Nissan and Daimler announced in 2010, the formation of a partnership in which the firms would share the cost of developing engines and small-car technologies with projected savings totaling $5.3 billion. As part of the arrangement, each firm will buy a 3.1% stake in the other.

A Prelude to Acquisition or Exit

Rather than acquire a company, a firm may choose to make a minority investment in another company. In exchange for the investment, the investing firm may receive board representation, preferred access to specific proprietary technology, and an option to purchase a controlling interest in the company. The investing firm is able to assess the quality of management, the cultural compatibility, and the viability of the other firm's technology without having to acquire a controlling interest in the firm. In mid-2012, American drugstore chain Walgreen Company (Walgreen) agreed to buy a 45% stake in Alliance Boots (Alliance), the European pharmacy retailer, for $6.7 billion in cash and stock, with an option to buy the remaining 55% for $9.5 billion in cash and stock sometime during the three years following closing. Walgreen can take advantage of Alliance Boots' operations in Europe and several emerging markets, while Alliance Boots gets a foothold in the United States. Similarly, Heineken, which already owns 42% of Asian Pacific Breweries, agreed to buy an additional 40% for $4.1 billion in the Singapore conglomerate in August 2012 as a play to enlarge its position in emerging markets. The deal also required Heineken to buy out the remaining shareholders before the end of 2012. Deals involving the gradual accumulation of control sometimes are referred to as creeping takeovers.

A parent wanting to exit a subsidiary may contribute the unit to a JV and negotiate as part of the deal a put or call option with the other partners. A *call option* gives the partners the right to purchase the unit, and the *put option* gives the parent the right to sell the unit to the other partners. GE negotiated a put option with Comcast in 2010 when GE announced that it would be contributing its NBCUniversal subsidiary to a JV corporation in which Comcast and GE would own 51% and 49% stakes, respectively (see Case Study 15.2 for more details).

Favorable Regulatory Treatment

As noted in Chapter 2, the Department of Justice has looked on JVs far more favorably than M&As, which result in a reduction in the number of firms. JVs increase the number of firms because the parents continue to operate while another firm is created. Project-oriented JVs often are viewed favorably by regulators. Regulatory authorities tend to encourage collaborative research, particularly when the research is shared among all the parties to the JV.

WHAT MAKES BUSINESS ALLIANCES SUCCESSFUL?

Success depends on synergy; cooperation; clarity of purpose, roles, and responsibilities; accountability; a win–win situation; compatible timeframes and financial expectations for the partners; and support from top management.[4] Each of these factors is discussed next.

Synergy

Successful alliances are those in which partners either complement existing strengths or offset significant weaknesses. Examples include economies of scale and scope; access to new products; distribution channels; and proprietary know-how. Successful alliances are often those in which the partners contribute a skill or resource in addition to or other than money. Such alliances often make good economic sense and, as such, are able to get financing.

Cooperation

A lack of cooperation contributes to poor communication and reduces the likelihood that alliance objectives will be realized. Firms with similar philosophies, goals, rewards, operating practices, and ethics are more likely to cooperate over the long run.

Clarity of Purpose, Roles, and Responsibilities

A purpose that is widely understood drives timetables, division of responsibility, commitments to milestones, and measurable results. Internal conflict and lethargic decision-making inevitably result from poorly defined roles and responsibilities of alliance participants.

Accountability

Once roles and responsibilities have been communicated, measurable goals to be achieved in identifiable timeframes should be established for all managers. Such goals should be tied directly to the key objectives for the alliance. Incentives should be in place to reward good performance with respect to goals, and those failing to perform should be held accountable.

[4]Kantor, 2002; Child and Faulkner, 1998; Lynch, 1990, 1993

Win–Win Situation

Alliance partners must believe they are benefiting from the activity for it to be successful. The Johnson & Johnson (J&J) alliance with Merck & Company in the marketing of Pepcid AC is a classic win–win situation. Merck contributed its prescription drug Pepcid AC to the alliance so that J&J could market it as an over-the-counter drug. With Merck as the developer of the upset-stomach remedy and J&J as the marketer, the product became the leader in this drug category. In contrast, the attempt by DaimlerChrysler, Ford, and GM to form an online auction network for parts failed, in part because of the partners' concern that they would lose competitive information.

Compatible Timeframes and Financial Expectations

The length of time an alliance agreement remains in force depends on the partners' objectives, the availability of resources, and the accuracy of the assumptions on which the alliance's business plans are based. Incompatible timeframes are a recipe for disaster: The management of a small Internet business may want to cash out within the next 18–24 months, whereas a larger firm may wish to gain market share over a number of years.

Support from the Top

Top management of the parents of a business alliance must involve themselves aggressively and publicly. Tepid support filters down to lower-level managers and proves to be demotivating. Managers focus their time on those activities that maximize their compensation, potentially diverting attention from the alliance.

ALTERNATIVE LEGAL FORMS OF BUSINESS ALLIANCES

The legal form of an alliance should follow the creation of a business strategy. Alliances may assume a variety of legal structures, including corporate, partnership, franchise, equity partnership, and written contract.[5] The five basic legal structures are discussed in detail in this section. Each has implications for taxation, control by the owners, ability to trade ownership positions, limitations on liability, duration, and ease of raising capital (Table 15.2).

---

[5] Technically, a "handshake" agreement is also an option. Given the inordinate risk associated with the lack of a written agreement, those seeking to create an alliance are encouraged to avoid this type of arrangement. However, in some cultures, insistence on a detailed written agreement may be viewed as offensive.

TABLE 15.2   Alternative Legal Forms Applicable to Business Alliances

Legal Form	Advantages	Disadvantages
CORPORATE STRUCTURES		
C Corporation	Continuity of ownership	Double taxation
	Limited liability	Inability to pass losses on to shareholders
	Provides operational autonomy	Relatively high setup costs, including charter and bylaws
	Provides for flexible financing	
	Facilitates tax-free merger	
Subchapter S	Avoids double taxation	Maximum of 100 shareholders
	Limited liability	Excludes corporate shareholders
		Must distribute all earnings
		Allows only one class of stock
		Lacks continuity of C corporation
		Difficult to raise large sums of money
Limited Liability Company (LLC)	Limited liability	Owners also must be active participants in the firm
	Owners can be managers without losing limited liability	Lacks continuity of a corporate structure
	Avoids double taxation	State laws governing LLC formation differ, making it difficult for LLCs doing business in multiple states
	Allows an unlimited number of members (i.e., owners)	Member shares are often illiquid because the consent of members is required to transfer ownership
	Allows corporate shareholders	
	Can own more than 80% of another company	
	Allows flexibility in allocating investment, profits, losses, and operational responsibilities among members	
	Duration set by owners	
	Can sell shares to "members" without SEC registration	
	Allows foreign corporations as investors	

(Continued)

TABLE 15.2 (Continued)

Legal Form	Advantages	Disadvantages
PARTNERSHIP STRUCTURES		
General Partnerships	Avoids double taxation	Partners have unlimited liability
	Allows flexibility in allocating investment, profits, losses, and operational responsibilities	Lacks continuity of corporate structure
	Life set by general partner	Partnership interests illiquid
		Partners jointly and severally liable
		Each partner has authority to bind the partnership to contracts
Private Limited Liability Partnerships[a]	Limits partner liability (except for general partner)	Partnership interests are illiquid
	Avoids double taxation	Partnership is dissolved if a partner leaves
	State laws consistent (covered under the Uniform Limited Partnership Act)	Private partnerships are limited to 35 partners
Master Limited Partnerships	Same as above	
	Units/shares are publicly traded and more liquid than other types of partnership interests	Unlike corporate dividends, failure to make quarterly distributions constitutes default
Franchise Alliances	Allows repeated application of a successful business model	Success depends on quality of franchise sponsor support
	Minimizes start-up expenses	Royalty payments (3–7% of revenue)
	Facilitates communication of common brand and marketing strategy	
Equity Partnerships	Facilitates close working relationship	Limited tactical and strategic control
	Potential prelude to merger	
	May preempt competition	
Written Contracts	Easy start-up	Limited control
	Potential prelude to merger	Lacks close coordination
		Potential for limited commitment

[a]Public limited partnerships may have an unlimited number of investors and must be registered with the SEC.

Corporate Structures

A corporation is a legal entity created under state law in the United States with an unending life and limited financial liability for its owners. Corporate legal structures include a generalized corporate form (also called a C-type corporation) and the Subchapter S (S-type) corporation. S-type corporations have tax advantages intended to facilitate the formation of small businesses.

C-Type Corporations

A JV corporation normally involves a stand-alone business whose income is taxed at the prevailing corporate tax rates. Corporations other than S-type corporations are subject to double taxation. Taxes are paid by the corporation when profits are earned, and again by the shareholders when the corporation issues dividends. Moreover, setting up a corporate legal structure may be more time consuming and costly than other legal forms because of legal expenses incurred in drafting a corporate charter and bylaws. Although the corporate legal structure has adverse tax consequences and may be more costly to establish, it does offer advantages over other legal forms. The four primary characteristics of a C-type corporate structure include managerial autonomy; continuity of ownership; ease of transferring ownership and raising money; and limited liability. These characteristics are discussed next.

Managerial autonomy most often is used when the JV is large or complex enough to require a separate or centralized management organization. The corporate structure works best when the JV requires some operational autonomy to be effective. The parent companies would continue to set strategy, but the JV's management would manage the day-to-day operations.

Unlike other legal forms, the corporate structure provides *continuity of ownership*, because it has an indefinite life. That is, it does not have to be dissolved due to the death of the owners or if an owner wishes to liquidate her ownership stake. A corporate legal structure may be warranted if the JV's goals are long-term and the parties choose to contribute cash directly to the JV. In return for the cash contribution, the JV partners receive stock in the new company, enabling a partner to cash out by selling his shares. Alternatively, the partner–shareholder can withdraw from active participation in the JV but remain a passive shareholder in anticipation of potential future appreciation of the stock. A corporate structure also facilitates a tax-free merger, since the stock of the acquiring firm can be exchanged for the stock or assets of another firm.

Under a C-type corporate structure, the *ease of transferring ownership* facilitates raising money. A corporate structure also may be justified if the JV is expected to have substantial future financing requirements. Such structures provide a broader array of financing options than other legal forms, including the ability to sell shares and issue corporate debentures and mortgage bonds. Selling new shares enables the corporation to raise funds while still retaining control if less than 50.1% of the corporation's shares are sold.

Finally, this legal form provides for *limited liability* in that a shareholder's liability is limited to the extent of their investment. However, an owner can be held personally liable if the owner injures someone directly or personally guarantees a bank loan or a business debt on which the firm defaults. Other exceptions include failing to deposit taxes withheld from employees' wages or committing intentional fraud that causes harm to the corporation or someone else. An owner also may be liable for failing to capitalize the corporation adequately or hold regular directors and shareholders meetings or for withholding information from other owners.

Subchapter S Corporations

A firm having 100 or fewer shareholders may qualify as an S-type corporation and be taxed as if it were a partnership and thus avoid double taxation. The members of a single family may be considered a single shareholder.[6] An ESOP maintained by an S corporation is not in violation of the requirement regarding the maximum number of shareholders because the S corporation contributes stock to the ESOP. The major disadvantages to S-type corporations are the exclusion of any corporate shareholders, the requirement to issue only one class of stock, the necessity of distributing all earnings to the shareholders each year and that no more than 25% of the corporation's gross income may be derived from passive income.

C corporations may convert to S corporations to eliminate double taxation on dividends. Asset sales within 10 years of the conversion are subject to capital gains taxes at the prevailing corporate income tax rate. After 10 years, such gains are tax-free to the S corporation but are taxable when distributed to shareholders, at their personal tax rates. In 2007, turnaround specialist Sam Zell, after taking the Tribune Company private, converted the firm to an S corporation to take advantage of the favorable tax status. Sales of assets acquired by an S corporation or after a 10-year period following conversion from one form of legal entity to an S corporation are taxed at the capital gains tax rate, which is generally more favorable than the corporate income tax rate.[7]

As discussed next, the limited liability company offers its owners the significant advantage of greater flexibility in allocating profits and losses and is not subject to the many restrictions of the S corporation. Consequently, the popularity of the S corporation has declined.

---

[6] A husband and wife would be treated as a single shareholder. *Family members* refers to those with a common ancestor, lineal descendants of the ancestor, and the spouses of such lineal descendants or common ancestor.

[7] The 10-year "built-in-gains" period is designed by the IRS to discourage C corporations from converting to S corporations to take advantage of the more favorable capital gains tax rates on gains realized by selling corporate assets. Gains on the sale of assets by C corporations are taxed at the prevailing corporate income tax rate rather than a more favorable capital gains tax rate.

Limited Liability Company (LLC)

Like a corporation, the LLC limits the liability of its owners (called *members*) to the extent of their investment. Like a limited partnership, the LLC passes through all of the profits and losses of the entity to its owners without itself being taxed. To obtain this favorable tax status, the IRS requires that the LLC adopt an organization agreement eliminating the characteristics of a C corporation: management autonomy, continuity of ownership or life, and free transferability of shares. Management autonomy is limited by placing decisions about major issues pertaining to the management of the LLC (e.g., mergers or asset sales) in the hands of all its members. LLC agreements require that they be dissolved in case of the death, retirement, or resignation of any member, thereby eliminating continuity of ownership or life. Free transferability is limited by making a transfer of ownership subject to the approval of all members.

Unlike S-type corporations, LLCs can own more than 80% of another corporation and have an unlimited number of members. Also, corporations as well as non-U.S. residents can own LLC shares. Equity capital is obtained through offerings to owners or members.[8] The LLC can sell shares or interests to members without completing the costly process of registering them with the SEC, which is required for corporations that sell their securities to the public. LLC shares are not traded on public exchanges. This arrangement works well for corporate JVs or projects developed through a subsidiary or affiliate. The parent corporation can separate a JV's risk from its other businesses while getting favorable tax treatment and greater flexibility in the allocation of revenues and losses among owners. Finally, LLCs can incorporate before an IPO, tax-free.

The LLC's drawbacks are evident if one owner decides to leave. All other owners must agree formally to continue the firm. Also, all the LLC's owners must take active roles in managing the firm. LLC interests are often illiquid, since transfer of ownership is subject to the approval of other members. LLCs must be set for a limited time, typically 30 years. Each state has different laws about LLC formation and governance, so an LLC that does business in several states might not meet the requirements in every state. LLCs are formed when two or more "persons" (i.e., individuals, LLPs, corporations, etc.) agree to file articles of organization with the Secretary of State's office. The most common types of firm to form LLCs are family-owned businesses, professional services firms such as lawyers, and companies with foreign investors.

Partnership Structures

Frequently used as an alternative to a corporation, partnership structures include general partnerships and limited partnerships.

---

[8]Capital is sometimes referred to as *interests* rather than *shares*, since the latter denotes something that may be freely traded.

General Partnerships

Under this legal structure, investment, profits, losses, and operational responsibilities are allocated to the partners. Because profits and losses are allocated to the partners, the partnership is not subject to tax. The partnership structure also offers substantial flexibility in how the profits and losses are allocated to the partners. Typically, a corporate partner forms a special-purpose subsidiary to hold its interest. This not only limits liability but also may facilitate disposition of the JV interest in the future. The partnership structure is preferable to the other options when the business alliance is expected to have short (three to five years) duration and if high levels of commitment and management interaction are necessary for short time periods.

The primary disadvantage of the general partnership is that all the partners have unlimited liability. Each partner is said to be jointly and severally liable for the partnership's debts. If one partner negotiates a contract resulting in a substantial loss, each partner must pay for a portion of the loss, based on a previously determined agreement on the distribution of profits and losses. Because each partner has unlimited liability for all the debts of the firm, creditors of the partnership may claim assets from one or more of the partners if the remaining partners are unable to cover their share of the loss. Another disadvantage is the ability of any partner to bind the business to a contract or other business deal. Consequently, if one partner purchases inventory at a price that the partnership cannot afford, the partnership is still obligated to pay. Partnerships also lack continuity, in that they must be dissolved if a partner dies or withdraws, unless a new partnership agreement can be drafted. To avoid this possibility, a partnership agreement should include a buy–sell condition or right of first refusal, allowing the partners to buy out a departing partner's interest so the business can continue. Finally, partnership interests may also be difficult to sell because of the lack of a public market, thus making it difficult to liquidate the partnership or to transfer partnership interests.

Limited Liability Partnerships (LLPs)

In an LLP, one or more of the partners can be designated as having limited liability as long as at least one partner has unlimited liability. Those who are responsible for the day-to-day operations of the partnership's activities, whose individual acts are binding on the other partners, and who are personally liable for the partnership's total liabilities are called *general partners.* Those who contribute only money and are not involved in management decisions are called *limited partners.* Usually limited partners receive income, capital gains, and tax benefits, whereas the general partner collects fees and a percentage of the capital gain and income.

Typical limited partnerships are in real estate; oil and gas; and equipment leasing, but they also are used to finance movies, R&D, and other projects. Public limited partnerships are sold through brokerage firms, financial planners, and other registered securities representatives. Public partnerships may have an unlimited number of investors, and their partnership plans must be filed with the SEC. Private limited partnerships have fewer than 35 limited partners, who each invest more than $20,000. Their plans do not have to be filed with the SEC. The sources of equity capital for limited partnerships are the funds supplied by the general and limited partners. The total amount of equity funds needed by the limited partnerships is typically committed when the partnership is formed; ventures that are expected to grow are not usually set up as limited partnerships. LLPs are very popular for accountants, physicians, attorneys, and consultants.

Master Limited Partnerships (MLPs)

MLPs are partnerships whose interests are separated into units that trade like shares of stock. Unlike common stock dividends paid by corporations, the failure to make quarterly payouts to investors is an act of default. Because of these mandatory payments, MLPs are used in industries with predictable cash flows, such as natural resources and real estate. To avoid being taxed as a corporation, an MLP can have only two of the four characteristics of a corporation: managerial autonomy, limited liability, an unlimited life, and freely traded shares. Generally, MLPs have freely traded shares and managerial autonomy but do not have unlimited life or unlimited liability for *all* owners, in that at least one partner has unlimited liability.

Franchise Alliance

Franchises typically involve a franchisee making an initial investment to purchase a license, plus additional capital investment for real estate, machinery, and working capital. For this investment, the franchisor provides training, site-selection assistance, and discounts resulting from bulk purchasing. Royalty payments for the license typically run 3–7% of annual franchisee revenue. Franchise success rates exceed 80% over a five-year period as compared with some types of start-ups, which have success rates of less than 10% after five years.[9] The franchise alliance is preferred when a given business format can be replicated many times. Moreover, franchise alliances are also appropriate when there needs to be a common, recognizable identity presented to customers of each of the alliance partners and close operational coordination is required. A franchise alliance also may be desirable when a common marketing program needs to be coordinated and implemented by a single partner. The franchisor and franchisee operate as separate entities, usually as corporations or LLCs. The four basic types of franchises are distributor (auto dealerships), processing (bottling plants), chain (restaurants), and area franchises (a geographic region is licensed to a new franchisee to subfranchise to others).

[9]Lynch, 1990

Equity Partnership

Such arrangements involve a company's purchase of stock (resulting in a less-than-controlling interest) in another company or a two-way exchange of stock by the two firms.[10] It is referred to as a partnership because of the equity ownership exchanged. Equity partnerships are used in purchaser–supplier relationships, technology development, marketing alliances; and when a larger firm makes an investment in a smaller firm to ensure its continued financial viability. In exchange for an equity investment, a firm often receives a seat on the board of directors and possibly an option to buy a controlling interest in the company. The equity partnership is most effective when there is a need to have a long-term or close strategic relationship, to preempt a competitor from making an alliance or acquisition, or as a prelude to a takeover.

Written Contract

The written contract is the simplest form of legal structure and is used most often with strategic alliances because it maintains an "arms-length" or independent relationship between the parties to the contract. The contract normally stipulates such things as how the revenue is divided, the responsibilities of each party, the duration of the alliance, and confidentiality requirements. No separate business entity is established for legal or tax purposes. The written contract most often is used when the business alliance is expected to last less than three years, frequent close coordination is not required, capital investments are made independently by each party to the agreement, and the parties have had little previous contact.

STRATEGIC AND OPERATIONAL PLANS

Before any deal-structuring issues are addressed, the prospective parties must agree on the basic strategic direction and purpose of the alliance as defined in the alliance's strategic plan, as well as the financial and nonfinancial goals established in the operation's plan. The strategic plan identifies the primary purpose or mission of the business alliance; communicates specific quantifiable targets, such as financial returns or market share and milestones; and analyzes the business alliance's strengths and weaknesses, opportunities and threats relative to the competition. Teams representing all parties to the alliance should be involved from the outset of the discussions in developing both a strategic plan and an operations plan for the venture. The operations plan (i.e., annual budget) should reflect the specific needs of the proposed business alliance and be written

---

[10]Such exchanges keep both parties committed to the success of the partnership. If the partnership fails, the value of each party's partnership interest declines, as could the ownership stake each partner has in the other firm.

by those responsible for implementing the plan. The operations plan is typically a one-year plan that outlines for managers what is to be accomplished, when it is to be accomplished, and what resources are required.

RESOLVING BUSINESS ALLIANCE DEAL-STRUCTURING ISSUES

The purpose of deal structuring in a business alliance is to allocate risks, rewards, resource requirements, and responsibilities among participants. Table 15.3 summarizes the key issues and related questions that need to be addressed as part of the business alliance deal-structuring process. This section discusses how these issues most often are resolved.

Scope

A basic question in setting up a business alliance involves which of the partners' products are included and which excluded from the business alliance. This question deals with defining the scope of the business alliance, that is, how broadly the alliance will be applied in pursuing its purpose. For example, an alliance whose purpose is to commercialize products developed by the partners could be broadly or narrowly defined in specifying what products or services are to be offered, to whom, in what geographic areas, and for what time period. Failure to define scope adequately can lead to situations in which the alliance may be competing with the products or services offered by the parent firms. With respect to both current and future products, the alliance agreement should identify who receives the rights to market or distribute products, manufacture products, acquire or license technology, or purchase products from the venture.

Duration

The participants need to agree on how long the business alliance is to remain in force. Participant expectations must be compatible. The expected longevity of the alliance is also an important determinant in the choice of a legal form. The corporate structure more readily provides for a continuous life than a partnership, because it is easier to transfer ownership interests. There is conflicting evidence on how long most business alliances actually last.[11] The critical point is that most business alliances have a finite life, corresponding to the time required to achieve their original strategic objectives.

---

[11] Mercer Management Consulting, in ongoing research, concludes that most JVs last only about three years (Lajoux, 1998), whereas Booz-Allen Hamilton (1993) reported an average lifespan of seven years.

TABLE 15.3   Business Alliance Deal-Structuring Issues

Issue	Key Questions
Scope	What products are included and what are excluded? Who receives rights to distribute, manufacture, acquire, or license technology or purchase future products or technology?
Duration	How long is the alliance expected to exist?
Legal Form	What is the appropriate legal structure—stand-alone entity or contractual?
Governance	How are the interests of the parent firms to be protected? Who is responsible for specific accomplishments?
Control	How are strategic decisions to be addressed? How are day-to-day operational decisions to be handled?
Resource Contributions and Ownership Determination	Who contributes what and in what form? Cash? Assets? Guarantees/loans? Technology including patents, trademarks, copyrights, and proprietary knowledge? How are contributions to be valued? How is ownership determined?
Financing Ongoing Capital Requirements	What happens if additional cash is needed?
Distribution	How are profits and losses allocated? How are dividends determined?
Performance Criteria	How is performance to the plan measured and monitored?
Dispute Resolution	How are disagreements resolved?
Revision	How will the agreement be modified?
Termination	What are the guidelines for termination? Who owns the assets on termination? What are the rights of the parties to continue the alliance activities after termination?
Transfer of Interests	How are ownership interests to be transferred? What are the restrictions on the transfer of interests? How will new alliance participants be handled? Will there be rights of first refusal, drag-along, tag-along, or put provisions?
Tax	Who receives tax benefits?
Management/Organization	How is the alliance to be managed?
Confidential Information	How is confidential information handled? How are employees and customers of the parent firms protected?
Regulatory Restrictions and Notifications	What licenses are required? What regulations need to be satisfied? What agencies need to be notified?

TABLE 15.4   Key Factors Affecting Choice of Legal Entity

Determining Factors: Businesses With	Should Select
High liability risks	C corporation, LLP, or LLC
Large capital/financing requirements	C corporation
Desire for continuity of existence	C corporation
Desire for managerial autonomy	C corporation
Desire for growth through M&A	C corporation
Owners who are also active participants	LLC
Foreign corporate investors	LLC
Desire to allocate investments, profits, losses, and operating responsibilities among owners	LLC and LLP
High pretax profits	LLC and LLP
Project focus/expected limited existence	LLP
Owners who want to remain inactive	LLP and C corporation
Large marketing expenses	Franchise
Strategies that are easily replicated	Franchise
Close coordination among participants not required	Written "arms-length" agreement
Low risk/low capital requirements	Sole proprietorship or partnership

Legal Form

Businesses that are growth oriented or intend eventually to go public through an IPO generally become a C corporation due to its financing flexibility, unlimited life, continuity of ownership, and ability to combine on a tax-free basis with other firms. With certain exceptions concerning frequency, firms may convert from one legal structure to a C corporation before going public. The nature of the business greatly influences the legal form chosen (Table 15.4).

Governance

In the context of an alliance, *governance* may be defined broadly as an oversight function providing for efficient, informed communication between two or more parent firms. The primary responsibilities of this oversight function are to protect the interests of the corporate parents, approve changes to strategy and annual operating plans, allocate resources needed to make the alliance succeed, and arbitrate conflicts among lower levels of management. Historically, governance of business alliances has followed either a quasi-corporate or a quasi-project approach. For example, the oil industry traditionally has managed alliances by establishing a board of directors to provide oversight of managers and to protect the interests of nonoperating owners. In contrast, in the pharmaceutical and automotive industries, where nonequity alliances are common, firms treat governance like project management by creating a steering committee that allows all participants to comment on issues confronting the alliance.

Resource Contributions and Ownership Determination

As part of the negotiation process, the participants must agree on a fair value for all tangible and intangible assets contributed to the business alliance. The valuation of partner contributions is important, in that it often provides the basis for determining ownership shares in the business alliance. The shares of the corporation or the interests in the partnership are distributed among the owners in accordance with the value contributed by each participant. The partner with the largest risk, the largest contributor of cash, or the person who contributes critical tangible or intangible assets generally is given the greatest equity share in a JV.

It is relatively easy to value tangible, or "hard" contributions, such as cash, promissory cash commitments, contingent commitments, stock of existing corporations, and assets and liabilities associated with an ongoing business in terms of actual dollars or their present values. A party that contributes hard assets, such as a production facility, may want the contribution valued in terms of the value of increased production rather than its replacement cost or lease value. The contribution of a fully operational, modern facility to a venture interested in being first to market with a particular product may provide far greater value than if the venture attempted to build a new facility because of the delay inherent in making the facility fully operational.

Intangible, or soft or in-kind = contributions, such as skills, knowledge, services, patents, licenses, brand names, and technology, are often much more difficult to value. Partners providing such services may be compensated by having the business alliance pay a market-based royalty or fee for such services.[12] Alternatively, contributors of intellectual property may be compensated by receiving rights to future patents or technologies developed by the alliance. Participants in the business alliance that contribute brand identities, which facilitate the alliance's entry into a particular market, may require assurances that they can purchase a certain amount of the product or service, at a guaranteed price, for a specific time period. Exhibit 15.1 illustrates how the distribution of ownership between General Electric and Vivendi Universal Entertainment may have been determined in the formation of NBCUniversal.

[12] If the royalties or fees paid by the alliance are below standard market prices for comparable services, the difference between the market price and what the alliance actually is paying may become taxable income to the alliance.

EXHIBIT 15.1   DETERMINING OWNERSHIP DISTRIBUTION IN A JOINT VENTURE

Vivendi Universal Entertainment contributed film and television assets valued at $14 billion to create NBCUniversal, a joint venture with TV station NBC, which was wholly owned by General Electric at that time. NBCUniversal was valued at $42 billion at closing. NBCUniversal's EBITDA was estimated to be $3 billion, of which GE contributed two-thirds; VUE accounted for the remaining one-third. EBITDA multiples for recent transactions involving TV media firms averaged 14 times EBITDA at that time. GE provided VUE an option to buy $4 billion in GE stock, assumed $1.6 billion in VUE debt, and paid the remainder of the $14 billion purchase price in the form of NBCUniversal stock. At closing, VUE converted the option to buy GE stock into $4 billion in cash. GE owned 80% of NBCUniversal and VUE 20%. How might this ownership distribution have been determined?

Solution

Step 1: **Estimate the total value of the joint venture**

$$\$3 \text{ billion} \times 14 = \$42 \text{ billion}$$

Step 2: **Estimate the value of assets contributed by each partner**

Reflecting the relative contribution of each partner to EBITDA (⅔ from GE; ⅓ from VUE), GE's contributed assets were valued at $28 billion (i.e., ⅔ of $42 billion) and VUE's at $14 billion (i.e., ⅓ of $42 billion).

Step 3: **Determine the form of payment**

$4.0 billion (GE stock)
$1.6 billion (assumed Vivendi debt)
<u>$8.4</u> billion (value of VUE's equity position in NBCUniversal = $14 − $4.0 − $1.6)
$14.0 billion (purchase price paid by GE to Vivendi for VUE assets)

Step 4: **Determine ownership distribution**

At closing, Vivendi chose to receive a cash infusion of $5.6 billion (i.e., $4 billion in cash in lieu of GE stock + $1.6 billion in assumed VUE debt). Thus,

$$\text{VUE's ownership of NBCUniversal} = (\$14 \text{ billion} - \$5.6 \text{ billion})/\$42 \text{ billion}$$
$$= \$8.4 \text{ billion}/\$42 \text{ billion}$$
$$= 0.2$$
$$\text{GE's ownership of NBCUniversal} = 1 - 0.2 = 0.8$$

Financing Ongoing Capital Requirements

The business alliance may fund capital requirements that cannot be financed internally by calling on the participants to make a capital contribution, issuing additional equity or partnership interests, or borrowing. If it is decided that the alliance should be able to borrow, the participants must agree on an appropriate financial structure for the enterprise. *Financial structure* refers to the amount of equity that will be contributed to the business alliance and how much debt it will carry. Alliances established through a written contract obviate the need for such a financing decision because each party to the contract finances its own financial commitments to the alliance. Project-based JVs, particularly those that create a separate corporation, sometimes sell equity directly to the public or though a private placement.

Owner or Partner Financing

The equity owners or partners may agree to make contributions of capital in addition to their initial investments in the enterprise. The contributions usually are made in direct proportion to their equity or partnership interests. If one party chooses not to make a capital contribution, the ownership interests of all the parties are adjusted to reflect the changes in their cumulative capital contributions. This adjustment increases the ownership interest of those making the contribution while reducing the interest of those not contributing.

Equity and Debt Financing

JVs formed as a corporation may issue different classes of either common or preferred stock. JVs established as partnerships raise capital through the issuance of limited partnership units to investors, with the sponsoring firms becoming general partners. When a larger company aligns with a smaller company, it may make a small equity investment in the smaller firm to ensure it remains solvent or to benefit from potential equity appreciation. Such investments often include an option to purchase the remainder of the shares, or at least a controlling interest, at a predetermined price if the smaller firm or the JV satisfies certain financial targets.

Control

Control is distinguishable from ownership by the use of agreements among investors or voting rights or by issuing different classes of shares. The most successful JVs are those in which one party is responsible for most routine management decisions, with the other parties participating in decision making only when the issue is fundamental to the business alliance. The alliance agreement must define what issues are to be considered fundamental to the alliance and address how they are to be resolved, either by majority votes or by veto rights given to one or more of the parties. Operational control should be placed with the owner best able to manage the JV. The owner who has the largest equity share but not operational control is likely to insist on being involved in the operation of the business alliance by having a seat on the board of directors or steering committee. The owner also may insist on having veto rights over such issues as changes in the alliance's purpose and scope, overall strategy, capital expenditures over a certain amount of money, key management promotions, salary increases applying to the general employee population, the amount and timing of dividend payments, buyout conditions, and restructuring.

Distribution Issues

Such issues relate to dividend policies and how profits and losses are allocated among the owners. The dividend policy determines the cash return each partner should receive. How the cash-flows of the venture will be divided generally depends on the initial equity contribution of each partner, ongoing equity contributions, and noncash contributions in the form of technical and managerial resources. Allocation of profits and losses normally follow directly from the allocation of shares or partnership interests. When the profits come from intellectual property rights contributed by one of the parties, royalties may be used to compensate the party providing the property rights. When profits are attributable to distribution or marketing efforts of a partner, fees and commission can be used to compensate the partners. Similarly, rental payments can be used to allocate profits attributable to specific equipment or facilities contributed by a partner.

Performance Criteria

The lack of adequate performance-measurement criteria can result in significant disputes among the partners and eventually contribute to the termination of the venture. Performance criteria should be both measurable and simple enough to be understood and used by the partners and managers at all levels and spelled out clearly in the business alliance agreement.

Dispute Resolution

How disputes are resolved reflects the choice of law provision, the definition of what constitutes an impasse, and the arbitration clause provided in the alliance agreement. The *choice of law provision* in the agreement indicates which states or country's laws have jurisdiction in settling disputes. This provision should be drafted with an understanding of the likely outcome of litigation in any of the participants' home countries or states and the attitude of these countries' or states' courts in enforcing choice-of-law provisions in the JV agreements. The *deadlock or impasse clause* defines events triggering dispute-resolution procedures. Such events should not be defined so narrowly that minor disagreements are subject to the dispute mechanism. Finally, an *arbitration clause* addresses disagreements by defining the type of dispute subject to arbitration and how the arbitrator will be selected.

Revision

Changing circumstances and partner objectives may prompt a need to revise alliance objectives. If one party to the agreement wishes to withdraw, the participants should have agreed in advance how the withdrawing party's ownership interest would be divided among the remaining parties. Moreover, a product or technology may be developed that was not foreseen when the alliance first was conceived. The alliance agreement should indicate that the rights to manufacture and distribute the product or technology might be purchased by a specific alliance participant.

Termination

A business alliance may be terminated due to the completion of a project, due to successful operations resulting in a merger of the partners, due to diverging partner objectives, or due to the failure of the alliance to achieve stated objectives. Termination provisions in the alliance agreement should include buyout clauses enabling one party to purchase another's ownership interests, prices of the buyout, and how assets and liabilities are to be divided if the venture fails or the partners elect to dissolve the operation. A JV may convert to a simple licensing arrangement, allowing the partner to leave without losing all benefits by purchasing rights to the product or technology.

Transfer of Interests

Alliance agreements often limit how and to whom parties to the agreements can transfer their interests. This is justified by noting that each party entered the agreement with the understanding of who its partners would be. In agreements that permit transfers under certain conditions, the partners or the JV itself may have *right of first refusal* (i.e., the party wishing to leave the JV first must offer its interests to other participants in the JV). Parties to the agreement may have the right to "put" (or sell) their interests to the venture, and the venture may have a call option (or right to purchase such interests). There also may be tag-along and drag-along provisions, which have the effect of a third-party purchaser acquiring not only the interest of the JV party whose interest it seeks to acquire but also the interests of other parties. A *drag-along* provision *requires* a party not otherwise interested in selling its ownership interest to the third party to do so. A *tag-along* provision gives a party to the alliance who was not originally targeted by the third party the *option* to join the targeted party in selling its interest to the third party.

Taxes

The primary tax concerns of the JV partners are to avoid the recognition of taxable gains on the formation of the venture and to minimize taxes on the distribution of its earnings. In addition to the double taxation of dividends discussed earlier, the corporate structure may have other adverse tax consequences. If the partner owns less than 80% of the alliance, its share of the alliance's results cannot be included in its consolidated income tax return. This has two effects. First, when earnings are distributed, they are subject to an intercorporate dividend tax, which can be 7% if the partner's ownership interest in the venture is 20% or more. Second, losses of the business alliance cannot be used to offset other income earned by the participant. For tax purposes, the preferred alternative to a corporate legal structure is to use a pass-through legal structure, such as a limited liability company or a partnership.

A partnership can be structured in such a way that some partners receive a larger share of the profits, whereas others receive a larger share of the losses. This flexibility in tax planning is an important factor stimulating the use of partnerships and LLCs. These entities can allocate to each JV partner a portion of a particular class of revenue, income, gain, loss, or expense. Services provided to the JV, such as accounting, auditing, legal, human resource, and treasury services, are not viewed by the IRS as being "at risk" if the JV fails. The JV should pay prevailing market fees for such services; otherwise such services may be taxable.

Management and Organizational Issues

Before a business alliance agreement is signed, the partners must decide what type of organizational structure provides the most effective management and leadership.

Steering or Joint Management Committee

Control of business alliances most often is accomplished through a steering committee, the ultimate authority for ensuring that the venture stays focused on the strategic objectives agreed to by the partners. To maintain good communication, coordination, and teamwork, the committee should meet at least monthly. The committee should provide operations managers with sufficient autonomy so that they can take responsibility for their actions and be rewarded for their initiative.

Methods of Dividing Ownership and Control

A common method of control is the *majority–minority* framework, which relies on identifying a clearly dominant partner, usually the one having at least a 50.1% ownership stake. In this scenario, the equity, control, and distribution of rewards reflect the majority–minority relationship. This type of structure promotes the ability to make rapid corrections, defines who is in charge, and is most appropriate for high-risk ventures, where quick decisions often are required. The major disadvantage of this approach is that the minority partner may feel powerless and become passive or alienated.

Another method of control is the *equal division of power* framework, which usually means that equity is split equally. This assumes that the initial contribution, distribution, decision making, and control are split equally. This approach helps keep the partners actively engaged in the management of the venture. It is best suited for partners sharing a strong common vision for the venture and possessing similar corporate cultures. However, the approach can lead to deadlocks and the eventual dissolution of the alliance.

Under the *majority rules* framework, the equity distribution may involve three partners. Two of the partners have large equal shares, whereas the third partner may have less than 10%. The minority partner is used to break deadlocks. This approach enables the primary partners to remain engaged in the enterprise without stalemating the decision-making process.

In the *multiple party* framework, no partner has control; instead, control resides with the management of the venture. Consequently, decision making can be nimble and made by those who understand the issues best. This framework is well suited for international ventures, where a country's laws may prohibit a foreign firm from having a controlling interest in a domestic firm. It is common for a domestic company to own the majority of the equity but for the operational control of the venture to reside with the foreign partner. In addition to a proportional split of the dividends paid, the foreign company may receive additional payments in the form of management fees and bonuses.

Regulatory Restrictions and Notifications

JVs may be subject to Hart-Scott-Rodino filing requirements because the parties to the JV are viewed as acquirers, and the JV as a target. For JVs between competitors, to get regulatory approval, competitors should be able to do something together that they could not do alone. Competitors can be relatively confident that a partnership will be acceptable to regulators if, in combination, they control no more than 20% of the market. Project-oriented ventures are looked at most favorably. Collaborative research is encouraged, particularly when the research is shared among all the parties to the alliance. Alliances among competitors are likely to spark a review by the regulators because they have the potential to result in price fixing and dividing up the market.

EMPIRICAL FINDINGS

Reflecting their flexibility and relatively low capital requirements, business alliances are becoming increasingly popular ways to implement business strategies. Under the right conditions, alliances can generate significant abnormal financial returns. Empirical evidence shows that JVs and strategic alliances often create value for their participants, with average announcement-date positive abnormal returns varying from 1% to 3%.[13]

[13]Chan et al. (1997); Das et al. (1998); Johnson et al. (2000); Kale et al. (2002)

Partners in JVs who are in the same industry (horizontal JVs) tend to share equally in wealth creation. The wealth increase is often much greater for horizontal alliances involving the transfer of technical knowledge than for nontechnical alliances.[14] For vertical JVs, suppliers experience a greater portion of the wealth created.[15] Firms with greater alliance experience enjoy a greater likelihood of success and greater wealth creation than those with little experience.[16]

Strategic alliances can have a salutary effect on the share prices of their suppliers and customers and a negative impact on the share prices of competitors. For alliances created to share technologies or develop new technical capabilities, suppliers benefit from increased sales to the alliance and customers benefit from using the enhanced technology developed by the alliance in their products. Competitors' share prices decline due to lost sales and earnings to the alliance.[17] The average large company has more than 30 alliances,[18] and the rate of formation of new alliances is accelerating, in part reflecting a loosening of antitrust regulatory policies with respect to business alliances.[19] However, despite rapid growth, studies show that as many as 60% of all business alliances fail to meet expectations.[20]

SOME THINGS TO REMEMBER

Business alliances may offer attractive alternatives to M&As. Motivations for alliances include risk sharing, access to new markets, new-product introduction, technology sharing, globalization, a desire to acquire (or exit) a business, and the perception that they are often more acceptable to regulators than M&As. Business alliances may assume a variety of legal structures: corporate, LLC, partnership, franchise, equity partnership, and written contract. Key deal-structuring issues include the alliance's scope, duration, legal form, governance, and control mechanism. The valuation of resource contributions ultimately determines ownership interests.

[14] Chan et al., 1997; Das et al., 1998

[15] Johnson et al., 2000

[16] Kale et al., 2002

[17] Chang, 2008

[18] Kalmbach and Roussel, 1999

[19] Robinson, 2002a

[20] Kalmbach and Roussel (1999) indicate that 61% of the alliances are viewed as either disappointments or outright failures. This figure substantiates earlier findings by Robert Spekman of the Darden Graduate School of Business Administration, that 60% of all ventures fail to meet expectations (Ellis, 1996). Klein (2004) reports that 55% of alliances fall apart within three years of their formation.

DISCUSSION QUESTIONS

15.1   What is a limited liability company? What are its advantages and disadvantages?

15.2   Why is defining the scope of a business alliance important?

15.3   Discuss ways of valuing tangible and intangible contributions to a JV.

15.4   What are the advantages and disadvantages of the various organizational structures that could be used to manage a business alliance?

15.5   What are the common reasons for the termination of a business alliance?

15.6   Google invested $1 billion for a 5% stake in America Online as part of a partnership that expands the firm's existing search engine deal to include collaboration on advertising, instant messaging, and video. Under the deal, Google would have the customary rights afforded a minority investor. What rights or terms do you believe Google would have negotiated in this transaction? What rights do you believe AOL might want?

15.7   ConocoPhillips (Conoco) announced the purchase of 7.6% of Lukoil's (a largely government-owned Russian oil and gas company) stock for $2.36 billion during a government auction of Lukoil's stock. Conoco would have one seat on Lukoil's board. As a minority investor, how could Conoco protect its interests?

15.8   Johnson & Johnson sued Amgen over their 14-year alliance to sell a blood-enhancing treatment called erythropoietin. The partners ended up squabbling over sales rights and a spin-off drug and could not agree on future products for the JV. Amgen won the right in arbitration to sell a chemically similar medicine that can be taken weekly rather than daily. What could these companies have done before forming the alliance to have mitigated the problems that arose after the alliance was formed? Why do you believe they may have avoided addressing these issues at the outset?

15.9   General Motors, the world's largest auto manufacturer, agreed to purchase 20% of Japan's Fuji Heavy Industries, Ltd., the manufacturer of Subaru vehicles, for $1.4 billion. Why do you believe that General Motors initially may have wanted to limit its investment to 20%?

15.10   Through its alliance with Best Buy, Microsoft is selling its products— including Microsoft Network (MSN) Internet access services and handheld devices, such as digital telephones, handheld organizers, and WebTV, that connect to the web—through kiosks in Best Buy's 354 stores nationwide. In exchange, Microsoft has invested $200 million in Best Buy. What do you believe were the motivations for this strategic alliance?

Answers to these Discussion Questions are available in the Online Instructor's Manual for instructors using this book.

CASE STUDY 15.1
Nokia Gambles on Microsoft in the Smartphone Wars

Key Points

- An alliance may represent a low-cost alternative to a merger or acquisition.
- Selecting an alliance partner must be done judiciously to avoid competing with a firm's own customers or partners, cannibalizing its own product offering, or unintentionally transferring proprietary information and technology.

Smartphones outsold personal computers for the first time in the fourth quarter of 2010. The Apple iPhone and devices powered by Google's Android operating system have won consumers with their sleek touchscreen software and with an army of developers creating applications for their devices. In just three years, they have captured the largest share of the market. These developments put Microsoft's core business, selling software for PCs, in jeopardy and have caused Finnish phone handset manufacturer Nokia to fall further behind in its efforts to compete with Apple and makers of Android-based devices in the smartphone market.

On February 11, 2011, Nokia's CEO, Stephen Elop, announced an alliance with Microsoft to establish a third major player in the intensely competitive smartphone market, currently dominated by Google and Apple. Under the deal, Nokia will adopt Windows Phone 7 (WP7) as its

principal smartphone operating system, replacing its own software, which has been losing market share. Nokia and Microsoft are betting that the carriers want an alternative system to iPhone and Android. While some WP7-based products were anticipated in 2011, a substantial increase in volume was not expected before 2013. Nokia could have partnered with Google, as have many handset manufacturers. However, it would require that the firm compete with the likes of Samsung, HTC, and Motorola—all makers of Android-powered smartphones.

Under the agreement with Microsoft, WP7 becomes Nokia's primary smartphone platform; Nokia also agreed to help introduce WP7-powered smartphones in new consumer and business markets throughout the world. The two firms will jointly market their products and integrate their mobile application online stores such that Microsoft's Marketplace (applications and media store) will absorb Nokia's current online applications and content store (Ovi). Nokia phones will use Microsoft's Bing search engine, Zune music store, and Xbox Live gaming center and will work with Microsoft on future services to expand the capabilities of mobile devices. However, the deal is not exclusive, for Microsoft will continue to have other hardware partners. Microsoft also agreed to invest about $1 billion in Nokia over a period of years to defray development and marketing costs.

The alliance enables Nokia to adopt new software (WP7) with an established community of developers but that has sold relatively poorly since its introduction in late 2010. With the phase-out of its discontinued Symbian operating system over a period of years, Nokia will be able to reduce substantially its own research and development and marketing budgets. Microsoft will also benefit from Nokia's extensive intellectual property portfolio in the mobile market to strengthen the WP7 system. For Microsoft, the deal represents a major opportunity to boost lagging sales in the mobile phone market and gives it access to Nokia's brand recognition.

Despite having been an early entrant into the smartphone business, Microsoft had been unable to gain significant market share. Over the years, Microsoft has struck deals with many of the world's best known cellphone manufacturers, including Motorola and HTC Corp. But these alliances were hampered either by execution problems or by an inability of Microsoft to prevent handset makers from shifting to other technologies, such as Google's Android operating system. For example, after failing to deliver mobile phone technology that would compete with Apple's and Google's innovative systems, Taiwanese handset manufacturer HTC lost interest in manufacturing smartphones based on what was then known as the Windows Mobile operating system and now makes many different Android phone models in addition to devices powered by WP7. Even though Microsoft's Mobility

software was substantially revamped and dubbed Windows Phone 7, it was only able to capture 2% market share in the fourth quarter of 2010 following its introduction early in the fall of that year.

Elop also announced that effective April 1, 2011, Nokia would be reorganized into two business units: smart devices and mobile phones. The smart devices unit would focus on manufacturing the new Windows Phone 7 devices. The smart devices business must compete in the smartphone market against the likes of those producing handsets powered by the Google operating system, Blackberry, and Apple, with only the Windows Phone 7–powered phone. The mobile phones operation would continue to develop phones for Nokia's mass market. The mass market feature-phone business represented Nokia's core business, in which the firm would produce large volumes of phones for the mass market differentiated largely by their features. While this market had proven lucrative for years, it is now under increasing pressure from mass-produced Chinese phones.

Investors expressed their disapproval of the deal, with Nokia's stock falling 11% on the announcement. Similarly, Microsoft's shares fell by 1% as investors expressed concern that the firm had teamed with a weak player in the smartphone market and that the two-year transition period before WP7-based smartphones would be sold in volume would allow only Android-based smartphones and iPhones to get further ahead.

The partnership faces many challenges. With Samsung, HTC, and LG having invested heavily in Android-powered devices, they have little incentive to commit to WP7-based devices. Their strategy seems to be to use the WP7 system as an alternative to Android in its negotiations with Google, threatening to shift resources to WP7. Furthermore, Nokia is a European company, and Europe is where it has greatest market share. However, Microsoft has had a checkered past with EU antitrust authorities, which sued the firm for alleged monopolies in its Windows and Office products. European companies have been much faster to adopt open-source solutions, often in an effort to replace Microsoft software.

The partnership does, however, have potential advantages. Nokia remains a powerhouse in feature phones, and, if it can successfully transition these devices to the WP7 operating system, it may be able to increase market penetration sharply. Android may be vulnerable due to a number of problems: platform fragmentation, inconsistent updates and versions across devices, and the operating system's becoming slower as it is called on to support more applications. WP7, at this time, has none of these problems. If customers become frustrated with Android, WP7 could gain significant share. As always, time will tell.

Discussion Questions

1. Conduct an external analysis of the smartphone marketplace (see Chapter 4).
2. Conduct an internal analysis of Nokia and Microsoft (see Chapter 4).
3. What alternatives to a partnership did Nokia and Microsoft have? Why was a partnership selected as the means of implementing Microsoft's strategy to expand into the smartphone market?
4. Who do you believe benefitted most from the partnership, Microsoft or Nokia, and why?

Solutions to these case study questions are provided in the Online Instructor's Manual for instructors using this book.

CASE STUDY 15.2
General Electric and Comcast Join Forces

Key Points

- Joint ventures are sometimes created if a business cannot be sold outright.
- Such JVs are viewed as a way of improving a firm's operations enabling the parent to exit the business eventually at a higher value.

In an effort to shore up its big finance business, severely weakened during the 2008 financial crisis, and to focus more on its manufacturing and infrastructure operations, General Electric (GE) sought to sell its media and entertainment business, NBCUniversal. GE's decision to sell also reflected the deteriorating state of the broadcast television industry and a desire to exit a business that never quite fit with its industrial side. NBC has been mired in fourth place among the major broadcast networks, and the economics of the broadcast television industry have deteriorated in recent years amid declining overall ratings and a reduction in advertising. In contrast, cable channels have continued to thrive because they rely on a steady stream of subscriber fees from cable companies such as Comcast. Moreover, while NBCUniversal was profitable in 2009, it was expected to go into the red in subsequent years.

Unable to find a buyer for the entire business at what GE believed was a reasonable price, GE sought other options, including combining the operation with another media business. After extended discussions, GE and Comcast announced a deal on December 2, 2009, to form a joint venture consisting of NBCUniversal and selected Comcast assets. Comcast is primarily a cable company and provider of programming content, with 24.3 million cable customers, 16.1 million high-speed Internet customers, and 7.8 million voice customers. Comcast hopes to diversify its holdings as it faces encroaching threats from online video and more aggressive competition from satellite and phone companies that offer subscription TV services, by adding more content on its video-on-demand offerings. Furthermore, by having an interest in NBCUniversal's digital properties, such as Hulu.com, Comcast expects to capitalize on any shift of its cable customers to viewing their favorite TV programs online by owning the program content.

Comcast's strategy is to integrate vertically by owning the content it distributes through its cable operations. Previous attempts to do this, such as AOL's acquisition of Time Warner in 2001, have ended in failure, largely because the cultures of the two firms did not mesh. Some media companies have merged successfully—for example, Time Warner's merger with Turner Broadcasting. Having learned from AOL's rush to achieve synergy, Comcast is allowing the NBCUniversal JV to operate independent of the parents and is sharing the risk with GE.

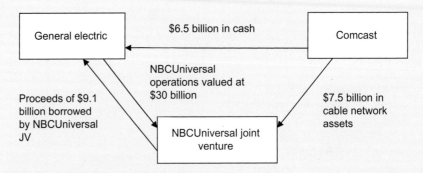

FIGURE 15.1   **NBCUniversal joint venture at closing.**

This joint venture transaction is noteworthy for its potential impact on limiting competition in the entertainment industry, its complex financial engineering, its multifaceted organizational structure, and as an exit strategy for GE from the media and entertainment business. Each of these considerations is discussed next.

The announcement raised significant concerns within the media and entertainment industry about the potential for limiting access to both content and distribution by increasing industry concentration. After receiving significant concessions, regulators approved the creation of the joint venture media giant on January 17, 2011. The U.S. Federal Communications Commission and the Department of Justice required Comcast and NBCUniversal to relinquish voting rights and board representation to Hulu, although they could continue to remain part owners. Furthermore, Comcast has to ensure what the FCC called "reasonable access" to its programming for its competitors, and the firm may not discriminate against programming that competes with its own offerings.

The deal reflected complicated financial engineering, involving both parties contributing assets to create a joint venture, agreeing on the total value of the endeavor, determining the value of each party's contributed assets to determine ownership distribution, and finally, determining how GE would be compensated. The joint venture transaction based on the value of the assets contributed by both parties was valued at $37.25 billion, consisting of GE's contribution of NBCUniversal, valued at $30 billion, and Comcast's contribution of cable network assets valued at $7.25 billion. The ownership interests were determined based on the value of the contributed assets and cash payments made to GE as described in Figure 15.1.

- In exchange for contributing NBCUniversal operations valued at $30 billion to the JV, GE received $15.6 billion in cash ($6.5 billion from Comcast + $9.1 billion borrowed by the NBCUniversal JV) + a 49% ownership interest in the NBCUniversal JV).

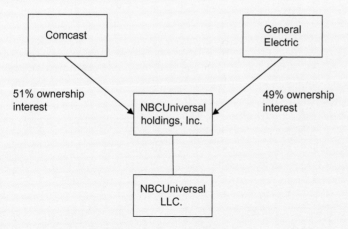

FIGURE 15.2 **NBCUniversal postclosing organization.**

- In exchange for contributing $7.5 billion in cable network assets to the JV and paying GE $6.5 billion in cash, Comcast received a 51% interest in the NBCUniversal JV.

Organizationally, the two parties own NBCUniversal indirectly through their ownership in a holding company (see Figure 15.2). As part of the deal, NBCUniversal Inc. was converted to a limited liability company (NBCUniversal Media LLC), which is a wholly owned subsidiary of NBCUniversal Holdings Inc., a corporation in which Comcast owns 51% of the outstanding shares and GE the remainder. NBCUniversal Holdings is the sole member (owner) in NBCUniversal Media LLC. By having the right to designate the majority of the board members of NBCUniversal Holdings, Comcast effectively controls the holding company and, in turn, NBCUniversal Media LLC. To maintain its status as a pass-through organization for tax purposes, NBCUniversal Media makes quarterly distributions to the holding company, which has no independent source of income, to meet its cash requirements. Among other things, these obligations include making cash distributions to Comcast and GE so that they can pay taxes due on the income generated by NBCUniversal Media. As long as GE retains at least a 20% ownership interest in the combined firms, it has certain approval rights over acquisitions, mergers, dissolution, bankruptcy, material expansion of the business, dividend payouts, new equity issues or repurchase, additional borrowing in excess of working capital requirements, loan guarantees, and other actions that could affect the value of its investment.

Finally, the deal enables General Electric to pursue a staged exit of NBCUniversal over a number of years. In doing so, GE hopes that the potential synergy with Comcast will increase substantially the value of its share of the joint venture. GE has redemption rights (a put option) during the six months beginning January 28, 2014, to redeem one-half of its interest in NBCUniversal Holdings. In the six months beginning on January 28, 2018, GE can redeem its remaining interest. Comcast is committed to funding $2.9 billion for each of the two redemptions, payable in cash and stock up to $5.8 billion to the extent NBCUniversal Media cannot fund the redemptions. The purchase price to be paid with any redemption by GE will be 120% of the "public market trading value" of NBCUniversal Holding, to be determined by an appraisal if the business is not yet publicly traded, less 50% of the "public market trading value" greater than $28.4 billion. After January 28, 2014, GE may transfer its interest to a third party, subject to Comcast's having the right of first offer (first refusal). Comcast has a call option to buy out GE after the same dates designated for GE's put option at the same price required under the put option.

In 2011, NBCUniversal Media had revenue of $19.3 billion, earnings before interest and taxes of $2.3 billion, and net income of $1.7 billion. While the financial outlook for the business has stabilized, the deal continues to be subject to the criticism that there is little overlap between Comcast and NBCUniversal Media's businesses to provide significant cost savings. Moreover, big media deals have a poor track record, as illustrated by the AOL Time Warner debacle. Comcast is placing a big bet that it will be able to combine content and distribution successfully and to grow the value of the consolidated businesses.

In contrast, General Electric may be more intent on exercising its option to sell its interests unless the fortunes of NBCUniversal Media improve dramatically in the coming years.

Discussion Questions

1. Speculate as to why GE may have found it difficult to manage NBCUniversal.
2. Why was the NBCUniversal joint venture used to borrow the $9.1 billion paid to GE? How might this impact the ongoing operation of NBCUniversal? What are the tradeoffs the partners are making in agreeing to fund a portion of the purchase price through NBCUniversal?
3. Speculate as to the potential circumstances in which either Comcast or GE would be likely to exercise their call or put options. Which party do you believe is likely to exercise their options first, and why?
4. What are the likely challenges Comcast and GE will have in integrating the various businesses that comprise the joint venture? Be specific.
5. Why did GE and Comcast choose to operate NBCUniversal as a limited liability company rather than as a corporation? Be specific.
6. Speculate as to why the partners chose to operate NBCUniversal through a holding company.

Solutions to these case study questions are found in the Online Instructor's Manual for instructors using this book.

Alternative Exit and Restructuring Strategies

Divestitures, Spin-Offs, Carve-Outs, Split-Offs, and Tracking Stocks

Experience is the name everyone gives to their mistakes.—**Oscar Wilde**

INSIDE M&A: THE WARNER MUSIC GROUP IS SOLD AT AUCTION

KEY POINTS

- In selling a business, a firm may choose either to negotiate with a single potential buyer, to control the number of potential bidders, or to engage in a public auction.
- The auction process often is viewed as the most effective way to get the highest price for a business to be sold; however, far from simple, an auction can be both a chaotic and a time-consuming procedure.
- Auctions may be most suitable for businesses whose value is largely intangible or for "hard-to-value" businesses.

In early 2011, the Warner Music Group (WMG), the third largest of the "big four" recorded-music companies, consisted of two separate businesses: one showing high growth potential and the other with declining revenues. Of WMG's $3 billion in annual revenue, 82% came from sales of recorded music, with the remainder attributed to royalty payments for the use of music owned by the firm. Of the two, only recorded music has suffered revenue declines, due to piracy, aggressive pricing of online music sales, and the bankruptcy of many record retailers and wholesalers. In contrast, music publishing has grown as a result of diverse revenue streams from radio, television, advertising, and other sources. Music publishing also is benefiting from digital music downloads and the proliferation of cellphone ringtones.

In 2004, Warner Music's parent at the time, Time Warner Inc., agreed to sell the business to a consortium led by THL Partners for $2.6 billion in cash. The group also included Edgar Bronfman, Jr. (the Seagram's heir, who also became the CEO of WMG), Bain Capital, and Providence Equity Partners. Having held the firm for seven years, a long time for private equity investors, its primary investors were seeking a way to cash out of the business, whose long-term fortunes appeared problematic. WMG's investors were also in a race with Terra Firma Capital Partners, owner of the venerable British record company EMI, which was expected to take EMI public or to sell the business to a strategic buyer. WMG's investors were concerned that, if EMI were to be sold before WMG, the firm's exit strategy would be compromised, because there was much speculation that the only logical buyer for WMG was EMI.

By the end of January 2011, WMG had solicited about 70 potential bidders and attracted unsolicited indications of interest from at least 20 others. As this group winnowed through the auction's three rounds, alliances among the bidders continually changed. In the ensuing auction, WMG's stock price jumped by 75% from $4.72 per share on January 20 to $8.25 per share, for a total market value of $3.3 billion on May 6, 2011.

In view of the differences between these two businesses, WMG was open to selling the firm in total or in pieces, contributing to the extensive bidder interest. Risk takers were betting on an eventual recovery in recorded-music sales, while risk-averse investors were more likely to focus on music publishing. Prior to the auction, WMG distributed confidentiality agreements to 37 suitors, with 10 actually submitting a preliminary bid by the deadline of February 22, 2011. Of the preliminary bids, four were for the entire company, three for recorded music, and three for music publishing. For the entire firm, prices ranged from a low bid of $6 per share to a high bid of $8.25 per share. For recorded music, bids ranged from a low of $700 million to a high of $1.1 billion. Music publishing bids were almost twice that of recorded music, ranging from a low of $1.45 billion to a high of $2 billion.

For bidders, the objective is to make it to the next round in the auction; for sellers, the objective is less about prices offered during the initial round and more about determining who is committed to the process and who has the financial wherewithal to consummate the deal. According to the firm's proxy pertaining to the sale, released on May 20, 2011, the subsequent bidding was characterized as a series of ever-changing alliances among bidders, with Access Industries submitting the winning bid. The sale appears to have been a success from the investors' standpoint, with some speculating that THL alone earned an internal rate of return (including dividends) of 34%.[1]

[1] De La Merced, 2011

CHAPTER OVERVIEW

Many corporations, particularly large, highly diversified organizations, are constantly looking for ways in which they can enhance shareholder value by changing the composition of their assets, liabilities, equity, and operations. These activities generally are referred to as *restructuring strategies*. Restructuring may embody both growth strategies and exit strategies. Growth strategies have been discussed elsewhere in this book. The focus in this chapter is on those strategic options allowing the firm to maximize shareholder value by redeploying assets through downsizing or refocusing the parent company. As such, this chapter discusses the myriad motives for exiting businesses, the various restructuring strategies for doing so, and why firms select one strategy over other options. In this context, equity carve-outs, spin-offs, divestitures, and split-offs are discussed separately rather than as a specialized form of a carve-out.[2] The chapter concludes with a discussion of what empirical studies say are the primary determinants of financial returns to shareholders resulting from undertaking the various restructuring strategies. Voluntary and involuntary restructuring and reorganization (both inside and outside the protection of bankruptcy court) also represent exit strategies for firms and are discussed in detail in Chapter 17. A review of Chapter 16 (including practice questions with answers) is available in the file folder entitled "Student Study Guide" on the companion website to this book (*http://booksite.elsevier.com/9780123854872*).

WHY DO FIRMS EXIT BUSINESSES?

Theories abound as to why corporations choose to exit certain businesses. Some of the most common are discussed next.

Increasing Corporate Focus

Managing highly diverse and complex portfolios of businesses is both time consuming and distracting and may result in funding those businesses with relatively unattractive investment opportunities with cash flows generated by units offering more favorable opportunities. Firms often choose to simplify their business portfolio by focusing on those units with the highest growth potential and by exiting those businesses that are not germane to the firm's core business strategy. Increasing focus often improves firm value by allocating limited resources better and by reducing competition for such resources within multidivisional firms.[3]

---

[2]In some accounting texts, divestitures (referred to as *sell-offs*), spin-offs, and split-offs are all viewed as different forms of equity carve-outs and discussed in terms of how they affect the parent firm's shareholders' equity for financial-reporting purposes.

[3]Fulghieri and Sevilir, 2011

Underperforming Businesses

Parent firms often exit businesses failing to meet or exceed the parent's hurdle-rate requirements. In May 2007, General Electric announced the sale of its plastics operations for $11.6 billion to Saudi Basic Industries as part of its strategy to sell lower-return units and move into faster-growing and potentially higher-return businesses, such as healthcare and water processing.

Regulatory Concerns

A firm with substantial market share purchasing a direct competitor may create antitrust concerns. Regulatory agencies still may approve the merger if the acquirer divests operations that, when combined with similar target firm businesses, are deemed to be anticompetitive.

Lack of Fit

Synergies anticipated by the parent among its businesses may not materialize. TRW's decision to sell its commercial and consumer information services businesses in 1997 came after years of trying to find a significant fit with its space and defense businesses.

Tax Considerations

Tax benefits may be realized through a restructuring of the business. Nursing home operator Sun Healthcare Systems (Sun) contributed its nursing home real estate operations to a Real Estate Investment Trust (REIT) in 2010 through a spin-off. Because REITs do not pay taxes on income that is distributed to shareholders, Sun was able to enhance shareholder value by eliminating the double taxation of income, once by the parent and again by investors when dividends are paid.

Raising Funds

Parent firms may choose to fund new initiatives or reduce leverage or other financial obligations through the sale or partial sale of units no longer considered strategic. In late 2010, British Petroleum completed a sale of oil and gas properties to Apache Corporation for $7 billion in order to finance a portion of the cleanup costs associated with the Gulf of Mexico oil well blowout. Pressured by activist shareholders, Chesapeake Energy Group announced in 2012 its intention to sell $11.5 billion to $14 billion in assets to reduce its leverage.

Worth More to Others

Others may view a firm's operating units as much more valuable than the parent and be willing to pay a premium price for such businesses. In early 2010,

GE completed the sale of its fire alarm and security systems unit at a substantial profit to United Technologies for $1.82 billion, to eliminate what it considered a noncore business. United Technologies desired to increase its focus in the security business and had acquired a series of home security firms.

Risk Reduction

A firm may reduce risk associated with a unit by selling or spinning-off the business. For example, major tobacco companies have been under pressure for years to divest or spin off their food businesses because of the litigation risk associated with their tobacco subsidiaries. Altria bowed to such pressure in 2007 with the spin-off of its Kraft Food operations.

Discarding Unwanted Businesses from Prior Acquisitions

Acquirers often find themselves with certain target firm assets that do not fit their primary strategy. These redundant assets may be divested to raise funds to help pay for the acquisition and to enable management to focus on integrating the remaining businesses into the parent without the distraction of having to manage nonstrategic assets. When Northrop Grumman acquired TRW in 2002, it announced it would retain TRW's space and defense businesses and divest operations not germane to Northrop's core defense business. Nestlé acquired Adams, Pfizer's chewing gum and confectionery business, in early 2003 for $4.6 billion, which Pfizer viewed as a noncore business acquired as part of its acquisition of Warner-Lambert in 2000.

Avoiding Conflicts with Customers

For years, many of the regional Bell operating companies (i.e., RBOCs) that AT&T spun off in 1984 have been interested in competing in the long-distance market, which would put them in direct competition with their former parent. Similarly, AT&T sought to penetrate the regional telephone markets by gaining access to millions of households by acquiring cable TV companies. In preparation for the implementation of these plans, AT&T announced in 1995 that it would divide the company into three publicly traded global companies, to avoid conflicts between AT&T's former equipment manufacturer and its main customers, the RBOCs.

Increasing Transparency

Firms may be opaque to investors due to their diverse business and product offerings. General Electric is an example, operating dozens of separate businesses in many countries. Even with access to financial and competitive information on each business, it is challenging for any analyst or investor to value properly such a diversified firm. By reducing its complexity, a firm may make it easier for investors to assess accurately its true value.

DIVESTITURES

A *divestiture* is the sale of a portion of a firm's assets to an outside party, generally resulting in a cash infusion to the parent. Such assets may include a product line, a subsidiary, or a division.

Motives for Divestitures

Divestitures often represent a way of raising cash. A firm may choose to sell an undervalued or underperforming operation that it determined to be nonstrategic or unrelated to the core business and to use the proceeds of the sale to fund investments in potentially higher-return opportunities, including paying off debt. Alternatively, the firm may choose to divest the undervalued business and return the cash to shareholders through either a liquidating dividend[4] or share repurchase. Moreover, an operating unit may simply be worth more if sold than if retained by the parent.

Corporate Portfolio Reviews

The parent conducts a financial analysis to determine if the business is worth more to shareholders if it is sold and the proceeds are either returned to the shareholders or reinvested in opportunities offering higher returns. Weighing the future of certain businesses with other opportunities, GE's portfolio of companies has been undergoing change since the current CEO, Jeffrey Immelt, took control in September 2001. Since then, GE has completed transactions valued at more than $160 billion in buying and selling various operating units.

To Sell or Not to Sell

An analysis undertaken to determine if a business should be sold involves a multistep process. These steps include determining the after-tax cash flows generated by the unit, an appropriate discount rate reflecting the risk of the business, the after-tax market value of the business, and the after-tax value of the business to the parent. The decision to sell or retain the business depends on a comparison of the after-tax value of the business to the parent with the after-tax proceeds from the sale of the business. These steps are outlined in more detail next.

---

[4] A liquidating dividend is a payment made to shareholders exceeding the firm's net income. It is a "liquidating" dividend because the firm must sell assets to make the payment.

Step 1: Calculating After-Tax Cash Flows

To decide if a business is worth more to the shareholder if sold, the parent must first estimate the after-tax cash flows of the business viewed on a stand-alone basis. This requires adjusting the cash flows for intercompany sales and the cost of services (e.g., legal, treasury, and audit) provided by the parent. *Intercompany sales* refers to operating unit revenue generated by selling products or services to another unit owned by the same parent. Intercompany sales should be restated to ensure they are valued at market prices.[5] Moreover, services provided by the parent to the business may be subsidized or at a markup over actual cost. Operating profits should be reduced by the amount of any subsidies and increased by any markup over what the business would have to pay if it purchased comparable services from sources outside of the parent firm.

Step 2: Estimating the Discount Rate

Once cash flows have been determined, a discount rate should be estimated that reflects the risk characteristics of the industry in which the business competes. The cost of capital of other firms in the same industry (or firms in other industries exhibiting similar profitability, growth, and risk characteristics) is often a good proxy for the discount rate of the business being analyzed.

Step 3: Estimating the After-Tax Market Value of the Business

The discount rate then is used to estimate the market value of the projected after-tax cash flows of the business determined in Step 1.

Step 4: Estimating the Value of the Business to the Parent

The after-tax equity value (EV) of the business as part of the parent is estimated by subtracting the market value of the business's liabilities (L) from its after-tax market value (MV) as a stand-alone operation. This relationship can be expressed as follows:

$$EV = MV - L$$

EV is a measure of the after-tax market value of the shareholder equity of the business, where the shareholder is the parent firm.

Step 5: Deciding to Sell

The decision to sell or retain the business is made by comparing the EV with the after-tax sale value (SV) of the business. Assuming other considerations do

---

[5] In vertically integrated firms such as steelmakers, much of the revenue generated by a firm's iron ore and coal operations comes from sales to the parent firm's steelmaking unit. The parent may value this revenue for financial-reporting purposes using transfer prices. If such prices do not reflect market prices, intercompany revenue may be artificially high or low, depending on whether the transfer prices are higher or lower than market prices.

not outweigh any after-tax gain on the sale of the business, the decision to sell or retain can be summarized as follows:

If SV > EV, divest.
If SV < EV, retain.

Although the sale value may exceed the equity value of the business, the parent may choose to retain the business for strategic reasons. The parent may believe that the business's products facilitate the sale of other products the firm offers. Amazon.com breaks even on the sale of Kindle e-book readers while expecting to make money on electronic books that will be downloaded via the Kindle. In another instance, the divestiture of one subsidiary of a diversified parent may increase operating expenses for other parent operations. In 2011, one reason given for Hewlett-Packard's decision not to sell its PC unit after publicly announcing its intention to do so was the potential for a one-time increase in expenses following the selloff of the unit.[6]

Timing of the Sale

Obviously, the best time to sell a business is when the owner does not need to sell or the demand for the business is greatest. The decision to sell also should reflect the broader financial environment. Selling when business confidence is high, stock prices are rising, and interest rates are low is likely to fetch a higher price for the unit. If the business to be sold is highly cyclical, the sale should be timed to coincide with the firm's peak-year earnings.

The Selling Process

Selling firms choose the selling process that best serves their objectives and influences the types of buyers that are attracted (e.g., strategic versus private equity).[7] The selling process may be reactive or proactive (Figure 16.1). *Reactive sales* occur when the parent is unexpectedly approached by a buyer, either for the entire firm or for a portion of the firm, such as a product line or subsidiary. If the bid is sufficiently attractive, the parent firm may choose to reach a negotiated settlement with the bidder without investigating other options. This may occur if the parent is concerned about potential degradation of its business, or that of a subsidiary, if its interest in selling becomes public knowledge. In contrast, *proactive sales* may be characterized as public or private solicitations. In a *public sale or auction*, a firm announces publicly that it is putting itself, a subsidiary, or a

---

[6]Such expenses included the need to establish new infrastructure and systems for information technology, support, sales, and distribution channels for other businesses that had been using the PC unit's infrastructure. In addition, other HP operating businesses would lose volume discounts on purchases of components enjoyed as a result of the huge volume of such purchases made by the PC business.

[7]Fidrmuc et al., 2012

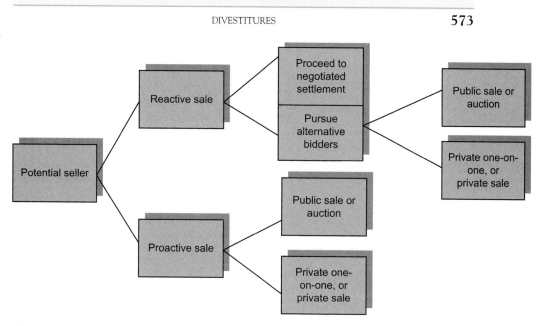

FIGURE 16.1   **The selling process.**

product line up for sale. In this instance, potential buyers contact the seller. This is a way to identify easily interested parties; however, this approach can also attract unqualified bidders (i.e., those lacking the resources necessary to complete the deal) or those seeking to obtain proprietary information through the due diligence process. In a *private or controlled sale,* the parent firm may hire an investment banker or undertake on its own to identify potential buyers to be contacted. Once a preferred potential buyer or list of what are believed to be qualified buyers has been compiled, contact is made.[8]

In either a public or a private sale, interested parties are asked to sign confidentiality agreements before being given access to proprietary information. The challenge for the selling firm is to manage efficiently this information, which can grow into thousands of pages of documents and spreadsheets, and to provide easy and secure access to all interested parties. Increasingly, such information is offered online through so-called *virtual data rooms* (VDRs).[9] In private sales, bidders may be asked to sign a standstill agreement requiring them not to make an

[8]See the discussion of the screening and contacting process in Chapter 5 for more details.

[9]The VDR is intended to replace the traditional paper-based data room and the challenges of keeping such information current and secure. Because the VDR is searchable electronically, bidders have easier and more rapid access to the specific information they are seeking. Since multiple parties can access the information simultaneously from anywhere in the world unaware of the presence of others, the VDR provides for more efficient and thorough due diligence. VDRs also allow for online questions and answers. The major limitations of the VDR are the expense and technical expertise required and the inability to meet in person the management of the unit to be sold.

TABLE 16.1   Choosing the Right Selling Process

Selling Process	Advantages/Disadvantages
One-on-One Negotiations (single bidder)	Enables seller to select the buyer with the greatest synergy.
	Minimizes disruptive due diligence.
	Limits the potential for loss of proprietary information to competitors.
	May exclude potentially attractive bidders.
Public Auction (no limit on number of bidders)	Most appropriate for small, private, or hard-to-value firms.
	May discourage bidders concerned about undisciplined bidding by uninformed bidders.
	Potentially disruptive due to multiple due diligences.
Controlled Auction (limited number of bidders)	Enables seller to select potential buyers with the greatest synergy.
	Sparks competition without the disruptive effects of public auctions.
	May exclude potentially attractive bidders.

unsolicited bid. Parties willing to sign these agreements are then asked to submit preliminary, nonbinding indications of interest (i.e., a single number or a bid within a range). Those parties submitting preliminary bids are then ranked by the selling company by size of the bid, form of payment, the ability of the bidder to finance the transaction, form of acquisition, and ease of doing the deal. A small number of those submitting preliminary bids are then asked to submit a legally binding best and final offer. At this point, the seller may choose to initiate an auction among the most attractive bids or to go directly into negotiating a purchase agreement with a single party.

Choosing the Right Selling Process

Selling firms attempt to manage the selling process in a manner that will realize the highest possible purchase price while maintaining the interest of potential acquirers. Selling firms may choose to negotiate with a single firm, to control the number of potential bidders, or to engage in a public auction (Table 16.1). Large firms often choose to sell themselves, major product lines, or subsidiaries through one-on-one negotiations with a single bidder deemed to have the greatest synergy with the selling firm. Such firms' sellers are concerned about the deleterious effects of making the sale public and the disruptive effects of allowing many firms to perform due diligence. This approach also may be adopted to limit the potential for losing bidders, who may also be competitors, from obtaining proprietary information as a result of due diligence.

An auction among a number of bidders may be undertaken to elicit the highest offer when selling smaller firms that are more difficult to value. Paradoxically, public auctions may actually discourage some firms from bidding due to the potential for overly aggressive bidding by relatively uninformed bidders to boost the bid price to excessive levels. The private or controlled sale among a small number of carefully selected bidders may spark competition to boost the selling price while minimizing the deleterious effects of public auctions. Pfizer's 2012 auction of its fast-growing baby food business is a recent example of a controlled auction. Pfizer sought bids from those it knew could benefit from the unit's exposure to emerging markets and had the financial wherewithal to pay a substantial premium. The auction process involving Swiss-based Nestlé and France's Groupe Danone went through several rounds before Nestlé's $11.85 billion bid was accepted by Pfizer. At 19.8 times EBITDA, the bid was considerably higher than that of the 15.7 multiple Nestlé paid for Gerber's baby food operations in 2007.

Approximately one-half of corporate M&A transactions involve one-on-one negotiations. The remaining transactions involve public or controlled auctions in which the sellers contacted an average of 10 potential bidders, with some contacting as many as 150. The financial returns to the selling firm's shareholders appear to be about the same regardless of the way in which the business is sold. However, for larger target firms, one-on-one negotiation is more common.[10] One-on-one negotiation may be superior to auctions when the target is large, because there are likely to be fewer potential buyers, which may result in a higher purchase price because the selling firm is able to share more value-enhancing proprietary information with the potential buyer. In an auction involving many bidders, the likelihood that such information could leak to competitors and be used to the competitive disadvantage of the selling firm is much higher.[11]

These findings seem at odds with the conventional wisdom that auctions should result, on average, in higher returns for selling-company shareholders on the presumption that more bidders are usually better than fewer bidders.[12] This conclusion is based on the premise that all bidders have access to the same information and have the financial ability to finance their bids. As previously noted, some qualified bidders may choose to refrain from bidding in an auction, concerned about overpaying for the target firm.

The mere fact that most transactions involve relatively few bidders does not suggest that the bidding process is not competitive.[13] In most cases, simply the threat of rival bids is sufficient to increase bids, even in one-on-one negotiations. Such latent competition tends to influence bid prices the most when market liquidity is greatest such that potential bidders have relatively inexpensive access to funds through borrowing or new equity issues. Ultimately, the premium a target firm receives over its current share price is influenced by a variety of factors relating to the deal and industry characteristics. Table 16.2 provides a

[10] Boone and Mulherin, 2009

[11] Subramanian, 2010

[12] Bulow and Klemperer, 2009

[13] Aktas et al., 2010

TABLE 16.2　Factors Affecting Purchase Price Premiums

Factor	Explanation
Net Synergy Potential	Purchase premiums are likely to increase the greater the magnitude of perceived net synergy (see Chapter 9). Net synergy often is the greatest in highly related firms.[a] Moreover, premiums are likely to be larger if most of the synergy is provided by the target.
Desire for Control	Buyers may pay more to gain control of firms exhibiting weak financial performance because of potential gains from making better business decisions (see Chapter 10).
Growth Potential	Targets displaying greater growth potential relative to competitors generally command higher premiums.[b]
Information Asymmetry (i.e., one bidder has more information than other bidders)	Informed bidders are likely to pay lower premiums because less informed bidders fear overpaying and either withdraw from or do not participate in the bidding process.[c]
Target Size	Buyers pay more for smaller targets due to the anticipated ease of integration.[d]
Target's Eagerness to Sell	Targets with a strong desire to sell typically receive lower premiums due to their relatively weak negotiating positions.[e]
Run-up in Preannouncement Target Share Price	Share price run-up causes bidders unsure of having adequate information to revalue their bids upward.[f]
Type of Purchase	Hostile transactions tend to command higher premiums than friendly transactions.[g]
Hubris	Excessive confidence may lead bidders to overpay.[h]
Type of Payment	Cash purchases usually require an increased premium to compensate target shareholders for the immediate tax liability they incur.[i] Bidders using overvalued shares often overpay for target firms.
Leverage	Highly leveraged buyers are disciplined by their lenders not to overpay; relatively unleveraged buyers often are prone to pay excessive premiums.[j]
Customer–Supplier Relationships	In vertical mergers, buyers substantially reliant on a target that is either a customer or a supplier and that has few alternatives will be forced to pay higher premiums than otherwise.[k]
Board Connections	Acquirers realize higher announcement-date returns in transactions in which the target and the acquirer's boards share a common director.[l]
Investor Consensus Around Target Share Price	If investors generally agree that the target's current share price is valued fairly, they are more likely to accept a smaller takeover premium in view of the firm's limited appreciation potential than if there is substantial disagreement among investors.[m]

(Continued)

V. ALTERNATIVE BUSINESS AND RESTRUCTURING STRATEGIES

TABLE 16.2   (Continued)

Factor	Explanation
Industry growth prospects	The magnitude of premiums varies substantially across industries, reflecting differences in expected growth rates.[n]

[a]Betton et al., 2009.
[b]Betton et al., 2008.
[c]Dionne et al., 2010.
[d]Moeller, 2005.
[e]Aktas et al., 2010.
[f]Betton et al., 2009.
[g]Moeller, 2005.
[h]Hayward et al., 1997.
[i]Betton et al., 2008.
[j]Gondhalekar et al. (2004) argue that highly leveraged buyers are monitored closely by their lenders and are less likely to overpay. Morellec and Zhdanov (2008) find that relatively unleveraged buyers often pay more for targets.
[k]Ahern, 2012.
[l]Cai and Sevilir, 2012. Having a board connection often improves the information flow such that the acquirer is less likely to overpay for the target firm.
[m]Chatterjee et al., 2012.
[n]Madura, Ngo, and Viale, 2012.

summary of those factors that have been found to be significant determinants of the magnitude of purchase price premiums.

Tax and Accounting Considerations for Divestitures

The divesting firm recognizes a gain or loss for financial-reporting purposes equal to the difference between the fair value of the payment received for the divested operation and its book value. For tax purposes, the gain or loss is the difference between the proceeds and the parent's tax basis in the stock or assets. Capital gains are taxed at the same rate as other business income.

SPIN-OFFS

A *spin-off* is a stock dividend paid by a firm to its current shareholders consisting of shares in an existing or newly created subsidiary. Such distributions are made in direct proportion to the shareholders' current holdings of the parent's stock. As such, the proportional ownership of shares in the subsidiary is the same as the stockholders' proportional ownership of shares in the parent firm. The new entity has its own management and operates independent of the parent company. Unlike the divestiture or equity carve-out (explained later in this chapter), the spin-off does not result in an infusion of cash to the parent company. Following the spin-off, the firm's shareholders own both parent company shares and shares in the unit involved in the spin-off.

While spin-offs may be less cumbersome than divestitures, they are by no means simple to execute. The parent firm must make sure that the unit to be spun-off is fully operational and legally disentangled from other parent opera-tions and that the parent has no ongoing liabilities associated with the spun-off unit. In early 2011, Motorola Inc., completed its ongoing restructuring effort by spinning off Motorola Mobility to its shareholders and renaming the remaining business Motorola Solutions. Motorola's board took action to ensure the financial viability of Motorola Mobility by buying back nearly all of its outstanding $3.9 billion debt and transferring as much as $4 billion in cash to Motorola Mobility. Furthermore, Motorola Solutions assumed the responsibility for the pension obligations of Motorola Mobility. If Motorola Mobility were to be forced into bankruptcy shortly after the breakup, Motorola Solutions could be held legally responsible for some of the business's liabilities.

Motives for Spin-Offs

In addition to the motives for exiting businesses discussed earlier, spin-offs provide a means of rewarding shareholders with a nontaxable dividend (if prop-erly structured). Parent firms with a low tax basis in a business may choose to spin off the unit as a tax-free distribution to shareholders rather than sell the business and incur a substantial tax liability. The unit, now independent of the parent, has its own stock to use for possible acquisitions. Finally, the managers of the business that is to be spun off have a greater incentive to improve the unit's performance if they own stock in the unit.

Tax and Accounting Considerations for Spin-Offs

If properly structured, a corporation can make a tax-free distribution to its shareholders of stock in a subsidiary in which it holds a controlling interest (i.e., a controlled subsidiary). Neither the distributing corporation (i.e., parent) nor its shareholders recognize any taxable gain or loss on the distribution. Such dis-tributions can involve a spin-off, a split-up (a series of corporate spin-offs often resulting in the dissolution of the firm), or a split-off (an exchange offer of sub-sidiary stock for parent stock). Split-ups and split-offs are explained in more detail later in this chapter.

To be tax free, such distributions must satisfy certain conditions. These include the following:

1. The parent must control the subsidiary(ies) to be spun-off, split-up, or split-off by owning at least 80% of each class of the unit's voting and nonvoting stock;
2. The distributing firm must distribute all of the stock of the controlled subsidiary;
3. Both the parent and the controlled subsidiary must remain in the same business following the distribution in which they were actively engaged for the five years prior to the distribution;
4. Shareholders of the parent must maintain a significant continuity of interest in both the parent and the subsidiary after the transaction; and

5. The transaction must be for a sound business purpose, such as profit improvement or to increase management focus, and not for tax avoidance.[14]

For financial-reporting purposes, the parent firm should account for the spin-off of a subsidiary's stock to its shareholders at book value, with no gain or loss recognized, other than any reduction in value due to impairment. The reason for this treatment is that the ownership interests are essentially the same before and after the spin-off.

EQUITY CARVE-OUTS

Equity carve-outs exhibit characteristics similar to spin-offs. Both result in the subsidiary's stock's being traded separately from the parent's stock. They also are similar to divestitures and IPOs, in that they provide cash to the parent. However, unlike the spin-off or the divestiture, the parent generally retains control of the subsidiary in a carve-out transaction. A potentially significant drawback to the carve-out is the creation of minority shareholders.

Motives for Equity Carve-Outs

Like divestitures, equity carve-outs provide an opportunity to raise funds for reinvestment in the subsidiary, paying off debt, or paying a dividend to the parent firm. Carve-outs also may be used if the parent has significant contractual obligations, such as supply agreements, with its subsidiary.[15] Moreover, a carve-out frequently is a prelude to a divestiture, since it provides an opportunity to value the business by selling stock in a public stock exchange. The stock created for purposes of the carve-out often is used in incentive programs for the unit's management and as an *acquisition currency* (i.e., form of payment) if the parent later decides to grow the subsidiary. The two basic forms of an equity carve-out are the initial public offering and the subsidiary equity carve-out.

Initial Public Offerings and Subsidiary Equity Carve-Outs

An *initial public offering* is the first offering to the public of common stock of a formerly privately held firm. The sale of the stock provides an infusion of cash to the parent. The cash may be retained by the parent or returned to shareholders. Computer game designer Zynga entered the public equity market for the first time on December 15, 2011, to raise about $1 billion. At $10 per share, the IPO valued the firm at $8.9 billion.

---

[14] A spin-off cannot be used to avoid the payment of taxes on capital gains that might have been incurred if the parent had chosen to sell a subsidiary in which it had a low tax basis.

[15] By retaining a controlling interest in the subsidiary, a parent can honor such obligations (Jain et al., 2011).

The *subsidiary carve-out* is a transaction in which the parent creates a wholly owned, independent subsidiary, with stock and a management team that are different from the parent's, and issues a portion of the subsidiary's stock to the public. Usually, only a minority share of the parent's ownership in the subsidiary is issued to the public. Although the parent retains control, the subsidiary's shareholder base may be different than that of the parent due to the public sale of equity. The cash raised may be retained in the subsidiary or transferred to the parent as a dividend, a stock repurchase, or an intercompany loan. An example of a subsidiary carve-out is the sale to the public by Phillip Morris in 2001 of 15% of its wholly owned Kraft subsidiary. Phillip Morris' voting power over Kraft was reduced only to 97.7% because Kraft had a dual-class share structure in which only low-voting shares were issued in the public stock offering.

Tax and Accounting Considerations for Equity Carve-Outs

Retention of at least 80% of the unit enables consolidation for tax purposes, and retention of more than 50% enables consolidation for financial-reporting purposes.[16] If the parent owns less than 50% but more than 20%, it must use the equity method for financial reporting. Below 20%, it must use the cost method.[17]

SPLIT-OFFS AND SPLIT-UPS

A *split-off* is similar to a spin-off, in that a firm's subsidiary becomes an independent firm and the parent firm does not generate any new cash. However, unlike a spin-off, the split-off involves an offer to exchange parent stock for stock in the parent firm's subsidiary at an exchange ratio determined by the parent firm.[18] Split-offs most often arise when a portion of the parent firm's shareholders prefer to own the shares of a subsidiary of the parent rather than the parent's shares. Split-offs normally are non–pro rata stock distributions, in contrast to spin-offs, which generally are pro rata (or proportional) distributions of shares. In a pro rata distribution, a shareholder owning 10% of the outstanding parent company stock would receive 10% of the subsidiary whose shares were distributed. A non–pro rata distribution takes the form of a tender or exchange offer in which shareholders can accept or reject the distribution.

---

[16]Allen and McConnell (1998) found a median retention of subsidiary shares of 69%, while Vijh (2002) found a median ownership stake of 72%.

[17]When the equity method is used to account for ownership in a company, the investor records the initial investment at cost and then periodically adjusts the value to reflect its proportionate share of income or losses generated by the company. The cost method requires recording the investment at cost, and dividends received are included in investment income.

[18]Split-offs tend to be less common than spin-offs because they require the parent to determine the relative value of the parent and subsidiary stock to calculate the exchange ratio and because shareholders may have difficulty in understanding the proposed exchange offer.

A *split-up* refers to a restructuring strategy in which a single company splits into two or more separately managed firms. Through a series of split-offs or spin-offs, shareholders of the original or parent firm may choose to exchange their shares in the parent firm for shares in the new companies. Following the split, the original firm's shares are cancelled, and it ceases to exist. Kraft Foods decision in 2011 to split in two represented the culmination of a series of major restructuring actions designed to boost shareholder value (see Case Study 16.1).

CASE STUDY 16.1
Kraft Foods Splits-Up in Its Biggest Deal Yet

Key Points

- Investors often evaluate a firm's performance in terms of how well it does as compared to its peers.
- Activist investors can force an underperforming firm to change its strategy radically.
- The Kraft decision to split its businesses is yet another example of the recent trend by highly diversified businesses to increase their product focus.

Following a successful career as CEO of PepsiCo's Frito-Lay, Irene Rosenfeld became the CEO of Kraft Foods in 2006. As the world's second-largest packaged foods manufacturer, behind Nestlé, Kraft had stumbled in its efforts to increase its global reach by growing in emerging markets. Its brands tended to be old, and the firm was having difficulty developing new, trendy products. Rosenfeld was tasked by its board of directors with turning the firm around. She reasoned that it would take a complete overhaul of Kraft, including organization, culture, operations, marketing, branding, and the product portfolio, to transform the firm.

In 2010, the firm made what at the time was viewed by top management as its most transformational move by acquiring British confectionery company Cadbury for $19 billion. While the firm became the world's largest snack company with the completion of the transaction, it was still entrenched in its traditional business, groceries. The company now owned two very different product portfolios.

Between January 2010 and mid-2011, Kraft's earnings steadily improved, powered by stronger sales. Kraft shares rose almost 25%, more than twice the increase in the S&P 500 stock index. However, it continued to trade throughout this period at a lower price-to-earnings multiple than such competitors as Nestlé and Groupe Danone. Some investors were concerned that Kraft was not realizing the promised synergies from the Cadbury deal. Activist investors (Nelson Peltz's Trian Fund and Bill Ackman's Pershing Square Capital Management) had discussions with Kraft's management about splitting the firm. This plan had the support of Warren Buffett, whose conglomerate, Berkshire Hathaway, was Kraft's largest investor at that time, with a 6% owner-ship interest.

To avert a proxy fight, Kraft's board and management announced on August 4, 2011, its intention to restructure the firm radically by separating it into two distinct businesses. Coming just 18 months after the Cadbury deal, investors were initially stunned by the announcement but appeared to avidly support the proposal avidly by driving up the firm's share price by the end of the day. The proposal entailed separating its faster-growing global snack food business from its slower-growing, more United States–centered grocery business. The separation was completed through a tax-free spin-off to Kraft Food shareholders of the grocery business on October 1, 2012. The global snack food business will be named Mondelez International, while the North American grocery business will retain the Kraft name.

Management justified the proposed split-up of the firm as a means of increasing focus, providing greater opportunities, and giving investors a choice between the faster-growing snack business and the slower-growing but more predictable grocery operation. Management also argued that the Cadbury acquisition gave the snack business scale to compete against such competitors as Nestlé and PepsiCo.

Discussion Questions

1. Speculate as to why Kraft chose not divest its grocery business and use the proceeds either to reinvest in its faster-growing snack business, to buy back its stock, or a combination of the two.
2. How might a spin-off create shareholder value for Kraft Foods' shareholders?
3. There is often a natural tension between so-called activist investors, interested in short-term profits, and a firm's management, interested in pursuing a longer-term vision. When is this tension helpful to shareholders, and when does it destroy shareholder value?

Answers to these questions are provided in the Online Instructors Manual for instructors using this textbook.

Motives for Split-Offs

Divestiture may not be an option for disposing of a business in which the parent owns less than 100% of the stock, because potential buyers often want to acquire all of a firm's outstanding stock. By acquiring less than 100%, a buyer inherits minority shareholders, who may disagree with the new owner's future business decisions. Best suited for disposing of a less-than-100% investment stake in a subsidiary, split-offs also reduce the pressure on the spun-off firm's share price because shareholders who exchange their stock are less likely to sell the new stock. Presumably, a shareholder willing to make the exchange believes

Transaction:

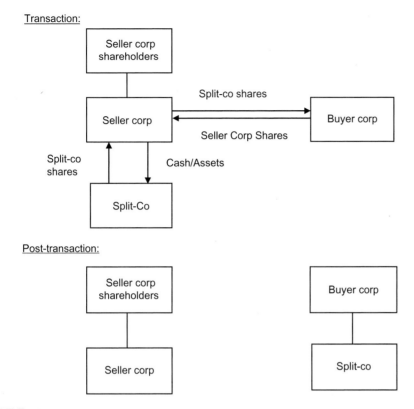

Post-transaction:

FIGURE 16.2   **"Cash-rich" split-off.**

the stock in the subsidiary has greater appreciation potential than the parent's stock. The exchange also increases the earnings per share of the parent firm by reducing the number of its shares outstanding, as long as the impact of the reduction in the number of shares outstanding exceeds the loss of the subsidiary's earnings. Split-offs are generally tax free to shareholders as long as they conform to the IRS requirements previously described for spin-offs. Finally, the split-off gives the parent shareholder the option to decide whether the shareholder wants to hold parent stock, split-off company stock, or a combination of both.

Cash-Rich Split-Offs

Cash-rich split-offs are variations of a conventional split-off and commonly occur when one firm owns stock in another. If a firm chooses to buy back its stock owned by another firm, it may exchange tax-free stock in a subsidiary it controls for its stock held by the other firm. Assume Buyer Corp owns stock in Seller Corp and Seller Corp wishes to buy back its stock (see Figure 16.2). To do so in a tax-free transaction, Seller Corp forms a new subsidiary (Split-Co) and transfers operating assets and liabilities and cash into the subsidiary in exchange for subsidiary stock. The subsidiary's assets can consist of up to 66% cash and 33% operating assets. The fair market value of the subsidiary must be approximately equal to the market value of Seller Corp's stock held by Buyer Corp. Seller Corp enters into a split-off in which it exchanges Split-Co stock for Seller stock held by Buyer Corp. Following the transaction, Split-Co becomes a wholly owned subsidiary of Buyer Corp. The transaction is tax free to both Seller Corp shareholders and Buyer Corp shareholders. The disadvantages of this deal is that it is complicated to execute and Buyer Corp must operate the acquired business for at least two years following closing.

News Corp. employed a tax-free, cash-rich split-off in reaching an agreement in early 2007 to buy Liberty Media's 19%—or $11 billion—stake in the media giant in exchange for News Corp.'s 38.6% stake in satellite TV firm DirecTV Group, $550 million in cash, and three sports TV channels. The cash and media assets were added to ensure that Liberty Media was exchanging its stake in News Corp. for "like-kind" assets of an equivalent or higher value to qualify as a tax-free exchange. Had the assets been divested, the two firms would have had to pay $4.5 billion in taxes due to likely gains on the sale.[19] Other recent cash-rich split-offs include Comcast/Time Warner Cable, Comcast/Liberty, KeySpan/Houston Exploration, Cox Communications/ Discovery Communications, and DST Systems/Janus Capital Group.

TRACKING STOCKS, TARGET STOCKS, AND LETTER STOCKS

Such stocks are separate classes of common stock of the parent firm. The parent divides its operations into two or more subsidiaries and assigns a common stock to each. Tracking stock is a class of common stock that links the shareholders' return to the subsidiary's operating performance. Tracking stock dividends rise or fall with the subsidiary's performance. Such stock represents an ownership interest in the parent rather than an ownership interest in the subsidiary. For voting purposes, holders of tracking stock with voting rights may vote their shares on issues related to the parent and not the subsidiary. The parent's board of directors and top management retain control of the subsidiary for which a tracking stock has been issued, since it is still legally part of the parent. Tracking stocks may be issued to current parent shareholders as a dividend, used as payment for an acquisition, or issued in a public offering.

Motives for Tracking Stocks

Tracking stock enables investors to value the different operations within a corporation based on their own performance. There is little empirical evidence that issuing a tracking stock for a subsidiary creates pure-play investment opportunities for investors, since the tracking stock tends to be correlated more with the

---

[19] Angwin and Drucker, 2006

parent's other outstanding stocks than with the stocks in the industry in which the subsidiary competes.[20] Tracking stocks provide the parent with another way of raising capital for a specific operation by selling a portion of the stock to the public and an alternative "currency" for making acquisitions. Stock-based incentive programs to attract and retain key managers also can be implemented for each operation with its own tracking stock.

Tax and Accounting Considerations for Tracking Stocks

For financial-reporting purposes, a distribution of tracking stock divides the parent firm's equity structure into separate classes of stock without a legal split-up of the firm. Unlike spin-offs, the IRS currently does not require that the business for which the tracking stock is created be at least five years old and that the parent retain a controlling interest in the business for the stock to be exempt from capital gains taxes. Unlike a spin-off or a carve-out, the parent retains complete ownership of the business. In general, a proportionate distribution by a company to its shareholders of the company's stock is tax free to shareholders.

Problems with Tracking Stocks

Few tracking stocks have been issued in recent years, perhaps due to inherent governance issues and their poor long-term performance. Conflicts among the parent's operating units often arise in determining how the parent's overhead expenses are allocated to the business units and what price one business unit is paid for selling products to other business units. Tracking stocks can stimulate shareholder lawsuits. The parent's board approves overall operating unit and capital budgets. Decisions made in support of one operating unit may appear to be unfair to those holding a tracking stock in another unit. Thus, tracking stocks can pit classes of shareholders against one another and lead to lawsuits. Tracking stocks also may not have voting rights. Further, the chances of a hostile takeover of a firm with a tracking stock are virtually zero because the firm is controlled by the parent.

COMPARING ALTERNATIVE EXIT AND RESTRUCTURING STRATEGIES

Table 16.3 summarizes the primary characteristics of each of the restructuring strategies discussed in this chapter. Note that divestitures and carve-outs provide cash to the parent, whereas spin-offs and split-ups do not. The parent remains in existence in all restructuring strategies. A new legal entity generally is created with each restructuring strategy. With the exception of the carve-out, the parent generally loses control of the division involved in the restructuring strategy. Only spin-offs, split-ups, and split-offs are generally not taxable to shareholders, if properly structured.

---

[20] D'Souza and Jacob, 2000

TABLE 16.3	Key Characteristics of Alternative Exit and Restructuring Strategies

	Alternative Strategies					
Characteristics	Divestitures	Equity Carve-Outs/IPOs	Spin-Offs	Split-Ups	Split-Offs	Tracking Stocks
Cash Infusion to Parent	Yes	Yes	No	No	No	Yes
Parent Ceases to Exist	No	No	No	Yes	No	No
New Legal Entity Created	Sometimes	Yes	Yes	Yes	No	No
New Shares Issued	Sometimes	Yes	Yes	Yes	Yes	Yes
Parent Remains in Control	No	Generally	No	No	No	Yes
Taxable to Shareholders	Yes	Yes	No	No	No	No

CHOOSING AMONG DIVESTITURE, CARVE-OUT, AND SPIN-OFF RESTRUCTURING STRATEGIES

Parent firms that engage in divestitures often are highly diversified in largely unrelated businesses and have a desire to achieve greater focus or to raise cash.[21] Those that use carve-out strategies usually operate businesses in related industries exhibiting some degree of synergy and have significant contractual obligations to the business and a desire to raise cash.[22] Consequently, the parent firm may pursue a carve-out rather than a divestiture or spin-off strategy to retain perceived synergy.[23] Evidence shows that the timing of the carve-out is influenced by when management sees its subsidiary's assets as overvalued.[24] Firms engaging in spin-offs often are diversified, but less so than those that are prone to pursue divestiture strategies and have little need to raise cash.[25] Table 16.4 identifies characteristics of parent firm operating units that are subject to certain types of restructuring activities.

The decision to exit a business is a two-stage process. The first stage involves the firm's deciding to exit a line of business or product line. The second stage entails selecting the appropriate exit strategy. Divestitures, carve-outs, and

[21] Bergh, Johnson, and Dewitt, 2007

[22] Jain et al., 2011

[23] Powers, 2001

[24] Powers, 2003; Chen and Guo, 2005

[25] John and Ofek, 1995; Kaplan and Weisbach, 1992

TABLE 16.4   Characteristics of Parent Company Operating Units That Undergo Divestiture, Carve-Out, or Spin-Off.

Exit/Restructuring Strategy	Characteristics of Operating Unit Subject to Exit/ Restructuring Strategy
Divestitures	• Usually unrelated to other businesses owned by the parent • Operating performance generally worse than the parent's performance • Slightly underperform their peers in the year before the announcement date • Generally sell at a lower price than carve-outs, measured by the ratio of market value to book assets
Carve-Outs	• Generally more profitable and faster growing than spun-off or divested businesses • Operating performance often exceeds parent's • Usually operate in industries characterized by the high ratio of market to book values • Generally outperform peers in the year before the announcement date
Spin-Offs	• Generally faster growing and more profitable than divested businesses • Most often operate in industries related to other industries in which the parent operates • Operating performance worse than parent's • Slightly underperform peers in the year before the announcement date

Sources: Ravenscroft and Scherer (1991), Cho and Cohen (1997), Hand and Skantz (1997), Kang and Shivdasani (1997), Powers (2001, 2003), Chen and Guo (2005), and Bergh (2007).

spin-offs are the most commonly used restructuring strategy when a parent corporation is considering exiting a business partially or entirely. The decision as to which of these three strategies to use is often heavily influenced by the parent firm's need for cash, the degree of synergy between the business to be divested or spun off and the parent's other operating units, and the potential selling price of the division.[26] However, these factors are not independent. Parent firms needing cash are more likely to divest or engage in an equity carve-out for operations exhibiting high selling prices relative to their synergy value. Parent firms not needing cash are more likely to spin off units exhibiting low selling prices and synergy with the parent. Parent firms with moderate cash needs are likely to engage in equity carve-outs when the unit's selling price is low relative to perceived synergy. Table 16.5 illustrates this two-stage procedure.

It may seem that a divestiture or carve-out would be preferable to a spin-off if the after-tax proceeds from the sale of an operating unit exceed its after-tax equity value to the firm. Unlike a spin-off, a divestiture or carve-out generates a cash infusion to the firm. However, a spin-off may create greater shareholder

[26] Powers, 2001

TABLE 16.5 Divestitures, Carve-Outs, and Spin-Offs: Selecting the Appropriate Restructuring Strategy

Stage 1 Considerations (Primary Motive for Restructuring)	Stage 2 Considerations		Appropriate Restructuring Strategy	Restructuring Strategy More Likely If Parent
	Need for Cash	Value of Business/Degree of Business Synergy		
Change Strategy/Increase Focus →	Needs Cash →	High Price/High Synergy	Carve-Out	Can retain synergy
		Low Price/High Synergy	Carve-Out	Can retain synergy
		High Price/Low Synergy	Divestiture	Can shield taxable gains[a]
		Low Price/Low Synergy	Divestiture	
	Little Need for Cash →	High Price/High Synergy	Carve-Out	Can retain synergy
		Low Price/High Synergy	Carve-Out	Can retain synergy
		High Price/Low Synergy	Spin-Off	Cannot shield potential gains
		Low Price/Low Synergy	Spin-Off	
Underperforming Businesses →	Needs Cash →	↑	Divestiture	Can shield taxable gains
	Little Need for Cash →	↑	Spin-Off	Cannot shield potential gains
Regulatory Concerns →		↑	Divestiture/Spin-Off	Carve-out not an option

Motive		Restructuring Type	Tax Treatment[a]
Lack of Fit	Needs Cash ──→	Divestiture	Can shield taxable gains
	Little Need for Cash ──→	Spin-Off	Cannot shield potential gains
Tax Considerations ──→		Spin-Off	Cannot shield potential gains
Raising Funds/Worth More to Others ──→		Divestiture	Can shield taxable gains
Risk Reduction ──→		Carve-Out	Can shield taxable gains
Moving Away from Core Business ──→		Divestiture/Carve-Out	Can shield taxable gains
Discarding Unwanted Businesses from Prior Acquisitions ──→		Divestiture	Can shield taxable gains
Avoiding Customer Conflicts	Need Cash ──→	Divestiture	Can shield taxable gains
	Little Need for Cash ──→	Spin-Off	Cannot shield taxable gains

[a] Parent can shield any taxable gains on the sale by offsetting such gains with losses incurred elsewhere in the consolidated firm.

wealth, for several reasons. First, a spin-off is tax-free to the shareholders if it is properly structured. The cash proceeds from an outright sale may be taxable to the parent to the extent a gain is realized. Also, management must be able to reinvest the after-tax proceeds at or above the firm's cost of capital. If management chooses to return the cash proceeds to shareholders, the shareholders incur a tax liability. Second, a spin-off enables the shareholders to decide when to sell their shares. Third, a spin-off may be less traumatic than a divestiture for an operating unit. The divestiture process can degrade value if it is lengthy: Employees leave, worker productivity suffers, and customers may not renew contracts.

DETERMINANTS OF RETURNS TO SHAREHOLDERS RESULTING FROM RESTRUCTURING STRATEGIES

Restructuring can create value by increasing parent firm focus, transferring assets to those who can operate them more efficiently, and mitigating agency conflicts and financial distress. The empirical support for this statement is discussed next in terms of pre- and post-announcement financial returns to shareholders by type of restructuring strategy.

Pre-announcement Abnormal Returns

Empirical studies indicate that the alternative restructure and exit strategies discussed in this chapter generally provide positive abnormal returns to the shareholders of the company implementing the strategy. This should not be surprising, since such actions often are undertaken to correct many of the problems associated with highly diversified firms, such as having invested in underperforming businesses, having failed to link executive compensation to the performance of the operations directly under their control, and being too difficult for investors and analysts to evaluate. Alternatively, restructuring strategies involving a divisional or asset sale may create value simply because the asset is worth more to another investor. Table 16.6 provides a summary of the results of selected empirical studies of restructuring activities.

Divestitures

Abnormal returns around the announcement date of the restructure strategy average 1.6% for sellers. Buyers average abnormal returns of about 0.5%.[27] While both sellers and buyers gain from a divestiture, most of the gain appears to accrue to the seller. How the total gain is divided ultimately depends on the relative bargaining strength of the seller and the buyer.

---

[27] Hanson and Song, 2000; John and Ofek, 1995; Sicherman and Pettway, 1992

TABLE 16.6   Returns to Shareholders of Firms
Undertaking Restructuring Strategies

Restructuring Strategy	Average Pre-announcement Abnormal Returns (%)
Divestitures[a]	1.6
Spin-Offs[b]	3.7
Tracking Stocks[c]	3.0
Equity Carve-Outs[d]	4.5

[a]*Lang et al. (1995); Allen (2000); Mulherin et al. (2000); Clubb et al. (2002); Ditmar et al. (2002); Bates (2005); Slovin et al. (2005)*
[b]*Michaely et al. (1995); Loh et al. (1995); J.P. Morgan (1995); Vroom et al. (1999); Mulherin et al. (2000); Davis et al. (2002); Maxwell et al. (2003); Veld (2004); McNeil et al. (2005); Harris et al. (2007); and Khorana et al. (2011)*
[c]*Logue et al. (1996); D'Souza et al. (2000); Elder et al. (2000); Chemmanur et al. (2000); Haushalter et al. (2001); Billet et al. (2004)*
[d]*Michaely et al. (1995); Allen et al. (1998); Vijh (1999); Mulherin et al. (2000); Prezas et al. (2000); Hulbert et al. (2002); Hogan et al. (2004); Wagner (2004)*

Increasing Focus of the Divesting Firm

The difficulty in managing diverse portfolios of businesses in many industries and the difficulty in accurately valuing these portfolios contributed to the breakup of conglomerates in the 1970s and 1980s. Of the acquisitions made between 1970 and 1982 by companies in industries unrelated to the acquirer's primary industry focus, 60% were divested by 1989. Abnormal returns earned by the shareholders of a firm divesting a business result largely from improved management of the assets that remain after the divestiture. With 75% of the divested units unrelated to the selling firm, these returns may be attributed to increased focus and the ability of management to understand fewer lines of business.[28] Divesting firms tend also to improve their investment decisions in their remaining businesses following divestitures by achieving levels of investment in core businesses comparable to those of their more focused peers.[29]

Transferring Assets to Those Who Can Use Them More Efficiently

Divestitures result in productivity gains by transferring assets from poorly managed sellers to acquirers that are, on average, better managed. Acquirer

[28] Petty, Keown, Scott, and Martin, 1993; John and Ofek, 1995

[29] Dittmar and Shivdasani, 2003

investors thus have a reasonable expectation that the acquirer can generate a higher financial return and bid up its share price.[30]

Resolving Differences between Management and Shareholders (Agency Conflicts)

Conflicts arise when management and shareholders disagree about major corporate decisions. What to do with the proceeds of the sale of assets can result in such a conflict, since they can be reinvested in the seller's remaining operations, paid to shareholders, or used to reduce the firm's outstanding debt. Abnormal returns on divestiture announcement dates tend to be positive when the proceeds are used to pay off debt[31] or are distributed to the shareholders.[32] Such results suggest shareholders mistrust management's ability to invest intelligently.

Mitigating Financial Distress

Not surprisingly, empirical studies indicate that firms sell assets when they need cash. The period before a firm announces asset sales often is characterized by deteriorating operating performance.[33] Firms that divest assets often have lower cash balances, cash flow, and bond credit ratings, than firms exhibiting similar growth, risk, and profitability characteristics.[34] Firms experiencing financial distress are more likely to utilize divestitures as part of their restructuring programs than other options, because they generate cash.[35]

Spin-Offs

At 3.7%, the average abnormal return to parent firm shareholders associated with spin-off announcements is more than twice the average excess return on divestitures. The difference in returns is smaller than it appears if we note that some portion of the total gain in wealth created by divestitures is shared with the buying firm's shareholders, who realize synergy in integrating the acquired firm into the buyer. In contrast, the jump in the parent firm's share price following the announcement of a spin-off reflects the total gain due to the spin-off. The gap between abnormal returns to shareholders from spin-offs versus divestitures also may be attributable to tax considerations. Spin-offs generally are tax-free,

---

[30] Using Tobin's Q-Ratios (i.e., the ratio of the market value of a firm to the cost of replacing the firm's assets) as a proxy for better-managed firms, Datta et al. (2003) found that announcement-period returns are highest for transactions in which the buyer's Q-Ratio is higher than the seller's. This implies that the assets are being transferred to a better-managed firm. Maksimovic and Phillips's (2001) findings also support this conclusion.

[31] Lang et al., 1995; Kaiser and Stouraitis, 2001

[32] Slovin et al., 2005

[33] Lang et al., 1995; Schlingemann et al., 2003

[34] Officer, 2007

[35] Nixon, Roenfeldt, and Sicherman, 2000; Ofek, 1993

while any gains on divested assets can be subject to double taxation. With spin-offs, shareholder value is created by increasing the focus of the parent by spinning off unrelated units, providing greater transparency, and transferring wealth from bondholders to shareholders.

Increasing Focus

Spin-offs that increase parent focus improve excess financial returns more than spin-offs that do not increase focus.[36] There is also a reduction in the diversification discount when a spin-off increases corporate focus, but not for those that do not.[37] Spin-offs of subsidiaries that are in the same industry as the parent firm do not result in positive announcement-date returns because they do little to enhance corporate focus.[38] Like divestitures, spin-offs contribute to better investment decisions by eliminating the tendency to use the cash flows of efficient businesses to finance investment in less efficient business units; parent firms also are more likely to invest in their attractive businesses after the spin-off.[39]

Achieving Greater Transparency (Eliminating Information Asymmetries)

Divestitures and spin-offs that tend to reduce a firm's complexity help to improve investors' ability to evaluate the firm's operating performance. By reducing complexity, financial analysts are better able to forecast earnings accurately.[40] Analysts tend to revise upward their earnings forecasts of the parent in response to a spin-off.[41]

Wealth Transfers

Evidence shows that spin-offs transfer wealth from bondholders to parent stockholders, for several reasons.[42] First, spin-offs reduce the assets available for liquidation in the event of business failure: Investors may view the firm's existing debt as riskier.[43] Second, the loss of the cash flow generated by the spin-off may result in less total parent cash flow to cover interest and principal repayments on the parent's current debt. Stockholders benefit from holding shares in

---

[36] Desai and Jain, 1997

[37] Burch and Nanda, 2001; Seoungpil and Denis, 2004

[38] Daley, Mehrotra, and Sivakumar, 1997

[39] Gertner, Powers, and Scharfstein, 2002

[40] Gilson et al., 2001

[41] Huson and MacKinnon, 2003

[42] Maxwell and Rao (2003) note that bondholders on average suffer a negative abnormal return of 0.8% in the month of the spin-off announcement. Stockholders experience an increase of about 3.6% during the same period.

[43] Assets actually pledged as collateral to current debt may not be spun-off without violating loan covenants.

the parent firm and shares in the unit spun-off by the parent, with the latter now separate from the parent, having the potential to appreciate in value.

Equity Carve-Outs

Investors view the announcement of a carve-out as the beginning of a series of restructuring activities, such as a reacquisition of the unit by the parent, a spin-off, a secondary offering, or an M&A. The sizeable announcement-date abnormal returns to parent firm shareholders averaging 4.5% reflect investor anticipated profit from these secondary events. These abnormal positive returns are realized when the parent firm retains a controlling interest after a carve-out announcement, allowing the parent to initiate these secondary actions.[44] Furthermore, these returns tend to increase with the size of the carve-out.[45] Announcement-date returns are significant for both parent firm stock and bond investors when the parent indicates that the majority of the proceeds resulting from the carve-out will be used to redeem debt.[46]

Managers use their inside information about the subsidiary's growth prospects to decide how much of the subsidiary to issue to the public. They are more inclined to retain a larger percentage of the business if they feel the unit's growth prospects are favorable.[47] Carve-outs may show poorer operating performance than their peers when their parents keep less than 50% of the subsidiary's equity. Either the parent chooses not to consolidate the carved-out unit due to its expected poor performance or it intends to transfer cash from minority-owned businesses through intercompany loans or dividends.[48] Value is created by increased parent focus, providing a source of financing, and resolving differences between the parent firm's management and shareholders (i.e., agency issues).

Increasing Focus

Parents and subsidiaries involved in carve-outs often are in different industries. Positive announcement-date returns tend to be higher for carve-outs of unrelated subsidiaries. This is consistent with the common observation that carve-outs are undertaken for businesses that do not fit with the parent's business strategy. It is unclear if operating performance improves following equity carve-outs.[49] Evidence has shown that both parents and carved-out subsidiaries

[44] Otsubo, 2009

[45] Allen and McConnell, 1998; Vijh, 2002

[46] The carve-out proceeds boost bondholder returns as current debt is repurchased. The reduction in outstanding debt means less interest expense is incurred and more cash is available for dividend payments and share repurchases of stock held by current shareholders. See Thompson and Apilado (2009).

[47] Powers, 2003

[48] Atanasov, Boone, and Haushalter, 2005

[49] Vijh, 2002

tend to improve their operating performance relative to their industry peers in the year following the carve-out.[50] However, other studies have shown that operating performance deteriorates.[51]

Providing a Source of Financing

Equity carve-outs can help to finance the needs of the parent or the subsidiary. Firms may use carve-outs to finance their high-growth subsidiaries.[52] Corporations tend to choose equity carve-outs and divestitures over spin-offs when the ratio of market value to book value and revenue growth of the carved-out unit are high, to maximize the cash proceeds of the sale of equity or asset sales.[53]

Resolving Agency Issues

There is evidence that investor reaction to the announcement of a carve-out is determined by how the proceeds are used. Firms announcing that the proceeds will be used to repay debt or pay dividends earn a 7% abnormal return, compared to minimal returns for those announcing that the proceeds will be reinvested in the firm.[54]

Tracking Stocks

Reflecting initial investor enthusiasm, a number of studies show that tracking stocks experience significant positive abnormal returns around their announcement date. Studies addressing the issue of whether the existence of publicly listed tracking shares increases the demand for other stock issued by the parent give mixed results.[55] However, there is some evidence that investors become disenchanted with tracking stocks over time, with excess shareholder returns averaging 13.9% around the date of the announcement that firms would eliminate their target stock issues.[56]

Post-Carve-Out and Post-Spin-Off Returns to Shareholders

Carve-outs and spin-offs are more likely to outperform the broader stock market indices because their share prices reflect speculation that they will be acquired rather than any improvement in the operating performance of the units. One-third of spin-offs are acquired within three years after the unit is spun

---

[50] Hulbert et al., 2002

[51] Powers et al., 2003; Boone, Haushalter, and Mikkelson, 2003

[52] Schipper and Smith, 1986

[53] Chen and Guo, 2005

[54] Allen and McConnell, 1998

[55] Clayton and Qian (2004) found evidence that parent shares rise following the issuance of publicly listed tracking stocks. However, Elder et al., (2000) find no evidence that tracking shares lead to greater interest in the parent's and other subsidiary shares.

[56] Billet and Vijh, 2004

off by the parent. Once those spin-offs that have been acquired are removed from the sample, the remaining spin-offs perform no better than their peers.[57] Spin-offs simply may create value by providing an efficient method of transferring corporate assets to acquiring companies.[58] The probability of acquisition is higher for units subject to a carve-out than for similar firms in the same industry.[59] Spin-offs involving parents and subsidiaries in different countries often show significant positive abnormal returns. The magnitude of the wealth gain accruing to holders of stock in the unit spun-off by the parent is higher in countries where takeover activity is high. This reflects the increased likelihood that the spun-off units will become takeover targets.[60]

Smaller spin-offs (i.e., those with a market cap of less than $200 million) tend to outperform larger ones (i.e., those with a market cap greater than $200 million).[61] This may be a result of a tendency of investors who are relatively unfamiliar with the business that is spun-off by the parent to undervalue the spin-off. Carve-outs that are largely independent of the parent (i.e., in which the parent tended to own less than 50% of the equity) tended to outperform the S&P 500 significantly.[62] The evidence for the long-term performance of tracking stocks is mixed.[63]

SOME THINGS TO REMEMBER

Divestitures, spin-offs, equity carve-outs, split-ups, and split-offs are commonly used restructuring and exit strategies to redeploy assets by returning cash or noncash assets through a special dividend to shareholders or to use cash proceeds to pay off debt. On average, these restructuring strategies create positive abnormal financial returns for shareholders around the announcement date because they tend to correct problems facing the parent. However, the longer-term performance of spin-offs, carve-outs, and tracking stocks is problematic.

DISCUSSION QUESTIONS

16.1. What are the advantages and disadvantages of tracking stocks to investors and the firm?

[57] Cusatis, Miles, and Woolridge, 1993

[58] McConnell, Ozbilgin, and Wahal, 2001

[59] Hulbert et al., 2002

[60] Harris and Glegg, 2007

[61] J.P. Morgan, 1999

[62] Annema et al., 2002

[63] Chemmanur and Paeglis (2000) found that the stock of parent firms tends to underperform the major stock indices, while the average tracking stock outperforms its industry stock index. However, Billett and Vijh (2004) found negative financial returns following the issue date for tracking stocks and positive but statistically insignificant returns for parents.

16.2. How would you decide when to sell a business?

16.3. What factors influence a parent firm's decision to undertake a spin-off rather than a divestiture or equity carve-out?

16.4. How might the form of payment affect the abnormal return to sellers and buyers?

16.5. How might spin-offs result in a transfer of wealth from bondholders to shareholders?

16.6. Explain how executing successfully a large-scale divestiture can be highly complex. This is especially true when the divested unit is integrated with the parent's functional departments and other units operated by the parent. Consider the challenges of timing, interdependencies, regulatory requirements, and customer and employee perceptions.

16.7. In an effort to increase shareholder value, USX announced its intention to split U.S. Steel and Marathon Oil into two separately traded companies.

The breakup gives holders of Marathon Oil stock an opportunity to participate in the ongoing consolidation within the global oil and gas industry. Holders of USX–U.S. Steel Group common stock (target stock) would become holders of newly formed Pittsburgh-based United States Steel Corporation. What other alternatives could USX have pursued to increase shareholder value? Why do you believe they pursued the breakup strategy rather than some of the alternatives?

16.8. Hewlett-Packard announced in 1999 the spin-off of its Agilent Technologies unit to focus on its main business of computers and printers. HP retained a controlling interest until mid-2000, when it spun off the rest of its shares in Agilent to HP shareholders as a tax-free transaction. Discuss the reasons why HP may have chosen a staged transaction rather than an outright divestiture or spin-off of the business.

16.9. After months of trying to sell its 81% stake in Blockbuster Inc., Viacom undertook a spin-off in mid-2004. Why would Viacom choose to spin-off rather than divest its Blockbuster unit? Explain your answer.

16.10. Since 2001, GE, the world's largest conglomerate, had been underperforming the S&P 500 stock index. In late 2008, the firm announced that it would spin-off its consumer and industrial unit. What do you believe are GE's motives for their proposed restructuring? Why do you believe they chose a spin-off rather than an alternative restructuring strategy?

Answers to these Chapter Discussion Questions are found in the Online Instructor's Manual for instructors using this book.

CASE STUDY 16.2
The Anatomy of a Reverse Morris Trust Transaction
The Pringles Potato Chip Saga[64]

Key Points

- Greater shareholder value may be created by exiting rather than operating a business.
- Deal structures can impose significant limitations on a firm's future strategies and tactics.

Following a rigorous portfolio review and an informal expression of interest in the Pringles brand by Diamond Foods (Diamond) in late 2009, Proctor & Gamble (P&G), the world's leading manufacturer of household products, believed that Pringles could be worth more to its shareholders if divested than if retained. Pringles is the iconic potato chip brand, with sales in 140 countries and operations in the United States, Europe, and Asia.

Diamond's executive management had long viewed the Pringles' brand as an attractive fit for their strategy of building, acquiring, and energizing brands. The acquisition of Pringles would triple the size of the firm's snack business and provide greater merchandising influence in the way in which its products are distributed. The merger would also give Diamond a substantial presence in Asia, Latin America, and Central Europe. The increased geographic diversity means the firm would derive almost one-half of its revenue from international sales

After extended negotiations, Diamond and P&G announced on April 15, 2011, their intent to merge P&G's Pringles subsidiary into Diamond in a transaction valued at $2.35 billion. The purchase price consisted of $1.5 billion in Diamond common stock, valued at $51.47 per share, and Diamond's assumption of $850 million in Pringles outstanding debt. The way in which the deal was structured enabled P&G shareholders to defer any gains they realize from the transaction and resulted in a one-time after-tax earnings increase for P&G of $1.5 billion due to the firm's low tax basis in Pringles.

The offer to exchange Pringles shares for P&G shares reduced the number of outstanding P&G common shares, partially offsetting the impact on P&G's earnings per share of the loss of Pringles earnings. Diamond agreed to issue one share of its common stock for each Pringles common share. The 29.1 million common shares issued by Diamond resulted in P&G shareholders participating in the exchange offer, owning a 57% stake in the combined firms, with Diamond's shareholders owning the remainder.

The deal was structured as a reverse Morris Trust acquisition, which combines a divisive reorganization (e.g., a spin-off or a split-off) with an acquisitive reorganization (e.g., a statutory

---

[64]The deal discussed in this case is for illustration only. Following the disclosure that Diamond Food's reported earnings were subject to substantial revision due to accounting irregularities, Proctor & Gamble invoked a material adverse change clause to terminate the purchase agreement in 2012.

merger) to allow a tax-free transfer of a subsidiary under U.S. law. The use of a divisive reorganization results in the creation of a public company that is subsequently merged into a shell subsidiary (i.e., a privately owned company) of another firm, with the shell surviving.

The structure of the deal involved four discrete steps, outlined in separation and transaction agreements signed by P&G and Diamond. These steps included the following: (1) the creation by P&G of a wholly owned subsidiary containing Pringles' assets and liabilities; (2) the recapitalization of the wholly owned Pringles subsidiary; (3) the separation of the wholly owned subsidiary through a split-off exchange offer; and (4) a merger with a wholly owned subsidiary of Diamond Foods. The separation agreement covered the first three steps, with the final step detailed in the transaction agreement.

Under the separation agreement, P&G contributed certain Pringles assets and liabilities to the Pringles Company, a newly formed wholly owned subsidiary of P&G. After P&G and Diamond reached a negotiated value for the Pringles Company equity of $1.5 billion, or $51.47 per share, the Pringles Company was subsequently recapitalized by issuing to P&G 29.1 million shares of Pringles Company stock. To complete the separation of Pringles from the parent firm, P&G distributed on the closing date Pringles shares to P&G shareholders participating in a share-exchange offer in which they agreed to exchange their P&G shares for Pringles shares.

In addition, the Pringles Company borrowed $850 million and used the proceeds to pay P&G a cash dividend and to acquire certain Pringles business assets held by P&G affiliates. Since P&G is the sole owner of the Pringles Company, the dividend is tax free to P&G because it is an intracompany transfer. If the exchange offer had not been fully subscribed, P&G would have distributed through a tax-free spin-off the remaining shares as a dividend to P&G shareholders.

The transaction agreement outlined the terms and conditions pertinent to completion of the merger with Diamond Foods. Immediately after the completion of the distribution, the Pringles Company merged with Merger Sub, a wholly owned shell subsidiary of Diamond, with Merger Sub's continuing as the surviving company. The shares of Pringles Company common stock distributed in connection with the split-off exchange offer automatically converted into the right to receive shares of Diamond common stock on a one-for-one basis. After the merger, Diamond, through Merger Sub, owned and operated Pringles (see Figure 16.3).

Prior to the merger, Diamond already had formidable antitakeover defenses in place as part of its charter documents, including a classified board of directors, a prohibition against stockholders' taking action by written consent (i.e., consent solicitation), and a requirement that stockholders give advance notice before raising matters at a stockholders' meeting. Following the merger, Diamond adopted a shareholder-rights

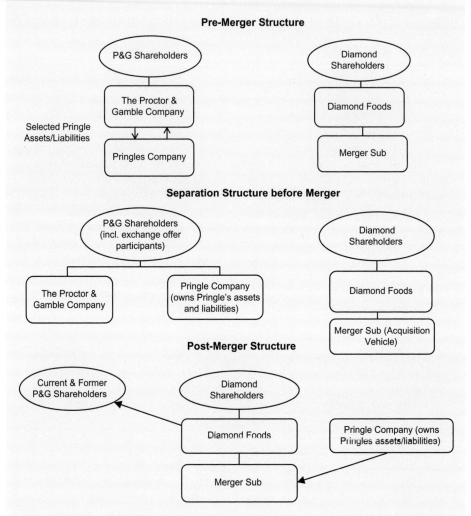

FIGURE 16.3   **Reverse Morris Trust.**

plan. The plan entitled the holder of such rights to purchase 1/100 of a share of Diamond's Series A Junior Participating Preferred Stock if a person or group acquires 15% or more of Diamond's outstanding common stock. Holders of this preferred stock (other than the person or group triggering their exercise) would be able to purchase Diamond common shares (flip-in poison pill) or those of any company into which Diamond is merged (flip-over poison pill) at a price of $60 per share. Such rights would expire in March 2015 unless extended by Diamond's board of directors.

Discussion Questions

1. The merger of Pringles and Diamond Foods could have been achieved as a result of a P&G spin-off of Pringles. Explain the details of how this might happen.
2. Speculate as to why P&G chose to split-off rather than spin-off Pringles as part of its plan to merge post with Diamond. Be specific.
3. Why was this transaction subject to the Morris Trust tax regulations?
4. How is value created for the P&G and Diamond shareholders in this type of transaction?
5. Why did the addition of the shareholder-rights plan by Diamond Foods following the merger with Pringles make sense given the type of deal structure used?

Solutions to this case study are found in the Online Instructors Manual for instructors using this book.

CASE STUDY 16.3
The Anatomy of a Spin-Off—Northrop Grumman Exits the Shipbuilding Business

Key Points

- There are many ways a firm can choose to separate itself from one of its operations.
- Which restructuring method is used reflects the firm's objectives and circumstances.

In an effort to focus on more attractive growth markets, Northrop Grumman Corporation (NGC), a global leader in aerospace, communications, defense, and security systems, announced that it would exit its mature shipbuilding business on October 15, 2010. Huntington Ingalls Industries (HII), the largest military U.S. shipbuilder and a wholly owned subsidiary of NGC, had been under pressure to cut costs amidst increased competition from competitors such as General Dynamics and a slowdown in orders from the U.S. Navy. Nor did the outlook for the shipbuilding industry look like it would improve any time soon.

Given the limited synergy between shipbuilding and HII's other businesses, HII's operations were largely independent of NGC's other units. NGC's management and board argued that their decision to separate from the shipbuilding business would enable both NGC and HII to focus on those areas they knew best. Moreover, given the shipbuilding business's greater ongoing capital requirements, HII would find it easier to tap capital markets directly rather than to compete with other NGC operations for financing. Finally, investors would be better able to value businesses (NGC and HII) whose operations were more focused.

After reviewing a range of options, NGC pursued a spin-off as the most efficient way to separate itself from its shipbuilding operations. If properly structured, spin-offs are tax free to shareholders. Furthermore, management argued that they could be completed in a timelier manner and were less disruptive to current operations than an outright sale of the business. The spin-off represented about one-sixth of NGC's $36 billion in 2010 revenue. Effective March 31, 2011, all of the outstanding stock of HII was spun off to NGC shareholders through a pro rata distribution to shareholders of record on March 30, 2011. Each NGC shareholder received one HII common share for every six shares of NGC common stock held.[65]

The spin-off process involved an internal reorganization of NGC businesses, a Separation and Distribution Agreement, and finally the actual distribution of HII shares to NGC shareholders. The internal reorganization and subsequent spin-off is illustrated in Figure 16.4. NGC (referred to as Current NGC) first reorganized its businesses such that the firm would become a holding company whose primary investments would include Huntington Ingalls Industries (HII)

and Northrop Grumman Systems Corporation (i.e., all other non-shipbuilding operations). HII was formed in anticipation of the spin-off as a holding company for NGC's shipbuilding business, which had been previously known as Northrop Grumman Shipbuilding (NGSB). NGSB was changed to Huntington Ingalls Industries Company following the spin-off. Reflecting the new organizational structure, Current NGC common stock was exchanged for stock in New Northrop Grumman Corporation. This internal reorganization was followed by the distribution of HII stock to NGC's common shareholders.

Following the spin-off, HII became a separate company from NGC, with NGC having no ownership interest in HII. Renamed Titan II, Current NGC became a direct, wholly owned subsidiary of HII and held no material assets or liabilities other than Current NGC's guarantees of HII performance under certain HII shipbuilding contracts (under way prior to the spin-off and guaranteed by NGC) and HII's obligations to repay intercompany loans owed to NGC. New NGC changed its name to Northrop Grumman Corporation. The board of

[65] The share-exchange ratio of one share of HII common for each six shares of NGC common was calculated by dividing HII's 48.8 million common shares (having a par value of $.01) by the 298 million NGC shares outstanding. Since fractional shares were created, shareholders owning 100 shares would be entitled to 16.6667 shares—100/6. In this instance, the shareholder would receive 16 HII shares and the cash equivalent of 0.6667 shares. The cash to pay for fractional shares came from the aggregation of all fractional shares, which were subsequently sold in the public market. The cash proceeds were then distributed to NGC shareholders on a pro rata basis and were taxable to the extent a taxable gain is incurred by the shareholder.

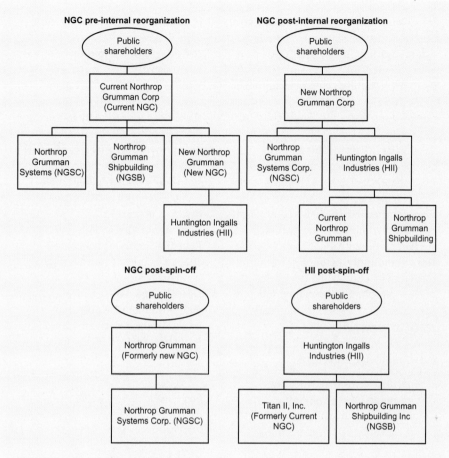

FIGURE 16.4   **Spin-off illustration.**

directors remained the same following the reorganization.

No gain or loss was incurred by common shareholders because the exchange of stock between the Current and New Northrop Grumman corporations did not change the shareholders' tax basis in the stock. Similarly, no gain or loss was incurred by shareholders with the distribution of HII's stock, since there was no change in the total value of their investment. That is,

the value of the HII shares were offset by a corresponding reduction in the value of NGC shares, reflecting the loss of HII's cash flows.

Before the spin-off, HII entered into a Separation and Distribution Agreement with NGC that governed the relationship between HII and NGC after completion of the spin-off and provided for the allocation between the two firms of assets, liabilities, and obligations (e.g., employee benefits, intellectual property, information technology, insurance, and tax-related assets and liabilities). The agreement also provided that NGC and HII each would indemnify (compensate) the other against any liabilities arising out of their respective businesses. As part of the agreement, HII agreed not to engage in any transactions, such as mergers or acquisitions, involving share-for-share exchanges that would change the ownership of the firm by more than 50% for at least two years following the transaction. A change in control could violate the IRS's "continuity of interest" requirement and jeopardize the tax-free status of the spin-off. Consequently, HII put in place certain takeover defenses to make takeovers difficult.

Discussion Questions

1. Speculate as to why Northrop Grumman used a spin-off rather than a divestiture, a split-off, or a split up to separate Huntington Ingalls from the rest of its operations. What were the advantages of the spin-off over the other restructuring strategies?

2. What is the likely impact of the spin-off on Northrop Grumman's share price immediately following the spin-off of Huntington Ingalls, assuming no other factors offset it?

3. Why do businesses that have been spun-off from their parent often immediately put antitakeover defenses in place?

4. Why would the U.S. Internal Revenue Service be concerned about a change of control of the spun-off business?

5. Describe how you, as an analyst, would estimate the potential impact of the Huntington Ingalls Industries spin-off on the long-term value of Northrop Grumman's share price.

Solutions to these questions are found in the Online Instructor's Manual available for instructors using this book.

Alternative Exit and Restructuring Strategies
Bankruptcy Reorganization and Liquidation

Success breeds disregard for the possibility of failure. —**Hyman P. Minsky**

INSIDE M&A: PHOTOGRAPHY ICON KODAK DECLARES BANKRUPTCY, A VICTIM OF CREATIVE DESTRUCTION

KEY POINTS

- Having invented the digital camera, Kodak knew that the longevity of its traditional film business was problematic.
- Concerned about protecting its core film business, Kodak was unable to reposition itself fast enough to stave off failure.
- Chapter 11 reorganization offers an opportunity to emerge as a viable business, save jobs, minimize creditor losses, and limit the impact on communities.

Economic historian Joseph Schumpeter described the free market process by which new technologies and deregulation create new industries, often at the expense of existing ones, as "creative destruction." In the short run, this process can have a highly disruptive impact on current employees whose skills are made obsolete; investors and business owners whose businesses are no longer competitive; and communities that are ravaged by increasing unemployment and diminished tax revenues. However, in the long run, the process tends to raise living standards by boosting worker productivity and increasing real income and leisure time; stimulating innovation; expanding the range of products and services offered, often at a lower price, to consumers; and increases tax revenues. Kodak is a recent illustration of this process.

Founded in 1880 by George Eastman, Kodak became the latest giant to fall in the face of advancing technology, announcing that it had filed for the protection of the bankruptcy court early in 2012. Kodak had established the market for camera film and then dominated the marketplace before suffering a series of setbacks over the last 40 years. First foreign competitors, most notably Fujifilm of Japan, undercut Kodak's film prices. Then the increased popularity of digital photography eroded demand for traditional film, eventually causing the firm to cease investment in its traditional film product in 2003. Although it had invented the digital camera, Kodak had failed to develop it further, announcing on February 12, 2012, that it would discontinue its production of such cameras. Kodak's failure to move aggressively into the digital world may have reflected its concern about cannibalizing its core film business. This concern may have ultimately destined the firm for failure.

Kodak closed 13 manufacturing plants and 130 processing labs and had reduced its workforce to 17,000 in 2011 from 63,000 in 2003. In recent years, the firm has undertaken a two-pronged strategy: expanding into the inkjet printer market and initiating patent lawsuits to generate royalty payments from firms allegedly violating Kodak digital patents. Kodak technologies are found in virtually all modern digital cameras, smartphones, and tablet computers. Kodak had raised $3 billion between 2003 and 2010 by reaching settlements with alleged patent infringement companies. But the revenue from litigation dried up in 2011.

With only one profitable year since 2004, the firm eventually ran out of cash. Its market value on the day it announced its bankruptcy filing had slumped to $150 million, compared to $31 billion in 1995. Kodak said it had $5.1 billion in assets and $6.8 billion in debt, rendering the firm insolvent. The Chapter 11 filing was made in the U.S. bankruptcy court in lower New York City and excluded the firm's non-U.S. subsidiaries. The objectives of the bankruptcy filing were to buy time to find buyers for some of its 1,100 digital patents; to continue to shrink its current employment; to reduce significantly its healthcare and pension obligations; and to renegotiate more favorable payment terms on its outstanding debt. Kodak had put the patents up for sale in August 2011 but did not receive any bids, since potential buyers were concerned that they would be required to return the assets by creditors if Kodak filed for bankruptcy protection. While the firm's pension obligations are well funded, the firm owes health benefits to 38,000 U.S. retirees, which in 2011 cost the firm $240 million.

Kodak also announced that it had obtained a $950 million loan from Citibank to keep operating during the bankruptcy process. Moreover, the firm filed new patent infringement suits in March 2012 against a number of competitors, including Fujifilm, Research in Motion (RIM), and Apple, in order to increase the value of its patent portfolios. However, a court ruled in mid-2012 that neither Apple nor RIM had infringed on Kodak patents. In early 2013, Kodak announced that it would put additional assets up for sale (including its camera film business, and heavy-duty commercial scanners and software businesses) since the sale of its remaining digital imaging patents raised only $525 million, much less than the nearly $2 billion the firm had expected. The sale of these businesses would cement Kodak's departure from its roots. In late September 2012, Kodak announced that it would suspend the production and sale of consumer inkjet printers. Kodak also received permission from the bankruptcy court judge to terminate the payment of retiree medical, dental, and life insurance benefits for 56,000 retirees at the end of 2012.

Kodak has to demonstrate viability to emerge from Chapter 11 as a reorganized firm or be acquired by another firm. The firm has pinned its remaining hopes for survival on selling commercial printing equipment and services, a business that generated about $2 billion in revenue in 2012 but that may lack the scale to sustain profitability. If it cannot demonstrate viability, Kodak will face liquidation. In either case, the outcome is a sad ending to a photography icon.

CHAPTER OVERVIEW

Bankruptcy and liquidation are alternative restructuring and exit strategies for failing firms. How reorganization and liquidation take place both inside and outside the protection of the bankruptcy court are examined in detail. This chapter also discusses common strategic options for failing firms and how to value such firms; the current state of bankruptcy-prediction models; and empirical studies of the performance of firms experiencing financial distress. A review of this chapter (including practice questions with answers) is available in the file folder entitled "Student Study Guide" on the companion website to this book (*http://booksite.elsevier.com/9780123854872*).

BUSINESS FAILURE

Failing firms may be subject to financial distress, as measured by declining asset values, liquidity, and cash flow. The term *financial distress* does not have a strict technical or legal definition. The term applies to a firm that is unable to meet its obligations or to a specific security on which the issuer has defaulted.[1] *Technical insolvency* arises when a firm is unable to pay its liabilities when due. *Legal insolvency* occurs when a firm's liabilities exceed the fair market value of its assets, since creditors' claims cannot be satisfied unless the firm's

---

[1] *Default* is defined by Moody's Credit Rating Agency as any delinquent payout of interest or principal, bankruptcy, receivership, or an exchange that reduces the value of what is owed; e.g., the issuer might offer bondholders a new security or combination of securities, such as preferred or common stock, or debt with a lower coupon worth less than what they are owed.

assets can be liquidated for more than the book value of the firm's liabilities. A federal legal proceeding designed to protect the technically or legally insolvent firm from lawsuits by its creditors until a decision can be made to close or continue to operate the firm is called *bankruptcy*. A firm is not bankrupt or in bankruptcy until it files, or its creditors file, a petition for reorganization or liquidation with the federal bankruptcy courts.[2]

Receivership can be an alternative to bankruptcy in which a court- or government-appointed individual (i.e., a receiver) takes control of the assets and affairs of a business to administer them according to the court's or government's directives. The purpose of a receiver may be to serve as a custodian while disputes between officers, directors, or stockholders are settled, or to liquidate the firm's assets. Under no circumstances can the firm's debt be discharged without the approval of the bankruptcy court. In most states, receivership cannot take effect unless a lawsuit is under way and the court has determined that receivership is appropriate. *Conservatorship* represents a less restrictive alternative to receivership. While the receiver is expected to terminate the rights of shareholders and managers, a conservator is expected merely to assume these rights temporarily. For example, in July 2008, the failing IndyMac Bank was taken into administrative receivership by the Federal Deposit Insurance Corporation, and the bank's assets and secured liabilities were transferred into a "bridge bank" called *IndyMac Federal Bank* until the assets could be liquidated. Also in September 2008, the CEO and the boards of the Federal National Mortgage Association and the Federal Home Loan Mortgage Corporation were dismissed, and the firms were put under the conservatorship of the Federal Housing Finance Agency while their asset portfolios were reduced.

A debtor firm and its creditors may choose to reach a negotiated settlement outside of bankruptcy, within the protection of the court, or through a prepackaged bankruptcy, which represents a blend of the first two options. The following sections discuss each of these options.

VOLUNTARY SETTLEMENTS OUTSIDE OF BANKRUPTCY

An insolvent firm and its creditors may agree to restructure the firm's obligations out of court to avoid the costs of bankruptcy proceedings, because this generally offers the best chance for creditors to recover the largest percentage of what they are owed and owners some portion of their investment in the firm. This process normally involves the debtor firm's requesting a meeting with its creditors. A committee of creditors is selected to analyze the debtor firm's

---

[2] The terms *liquidity* and *solvency* often are used inappropriately. *Liquidity* is the ability of a business to have sufficient cash on hand (as opposed to tied up in receivables and inventory) to meet its immediate obligations without having to incur significant losses in selling assets. *Insolvency* means that a firm cannot pay its bills under any circumstances. A liquid business is more likely to be solvent (i.e., able to pay its bills); however, not all businesses that are liquid are solvent, and not all solvent businesses have adequate liquidity.

financial position and recommend a course of action: whether the firm continues to operate or is liquidated.

Voluntary Settlements Resulting in Continued Operation

Plans to restructure the debtor firm developed cooperatively with creditors commonly are called *workouts*, arrangements outside of bankruptcy by a debtor and its creditors for payment or rescheduling of payment of the debtor's obligations. Because of the firm's weak financial position, the creditors must be willing to restructure the insolvent firm's debts to enable it to sustain its operations. *Debt restructuring* involves concessions by creditors that lower an insolvent firm's payments so that it may remain in business. Restructuring normally is accomplished in three ways: via an extension, a composition, or a debt-for-equity swap. An *extension* occurs when creditors agree to lengthen the period during which the debtor firm can repay its debt. Creditors often agree to suspend temporarily both interest and principal repayments. A *composition* is an agreement in which creditors agree to receive less than the full amount they are owed. A *debt-for-equity swap* occurs when creditors surrender a portion of their claims on the firm in exchange for an ownership position in the firm. If the reduced debt service payments enable the firm to prosper, the value of the stock in the long run may far exceed the amount of debt the creditors were willing to forgive.

Exhibit 17.1 depicts a debt restructure that enables the firm to continue operation by converting debt to equity. Although the firm, Survivor Inc., has positive earnings before interest and taxes, they are not enough to meet its interest payments. When principal payments are considered, cash flow becomes negative, rendering the firm technically insolvent. As a result of the restructuring of the firm's debt, Survivor Inc., is able to continue to operate; however, the firm's lenders now have a controlling interest in the firm. Note that the same type of restructuring could take place either voluntarily outside the courts or as a result of reorganizing under the protection of the bankruptcy court. The latter scenario is discussed later in this chapter.

Voluntary Settlement Resulting in Liquidation

If the creditors conclude that the insolvent firm's situation cannot be resolved, liquidation may be the only acceptable course of action. Liquidation can be conducted outside the court in a private liquidation or through the U.S. bankruptcy court. If the insolvent firm is willing to accept liquidation and all creditors agree, legal proceedings are not necessary. Creditors normally prefer private liquidations, to avoid lengthy and costly litigation. Through a process called an *assignment*, a committee representing creditors grants the power to liquidate the firm's assets to a third party, called an *assignee* or *trustee*. The responsibility of the assignee is to sell the assets as quickly as possible while obtaining the best possible price. The assignee distributes the proceeds of the asset sales to the creditors and the firm's owners if any monies remain.

EXHIBIT 17.1 SURVIVOR INC., RESTRUCTURES ITS DEBT

Survivor Inc., currently has 400,000 shares of common equity outstanding at a par value of $10 per share. The current rate of interest on its debt is 8%, and the debt is amortized over 20 years. The combined federal, state, and local tax rate is 40%. The firm's cash flow and capital position are shown in Table 17.1. Assume that bondholders are willing to convert $5 million of debt to equity at the current par value of $10 per share. This necessitates that Survivor Inc., issue 500,000 new shares. These actions result in positive cash flow, a substantial reduction in the firm's debt–to–total capital ratio, and a transfer of control to the bondholders. The former stockholders now own only 44.4% (4 million/9 million) of the company. The revised cash flow and capital position are shown in Table 17.2.

TABLE 17.1   Cash Flow and Capital Position

Income and Cash Flow		Total Capital	
Earnings Before Interest and Taxes	$500,000	Debt	$10,000,000
Interest	$800,000	Equity	$4,000,000
Earnings before Taxes	$(300,000)	Total	$14,000,000
Taxes	$120,000		
Earnings after Taxes	$(180,000)	Debt/Total Capital	71.4%
Depreciation	$400,000		
Principal Repayment	$(500,000)		
Cash Flow	$(280,000)		

TABLE 17.2   Revised Cash Flow and Capital Position

Income and Cash Flow		Total Capital	
Earnings before Interest and Taxes	$500,000	Debt	$5,000,000
Interest	$400,000	Equity	$9,000,000
Earnings before Taxes	$100,000	Total	$14,000,000
Taxes	$40,000		
Earnings after Taxes	$60,000	Debt/Total Capital	35.7%
Depreciation	$400,000		
Principal Repayment	$(250,000)		
Cash Flow	$210,000		

REORGANIZATION AND LIQUIDATION IN BANKRUPTCY

In the absence of a voluntary settlement out of court, the debtor firm may seek protection from its creditors by initiating bankruptcy or may be forced into bankruptcy by its creditors. When the debtor firm files the petition with the bankruptcy court, the bankruptcy is said to be *voluntary*. When creditors do the filing, the action is said to be *involuntary*. Once a bankruptcy petition is filed, the debtor firm is protected from any further legal action related to its debts until the bankruptcy proceedings are completed. The filing of a petition triggers an *automatic stay* once the court accepts the request, which provides a period suspending all judgments, collection activities, foreclosures, and repossessions of property by the creditors on any debt or claim that arose before the filing of the bankruptcy petition.

The Evolution of U.S. Bankruptcy Laws and Practices

U.S. bankruptcy laws focus on rehabilitating and reorganizing debtors in distress. Except for Chapter 12, all the chapters of the present Bankruptcy Code are odd-numbered. Chapters 1, 3, and 5 cover matters of general application, while Chapters 7, 9, 11, 12, and 13 concern liquidation (business or nonbusiness), municipality bankruptcy, business reorganization, family farm debt adjustment, and wage-earner or personal reorganization, respectively. Chapter 15 applies to international cases.

The Bankruptcy Reform Act of 1978 changed the bankruptcy laws substantially by adding a strong business reorganization mechanism, referred to as Chapter 11 of the U.S. Bankruptcy Code. The 1978 law also broadened the conditions under which companies could file so that a firm could declare bankruptcy without waiting until it was insolvent. The Bankruptcy Reform Act of 1994 contained provisions to expedite bankruptcy proceedings and to encourage individual debtors to use Chapter 13 to reschedule their debts rather than use Chapter 7 to liquidate.

On April 19, 2005, the Bankruptcy Abuse Prevention and Consumer Protection Act (BAPCPA) became law. While the new legislation affects primarily consumer filings, BAPCPA affects business filers as well, with the heaviest influence on smaller businesses (i.e., those with less than $2 million in debt). BAPCPA changed this process by (1) reducing the maximum length of time during which debtors have an exclusive right to submit a plan; (2) shortening the time that debtors have to accept or reject leases; and (3) limiting compensation under key employee retention programs. Prior to BAPCPA, a debtor corporation had the opportunity to request a bankruptcy judge to extend the period for submission of the plan of reorganization as long as it could justify its request. Once the judge ruled that the debtor had been given sufficient time, any creditor could submit a reorganization plan. The new law caps the exclusivity period at 18 months from the day of the bankruptcy filing. The debtor then has an additional two months to win the creditors' acceptance of the plan, thereby providing a *debtor-in-position* a maximum of 20 months before creditors can submit their reorganization plans.

Finally, Chapter 15 was added to the U.S. Bankruptcy Code by BAPCPA of 2005 to reflect the adoption of the Model Law on Cross-Border Insolvency passed by the United Nations Commission on International Trade Law (UNCITRAL) in 1997. The purpose of UNCITRAL is to provide for better coordination among legal systems for cross-border bankruptcy cases. Chapter 15 is discussed in more detail later in this chapter.

Filing for Chapter 11 Reorganization

Chapter 11 reorganization may involve a corporation, a sole proprietorship, or a partnership. Since a corporation is viewed as separate from its owners (i.e., the shareholders), the Chapter 11 bankruptcy of a corporation does not put the personal assets of the stockholders at risk, other than the value of their investment in the firm's stock. In contrast, sole proprietorships and owners are not separate; a bankruptcy case involving a sole proprietorship includes both the business and personal assets of the owner–debtor. Like a corporation, a partnership exists as an entity separate from its partners. In a general partnership bankruptcy case, since the partners are personally responsible for the debts and obligations of the partnership, they may be sued such that their personal assets are used to pay creditors, forcing the partners to file for bankruptcy.

Figure 17.1 summarizes the process for filing for reorganization under Chapter 11. The process begins by filing in a federal bankruptcy court. In the case of an involuntary petition, a hearing must be held to determine whether the firm is insolvent. If the firm is found to be insolvent, the court enters an *order for relief*, which initiates the bankruptcy proceedings. On the filing of a reorganization petition, the filing firm becomes the *debtor-in-possession* of all the assets and has a maximum of 20 months to convince creditors to accept its reorganization plan, after which the creditors can submit their own proposal. In the case of fraud, creditors may request that the court appoint a trustee instead of the debtor to manage the firm during the reorganization period.

The U.S. Trustee (the bankruptcy department of the U.S. Justice Department) appoints one or more committees to represent the interests of creditors and shareholders. The purpose of these committees is to work with the debtor-in-possession to develop a reorganization plan for exiting Chapter 11. Creditors and shareholders are grouped according to the similarity of claims. In the case of creditors, the plan must be approved by holders of at least two-thirds of the dollar value of the claims as well as by a simple majority of the creditors in each group. In the case

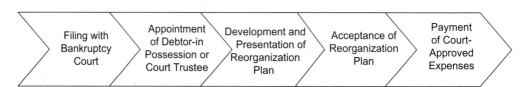

FIGURE 17.1 **Procedures for reorganizing during bankruptcy.**

of shareholders, two-thirds of those in each group (e.g., common and preferred shareholders) must approve the plan. Following acceptance by creditors, bondholders, and stockholders, the bankruptcy court also must approve the reorganization plan. Even if creditors or shareholders vote to reject the plan, the court is empowered to ignore the vote and approve the plan if it finds the plan fair to creditors and shareholders as well as feasible. Finally, the debtor-in-possession is responsible for paying the expenses approved by the court of all parties whose services contributed to the approval or disapproval of the plan.

Implementing Chapter 7 Liquidation

If the bankruptcy court determines that reorganization is infeasible, the failing firm may be forced to liquidate. According to the Administrative Office of the U.S. Courts, about 70% of bankruptcy filings are Chapter 7 filings rather than Chapter 11 reorganization. The prevalence of Chapter 7 liquidations may be a result of the tendency of secured creditors to force debtor firms into liquidation to recover what they are owed by selling off the collateral underlying their loans, often at the expense of unsecured creditors and equity investors.

Under Chapter 7, a trustee is given the responsibility to liquidate the firm's assets, keep records, examine creditors' claims, disburse the proceeds, and submit a final report on the liquidation. The priority in which the claims are paid is stipulated in Chapter 7 of the Bankruptcy Reform Act, which must be followed by the trustee when the firm is liquidated.[3] All secured creditors are paid when the firm's assets that were pledged as collateral are liquidated.[4] If the proceeds of the sale of these assets are inadequate to satisfy all of the secured creditors' claims, they become unsecured (general) creditors for the amount that was not recovered. If the proceeds of the sale of pledged assets exceed secured creditors' claims, the excess proceeds are used to pay general creditors. Liquidation under Chapter 7 does not mean that all employees lose their jobs. When a large firm enters Chapter 7 bankruptcy, a division of the company may be sold intact to other companies during the liquidation.

Exhibit 17.2 describes how a legally bankrupt company could be liquidated. In this illustration, the bankruptcy court, owners, and creditors could not agree on an appropriate reorganization plan for DOA Inc. Consequently, the court

---

[3] Chapter 7 distributes the liquidation proceeds according to the following priorities: (1) administrative claims (e.g., lawyers' fees, court costs, accountants' fees, trustees' fees, and other costs necessary to liquidate the firm's assets); (2) statutory claims (e.g., tax obligations, rent, consumer deposits, and unpaid wages and benefits owed before the filing, up to some threshold); (3) secured creditors' claims; (4) unsecured creditors' claims; and (5) equity claims.

[4] Fully secured creditors, such as bondholders and mortgage lenders, have a legally enforceable right to the collateral securing their loans or the equivalent value. A creditor is fully secured if the value of the collateral for its loan to the debtor equals or exceeds the amount of the debt. For this reason, fully secured creditors are not entitled to participate in any distribution of liquidated assets that the bankruptcy trustee might make.

EXHIBIT 17.2 LIQUIDATION OF DOA INC. UNDER CHAPTER 7

DOA has the balance sheet in Table 17.3. The only liability that is not shown on the balance sheet is the cost of the bankruptcy proceedings, which is treated as an expense and is not capitalized. The sale of DOA's assets generates $5.4 million in cash. The distribution of the proceeds is displayed in Table 17.4. Note that the proceeds are distributed in accordance with the priorities stipulated in current commercial bankruptcy law and that the cost of administering the bankruptcy totals 18% (i.e., $972,000 ÷ $5,400,000) of the proceeds from liquidation. Once all prior claims have been satisfied, the remaining proceeds are distributed to the unsecured creditors. The pro rata (proportional) settlement percentage of 27.64% is calculated by dividing funds available for unsecured creditors by the amount of unsecured creditor claims (i.e., $1,368 ÷ $4,950). The shareholders receive nothing because not all unsecured creditor claims have been satisfied (Table 17.5).

TABLE 17.3 DOA Balance Sheet

Assets		Liabilities	
Cash	$35,000	Accounts Payable	$ 750,000
Accounts Receivable	$2,300,000	Bank Notes Payable	$3,000,000
Inventories	$2,100.000	Accrued Salaries	$720,000
Total Current Assets	$4,435,000	Unpaid Benefits	$140,000
Land	$1,500,000	Unsecured Customer Deposits	$300,000
Net Plant and Equipment	$2,000,000	Taxes Payable	$400,000
Total Fixed Assets	$3,500,000	Total Current Liabilities	$5,310,000
Total Assets	$7,935,000	First Mortgage	$2,500,000
		Unsecured Debt	$200,000
		Total Long-Term Debt	$2,700,000
		Preferred Stock	$50,000
		Common Stock	$100,000
		Paid in Surplus	$500,000
		Retained Earnings	$(725,000)
		Total Stockholders' Equity	$ (75,000)
		Total Shareholders' Equity and Total Liabilities	$7,935,000

TABLE 17.4 Distribution of Liquidation Proceeds

Proceeds from Liquidation	$5,400,000
Expenses of Administering Bankruptcy	$972,000
Salaries Owed Employees	$720,000
Unpaid Employee Benefits	$140,000
Unsecured Customer Deposits	$300,000
Taxes	$400,000
Funds Available for Creditors	$2,868,000
First Mortgage (from sale of fixed assets)	$1,500,000
Funds Available for Unsecured Creditors	$1,368,000

TABLE 17.5 Pro Rata Distribution of Funds among Unsecured Creditors

Unsecured Creditor Claims	Amount	Settlement at 27.64%
Unpaid Balance from First Mortgage	$1,000,000	$276,400
Accounts Payable	$750,000	$207,300
Notes Payable	$3,000,000	$829,200
Unsecured Debt	$200,000	$55,280
Total	$4,950,000	$1,368,000

ordered that the firm be liquidated in accordance with Chapter 7. Note that this illustration would differ from a private or voluntary out-of-court liquidation in two important respects. First, the expenses associated with conducting the liquidation would be lower because the liquidation would not involve extended legal proceedings. Second, the distribution of proceeds could reflect the priority of claims negotiated between the creditors and the owners that differs from that set forth in Chapter 7 of the Bankruptcy Reform Act.

Section 363 Sales from Chapter 11

So-called 363 sales have become popular in recent years when time is critical. Section 363 bankruptcies allow a firm to enter a court-supervised sale of assets—usually an auction—as the best means of protecting the value of such assets. Unlike typical bankruptcies, firms may emerge in as little as 30–60 days. The auction process starts with a prospective buyer's setting the initial purchase price and terms as well as negotiating a *topping fee* to be paid if it is not successful in buying the assets. Often referred to as a *stalking horse*, the identity of the initial bidder may be concealed. The purpose of the stalking horse is to set a value for the business and to generate interest in the coming auction. *Credit bids* occur when secured creditors propose to buy the assets. Such bidders can bid up to the amount of the debt owed before offering any cash.[5] Creditors opposing the sale have only 10–20 days to file objections to the court, although the period may be shortened to as little as a few days by the bankruptcy judge. The bankruptcy judge decides how the proceeds of the auction are distributed among secured creditors. Some of the most high-profile 363 cases included the General Motors and Chrysler bankruptcies in 2008.

Chapter 15: Dealing with Cross-Border Bankruptcy

The purpose of Chapter 15 of the U.S. Bankruptcy Code is to provide mechanisms for resolving insolvency cases involving assets, lenders, and other parties in various countries. A Chapter 15 case is secondary to the primary proceeding brought in another country, which is typically the debtor's home country. As an alternative to Chapter 15, the debtor may proceed with a Chapter 7 or Chapter 11 case in the United States. As part of a Chapter 15 proceeding, the U.S. Bankruptcy Court may authorize a trustee to act in a foreign country on its behalf.

The foreign trustee has the right to petition the U.S. court system for resolving insolvency issues. The petition gives the court the authority to issue an order recognizing the foreign proceeding as either a foreign main proceeding or a foreign non-main proceeding. A *foreign main proceeding* is a proceeding in a country where the debtor's main interests are located; a *foreign non-main proceeding* is a proceeding in a country where the debtor has a business not representing their primary holdings. If the proceeding is recognized as a foreign main proceeding, the court imposes an automatic stay on assets in dispute in the United States and authorizes the foreign representative to operate the debtor's business.[6]

Motivations for Filing for Bankruptcy

Although most companies that file for bankruptcy do so because of their deteriorating financial position, companies also seek bankruptcy protection to enhance negotiating leverage, avoid litigation, and limit exposure to potential future liabilities. Texaco used the threat of bankruptcy in the early 1990s as a negotiating ploy to reduce the amount of court-ordered payments to Occidental Petroleum resulting from the court's finding that Texaco had

---

[5] In 2010, creditors outbid an investor group to acquire the *Philadelphia Inquirer* for an amount equal to $318 million, about one-half of what they were owed by the newspaper.

[6] Chapter 15 also gives foreign creditors the right to participate in U.S. bankruptcy cases and prohibits discrimination against foreign creditors. The Chapter 15 proceeding attempts to promote collaboration between U.S. and foreign courts, since the participants in the proceeding must cooperate fully.

intervened improperly in a pending merger. In 2001, LTV sold its plants while in bankruptcy to W.L. Ross and Company, which restarted the plants in 2002 in a new company named the International Steel Group. By simply buying assets, ISI eliminated its obligation to pay pension, healthcare, or insurance liabilities, which remained with LTV. More recently, a bankruptcy judge in late 2004 approved a settlement enabling two subsidiaries of the energy giant Halliburton to emerge from bankruptcy and to limit their exposure to potential future asbestos claims by establishing a $4.2 billion trust fund to pay such claims. Delphi, the ailing auto parts manufacturer, used its bankrupt status to threaten to rescind union contracts, to gain wage and benefit reductions from employees in 2007.

The High Cost of Bankruptcy

Efforts to contain costs have prompted a greater use of auctions and other market-based techniques. These include *prepackaged bankruptcies* with a reorganization plan in place at the time of the bankruptcy filing, acquisition of distressed debt by investors willing to support the proposed plan of reorganization, and voluntary auction-based sales while a firm is under the protection of Chapter 11. Despite the increasing use of innovative ways of expediting the bankruptcy process, the cost of professional services remains high. While large and complex, fees paid to bankruptcy advisors, such as appraisers, investment bankers, and lawyers, since the Lehman Brothers liquidation began in 2008 are estimated to have exceeded $900 million by the end of 2012.

Prepackaged Bankruptcies

Under a *prepackaged bankruptcy*, the debtor negotiates with creditors well in advance of filing for a Chapter 11 bankruptcy. Because there is general approval of the plan before the filing, the formal Chapter 11 reorganization that follows generally averages only a few months and results in substantially lower legal and administrative expenses.[7] Prepackaged bankruptcies are often a result of major creditors' anticipating a potential liquidation in bankruptcy as occurring at fire sale prices.[8] Such bankruptcy proceedings work best when a limited number of sophisticated secured creditors are involved, enabling the negotiations to proceed rapidly.[9]

---

[7] Altman, 1993; Betker, 1995; Tashjian, Lease, and McConnell, 1996

[8] Eckbo and Thorburn, 2008

[9] The notion that acquirer returns are enhanced if targets are acquired at fire sale prices is disputed by Ang and Mauck (2011), who find that the acquisition of distressed firms does not lead to superior performance. Acquirers overpay, since they often compare the target's current distressed share price to the previous 52-week high. Hence, the target's distressed price does not necessarily represent a discount from the target's true intrinsic value but, rather, a discount from the firm's previous high.

In a true prepackaged bankruptcy, creditors approve a reorganization plan before filing for bankruptcy. The bankruptcy court then approves the plan and the company emerges from bankruptcy quickly. Minority creditors often are required by the court to accept a plan of reorganization. The confirmation of such a plan over the objections of one or more classes of creditors sometimes is referred to as a *cram down*.

On November 4, 2010, U.S. movie studio Metro-Goldwyn-Mayer filed a prepackaged Chapter 11 bankruptcy in New York that had the approval of nearly all of its creditors. The week before, creditors had approved a plan to forgive more than $4 billion in debt for ownership stakes in the restructured studio and to replace existing management. The bankruptcy was approved the following month, with the reorganized firm emerging from court protection having raised $600 million in new financing.

ALTERNATIVE OPTIONS FOR FAILING FIRMS

A failing firm's strategic options are to merge with another firm, reach an out-of-court voluntary settlement with creditors, or file for Chapter 11 bankruptcy.[10] Note that the prepackaged bankruptcy discussed earlier in this chapter constitutes a blend of the second and third options. The firm may liquidate voluntarily as part of an out-of-court settlement, or be forced to liquidate under Chapter 7 of the Bankruptcy Code. Table 17.6 summarizes the implications of each option. The choice of which option to pursue is critically dependent on which provides the greatest net present value for creditors and shareholders. To evaluate these options, the firm's management needs to estimate the going concern, selling price, and liquidation values of the firm.

Merging with another Firm

If the failing firm's management estimates that the sale price of the firm is greater than the going-concern or liquidation value, management should seek to be acquired by or to merge with another firm. In an essentially make-versus-buy decision,[11] firms in the same industry may be inclined to acquire the failing firm, even if there is little operating synergy, if they are able to acquire assets at distressed prices that can be used in their operations.[12]

---

[10] Gormley and Matsa (2011) argue that when firms with weak governance mechanisms, and entrenched managers face financial distress, they sometimes make large, often unrelated, acquisitions with relatively high operating cash flows in an effort to grow their way out of their predicament. Such deals often destroy value for acquirer shareholders.

[11] Make-versus-buy decisions reflect the option of a firm to develop an asset on its own or to obtain it by acquiring another firm that already owns the desired asset.

[12] Almeida et al., 2011

TABLE 17.6   Alternative Strategies for Failing Firms

Assumptions	Options: Failing Firm	Outcome: Failing Firm
Selling Price is Greater Than the Going-Concern or Liquidation Value	1. Is acquired by another firm 2. Merges with another firm	1. Continues as subsidiary of acquirer 2. Merges into acquirer and ceases to exist
Going-Concern Value is Greater Than the Sale or Liquidation Value	1. Reaches out-of-court settlement with creditors 2. Seeks bankruptcy protection under Chapter 11 3. Seeks prepackaged settlement with primary creditors before entering Chapter 11	1. Continues with debt for equity swap, extension, and composition 2. Continues in reorganization
Liquidation Value is Greater Than the Sale or Going-Concern Value	1. Reaches out-of-court settlement with creditors 2. Liquidates under Chapter 7	1. Ceases to exist; assignee liquidates assets and distributes proceeds, reflecting the terms of the negotiated settlement with creditors 2. Ceases to exist; trustee supervises liquidation and distributes proceeds according to statutory priorities

If there is a strategic buyer, management must convince the firm's creditors that they will be more likely to receive what they are owed and shareholders are more likely to preserve share value if the firm is acquired rather than liquidated or allowed to remain independent. In some instances, buyers are willing to acquire failing firms only if their liabilities are reduced through the bankruptcy process. Hence, it may make sense to force the firm into bankruptcy to have some portion of its liabilities discharged during the process of Chapter 11 reorganization.[13] Alternatively, the potential buyer could reach agreement in advance of bankruptcy reorganization with the primary creditors (i.e., a prepackaged bankruptcy) and employ the bankruptcy process to achieve compliance from the minority creditors.

Sales within the protection of Chapter 11 reorganization may be accomplished either by a negotiated private sale to a particular purchaser or through a public auction. The latter is often favored by the court, since the purchase price is more likely to reflect the true market value of the assets. Generally, a public

[13] To protect it from litigation, Washington Construction Group required Morrison Knudsen Corporation to file for bankruptcy as a closing condition in the agreement of purchase and sale in 2000.

auction can withstand any court challenge by creditors questioning whether the purchaser has paid fair market value for the failing firm's assets. In 2005, Time Warner Inc., and Comcast Corp reached an agreement to buy bankrupt cable operator Adelphia Communications Corp while in Chapter 11 for nearly $18 billion. Time Warner and Comcast paid Adelphia bondholders and other creditors in cash and warrants for stock in a new company formed by combining Time Warner's cable business and Adelphia. Bidders tend to overpay for firms purchased out of Chapter 11, with such strategies benefiting the target firm but not acquirer shareholders. In most cases, the acquirers fail to restructure the target firms successfully.[14]

Reaching an Out-of-Court Voluntary Settlement with Creditors

The going-concern value of the firm may exceed the sale or liquidation value. Management must be able to demonstrate to creditors that a restructured or downsized firm would be able to repay its debts if creditors were willing to accept less, extend the maturity of the debt, or exchange debt for equity. In what is known as the *holdout problem*, smaller creditors have an incentive to attempt to hold up the agreement unless they receive special treatment, making an out-of-court voluntary settlement difficult to achieve. Consensus may be accomplished by paying all small creditors 100% of what they are owed and the larger creditors an agreed-on percentage. Other factors limiting voluntary settlements, such as a debt-for-equity swap, include a preference by some creditors for debt rather than equity and the lack of the necessary information to enable proper valuation of the equity offered to the creditors. Because of these factors, there is some evidence that firms attempting to restructure outside of Chapter 11 bankruptcy have more difficulty in reducing their indebtedness than those that negotiate with creditors while under the protection of Chapter 11.[15]

Voluntary and Involuntary Liquidations

The failing firm's management, shareholders, and creditors may agree that the firm is worth more in liquidation than in sale or as a continuing operation. If management cannot reach agreement with its creditors on a private liquidation, the firm may seek Chapter 7 liquidation. The proceeds of a private liquidation are distributed in accordance with the agreement negotiated with creditors, while the order in which claimants are paid under Chapter 7 is set by statute.

The Increasing Role of Hedge Funds in the Bankruptcy Process

Hedge funds can pursue activist strategies because of their focus on achieving high financial returns and because they are not limited by having other business

[14]Clark and Ofek, 1994

[15]Gilson, 1997

relationships with the debtor firm. Banks, mutual funds, and pension funds often have potential conflicts of interest with the debtor firm ranging from meeting their capital needs to managing the firm's pension fund assets. Unlike pension and mutual funds, hedge funds also are able to hold large concentrations of illiquid investments that strengthen their influence in negotiating with secured creditors.

Hedge funds play a key role in financing debtor firms in Chapter 11 by providing debtor-in-position (DIP) financing and acquiring equity stakes in such businesses. Hedge funds use the offer of DIP financing to bargain for seats on the debtor firm's board of directors and for receiving an ownership stake when the firm emerges from bankruptcy. DIP loans often convert to equity ownership, because they frequently allow for debt-for-equity swaps. Hedge funds also can acquire a controlling interest through so-called loan-to-own strategies and by acquiring unsecured debt in order to serve on the unsecured creditor or equity committees.

Under a loan-to-own strategy, a hedge fund acquires the debt of a failing firm and converts the debt into a controlling equity stake. That is, the hedge fund buys the debt at depressed prices, forces the distressed firm into Chapter 11, and converts the debt at book value to equity in a debt-for-equity swap, resulting in a controlling stake in the firm when the firm emerges from bankruptcy. The emergence from Chapter 11 is accomplished under section 363(k) of the Bankruptcy Code, which gives debtors the right to bid on the firm in a public auction sale. During the auction, the firm's debt is valued at face value rather than market value, discouraging other bidders other than the hedge fund, which acquired the debt prior to bankruptcy at distressed levels. By buying unsecured debt, hedge funds play an important role in affecting the balance of power between the debtor firm and secured creditors. Reorganizations in which hedge funds have substantial representation on unsecured creditor committees exhibit higher recovery rates for unsecured creditors and equity owners due to the ability of hedge funds to offset the tendency of secured creditors to push for liquidation.[16]

FAILING FIRMS AND SYSTEMIC RISK

In response to the meltdown in global financial markets in 2008 and 2009, the U.S. Congress passed the Dodd-Frank Wall Street Reform and Consumer Protections Act of 2010 (Dodd-Frank). Among other things, the act created a new government authority to dismantle financial services firms whose demise would endanger the U.S. financial system and economy. The objectives of this new authority, called the Orderly Liquidation Authority (OLA), are to ensure that losses resulting from the speedy liquidation of a firm are borne primarily by the firm's shareholders and creditors, to minimize the loss of taxpayer funds, and to penalize current management. The OLA is solely a liquidation remedy and,

[16] Jiang et al., 2012

unlike Chapter 11 of the U.S. Bankruptcy Code, does not allow for reorganization or rehabilitation as an option. The order in which claimants are paid during liquidation is similar to that defined under Chapter 7, except that the government puts itself first.

The OLA applies to U.S. bank holding companies and non-bank financial firms supervised by the Federal Reserve Board of Governors (the Fed). The OLA also applies to companies engaged predominantly in activities that the Fed determines are financial in nature, subsidiaries of such companies (other than insured depositor institutions or insurance companies), and brokers and dealers registered with the SEC and a member of the Securities Investor Protection Corporation (SIPC), a fund designed to insure clients against broker/dealer fraud. The liquidation of insured depository institutions will continue to be the responsibility of the FDIC under the agency's current mandate. While insurance companies will continue to be subject to state regulation, their holding companies and unregulated affiliates are covered by the OLA.

The advantages of the OLA are that it provides the government with both the authority and a clear process for expeditiously winding down failing firms that are deemed a risk to the financial system. However, the resolution process for dealing with failing, systemically risky firms can itself destabilize the financial system, since the process could panic investors and lenders. Furthermore, the OLA is applicable only to firms whose operations are wholly domestic, since there is currently no cross-border mechanism for resolving issues involving banks operating in multiple countries. Consequently, large, multinational banks will be unaffected by the OLA.

PREDICTING CORPORATE DEFAULT AND BANKRUPTCY

The accuracy of bankruptcy-prediction models has improved over the years with better financial reporting required under the Sarbanes-Oxley Act of 2002[17] and the development of more robust statistical models. However, the widespread defaults during the 2008 and 2009 global recession underscore the need for further research.

Alternative Models

A review of 165 bankruptcy-prediction studies published from 1930 to 2006 examined how modeling trends have changed by decade. Discriminant analysis was the primary method used to develop models in the 1960s and 1970s. However, the primary modeling methods shifted by the 1980s to logit analysis and neural networks. While the number of factors used in building the models varied by decade, the average model used about 10 variables. In analyzing model accuracy, multivariate discriminant analysis and neural networks seem

[17] Kwak et al., 2012

to be the most promising, and increasing the number of variables in the model does not guarantee greater accuracy. Interestingly, two-factor models often are as accurate as models with as many as 21 factors.[18]

An international study analyzed the findings and methodologies used in 46 studies applied in 10 countries from 1968 to 2003. The study found that bankruptcy-prediction models typically used financial ratios to predict business failure, with about 60% of the studies reviewed using only financial ratios. The remaining studies used both financial ratios and other information. The financial ratios typically included measures of liquidity, solvency, leverage, profitability, asset composition, firm size, and growth rate. Also included were macroeconomic, industry-specific, location, and firm-specific variables. This study concluded that the predictive accuracy of the various types of models investigated was very similar, correctly identifying failing firms about 80% of the time for firms in the sample employed in estimating the models. However, accuracy dropped substantially for out-of-sample predictions.[19]

Documenting potential problems with bankruptcy-prediction models, researchers have found that model results often vary by industry and time period. Model accuracy also tends to decline when applied to periods different from those employed to develop the models (i.e., in sample versus out-of-sample predictions). Moreover, applying models to industries other than those used to develop the models often results in greatly diminished accuracy.[20]

In view of the extensive literature on the subject, the following subsections discuss categories of models that differ by methodology and choice of variables used to predict bankruptcy. The intent of these subsections is to provide an overview of the state of such models.[21]

Models that Differ by Methodology

Bankruptcy-prediction models tend to fall into three major categories: credit-scoring, structural, and reduced-form models.

Credit-Scoring Models

One of the earliest (1960s) quantitative efforts to predict bankruptcy relied on discriminant analysis to distinguish between bankrupt and nonbankrupt firms.[22] Discriminant analysis uses a combination of independent variables to assign a score (i.e., a Z score) to a particular firm. This score then is used to distinguish between bankrupt and nonbankrupt firms by using a cutoff point. The likelihood

[18] Bellovary, Giacomino, and Akers, 2007

[19] Aziz and Dar, 2006

[20] Grice and Dugan, 2001

[21] For a more rigorous discussion of bankruptcy-prediction models, see Jones and Hensher (2008)

[22] Altman, 1968

of default for firms with low Z scores is less than for firms with high Z scores. The most significant financial ratios for predicting default are earnings before income and taxes as a percentage of total assets and the ratio of sales to total assets. The limitation of this approach is that it captures a firm's financial health at a moment in time and does not reflect changes in a company's financial ratios over time. Tests of this methodology applied to more recent samples found that the earlier model's ability to classify bankrupt companies correctly fell from 83.5% to 57.8%.[23]

To compensate for the shortcomings of the discriminant model, analysts developed models to predict the probability that a firm would default over some future period. The model postulated that the default rate depended not only on the firm's current financial ratios but also on such forward-looking market variables as market capitalization, abnormal financial returns, and the volatility of such financial returns. The only financial ratios with significant predictive power are earnings before interest and taxes to total liabilities and the market value of equity to total liabilities.[24]

Structural Models

Structural models of credit risk assume that firms default when they violate a debt covenant, cash flow falls short of required debt payments, or shareholders decide that servicing the debt is no longer in their best interests. Structural models employ logit or probit regression models that provide a conditional probability that an observation belongs to a specific category and do not require assumptions as restrictive as discriminant analysis. The logit model yields a score between 0 and 1, which gives the probability that the firm will default.[25]

Reduced-Form Models

In contrast to structural models, reduced-form models use market prices of the distressed firm's debt as the only source of information about the firm's risk. Such prices are a proxy for the variables used in the structural models. Although easier to estimate, such models lack a specific link between credit risk and the firm's assets and liabilities and assume that the timing of default is random, in that investors with incomplete data do not know how far the firm is from default.[26]

Other Modeling Methods

While statistical discriminant analysis and probit or logit methods dominate the literature, they are not the only techniques used in bankruptcy prediction. Neural networks use artificial intelligence that attempts to mimic the way a human brain works and are particularly effective when a large database of prior

---

[23] Grice and Ingram, 2001

[24] Li, 2012; Shumway, 2001

[25] A partial list of structural credit risk models includes the following: Kim et al., 1993; Leland, 1994; Longstaff et al., 1995; and Hsu et al., 2002

[26] See Jarrow and Turnbull (1995) for examples of reduced-form models.

examples exists.[27] The cumulative sums (CUSUM) method represents a class of models that account for serial correlation (i.e., interdependencies) in the data and that incorporate information from more than one period.[28] The options-based approach to bankruptcy prediction builds on option-pricing theory to explain business bankruptcy, relying on such variables as firm volatility to predict default.[29]

Models Differing in Choice of Variables Used to Predict Bankruptcy

Accounting data are sometimes used to predict credit ratings, which serve as proxies for the probability of default.[30] Other analysts argue that the probability of failure depends on the length of the time horizon considered[31] or demonstrate a correlation between default rates and loss in the event of default and the business cycle.[32] Shocks, such as recession and credit crunches contribute to default by affecting firm assets or cash flow negatively.[33] Other studies use net worth as a key factor affecting a firm's ability to raise funds in a liquidity crisis[34] or equity returns and debt service ratios as measures of distress.[35]

VALUING DISTRESSED BUSINESSES

The intent of this section is to discuss ways of incorporating the impact of potential financial distress, default, and ultimately bankruptcy on the value of the firm. Historical performance may prove a poor guide to determining the future financial performance of businesses experiencing declining revenue and profitability, since it is unclear when or if they will recover.

Standard DCF methods attempt to adjust for financial distress by increasing the discount rate. Since the bulk of the firm's total value will come from its terminal value, this adjustment implies that the firm will be able to generate cash flows in perpetuity despite its weakened state. Consequently, it is likely that the value of the firm will be overstated. To adjust DCF estimates, it is necessary to estimate the likelihood and cost of financial distress. In practice, it is extremely difficult to estimate the probability of a bankruptcy. Not only do we need to

---

[27] Platt et al., 1999

[28] Kahya and Theodosiou, 1999

[29] Charitou and Trigeorgis, 2000

[30] Blume, Lim, and MacKinlay, 1998; Molina, 2006; Avramov et al., 2006

[31] Duffie, Saita, and Wang, 2007

[32] Altman et al., 2003

[33] Hennessy and Whited, 2007; Anderson and Coverhill, 2007

[34] White, 1989

[35] Gilson, John, and Lang, 1990; Asquith, Gertner, and Scharfstein, 1994

estimate the probability of a specific outcome annually but also the cumulative probability of that outcome, since a firm experiencing distress in one year is likely to continue to experience distress in subsequent years. Thus, the effect of financial distress tends to accumulate because a firm may be less able to reinvest such that future cash flows are reduced below what they would have been, had the firm not experienced financial distress.

A common approach to valuing distressed firms is the adjusted present value, or APV, method (see Chapter 14). The APV method requires the estimation of the value of the firm without debt by discounting the projected cash flows by the unlevered cost of equity; calculating the present value of interest tax savings at the unlevered cost of equity (since these tax benefits are subject to the same risk as the cash flows of an unlevered firm); and the estimation of the probability and cost of financial distress. Table 17.7 illustrates the inclusion of financial distress in the valuation of the McClatchy Company using the APV method. The McClatchy Company is a United States–based newspaper publisher owning 30 daily newspapers and 43 non-daily newspapers in 29 regional markets. The company also owns local websites offering a variety of content, engages in direct marketing and direct mail operations, and has minority interests in a series of digital businesses. The entire newspaper industry has been experiencing long-term erosion in its readership base and a subsequent decline in advertising revenue. The decline in revenues was exacerbated by the 2008–2009 recession. The model assumes that the deterioration in revenues would continue through 2013 before showing a modest improvement in 2014–2015 as the firm transformed itself from primarily a print business to a digital media business. The key assumption in calculating the terminal value is an assumed 3% growth in cash flow in perpetuity.

As of March 10, 2010, the major credit-rating agencies rated the firm below investment grade. Such firms carry a B− credit rating and have an estimated cumulative probability of default of about 42% (see Table 14.2 in Chapter 14). Table 17.7 adjusts the value of the firm for the expected cost of bankruptcy, ranging from 15% to 40% of the firm's APV. The cost of bankruptcy is assumed to be included in the cost of financial distress. The value of the firm's share price varies from a high of $5.85 (at 15%) to a low of $1.55 (at 40%). The firm's price per share of $5.19 at the time of the valuation suggests that investors believed the impact of financial distress was limited. See Chapter 14 for a detailed discussion of estimating the probability and cost of financial distress. The Excel model underlying Table 17.7 is available on the companion website to this book in a file entitled "Excel-Based Model to Value Firms Experiencing Financial Distress."

EMPIRICAL STUDIES OF FINANCIAL DISTRESS

Many of the quantitative studies of firms in financial distress reveal an array of sometimes-surprising results. These are discussed next.

TABLE 17.7 Present Value of McClatchy Company Using the Adjusted Present Value Method

	2010	2011	2012	2013	2014	2015
COMPANY DATA: McCLATCHY						
Price/Share on March 10, 2010	$5.19					
Fully Diluted Shares Outstanding	84,470,000					
Market Value (MV) of Equity March 10, 2010	$438,399,300	$650,896,030	$854,892,890	$1,054,809,813	$1,307,204,929	$1,616,136,550
Market Value (MV) of Debt March 10, 2010[a]	$740,249,905	$666,224,915	$599,602,423	$539,642,181	$485,677,963	$437,110,166
Ratio of MV of Debt to MV of Equity	1.69	1.02	0.70	0.51	0.37	0.27
Weighted Average Maturity of McClatchy Debt	9.6 years					
McClatchy Credit Rating	B –					A
GENERAL ASSUMPTIONS						
Comparable-Company Unlevered Beta[b]	1.1344					
10-Year Treasury Bond Rate (%)	3.65					
Cumulative Probability of Default for Firm Rated B – [c]	0.4212					
Equity Premium	0.055					
McCLATCHY COMPANY ASSUMPTIONS						
Price-Earnings Ratio	6.00	4.00	4.00	4.00	5.00	6.00
Target Debt/Equity Ratio for 2015	0.33					
Ratio of Implied Target Debt to Total Capital for 2015[d]	0.25					

(Continued)

TABLE 17.7 (Continued)

	2010	2011	2012	2013	2014	2015
Current Cost of Debt[e]	10 65					0.08
Expected Cost of Financial Distress (% of Firm Value)	0.15–0 40					
Terminal-Period Growth Rate	0 03					
Unlevered Cost of Equity (2011–2015)[f]	0.0989					
Terminal-Period WACC[g]	0.0862					
Revenue	$1,471,584,000	$1,398,004,800	$1,342,084,608	$1,315,242,916	$1,328,395,345	$1,354,963,252
Net Income (3.8% of Revenue)	$54,090,000	$53,124,182	$50,999,215	$49,979,231	$50,479,023	$51,488,604
Depreciation (8% of Revenue)	$142,889,000	$111,840,384	$107,366,769	$105,219,433	$106,271,628	$108,397,060
Change in Working Capital (3.5% of Revenue)	$73,579,000	$48,930,168	$46,972,961	$46,033,502	$46,493,837	$54,198,530
Gross Capital Spending	$13,574,000	$13,980,048	$20,131,269	$26,304,858	$33,209,884	$33,874,081
Principal Repayments	$64,200,000	$74,024,991	$66,622,491	$59,960,242	$53,964,218	$48,567,796
Dividends Paid	$14,905,000	$10,905,000	$5,905,000	$5,905,000	$5,905,000	$5,905,000
Equity Cash Flow	$30,721,000	$17,124,360	$18,734,262	$16,995,061	$17,177,712	$17,340,256
Interest Expense	$107,353,000	$96,617,700	$86,955,930	$78,260,337	$70,434,303	$63,390,873
Tax Shield (40% of Interest Expense)	$42,941,200	$38,647,080	$34,782,372	$31,304,135	$28,173,721	$25,356,349

ADJUSTED PRESENT VALUE

PV Equity Cash Flow at 9.89%	$2,026,598
PV Terminal Value	$1,445,999,847
Total PV	$1,448,026,445
Plus: PV of Tax Shield	$3,868,418

	15%	20%	25%	30%	35%	40%
Adjusted Present Value of Firm	$1,451,894,863					
Less: Expected Cost of Financial Distress at 15%	$217,784,229					
Expected Cost of Financial Distress at 20%		$290,378,973				
Expected Cost of Financial Distress at 25%			$362,973,716			
Expected Cost of Financial Distress at 30%				$435,568,459		
Expected Cost of Financial Distress at 35%					$508,163,202	
Expected Cost of Financial Distress at 40%						$580,757,945
Less: Market Value of Debt	$740,249,837	$740,249,837	$740,249,837	$740,249,837	$740,249,837	$740,249,837
Equals: Equity Value	$493,860,796	$421,266,053	$348,671,310	$276,076,567	$203,481,824	$130,887,081
Equals: Equity Value per Share	$5.85	$4.99	$4.13	$3.27	$2.41	$1.55

[a] Market value of debt = Interest expense $\times$ $\{[1 - 1/(1 + i^n)(1 + i)] + Face\ value\ of\ debt/(1 + i)^n = \$107,353,000 \times \{[1 - 1/(1.1065)^{9.6}]/(1.1065)] + 1,796,436,000/(1.1065)^{9.6} = 60,298,095 + 679,951,810 = \$740,249,905$

[b] Comparable company unlevered beta = Comparable company levered beta/[1 + (1−marginal tax rate) × (comparable company debt/equity)]=1.924/[1 + (1 − 0.4) × 1.16] = 1.1344 (based on top-10 U.S. newspapers in terms of market capitalization).

[c] See Table 13.9 in Chapter 13.

[d] Implied debt-to-total capital ratio = (D/E)/(1 + D/E) = 0.33/1.33 = 0.25

[e] Cost of debt equals the risk-free rate of 3.65% plus a 7% default spread based on McClatchy's rating of B − from S&P.

[f] Unlevered cost of equity = 0.0365 + 1.1344(0.055) = 0.0989

[g] Terminal period WACC = 0.25 × (1 − 0.4) × 0.08 + 0.75 × 0.0989 = 0.012 + 0.0742 = 0.0862

Attractive Returns to Firms Emerging from Bankruptcy are Often Temporary

When firms emerge from bankruptcy, they often cancel the old stock and issue new common stock. Empirical studies show that such firms often experience attractive financial returns to holders of the new stock immediately following the announcement that the firm is emerging from bankruptcy.[36] However, long-term performance often deteriorates, with some studies showing that 40% of the firms studied experiencing operating losses in the three years after emerging from Chapter 11. Almost one-third subsequently filed for bankruptcy or had to restructure their debt. After five years, about one-quarter of all firms that reorganized were liquidated or merged or refiled for bankruptcy.[37] The most common reason for firms having to file for bankruptcy again is excessive debt.

Returns to Financially Distressed Stocks are Unexpectedly Low

As a class, distressed stocks offer low financial rates of return despite their high risk of business failure.[38] In theory, one would expect such risky assets to offer financial returns commensurate with risk. The low financial return for distressed stocks tends to be worse for stocks with low analyst coverage, institutional ownership, and price per share. Factors potentially contributing to these low returns could include unexpected events, valuation errors by uninformed investors, and the characteristics of distressed stocks. Unexpected events include the economy's being worse than expected. Valuation errors include investors' not understanding the relationship between variables used to predict failure and the risk of failure and therefore not having fully discounted the value of stocks to offset this risk. The characteristics of failing firms are such that some investors may have an incentive to hold such stocks despite their low returns. For example, majority owners of distressed stocks can benefit by having other firms in which they have an ownership stake buy the firm's output or assets at bargain prices. Consequently, the benefits from having control could exceed the low returns associated with financially distressed stocks.

Low returns to financially distressed stocks also may be related to the future potential for asset recovery. If expected recovery rates are high, the distressed firm's shareholders may deliberately trigger default by missing payments if they believe they can recover a significant portion of the value of their shares through renegotiation of credit terms with lenders. Consequently, the lower perceived risk of such shares would result in commensurately lower financial returns.[39]

[36] Alderson et al., 1996; Eberhart et al., 1999

[37] Hotchkiss, 1995; France, 2002

[38] Campbell et al., 2008

[39] Garlappi et al., 2011

IPOs are More Likely to Experience Bankruptcy than are Established Firms

Firms that have recently undergone IPOs tend to experience a much higher incidence of financial distress and bankruptcy than more established firms.[40] These findings are consistent with other studies showing that a portfolio of IPOs performs well below the return on the S&P 500 stock index for up to five years after the firms go public.[41] Some observers attribute this underperformance to the limited amount of information available on these firms.[42]

Financially Ailing Firms can be Contagious

A contagion in this context describes the spread of financial distress of one firm to other firms. A declaration of bankruptcy by one firm can impact rival firms and suppliers negatively. The extent to which this may happen depends on whether the factors contributing to financial distress are affecting all firms within an industry or relate to a specific firm. The effects of financial distress may also differ depending on the degree to which an industry is concentrated. Studies show that stock prices of peers react negatively to a competitor's bankruptcy in most industries; however, peer share prices may increase whenever a competitor declares bankruptcy in highly concentrated industries. The latter reflects the likelihood that the remaining competitors in concentrated industries will gain market share, enabling them to benefit from increased economies of scale and pricing power.[43] Furthermore, firms experiencing financial distress or in Chapter 11 are likely to experience declining sales and in turn to reduce their demand for raw materials and services from suppliers. When such firms represent important customers, suppliers often experience significant declines in valuations.[44]

There also is evidence that industry bankruptcies raise the cost of borrowing and reduce the access to credit of other industry participants by reducing the value of the collateral used to secure debt financing.[45] Specifically, firms experiencing financial distress are forced to sell assets and reduce their purchases of similar assets, putting downward pressure on the value of such assets. Consequently, firms owning similar assets whose value has fallen will be forced to borrow less, pay more for credit, or both.

---

[40] Beneda, 2007

[41] Aggarwal et al., 1990; Ritter, 1991; and Loughran et al., 1994

[42] Grinblatt et al., 2002

[43] Lang and Stulz, 1992

[44] Hertzel, Li, Officer, and Rodgers, 2008

[45] Benmelech and Bergman, 2011

SOME THINGS TO REMEMBER

Bankruptcy is designed to protect the technically or legally insolvent firm from lawsuits by its creditors until a decision is made to liquidate or reorganize the firm. Absent a voluntary settlement out of court, the debtor firm may voluntarily seek protection from its creditors by initiating bankruptcy or be forced involuntarily into bankruptcy by its creditors.

DISCUSSION QUESTIONS

17.1 Why would creditors make concessions to a debtor firm? Give examples of common types of concessions. Describe how these concessions affect the debtor firm.

17.2 Although most companies that file for bankruptcy do so because of their deteriorating financial position, companies increasingly are seeking bankruptcy protection to avoid litigation. Give examples of how bankruptcy can be used to avoid litigation.

17.3 What are the primary options available to a failing firm? What criteria might the firm use to select a particular option? Be specific.

17.4 Describe the probable trend in financial returns to shareholders of firms that emerge from bankruptcy. To what do you attribute these trends? Explain your answer.

17.5 Identify at least two financial or non-financial variables that have been shown to affect firm defaults and bankruptcies. Explain how each might affect the likelihood the firm will default or seek Chapter 11 protection.

17.6 On June 25, 2008, JHT Holdings, Inc., a Kenosha, Wisconsin–based package delivery service, filed for bankruptcy. The firm had annual revenues of $500 million. What would the firm have to demonstrate for its petition to be accepted by the bankruptcy court?

17.7 Dura Automotive emerged from Chapter 11 protection in mid-2008. The firm obtained exit financing consisting of a $110 million revolving-credit facility, a $50 million European first-lien term loan, and an $84 million U.S. second-lien loan. The reorganization plan specified how a portion of the proceeds of these loans would be used. What do you believe might be typical stipulations in reorganization plans for using such funds? Be specific.

17.8 What are the primary factors contributing to business failure? Be specific.

17.9 In recent years, hedge funds engaged in so-called loan-to-own pre-bankruptcy investments, in which they acquired debt from distressed firms at a fraction of face value. Subsequently, they moved the company into Chapter 11, intent on converting the acquired debt to equity in a firm with sharply reduced liabilities. The hedge fund also provided financing to secure its interest in the business. The emergence from Chapter 11 was typically accomplished under section 363(k) of the Bankruptcy Code, which gives debtors the right to bid on the firm in a public auction sale. During the auction, the firm's debt was valued at face value rather than market value, discouraging bidders other than the hedge fund, which acquired the debt prior to bankruptcy at distressed levels. Without competitive bidding, there was little chance of generating additional cash for the general creditors. Is this an abuse of the Chapter 11 bankruptcy process? Explain your answer.

17.10 American Home Mortgage Investments filed for Chapter 11 bankruptcy in late 2008. The company indicated that it chose this course of action because it represented the best means of preserving the firm's assets. W.L. Ross and Company agreed to provide the firm $50 million in debtor-in-possession financing to meet its anticipated cash needs while in Chapter 11. Comment on the statement that bankruptcy provides the best means of asset preservation. Why would W.L. Ross and Company lend money to a firm that had just filed for bankruptcy?

Answers to these Chapter Discussion Questions are found in the Online Instructor's Manual for instructors using this book.

QUESTIONS FROM THE CFA CURRICULUM

17.11 An investor worried that a company may go bankrupt would most likely examine its:
  a. Current ratio
  b. Return on equity
  c. Debt-to-equity ratio
Source: CFA Institute, 2011, Understanding the Balance Sheet, Reading 33, question 21.

17.12 An analyst has calculated a ratio using as the numerator the sum of operating cash flow, interest, and taxes, and as the denominator the amount of interest. What is this ratio, what does it measure, and what does it indicate?
  a. This ratio is an interest coverage ratio, measuring a company's ability to meet its interest obligations and indicating a company's solvency.
  b. This ratio is an effective tax ratio, measuring the amount of a company's operating cash flow used for taxes and indicating a company's efficiency in tax management.
  c. This ratio is an operating profitability ratio, measuring the operating cash flow generated accounting for taxes and interest and indicating the company's liquidity.
Source: CFA Institute, 2011, Understanding the Cash Flow Statement, Reading 34, question 23.

17.13 In general, a creditor would consider a decrease in which of the following ratios to be positive news?
   a. Interest coverage ratio
   b. Debt-total assets
   c. Return on assets

Source: CFA Institute, 2011, Financial Analysis Techniques, Reading 35, question 20.

Answers to questions from the CFA curriculum are available in the Online Student Companion website to this book in a file folder entitled CFA Cuirriculum Questions and Solutions.

CASE STUDY 17.1
Blockbuster Acquired by Dish Network in a Section 363 Sale

Key Points

- Section 363 auctions are an increasingly common means of preserving asset value when failing firms are hemorrhaging cash flow.
- Such sales allow buyers to purchase assets at potentially bargain prices.
- While not without risk, 363 sales are often viewed as a more efficient way to exit bankruptcy than via a more conventional reorganization plan.

Despite facing challenges reminiscent of a Hollywood movie thriller, Blockbuster, the movie rental giant, went from a mundane prepackaged bankruptcy agreement to acknowledging its own insolvency to facing the real possibility of liquidation in the span of six months. What follows is a discussion of the sometimes-unpredictable twists and turns of a highly contentious Section 363 bankruptcy filing.

Blockbuster had been in a downward spiral years before approaching its creditors for a negotiated reduction in its debt burden in mid-2010.

The ability to download movies via the Internet had come to dominate the video rental business, thanks largely to DVD rental provider Netflix Inc. and video-on-demand services from cable providers. Blockbuster was forced to file for bankruptcy for its North American operations on September 23, 2010, with 5,600 stores, including 3,300 in the United States. The fate of 29,000 employees and hundreds of creditors hung in the balance.

Prior to the firm's petition for protection under Chapter 11 of the U.S. Bankruptcy Code, Blockbuster had reached an agreement with its major creditors on a so-called prepackaged reorganization plan that would have left the firm with $400 million in new senior debt as it emerged from bankruptcy as an ongoing business. This amounted to about 27% of its outstanding prepetition debt of $1.46 billion.

The circumstances changed unexpectedly when famed billionaire investor Charles Icahn bought 31% of the firm's existing senior notes in late

September, making him a major creditor and a key participant on the creditor committee in the subsequent negotiations. Icahn and Blockbuster had had a tumultuous history together. He had purchased shares in Blockbuster in 2004. The next year, following a bitter proxy battle, he won three seats on the firm's board of directors. Eventually, Icahn was able to oust then–board Chairman John Antioco. In 2010, due to increasing demands on his time, Icahn stepped down from the board and sold his shares in Blockbuster.

By buying such a large percentage of the outstanding debt, Icahn, as a major creditor, was able to submit his own plan for revamping Blockbuster. His proposal was to eliminate Blockbuster's debt when it emerged from bankruptcy, and it represented a radically different approach from the prepackaged plan that Blockbuster had negotiated with other creditors. His proposal involved swapping senior secured notes for equity in a recapitalized company, with the senior subordinated note holders, preferred, and common shareholders completely wiped out. Unsecured shareholders were to receive warrants to buy up to 3% of the new firm's equity. Financing to meet the firm's immediate cash flow needs would come from a $375 million debtor-in-possession (DIP) loan from a group of the senior note holders. Such lenders' credit claims are given a much higher payment priority than those of other creditors in the event of the firm's liquidation and, as such, are often viewed as relatively low risk.

Movie studio creditors, critical suppliers to Blockbuster, supported the plan because they were promised payments for what they were owed on a priority basis out of the operating cash flows once the firm emerged from bankruptcy. Senior secured note holders, owning 80.1% of the firm's debt, also were willing to accept the Icahn proposal. With the blessing of its major creditors, Blockbuster undertook an expensive but unsuccessful advertising campaign in late 2010 in an attempt to restore growth, with lenders providing an additional $30 million. Despite the ad campaign, sales continued to decline. The firm waited until late January 2011 to tell the movie studios and other creditors about its deteriorating cash position. Already technically insolvent, the firm was fast running out of cash.

Having missed several performance milestones in the prepackaged (but never filed) reorganization plan, Blockbuster was in default on its DIP loan, even though it had never utilized any of the funds. By defaulting, the firm violated a covenant that allowed senior note holders to include $125 million of their securities as part of the DIP loan. This action gave them the same high-priority position as that afforded a DIP lender.

Blockbuster feared that it would be liquidated if it were acquired by Icahn, and it accelerated efforts to conduct a 363(k) auction for selling the firm's assets in the hope it could emerge from bankruptcy as a going concern. On February 21, 2011, Blockbuster filed a motion with the U.S. Bankruptcy Court seeking authorization to conduct an auction for selling the company's assets, which would be conducted under the Court's supervision and in accordance with Section 363 of the U.S. Bankruptcy Code. Following approval by the Court, Blockbuster initiated the bidding process. The auction allowed for a 30-day period during which potential bidders could perform due diligence. At the end of this period, interested parties would have one week to submit bids, with the winning bid to be announced shortly following the close of the auction.

On April 5, five different bidding groups submitted bids. The financial buyers included the consortium led by Icahn (which included liquidator Great American Group); a group led by Monarch Investors; and a group consisting of liquidators Gordon Brothers and Hilco Merchant Resources. Hedge funds and investor groups specializing in restructuring and liquidation often buy distressed debt at a deep discount, acquire the failing firm's assets through a credit bid (i.e., exchanging what they are owed for the firm's assets), and liquidate the assets at a price in excess of what they paid for the debt. The other bidders included South Korea's SK Telecom Co. and satellite television provider Dish Network. Both were interested in Blockbuster because of potential synergy with their current operations.

The strategies of Icahn, Monarch, and the Gordon Brothers appeared to be similar: close the Blockbuster stores, liquidate the inventories, and sell the digital download business. In contrast, SK Telecom and Dish offered the prospect of Blockbuster's emerging from bankruptcy as a reorganized but going concern. Dish believed the chain's brand could be valuable for its video-on-demand services. Dish also saw an opportunity to sell subscriptions through Blockbuster's stores and believed the Blockbuster buyout could give it some leverage in negotiating future business with movie studios.

Dish submitted the winning bid of $320 million. Of that figure, $125 million was to repay the senior notes that had been "rolled up" into the DIP loan, with 75% of the rest of the proceeds paid to noteholders and 25% to the holders of administrative claims. Senior noteholders were expected to receive about 26% of their claims and unsecured lenders about 19% of their claims, with preferred and common shareholders receiving nothing. Dish assumed $11.5 million in debt to the movie studios. The bankruptcy judge overruled 111 objections from landlords, business partners, and other creditors about the amounts Blockbuster proposed to pay them under contracts on which it had defaulted.

Discussion Questions

1. What are the primary objectives of the bankruptcy process?
2. What types of businesses are most appropriate for Chapter 11 reorganization, Chapter 7 liquidation, or a Section 363 sale?
3. The Blockbuster case study illustrates the options available to the creditors and owners of a failing firm. How do you believe creditors and owners might choose

among the range of available options? Explain your answer.

4. Financial buyers such as hedge funds clearly are motivated by the potential profit they can make by buying distressed debt. Their actions may have both a positive and a negative impact on parties to the bankruptcy process. Identify how parties to a bankruptcy may be helped or hurt by the actions of the hedge funds.

5. Do you believe that a strategic bidder like Dish Network has an inherent advantage over a financial bidder in a 363 auction? Explain your answer.

6. Speculate as to why Blockbuster filed a motion with the Court to initiate a Section 363 auction rather than to continue to negotiate a reorganization plan with its creditors to exit Chapter 11.

Answers to these Case Study questions are found in the Online Instructor's Manual available for instructors using this book.

CASE STUDY 17.2
The Deal from Hell: The Tribune Company Emerges from Chapter 11

Key Points

- Tribune Company's LBO failed because it was structured without any margin for error.
- Large secured creditors failing to recover what they are owed often exchange their debt for equity in the restructured company.
- The extreme length of time in Chapter 11 reflected the absence of prenegotiation with creditors due to the firm's rapid entry into bankruptcy, the deal structure's complexity, and fraud allegations.

Four years after its ill-fated leveraged buyout left the media firm with an unsustainably large debt load, Tribune Company (Tribune) emerged from Chapter 11 bankruptcy on December 31, 2012. Founded in 1847, Tribune publishes some of the best-known newspapers in the United States, such as the *Los Angeles Times*, the *Baltimore Sun*, and the *Chicago Tribune*. The firm also owns WGN in Chicago and 22 other television stations as well as the WGN radio station. Over the years the firm has spent hundreds of millions of dollars in an attempt to become a diversified media company.

The bankruptcy court judge approved a reorganization plan that left the firm in the hands of a new ownership group consisting largely of former creditors and hedge funds that had acquired some of the firm's outstanding debt. The largest owners included Oaktree Capital Management, JPMorgan Chase, and Angelo, Gordon

& Co., a firm that specializes in investing in distressed companies. Senior lenders now own 91% of the firm's shares in exchange for forgiving their credit claims. This group held most of Tribune's senior debt and worked with the company and the committee representing unsecured creditors to create a reorganization plan acceptable to the bankruptcy court judge. Court documents indicated that the restructured firm was valued at about 40% of its $8.2 billion valuation when it was taken private in 2007. The firm's broadcast business had an estimated value of $2.85 billion, and its publishing businesses were valued at $623 million, bringing the firm's total value to $3.47 billion.

While the reorganization plan shielded JPMorgan and other lenders from lawsuits related to the leveraged buyout, it did allow junior creditors to file lawsuits against other parties involved in the LBO transaction. These could include Sam Zell (a well-known real estate investor), other Tribune officers and directors, and Tribune stockholders who sold their shares in the buyout. Junior creditors who led the opposition to the final reorganization plan alleged that the larger creditors that financed the LBO transaction were well aware of the Tribune's precarious financial position in 2007 and that they were largely escaping any punitive action stemming from their alleged fraudulent activities. The junior creditors believed that the large lenders expected that the firm would become insolvent once the transaction was completed, prompting some to sell loans made to the Tribune.

To understand these allegations it is necessary to recognize the extent of the financial engineering underlying this transaction. The deal was predicated on achieving the highest leverage possible and quickly paying down the debt through asset sales and expected tax savings. However, the timing of the transaction could not have been worse, closing at a time when newspapers nationwide were beset by declines in their subscriber base and advertising revenue.

Despite these considerations, Tribune seemed ripe for a takeover, with its share price having lagged well behind that of other media companies. This also was one of the most active periods in decades for LBO transactions. With interest rates at near-record lows, prices paid for LBO targets soared. While the firm's cash flows from newspapers were declining, operating cash flow from its other media operations had been relatively stable in recent years. With profit margins on loans squeezed, lenders were trying to offset declining interest earnings by generating additional fee income that would result from originating loans and later selling them to other investors.

On April 2, 2007, Tribune announced that the firm's publicly traded shares would be acquired in a transaction valued at $8.2 billion. The deal was implemented in a two-stage transaction in which Sam Zell acquired a controlling 51% interest in the first stage, followed by a backend merger in the second stage in which the remaining outstanding Tribune shares were acquired. In the first stage,

Tribune initiated a cash tender offer for 51% of total shares for $34 per share, totaling $4.2 billion. The tender was financed using $250 million of the $315 million provided by Sam Zell in the form of subordinated debt plus additional borrowing to cover the balance. Stage 2 was triggered when the deal received regulatory approval. During this stage, an employee stock ownership plan (ESOP) bought the rest of the shares at $34 a share (totaling about $4 billion), with Zell providing the remaining $65 million of his pledge. Over time, the ESOP would hold all of the remaining stock. Furthermore, Tribune was converted from a C corporation to a subchapter S corporation, allowing the firm to avoid corporate income taxes, except on gains resulting from the sale of assets held less than 10 years after the conversion from a C to an S corporation.

The purchase of Tribune's stock was financed almost entirely with debt, with Zell's equity contribution amounting to less than 4% of the purchase price. The Tribune ended up with $13 billion in debt (including the $5 billion it currently held). At this level, the firm's debt was 10 times EBITDA, more than 2.5 times that of the average media company. Annual interest and principal repayments reached $800 million (almost three times their preacquisition level), about 62% of the firm's previous EBITDA cash flow of $1.3 billion. The conversion of the Tribune into a subchapter S corporation eliminated the firm's current annual tax liability of $348 million. Such entities pay no corporate income tax, but must pay all profit directly to shareholders, who then pay taxes on these distributions. Since the ESOP was the sole shareholder, the Tribune was expected to be largely tax exempt, given that ESOPs are not taxed. In an effort to reduce the firm's debt burden, the Tribune tried unsuccessfully to sell certain assets. While the Tribune was able to sell the Chicago Cubs, Wrigley Field, and the firm's 25% stake in Comcast's SportsNet for $845 million, the price was about 15% less than expected.

At the closing in late December 2007, Sam Zell described the takeover of the Tribune Company as "the transaction from hell." His comments were prescient, in that what had appeared to be a cleverly crafted deal from a tax standpoint was unable to withstand the credit malaise of 2008. The end came swiftly when the 161-year-old Tribune filed for bankruptcy on December 8, 2008, to conserve its rapidly dwindling cash flow.

Those benefiting from the deal included the Tribune's public shareholders, such as the Chandler family, which owed 12% of the Tribune as a result of its prior sale of the *Times Mirror* to Tribune, and Dennis Fitzsimons, the firm's former CEO, who received $17.7 million in severance and $23.8 million for his holdings of Tribune shares. Citigroup and Merrill Lynch received $35.8 million and $37 million, respectively, in advisory fees. Morgan Stanley received $7.5 million for writing a fairness opinion letter. Finally, Valuation Research Corporation received $1 million for an opinion indicating that Tribune could satisfy its loan covenants.

What appeared to be one of the most complex deals of 2007, designed to reap huge tax advantages and to use as much debt as possible, soon became a victim of the downward-spiraling economy, the credit crunch, and its own leverage. Ironically, those who constructed what appeared on paper to be a very shrewd deal had failed to include in their planning the potential for a slowing economy, let alone one of the worst recessions in U.S. history. For this highly leveraged deal to have worked, everything would have had to go according to plan, a plan that did not seem to include any contingencies.

Discussion Questions

1. To what extent do you believe the factors contributing to Tribune's bankruptcy were beyond the control of current management? To what extent do you believe past mismanagement may have contributed to the bankruptcy?

2. Comment on the fairness of the bankruptcy process to shareholders, lenders, employees, communities, government, etc. Be specific.

3. Describe the firm's strategy to finance the transaction.

4. Comment on the fairness of this transaction to the various stakeholders involved. How would you apportion the responsibility for the eventual bankruptcy of Tribune among Sam Zell and his advisors, the Tribune board, and the largely unforeseen collapse of the credit markets in late 2008? Be specific.

5. Why do the bankruptcy courts allow investors such as hedge funds to buy deeply discounted debt from creditors and later exchange such debt at face value for equity in the newly restructured firm?

Solutions to these case study questions are found in the Online Instructor's Manual for instructors using this book.

Cross-Border Mergers and Acquisitions
Analysis and Valuation

Courage is not the absence of fear. It is doing the thing you fear the most. **—Rick Warren**

INSIDE M&A: SABMILLER ACQUIRES AUSTRALIA'S FOSTER'S BEER

KEY POINTS

- Properly executed cross-border acquisitions can transform regional businesses into global competitors.
- Management must be nimble to exploit opportunistic acquisitions.

With the end of apartheid in South Africa in 1994, South African Breweries (SAB) moved from a sprawling conglomerate consisting of beer, soda bottling, furniture, apparel, and other businesses to a focus on beverages only. Seeking to expand beyond South Africa's borders, SAB executives studied the global practices of multinational corporations like Unilever and IBM to adopt what they believed were best practices before undertaking strategic acquisitions in Africa and elsewhere. The firm's overarching objective was to create a global brand. After a series of cross-border transactions, SAB's international operations accounted for more than 40% of its annual sales by 2001. In a transformational transaction, SAB bought Miller Brewery from Philip Morris for $5.6 billion in 2002 and renamed the combined companies SABMiller. Since then it has filled out its global portfolio, adding breweries in Latin America, Asia, and Africa.

During the last decade, the global beer industry experienced increasing consolidation. Following InBev's acquisition of Anheuser-Busch for $56 billion In 2008 and Heineken's purchase of Mexico's FEMSA Cerveza in 2010, the top four breweries (i.e., Anheuser-Busch InBev, SABMiller, Heineken, and Carlsberg) controlled more than 50% of the global beer market, up from 20% in the late 1990s.

In 2011, SABMiller's annual revenue exceeded $31 billion, just behind the industry leader, Anheuser-Busch InBev. About 70% of SABMiller's revenue is in emerging markets. With the number of sizeable independent and profitable breweries declining rapidly, SAB moved to acquire the Foster's Group, Australia's largest brewer, with more than 50% of the domestic beer market. SABMiller believed the timing was right because both Anheuser-Busch InBev, and Heineken were saddled with too much debt from their recent acquisitions to submit serious bids.

The firm's initial bid on June 21, 2011, valued the target at AU$9.5 billion (US$9.7 billion), or AU$4.90 per share (U$5); however, Foster's dismissed the offer as too low. On August 17, 2011, SABMiller adopted a hostile strategy when it went directly to Foster's' shareholders with a tender offer. To win the backing of its shareholders, Foster's said in late August that it would pay out at least AU$525 million (US$536) to shareholders through a share buyback or dividend. To counter this move, SABMiller said that it would reduce its purchase price by the amount of any dividend paid to shareholders or share buyback undertaken by Foster's.

The acrimonious takeover battle came to an end on September 1, 2012, as SABMiller offered to raise its cash bid by 20 cents to AU$5.10 (US$5.20). As part of the deal, Foster's made a one-time payment of AU$.43 per share (US$.44) to its shareholders. The total value, including the value of assumed debt, was AU$11.5 billion (US$11.7). SABMiller now holds about 12% of the global beer market, second to Anheuser-Busch InBev's 25%. Foster's has one of the highest profit margins of any large brewery worldwide, reflecting its greater-than-50% market share in Australia. While synergies would appear to be limited, SABMiller's reputation for aggressive cost cutting could result in profit improvements. SABMiller also received tax loss carryforwards totaling AU$817 million (US$833 million) resulting from the spin-off by the Foster Group of its wine operations in 2010. The acquisition is expected to be accretive after the first full year of operation.

CHAPTER OVERVIEW

Cross-border M&As have become increasingly important in recent years.[1] Reflecting this trend, the current chapter addresses the challenges of M&A deal structures, financing, valuation, and execution in both developed and emerging countries. Throughout the chapter, the term *local country* refers to the target's country of residence, while *home country* refers to the acquirer's country of residence. *Developed countries* are those having significant and sustainable per capita

[1] Erel et al., 2012

economic growth, globally integrated capital markets, a well-defined legal system, transparent financial statements, currency convertibility, and a stable government. According to the World Bank, *emerging countries* have a growth rate in per capita gross domestic product significantly below that of developed countries and often lack many of the characteristics defining developed countries.

Foreign investment has traditionally flowed from developed to developing countries; however, in recent years there has been a trend toward capital flowing from emerging market investors to developed countries.[2] In 2010, almost one-third of foreign direct investment flowing from emerging markets to developed countries consisted of M&As, while less than one-fourth of capital flowing into emerging-market countries was composed of M&As.[3] Moreover, according to Dealogic, cross-border M&A deals between emerging-market buyers and sellers have averaged 12% of total cross-border M&A volume during the three-year period ending in 2011. Special attention in this chapter is given to dealing with cross-border M&As involving emerging countries. A chapter review (including practice questions with answers) is available in the file folder entitled "Student Study Guide" on the companion website to this book (*http://booksite.elsevier.com/9780123854872*).

GLOBALLY INTEGRATED MARKETS VERSUS SEGMENTED CAPITAL MARKETS

The world's economies have become more interdependent since WWII due to expanding international trade. Financial markets have displayed similar interdependence or global integration such that fluctuations in financial returns in one country's equity markets impact returns in other countries' equity markets. Factors contributing to the long-term integration of global capital markets include the reduction in trade barriers, the removal of capital controls, the harmonization of tax laws, floating exchange rates, and the free convertibility of currencies. Improving accounting standards and corporate governance also encourage cross-border capital flows. Transaction costs associated with foreign investment portfolios have also fallen because of advances in information technology and competition. Multinational companies can now more easily raise funds in both domestic and foreign capital markets.

These developments represent a mixed blessing for the world's economies. *Globally integrated capital markets* provide foreigners with unfettered access to local capital markets and provide local residents access to foreign capital markets and ultimately a lower cost of capital. However, they also transmit disruptions rapidly in capital markets in major economies throughout the world, as evidenced by the global meltdown in the equity and bond markets in 2008 and 2009.

[2]Chari et al., 2012
[3]Rabbiosi et al., 2012

Unlike globally integrated capital markets, *segmented capital markets* exhibit different bond and equity prices in different geographic areas for identical assets in terms of risk and maturity. Arbitrage should drive the prices in different markets to be the same (when expressed in the same currency), since investors sell those assets that are overvalued to buy those that are undervalued. Segmentation arises when investors are unable to move capital from one market to another due to capital controls, prefer to invest in their local markets, or have better information about local rather than more remote firms.[4] Investors in segmented markets bear a higher level of risk by holding a disproportionately large share of their investments in their local market as opposed to the level of risk if they invested in a globally diversified portfolio. Reflecting this higher level of risk, investors and lenders in such markets require a higher rate of return on local market investments than if investing in a globally diversified portfolio of stocks. As such, the cost of capital for firms in segmented markets, having limited access to global capital markets, often is higher than the global cost of capital.

MOTIVES FOR INTERNATIONAL EXPANSION

Firms expand internationally for a variety of reasons. These are discussed next.

Geographic and Industrial Diversification

Firms may diversify by investing in different industries in the same country, the same industries in different countries, or different industries in different countries. Firms investing in industries or countries whose economic cycles are not highly correlated may lower the overall volatility in their consolidated earnings and cash flows and, in turn, reduce their cost of capital.[5]

Accelerating Growth

Foreign markets represent an opportunity for domestic firms to grow. Large firms experiencing slower growth in their domestic markets have a greater likelihood of making foreign acquisitions, particularly in rapidly growing emerging markets.[6] U.S. firms have historically invested in potentially higher-growth foreign markets. Similarly, the United States represents a large, growing, and politically stable market. Consequently, foreign firms have increased their exports to and direct investment (including M&As) in the United States.

---

[4]Kang, 2008

[5]Studies show that diversified international firms often exhibit a lower cost of capital than do firms whose investments are not well diversified (Chan et al., 1992; Stulz, 1995a, 1995b; Stulz et al., 1995; and Seth et al., 2002).

[6]Graham, Martey, and Yawson, 2008

Industry Consolidation

Excess capacity in many industries often drives M&A activity, as firms strive to achieve greater economies of scale and scope as well as pricing power with customers and suppliers. The highly active consolidation in recent years in the metals industries (e.g., steel, nickel, and copper) represents an excellent example of this global trend. Global consolidation also is common in the financial services; media; oil and gas; telecommunications; and pharmaceuticals industries.

Utilization of Lower Raw Material and Labor Costs

Emerging markets offer low labor costs, access to inexpensive raw materials, and low levels of regulation. Shifting production overseas allows firms to reduce operating expenses and become more competitive globally. The benefit of lower labor costs is overstated because worker productivity in emerging countries tends to be significantly lower than in more developed countries.

Leveraging Intangible Assets

Firms with expertise, brands, patents, copyrights, and proprietary technologies seek to grow by exploiting these advantages in emerging markets. Foreign buyers may seek to acquire firms with intellectual property so that they can employ such assets in their own domestic markets.[7] Firms with a reputation for superior products in their home markets might find that they can apply this reputation successfully in foreign markets (e.g., Coca-Cola and McDonald's). Firms seeking to leverage their capabilities are likely to acquire controlling interests in foreign firms.[8] However, as Wal-Mart discovered, sometimes even a widely recognized brand name is insufficient to overcome the challenges of foreign markets.

Minimizing Tax Liabilities

Firms in high-tax countries may shift production and reported profits by building or acquiring operations in countries with more favorable tax laws. Evidence supporting the notion that such strategies are common is mixed, with more recent studies showing a greater tendency of firms to shift their investments from high-tax countries to lower-tax countries and to pursue M&A transactions, in part due to their favorable tax consequences.[9]

[7] Eun, Kolodny, and Scherage, 1996; Morck and Yeung, 1991
[8] Ferreira and Tallman, 2005
[9] Zodrow (2010), Overesch (2009), and Servaes et al., (1994) found a positive correlation between cross-border investment (including mergers and acquisitions) and differences in tax laws. However, Manzon et al., (1994) and Dewenter (1995) found little correlation.

Avoiding Entry Barriers

Quotas and tariffs on imports imposed by governments to protect domestic industries often encourage foreign direct investment. Foreign firms may acquire existing facilities or start new operations in the country imposing the quotas and tariffs to circumvent such measures.

Fluctuating Exchange Rates

Changes in currency values have a significant impact on where and when foreign direct investments are made. The appreciation of foreign currencies relative to the dollar reduces the overall cost of investing in the United States. The impact of exchange rates on cross-border transactions has been substantiated in a number of studies.[10]

Following Customers

Often suppliers are encouraged to invest abroad to satisfy better the immediate needs of their customers. For example, auto parts suppliers worldwide have setup operations next to large auto manufacturing companies in China.

COMMON INTERNATIONAL MARKET ENTRY STRATEGIES

The method of market entry chosen by a firm reflects the firm's risk tolerance, perceived risk, competitive conditions, and overall resources. Common entry strategies include mergers and acquisitions, greenfield or solo ventures, joint ventures, export, and licensing. Figure 18.1 summarizes the factors influencing the choice of entry strategy.

In a greenfield or solo venture, a foreign firm starts a new business in the local country, enabling the firm to control technology, production, marketing, and product distribution. Firms with significant intangible assets (e.g., proprietary know-how) are frequently able to earn above-average returns, which can be leveraged in a greenfield or start-up venture.[11] However, the firm's total investment is at risk. M&As can provide quick access to a new market; however, they often are expensive, complex to negotiate, subject to myriad regulatory requirements, and beset by intractable cultural issues. Joint ventures allow firms to share the risks and costs of international expansion, develop new capabilities, and gain access to important resources, but often fail due to conflict between partners.[12]

---

[10] Erel et al., 2012; Georgopoulos, 2008; Feliciano et al., 2002; Vasconcellos et al., 1998; Harris et al., 1991; Vasconcellos, Madura, and Kish, 1990
[11] Brouthers et al., 2000
[12] Zahra et al., 1994

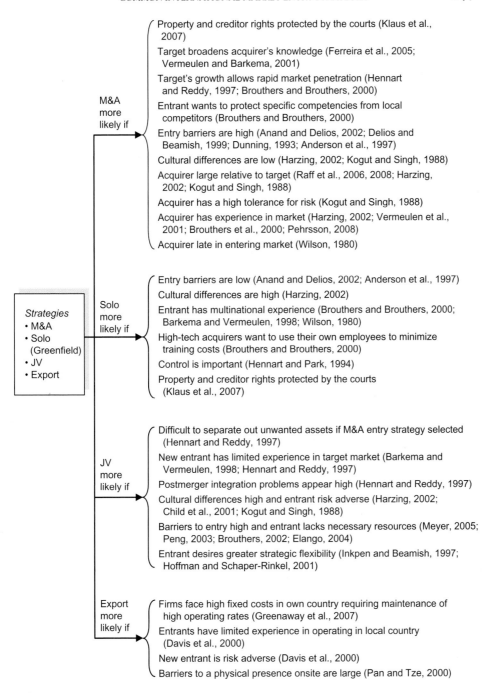

FIGURE 18.1 **Alternative market entry strategies.**

Exporting does not require the expense of establishing local operations; however, exporters must establish some means of marketing and distributing their products at the local level. The disadvantages of exporting include high transportation costs, exchange rate fluctuations, and possible tariffs placed on imports into the local country. Moreover, the exporter has limited control over the marketing and distribution of its products in the local market.

Licensing allows a firm to purchase the right to manufacture and sell another firm's products within a specific country or set of countries. The licensor is normally paid a royalty on each unit sold. The licensee takes the risks and makes the investments in facilities for manufacturing, marketing, and distribution of goods and services, making licensing possibly the least costly form of international expansion. Licensing is a popular entry mode for smaller firms with insufficient capital and limited brand recognition.[13] Disadvantages include the lack of control over the manufacture and marketing of the firm's products in other countries. Licensing often is the least profitable entry strategy because the profits must be shared between the licensor and the licensee. Finally, the licensee may learn the technology and sell a similar competitive product after the license expires.

STRUCTURING CROSS-BORDER DEALS

This section provides an abbreviated discussion of those aspects of deal structuring discussed in Chapters 11 and 12 most applicable to cross-border transactions.

Acquisition Vehicles

Non-U.S. firms seeking to acquire U.S. companies often use C corporations rather than limited liability companies or partnerships to acquire the shares or assets of U.S. targets. They are relatively easy to organize quickly, since all states permit such structures and no prior government approval is required. There is no limitation on non-U.S. persons or entities acting as shareholders in U.S. corporations, except for certain regulated industries. A limited liability company is attractive for JVs in which the target would be owned by two or more unrelated parties, corporations, or nonresident investors. While not traded on public stock exchanges, LLC shares can be sold freely to members. This facilitates the parent firm's operating the acquired firm as a subsidiary or JV. A partnership may have advantages for investors from certain countries (e.g., Germany), where income earned from a U.S. partnership is not subject to taxation. A holding company structure enables a foreign parent to offset gains from one subsidiary with losses generated by another, serves as a platform for future acquisitions, and provides the parent with additional legal protection in the event of lawsuits.

[13] Hitt and Ireland, 2000

U.S. companies acquiring businesses outside the United States encounter obstacles atypical of domestic acquisitions. These include investment and exchange control approvals, tax clearances, clearances under local competition (i.e., antitrust) laws, and unusual due diligence problems. Other problems involve the necessity of agreeing on an allocation of the purchase price among assets located in various jurisdictions and compliance with local law relating to the documentation necessary to complete the transaction. Much of what follows also applies to non-U.S. firms acquiring foreign firms.

The laws governing foreign firms have an important impact on the choice of acquisition vehicle, since the buyer must organize a local company to hold acquired shares or assets in a way that meets local-country law. In common-law countries (e.g., the United Kingdom, Canada, Australia, India, Pakistan, Hong Kong, Singapore, and other former British colonies), the acquisition vehicle will be a corporation-like structure, which is similar to those in the United States. In civil-law countries (which include Western Europe, South America, Japan, and Korea), the acquisition will be in the form of a share company or limited liability company. *Civil law* is synonymous with *codified law*, *continental law*, or the *Napoleonic Code*. Practiced in some Middle Eastern Muslim countries and some countries in Southeast Asia (e.g., Indonesia and Malaysia), Islamic law is based on the Koran.

In the European Union, there is no overarching law or EU directive requiring a specific corporate form. Rather, corporate law is the responsibility of each member nation. In many civil-law countries, smaller enterprises often use a limited liability company, while larger enterprises, particularly those with public shareholders, are referred to as *share companies*. The rules applicable to limited liability companies tend to be flexible and are particularly useful for wholly owned subsidiaries. In contrast, share companies are subject to numerous restrictions and securities laws. However, their shares trade freely on public exchanges.

Share companies are more regulated than U.S. corporations. They must register with the commercial registrar in the location of their principal place of business. Bureaucratic delays from several weeks to several months between the filing of the appropriate documents and the organization of the company may occur. Most civil-law countries require that there be more than one shareholder. Usually there is no limitation on foreigners acting as shareholders. Limited liability companies outside the United States are generally subject to fewer restrictions than share companies. A limited liability company typically is required to have more than one quota holder (i.e., investor). In general, either domestic or foreign corporations or individuals may be quota holders in the LLC.[14]

Form of Payment

U.S. target shareholders often receive cash rather than shares in cross-border deals.[15] Shares and other securities require registration with the Securities and

[14] For an excellent discussion of corporate structures in common-law and civil-law countries, see Truitt (2006).
[15] Ceneboyan, Papaioannou, and Travlos, 1991

Exchange Commission and compliance with all local securities (including state) laws if they are resold in the United States. Acquirer shares often are less attractive to potential targets because of the absence of a liquid market for resale or because the acquirer is not recognized by the target firm's shareholders.

Form of Acquisition

Share acquisitions are generally the simplest form of acquisition in cross-border deals, because all target assets and liabilities transfer to the acquirer by "rule of law." Asset purchases result in the transference of all or some of the assets of the target firm to the acquirer. The major disadvantage of a share purchase is that all the target's known and unknown liabilities transfer to the buyer. When the target is in a foreign country, full disclosure of liabilities is limited: Some target assets transfer with tax liens or other associated liabilities. Asset sales often are more complicated in foreign countries when the local law requires that the target firm's employees automatically become the acquirer's employees. Mergers are not legal or practical in all countries, often due to the requirement that minority shareholders agree with the will of the majority vote.

Tax Strategies

Tax-free reorganizations, or mergers, are often used by foreign acquirers of U.S. firms. The target firm merges with a U.S. subsidiary of the foreign acquirer in a statutory merger under state laws. To qualify as a U.S. corporation for tax purposes, the foreign firm must own at least 80% of the stock of the domestic subsidiary. As such, the transaction can qualify as a Type-A tax-free reorganization (see Chapter 12).

Another form of deal structure is the taxable purchase, which involves the acquisition by one company of the shares or assets of another, usually in exchange for cash or debt. Target firm shareholders recognize a taxable gain or loss on the exchange. The forward triangular merger is the most common form of taxable transaction. The target company merges with a U.S. subsidiary of the foreign acquirer, with shareholders of the target firm receiving acquirer shares as well as cash, although cash is the predominant form of payment. This structure is useful when some target company shareholders want shares while others want cash.

Hybrid transactions represent a third form of transaction used in cross-border transactions. This type of structure affords the U.S. target corporation and its shareholders tax-free treatment while avoiding the issuance of shares of the foreign acquirer. A hybrid transaction may be taxable to some target shareholders and tax-free to others. To structure hybrid transactions, some target company shareholders may exchange their common shares for a nonvoting preferred stock while the foreign acquirer or its U.S. subsidiary buys the remaining common stock for cash. This transaction is tax-free to target company shareholders taking preferred stock and taxable to those selling their shares for cash.[16]

[16]For an excellent discussion of the different tax laws in various countries, see PricewaterhouseCoopers (2010).

FINANCING CROSS-BORDER DEALS

Debt is most often used to finance cross-border transactions. Sources of financing exist in capital markets in the acquirer's home, the target's local country, or in some third country. Domestic capital sources available to cross-border acquirers include banks willing to provide bridge financing and lines of credit, bond markets, and equity markets.

Debt Markets

Commonly used to finance cross-border deals, Eurobonds are debt instruments expressed in terms of U.S. dollars or other currencies and sold to investors outside the country in whose currency they are denominated. A typical Eurobond transaction could be a dollar-denominated bond issued by a French firm through an underwriting group. The underwriting group could comprise the overseas affiliate of a New York commercial bank, a German commercial bank, and a consortium of London banks. Bonds issued by foreign firms and governments in local markets have existed for many years. Such bonds are issued in another country's domestic bond market, denominated in its currency, and subject to that country's regulations.[17]

Equity Markets

The American Depository Receipt (ADR) market evolved as a means of enabling foreign firms to raise funds in U.S. equity markets. ADRs represent the receipt for the shares of a foreign-based corporation held in a U.S. bank, entitling the holder to all dividends and capital gains. The acronyms ADS and ADR often are used interchangeably. The Euroequity market reflects equity issues by a foreign firm tapping a larger investor base than the firm's home equity market.[18]

Sovereign Funds

Sovereign wealth funds (SWFs) are government-backed or government-sponsored investment funds whose function is to invest accumulated reserves of foreign currencies. For years, such funds, in countries that had accumulated

---

[17] Bonds of a non-U.S. issuer registered with the SEC for sale in the U.S. public bond markets are called *yankee bonds*. Similarly, a U.S. company issuing a bond in Japan would be issuing a *samurai bond*.

[18] If the acquirer is not well known in the target's home market, target shareholders may be able to sell the shares only at a discount in their home market. The buyer may have to issue shares in its home market or possibly in the international equities market and use the proceeds to acquire the target for cash. Alternatively, the acquirer may issue shares in the target's market to create a resale market for target shareholders or offer target shareholders the opportunity to sell the shares in the buyer's home market through an investment banker.

huge quantities of dollars, would reinvest these funds in U.S. Treasury securities. However, in recent years, such funds have become more sophisticated, increasingly taking equity positions in foreign firms and diversifying their currency holdings. Collectively, the sovereign funds controlled about $4.62 trillion in assets worldwide in 2011.[19] In addition to providing a source of capital, sovereign wealth funds, as politically connected large investors, may contribute to the value of a firm in which they invest by providing access to the SWF's home market and to government-related contracts.[20]

PLANNING AND IMPLEMENTING CROSS-BORDER TRANSACTIONS IN EMERGING COUNTRIES

Entering emerging economies poses challenges not generally encountered in developed countries.

Political and Economic Risks

Political and economic risks are often interrelated. Examples of political and economic risk include excessive local government regulation, confiscatory tax policies, restrictions on cash remittances, currency inconvertibility, restrictive employment policies, expropriation of assets of foreign firms, civil war or local insurgencies, and corruption. Another, sometimes overlooked challenge is the failure of the legal system in an emerging country to honor contracts.[21]

Unexpected changes in exchange rates can influence the competitiveness of goods produced in the local market for export to the global marketplace. Changes in exchange rates alter the value of assets invested in the local country and earnings repatriated from the local operations to the parent firm in the home country. Not surprisingly, the degree of economic and political freedom correlates positively with foreign direct investment. When property rights are respected and earnings repatriation is unrestricted, foreigners are inclined to invest in the local country.[22]

Sources of Information for Assessing Political and Economic Risk

Information sources include consultants in the local country, joint venture partners, a local legal counsel, or appropriate government agency, such as the

---

[19] M. Miller, May 2012
[20] Sojli and Tham, 2010
[21] Khanna, Palepu, and Sinha, 2005
[22] Bengoa and Sanchez-Robles (2003) and Berggren and Jordahl (2005) demonstrate a strong positive relationship between foreign direct investment and the Heritage Foundation's Freedom Index. This index contains about 50 variables divided into 10 categories, measuring various aspects of economic and political freedoms.

U.S. Department of State. Other sources of information include the major credit-rating agencies, such as Standard & Poor's, Moody's, and Fitch IBCA. Trade magazines, such as *Euromoney* and *Institutional Investor*, provide overall country-risk ratings updated semiannually. The Economic Intelligence Unit also provides numerical risk scores for individual countries. The *International Country Risk Guide*, published by the Political Risk Services Group, offers overall numerical risk scores for individual countries as well as separate scores for political, financial, and economic risks.

Using Insurance to Manage Risk

The decision to buy insurance depends on the size of the investment and the level of risk. Parties have a variety of sources from which to choose. For instance, the export credit agency in a variety of countries, such as Export Import Bank (United States), SACE (Italy), and Hermes (Germany), may offer coverage for companies based within their jurisdictions. The Overseas Private Investment Corporation is available to firms based in the United States, while the World Bank's Multilateral Investment Guarantee Agency is available to all firms.

Using Options and Contract Language to Manage Risk

When adequate due diligence is impractical, acquirers may include a put option in the purchase agreement, enabling the buyer to require the seller to repurchase shares from the buyer at a predetermined price under certain circumstances. Alternatively, the agreement could include a clause requiring a purchase price adjustment. However, there is always the risk that such conditions will not be honored by all parties to the contract.

HOW ARE CROSS-BORDER TRANSACTIONS VALUED?

Cross-border deals require converting cash flows from one currency to another. Also, discount rates may be adjusted for risks not found when the acquirer and the target are in the same country.

Converting Foreign Target Cash Flows to Acquirer Domestic Cash Flows

Cash flows of the target firm can be expressed in its own currency, including expected inflation (i.e., nominal terms), its own currency without inflation (i.e., real terms), or the acquirer's currency. Real cash flow valuation adjusts all cash flows for inflation and uses real discount rates. M&A practitioners utilize nominal cash flows, except when inflation rates are high. Under these circumstances, real cash flows are preferable. Real cash flows are determined by dividing the nominal cash flows by the country's gross domestic product deflator or some other broad measure of inflation. Future real cash flows are estimated by dividing future nominal cash flows by the current GDP deflator,[23] increased by the expected rate of inflation. Real discount rates are determined by subtracting the expected rate of inflation from nominal discount rates.[24]

It is simpler to project the target's aggregate cash flows (rather than each component separately) in terms in its own currency and then convert the cash flows into the acquirer's currency. This requires estimating future exchange rates between the target (local) and the acquirer's (home) currencies, which are affected by interest rates and expected inflation in the two countries. The current rate at which one currency can be exchanged for another is called the *spot exchange rate*. Conversion to the acquirer's currency can be achieved by using future spot exchange rates, estimated either from relative interest rates (the interest rate parity theory) in each country or by the relative rates of expected inflation (the purchasing power parity theory).

When Target Firms are in Developed (Globally Integrated) Capital Market Countries

For developed countries, the interest rate parity theory provides a useful framework for estimating *forward currency exchange rates* (i.e., future spot exchange rates). Consider a U.S. acquirer's valuation of a firm in the European Union (EU), with projected cash flows expressed in terms of euros. The target's cash flows can be converted into dollars by using a forecast of future dollar-to-euro spot rates. The *interest rate parity theory* relates forward (future) spot exchange rates to differences in interest rates between two countries adjusted by the spot rate. Therefore, the dollar/euro exchange rate $(\$/€)_n$ (i.e., the future, or forward, exchange rate), n periods into the future, is expected to appreciate (depreciate) according to the following relationship:

$$(\$/€)_n = \{(1 + R_{\$n})^n / (1 + R_{€n})^n\} \times (\$/€)_0 \qquad (18.1)$$

Similarly, the euro-to-dollar exchange rate $(€/\$)_n$, n periods into the future, would be expected to appreciate (depreciate) according to the following relationship:

$$(\$/€)_n = \{(1 + R_{\$n})^n / (1 + R_{€n})^n\} \times (\$/€)_0 \qquad (18.2)$$

Note that $(\$/€)_0$ and $(€/\$)_0$ represent the spot rate for the dollar-to-euro and euro-to-dollar exchange rates, respectively; $R_{\$n}$ and $R_{€n}$ represent the interest

---

[23] The GDP deflator is the ratio of current dollar GDP to real or constant-dollar GDP and measures the percent change in prices between the current period and some prior "base" period.

[24] Nominal (real) cash flows should give the same NPVs if the expected rate of inflation used to convert future cash flows to real terms is the same inflation rate used to estimate the real discount rate.

rate in the United States and the European Union, respectively. Equations (18.1) and (18.2) imply that if U.S. interest rates rise relative to those in the European Union, investors will buy dollars with euros at the current spot rate and sell an equivalent amount of dollars for euros in the forward (future) market n periods into the future in anticipation of converting their dollar holdings back into euros. According to this theory, the dollar-to-euro spot rate will appreciate and the dollar-to-euro forward rate will depreciate until any profit due to the difference in interest rates is eliminated.[25]Exhibit 18.1 illustrates how to convert a target company's nominal free cash flows to the firm (FCFF) expressed in euros (i.e., the local country or target's currency) to those expressed in dollars (i.e., home country or acquirer's currency).

When Target Firms are in Emerging (Segmented) Capital Market Countries

Cash flows are converted, as before, using the interest rate parity theory or the purchasing power parity theory. The latter is used if there is insufficient information about interest rates in the emerging market. The *purchasing power parity*

EXHIBIT 18.1 CONVERTING EURO-DENOMINATED INTO DOLLAR-DENOMINATED FREE CASH FLOWS TO THE FIRM USING THE INTEREST RATE PARITY THEORY

	2012	2013	2014
Target's Euro-Denominated FCFF Cash Flows (Millions)	€124.5	€130.7	€136.0
Target Country's Interest Rate (%)	4.50	4.70	5.30
U.S. Interest Rate (%)	4.25	4.35	4.55
Current Spot Rate ($/€) = 1.2044			
Projected Spot Rate ($/€)	1.2015	1.1964	1.1788
Target's Dollar-Denominated FCFF Cash Flows (Millions)	$149.59	$156.37	$160.32

Note: Calculating the projected spot rate using Eq. (18.1):

$$(\$/€)_{2012} = \{(1.0425)/(1.0450)\} \times 1.2044 = 1.2015$$
$$(\$/€)_{2013} = \{(1.0435)^2/(1.0470)^2\} \times 1.2044 = 1.1964$$
$$(\$/€)_{2014} = \{(1.0455)^3/(1.0530)^3\} \times 1.2044 = 1.1788$$

[25]Equilibrium between forward exchange rates and spot rates adjusted for the ratio of U.S. interest rates to those in Eurozone countries will in practice be restored by a combination of appreciating dollar-to-Euro spot rates, depreciating dollar-to-Euro forward rates, and declining U.S. interest rates and increasing Eurozone interest rates. Interest rates on U.S. bonds decline as the investors bid up their prices, and interest rates on comparable Eurozone bonds increase as investors sell these bonds and invest the proceeds in the United States.

theory states that the percentage difference in the forward rate relative to the spot rate should, over time, equal the difference in expected inflation rates between countries. That is, one currency appreciates (depreciates) with respect to another currency according to the expected relative rates of inflation between the two countries such that an identical good in each country will have the same price. To illustrate, the dollar/Mexican peso exchange rate, $(\$/peso)_n$, and the Mexican peso/dollar exchange rate, $(peso/\$)_n$, n periods from now (i.e., future exchange rates) is expected to change according to the following relationships:

$$(\$/peso)_n = [(1 + P_{us})^n/(1 + P_{mex})^n] \times (\$/peso)_0 \qquad (18.3)$$

and

$$(peso/\$)_n = [(1 + P_{mex})^n/(1 + P_{us})^n] \times (peso/\$)_0 \qquad (18.4)$$

where P_{us} and P_{mex} are the expected inflation rates in the United States and Mexico, respectively, and $(\$/peso)_0$ and $(peso/\$)_0$ are the dollar-to-peso and peso-to-dollar spot exchange rates, respectively. If prices in the United States are expected to rise faster than those in Mexico for the same goods and services, other things equal, holders of pesos will buy dollars to purchase U.S. goods and services before they rise in price and sell an equivalent amount of dollars for pesos in the forward exchange market before the dollar depreciates. This causes the dollar/peso spot rate to decline (i.e., the dollar to appreciate against the peso) and the forward dollar/peso exchange rate to increase (i.e., the dollar to depreciate against the peso). See Exhibit 18.2 for an illustration of how this might work in practice.

Selecting the Correct Marginal Tax Rate

Most foreign firms pay only a small token tax if they bring their after-tax profits back to their home country. U.S. firms must pay the difference between the U.S. tax rate and the tax that they have already paid. For example, French and U.S. firms investing in Ireland pay a corporate tax of only 12.5%. The French firm can then repatriate its after-tax profit to France by paying less than 5% on those repatriated profits. The U.S. firm has to pay the 22.5% difference between the U.S. 35% corporate tax and the 12.5% Irish tax. The huge difference provides a major incentive for U.S. firms to retain foreign-earned profits outside the United States.

The selection of the right marginal tax rate for valuation purposes thus depends on where the bulk of taxes is actually paid. If the acquirer's country makes foreign income exempt from further taxation once taxed in the foreign country, the correct tax rate would be the marginal tax rate in the foreign country because that is where taxes are paid. Otherwise, the correct tax rate should be the acquirer's country rate if it is higher than the target's country rate and taxes paid in a foreign country are deductible from the taxes owed by the acquirer in its home country.

EXHIBIT 18.2 CONVERTING PESO-DENOMINATED INTO DOLLAR-DENOMINATED FREE CASH FLOWS TO THE FIRM USING THE PURCHASING POWER PARITY THEORY

	2012	2013	2014
Target's Peso-Denominated FCFF Cash Flows (Millions of Pesos)	P1,050.5	P1,124.7	P1,202.7
Current Mexican Expected Inflation Rate = 6%			
Current U.S. Expected Inflation Rate = 4%			
Current Spot Rate ($/Peso) = 0.0877			
Projected Spot Rate ($/Peso)	0.0860	0.0844	0.0828
Target's Dollar-Denominated FCFF Cash Flows (Millions of $)	$90.34	$94.92	$99.58

Note: Calculating the projected spot rate using Eq. (18.3):

$$(\$/Peso)_{2012} = \{(1.04)/(1.06)\} \times 0.0877 = 0.0860$$

$$(\$/Peso)_{2013} = \{(1.04)^2/(1.06)^2\} \times 0.0877 = 0.0844$$

$$(\$/Peso)_{2014} = \{(1.04)^3/(1.06)^3\} \times 0.0877 = 0.0828$$

Estimating the Cost of Equity in Cross-Border Transactions

The capital asset pricing model or a multifactor model (e.g., CAPM plus a firm size adjustment) often are used in developed countries with liquid capital markets.[26] For emerging nations, estimating the cost of equity is more complex, with at least 12 separate approaches employed.[27] Each method attempts to adjust the discount rate for potential capital market segmentation and specific country risks. Still other methods attempt to include emerging-country risk by adjusting projected cash flows. In either case, the adjustments often appear arbitrary.

Developed economies seem to exhibit little differences in the cost of equity, due to the relatively high integration of their capital markets with the global capital market. Thus, adjusting the cost of equity for specific country risk does not seem to make any significant difference.[28] For emerging-market countries, the existence of segmented capital markets, political instability, limited liquidity, currency fluctuations, and currency inconvertibility seems to make adjusting the target firm's cost of equity for these factors desirable but often impractical.[29]

The following discussion incorporates the basic elements of valuing cross-border transactions, distinguishing between the different adjustments made

[26] Graham and Harvey, 2001

[27] Harvey, 2005

[28] Koedijk et al., 2000; Koedijk et al., 2002; Mishra et al., 2001; Bodnar et al., 2003

[29] Bodnar et al., (2003)

when investing in developed and emerging countries. Nonetheless, considerable debate continues in this area.

Estimating the Cost of Equity in Developed (Globally Integrated) Countries

What follows is a discussion of how to adjust the basic CAPM formulation for valuing cross-border transactions when the target is located in a developed country. The discussion is similar to the capital asset pricing model formulation (CAPM) outlined in Chapter 7, except for the use of either national or globally diversified stock market indices in estimating beta and calculating the equity market risk premium.

Estimating the Risk-Free Rate of Return (Developed Countries)

The risk-free rate generally is the local country's government (or sovereign) bond rate whenever the projected cash flows for the target firm are expressed in local currency.[30] Risk-free rates usually are U.S. Treasury bond rates if projected cash flows are in dollars.

Adjusting CAPM for Risk (Developed Countries)

The equity premium, the difference between the return on a well-diversified portfolio and the risk-free return, is the additional return required by investors to buy stock. When capital markets are fully integrated, equity investors hold globally diversified portfolios, resulting in a high correlation between individual country equity indices and global indices. Therefore, an equity premium may be estimated by regressing the firm's share price against a well-diversified portfolio of U.S. equities, another developed country's equity portfolio, or a global equity portfolio.[31]

The CAPM also should be adjusted for the size of the firm, which serves as a proxy for factors such as smaller firms being subject to higher default risk and generally being less liquid than large capitalization firms. See Table 7.1 in

---

[30] The debt crises in many developed countries in 2010 and 2011 suggest that using a government bond rate as a risk-free rate in countries not having their own currencies (e.g., Eurozone countries) is questionable. Such countries cannot repay their debt by simply printing money. In July 2012, the Spanish government's 10-year bond rate was 6.95% and the cost of default insurance (i.e., the amount investors pay others to insure against default) was 564 basis points, or 5.64%. Known as the *credit default swap* (CDS) rate, this figure is the difference between a bond rate and a presumed risk-free rate, which in Europe was the German government bond rate. To investors, the implied risk-free return on 10-year Spanish debt was 1.31% (i.e., 6.95% − 5.64%), assuming the German government will not default. Alternatively, either the U.S. Treasury bond rate adjusted for differences in inflation between countries [see Eq. (18.6)] or a large corporation's borrowing rate within the local country could be used as a risk-free rate.

[31] In the United States, an example of a well-diversified portfolio is the Standard & Poor's 500 stock index (S&P 500); in the global capital markets, the Morgan Stanley Capital International World Index (MSCI) is commonly used as a proxy for a well-diversified global equity portfolio.

Chapter 7 for estimates of the amount of the adjustment to the cost of equity to correct for firm size, as measured by market value.

Global CAPM Formulation (Developed Countries)

In globally integrated markets, systematic risk is defined relative to the rest of the world. An asset has systematic risk only to the extent that the performance of the asset correlates with the overall world economy. When using a global equity index, the CAPM often is called the *global* or *international capital asset pricing model*. If the target firm's risk is similar to that faced by the acquirer, the acquirer's cost of equity may be used to discount the target's cash flows.

The global capital asset pricing model for the target firm may be expressed as follows:

$$k_{e,\text{dev}} = R_f + \beta_{\text{devfirm,global}}(R_m - R_f) + \text{FSP} \tag{18.5}$$

where

$k_{e,\text{dev}}$ = required return on equity for a firm operating in a developed country
R_f = local country's risk-free financial rate of return if cash flows are measured in the local country's currency or the U.S. Treasury bond rate if in dollars
$(R_m - R_f)$ = difference between the expected return on the global market portfolio (i.e., MSCI), the U.S. equity index (S&P 500), or a broadly defined index in the target's local country and R_f. This difference is the equity premium, which should be approximately the same when expressed in the same currency for countries with globally integrated capital markets.
$\beta_{\text{devfirm,global}}$ = measure of nondiversifiable risk with respect to a globally diversified equity portfolio or a well-diversified country portfolio highly correlated with the global index Alternatively, $\beta_{\text{devfirm,global}}$ may be estimated indirectly, as illustrated in Eq. (18.7).
FSP = firm size premium, reflecting the additional return smaller firms must earn relative to larger firms to attract investors

An analyst may wish to value the target's future cash flows in both the local and home currencies. The Fisher Effect allows the analyst to convert a nominal cost of equity from one currency to another. Assuming the expected inflation rates in the two countries are accurate, the real cost of equity should be the same in both countries.

Applying the Fisher Effect

The so-called Fisher Effect states that nominal interest rates can be expressed as the sum of the real interest rate (i.e., interest rates excluding inflation) and the anticipated rate of inflation. The Fisher effect can be shown for the United States and Mexico as follows:

$$(1 + i_{\text{us}}) = (1 + r_{\text{us}})(1 + P_{\text{us}}) \text{ and } (1 + r_{\text{us}}) = (1 + i_{\text{us}})/(1 + P_{\text{us}})$$
$$(1 + i_{\text{mex}}) = (1 + r_{\text{mex}})(1 + P_{\text{mex}}) \text{ and } (1 + r_{\text{mex}}) = (1 + i_{\text{mex}})/(1 + P_{\text{mex}})$$

If real interest rates are constant among all countries, nominal interest rates among countries will vary only by the difference in the anticipated inflation rates. Therefore,

$$(1 + i_{us})/(1 + P_{us}) = (1 + i_{mex})/(1 + P_{mex}) \qquad (18.6)$$

where

i_{us} and i_{mex} = nominal interest rates in the United States and Mexico, respectively
r_{us} and r_{mex} = real interest rates in the United States and Mexico, respectively
P_{us} and P_{mex} = anticipated inflation rates in the United States and Mexico, respectively

If the analyst knows the Mexican interest rate and the anticipated inflation rates in Mexico and the United States, solving Eq. (18.6) provides an estimate of the U.S. interest rate (i.e., $i_{us} = [(1 + i_{mex}) \times (1 + P_{us})/(1 + P_{mex})] - 1$). Exhibit 18.3 illustrates how the cost of equity estimated in one currency is converted easily to the cost in another using Eq. (18.6). Although the historical equity premium in the United States is used in calculating the cost of equity, the historical U.K. or MSCI premium also could have been employed.

Estimating the Cost of Equity in Emerging (Segmented) Capital Market Countries

If capital markets are segmented, the global capital asset pricing model must reflect the tendency of investors in individual countries to hold local country rather than globally diversified equity portfolios. Consequently, equity premiums differ among countries, reflecting the nondiversifiable risk associated with each country's equity market index. What follows is a discussion of how to adjust the basic CAPM formulation for valuing cross-border deals when the target is located in an emerging country.

Estimating the Risk-Free Rate of Return (Emerging Countries)

Data limitations often preclude using the local country's government bond rate as the risk-free rate. If the target firm's cash flows are in terms of local currency, the U.S. Treasury bond rate often is used to estimate the risk-free rate. To create a local nominal interest rate, the Treasury bond rate should be adjusted for the difference in the anticipated inflation rates in the two countries using Eq. (18.6). Alternatively, the risk-free rate can be estimated using the buildup method as the sum of the expected inflation rate and the expected real rate. The analyst can add the expected inflation rate for the country to the U.S. Treasury inflation-adjusted bond rate (i.e., Treasury inflation-protected securities, or TIPS). For example, the expected inflation rate for Angola in June 2012 was 12%, and the 5-year rate on 10-year U.S. treasury inflation-indexed securities (the real

EXHIBIT 18.3 CALCULATING THE TARGET FIRM'S COST OF EQUITY IN BOTH HOME AND LOCAL CURRENCIES

Acquirer, a U.S. multinational firm, is interested in purchasing Target, a small U.K.-based competitor, with a market value of €550 million, or about $1 billion. The current risk-free rate of return for U.K., 10-year government bonds is 4.2%. The anticipated inflation rates in the United States and the United Kingdom are 3% and 4%, respectively. The size premium is estimated at 1.2%. The historical equity risk premium in the United States is 5.5%.[a] Acquirer estimates Target's β to be 0.8, by regressing Target's historical financial returns against the S&P 500. What is the cost of equity $(k_{e,uk})$ that should be used to discount Target's projected cash flows when they are expressed in terms of British pounds (i.e., local currency)? What is the cost of equity $(k_{e,us})$ that should be used to discount Target's projected cash flows when they are expressed in terms of U.S. dollars (i.e., home currency)?[b]

$k_{e,uk}$[see Eq. (18.5)] = $0.042 + 0.8 \times (0.055) + 0.012 = 0.098 = 9.80\%$

$k_{e,us}$[see Eq. (18.6)] = $[(1 + 0.098) \times (1 + 0.03)/(1 + 0.04)] - 1 = 0.0875 \times 100 = 8.75\%$

---

[a] The U.S. equity premium or the U.K. equity premium could have been used, since equity markets in either country are highly correlated.

[b] The real rate of return is the same in the United Kingdom (r_{uk}) and the United States (r_{us}). $r_{uk} = 9.8\%$ − 4.0% = 5.8%, and $r_{us} = 8.8\% - 3.0\% = 5.8\%$.

rate) was 2.38%.[32] Therefore, the estimated risk-free rate for Angolan government bonds at that time was 14.38%.

Adjusting CAPM for Risk (Emerging Countries)

Systematic risk for a firm operating primarily in its emerging country's home market, whose capital market is segmented,[33] is measured mainly with respect to the country's equity market index $(\beta_{emfirm,country})$ and to a lesser extent with respect to a globally diversified equity portfolio $(\beta_{country,global})$. The emerging-country firm's global beta $(\beta_{emfirm,global})$ can be adjusted to reflect the relationship with the global capital market as follows:

$$\beta_{emfirm,global} = \beta_{emfirm,country} \times \beta_{country,global} \tag{18.7}$$

[32] The five-year TIPS rate is used because the TIPS rate in June 2012 was an artificially low − 1.5% (a 0.98% nominal rate less the 2.48% change in the CPI) due to efforts by the U.S. Federal Reserve to reduce U.S. Treasury bond rates through "Operation Twist."

[33] An analyst can determine if a country's equity market is segmented from the global equity market if the two markets are relatively uncorrelated. This implies that the local country's equity premium differs from the global equity premium, reflecting the local country's systematic risk.

The value of $\beta_{\text{emfirm,country}}$ is estimated by regressing historical returns for the local firm against returns for the country's equity index.[34] The value of $\beta_{\text{country,global}}$ can be estimated by regressing the financial returns for the local-country equity index (or for an index in a similar country) against the historical financial returns for a global equity index.[35] Due to the absence of historical data in many emerging economies, the equity risk premium often is estimated using the prospective method implied in the constant-growth valuation model. As shown in Eq. (7.14) in Chapter 7, this formulation provides an estimate of the present value of dividends growing at a constant rate in perpetuity. That is, dividends paid in the current period (d_0) are grown at a constant rate of growth (g) such that d_1 equals $d_0(1 + g)$.

Assuming the stock market values stocks correctly and we know the present value of a broadly defined index in the target firm's country (P_{country}) or in a similar country, dividends paid annually on this index in the next period (d_1), and the expected dividend growth (g), we can estimate the expected return (R_{country}) on the stock index as follows:

$$P_{\text{country}} = d_1/(R_{\text{country}} - g) \text{ and } R_{\text{country}} = (d_1/P_{\text{country}}) + g \qquad (18.8)$$

From Eq. (18.8), the equity risk premium for the local country's equity market is $R_{\text{country}} - R_f$, where R_f is the local country's risk-free rate of return. Exhibit 18.4 illustrates how to calculate the cost of equity for a firm in an emerging country in the absence of perceived significant country or political risk not captured in the beta or equity risk premium. Note that the local country's risk-free rate of return is estimated using the U.S. Treasury bond rate adjusted for the expected inflation in the local country relative to the United States. This converts the U.S. Treasury bond rate into a local-country nominal interest rate.

Adjusting the CAPM for Country or Political Risk

A country's equity premium may not capture all the events that could jeopardize a firm's ability to operate, such as political instability, limits on repatriation of earnings, capital controls, and the levying of confiscatory or discriminatory taxes. Such factors could increase the firm's likelihood of default. Unless the analyst includes the risk of default by the firm in projecting a local

---

[34] Absent sufficient data, $\beta_{\text{emfirm,country}}$ may be estimated using the beta for a similar local or foreign firm.

[35] Alternatively, a more direct approach is to regress the local firm's historical returns against the financial returns for a globally diversified portfolio of stocks to estimate $\beta_{\text{emfirm,global}}$. Furthermore, the β between a similar local or foreign firm and the global index could be used for this purpose.

EXHIBIT 18.4 CALCULATING THE TARGET FIRM'S COST OF EQUITY FOR FIRMS IN EMERGING COUNTRIES

Assume next year's dividend yield on an emerging country's stock market is 5% and that earnings for the companies in the stock market index are expected to grow by 6% annually in the foreseeable future. The country's global beta ($\beta_{country,global}$) is 1.1. The U.S Treasury bond rate is 4%, and the expected inflation rate in the emerging country is 4%, compared to 3% in the United States. Estimate the country's risk-free rate (R_f), the return on a diversified portfolio of equities in the emerging country ($R_{country}$), and the country's equity risk premium ($R_{country} - R_f$). What is the cost of equity in the local currency for a local firm ($k_{e,em}$) whose country beta ($\beta_{emfirm,country}$) is 1.3?

Solution

$$R_f = [(1 + 0.04)((1 + 0.04)/(1 + 0.03)) - 1] = 0.0501 \times 100 = 5.01\%$$
$$R_{country}[\text{see Eq. (18.8)}] = 5.00 + 6.00 = 11.00\%$$
$$R_{country} - R_f = 11.00 - 5.01 = 5.99\%$$
$$\beta_{emfirm,global}[\text{see Eq. (18.7)}] = 1.3 \times 1.1 = 1.43$$
$$k_{e,em} = 5.01 + 1.43(5.99) = 13.58\%$$

firm's cash flows, the expected cash flow stream would be overstated to the extent that it does not reflect the costs of financial distress.

If the U.S. Treasury bond rate is used as the risk-free rate in calculating the CAPM, adding a country risk premium to the basic CAPM estimate is appropriate. The country risk premium (CRP) often is measured as the difference between the yield on the country's sovereign or government bonds and the U.S. Treasury bond rate of the same maturity. The difference, or "spread," is the additional risk premium that investors demand for holding the emerging country's debt rather than U.S. Treasury bonds.[36] Standard & Poor's (*www.standardandpoors.com*), Moody's Investors Service (*www.moodys.com*), and Fitch IBCA (*www.fitchratings.com*) provide sovereign bond spreads. In practice, the sovereign bond spread is computed from a bond with the same maturity as the U.S. benchmark 10-year Treasury bond used to compute the risk-free rate for calculating the cost of equity.

---

[36] A country risk premium should not be added to the cost of equity if the risk-free rate is the country's sovereign or government bond rate, since the effects of specific country or political risk would be reflected already.

Global CAPM Formulation (Emerging Countries)

To estimate the cost of equity for a firm in an emerging economy ($k_{e,em}$), Eq. (18.5) can be modified for specific country risk as follows:

$$k_{e,em} = R_f + \beta_{emfirm,global}(R_{country} - R_f) + FSP + CRP \qquad (18.9)$$

where

R_f = local risk-free rate or the U.S. Treasury bond rate converted to a local nominal rate if cash flows are in the local currency [see Eq. (18.6)] or to the U.S. Treasury bond rate if cash flows are in dollars

$(R_{country} - R_f)$ = difference between expected return on a well-diversified equity index in the local country or a similar country and the risk-free rate

$\beta_{emfirm,global}$ = emerging country firm's global beta [see Eq. (18.7)]

FSP = firm size premium, reflecting the additional return that smaller firms must earn relative to larger firms to attract investors

CRP = specific country risk premium, expressed as the difference between the local country's (or a similar country's) government bond rate and the U.S. Treasury bond rate of the same maturity. Add to the CAPM estimate only if the U.S. Treasury bond rate is employed as a proxy for the local country's risk-free rate.

Estimating the Local Firm's Cost of Debt in Emerging Markets

The cost of debt for an emerging market firm (i_{emfirm}) should be adjusted for default risk due to events related to the country and those specific to the firm. When a local corporate bond rate is not available, the cost of debt for a specific local firm may be estimated by using an interest rate in the home country (i_{home}) that reflects a level of creditworthiness comparable to that of the firm in the emerging country. The country risk premium is added to the appropriate home country interest rate to reflect the impact of such factors as political instability on i_{emfirm}. Therefore, the cost of debt can be expressed as follows:

$$i_{emfirm} = i_{home} + CRP \qquad (18.10)$$

Most firms in emerging markets are not rated; to determine which home-country interest rate to select, it is necessary to assign a credit rating to the local firm. This "synthetic" credit rating is obtained by comparing financial ratios for the target firm to those used by U.S. rating agencies. The estimate of the unrated firm's credit rating may be obtained by comparing interest coverage ratios used by Standard & Poor's to the firm's interest coverage ratio to determine how S&P would rate the firm. Exhibit 18.5 illustrates how to calculate the cost of emerging-market debt.

Exhibit 18.6 illustrates the calculation of WACC in cross-border transactions. Note the adjustments made to the estimate of the cost of equity for firm size

ESTIMATING THE COST OF DEBT IN EMERGING-MARKET COUNTRIES

Assume that a firm in an emerging market has annual operating income before interest and taxes of $550 million and annual interest expenses of $18 million. This implies an interest coverage ratio of 30.6 (i.e., $550 ÷ $18). For Standard & Poor's (S&P), this corresponds to an AAA (or triple A) rating. According to S&P, default spreads for AAA firms are 0.85 currently. The current interest rate on U.S. triple A–rated bonds is 6.0 %. Assume further that the country's government bond rate is 10.3% and that the U.S. Treasury bond rate is 5%. Assume that the firm's marginal tax rate is 0.4. What is the firm's cost of debt before and after tax?

Solution

$$\text{Cost of debt before taxes [see Eq. (18.10)]} = 6.0 + (10.3 - 5.0) = 11.3\%$$
$$\text{After-tax cost of debt} = 11.3 \times (1 - 0.4) = 6.78\%$$

and country risk. Note also the adjustment made to the local borrowing cost for country risk. The risk-free rate of return is the U.S. Treasury bond rate converted to a local nominal rate of interest.

Table 18.1 summarizes methods commonly used for valuing cross-border M&As for developed-country and emerging-country firms. The WACC calculation assumes that the firm uses only common equity and debt financing. Note that the country risk premium is added to both the cost of equity and the after-tax cost of debt in calculating the WACC for a target firm in an emerging country, if the U.S. Treasury bond rate is used as the risk-free rate of return. The analyst should avoid adding the country risk premium to the cost of equity if the risk-free rate used to estimate the cost of equity is the local country's government bond rate. References to home and local countries in Table 18.1 refer to the acquirer and the target's countries, respectively.

Evaluating Risk Using Scenario Planning

With countries like China and India growing at near-double-digit rates, the future may be too dynamic to rely on discounted cash flows. As an alternative to adjusting the target's cost of capital, the acquirer may incorporate risk into the valuation by considering different economic scenarios for the emerging country. Variables defining alternative scenarios could include GDP growth, inflation rates, interest rates, and foreign exchange rates. For example, a best-case scenario can be based on projected cash flows, assuming the emerging market's economy grows at a moderate real growth rate of 2% per annum for the next five years. Alternative scenarios could assume a one- to two-year recession. A third scenario could assume a dramatic devaluation of the country's currency. The NPVs are

EXHIBIT 18.6 ESTIMATING THE WEIGHTED AVERAGE COST OF CAPITAL IN CROSS-BORDER TRANSACTIONS

Acquirer Inc., a U.S.-based corporation, wants to purchase Target Inc., Acquirer's management believes that the country in which Target is located is segmented from global capital markets because the beta estimated by regressing the financial returns on the country's stock market with those of a global index is significantly different from 1.

Assumptions: The current U.S. Treasury bond rate (R_{us}) is 5%. The expected inflation rate in the target's country is 6% annually, as compared to 3% in the United States. The country's risk premium (CRP) provided by Standard & Poor's is estimated to be 2%. Based on Target's interest coverage ratio, its credit rating is estimated to be AA. The current interest rate on AA-rated U.S. corporate bonds is 6.25%. Acquirer Inc., receives a tax credit for taxes paid in a foreign country. Since its marginal tax rate is higher than Target's, Acquirer's marginal tax rate of 0.4 is used in calculating WACC. Acquirer's pretax cost of debt is 6%. The firm's total capitalization consists only of common equity and debt. Acquirer's projected debt–to–total capital ratio is 0.3.

Target's beta and the country beta are estimated to be 1.3 and 0.7, respectively. The equity premium is estimated to be 6% based on the spread between the prospective return on the country's equity index and the estimated risk-free rate of return. Given Target Inc.,'s current market capitalization of $3 billion, the firm's size premium (FSP) is estimated at 1.0 (see Table 7.1 in Chapter 7). What is the appropriate weighted average cost of capital Acquirer should use to discount target's projected annual cash flows, expressed in its own local currency?

Solution

$$k_{e,em}[\text{see Eq. (18.9)}] = \{[(1 + 0.05) \times (1 + 0.06)/(1 + 0.03)] - 1\} \times 100^a$$
$$+ 1.3 \times 0.7 \ (6.0) + 1.0 + 2.0 = 16.52\%$$
$$i_{local}[\text{see Eq. (18.10)}] = 6.25 + 2.0 = 8.25\%$$
$$\text{wacc}_{em}[\text{see Eq. (7.4)}] = 16.52 \times (1 - 0.3) + 8.25 \times (1 - 0.4) \times 0.3 = 13.05\%$$

[a] Note that the expression $\{[(1 + 0.05) \times (1 + 0.06)/(1 + 0.03)] - 1\} \times 100$ represents the conversion of the U.S. Treasury bond rate to a local nominal rate of interest using Eq. (18.6). Also note that 1.3×0.7 results in the estimation of the target's global beta, as indicated in Eq. (18.7).

weighted by subjectively determined probabilities. The actual valuation of the target firm reflects the expected value of the three scenarios.[37]

[37] Note that if a scenario approach is used to incorporate risk in the valuation, there is no need to modify the discount rate for perceived political and economic risk in the local country. See Chapter 8 for how to use decision trees.

TABLE 18.1   Common Methodologies for Valuing Cross-Border Transactions

Developed Countries (Integrated Capital Markets)	Emerging Countries (Segmented Capital Markets)
Step 1. Project and Convert Cash Flows	**Step 1. Project and Convert Cash Flows**
a. Project target's cash flows in local currency. b. Convert local cash flows into acquirer's home currency, employing forward exchange rates projected using interest rate parity theory.	a. Project target's cash flows in local currency. b. Convert local cash flows into acquirer's home currency, using forward exchange rates. Project exchange rates, using purchasing power parity theory if little reliable data on interest rates available.
Step 2. Adjust Discount Rates	**Step 2. Adjust Discount Rates**
$k_{e,dev} = R_f + \beta_{devfirm,global}{}^a (R_m - R_f) + FSP$ $i = \text{cost of debt}^c$ $WACC = k_e W_e + i(1-t) \times W_d$	$k_{e,em} = R_f + \beta_{emfirm,global}{}^a (R_{country} - R_f)^b + FSP + CRP$ $i_{local} = i_{home} + CRP$ $WACC = k_e W_e + i_{local}(1-t) \times W_d$
a. R_f is the long-term government bond rate in the home country. b. $\beta_{devfirm,global}$ is nondiversifiable risk associated with a well-diversified global, U.S., or local-country equity index. c. R_m is the return on a well-diversified U.S., local, or global equity index. d. FSP is the firm size premium. e. t is the appropriate marginal tax rate. f. W_e is the acquirer's target equity–to–total capital ratio, and W_d is $1 - W_e$.	a. R_f is the long-term government bond rate in the local country or the U.S. Treasury bond rate converted to a local nominal rate if cash flows in local currency or if cash flows in dollars, the U.S. Treasury bond rate. Note that if the local risk-free rate is used, do *not* add CRP. b. $\beta_{emfirm,global}$ is nondiversifiable risk associated with target's local-country β and local country's global β. c. $R_{country}$ is the return on a diversified local equity index or a similar country's index. d. CRP is the country risk premium. e. i_{home} is the home-country cost of debt. f. i_{local} is the local-country cost of debt.

$^a\beta$ *may be estimated directly for firms whose business is heavily dependent on exports or operating in either developing or emerging countries by regressing directly the firm's historical financial returns against returns on a well-diversified global equity index. For firms operating primarily in their home markets, β may be estimated indirectly by using Eq. (18.7).*
$^b(R_{country} - R_f)$ *also could be the equity premium for well-diversified U.S. or global equity indices if the degree of local segmentation is believed to be small.*
^{c}*For developed countries, either the home-country or local-country cost of debt may be used. There is no need to add a country risk premium as would be the case in estimating a local emerging country's cost of debt.*

While building risk into the projected cash flows is equivalent to adjusting the discount rate in applying the DCF method, it also is subject to making arbitrary or highly subjective adjustments. What are the appropriate scenarios to be simulated? How many such scenarios are needed to incorporate risk adequately into the projections? What is the likelihood that each scenario will occur? The primary advantage of adopting a scenario approach is that it forces the analyst to evaluate a wider range of possible outcomes. The major disadvantages are the substantial additional effort required and the degree of subjectivity in estimating probabilities.

EMPIRICAL STUDIES OF CROSS-BORDER TRANSACTIONS

While cross-border M&As occur for reasons similar to domestic transactions, cross-border deals generally involve additional costs and complexities due to geographical and cultural differences; differences in corporate governance and stakeholder protections; underdeveloped capital markets in emerging economies, and currency fluctuations. The latter factors often enable acquirers having higher per-share valuations and appreciating currencies to purchase target firms that are comparatively inexpensive in terms of their local currencies.

Erel, Liao, and Weisbach (2012) in a sample of 56,978 cross-border M&As between 1990 and 2007 found that 80% of completed deals targeted a non-U.S. firm and 75% involved non-U.S. acquirers. Moreover, the vast majority of the deals involved private firms as either the target firm or the acquiring firm. Cultural and political compatibility seemed to be important in determining the geographic location of firms involved in cross-border transactions. M&As are more likely to occur between firms located in countries that commonly trade with one another and are relatively close geographically. Familiarity with a country's legal institutions and customs and values contributes to higher announcement-date returns in cross-border deals[38] due to the greater likelihood of realizing potential synergies.[39]

International Diversification May Contribute to Higher Financial Returns

Empirical studies suggest that international diversification may increase financial returns by reducing risk if economies are relatively uncorrelated.[40] Higher financial returns from international diversification may also be due to economies of scale and scope; geographic location advantages associated with being nearer customers; increasing the size of the firm's served market; and learning new technologies.[41] There is significant controversy about whether returns are higher for multinational companies that diversify across countries[42] or across industries.[43] Buyers of targets in segmented markets realize larger abnormal returns than if they were to buy firms in globally integrated countries, since targets in segmented markets benefit from the acquirer's lower cost of capital.[44]

---

[38] Ahern et al., 2013
[39] Capron and Guillén, 2009
[40] Delos and Beamish, 1999; Tang and Tikoo, 1999; Madura and Whyte, 1990
[41] Zahra et al., 2000
[42] Isakov et al., 2002
[43] Diermeier et al., 2001
[44] Francis et al., 2008

Returns for Cross-Border Deals are Generally Consistent with Those for Domestic Deals

Like domestic takeovers, shareholders of target firms in cross-border M&As earn substantial abnormal returns. Such returns for shareholders of U.S. targets of foreign buyers range from about 23%[45] to about 40%.[46] Cross-border acquirers on average exhibit 1.5% abnormal returns around the announcement date of the transaction, slightly higher than the 1.43% abnormal returns received by domestic acquirers (see Chapter 1). However, cross-border deals involving public acquirers and large public targets often experience financial returns that are zero to somewhat negative, particularly when such transactions are paid for with acquirer equity.[47] This is consistent with the greater complexity of integrating large transactions and the tendency of public acquirers using overvalued stock to overpay for the target firm.

Acquirers of targets in emerging countries often earn abnormal returns of 1.65% to 3.1%, well in excess of the average cross-border or domestic deal. This improvement may be attributable to the achievement of control, improved governance practices, the elimination of minority shareholders, and the encouragement of investment in the target by the parent.[48]

Improving Corporate Governance Creates Significant Shareholder Value

Abnormal financial returns to acquirers are greater if the acquirer is from a country with stronger governance control of a target in a country with weaker governance standards. Having control enables the acquirer to impose its stricter management practices and shareholder protections on the target, often resulting in better long-term operating performance.[49] Similarly, cross-border deals made by emerging country acquirers are associated with positive abnormal returns of 1.1 % on the announcement date when the target firm is located in a country whose governance and shareholder protections are viewed as stronger than in the acquirer's home country. Investors see the acquirer adopting the governance practices of the target firms.[50]

Foreign Institutional Ownership may Promote Cross-Border M&A Activity

Cross-border deals often involve significant foreign institutional ownership intent on facilitating a change in control in firms located in countries

---

[45] Kuipers et al., 2003

[46] Seth et al, 2000; Eun et al., 1996; Servaes et al., 1994; Harris et al., 1991

[47] Ellis et al., 2011

[48] Chari et al., 2004

[49] Erel et al., 2012; Yen et al., 2010; Martynova et al., 2008b; Moeller et al., 2005; Rossi and Volpin, 2004; Bris et al., 2004

[50] Bhagat et al., 2011

having weak corporate governance or legal institutions.[51] The foreign institutional investors facilitate change-of-control deals by serving as intermediaries between buyers and sellers and by supplying information not publicly available. In doing so, the institutional investors hope to raise the value of their investments.

SOME THINGS TO REMEMBER

Motives for international corporate expansion include a desire to accelerate growth, to achieve diversification, to consolidate industries, and to exploit natural resources and lower labor costs available elsewhere. Other motives include applying a firm's brand name or intellectual property in new markets, minimizing tax liabilities, following customers, and avoiding tariffs and import barriers. Alternative entry strategies include exporting, licensing, alliances or joint ventures, solo ventures or greenfield operations, as well as M&As. The basic differences between within-country and cross-border valuation methods is that the latter involves converting cash flows from one currency to another and adjusting the discount rate for risks common in cross-border deals.

DISCUSSION QUESTIONS

18.1 Discuss the circumstances under which a non-U.S. buyer may choose as its acquisition vehicle a U.S. corporate structure; a limited liability company; a partnership.

18.2 What factors influence the selection of which tax rate to use (i.e., the target's or the acquirer's) in calculating the weighted-average cost of capital in cross-border transactions?

18.3 Discuss adjustments commonly made in estimating the cost of debt in emerging countries.

18.4 Find an example of a recent cross-border transaction in the business section of a newspaper. Discuss the challenges an analyst might face in valuing the target firm.

18.5 Discuss the various types of adjustments for risk that might be made to the global CAPM before valuing a target firm in an emerging country. Be specific.

18.6 Do you see the growth in sovereign wealth funds as important sources of capital to the M&A market or as a threat to the sovereignty of the countries in which they invest?

18.7 What factors contribute to the increasing integration of the global capital markets?

[51] Ferreira et al., 2010

18.8 Give examples of economic and political risk that you could reasonably expect to encounter in acquiring a firm in an emerging economy. Be specific.

18.9 During the 1980s and 1990s, changes in the S&P 500 (a broadly diversified index of U.S. stocks) were about 50% correlated with the MSCI EAFE Index (a broadly diversified index of European and other major industrialized countries' stock markets). In recent years, the correlation has increased to more than 90%. Why? If an analyst wishes to calculate the cost of equity, which index should he or she use in estimating the equity risk premium?

18.10 Comment on the following statement: "The conditions for foreign buyers interested in U.S. targets could not be more auspicious. The dollar is weak, M&A financing is harder to come by for financial sponsors (private equity firms), and many strategic buyers in the United States are hard-pressed to make acquisitions at a time when earnings targets are being missed."

Answers to these Chapter Discussion Questions are found in the Online Instructor's Manual for instructors using this book.

QUESTIONS FROM THE CFA CURRICULUM

18.11
  a. List reasons that an international extension of the CAPM is problematic.
  b. In an international extension of the CAPM, why would the optimal portfolio differ from the world market portfolio, as suggested by the traditional CAPM, even if the markets are fully efficient?
  Source: CFA Institute 2011 International Asset Pricing, Reading 68, question 14.

18.12 Assume that the Eurozone risk-free interest rate on bonds with one year to maturity is 4.78% and that the U.S. risk-free interest rate on one-year bonds is 3.155%. The current exchange rate is $.90 per euro. Assume that the United States is the domestic country.
  a. Calculate the one-year forward exchange rate.
  b. Is the euro trading at forward premium on discount?
  c. Is your answer to part b consistent with interest rate parity? Explain
  Source: CFA Institute 2011 International Asset Pricing, Reading 68, question 8.

Answers to questions from the CFA curriculum are available in the Online Student Companion website to this book in a file folder entitled CFA Sample Exam Questions and Solutions.

CASE STUDY 18.1
Nestlé Buys Majority Ownership Stake in Chinese Candy Maker

Key Points

- Acquisition often is a more desirable option to a startup in a foreign country.
- Cross-border acquisitions require substantial patience.
- The size of the Chinese consumer market makes growth potential highly attractive.

After being in negotiations for two years, Swiss giant Nestlé, the world's largest food company, announced on July 15, 2011, that it had reached an agreement to pay $1.7 billion for a 60% interest in candy maker Hsu Fu Chi International. The remainder of the firm would be owned by the founding Hsu family. This transaction constituted the biggest deal yet for Nestlé in China and one of the biggest in China by a foreign firm. The deal represents Nestlé's second major purchase in China in 2011, after the firm agreed to buy 60% of the Yinlu Foods Group in April.

The agreement called for Nestlé initially to buy 43.5% of the firm's shares from independent shareholders (i.e., nonfounding family and noninstitutional investors) for 4.35 Singapore dollars (equivalent to $3.56 per share), a 24.7 % premium over the six months ending on July 1, 2011, and a 16.5% stake from the Hsu family. Hsu Fu Chi's current CEO and chairman, Mr. Hsu Chen, would continue to manage the firm. Nestlé paid 3.3 times revenue, as compared to 2.4 times what U.S. food manufacturer Kraft Foods paid for British candy

company Cadbury in 2010. However, the deal was less expensive than Mars' takeover of Wrigley at 4.2 times sales in 2008 and Danone's purchase of Dutch rival Numico for 4.5 times sales in 2007. Nestlé justified the multiple of revenue it paid by noting that the investment in Hsu Fu Chi provides an opportunity to become the top player in this high-growth market. In addition, Hsu Fu Chi provides a platform for future acquisitions that could in concept be relatively easily added to its Chinese confectionary operations.

Despite having had a presence in China for more than 20 years, Nestlé has found it difficult to grow its distribution system organically (i.e., by reinvesting in its existing operations). As of 2010, Nestlé operated 23 plants and two research centers with more than 14,000 employees in the country, with annual sales of $3.3 billion. Nestlé's existing product portfolio in China at that time included culinary products, instant coffee, bottled water, milk powder, and other products for the food service industry. With the addition of Hsu Fu Chi, Nestlé's sales in China jumped to $4.2 billion. Nevertheless, its market share in the food business still lagged that of rivals Unilever and Danone. With its revenues in China growing at 8% to 10% annually, Nestlé has stated publicly that it intends to derive at least 45% of its total annual revenue from emerging countries by the end of the decade, as compared to about one-third in 2010.

Founded in 1992, Hsu Fu Chi has four factories and 16,000 employees in China and is the leading manufacturer and distributor of confectionery products in China. With an estimated 6.6% market share and annual sales of $800 million, the firm makes chocolate, candies, and pastries popular in China and had annual sales of $800 million at the time of the transaction. Profits rose 31% in 2010 to $93 million. Located in the southern Chinese city of Dongguan, the firm operates an extensive distribution network and has numerous retail outlets, which should facilitate the distribution and sale of Nestlé products in China. Hsu Fu's annual revenue is growing three times faster than Nestlé's global annual sales. The firm's direct distribution network forms a large barrier to entry for competitors.

With Hsu Fu Chi listed on the Singapore stock exchange, the deal helped unlock value for Hsu Fu Chi's independent shareholders. As with many Singapore-listed Chinese firms, Hsu Fu Chi's independent shareholders had seen little appreciation of their holdings in recent years and had found it difficult to sell their shares, given the limited daily trading volume in the market for the firm's shares. Daily trading volume in the shares averaged about 0.1% of the firm's market cap. Despite having similar profit margins, Hsu Fu Chi traded at a ratio of 22 times trailing earnings, compared with 28 for comparable firms.

With the founding family owing 57% of the shares and Baring Private Equity Asia owning 15%, there were few independent shareholders to whom to sell shares. As the controlling shareholder, the founding family had little incentive to buy out the minority shareholders except at a significant discount from what investors believe is the firm's true value in order to take the firm private by buying out the public shareholders. Consequently, the independent shareholders had ample reason to support the Nestlé proposal. Hsu Fu Chi, which currently generates all of its revenue in China, may need Nestlé to expand overseas. The firm has stated that it wants to enter the international market, but it may not have the requisite resources to do so. Nestlé's strong international network and name recognition may make such expansion possible.

Discussion Questions

1. What were Nestlé's motives for acquiring Hsu Fu Chi? What were the firm's alternatives to acquisition, and why do you believe they may not have been pursued?

2. What alternatives did the majority shareholders in Hsu Fu Chi have for growing the firm? Speculate as to why they may have chosen to sell a controlling interest to Nestlé?

3. Speculate as to why Nestlé used cash rather than its stock to acquire its ownership interest in Hsu Fu Chi.

4. Why do you believe the independent and noninstitutional shareholders in Hsu Fu Chi, whose shares were listed on the Singapore stock exchange, were willing to sell to Nestlé? What were their other options?

5. Nestlé is assuming that it will be able to grow its share of the Chinese confectionary market by a combination of expanding its existing Chinese operations (so-called organic growth) and acquiring regional candy and food manufacturers. What obstacles do you believe Nestlé could encounter in its efforts to expand in China?

6. Do you believe that multiples of revenue paid by other food companies is a good means of determining the true value of Hsu Fu Chi? Why? Why not?

7. Despite having similar profit margins, Hsu Fu Chi traded at a ratio of 22 times trailing earnings, compared with 28 for comparable firms. Why do you believe Hsu Fu Chi's share price on the Singapore stock market sold at a 21% discount from the share price of other firms?

Solutions to these questions are found in the Online Instructor's Manual available to instructors using this book.

CASE STUDY 18.2
A Tale of Two International Strategies: The Wal-Mart and Carrefour Saga

Key Points

- Integrating foreign target companies and introducing improved operating and governance can be a daunting task.
- What works in the acquirer's country may not be transferable to the target's local market.

Wal-Mart began expanding aggressively outside the United States in the 1990s. Its principal international rival at that time was French retail chain Carrefour. After opening the world's first superstore in 1963, Carrefour spent the next four decades expanding its grocery and general merchandise stores across Europe, South America, and Asia.

While the chain grew rapidly through the 1990s, Carrefour has experienced difficult times in recent years. Carrefour shares have plunged more than two-thirds since 2007. Though having about the same number of retail locations (9,667 for Wal-Mart compared to 9,631 for Carrefour), Carrefour fell far behind Wal Mart's $467 billion in fiscal 2011 revenue. Wal-Mart's international sales of $109 billion in 28 countries outside the U.S. almost exceed Carrefour's total $114 billion in annual revenue, including sales in France. Wal-Mart's operating margins of 7.5% are 2 percentage points higher than comparably defined Carrefour margins. Net income per employee for Wal-Mart was $7,804 per employee, versus Carrefour's $1,260.

To understand how Carrefour floundered, we need to look at the global strategies of the two firms. Intended to offset sluggish growth in

France, Carrefour expanded too rapidly internationally as it entered 24 countries during the 10 years ending in 2004. While it succeeded in China, with annual revenue totaling $5.8 billion, it fell short in a number of other countries. Since 2000, Carrefour has sold off operations in 10 countries, including Mexico, Russia, Japan, and South Korea. The firm also has announced that it will withdraw from other countries.

Wal-Mart has shown considerable success in growing its international operations. Having expanded at a more disciplined pace than Carrefour, Wal-Mart enjoyed greater success in expanding in Mexico, South America, and Asia. Unlike Carrefour, Wal-Mart was able to finance its international growth from cash generated from its domestic U.S. operations. For Carrefour, revenue from its French-based stores, which account for 43% of its annual revenue, was largely stagnant. Moreover, sales also were slumping throughout the rest of Europe, which contributes about one-third of Carrefour's sales.

This success has not come without considerable challenges. The year 2006 marked the most significant retrenchment for Wal-Mart since it undertook its international expansion in the early 1990s. In May 2006, Wal-Mart announced that it would sell its 16 stores in South Korea. In July 2006, the behemoth announced that it was selling its operations in Germany to German retailer Metro AG. Wal-Mart, which had been trying to make its German stores profitable for eight years, announced a pretax $1 billion loss on the sale. The firm apparently underestimated the ferocity of German competitors, the frugality of German shoppers, and the extent to which regulations, cultural differences, and labor unions would impede its ability to apply in Germany what had worked so well in the United States. Wal-Mart has not been alone in finding the German discount market challenging. Nestlé SA and Unilever are among the large multinational retailers that had to change the way they do business in Germany. France's Carrefour SA, Wal-Mart's largest competitor worldwide, diligently avoided Germany.

After opening its first store in mainland China in 1996, Wal-Mart faced the daunting challenge of the country's bureaucracy and a distribution system largely closed to foreign firms. In late 2011, Chinese officials required the firm to close 13 stores due to allegations of mislabeling pork as organic. Wal-Mart also has had difficulty in converting firms used to their own way of doing things to the "Wal-Mart way." Specifically, it has taken the firm more almost four years to integrate the 100-plus stores of Trust-Mart, a Chinese chain it acquired in 2007. Overall, Wal-Mart realized its first profit in 2008, a dozen years after it first entered the country.

In India, Wal-Mart is still waiting for the government to ease restrictions on foreign firms wanting to enter the retail sector, which is currently populated with numerous small merchants. Efforts to implement reforms allowing foreign retailers to own a majority holding in local supermarket chains were halted due to a firestorm of public protest. At the end of 2011, Wal-Mart has no retail presence in the country. Nor does Wal-Mart have a retail presence in Russia, where, unlike in India, foreign retailers are welcome but corruption is rife. The combination of corruption, bureaucracy, and administrative processes has discouraged Wal-Mart from making acquisitions in Russia, even though there have been opportunities to do so.

Despite these missteps, Wal-Mart would appear to be well on its way to diversifying its business from the more mature U.S. market to faster-growing emerging markets. With the announcement in late 2010 of its controlling interest in South African retailer Massmart Holdings, more than one-half of all Wal-Mart stores are now located outside of the United States. Massmart gives Wal-Mart entry into sub-Saharan Africa, a region that has been largely ignored by the firm's primary international competitors, France's Carrefour SA, Germany's Metro AG, and the United Kingdom's Tesco PLC. South Africa has embraced shopping malls for years, and an increasingly affluent middle class has emerged since the demise of apartheid. South Africa also has little regulatory oversight. Furthermore, there is an established infrastructure of roads, ports, and warehouses, as well as effective banking and telecommunications systems. While the country has a relatively small population of 50 million, it provides access to the entire region. However, the country is not without challenges, including well-organized and sometimes violent labor unions, a high crime rate, and a 25% unemployment rate.

Wal-Mart's past mistakes have taught it to make adequate allowances for significant cultural differences. With respect to Massmart Holdings, there appears to be no immediate plans to rebrand the chain. The first changes customers will see will be the introduction of new products, including private-label goods and the sale of more food in the stores. Wal-Mart also has publicly committed to honoring current union agreements and to work constructively with the unions in the future. Current Massmart management also will remain in place.

Its decision to buy less than 100% of Massmart's outstanding shares reflected a desire by institutional investors in Massmart to retain exposure to the region and by the South African government to continue to have Massmart listed on the South African stock exchange. As one of the nation's largest companies, it provides significant name recognition for investors and a sense of national pride. Wal-Mart has a history of structuring its international operations to meet the demands of each region. For example, Wal-Mart owns 100% of its Asda operations in the United Kingdom and 68% of Wal-Mart de Mexico.

Discussion Questions

1. Wal-Mart's missteps in Germany may represent an example of the limitations of introducing what works in one market into another. To what extent do you believe that Wal-Mart's failure represented a

strategic error? To what extent did the firm's lack of success represent an implementation error?

2. In what ways does the Massmart acquisition reflect lessons learned by Wal-Mart from its previous international market entries? Be specific.

3. Given the challenges of international market entry and the probable substantial delay in experiencing a return on investment, do you believe that Wal-Mart should slow its pace of international expansion or even avoid it altogether? Explain your answer.

4. In your judgment, what criteria should Wal-Mart employ in selecting other foreign markets to enter? Be specific.

Solutions to these questions are found in the Online Instructor's Manual available to instructors using this book.

References

Acharya, V. V., Franks, J., & Servaes, H. (2007). Private equity: Boom or bust? *Journal of Applied Corporate Finance, 19*(Fall), 44–53.

Acharya, V. V., & Kehoe, C. (2010). Board directors and experience: A lesson from private equity. *Perspectives on Corporate Finance*, McKinsey & Company, Number 35, Spring 2010.

AC Nielsen, Retailer Support Is Essential for New Product Success. www.bases.com/news/news112002.html.

Adams, R., & Ferreira, D. (2007). A theory of friendly boards. *Journal of Finance, 62*, 217–250.

Adegoke, Y. (2008). YouTube Rolls out Sponsored Videos in Revenue Drive. *Reuters.*

Adolph, G. (2006). *Mergers: Back to happily ever after. Strategy and business.* New York: Booz Allen Hamilton.

Aggarwal, R., Erel, I., Stulz, R., & Williamson, R. (2007). *Differences in governance practices between U.S. and foreign firms: Measurement, causes, and consequences.* NBER Working Paper 13288 August.

Aggarwal, R., & Rivoli, P. (1990). Fads in the initial public offering market. *Financial Management, 19*, 45–57.

Aggdata.com. (2008). www.aggdata.com/business/fortune_500.

Agrawal, A., Ferrer, C., & West, A. (2011, May). When Big Acquisitions Pay Off. *McKinsey Quarterly.*

Agrawal, A., Jaffe, J. F., & Mandelker, G. N. (1992). The post-merger performance of acquiring firms: A reexamination of an anomaly. *Journal of Finance, 47*, 1605–1621.

Agrawal, A., & Nasser, T. (2012). Insider trading in takeover targets. *Journal of Corporate Finance, 18*, 598–625.

Agrawal, T. N. (2012). Insider trading in takeover targets. *Journal of Corporate Finance, 18*, 598–625.

Ahern, K. (2012). Bargaining power and industry dependence in mergers. *Journal of Financial Economics, 103*, 530–550.

Ahern, K., Daminelli, D., & Fracassi, C. (2013). *Lost in translation? The effect of cultural values on mergers around the world.*

Ahern, K., & Harford, J. (2010, March 12). The Importance of Industry Links in Merger Waves. Ross School of Business paper, AFA 2011; Denver Meetings Paper, available at SSRN: http://ssrn.com/abstract=1522203.

Akbulut, M. (2013). Do overvaluation-driven stock acquisitions really benefit acquirer shareholders? *Journal of Financial and Quantitative Analysis*, forthcoming.

Akbulut, M., & Matsusaka, J. (2010). 50+ Years of diversification announcements. *Financial Review, 45*, 231–262.

Akdogu, E. (2011). Value-maximizing managers, value-increasing mergers, and overbidding. *Journal of Financial and Quantitative Analysis, 46*, 83–110.

Akhigbe, A., Borde, S. F., & Whyte, A. M. (2000). The source of gains to targets and their industry rivals: Evidence based on terminated merger proposals. *Financial Management, 29*(Winter), 101–118.

Aktas, N., de Bodt, E., & Roll, R. (2009). Learning, hubris, and corporate serial acquisitions. *Journal of Corporate Finance, 15*, 523–626.

Aktas, N., de Bodt, E., & Roll, R. (2010). Negotiations under the threat of an auction. *Journal of Financial Economics, 98*, 241–255.

Aktas, N., de Bodt, E., & Roll, R. (2013). Learning from repetitive acquisitions: Evidence from the time between deals. *Journal of Financial Economics.*

Alderson, M. J., & Betker, B. L. (1999). Assessing post-bankruptcy performance: An analysis of reorganized firms' cash flows. *Financial Management, 28*(Summer), 68–82.

Alexandridis, G., Fuller, K., Terhaar, L., & Travlos, N. (2013). Deal size, acquisition premia, and shareholder gains. *Journal of Corporate Finance, 20*, 1–13.

Allen, J. (2001). Private information and spin-off performance. *Journal of Business, 74*, 281–306.

Allen, J., & McConnell, J. J. (1998). Equity carve-outs and managerial discretion. *Journal of Finance, 53,* 163–186.

Allen, P. (2000). Corporate equity ownership, strategic alliances, and product market relationships. *Journal of Finance, 55,* 2791–2816.

Alli, K. L., & Thompson, D. J. (1991). The value of the resale limitation on restricted stock: An option theory approach. *Valuation, 36,* 22–34.

Almeida, H., Campello, M., & Hackbarth, D. (2011). Liquidity mergers. *Journal of Financial Economics, 102,* 526–558.

Almeida, H., & Philippon, T. (2007). The risk-adjusted cost of financial distress. *Journal of Finance, 62,* 2557–2586.

Altman, E. I. (1968). Financial ratios, discriminant analysis and the prediction of corporate bankruptcy. *Journal of Finance, 23,* 509–609.

Altman, E. I. (1993). *Corporate financial distress and bankruptcy* (2nd ed.). New York: Wiley.

Altman, E. I. (2007). Global debt markets in 2007: A new paradigm or great credit bubble. *Journal of Applied Corporate Finance, Summer,* 17–31.

Altman, E. I., Brady, B., Resti, A., & Sironi, A. (2005). The link between default and recovery rates: Theory, empirical evidence and implications. *Journal of Business, 78,* 2203–2227.

Altman, E. I., & Kishore, V. (2001). *The default experience of U.S. bonds.* Salomon Center: New York Working Paper.

Altman, E. I., & Kishore, V. M. (1996). Almost everything you wanted to know about recoveries on defaulted bonds. *Financial Analysts Journal, November/December,* 57–64.

American Bar Association, (2006). *Mergers and acquisitions: Understanding antitrust issues* (2nd ed.). Chicago: Illinois.

Ammann, M., Hoechle, D., & Schmid, M. (2012). Is there really no conglomerate discount? *Journal of Business Finance and Accounting, 39,* 264–288.

Anand, J., & Delios, A. (2002). Absolute and relative resources as determinants of international acquisitions. *Journal of Strategic Management, 23,* 119–134.

Anderson, R., & Reeb, M. (2003). Founding-family ownership and firm performance: Evidence from the S&P 500. *Journal of Finance, 58,* 1301–1329.

Anderson, R. W., & Coverhill, A. (2007). *Liquidity and capital structure.* Center for Economic Policy Research: Working Paper No. 6044.

Anderson, U., Johanson, J., & Vahlne, J. E. (1997). Organic acquisitions in the international process of the business firm. *Management International Review, 37,* 67.

Andersen Consulting, (1999). *Global survey acquisition and alliance integration.* Chicago. Andersen Consulting.

Andrade, G., & Kaplan, S. (1998). How costly is financial (not economic) distress? Evidence from highly leveraged transactions that become distressed. *Journal of Finance, 53,* 1443–1493.

Andreou, P., Doukas, J., Louca, C., & Malmendier, U. (2010). *Managerial overconfidence and the diversification discount.* Working Paper, Cyprus University of Technology, Limmasol, Cyprus.

Ang, J., & Kohers, N. (2001). The takeover market for privately held companies: The U.S. experience. *Cambridge Journal of Economics, 25,* 723–748.

Ang, J., & Mauck, N. (2011). Fire sale acquisitions, myth vs. reality. *Journal of Banking and Finance, 35,* 532–543.

Ang, J. S., & Cheng, Y. (2006). Direct evidence on the market-driven acquisition theory. *Journal of Financial Research, 29,* 199–216.

Angwin, J., & Drucker, J. (2006). How news corp. and liberty media can save $4.5 billion. *Wall Street Journal,* A3.

Annema, A., Fallon, W. C., & Goedhart, M. H. (2002). When Carve-outs Make Sense. McKinsey Quarterly 2; http://www.mckinseyquarterly.com/home.aspx.

Annema, A., & Goedhart, M. H. (2006). Betas: Back to Normal. McKinsey Quarterly; http://www.mckinseyquarterly.com/home.aspx.

Association for Financial Professionals. (2011, March). *AFP survey of current trends in estimating and applying the cost of capital.* Report of Survey Results. Bethesda, MD.

Aschwald, K. F. (2000). Restricted stock discounts decline as result of one-year holding period. *Shannon Pratt's Business Valuation Update, May*, 1–5.

Asker, J., Farre-Mensa, J., & Ljungqvist, A. (2010). *Does the stock market harm investment incentives?* New York University Working Paper.

Aspatore Staff, (2006). *M&A negotiations: Leading lawyers on negotiating deals: Structuring contracts and resolving merger and acquisition disputes.* Boston: Aspatore Books.

Asquith, P., Gerther, R., & Scharfstein, D. (1994). Anatomy of financial distress: An examination of junk bond issuers. *Quarterly Journal of Economics, 109*, 625–658.

Astrachan, J. H., & Shanker, M. C. (2003). Family businesses contributions to the U.S. economy: A closer look. *Family Business Review, 15*, 211–219.

Atanassov, J. (2013). Do hostile takeovers stifle innovation? Evidence from antitakeover legislation and corporate patenting. *Journal of Finance, 68*, 1097–1131.

Atanasov, V., Boone, A., & Haushalter, D. (2010). Is there shareholder expropriation in the U.S.? An analysis of publicly traded subsidiaries. *Journal of Financial and Quantitative Analysis, 5*, 1–26.

Auerbach, A. J., & Poterba, J. (1987). Tax loss carry-forwards and corporate tax incentives. In F. Martin (Ed.), *The effect of taxation on capital accumulation.* Chicago: University of Chicago Press.

Avramov, D., Chordia, T., Jostova, G., & Philipov, A. (2009). Credit ratings and the cross-section of stock returns. *Journal of Financial Markets, 12*, 469–499.

Axelson, U., Jenkinson, T., Stromberg, P., & Weisbach, M. (2009). Leverage and Pricing in Buyouts: An Empirical Analysis, http://ssrn.com/abstract=1344023, 2009.

Ayers, B. C., Lefanowicz, C. E., & Robinson, J. R. (2003). Shareholder taxes in acquisition premiums: The effect of capital gains taxation. *Journal of Finance, 58*, 2783–2801.

Aziz, M. A., & Dar, H. A. (2006). Predicting corporate bankruptcy: Where we stand. *Corporate Governance, 6*(1), 18–33.

Bailey, W., Li, H., Mao, C., & Zhong, R. (2003). Regulation fair disclosure and earnings information: Market, analyst, and corporate responses. *Journal of Finance, 58*, 2487–2514.

Baker, G., & Smith, G. (1998). *The new financial capitalists.* Cambridge, UK: Cambridge University Press.

Ball, M. (1997). How a spin-off could lift your share value. *Corporate Finance, May*, 23–29.

Bao, J., & Edmans, A. (2011). Do investment banks matter for M&A returns? *Review of Financial Studies, 24*, 2286–2315.

Barbopoulos, L., & Sudarsanam, S. (2012). Determinants of earnout as acquisition payment currency and bidder's value gains. *Journal of Banking and Finance, 30*, 678–694.

Barkema, H. G., & Schijven, M. (2008). How do firms learn to make acquisitions? A review of past research and an agenda for the future. *Journal of Management, 34*, 594–634.

Barkema, H. G., & Vermeulen, F. (1998). International expansion through start-up or acquisition: A learning perspective. *Journal of the Academy of Management, 41*, 7–26.

Barnett, T. R. (2008). Message from the AAG, U.S. department of justice. *Antitrust Division Update, Spring.*

Barrett, P., Burton, K. & Kishan, S. (2011). The Rajaratnam conviction: How big a victory?. *Bloomberg Businessweek*, May 11, p. 27.

Bates, T. W. (2005). Asset sales, investment opportunities, and the use of proceeds. *Journal of Finance, 60*, 105–135.

Baugess, S., Slovin, M., & Sushka, M. (2012). Large shareholder diversification, corporate risk taking, and the benefits of changing to differential voting rights. *Journal of Banking & Finance, 36*, 1244–1253.

Bebchuk, L., Coates, J., & Subramanian, G. (2002). The powerful anti-takeover force of staggered boards: Theory, evidence, and policy. *Stanford Law Rev, 54*, 887–951.

Bebchuk, L. J., Coates, J. C., IV, & Subramanian, G. (2003). *The powerful antitakeover force of staggered boards.* Harvard Law School and NBER: Working Paper.

Bebchuk, L., Cohen, A., & Ferrell, A. (2009). What matters in corporate governance. *Review of Financial Studies, 22*, 783–827.

Bebchuk, L., Cohen, A., & Wang, C. (2010). Learning and the disappearing association between governance and returns. *Journal of Financial Economics, 102*, 199–221.

Bekaert, G., & Harvey, C. R. (2000). Foreign speculators and emerging equity markets. *Journal of Finance, 55,* 565–613.

Bekier, M. M., Bogardus, A. J., & Oldham, T. (2001). Why mergers fail. *McKinsey Quarterly, 4*(3)

Bellovary, J. L., Giacomino, D. E., & Akers, M. D. (2007). A review of bankruptcy prediction studies: 1930 to the present. *Journal of Financial Education, Winter,* 262–298.

Benmelech, E., & Bergman, N. (2011). Bankruptcy and the collateral channel. *Journal of Finance, 66,* 337–378.

Ben-Amar, W., & Andre, P. (2006). Separation of ownership from control and acquiring firm performance: The case of family ownership in Canada. *Journal of Business Finance and Accounting, 33,* 517–543.

Beneda, N. (2007). Performance and distress indicators of new public companies. *Journal of Asset Management, 8,* 24–33.

Bengoa, M., & Sanchez-Robles, B. (2003). Foreign direct investment, economic freedom and growth. *European Journal of Political Economy, 19,* 529–545.

Bennedsen, M., Nielsen, K., Perez-Gonzalez, F., & Wolfenson, D. (2007). Inside the family firm: The role of families in succession decisions and performance. *Quarterly Journal of Economics, 122,* 647–691.

Berfield, S. (2011). The fall of the house of busch. *Bloomberg Businessweek,* July 17, pp. 22–24.

Berger, P. G., & Ofek, E. (1995). Diversification's effect on firm value. *Journal of Financial Economics, 37,* 39–65.

Berggren, N., & Jordahl, H. (2005). Does free trade reduce growth? Further testing using the economic freedom index. *Public Choice, 22,* 99–114.

Bergh, D., Johnson, R., & Dewitt, R. L. (2007). Restructuring through spin-off or sell-off: Transforming information asymmetries into financial gain. *Strategic Management Journal, 29,* 133–148.

Berk, J. B. (1995). A critique of size-related anomalies. *The Review of Financial Studies, 8,* 275–286.

Berman, D. K., & Sender, H. (2006). Back-story of kinder LBO underscores web of ethical issues such deals face. *Wall Street Journal,* A6.

Bernard, V., Healy, P., & Palepu, K. G. (2000). *Business analysis and valuation* (2nd ed.). Georgetown, TX: Southwestern College Publishing Company.

Best, R., & Hodges, C. W. (2004). Does information asymmetry explain the diversification discount? *Journal of Financial Research, 27*(Summer), 235–249.

Betker, B. (1995). An empirical examination of prepackaged bankruptcy. *Financial Management, Spring,* 3–18.

Betton, S., Eckbo, B., & Thorburn, K. (2008). Corporate takeovers. In B. (2008). Eckbo (Ed.), *Handbook of corporate finance: Empirical corporate finance* (Vol. 2, pp. 291–430). North-Holland: Elsevier.

Betton, S., Eckbo, B., & Thorburn, K. (2009). Merger negotiations and the toehold puzzle. *Journal of Financial Economics, 91,* 158–178.

Bhagat, S., Dong, M., Hirshleifer, D., & Noah, R. (2005). Do tender offers create value? New methods and evidence. *Journal of Financial Economics, 76,* 3–60.

Bhagat, S., Malhotra, S., & Zhu, P. (2011). Emerging country cross-border acquisitions: Characteristics, acquirer returns, and cross-sectional determinants. *Emerging Markets Review, 12,* 250–271.

Bhattacharyya, S., & Nain, A. (2011). Horizontal acquisitions and buying power. *Journal of Financial Economics, 99,* 97–115.

Bigelli, M., & Mengoli, S. (2004). Sub-optimal acquisition decision under a majority shareholder system. *Journal of Management Governance, 8,* 373–403.

Billett, M. T., & Qian, Y. (2008). Are overconfident managers born or made? Evidence of self-attribution bias from frequent acquirers. *Management Science, 54,* 1036–1055.

Billett, M. T., & Vijh, A. M. (2004). The wealth effects of tracking stock restructurings. *Journal of Financial Research, 27*(Winter), 559–583.

Billett, M. T., & Xue, H. (2007). The takeover deterrent effect of open market share repurchases. *Journal of Finance, 62,* 1827–1851.

Billett, M. T., King, T. -H. D., & Mauer, D. C. (2004). Bondholder wealth effects on mergers and acquisitions: New evidence from the 1980s and 1990s. *Journal of Finance, 59,* 107–135.

Billett, M. T., Jiang, Z., & Lie, E. (2010). The effect of change in control covenants on takeovers: Evidence from leveraged buyouts. *Journal of Corporate Finance, 16*, 1–15.

Black, E. L., Carnes, T. A., & Jandik, T. (2007). International accounting diversity and the long-term success of cross-border mergers and acquisitions. *Journal of Business Finance and Accounting, 34*, 139–168.

Bloomberg.com. (2000). *Glaxo, SmithKline Agree to Merge* (January 18).

Blouin, J., Core, J., & Guay, W. (2010). Have the tax benefits of debt been overestimated? *Journal of Financial Economics, 98*, 195–213.

Blume, M. E., Lim, F., & MacKinlay, A. C. (1998). The declining credit quality of U.S. corporate debt: Myth or reality? *Journal of Finance, 53*, 1389–1413.

Bodnar, G., Dumas, B., & Marston, R. (2003). *Cross-border valuations: The international cost of capital.* NBER Working Paper Series No. 10115.

Boehmer, E. (2000). Business groups, bank control, and large shareholders: An analysis of German takeovers. *Journal of Financial Intermediation, 9*, 117–148.

Bogle, J. C. (2007). Reflections on "Toward a Common Sense and Common Ground," 33 Iowa J. Corp. L. 31, 31.

Bogler, D. (1996). Post-takeover stress disorder, summary of a PA consulting study. *Financial Times*, 11.

Boone, A. L., & Mulherin, J. H. (2007). How are firms sold? *Journal of Finance, 62*, 847–875.

Boone, A. L., & Mulherin, J. H. (2009). Is there one best way to sell a firm? Auctions versus negotiations and controlled sales. *Journal of Applied Corporate Finance, 21*, 28–37.

Boone, A. L., & Mulherin, J. H. (2011). Do private equity consortiums facilitate collusion in takeover bidding? *Journal of Corporate Finance, 17*, 1475–1495.

Boone, A. L., Haushalter, D., & Mikkelson, W. (2003). An investigation of the gains from specialized equity claims. *Financial Management, 32*, 67–83.

Boot, A. W. A., Gopalan, R., & Thakor, A. V. (2008). Market liquidity, investor participation, and managerial autonomy: Why do firms go private. *Journal of Finance, 63*, 2013–2059.

Booz-Allen, , & Hamilton, (1993). *A practical guide to alliances: Leapfrogging the learning curve.* Los Angeles: Booz-Allen & Hamilton.

Borden, A. M. (1987). *Going private.* New York: Law Journal Seminar Press.

Boston Consulting Group, (1985). *The strategy development process.* Boston: The Boston Consulting Group.

Boston Consulting Group. (2003). *Weak Economy Is Ideal Time for Mergers and Acquisitions.* July 10, www.srimedia.com/artman/ppublish/printer_657.shtml.

Boucly, Q., Sraer, D., & Thesmar, D. (2011). Growth LBOs. *Journal of Financial Economics, 102*, 432–453.

Boulton, T., Smart, S., & Zutter, J. (2010). Acquisition activity and IPO underpricing. *Financial Management, 39*, 1521–1546.

Bouzgarrou, H., & Navatte, P. (2013). Ownership structure and acquirer's performance: Family versus non-family firms. *International Review of Financial Analysis, 27*, 123–134.

Boyle, G. W., Carer, R. B., & Stover, R. D. (1998). Extraordinary anti-takeover provisions and insider ownership structure: The case of converting savings and loans. *Journal of Financial and Quantitative Analysis, 33*, 291–304.

Brakman, S., Garretsen, H., & Van Marrewijk, C. (2005). *Cross-border mergers and acquisitions: On revealed comparative advantage and merger waves.* SESifo Working Paper No. 1602, Category 10: Empirical and Theoretical Methods.

Branch, B. (2002). The costs of bankruptcy: A review. *International Review of Financial Analysis, 11*, 39–57.

Brav, A. (2009). Access to capital, capital structure, and the funding of the firm. *Journal of Finance, 64*, 263–308.

Brav, A., Jiang, W., Partnoy, F., & Thomas, R. (2008). Hedge fund activism, corporate governance, and firm performance. *Journal of Finance, 63*, 1729–1775.

Brealey, R. A., & Myers, S. C. (1996). *Principles of corporate finance* (5th ed.). New York: McGraw-Hill.

Brealey, R. A., & Myers, S. C. (2003). *Principles of corporate finance* (7th ed.). New York: McGraw-Hill.

Briel, R. (2010). YouTube: Profitable in 2010, Broadband TV News, March, 3, www.broadbanktvnew. com/2010/03/05/youtube-proffitable-in-2010/

Brigham, E. F., & Ehrhardt, M. C. (2005). *Financial management. Theory and practice*. Mason, OH: Thomson-Southwestern Publishing.

Brigida, M., & Madura, J. (2012). Sources of target stock price run-up prior to acquisitions. *Journal of Economics and Business, 64*, 185–198.

Bris, A., & Cabolis, C. (2008). Adopting better corporate governance: Evidence from cross-border mergers. *Journal of Corporate Finance, 14*, 214–240.

Brookings Institute. (2000). *Antitrust Goes Global* (November).

Brophy, D. J., Ouimet, P. P., & Sialm, C. (2009). Hedge funds as investors of last resort. *The Review of Financial Studies, 22*, 541–574.

Brouthers, K. D. (2002). Institutional, cultural, and transaction cost influences on entry mode choice and performance. *Journal of International Business Studies, 33*, 203–221.

Brouthers, K. D., & Brouthers, L. E. (2000). Acquisition, greenfield start-up: Institutional, cultural, and transaction cost influences. *Strategic Management Journal, 21*, 89–97.

Brouthers, K. D., van Hastenburg, P., & van de Ven, J. (1998). If most mergers fail, why are they so popular? *Long-Range Planning, 31*, 347–353.

Browning, L., & Byrnes, N. (2011, August 31). Motorola deal offers google tax, patent benefits, *Reuters*.

Brunnermeier, M. (2009). Deciphering the liquidity and credit crunch of 2007–2008. *Journal of Economic Perspectives, 23*, 77–100.

Bryan-Low, C. (2005). European telecoms vie for emerging markets. *Wall Street Journal*, B2.

Bulow, J., & Klemperer, P. (2009). Why do sellers usually prefer auctions? *American Economic Review, 99*, 1544–1575.

Burch, T. R., & Nanda, V. (2001). Divisional diversity and the conglomerate discount: Evidence from spin-offs. *Journal of Financial Economics, 70*, 233–257.

Burch, T. R., Nanda, V., & Silveri, S. (2012). Taking stock or cashing in? Shareholder style preferences, premiums, and method of payment. *Journal of Empirical Finance, 19*, 558–582.

Burkhart, M., Gromb, D., & Panunzi, F. (1997). Larger shareholders, monitoring and the value of the firm. *Quarterly Journal of Economics*, 693–728.

Burrus, A., & McNamee, M. (2002). Evaluating the rating agencies. *Business Week, 8*, 39–40.

Business Week. (2000). *Jack's Risky Last Act* 40–45.

Business Week. (2001). *A Merger's Bitter Harvest* 112.

Business Week. (2008). *Easygoing Trustbusters* 8.

Bygrave, W. D., & Timmons, J. A. (1992). *Venture capital at the crossroads*. Boston: Harvard Business School Press.

Byrd, J., & Hickman, K. (1992). Do outside directors monitor managers? Evidence from tender offer bids. *Journal of Financial Economics, 32*, 195–207.

Cai, Y., & Sevilir, M. (2012). Board connections and M&A connections. *Journal of Financial Economics, 103*, 327–349.

Cai, J., Song, M., & Walkling, R. (2011). Anticipation, acquisitions, and bidder returns: Industry shocks and the transfer of information across rivals. *Review of Financial Studies, 24*, 2242–2282.

Cakici, N. G., & Tandon, K. (1996). Foreign acquisitions in the U.S: Effects on shareholder wealth of foreign acquiring firms. *Journal of Banking and Finance, 20*, 307–329.

Campa, J., & Simi, K. (2002). Explaining the diversification discount. *Journal of Finance, 57*, 135–160.

Campbell, A., Sadler, D., & Koch, R. (1997). *Breakup! When companies are worth more dead than alive*. Oxford, England: Capstone.

Campbell, J. Y., Hilscher, J., & Szilagyi, J. (2008). In search of distress risk. *Journal of Finance, 63*, 2899–2939.

Cao, J. X. (2008). An Empirical Study of LBOs and Takeover Premium; http://ssrn.com/abstrat=1100059 February 10, Available at SSRN.

Cao, J., & Lerner, J. (2009). The success of reverse leveraged buyouts. *Journal of Financial Economics, 91*, 139–157.

Caprio, L., Croci, E., & Del Giudice, A. (2011). Ownership structure, family control, and acquisition decisions. *Journal of Corporate Finance, 17*, 1636–1657.

Capron, L., & Guillén, M. (2009). National corporate governance institutions and post-acquisition target reorganization. *Strategic Management Journal, 30*(8), 803–833.

Capron, L., & Shen, J. C. (2007). Acquisitions of private versus public firms: Private information, target selection, and acquirer returns. *Strategic Management Journal, 28*, 891–911.

Carey, D. C., & Ogden, D. (2004). *The human side of M&A*. Oxford, England: Oxford University Press.

Carleton, J. R., & Lineberry, C. S. (2004). *Achieving post-merger success*. New York: Wiley.

Carow, K. A., & Roden, D. M. (1998). Determinants of the stock price reaction to leveraged buyouts. *Journal of Economics and Finance, 22*(Spring), 37–47.

CCH Tax Law Editors, (2005). *U.S. master tax code*. New York: Commerce Clearinghouse.

Ceneboyan, A. S., Papaioannou, G. J., & Travlos, N. (1991). Foreign takeover activity in the U.S. and wealth effects for target firm shareholders. *Financial Management, 31*, 58–68.

Chaffee, D. B. (1993). Option pricing as a proxy for discount for lack of marketability in private company valuation. *Business Valuation Review, 20*, 182–188.

Chakrabarti, A. (1990). Organizational factors in post-acquisition performance. *IEEE Transactions in Engineering Management EM-37, 135*, 259–266.

Chakrabarti, R., Jayaraman, N., & Mukherjee, S. (2009). Mars–venus marriages: Culture and cross-border M&A. *Journal of International Business Studies, 40*, 216–236.

Chan, K. C., Karolyi, G. A., & Stulz, R. M. (1992). Global financial markets and the risk premium of U.S. equity. *Journal of Financial Economics, 32*, 137–167.

Chan, S. H., Kensinger, J. W., Keown, A. J., & Martin, J. D. (1997). Do strategic alliances create value? *Journal of Financial Economics, 46*, 199–221.

Chang, S. (1998). Takeovers of privately held targets, methods of payment, and bidder returns. *Journal of Finance, 53*, 773–784.

Chang, S. C. (2008). *How do strategic alliances affect suppliers, customers, and rivals?* Working Paper Series, Social Science Research Network: February 1.

Chaochharia, V., & Grinstein, Y. (2007). Corporate governance and firm value: The impact of the 2002 governance rules. *Journal of Finance, 62*, 1789–1825.

Chaplinsky, S., & Ramchand, L. (2000). The impact of global equity offers. *Journal of Finance*, 2767–2789.

Chapman, T. L., Dempsey, J. J., Ramsdell, G., & Bell, T. E. (1998). Purchasing's big moment—after a merger. *McKinsey Quarterly, 1*, 56–65.

Chari, A., Chen, W., & Dominquez, K. (2012). Foreign ownership and firm performance: Emerging market acquisitions in the United States. *IMF Economic Review, 60*, 1–42.

Chari, A., Ouiment, P., & Tesar, L. (2010). The value of control in emerging markets. *Review of Financial Studies, 23*, 1741–1770.

Charitou, A., & Trigeorgis, L. (2008). Bankruptcy prediction and structural credit risk models Jones & D. Hensher (Eds.), *Credit risk modeling* (pp. 154–174). Cambridge, England: Cambridge University Press.

Chatterjee, R. A., & Aw, M. S. B. (2004). The performance of UK: Firms acquiring large cross-border and domestic takeover targets. *Applied Financial Economics, 14*, 337–349.

Chatterjee, S., John, K., & Yan, A. (2012). Takeovers and divergence of investor opinion. *Review of Financial Studies, 25*, 227–276.

Chatterjee, S., & Yan, A. (2008). Using innovative securities under asymmetric information: Why do some firms pay with contingent value rights? *Journal of Financial and Quantitative Analysis, 43*, 1001–1035.

Chemmanur, T., & Jiao, Y. (2012). Dual-class IPOs: A theoretical analysis. *Journal of Banking & Finance, 36*, 305–319.

Chemmanur, T., & Paeglis, I. (2001). Why issue tracking stock? Insights from a comparison with spin-offs and carve-outs. *Journal of Applied Corporate Finance, 14*, 102–114.

Chen, D. (2012). Classified boards, the cost of debt, and firm performance. *Journal of Banking and Finance, 36*, 3346–3365.

Chen, H. L., & Guo, R. J. (2005). On corporate divestitures. *Review of Quantitative Finance and Accounting, 25*, 399–421.

Chen, L. (2010). The use of independent fairness opinions and the performance of acquiring firms. *Journal of Accounting, Auditing, and Finance, 25,* 323–349.

Cheng, C. S., Liu, C. S., & Schaefer, T. F. (1996). Earnings permanence and the incremental information content of cash flow from operations. *Journal of Accounting Research, Spring,* 173–181.

Child, J., & Faulkner, D. (1998). *Strategies of cooperation: Managerial alliances, networks, and joint ventures.* Oxford, UK: Oxford University Press.

Child, J., Faulkner, D., & Pitkethley, R. (2001). *The management of international acquisitions.* Oxford, UK: Oxford University Press.

Cho, M. H., & Cohen, M. A. (1997). The economic causes and consequences of corporate divestiture. *Managerial and Decision Economics, 18,* 367–374.

Christofferson, S. A., McNish, R. S., & Sias, D. L. (2004). Where mergers go wrong. *McKinsey Quarterly;* https://www.mckinseyquarterly.com/home.aspx.

Chung, J. (2011, August 3). Leveraged Buyouts of Private Companies. http://ssrn.com/abstract=1904342.

Claessens, S., Djankov, S., Fan, J., & Lang, H. P. I. (2002). Disentangling the incentive and entrenchment effects of large shareholders. *Journal of Finance, 57,* 2741–2771.

Clark, K., & Ofek, E. (1994). Mergers as a means of restructuring distressed firms: An empirical investigation. *Journal of Financial and Quantitative Analysis, 29,* 541–565.

Clifford, C. (2008). Value creation or destruction: Hedge funds as shareholder activists. *Journal of Corporate Finance, 14,* 323–336.

Clubb, C., & Stouraitis, A. (2000). The significance of sell-off profitability in explaining the market reaction to divestiture announcements. *Journal of Banking and Finance, 26,* 671–688.

Coates, J. C. (2001). Explaining variation in takeover defenses: Blame the lawyers. *California Law Review, 89,* 1376.

Cohn, J. B., Mills, L. F., & Towery, E. M. (2011). The Evolution of Capital Structure and Operating Performance after Leveraged Buyouts: Evidence from U.S. Corporate Tax Returns; http://ssrn.com/abstract=1764406.

Colak, G., & Whited, T. (2007). Spin-offs, divestitures, and conglomerate investment. *The Review of Financial Studies, 20,* 557–595.

Coles, J. L., Daniel, N. D., & Naveen, L. (2008). Boards: Does one size fit all? *Journal of Financial Economics, 87,* 329–356.

Comment, R. (2012). Revisiting the illiquidity discount for private companies: A new (and "skeptical") restricted stock study. *Journal of Applied Corporate Finance, 23,* 80–92.

Comment, R., & Schwert, G. W. (1995). Poison or placebo: Evidence on the deterrence and wealth effects of modern anti-takeover measures. *Journal of Financial Economics, 39,* 3–43.

Cooper, S., & Lybrand, (1996). Most acquisitions fail, C&L study says. *Mergers & Acquisitions, 47*(2) (Report 7).

Corkery, M. (2012). Pension funds increasing their ties. *Wall Street Journal,* February 12, pp. C1–C2.

Cornaggia, K., Franzen, L., & Simin, T. (2012). *Bringing leased assets onto the balance sheet.* Loyola Marymount University Working Paper.

Cornelli, F., Kominek, Z., & Ljungqvist, A. (2013). Monitoring managers: does it matter? *Journal of Finance* (Forthcoming).

Cornett, M., Tanyeri, B., & Tehranian, H. (2011). The effect of merger anticipation on bidder and target firm announcement period returns. *Journal of Corporate Finance, 17,* 595–611.

Cossey, B. (1991). Systems assessment in acquired subsidiaries. *Accountancy,* 98–99.

Cremers, M., & Nair, V. (2005). Governance mechanisms and equity prices. *Journal of Finance, 60,* 2859–2894.

Cremers, M. K. J., Nair, V. B., & Wei, C. (2004). *The impact of shareholder control on bondholders.* Yale University and New York University: Working Paper.

Creswell, J. (2001). Would you give this man your company? *Fortune,* 127–129.

Cronqvist, H., & Nilsson, M. (2003). Agency costs of controlling minority shareholders. *Journal of Fiancial and Quantitative Analysis, 38,* 695–719.

Cumming, D., Siegel, D., & Wright, M. (2007). Private equity, leveraged buyouts and governance. *Journal of Corporate Finance, 13,* 439–460.

Cunat, V., Gine, M., & Guadalupe, M. (2012). The vote is cast: The effect of corporate governance on shareholder value. *Journal of Finance, 67*, 1943–1977.

Cusatis, P. J., Miles, J. A., & Randall Woolridge, J. (1993). Restructuring through spin-offs. *Journal of Financial Economics, 33*, 293–311.

Cyree, K. B., & Walker, M. M. (2008). The determinants and survival of reverse mergers versus IPOs. *Journal of Economics and Finance, 32*, 176–194.

Daley, L., Mehrotra, V., & Sivakumar, R. (1997). Corporate focus and value creation, evidence from spin-offs. *Journal of Financial Economics, 45*, 257–281.

Dalton, D. R. (2006). CEO tenure, boards of directors, and acquisition performance. *Journal of Business Research, 60*, 331–338.

Dalton, D. R., & Dalton, C. M. (2007). Sarbanes-oxley and the guideline of the listing exchanges: What have we wrought? *Business Horizons, 50*, 93–100.

Damodaran, A. (2001). *The dark side of valuation*. New York: Prentice-Hall.

Damodaran, A. (2002). *Investment valuation: Tools and techniques for determining the value of any asset* (2nd ed.). New York: Wiley.

Das, S., Sen, P. K., & Sengupta, S. (1998). Impact of strategic alliances on firm valuation. *Academy of Management Journal, 41*, 27–41.

Datta, S., Iskandar-Datta, M., & Raman, K. (2003). Value creation in corporate asset sales: The role of managerial performance and lender monitoring. *Journal of Banking and Finance, 27*, 351–375.

Davis, A., & Leblond, M. (2002). *A spin-off analysis: Evidence from new and old economies*, Working Paper. Queen's University: available by e-mail from adavis@business.queensu.ca.

Davis, G., & Kim, H. (2007). Business ties and proxy voting by mutual funds. *Journal of Financial Economics, 85*, 552–570.

Davis, P. S., Desai, A. B., & Francis, J. D. (2000). Mode of international entry: An isomorphian perspective. *Journal of International Business Studies, 31*, 239–258.

Davis, S. J., Haltiwanger, J., Jarmin, R., Lerner, J., & Miranda, J. (2011). *Private equity and employment*. National Bureau of Economic Research, Working Paper 17399.

Dechow, P. M. (1994). Accounting earnings and cash flows as measures of firm performance: The role of accounting accruals. *Journal of Accounting and Economics, 18*, 3–42.

De La Merced, M. J. (2011, May 6). Dealbook, New York Times.

Delios, A., & Beamish, P. S. (1999). Geographic scope, product diversification, and the corporate performance of Japanese firms. *Strategic Management Journal, 20*, 711–727.

DeLong, G. (2003). Does long-term performance of mergers match market expectations? *Financial Management, Summer*, 5–25.

De Mdedt, J., & Van Hoey, M. (2008). Integrating Steel Giants: An Interview with the Arcelor-Mittal Post-Merger Managers, McKinsey and Company www.mckinseyquarterly.com.

DeMong, R., Harris, I., & Williams, S. (2011). Financial and legal advisors in merger and acquisition transactions. *International Journal of Business, Humanities, and Technology, 1*, 1–13.

Demsetz, H., & Lehn, K. (1996). The structure of corporate ownership: Causes and consequences. *Journal of Political Economy, 93*, 1155–1177.

Deogun, N., & Lipin, S. (2000). Big Mergers in '90s Prove Disappointing to Shareholders. Salomon Smith Barney study, quoted in *Wall Street Journal* C12.

De Pamphilis, D. (2001). Managing growth through acquisition: Time-tested techniques for the entrepreneur. *International Journal of Entrepreneurship and Innovation, 2*(3), 195–205.

DePamphilis, D. (2010). *M&A basics: All you need to know*. Boston: Elsevier.

DePamphilis, D. (2010). *M&A negotiations and deal structuring: All you need to know*. Boston: Elsevier.

DePamphilis, D. (2011). Upstart graphics: Mergers and acquisitions issues. In P. Westhead, M. Wright & G. McElwee (Eds.), *Entrepreneurship: Perspectives and cases* (pp. 401–410). London: Prentice Hall.

Desai, H., & Jain, P. (1997). Firm performance and focus: Long-run stock market performance following spin-offs. *Journal of Financial Economics, 54*, 75–101.

De Visscher, F. M., Arnoff, C. E., & Ward, J. L. (1995). *Financing transitions: Managing capital and liquidity in the family business*. Marietta, GA: Business Owner Resources.

Dewenter, K. L. (1995). Does the market react differently to domestic and foreign takeover announcements? Evidence from the U.S. chemical and retail industries. *Journal of Financial Economics, 37*, 421–441.

Dichev, I. (1998). Is the risk of bankruptcy a systematic risk? *Journal of Finance, 53*, 1141–1148.

Diermeier, J., & Solnik, B. (2001). Global pricing of equity. *Financial Analysts Journal, 57*, 17–47.

Dimson, E., March, P., & Staunton, M. (2002). *Triumph of the optimists*. Princeton, NJ: Princeton University Press.

Dimson, E., March, P., & Staunton, M. (2003). Global evidence on the equity risk premium. *Journal of Applied Corporate Finance, 15*(Fall), 27–38.

Dionne, G., La Haye, M., & Bergeres, A. (2010). Does asymmetric information affect the premium in mergers and acquisitions? Interuniversity Research Center on Enterprise Networks, Logistics and Transportation and Department of Finance, HEC Montreal, H3T 2A7.

Dittmar, A., Li, D., & Nain, A. (2012). It pays to follow the leader: Acquiring targets picked by private equity. *Journal of Financial and Quantitative Analysis, 47*, 901–931.

Dittmar, A., & Shivdasani, A. (2003). Divestitures and divisional investment policies. *Journal of Finance, 58*, 2711–2744.

Dolly King, T., & Wen, M. (2011). Shareholder governance, Bondholder governance, and managerial risk-taking. *Journal of Banking and Finance, 35*, 512–531.

Dong, M., Hirshleifer, D., Richardson, S., & Teoh, S. H. (2006). Does investor misvaluation drive the takeover market? *Journal of Finance, 61*, 725–762.

Down, J. W. (1995). The M&A game is often won or lost after the deal. *Management Review Executive Forum, 10*, 6–9.

Draper, P., & Paudyal, K. (2006). Acquisitions: Private versus public. *European Financial Management, 12*, 57–80.

Drucker, J., & Silver, S. (2006). Alcatel stands to reap tax benefits on merger. *Wall Street Journal April, 26*, C3.

D'Souza, J., & Jacob, J. (2000). Why firms issue targeted stock. *Journal of Financial Economics, 56*, 459–483.

Duchin, R., & Schmidt, B. (2013). Riding the merger wave: Uncertainty, reduced monitoring, and bad acquisitions. *Journal of Financial Economics, 107*, 69–88.

Duff, X., & Phelps, Y. (2010). Risk premium report—risk study. In S. Pratt & R. Grabowski (Eds.), *Cost of capital: Applications and examples* (4th ed.). New York: John Wiley & Sons.

Duffie, D., Saita, L., & Wang, K. (2007). Multi-period corporate default prediction with stochastic covariates. *Journal of Financial Economics, 83*, 635–665.

Dumontier, P., & Pecherot, B. (2001). *Determinants of returns to acquiring firms around tender offer announcement dates: The French evidence*. ESA Université de Grenoble: Working Paper.

Dunning, J. (1993). *Multinational enterprises and the global economy*. Reading, MA: Addison-Wesley.

Duru, A., Wang, D., & Zhao, Y. (2013). Staggered boards, corporate opacity, and firm value. *Journal of Banking and Finance, 37*, 341–360.

Dutordoir, M., Roosenboom, P., & Vasconcellos, M. (2010, May 17). Synergies disclosure in mergers and acquisitions. Erasmus University Working Paper, *Social Science Research Network*. http://ssrn.com/abstract=1571546.

Dutta, S., Iskandar-Dutta, M., & Raman, K. (2001). Executive compensation and corporate acquisition decisions. *Journal of Finance, 56*, 2299–2396.

Dutta, S., Shantanu, X., & Vijay Jog, Y. (2009). The long-term performance of acquiring firms: A re-examination of an anomaly. *Journal of Banking and Finance, 33*, 1400–1412.

Dyck, A., & Zingales, L. (2004). Control premiums and the effectiveness of corporate governance systems. *Journal of Applied Finance, 16*(Spring–Summer), 51–72.

Eberhart, A. C., Altman, E. I., & Aggarwal, R. (1999). The equity performance of firms emerging from bankruptcy. *Journal of Finance, 54*, 1855–1868.

Eckbo, B., & Thorburn, K. S. (2008). Automatic bankruptcy auctions and fire-sales. *Journal of Financial Economics, 89*, 404–422.

Eckbo, E., & Thorburn, K. S. (2000). Gains to bidder firms revisited: Domestic and foreign acquisitions in Canada. *Journal of Financial and Quantitative Analysis, 35*(March), 1–25.

Economist. (2006a). Battling for Corporate America XX 69–71.

Economist. (2006b). A Survey of the World Economy XX 12.

Economist. (2011, September 22). Why Global Stock Markets Have Become More Correlated.

Edmans, A., Goldstein, I., & Jiang, W. (2012). The real effects of financial markets: The impact on takeovers. *Journal of Finance, 67,* 933–971.

Elango, B., & Rakeh, B. (2004). The influence of industry structure on the entry mode choice of overseas entrants in manufacturing industries. *Journal of International Management, 10,* 107–124.

Elder, J., & Westra, P. (2000). The reaction of security prices to tracking stock announcements. *Journal of Economics and Finance, 24,* 36–55.

Elkamhi, R., Ericsson, J., & Parsons, C. (2012). The cost of financial distress and the timing of default. *Journal of Financial Economics, 105,* 62–81.

Harvard Business Review, 74(8)

Ellis, J., Moeller, S. B., Schlingemann, F. P., & Stulz, R. M. (2011). *Globalization, governance, and the returns to cross-border acquisitions,* NBER Working Paper No. 16676.

Ellison, S. (2006). Clash of cultures exacerbates woes for Tribune Co. *Wall Street Journal,* 1.

Emory, J. D. (2001). The value of marketability as illustrated in initial public offerings of common stock. *Business Valuation Review, 20,* 21–24.

Engel, E., Hayes, R., & Xang, X. (2004). The Sarbanes-Oxley act and firms' going private decisions. *Journal of Accounting and Economics, 44,* 116–145.

Erel, I., Liao, R., & Weisbach, M. (2012). Determinants of cross-border mergers and acquisitions. *Journal of Finance, 67,* 1045–1082.

Ertimur, Y., Ferri, F., & Stubben, S. (2010). Board of directors responsiveness to shareholders: Evidence from shareholder proposals. *Journal of Corporate Finance, 16,* 53–72.

Eun, C. S., Kolodny, R., & Scherage, C. (1996). Cross-border acquisition and shareholder wealth: Tests of the synergy and internationalization hypotheses. *Journal of Banking and Finance, 20,* 1559–1582.

Faccio, M., & Lang, L. H. P. (2002). The ultimate ownership of Western European corporations. *Journal of Financial Economics, 65,* 365–395.

Faccio, M., Lang, L., & Young, L. (2001). Dividends and expropriation. *American Economic Review, 91,* 54–78.

Faccio, M., & Masulis, R. (2005). The choice of payment method in European mergers and acquisitions. *Journal of Finance, 60,* 1345–1388.

Faccio, M., McConnell, J., & Stolin, D. (2006). Returns to acquirers of listed and unlisted companies. *Journal of Financial and Quantitative Analysis, 47,* 197–220.

Factset Mergerstat Review. (2011) http://www.bvresources.com/bvstore/selectbook.asp?pid=PUB259.

Faleye, O. (2004). Cash and corporate control. *Journal of Finance, 59,* 2041–2060.

Fama, E. F. (1998). Market efficiency, long-term returns, and behavioral finance. *Journal of Financial Economics, 47,* 427–465.

Fama, E. F., & French, K. R. (2006). The value premium and the CAPM. *Journal of Finance, 61,* 2163–2185.

Farzad, R. (2006). Fidelity's divided loyalties. *Business Week, 12.*

Fauver, L., Houston, J., & Narango, A. (2003). Capital market development, international integration, and the value of corporate diversification: A cross-country analysis. *Journal of Financial and Quantitative Analysis, 38,* 138–155.

Federal Reserve Bulletin. (2003). Board of Governors, U.S. Federal Reserve System: 33 December.

Federal Trade Commission. (1999a). Merger Guidelines; www.ftc.com.

Federal Trade Commission, Bureau of Competition. (1999b). *A study of the commission's divestiture process.*

Fee, C., Hadlock, C., & Pierce, J. (2012). What happens in acquisitions? Evidence from brand ownership changes and advertising investment. *Journal of Corporate Finance, 18,* 584–597.

Feliciano, Z., & Lipsey, R. E. (2002). *Foreign entry into U.S. manufacturing by takeovers and the creation of new firms.* National Bureau of Economic Research: Cambridge, MA, Working Paper 9122.

Fernandez, P., Aguirreamalloa, J., & Corres, L. (2012). Market Risk Premium Used in 82 Countries in 2012: A Survey of 7192 Answers. http://ssrn.com/abstract=2084213.

Ferreira, M., Massa, M., & Matos, P. (2010). Shareholders at the gate? Institutional investors and cross-border mergers and acquisitions. *Review of Financial Studies, 23,* 601–644.

Ferreira, M., Ornelas, E., & Turner, J. (2010). *Unbundling ownership and control.* Working Paper, London School of Economics.

Ferreira, M. P., & Tallman, S. B. (2005). *Building and leveraging knowledge capabilities through cross-border acquisitions*. Presentation to the Academy of Management Meeting.

Ferri, R. (2012). The total economy portfolio. *Forbes, June 25*, 174–175.

Fich, E. M., Tran, A. L., & Walkling, R. A. (2013). On the importance of golden parachutes. *Journal of Financial and Quantitative Analysis* (forthcoming).

Fidrmuc, J., Roosenboom, P., Paap, R., & Teunissen, T. (2012). One size does not fit all: Selling firms to private equity versus strategic acquirers. *Journal of Corporate Finance, 18*, 828–849.

Field, L. C., & Karpoff, J. M. (2002). Takeover defenses of IPO firms. *Journal of Finance, 57*, 1629–1666.

Fields, L. P., & Mais, E. L. (1991). The valuation effects of private placements of convertible debt. *Journal of Finance, 46*, 1925–1932.

Financial Times. (1996). Bugged by Failures (April 8), 8.

Finnerty, J. D. (2002). *The impact of transfer restrictions on stock prices*. Analysis Group/Economics: Cambridge, MA; Working Paper.

Finnerty, J. D., Jiao, J., & Yan, A. (2012). Convertible securities in merger transactions. *Journal of Banking and Finance, 36*, 275–289.

Foley, L. L. P., & Lardner (2007). *What private companies and non-profits need to know about SOX*. Report presented at Foley and Lardner's 2004 National Directors Institute Meeting, Chicago.

Forte, G., Iannotta, G., & Vavone, M. (2010). The banking relationship's role in the choice of target's advisor in mergers and acquisitions. *European Financial Management, 16*, 686–701.

France, M. (2002). Bankruptcy reform won't help telecom. *Business Week, 40*.

Francis, B., Hasan, I., & Sun, X. (2008). Financial market integration and the value of global diversification: Evidence for U.S. acquirers in cross-border mergers and acquisitions. *Journal of Banking and Finance, 32*, 1522–1540.

Franks, J., & Mayer, C. (1996). Hostile takeovers and the correction of managerial failure. *Journal of Financial Economics, 40*, 163–181.

Franks, J., Mayer, C., Volpin, P., & Wagner, H. (2012). The life cycle of family ownership: International evidence. *Review of Financial Studies, 25*, 1675–1712.

Frazoni, F., Nowak, E., & Phalippou, L. (2012). Private equity performance and liquidity risk. *Journal of Finance, 67*, 2341–2373.

Frick, K. A., & Torres, A. (2002). Learning from high-tech deals. *McKinsey Quarterly, 1*, 2.

Fulghieri, P., & Sevilir, M. (2011). Mergers, spin-offs, and employee incentives. *Review of Financial Studies, 24*, 2207–2241.

Fuller, K., Netter, J., & Stegemoller, M. A. (2002). What do returns to acquiring firms tell us? Evidence from firms that make many acquisitions. *Journal of Finance, 57*, 1763–1793.

Furfine, C., & Rosen, R. (2011). Mergers increase default risk. *Journal of Corporate Finance, 17*, 832–849.

Gantchev, N. (2013). The costs of shareholder activism: Evidence from a sequential decision model. *Journal of Financial Economics* (forthcoming).

Gao, H., Harford, J., & Li, K. (2010). *Determinants of corporate cash policy: A comparison of private and public firms*, University of Washington Working Paper.

Garcia-Feijoo, L., Madura, J., & Ngo, T. (2012). Impact of industry characteristics on the method of payment in mergers. *Journal of Economics and Business, 64*, 261–274.

Garlappi, L., & Yan, H. (2011). Financial distress and the cross section of equity returns. *Journal of Finance, 66*, 789–822.

Gaspara, J. M., & Massa, P. (2005). Shareholder investment horizons and the market for corporate control. *Journal of Financial Economics, 76*, 135–165.

Gell, J., Kengelbach, J., & Roos, A. (2008). *The return of the strategist: Creating value with M&A in downturns*. Boston: Boston Consulting Group.

Georgopoulos, G. (2008). Cross-border mergers and acquisitions: Do exchange rates matter? Some evidence for Canada. *Canadian Journal of Economics, 41*, 450–474.

Gertner, R., Powers, E., & Scharfstein, D. (2002). Learning about internal capital markets from corporate spin-offs. *Journal of Finance, 57*, 2479–2506.

Ghosh, A. (2004). Increasing market share as a rationale for corporate acquisitions. *Journal of Business, Finance, and Accounting, 31*, 78–91.

Ghosh, A., & Lee, C. W. J. (2000). Abnormal returns and expected managerial performance of target firms. *Financial Management, 29*(Spring), 40–52.

Gillan, S., & Starks, L. (2007). The evolution of shareholder activism in the United States. *Journal of Applied Corporate Finance, 19*, 55–73.

Gillette, F. (2011). The rise and inglorious fall of myspace. *Bloomberg Businessweek, July 3*, 54–57.

Gilson, S. (1997). Transactions costs and capital structure choice: Evidence from financially distressed firms. *Journal of Finance, 52*(March), 161–196.

Gilson, S. C., Healy, P. M., Noe, C. F., & Palepu, L. G. (2001). Analyst specialization and conglomerate stock breakups. *Journal of Accounting Research, 39*, 565–582.

Gilson, S., John, K., & Lang, L. H. (1990). Troubled debt restructuring: An empirical study of private reorganization of firms in default. *Journal of Financial Economics, 27*, 315–353.

Goktan, M. S., & Kieschnick, R. (2012). A target's perspective on the effects of ATPs in takeovers after recognizing its choice in the process. *Journal of Corporate Finance, 18*, 1088–1103.

Goldblatt, H. (1999). Merging at internet speed. *Fortune, November 8*, 164–165.

Golubov, A., Petmezas, D., & Travlos, N. (2011). When it pays to pay your investment banker: New evidence on the role of financial advisors in M&As. *Journal of Finance and Quantitative Analysis, 38*, 475–501.

Gomes-Casseres, B., Hagedoorn, J., & Jaffe, A. (2006). Do alliances promote knowledge transfers? *Journal of Financial Economics, 80*, 5–33.

Gompers, P. A., Ishii, J., & Metrick, A. (2010). Extreme governance: An analysis of U.S. dual-class companies in the United States. *Review of Financial Studies, 23*, 1051–1088.

Gondhalekar, V., Sant, R., & Ferris, S. (2004). The price of corporate acquisition: Determinants of takeover premia. *Applied Economics Letters, 11*, 735–739.

Gordon, J. N. (2007). The rise of independent directors in the Unites States, 1950–2005: Of shareholder value and stock market prices. *Stanford Law Review, 1465*, 1472–1476.

Gormley, T. A., & Matsa, D. A. (2011). Growing out of trouble? Corporate responses to liability risk. *Review of Financial Studies, 25*, 2781–2821.

Gorton, G., Kahl, M., & Rosen, R. J. (2009). Eat or be eaten: A theory of mergers and firm size. *Journal of Finance, 64*, 1291–1344.

Gottschalg, O. (2012). Bain or blessing? *The Economist, January 28*, pp. 73–74.

Goyal, V. K., & Park, C. W. (2002). Board leadership structure and CEO turnover. *Journal of Corporate Finance, 8*, 49–66.

Graham, J. R. (2000). How big are the tax benefits of debt? *Journal of Finance, 55*, 1901–1941.

Graham, J. R., & Harvey, C. R. (2001). The theory and practice of corporate finance: Evidence from the field. *Journal of Financial Economics, 60*, 187–243.

Graham, J., Lemmon, M., & Wolf, J. (2002). Does diversification destroy firm value? *Journal of Finance, 57*, 695–720.

Graham, M., Martey, E., & Yawson, A. (2008). Acquisitions from UK firms into emerging markets. *Global Finance Journal, 19*, 56–71.

Greenaway, D., & Kneller, R. (2007). Firm heterogeneity, exporting, and foreign direct investment. *Economic Journal, Deposition/Interrogatory Review, 117*, 134–161.

Greenwood, R., & Schor, M. (2007). *Hedge fund investor activism and takeovers*. Working Paper. Harvard Business School: Cambridge, MA.

Grice, S., & Dugan, M. (2001). The limitations of bankruptcy prediction models: Some cautions for the researcher. *Review of Quantitative Finance and Accounting, 17*, 151–166.

Grice, S., & Ingram, R. (2001). Tests of the generalizability of Altman's Bankruptcy prediction model. *Journal of Business Research, 54*, 53–61.

Grinblatt, M., & Titman, S. (2002). *Financial markets and corporate strategy* (2nd ed.). New York: McGraw-Hill.

Groh, A., & Gottschaig, O. (2006). *The risk-adjusted performance of U.S. Buyouts*. Paris: HEC.

Gu, F., & Lev, B. (2011). Overpriced shares, Ill-advised acquisitions, and goodwill impairment. *The Accounting Review, 86*, 1995–2022.

Gugler, K., Mueller, D. C., Yurtoglu, B. B., & Zulehner, C. (2003). The effects of mergers: An international comparison. *International Journal of Industrial Organization, 21*(5), 625–653. (May 2003).

Gugler, K., Mueller, D., & Weichselbaumer, M. (2012). The determinants of merger waves: An international perspective. *International Journal of Industrial Organization, 30,* 1–15.

Guo, S., Hotchkiss, E. S., & Song, W. (2011). Do buyouts (still) create value? *Journal of Finance, 66,* 479–517.

Guo, R. J., Kruse, T. A., & Nohel, T. (2008). Undoing the powerful anti-takeover force of staggered boards. *Journal of Corporate Finance, 14,* 274–288.

Gurung, A., & Lerner, J. (2008). *The global economic impact of private equity.* Cambridge, MA: World Economic Forum and Harvard Business School.

Habbershon, T. G., & Williams, M. L. (1999). A resource-based framework for assessing the strategic advantages of family firms. *Family Business Review, 12,* 1–26.

Hackbarth, D., & Morellec, E. (2008). Stock returns in mergers and acquisitions. *Journal of Finance, 63,* 1213–1252.

Hall, B. (1992). *Investment and research and development at the firm level: Does the source of financing matter?* National Bureau of Economic Research: Working Paper No. 4096.

Hall, L. S., & Polacek, T. C. (1994). Strategies for obtaining the largest valuation discounts. *Estate Planning,* 38–44.

Hamel, G. C., & Prahalad, C. K. (1994). *Competing for the future.* Cambridge, MA: Harvard Business School Press.

Hanouna, P., Sarin, A., & Shapiro, A. (2001). *The value of corporate control: Some international evidence.* Marshall School of Business, University of Southern California: Los Angeles; Working Paper.

Hanson, R. C., & Song, M. H. (2000). Managerial ownership, board structure, and the division of gains. *Journal of Corporate Finance, 6,* 55–70.

Hao, K. Y., & Jaffe, A. B. (1993). The impact of corporate restructuring on industrial research and development. *Brookings Papers on Economic Activity, 1,* 275–282.

Harding, D., & Rovit, S. (2004). *Mastering the merger: Four critical decisions that make or break the deal.* Cambridge, MA: Harvard Business School Press.

Harford, J. (1999). Corporate cash reserves and acquisitions. *Journal of Finance, 54,* 1969–1997.

Harford, J. (2005). What drives merger waves? *Journal of Financial Economics, 77,* 529–560.

Harford, J., & Kolasinski, A. (2012, January 20). Do Private Equity Sponsors Sacrifice Long-Term Value for Short-Term Profit? Evidence from a Comprehensive Sample of Large Buyout and Exit Outcomes, http://ssrn.com/abstract=1785927.

Harper, N. W., & Schneider, A. (2004). Where mergers go wrong. *McKinsey Quarterly, Number 2.*

Harris, O., & Glegg, C. (2007). The wealth effects of cross-border spin-offs. *Journal of Multinational Financial Management, 18,* 461–476.

Harris, R. S., Jenkinson, T., & Kaplan, S. N. (2011, September 22). *Private equity performance: What do we know?* NBER Working Paper 17874.

Harris, R. S., & Ravenscraft, D. (1991). The role of acquisitions in foreign direct investment: Evidence from the U.S. stock market. *Journal of Finance, 46,* 825–844.

Hartman, T. E. (2005). The costs of being public in the Era of Sarbanes-Oxley. *Foley & Lardner LLP Annual Survey.*

Harvey, C. R. (2005). *Twelve ways to calculate the international cost of capital.* Duke University and National Bureau of Economic Research Working Paper, October 14.

Harzing, A. W. (2002). Acquisitions versus greenfield investments: International strategy and management of entry modes. *Strategic Management Journal, 23,* 211–227.

Hayes, R. H. (1979). The human side of acquisitions. *Management Review, 41,* 41–46.

Hayward, M., & Hambrick, D. (1997). Explaining the premiums paid for large acquisitions: Evidence of CEO hubris. *Administrative Science Quarterly, 35,* 621–633.

Heflin, F., Subramanyam, K., & Zhang, Y. (2001). Regulation FD and the financial information environment: Early evidence. *Accounting Review, 78,* 1–37.

Hennart, J. F., & Park, Y. R. (1993). Location, governance, and strategic determinants of Japanese manufacturing investment in the United States. *Journal of Strategic Management, 15,* 419–436.

Hennart, J. F., & Reddy, S. (1997). The choice between mergers, acquisitions, and joint ventures: The case of Japanese investors in the United States. *Strategic Management Journal, 18,* 1–12.

Hennessy, C. A., & Whited, T. M. (2007). How costly is external financing? Evidence from a structural estimation. *Journal of Finance, 62*, 1705–1745.

Henry, D. (2001). The numbers game. *Business Week, May 14*, 100–103.

Henry, D. (2002). Mergers: Why most big deals don't pay off. *Business Week, October 14*, 60–64.

Henry, D. (2003). A fair deal—but for whom. *Business Week, September 11*, 108–109.

Heron, R., & Lie, E. (2002). Operating performance and the method of payment in takeovers. *Journal of Financial and Quantitative Analysis, 37*, 137–155.

Hertzel, M. G., Li, Z., Officer, M. S., & Rodgers, K. J. (2008). Inter-firm linkages and the wealth effects of financial distress along the supply chain. *Journal of Financial Economics, 87*, 374–387.

Hertzel, B. M., & Smith, R. L. (1993). Market discounts and shareholder gains for placing equity privately. *Journal of Finance, 48*, 459–485.

Hillyer, C., & Smolowitz, I. (1996). Why do mergers fail to achieve synergy? *Director's Monthly*, January, p. 13.

Himmelberg, C. P., & Petersen, B. C. (1994). R&D and internal finance: A panel study of small firms in high-tech industries. *Review of Economics and Statistics, 76*, 38–51.

Hitt, J. M. A., & Ireland, R. D. (2000). The intersection of entrepreneurship and strategic management research. In D. Sexton & H. Landstrom (Eds.), *The Blackwell handbook of entrepreneurship*. Oxford, UK: Blackwell.

Hoechle, D., Schmid, M., Walter, I., & Yermack, D. (2012). How much of the diversification discount can be explained by poor corporate governance? *Journal of Financial Economics, 103*, 41–60.

Hoffman, W. H., & Schaper-Rinkel, W. (2001). Acquire or ally?—a strategic framework for deciding between acquisition and cooperation. *Management International Review, 41*, 131–159.

Hogan, K. M., & Olson, G. T. (2004). The pricing of equity carve-outs during the 1990s. *Journal of Financial Research, 27*(Winter), 521–537.

Holthausen, R. W., & Larker, D. F. (1996). The financial performance of reverse leveraged buyouts. *Journal of Financial Economics, 42*, 293–332.

Horton, T. (2011). The new United States horizontal merger guidelines: Devolution, evolution, or counterrevolution? *Journal of European Competition Law and Practice, 2*, 158–164.

Hotchkiss, E. S. (1995). The post-emergence performance of firms emerging from Chapter 11. *Journal of Finance, 50*, 3–21.

Hotchkiss, E., Qian, J., & Song, W. (2005). *Holdup, renegotiation, and deal protection in mergers* Boston College: Working Paper.

Houston, J., James, C., & Ryngaert, M. (2001). Where do merger gains come from? *Journal of Financial Economics, 60*, 285–331.

Hsu, J. C., Saa-Requejo, J., & Santa-Clara, P. (2002). *Bond pricing and default risk*. UCLA Working Paper.

Huang, J., Pierce, J., & Tsyplakov, S. (2011). Post-merger integration duration and leverage dynamics of mergers: Theory and evidence, http://ssrn.com/sol3/delivery.cfm?abstractid=1787265.

Hulburt, H. M., Miles, J. A., & Wollridge, J. R. (2002). Value creation from equity carve-outs. *Financial Management, 31*(Spring), 83–100.

Hunt, P. (2003). *Structuring mergers and acquisitions: A guide to creating shareholder value*. New York: Aspen.

Hunter, W., & Jagtiani, J. (2003). An analysis of advisor choice, fees, and effort in mergers and acquisitions. *Review of Financial Economics, 12*, 65–81.

Hurter, W. H., Petersen, J. R., & Thompson, K. E. (2005). *Merger, acquisitions, and 1031 tax exchanges*. New York: Lorman Education Services.

Huson, M. R., & MacKinnon, G. (2003). Corporate spin-offs and information asymmetry between investors. *Journal of Economics and Management Strategy, 9*, 481–501.

Hyland, D., & Diltz, J. (2002). Why firms diversify: An empirical examination. *Financial Management, 31*, 51–81.

Ibbotson, R., Kaplan, P., & Peterson, J. (1997). Estimate of small stock betas are much too low. *Journal of Portfolio Management Summer*, 104–111.

Ibbotson Associates, (2002). *Stock, bonds, bills, and inflation, valuation edition yearbook*. Chicago: Ibbotson Associates Inc.

Inkpen, A. C., & Beamish, P. W. (1997). Knowledge, bargaining power, and the instability of international joint ventures. *Academy of Management Review, 22*, 177–202.

Isakov, D., & Sonney, F. (2002). *Are parishioners right? On the relative importance of industrial factors in international stock returns.* HEC-University of Geneva: Working Paper.

Ismail, A. (2010). Are good financial advisors really good? The performance of investment banks in the M&A market. *Review of Quantitative Finance and Accounting, 35*, 411–429.

Ismail, A. (2011). Does management's forecast of merger synergies explain the premium paid, method of payment, and management motives? *Financial Management, Winter, 879*–910.

Ismail, A., & Krause, A. (2010). Determinants of the method of payment in mergers and acquisitions. *The Quarterly Review of Economics and Finance, 50*, 471–484.

Jaffe, A. B., & Trajtenberg, M. (2002). *Patents, citations, and innovations: A window on the knowledge economy.* Cambridge, MA: MIT Press.

Jain, B., Kini, O., & Shenoy, J. (2011). Vertical divestitures through equity carve-outs and spin-offs: A product markets perspective. *Journal of Financial Economics, 100*, 594–615.

Jarrow, R., & Turnbull, S. (1995). Pricing derivative on financial securities subject to credit risk. *Journal of Finance, 50*, 1449–1470.

Jenkinson, T., & Stucke, R. (2011). Who benefits from the leverage in LBOs? http://ssrn.com/abstract=1777266.

Jensen, M. C. (1986). Agency costs of free cash flow, corporate finance, and takeovers. *American economic association papers and proceedings* (May) (323–329).

Jensen, M. C. (2005). Agency costs of overvalued equity. *Financial Management, 34*(Spring), 5–19.

Jeon, J. Q., & Ligonb, J. A. (2011). How much is reasonable? The size of termination fees in mergers and acquisitions. *Journal of Corporate Finance, 17*, 959–981.

Jiang, W., Li, K., & Wang, W. (2012). Hedge funds and Chapter 11. *Journal of Finance, 67*, 513–560.

Jindra, J., & Walkling, R. (2004). Arbitrage spreads and the market pricing of proposed acquisitions. *Journal of Corporate Finance, 10*, 495–526.

John, K., & Ofek, E. (1995). Asset sales and increase in focus. *Journal of Financial Economics, 37*, 105–126.

Johnson, B. (1999). Quantitative support for discounts for lack of marketability. *Business Valuation Review, 132*.

Johnson, S. A., & Houston, M. B. (2000). A re-examination of the motives and gains in joint ventures. *Journal of Financial and Quantitative Analysis, 35*, 67–85.

Jones, S., & Hensher, D. (2008). *Advances in credit risk modeling and corporate bankruptcy prediction.* Cambridge, England: Cambridge University Press.

Kahle, K., & Walkling, R. (1996). The impact of industry classification on financial research. *Journal of Financial and Quantitative Analysis, 31*, 309–335.

Kahya, E., & Theodosiou, P. (1999). Predicting corporate financial distress: A time-series cusum methodology. *Review of Quantitative Finance and Accounting, 13*, 323–345.

Kaiser, K. M. J., & Stouraitis, A. (2001). Revering corporate diversification and the use of the proceeds from asset sales: The case of thorn emi. *Financial Management, 30*, 63–101.

Kale, P., Dyer, J. H., & Singh, H. (2002). Alliance capability, stock market response, and long-term alliance success: The role of the alliance function. *Strategic Management Journal, 23*(August), 747–767.

Kalmbach,Jr. C., & Roussel, C. (1999). *Dispelling the myths of alliances.* Andersen Consulting: Available at www.accenture.com/xd/xd.asp?it=enWeb&xd=ideas/outlook/special99/over_special_intro.xml.

Kamar, E., Karaca-Mandic, P., & Talley, E. (2009). Going-private decisions and the Sarbanes-Oxley Act of 2002: A cross-country analysis. *Journal of Law, Economics, and Organization, 25*, 107–133.

Kang, J. K., & Kim, J. M. (2008). The geography of block acquisitions. *Journal of Finance, 63*, 2817–2858.

Kang, J. K., & Shivdasani, A. (1997). Corporate restructuring during performance declines in Japan. *Journal of Financial Economics, 46*, 29–65.

Kantor, R. M. (2002). Collaborative advantage: The art of alliances: *Harvard Business Review on Strategic Alliances.* Cambridge, MA: Harvard Business School Press.

Kaplan, P., & Peterson, J. (1998). Full information industry betas. *Financial Management, 27*, 85–93.

Kaplan, S. N. (1988). *Management buyouts: Efficiency gains or value transfers.* University of Chicago: Working Paper 244.

Kaplan, S. N. (1989). The effects of management buyouts on operating performance and value. *Journal of Financial Economics, 24*, 217–254.

Kaplan, S. N. (1989). Management buyouts: Efficiency gains or value transfers. *Journal of Finance, 3*, 611–632.

Kaplan, S. N. (1991). The staying power of leveraged buyouts. *Journal of Financial Economics, 29*, 287–313.

Kaplan, S. N. (1997). The evolution of U.S. corporate governance: We are all Henry Kravis now. *Journal of Private Equity, Fall*, 7–14.

Kaplan, S. N. (2012). How to think about private equity. *The Journal of the American Enterprise Institute.*

Kaplan, S. N., & Schoar, A. (2005). Returns, persistence and capital flows. *Journal of Finance, 60*, 1791–1823.

Kaplan, S. N., & Stromberg, P. (2009). Leveraged buyouts and private equity. *Journal of Economic Perspectives, 23*, 121–146.

Kaplan, S. N., & Weisbach, M. S. (1992). The success of acquisitions: Evidence from divestitures. *Journal of Finance, 47*, 107–138.

Karpoff, J. M. (2001). *The impact of shareholder activism on target companies: A survey of empirical findings.* University of Washington: Working Paper.

Karpoff, J. M., & Malatesta, P. H. (1989). The wealth effects of second-generation state takeover legislation. *Journal of Financial Economics, 25*, 291–322.

Karpoff, J. M., & Walkling, R. A. (1996). Corporate governance and shareholder initiatives: Empirical evidence. *Journal of Financial Economics, 42*, 365–395.

Katz, S. (2008). *Earnings quality and ownership structure: The role of private equity sponsors.* NBER Working Paper No. W14085.

Kedia, S., Ravid, S., & Pons, V. (2011). When do vertical mergers create value? *Financial Management, Winter*, 845–877.

Kedia, S., & Zhou, X. (2011). Local market makers, liquidity and market quality. *Journal of Financial Markets, 14*, 540–567.

Kennedy, K., & Moore, M. (2003). *Going the distance: Why some companies dominate and others fail.* Upper Saddle River, NJ: Prentice-Hall.

Khanna, T., Palepu, K., & Sinha, J. (2005). Strategies that fit emerging markets. *Harvard Business Review, 83*, 63–74.

Khorana, A., Shivdasani, A., Stendevad, C., & Sanzhar, S. (2011). Spin-offs: Tackling the conglomerate discount. *Journal of Applied Corporate Finance, 23*, 90–102.

Kim, I. J., Ramaswamy, K., & Sundaresan, S. (1993). Does default risk in coupons affect the valuation of corporate bonds? A contingent claims model. *Financial Management, 22*, 117–131.

Kini, I., Kracaw, W., & Mian, S. (2004). The nature of discipline by corporate takeovers. *Journal of Finance, 59*, 1511–1552.

Kisgen, D. J., Qian, J., & Song, W. (2009). Are fairness opinions fair? The case of mergers and acquisitions. *Journal of Financial Economics, 91*, 178–207.

Klaus, M., Estrin, S., Bhaumik, S., & Peng, M. (2008). Institutions, resources, and entry strategies in emerging countries. *Strategic Management Journal, 31*, 61–80.

Klein, A., & Zur, E. (2009). Entrepreneurial shareholder activism: Hedge funds and other private investors. *Journal of Finance.*

Klein, K.E. (2004). Urge to merge? Take care to beware. *Business Week*, July 1, p. 68.

Koedijk, K., Kool, C., Schotman, P., & Van Kijk, M. (2002). *The cost of capital in international markets: Local or global.* Centre for Economic Policy Research: Working Paper.

Koedijk, K., & Van Dijk, M. (2000). *The cost of capital of cross-listed firms, rotterdam.* Erasmus University: Working Paper.

Koeplin, J., Sarin, A., & Shapiro, A. C. (2000). The private equity discount. *Journal of Applied Corporate Finance, 12*, 94–101.

Kogut, B., & Singh, H. (1988). The effect of national culture on the choice of entry mode. *Journal of International Business Studies, 19*, 411–432.

Kohers, N., & Ang, J. (2000). Earnouts in mergers: Agreeing to disagree and agreeing to stay. *Journal of Finance, 73*, 445–476.

Koller, T., Goedart, M., & Wessels, D. (2010). *Valuation: Measuring and managing the value of companies.* New York: John Wiley & Sons.

Korteweg, A (2010). The net benefits to leverage. *Journal of Finance, 65,* 2137–2170.

KPMG. (2006a). When hedge funds start to look like private equity firms. *Global M&A Spotlight* (Spring).

KPMG. (2006b). Mergers and acquisitions. *2006 M&A Outlook Survey.*

Kranhold, K. (2006). GE's water unit remains stagnant as it struggles to integrate acquisitions. *Wall Street Journal,* August 23, p. C2.

Krishnan, C. N. V., Masulis, R. W., Thomas, R. S., & Thompson, R. B. (2012). Stakeholder litigation in mergers and acquisitions. *Journal of Corporate Finance, 18,* 1248–1268.

Kuipers, D., Miller, D., & Patel, A. (2009). The legal environment and corporate valuation: Evidence from cross-border mergers. *International Review of Economics and Finance, 18,* 552–567.

Kwak, W., Cheng, X., & Ni, J. (2012). Predicting bankruptcy after the Sarbanes-Oxley act using logit analysis. *Journal of Business & Economics Research, 10,* 521–532.

Lajoux, A. R. (1998). *The art of M&A integration.* New York: McGraw-Hill.

Lang, L., & Stulz, R. M. (1992). Contagion and competitive intra-industry effects of bankruptcy announcements. *Journal of Financial Economics, 81,* 45–60.

Lang, L., Poulsen, A., & Stulz, R. (1995). Asset sales, firm performance, and the agency costs of managerial discretion. *Journal of Financial Economics, 37,* 3–37.

La Porta, R., Lopez-de-Sklanes, F., Schleifer, A., & Vishny, R. (2002). Investor protection and corporate valuation. *Journal of Finance, 57,* 1147–1170.

Lattman, P., & de la Merced, M. J. (2010). September 1. Old GM being sold in parts. *New York Times,* p. 23.

Leeth, J. D., & Rody Borg, J. (2000). The impact of takeovers on shareholders' wealth during the 1920s merger wave. *Journal of Financial and Quantitative Analysis, 35,* 29–38.

Lehn, K. M., & Zhao, M. (2006). CEO turnover after acquisitions: Are bad bidders fired? *Journal of Finance, 61,* 1383–1412.

Leland, H. E. (1994). Corporate debt value, bond covenants, and optimal capital structure. *Journal of Finance, 49,* 1213–1252.

Le Nadant, A. L., & Perdreau, F. (2012). *Do private equity firms foster innovation? Evidence from French LBOs.* Working Paper, University de Caen.

Lerner, J., Shane, H., & Tsai, A. (2003). Do equity financing cycles matter? *Journal of Financial Economics, 67,* 411–446.

Lerner, J., Sorensen, M., & Stromberg, P. (2011). Private equity and long-run investment: The case of innovation. *Journal of Finance, 66,* 445–477.

Leuz, C., Triantis, A., & Wang, T. Y. (2008). Why do firms go dark? Causes and economic consequences of voluntary SEC deregistrations. *Journal of Accounting and Economics, 45,* 181–208.

Levine, D. M., Berenson, M. L., & Stephan, D. (1999). *Statistics for managers* (2nd ed.). New York: Prentice-Hall.

Levit, D., & Malenko, N. (2012). Non-binding voting for shareholder proposals. *Journal of Finance, 66,* 1579–1614.

Li, J. (2012). Prediction of corporate bankruptcy from june 2008 through 2011. *Journal of Accounting and Finance, 12,* 31–42.

Lichtenberg, F. R., & Siegel, D. (1990). The effects of lbos on productivity and related aspects of firm behavior. *Journal of Financial Economics, 27,* 165–194.

Lim, S. C., Mann, S. C., & Mihov, V. T. (2004, December 1). Market Evaluation of Off-Balance Sheet Financing: You Can Run but You Can't Hide. EFMA Basel Meetings Paper.

Linck, J., Netter, J., & Yang, T. (2009). The effects and unintended consequences of the Sarbanes-Oxley act on the supply and demand for directors. *The Review of Financial Studies, 22,* 3287–3328.

Linn, S. C., & Switzer, J. A. (2001). Are cash acquisitions associated with better post-combination operating performance than stock acquisitions? *Journal of Banking and Finance, 25,* 1113–1138.

Lins, K. (2003). Equity ownership and firm value in emerging markets. *Journal of Financial and Quantitative Analysis, 38,* 159–184.

Lins, K., & Servaes, H. (1999). International evidence on the value of corporate diversification. *Journal of Finance, 54*, 2215–2239.

Listokin, Y. (2009). Corporate voting versus market price setting. *American Law and Economics Review, 11*, 608–637.

Liu, J., Nissim, D., & Thomas, J. K. (2002). Equity valuation using multiples. *Journal of Accounting Research, 40*(1), 135–172.

Liu, J., Nissim, D., & Thomas, J. (2007). Is cash flow king in valuations? *Financial Analysts Journal, 63*, 56–65.

Logue, D. E., Seward, J. K., & Walsh, J. W. (1996). Rearranging residual claims: A case for targeted stock. *Financial Management, 25*, 43–61.

Loh, C., Bezjak, J. R., & Toms, H. (1995). Voluntary corporate divestitures as an anti-takeover mechanism. *Financial Review, 30*, 21–24.

Longstaff, F. A. (1995). How can marketability affect security values? *Journal of Finance, 50*, 1767–1774.

Longstaff, F. A., & Schwartz, E. S. (1995). A simple approach to valuing risky fixed and floating rate debt. *Journal of Finance, 50*, 789–819.

Lord, M. D., & Ranft, A. L. (2000). Acquiring new knowledge: The role of retaining human capital in acquisitions of high-tech firms. *Journal of High-Technology Management Research, 11*, 295–320.

Lott, T. (2007). *Career guide to investment banking* (6th ed.). New York: Vault.

Loughran, T., & Ritter, J. (2002). Why don't issuers get upset about leaving money on the table in IPOs? *Review of Financial Studies, 15*, 413–443.

Loughran, T., Anand, M., & Vijh, A. (1997). Do long-term shareholders benefit from corporate acquisitions? *Journal of Finance, 22*, 321–340.

Loughran, T., Ritter, J., & Rydqvist, K. (1994). Initial public offerings: International insights. *Pacific Basin Finance Journal, 2*, 165–199.

Lynch, R. P. (1990). *The practical guide to joint ventures and corporate alliances*. New York: Wiley.

Lynch, R. P. (1993). *Business alliance guide: The hidden competitive weapon*. New York: Wiley.

Lyon, J. D., Barber, B. M., & Tsai, C. L. (1999). Improved methods for tests of long-run abnormal stock returns. *Journal of Finance, 54*, 165–201.

Morgan, J. P. (1999). *Monitoring spin-off Performances*. New York: Morgan Markets.

Madura, J., & Ngo, T. (2012). Determinants of the medium of payment used to acquire privately held targets. *Journal of Economics and Finance, 36*, 424–442.

Madura, J., Ngo, T., & Viale, A. (2012). Why do merger premiums vary across industries and over time? *The Quarterly Review of Economics and Finance, 52*, 49–62.

Madura, J., & Whyte, A. (1990). Diversification benefits of direct foreign investment. *Management International Review, 30*, 73–85.

Maguire, S., & Phillips, N. (2008). Citibankers at citigroup: A study of the loss on institutional trust after a merger. *Journal of Management Studies, 45*, 372–401.

Maksimovic, V., & Phillips, G. M. (2001). The market for corporate assets: Who engages in mergers and asset sales and are there efficiency gains? *Journal of Finance, 56*, 332–355.

Maksimovic, V., Phillips, G., & Prabhala, N. R. (2011). Post-merger restructuring and the boundaries of the firm. *Journal of Financial Economics, 102*, 317–343.

Maksimovic, V., Phillips, G., & Yang, L. (2013). Private and public merger waves. *Journal of Finance* (forthcoming).

Malatesta, P. H., & Walkling, R. A. (1988). Poison pills securities: Stockholder wealth, profitability and ownership structure. *Journal of Financial Economics, 20*, 347–376.

Malekzadeh, A. R., McWilliams, V. B., & Sen, N. (1998). Implications of CEO structural and ownership power, ownership, and board composition on the market's reaction to antitakeover charter amendments. *Journal of Applied Business Research, 14*, 53–62.

Malekzadeh, A. R., & Nahavandi, A. (1990). Making mergers work by managing cultures. *Journal of Business Strategy, 11*, 55–57.

Mallea, J. (2008). *A review of mergers of equals*. http://FactSetmergermetrics.com.

Malmendier, U., & Tate, G. (2008). Who makes acquisitions? CEO overconfidence and the market's reaction. *Journal of Financial Economics, 89*, 20–43.

Malmendier, U., Tate, G., & Yan, J. (2011). Overconfidence and early-life experiences: The impact of managerial traits on corporate financial policies. *Journal of Finance, 66,* 1687–1733.

Manzon, K. G. K., Sharp, D. J., & Travlos, N. (1994). An empirical study of the consequences of U.S. tax rules for international acquisitions by U.S. firms. *Journal of Finance, 49,* 1893–1904.

Maquierira, C. P., Megginson, W. L., & Nail, L. A. (1998). Wealth creation versus wealth redistributions in pure stock-for-stock mergers. *Journal of Financial Economics, 48,* 3–33.

Markides, C., & Oyon, D. (1998). International acquisitions: Do they create value for shareholders? *European Management Journal, 16,* 125–135.

Marks, M. L. (1996). *From turmoil to triumph: New life after mergers, acquisitions, and downsizing.* Lanham, MD: Lexington Books.

Marquez, R., & Singh, R. (2013). The economics of club bidding and value creation. *Journal of Financial Economics* (forthcoming).

Martynova, M., & Renneboog, L. (2008). A century of corporate takeovers: What have we learned and where do we stand? *Journal of Banking and Finance, 32,* 2148–2177.

Martynova, M., & Renneboog, L. (2008). Spillover of corporate governance standards in cross-border mergers and acquisitions. *Journal of Corporate Finance, 14,* 200–223.

Massari, M., Monge, V., & Zanetti, L. (2006). Control premium in the presence of rules imposing mandatory tender offers: Can it be measured? *Journal of Management and Governance, 22,* 101–110.

Masulis, R. W., Wang, C., & Xie, F. (2009). Agency problems in dual-class companies. *Journal of Finance, 64,* 1697–1727.

Masulis, R. W., Wang, C., & Xie, F. (2007). Corporate governance and acquirer returns. *Journal of Finance, 62,* 1851–1890.

Masulis, R. W., & Nahata, R. (2011). Venture capital conflicts of interest: Evidence from acquisitions of venture-backed firms. *Journal of Financial and Quantitative Analysis, 46,* 395–420.

Maxwell, W. F., & Rao, R. P. (2003). Do spin-offs expropriate wealth from bondholders? *Journal of Finance, 58*(5), 2087–2108.

McConnell, J. J., & Nantell, T. J. (1985). Corporate combinations and common stock returns: The case of joint ventures. *Journal of Finance, 40*(June), 519–536.

McConnell, J. J., Ozbilgin, M., & Wahal, S. (2001). Spin-offs: Ex ante. *Journal of Business, 74,* 245–280.

McCoy, K. & Chu, K. (2011). Merger of U.S. and Chinese firms is a cautionary tale. *USA Today,* December 26, p. 6.

McNamara, G., Dykes, B. J., & Haleblian, J. (2008). The performance implications of participating in an acquisition wave. *Academy of Management Journal, 51,* 744–767.

McNeil, C. R., & Moore, W. T. (2005). Dismantling internal capital markets via spin-off: Effects on capital allocation efficiency and firm valuation. *Journal of Corporate Finance, 11,* 253–275.

Megginson, W. L., Morgan, A., & Nail, L. (2003). The determinants of positive long-term performance in strategic mergers: Corporate focus and cash. *Journal of Banking and Finance, 28,* 523–552.

Mercer, C. (1997). *The management panning study: Quantifying marketability discounts.* New York: Peabody.

Mercer Management Consulting. 1998, 1995, and 1997 Surveys. (2000). Cited In: A.R. Lajoux (Ed.), *The art of M&A integration.* McGraw-Hill: New York.

Metrick, A., & Yasuda, A. (2010). The economics of private equity funds. *The Review of Financial Studies, 23,* 2303–2341.

Meuleman, M., & Wright, M. (2007). *Industry concentration, syndication networks and competition in the UK private equity market.* CMBOR Working Paper.

Meuleman, M., Amess, K., Wright, M., & Scholes, L. (2009). Agency, strategic entrepreneurship, and the performance of private equity-backed buyouts. *Entrepreneurship Theory and Practice, 33,* 213–239.

Meyer, K. E., Estrin, S., & Bhaumik, S. (2005). *Institutions and business strategies in emerging economies: A study of entry mode choice.* London Business School: Working Paper.

Michaely, R., & Shaw, W. H. (1995). The choice of going public: Spin-offs vs. Carve-outs. *Financial Management, 24,* 15–21.

Miller, M. (2012). The rich get richer. *The Deal,* May 12, p. 38.

Miller, W. (2010). *Value maps: Valuation tools that unlock business wealth.* New York: Wiley.

Mishra, D., & O'Brien, T. (2001). A comparison of cost of equity estimates of local and global CAPMs. *Financial Review, 36*, 27–48.

Mitchell, D. (1998). Survey conducted by economist intelligence unit. In A. R. Lajoux (Ed.), *The art of M&A integration* (pp. 226–228). New York: McGraw-Hill.

Mitchell, M. L., & Mulherin, J. H. (1996). The impact of industry shocks on takeover and restructuring activity. *Journal of Financial Economics, 41*, 193–229.

Mitchell, M. L., & Pulvino, T. C. (2001). Characteristics of risk and return in arbitrage. *Journal of Finance, 56*, 2135–2175.

Mitchell, M., Pulvino, T., & Stafford, E. (2004). Price pressure around mergers. *Journal of Finance, 59*, 31–63.

Moeller, T. (2005). Let's make a deal! How shareholder control impacts merger payoffs. *Journal of Financial Economics, 76*, 167–190.

Moeller, S. B., Schlingemann, F. P., & Stulz, R. M. (2004). Firm size and the gains from acquisitions. *Journal of Financial Economics, 73*, 201–228.

Moeller, S. B., & Schlingemann, P. (2005). Global diversification and bidder gains: A comparison between cross-border and domestic acquisitions. *Journal of Banking and Finance, 29*, 533–564.

Moeller, S. B., Schlingemann, F. P., & Stulz, R. M. (2005). Wealth destruction on a massive scale? A study of the acquiring firm returns in the recent merger wave. *Journal of Finance, 60*, 757–782.

Moeller, S. B., Schlingemann, F. P., & Stulz, R. M. (2007). How do diversity of opinion and information asymmetry affect acquirer returns? *Review of Financial Studies, 20*, 2047–2078.

Molina, C. A. (2006). Are firms unleveraged? An examination of the effect of leverage on default probabilities. *Journal of Finance, 60*, 1427–1459.

Moonchul, K., & Ritter, J. R. (1999). Valuing IPOs. *Journal of Financial Economics, 53*, 409–437.

Morck, R., Schleifer, A., & Vishny, R. W. (1990). Do managerial objectives drive bad acquisitions? *Journal of Finance, 45*, 31–48.

Morck, R., & Yeung, B. (1991). Why investors value multinationality. *Journal of Business, 64*, 165–188.

Morck, R., & Yeung, B. (2000). Inherited wealth, corporate control, and economic growth: The Canadian experience. In R. Morck (Ed.), *Concentrated corporate ownership* (pp. 319–369). Cambridge, MA: National Bureau of Economic Research.

Moroney, R. E. (1973). Most courts overvalue closely held stocks. *Taxes*, March, pp. 144–154.

Mulherin, J. H., & Boone, A. L. (2000). *Comparing acquisitions and divestitures*. Social Science Research Network 38 Working Paper Series.

Mulherin, J. H., & Poulsen, A. B. (1998). Proxy contests and corporate change: Implications for shareholder wealth. *Journal of Financial Economics, 47*, 279–313.

Mun, J. (2006). *Modeling risk: Applying monte carlo simulation, real option analysis, forecasting, and optimization*. New York: Wiley.

Murray, M. (2001). GE's honeywell deal is more than the sum of airplane parts. *Wall Street Journal*, April 5, p. B6.

Navarro, E. (2005). *Merger control in the EU: Law, economics, and practice* (2nd ed.). Oxford, UK: Oxford University Press.

Nenova, T. (2003). The value of corporate voting rights and control: A cross-country analysis. *Journal of Financial Economics, 68*, 325–351.

Netter, J., Stegemoller, M., & Wintoki, M. (2011). Implications of data screens on merger and acquisition analysis: A large sample study of mergers and acquisitions. *Review of Financial Studies, 24*, 2316–2357.

Newbould, G. D., Chatfield, R. E., & Anderson, R. F. (1992). Leveraged buyouts and tax incentives. *Financial Management, 21*, 1621–1637.

Nixon, T. D., Roenfeldt, R. L., & Sicherman, N. W. (2000). The choice between spin-offs and sell-offs. *Review of Quantitative Finance and Accounting, 14*, 277–288.

Oded, A., Michel, A., & Weinstein, S. (2011). Distortion in corporate valuation: Implications for capital structure changes. *Managerial Finance, 37*, 681–696.

Ofek, E. (1993). Capital structure and firm response to poor performance: An empirical analysis. *Journal of Financial Economics, 34*, 3–30.

Ofek, E. (1994). Efficiency gains in unsuccessful management buyouts. *Journal of Finance, 49*, 627–654.

Offenberg, D. (2009). Firm size and the effectiveness of the market for corporate control. *Journal of Corporate Finance, 15*, 66–79.

Offenberg, D., & Officer, M. S. (2012). *Payments to executive of target firms in mergers: Tests using newly available data.* Working Paper, Loyola Marymount University.

Offenberg, D., & Pirinsky, C. (2012). *How do acquirers choose between mergers and tender offers?* Working Paper, Loyola Marymount University.

Officer, M. S. (2003). Termination fees in mergers and acquisitions. *Journal of Financial Economics, 69*, 431–467.

Officer, M. S. (2004). Collars and renegotiation in mergers and acquisitions. *Journal of Finance, 59*, 2719–2743.

Officer, M. S. (2007). The price of corporate liquidity: Acquisition discounts for unlisted targets. *Journal of Financial Economics, 83*, 571–593.

Officer, M. S., Ozbas, O., & Sensoy, B. A. (2008). Club deals in leveraged buyouts. *Journal of Financial Economics, 98*, 214–240.

Officer, M. S., Poulsen, A. B., & Stegemoller, M. (2009). Information asymmetry and acquirer returns. *Review of Finance, 13*, 467–493.

Oliver, R. P., & Meyers, R. H. (2000). Discounts seen in private placements of restricted stock. In R. F. Reilly & R. P. Schweihs (Eds.), *Handbook of advanced business valuation.* New York: McGraw-Hill. (Ch. 5).

Opler, T., & Titman, S. (1993). The determinants of leveraged buyout activity: Free cash flow vs. financial distress costs. *Journal of Finance, 48*, 1985–2000.

Oppenheimer & Company, (1981). *The sum of the parts.* New York: Oppenheimer & Company.

Otsubo, M. (2009). Gains from equity carve-outs and subsequent events. *Journal of Business, 62*, 1207–1213.

Overesch, M. (2009). The effects of multinational profit-shifting activities on real investment. *National Tax Journal, 62*, 5–23.

Palepu, K. G., Healy, P. M., & Bernard, V. L. (2004). *Business analysis and valuation* (3rd ed.). Skokie, IL: Thomson.

Palter, R. N., & Srinivasan, D. (2006). Habits of the busiest acquirers. *McKinsey Quarterly;* https://www.mckinseyquarterly.com/home.aspxy.

Pan, Y., Li, S., & Tse, D. (1999). The impact of order and mode of entry on profitability and market share. *Journal of International Business Studies, 30*, 81–104.

Pan, Y., & Tse, D. K. (2000). The hierarchical model of market entry modes. *Journal of International Business Studies, 31*, 535–554.

Parfomak, P. (2011). Keeping American pipelines safe and secure: Key issues in congress. *Congressional Research Service, 7–5700.*

Park, W., & Sonenshine, R. (2012). Impact of horizontal mergers on research & development and patenting: Evidence from major challenges in the U.S. *Journal of Industry and Competitive Trade, 12*, 143–167.

Pehrsson, A. (2008). Strategy antecedents of mode of entry into foreign markets. *Journal of Business Research, 61*, 132–140.

Peng, M. W. (2003). Institutional transitions and strategic choices. *Academy of Management Review, 28*, 275–296.

Perez-Gonzalez, F. (2006). Inherited control and firm performance. *American Economic Review, 96*, 1559–1588.

Pergola, T. M. (2005). Management entrenchment: Can it negate the effectiveness of recently legislated governance reforms? *Journal of American Academy of Business, 6*, 177–185.

Petmezas, D. (2009). What drives acquisitions? Market valuations and bidder performance. *Journal of Multinational Financial Management, 19*, 54–74.

Petty, J. W., Keown, A. J., Scott, D. F., Jr., & Martin, J. D. (1993). *Basic financial management* (6th ed.). Englewood Cliffs, NJ: Prentice-Hall. (p. 798).

Phan, P. H. (1995). Organizational restructuring and economic performance in leveraged buyouts: An ex post study. *Academy of Management Journal, 38*, 704–739.

Pinkowitz, L. (2002). *The market for corporate control and corporate cash holdings*. Georgetown University: Working Paper.

Platt, D., Platt, B., & Yang, Z. (1999). Probabilistic neural networks in bankruptcy prediction. *Journal of Business Research, 44*, 67–74.

Porter, M. E. (1985). *Competitive advantage*. New York: Free Press.

Poulsen, A., & Stegemoller, M. (2002). *Transitions from private to public ownership*. University of Georgia: Working Paper.

Powers, E. A. (2001). *Spinoffs, selloffs, and equity carve-outs: An analysis of divestiture method choice*. Social Science Research Network 2–4.Working Paper Series.

Powers, E. A. (2003). Deciphering the motives for equity carve-outs. *Journal of Financial Research, 26*(1), 31–50. (Spring).

Pratt, S., & Niculita, A. (2008). *Valuing a business: The analysis and appraisal of closely held businesses*. New York: McGraw-Hill.

Prezas, A., Tarmicilar, M., & Vasudevan, G. (2000). The pricing of equity carve-outs. *Financial Review, 35*, 123–138.

PriceWaterhouseCoopers, Mergers and Acquisitions, (2010). *PriceWaterhouseCoopers, mergers and acquisitions 2010: A global tax guide*. New York: Wiley.

Rabbiosi, L., Elia, S., & Bertoni, F. (2012). Acquisitions by EMNCs in developed markets: An organizational learning perspective. *Management International Review, 52*, 192–212.

Raff, H., Ryan, M., & Staehler, F. (2006). *Asset ownership and foreign-market entry*. CESifo Working Paper No. 1676, Category 7: Trade Policy, February.

Rappaport, A. (1990). The staying power of the public corporation. *Harvard Business Review, 76*, 1–4.

Rau, P. R., & Vermaelen, T. (1998). Glamour, value, and the post-acquisition performance of acquiring firms. *Journal of Financial Economics, 49*, 223–253.

Rau, R. (2000). Investment bank market share, contingent fee payments, and the performance of acquiring firms. *Journal of Financial Economics, 56*, 293–324.

Ravenscraft, D., & Scherer, F. (1987). Life after takeovers. *Journal of Industrial Economics, 36*, 147–156.

Ravenscraft, D., & Scherer, F. (1988). Mergers and managerial performance. In J. Coffee, L. Lowenstein & S. R. Ackerman (Eds.), *Knights and targets* (pp. 194–210). New York: Oxford University Press.

Ravenscraft, D. J., & Scherer, F. M. (1991). Divisional sell-off: A Hazard function analysis. *Managerial and Decision Economics, 12*, 429–438.

Rehm, W., Uhlaner, R., & West, A. (2012, January). Taking a longer-term look at M&A value creation. McKinsey Quarterly http://www.mckinseyquarterly.com/article_print.aspx?L2=5&L3=4&ar=2916.

Renneboog, L., Simons, T., & Wright, M. (2007). Why do public firms go private in the U.K.? *Journal of Corporate Finance, 13*, 591–628.

Renneboog, L., & Szilagyi, P. (2007). Corporate restructuring and bondholder wealth. *European Financial Management, 14*, 792–819.

Rhodes-Kropf, M., & Viswanathan, S. (2004). Market valuation and merger waves. *Journal of Finance, 59*.

Ritter, J. (1991). The long-run performance of initial public offerings. *Journal of Finance, 46*, 3–27.

Robinson, A. (2002). Is corporate governance the solution or the problem? *Corporate Board, 23*, 12–16.

Robinson, D. T. (2002b). *Strategic alliances and the boundaries of the firm*. Columbia University: Working Paper.

Robinson, D. T., & Sensoy, B. A. (2011). *Cyclicality, performance measurement, and cash flow liquidity in private equity*. NBER Working Paper 17428. National Bureau of Economic Research.

Romano, R. (2001). Less is more: Making institutional investor activism a valuable mechanism of corporate governance. *Yale Journal of Regulation, 18*, 174–251.

Ross, S., Westerfield, R., & Jordan, B. (2009). *Fundamentals of corporate finance* (9th ed.). New York: McGraw-Hill.

Rossi, S., & Volpin, P. F. (2004). Cross-country determinants of mergers and acquisitions. *Journal of Financial Economics, 74*, 277–304.

RSM McGladrey, Inc. (2011). Maximizing Investments in an Evolving Market. *Managing Portfolio Investments Survey*, Los Angeles.

Ruback, R. S. (2002). Capital cash flows: A simple approach to valuing risky cash flows. *Financial Management Summer*, 85–103.

Ryngaert, M. (1988). The effects of poison pill securities on stockholder wealth. *Journal of Financial Economics, 20*, 377–417.

Sanderson, S., & Uzumeri, M. (1997). *The innovative imperative: Strategies for managing products, models, and families*. Burr Ridge, IL: Irwin Professional.

Scherreik, S. (2002). Gems among the trash. *Business Week, XX*, 112–113.

Schipper, K., & Smith, A. (1986). A comparison of equity carve-outs and equity offerings: Share price effects and corporate restructuring. *Journal of Financial Economics, 15*, 153–186.

Schleifer, A., & Vishny, R. W. (2003). Stock market–driven acquisitions. *Journal of Financial Economics, 70*, 295–311.

Schmid, R. E. (2001). Post office, fedex become partners. *Orange County Register* Business Section p. 2.

Schultes, R. (2010). AB InBev shines in tough times. *Wall Street Journal*, November 12, p. C7.

Schweiger, D. M. (2002). *M&A integration: Framework for executives and managers*. New York: McGraw-Hill.

Schwert, G. (2000). Hostility in takeovers: In the eyes of the bidder? *Journal of Finance, 55*, 2599–2640.

Selim, G. (2003). *Mergers, acquisitions and divestitures: Control and audit best practices*. New York: Institute of Internal Auditing Research Foundation.

Sender, H. (2006). High-risk debt still has allure for buyout deals. *Wall Street Journal*, p. C2.

Seoungpil, A., & Denis, D. J. (2004). Internal capital market and investment policy: Evidence of corporate spin-offs. *Journal of Financial Economics, 71*, 489–516.

Servaes, H., & Zenner, M. (1994). Taxes and the returns to foreign acquisitions in the U.S. *Financial Management, 23*, 42–56.

Seth, A., Song, K. P., & Petit, R. (2000). Synergy, managerialism or hubris: An empirical examination of motives for foreign acquisitions of U.S. firms. *Journal of International Business Studies, 31*, 387–405.

Seth, A., Song, K. P., & Petit, R. (2002). Value creation and destruction in cross-border acquisitions: An empirical analysis of foreign acquisitions of U.S. firms. *Strategic Management, 23*, 921–940.

Shahrur, H. (2005). Industry structure and horizontal takeovers: Analysis of wealth effects on rivals, suppliers, and corporate customers. *Journal of Financial Economics, 76*, 61–98.

Shapovalova, K., & Subbotin, A. (2011). *Value and size puzzles: A survey*, http://papers.ssrn.com/sol3/papers.cfm?abstract_id=1770626.

Sherman, A. (2006). *Mergers and acquisitions from A to Z: Strategic and practical guidance for small- and middle-market buyers and sellers* (2nd ed.). New York: AMACOM.

Sherman, D. H., & David Young, S. (2001). Tread lightly through these accounting minefields. *Harvard Business Review, July-August*, 129–137.

Shin, H. H., & Stulz, R. (1998). Are internal capital markets efficient? *Quarterly Journal of Economics, 113*, 531–552.

Shivdasani, A. (1993). Board composition, ownership structure, and hostile takeovers. *Journal of Accounting and Economics, 16*, 167–198.

Shumway, T. (2001). Forecasting bankruptcy more accurately: A simple hazard model. *Journal of Business, 74*, 101–124.

Shuttleworth, R. (2004). *Twelve keys to venture capital tech coast angels*; http://techcoastangels.com.

Sicherman, N. W., & Pettway, R. H. (1992). Wealth effects for buyers and sellers for the same divested assets. *Financial Management, 21*, 119–128.

Silber, W. L. (1991). Discounts on restricted stocks: The impact of illiquidity on stock prices. *Financial Analysts Journal, 47*, 60–64.

Singh, H., & Montgomery, C. (2008). Corporate acquisition strategies and economic performance. *Strategic Management Journal, 8*, 377–386.

Sirower, M. (1997). *The synergy trap*. New York: Free Press.

Skantz, T., & Marchesini, R. (1987). The effect of voluntary corporate liquidation on shareholder wealth. *Journal of Financial Research, 10*(Spring), 65–75.

Sloan, R. G. (1996). Do stock prices fully reflect information in accruals and cash flows about future earnings? *Accounting Review, 71*, 289–315.

Slovin, M. B., Sushka, M. E., & Polonchek, J. A. (2005). Methods of payment in asset sales: Contracting with equity versus cash. *Journal of Finance, 60*, 2385–2407.

Smith, A. (1990). Corporate ownership structure and performance: The case of management buy-outs. *Journal of Financial Economics, 27*, 143–164.

Sojli, E., & Tham, W. (2010). The impact of foreign government investments: Sovereign wealth fund investments in the U.S. In J. Cosset & N. Boubakri (Eds.), *Institutional investors in global capital markets (International Finance Review, 12)*. U.K: Emerald Group Publishing Limited.

Srikant, D., Frankel, R., & Wolfson, M. (2001). Earnouts: The effects of adverse selection and agency costs on acquisition techniques. *Journal of Law, Economics, and Organization, 17*, 201–238.

Standard Research Consultants, (1983). Revenue ruling 77-287 revisited. *SRC Quarterly Reports, Spring*, 1–3.

Stout, L. A. (2002). Do antitakeover defenses decrease shareholder wealth? The ex post/ex ante valuation problem. *Stanford Law Review, 55*, 845–861.

Stromberg, P. (2008). The new demography of private equity. Globalization of alternative investments. *The Global Economic Impact of Private Equity Report*. World Economic Forum 1 3–26. Working Paper.

Stromberg, P., Hotchkiss, E., & Smith, D. (2011, April 7). *Private equity and the resolution of financial distress* http://ssrn.com/sol3/papers.cfm?abstract_1787446.

Stulz, R. M. (1995). Globalization of the capital markets and the cost of capital: The case of nestle. *Journal of Applied Corporate Finance, 8*, 30–38.

Stulz, R. M. (1995). The cost of capital in internationally integrated markets: The case of nestle. *European Financial Management, 1*, 11–22.

Stulz, R. M., & Wasserfallen, W. (1995). Foreign equity invest restrictions, capital flight, and shareholder wealth maximization: Theory and evidence. *Review of Financial Studies, 8*, 1019–1057.

Subramanyam, A. (2010). The cross-section of expected returns: What have we learnt from the past twenty-five years of research? *European Financial Management, 16*, 27–43.

Subramanian, G. (2010). *Negotiauctions: Deal-making strategies for a competitive market place*. New York: W.W. Norton.

Sweeney, P. (2005). Gap. *Financial Executives Magazine*, 33–40.

Tang, C. Y., & Tikoo, S. (1999). Operational flexibility and market valuation of earnings. *Strategic Management Journal, 20*, 749–761.

Tashjian, E., Lease, R., & McConnell, J. J. (1996). Prepacks: An empirical analysis of prepackaged bankruptcies. *Journal of Financial Economics, 40*, 135–162.

Thompson Financial Securities Data Corporation. (2000). The world's urge to merge. *Press release*, January 5.

Thompson, T. H., & Apilado, V. (2009). An examination of the impact of equity carve-outs on stockholder and bondholder wealth. *Journal of Economics and Business, 61*, 376–391.

Titman, S., & Martin, J. (2010). *Valuation: The art and science of corporate investment decisions* (2nd ed.). Boston: Prentice-Hall. (pp. 144–147).

Travlos, N. G., & Cornett, M. N. (1993). Going private buyouts and determinants of shareholders' returns. *Journal of Accounting, Auditing and Finance, 8*, 1–25.

Truitt, W. B. (2006). *The corporation*. Westport, CT: Greenwood Press.

Tykova, T., & Borell, M. (2011, November 2). Do private equity owners increase risk of financial distress and bankruptcy? papers.ssrn.com/sol13/papers.cfm?abstract_1987639.

Uhlaner, R. T., & West, A. S. (2008). Running a winning M&A shop. *McKinsey Quarterly* mckinsey-quarterly.com.

United States v. Primestar, L.P., 58 Fed Register, 33944, June 22, 1993 (Proposed Final Judgment and Competitive Impact Study).

U.S. Attorney General. (2000). Global Antitrust Regulation: Issues and Solutions. *Final Report of the International Competition Policy Advisory Committee*.

U.S. Department of Justice. (1999). Antitrust division www.usdoj.gov.

U.S. General Accountability Office. (2008). *Private Equity: Real Growth in Leveraged Buyouts Exposes Risk*. GAO-08-885.

U.S. Securities and Exchange Commission. (2012, July 13). *Work Plan for the Consideration of Incorporating International Financial Reporting Standards in the Financial Reporting System for U.S. Issuers*, Final Staff Report, Office of the Chief Accountant.

U.S. Small Business Administration. (1999). *Financial Difficulties of Small Businesses and Reasons for Their Failure Office of Advocacy*, RS 188.

U.S. Small Business Administration. (2003). *State Small Business Profile*. Office of Advocacy: RS 203.

Uysal, V. (2011). Deviation from the target capital structure and acquisition choices. *Journal of Financial Economics, 102,* 602–620.

Vachon, M. (1993). Venture capital reborn. *Venture Capital Journal,* p. 32.

Vasconcellos, G. M., & Kish, R. J. (1998). Cross-border mergers and acquisitions: The European–U.S. experience. *Journal of Multinational Financial Management, 8,* 173–189.

Vasconcellos, G. M., Madura, J., & Kish, R. J. (1990). An empirical investigation of factors affecting cross-border acquisitions: U.S. versus non-U.S. experience. *Global Finance Journal, 1,* 173–189.

Veld, C., & Veld-Merkoulova, Y. (2004). Do spin-offs really create value? *Journal of Banking and Finance, 28,* 1111–1135.

Vermeulen, F., & Barkema, H. G. (2001). Learning through acquisitions. *Journal of the Academy of Management, 44,* 457–476.

Vijh, A. M. (1999). Long-term returns from equity carve-outs. *Journal of Financial Economics, 51,* 273–308.

Vijh, A. M. (2002). The positive announcement period returns of equity carve-outs: Asymmetric information or divestiture gains. *Journal of Business, 75,* 153–190.

Villalonga, B. (2004). Diversification discount or premium? New evidence from the business information tracking series. *Journal of Finance, 59,* 479–506.

Villalonga, B., & Amit, R. (2006). How do family ownership, control, and management affect firm value? *Journal of Financial Economics, 80,* 385–417.

de Vroom, H. J., & van Frederikslust, R. (1999). *Shareholder wealth effects of corporate spinoffs: The worldwide experience 1990–1998*. SSRN Working Paper Series, August 9.

Wagner, H. F. (2004). *The equity carve-out decision*. University of Munich: Working Paper.

Walsh, J. P., & Ellwood, J. W. (1991). Mergers, acquisitions, and the pruning of managerial deadwood. *Strategic Management Journal, 12,* 201–217.

Weifeng, W., Zhaoguo, Z., & Shasa, Z. (2008). Ownership structure and the private benefits of control: An analysis of chinese firms. *Corporate Governance, 8,* 286–298.

Weir, C., Jones, P., & Wright, M. (2007). *Public to private transactions, private equity and performance in the UK: An empirical analysis of the impact of going private*. Working Paper, Nottingham University, UK.

Weir, C., Liang, D., & Wright, M. (2005). Incentive effects, monitoring mechanisms and the threat from the market for corporate control: An analysis of the factors affecting public to private transactions in the U.K. *Journal of Business Finance and Accounting, 32,* 909–944.

White, M. (1989). The corporate bankruptcy decision. *Journal of Economic Perspectives, 3,* 129–152.

White, E., & Joann, S. (2007). Companies trim executive perks to avoid glare. *Wall Street Journal,* 13 p. A1.

Wilson, B. D. (1980). The propensity of multinational companies to expand through acquisitions. *Journal of International Business Studies, 11,* 59–64.

Wiltbank, R., & Boeker, W. (2007). Returns to Angel Investors in Groups. Marian Ewing Foundation and Angel Capital Education Foundation, November.

Wright, M., Burros, A., Ball, R., Scholes, L., Meuleman, M., & Amess, K. (2008). The Implications of Alternative Investment Vehicles for Corporate Governance: A Survey of Empirical Research. Organization for Economic Cooperation and Development; www.oecd,org/daf/corporate-affairs.

Wright, M. N. W., & Robbie, K. (1996). The longer-term effects of management-led buyouts. *Journal of Entrepreneurial and Small Business Finance, 5,* 213–234.

Wruck, K. H. (1989). Equity ownership concentration and firm value: Evidence from private equity financing. *Journal of Financial Economics, 23,* 3–28.

Wruck, K. H., & Yilin, W. (2009). Relationships, corporate governance, and performance: Evidence from private placements of common stock. *Journal of Corporate Finance, 15,* 30–47.

Wu, Y. L. (2004). The choice of equity-selling mechanisms. *Journal of Financial Economics, 74*, 93–119.

Wulf, J. (2004). Do CEOs in mergers trade power for premium? Evidence from mergers of equals. *Journal of Law and Organization, 20*, 60.

Wulf, J., & Rajan, R. (2003). *The flattening firm: Evidence from panel data on the changing nature of corporate hierarchies*. University of Chicago: Working Paper.

Yago, G., & Bonds, J. (1991). *How high-yield securities restructured corporate America*. New York: Oxford University Press.

Yen, T., & Andre, P. (2010). *Long-term operating performance of acquiring firms in emerging markets: The corporate governance issue*, August 22, 2010, http://ssrn.com/abstract=1663287.

Yermack, D. (1996). Higher market valuation of companies with a small board size. *Journal of Financial Economics, 40*, 185–211.

Zahra, S., & Elhagrasey, G. (1994). Strategic management of international joint ventures. *European Management Journal, 12*, 83–93.

Zahra, S. A., Ireland, R. D., & Hitt, M. A. (2000). International expansion by new venture firms: International, mode of market entry, technological learning and performance. *Academy of Management Journal, 19*, 244–257.

Zingales, L. (1995). What determines the value of corporate control? *The Quarterly Journal of Economics, 110*, 1047–1073.

Zodrow, G. (2010). Capital mobility and national tax competition. *National Tax Journal, 63*, 865–902.

Zola, M., & Meier, D. (2008). What is M&A performance? *Academy of Management Perspectives, 22*, 55–77.

Zuckerman, G., Sender, H., & Patterson, S. (2007). Hedge fund crowd sees more green as fortress hits jackpot with IPO. *Wall Street Journal*, p. A1.

Glossary

Abnormal return The return to shareholders due to nonrecurring events that differs from what would have been predicted by the market. It is the return due to an event such as a merger or an acquisition.

Acquirer A firm that attempts to acquire a controlling interest in another company.

Acquisition The purchase by one company of a controlling ownership interest in another firm, a legal subsidiary of another firm, or selected assets of another firm.

Acquisition vehicle The legal structure used to acquire another company.

Arbitrageurs (arbs) In the context of M&As, arbs are speculators who attempt to profit from the difference between the bid price and the target firm's current share price.

Asset impairment An asset is said to be impaired according to FASB Statement 142 if its fair value falls below its book or carrying value.

Asset purchases Transactions in which the acquirer buys all or a portion of the target company's assets and assumes all, some, or none of the target's liabilities.

Asymmetric information Information about a firm that is not equally available to managers as well as shareholders.

Back-end merger The merger following either a single- or two-tier tender offer consisting of either a long-form or short-form merger, with the latter not requiring a target firm shareholder vote.

Bankruptcy A federal legal proceeding designed to protect the technically or legally insolvent firm from lawsuits by its creditors until a decision can be made either to shut down or to continue to operate the firm.

Bear hug A takeover tactic involving the mailing of a letter containing an acquisition proposal to the board of directors of a target company without prior warning and demanding a rapid decision.

Beta A measure of nondiversifiable risk or the extent to which a firm's (or asset's) return changes because of a change in the market's return.

Boot The nonequity portion of a purchase price.

Breakup fee A fee that will be paid to a potential acquirer if a target firm decides to accept an alternative bid. Also called a *termination fee*.

Bridge financing Temporary unsecured short-term loans provided by investment banks to pay all or a portion of the purchase price and meet immediate working capital requirements until permanent or long-term financing is found.

Business alliance A generic term referring to all forms of business combinations other than mergers and acquisitions.

Business strategy or model That portion of a business plan detailing the way the firm intends to achieve its vision.

Buyout Change in controlling interest in a corporation.

Capital asset pricing model A framework for measuring the relationship between expected risk and return.

Capitalization multiple The multiple estimated by dividing 1 by the estimated discount or capitalization rate that can be used to estimate the value of a business by multiplying it by an indicator of value, such as free cash flow.

Capitalization rate The discount rate used by practitioners if the cash flows of a firm are not expected to grow or are expected to grow at a constant rate indefinitely.

Cash-for-assets An acquisition in which the acquirer pays cash for the seller's assets and may choose to accept some or all of the seller's liabilities.

Cash-out statutory merger A merger in which the shareholders of the selling firm receive cash or some form of nonvoting investment (e.g., debt or nonvoting preferred or common stock) for their shares.

Certificate of incorporation A document received from the state once the articles of incorporation have been approved.

Classified board election An antitakeover defense involving the separation of a firm's board into several classes, only one of which is up for election at any one point in time. Also called a *staggered board*.

Closing The phase of the acquisition process in which ownership is transferred from the target to the acquiring firm in exchange for some agreed-on consideration following the receipt of all necessary shareholder, regulatory, and third-party approvals.

Closing conditions Stipulations that must be satisfied before closing can take place.

Collar agreement An arrangement providing for certain changes in the share exchange ratio contingent on the level of the acquirer's share price around the effective date of the merger.

Common-size financial statements Financial statements calculated by taking each line item as a percentage of revenue.

Composition An agreement in which creditors consent to settling for less than the full amount they are owed.

Confidentiality agreement A mutually binding accord defining how information exchanged among the parties may be used and the circumstances under which the discussions may be made public. Also known as a *nondisclosure agreement*.

Conglomerate mergers Transactions in which the acquiring company purchases firms in largely unrelated industries.

Consent decree Requires the merging parties to divest overlapping businesses or restrict anticompetitive practices.

Consent solicitation A process enabling dissident shareholders in certain states to obtain shareholder support for their proposals by simply obtaining their written consent.

Consolidation A business combination involving two or more companies joining to form a new company, in which none of the combining firms survive.

Constant-growth model A valuation method that assumes that cash flow will grow at a constant rate.

Contingent value rights (CVR) Commitments by an issuing company to pay additional cash or securities to the holder of the CVR if the share price of the issuing company falls below a specified level at some future date.

Control premium The excess over a target's current share price the acquirer is willing to pay to gain a controlling interest. A pure control premium is one in which the anticipated synergies are small and the perceived value of the purchase is in gaining control to direct the activities of the target firm.

Corporate bylaws Rules governing the internal management of a corporation that are determined by the corporation's founders.

Corporate charters A state license defining the powers of a firm and the rights and responsibilities of its shareholders, board of directors, and managers. The charter consists of articles of incorporation and a certificate of incorporation.

Corporate governance The systems and controls in place to protect the rights of corporate stakeholders.

Corporate restructuring Actions taken to expand or contract a firm's basic operations or fundamentally change its asset or financial structure.

Cost leadership A strategy designed to make a firm the cost leader in its market by constructing efficient production facilities, tightly controlling overhead expense, and eliminating marginally profitable customer accounts.

Cram down A legal reorganization occurring whenever one or more classes of creditors or shareholders approve, even though others may not.

Cumulative voting rights In an election for a board of directors, each shareholder is entitled to as many votes as equal the number of shares the shareholder owns multiplied by the number of directors to be elected. Furthermore, the shareholder may cast all of these votes for a single candidate or any two or more of them.

Debt-for-equity swap Creditors surrender a portion of their claims on a firm in exchange for an ownership position in the firm.

Debtor-in-possession On the filing of a reorganization petition, the firm's current management remains in place to conduct the ongoing affairs of the firm.

Destroyers of value Factors that can reduce the future cash flow of combined companies.

Discounted cash flow The conversion of future to current cash flows by applying an appropriate discount rate.

Discount rate The opportunity cost associated with investment in a firm used to convert the projected cash flows to present values.

Diversifiable risk The risk specific to an individual firm, such as strikes and lawsuits.

Diversification A strategy of buying firms outside of the company's primary line of business.

Divestiture The sale of all or substantially all of a company or product line to another party for cash or securities.

Dual class recapitalization A takeover defense whereby a firm issues multiple classes of stock in which one class has voting rights that are 10 to 100 times those of another class. Such stock is also called *supervoting stock*.

Due diligence The process by which an acquirer seeks to determine the accuracy of a target's financial statements, evaluate the firm's operations, validate valuation assumptions, determine fatal flaws, and identify sources and destroyers of value.

Earnouts Payments to a seller based on the acquired business's achieving certain profit or revenue targets.

Economic value The present value of a firm's projected cash flows.

Economies of scale The spreading of fixed costs over increasing production levels.

Economies of scope The use of a specific set of skills or an asset currently used to produce a specific product to produce related products.

Effective control Control achieved when one firm has purchased another firm's voting stock, it is not likely to be temporary, there are no legal restrictions on control (such as from a bankruptcy court), and there are no powerful minority shareholders.

Employee stock ownership plan (ESOP) A trust fund or plan that invests in the securities of the firm sponsoring the plan on behalf of the firm's employees. Such plans are generally defined contribution employee-retirement plans.

Enterprise cash flow Cash available to shareholders and lenders after all operating obligations of a firm have been satisfied.

Enterprise value Viewed from the liability side of the balance sheet, it is the sum of the market or present value of a firm's common equity plus preferred stock and long-term debt. For simplicity, other long-term liabilities are often excluded from the calculation. From the perspective of the asset side of the balance sheet, it is equal to cash plus the market value of current operating and nonoperating assets less current liabilities plus long-term assets.

Equity carve-out A transaction in which a parent firm issues to the public a portion of its stock or that of a subsidiary.

Equity cash flow Cash available to common shareholders after all operating obligations of a firm have been satisfied.

Equity premium The rate of return in excess of the risk-free rate that investors require to invest in equities.

Excess returns See *abnormal returns*.

Exchange offer A tender offer involving a share-for-share exchange.

Extension Creditor agreement to lengthen the period during which the debtor firm can repay its debt and, in some cases, to temporarily suspend both interest and principal repayments.

Fair market value The cash or cash-equivalent price a willing buyer would propose and a willing seller would accept for a business if both parties have access to all relevant information.

Fairness opinion letter A written and signed third-party assertion certifying the appropriateness of the price of a proposed deal involving a tender offer, merger, asset sale, or leveraged buyout.

Fair value An estimate of the value of an asset when no strong market exists for a business or it is not possible to identify the value of substantially similar firms.

Financial buyer Acquirers that focus on relatively short-to-intermediate financial returns and typically use large amounts of debt to finance their acquisitions.

Financial sponsor An investor group providing equity financing in leveraged buyout transactions.

Financial synergy The reduction in the cost of capital as a result of more stable cash flows, financial economies of scale, or a better matching of investment opportunities with available funds.

Fixed or constant share-exchange agreement An exchange agreement in which the number of acquirer shares exchanged for each target share is unchanged between the signing of the agreement of purchase and the sale and closing.

Fixed-value agreement The value of the price per share is fixed by allowing the number of acquirer shares issued to vary to offset fluctuations in the buyer's share price.

Flip-in poison pill Shareholders' rights plan in which the shareholders of the target firm can acquire stock in the target firm at a substantial discount.

Flip-over poison pill Shareholders' rights plan in which the target firm's shareholders may convert such rights to acquire stock of the surviving company at a substantial discount.

Form of acquisition The determination of what is being acquired (i.e., stock or assets) and the way in which ownership is transferred.

Form of payment A means of payment: cash, common stock, debt, or some combination. Some portion of the payment may be deferred or dependent on the future performance of the acquired entity.

Forward triangular merger The acquisition subsidiary being merged with the target and the acquiring subsidiary surviving.

Free cash flow The difference between cash inflows and cash outflows, which may be positive, negative, or zero.

Friendly takeover Acquisition when the target's board and management are receptive to the idea and recommend shareholder approval.

General partner An individual responsible for the daily operations of a limited partnership.

Globally integrated capital markets Capital markets providing foreigners with unfettered access to local capital markets; and local residents to foreign capital markets.

Going concern value The value of a company defined as the firm's value in excess of the sum of the value of its parts.

Going private The purchase of the publicly traded shares of a firm by a group of investors.

Golden parachutes Employee severance arrangements that are triggered whenever a change in control takes place.

Goodwill The excess of the purchase price over the fair value of the acquired net assets on the acquisition date.

Go-shop provision A provision allowing a seller to continue to solicit other bidders for a specific time period after an agreement has been signed but before closing. However, the seller that accepts another bid must pay a breakup fee to the bidder with which it had a signed agreement.

Hedge fund Private investment limited partnerships (for U.S. investors) or offshore investment corporations (for non-U.S. or tax-exempt investors) in which the general partner has made a substantial personal investment.

Highly leveraged transactions Transactions involving a substantial amount of debt relative to the amount of equity invested.

Holding company A legal entity often having a controlling interest in one or more companies.

Horizontal merger A combination of two firms within the same industry.

Hostile takeover Acquisition when the initial bid was unsolicited, the target was not seeking a merger at the time of the approach, the approach was contested by the target's management, and control changed hands.

Hostile tender offer A tender offer that is unwanted by the target's board.

Hubris An explanation for takeovers that attributes a tendency to overpay to excessive optimism about the value of a deal's potential synergy; or excessive confidence in management's ability to manage the acquisition.

Impaired asset As defined by FASB, a long-term asset whose fair value falls below its book or carrying value.

Implementation strategy The way in which a firm chooses to execute a business strategy.

Indemnification A common contractual clause requiring a seller to indemnify or absolve the buyer of liability in the event of misrepresentations or breaches of warranties or covenants. Similarly, the buyer usually agrees to indemnify the seller. In

effect, it is the reimbursement to the other party for a loss for which it was not responsible.

Interest rate parity theory A theory that relates forward or future spot exchange rates to differences in interest rates between two countries adjusted by the spot rate.

Investment bankers Advisors who offer strategic and tactical advice and acquisition opportunities; screen potential buyers and sellers; make initial contact with a seller or buyer; and provide negotiation support, valuation, and deal-structuring advice.

Involuntary bankruptcy A situation in which creditors force a debtor firm into bankruptcy.

Junk bonds High-yield bonds either rated by the credit-rating agencies as below investment grade or not rated at all.

Legal form of the selling entity Whether the seller is a C or Subchapter S corporation, a limited liability company, or a partnership.

Legal insolvency When a firm's liabilities exceed the fair market value of its assets.

Letter of intent Preliminary agreement between two companies intending to merge that stipulates major areas of agreement between the parties.

Leveraged buyout Purchase of a company financed primarily by debt.

Liquidation The value of a firm's assets sold separately less its liabilities and expenses incurred in breaking up the firm.

Liquidity discount The discount or reduction in the offer price for the target firm made by discounting the value of the target firm estimated by examining the market values of comparable publicly traded firms to reflect the potential loss in value when sold due to the illiquidity of the market for similar types of investments. The liquidity discount also is referred to as a *marketability discount*.

Management buyout A leveraged buyout in which managers of the firm to be taken private are also equity investors in the transaction.

Management entrenchment theory A theory that managers use a variety of takeover defenses to ensure their longevity with the firm.

Management preferences The boundaries or limits that senior managers of an acquiring firm place on the acquisition process.

Managerialism theory A theory espousing that managers acquire companies to increase the acquirer's size and their own remuneration.

Marketability risk The risk associated with an illiquid market for a specific stock. Also called *liquidity risk*.

Maximum offer price The sum of the minimum price plus the present value of net synergy.

Merger A combination of two or more firms in which all but one legally cease to exist.

Merger–acquisition plan A specific type of implementation strategy that describes in detail the motivation for the acquisition and how and when it will be achieved.

Merger arbitrage An investment strategy that attempts to profit from the spread between a target firm's current share price and a pending takeover bid.

Merger of equals A merger framework usually applied whenever the merger participants are: comparable in size, competitive position, profitability, and market capitalization.

Minimum offer price The target's stand-alone or present value or its current market value.

Minority discount The reduction in the value of minority investors' investment in a firm because they cannot direct the activities of the firm.

Minority investment A less-than-controlling interest in another firm.

Net asset value The difference between the fair market value of total identifiable acquired assets and the value of acquired liabilities.

Net debt The market value of debt assumed by the acquirer less cash and marketable securities on the books of the target firm.

Net operating loss carryforward and carrybacks Provisions in the tax laws allowing firms to use accumulated net tax losses to offset income earned over a specified number of future years or recover taxes paid during a limited number of prior years.

Net purchase price Total purchase price plus other assumed liabilities less the proceeds from the sale of discretionary or redundant target assets.

Net synergy The difference between estimated sources of value and destroyers of value.

Nondiversifiable risk Risk generated by factors that affect all firms, such as inflation and war.

One-tiered offer A bidder announces the same offer to all target shareholders.

Operating synergy Increased value resulting from a combination of businesses due to such factors as economies of scale and scope.

Payment-in-kind (PIK) notes Equity or debt that pays dividends or interest in the form of additional equity or debt.

Poison pills A new class of securities issued as a dividend by a company to its shareholders, giving shareholders rights to acquire more shares at a discount.

Postclosing organization The organizational and legal framework used to manage the combined businesses following the completion of the transaction.

Private corporation A firm whose securities are not registered with state or federal authorities.

Private equity fund Limited partnerships in which the general partner has made a substantial personal investment.

Pro forma financial statements A form of accounting that presents financial statements in a way that purports to describe a firm's current or projected performance more accurately.

Proxy contest An attempt by dissident shareholders to obtain representation on the board of directors or to change a firm's bylaws.

Purchase accounting A form of accounting for financial reporting purposes in which the acquired assets and assumed liabilities are revalued to their fair market value on the date of acquisition and recorded on the books of the acquiring company.

Purchasing power parity theory The theory stating that one currency will appreciate (depreciate) with respect to another currency according to the expected relative rates of inflation between the two countries.

Purchase premium The excess of an offer price over the target's current share price, which reflects both the value of expected synergies and the amount necessary to obtain control.

Pure control premium The value an acquirer believes can be created by replacing incompetent management or changing the strategic direction of a firm.

Pure play A firm whose products or services focus on a single industry or market.

Real options Management's ability to adopt and later revise corporate investment decisions.

Reverse breakup fee Fee paid to a target firm in the event the bidder wants to withdraw from a signed contract.

Reverse merger Process by which a private firm goes public by merging with a public firm, with the public firm surviving.

Reverse triangular merger The merger of a target with a subsidiary of the acquiring firm, with the target surviving.

Risk-free rate of return The return on a security with an exceedingly low probability of default, such as U.S. Treasury securities, and minimal reinvestment risk.

Risk premium The additional rate of return in excess of the risk-free rate that investors require to purchase a firm's equity. Also called the *equity premium*.

Secured debt Debt backed by the borrower's assets.

Segmented capital markets Capital markets exhibiting different bond and equity prices in different geographic areas for identical assets in terms of risk and maturity.

Share-exchange ratio The number of shares of an acquirer's stock to be exchanged for each share of the target's stock.

Shareholders' interest theory The presumption that management resistance to proposed takeovers is a good bargaining strategy to increase the purchase price for the benefit of the target firm shareholders.

Shell corporation A company that is incorporated but has no significant assets or operations.

Sources of value Factors increasing the cash flow of combined companies.

Spin-off A transaction in which a parent creates a new legal subsidiary and distributes shares it owns in the subsidiary to its current shareholders as a stock dividend.

Split-off A variation of a spin-off in which some parent company shareholders receive shares in a subsidiary in return for relinquishing their parent company shares.

Split-up A transaction in which a parent firm splits its assets between two or more subsidiaries and the stock of each subsidiary is offered to its shareholders in exchange for their parent firm shares.

Staggered board election A takeover defense involving the division of a firm's directors into a number of different classes, with no two classes up for reelection at the same time. Also called a *classified board*.

Stand-alone business A business whose financial statements reflect all the costs of running the business and all the revenues generated by the business.

Standstill agreement A contractual arrangement in which an acquirer agrees not to make any further investments in the target's stock for a stipulated period.

Statutory merger The combination of the acquiring and target firms, in which one firm ceases to exist, in accordance with the statutes of the state in which the combined businesses will be incorporated.

Stock-for-stock statutory merger A merger in which the seller receives acquirer shares in exchange for its shares (with the seller shares subsequently cancelled); also called a *stock swap merger*.

Stock purchases The exchange of a target's stock for cash, debt, or the stock of the acquiring company.

Strategic buyer An acquirer primarily interested in increasing shareholder value by realizing long-term synergies.

Subsidiary carve-out A transaction in which the parent creates a wholly owned independent legal subsidiary, with stock and a management team different from the parent's, and issues a portion of the subsidiary's stock to the public.

Supermajority rules A takeover defense requiring a higher level of approval for amending a charter or for certain types of transactions, such as a merger or an acquisition.

Super voting stock A class of voting stock having voting rights many times those of other classes of stock.

Synergy The notion that the value of combined enterprises will exceed the sum of their individual values.

Takeover Generic term referring to a change in the controlling ownership interest of a corporation.

Takeover defenses Protective devices put in place by a firm to frustrate, slow down, or raise the cost of a takeover.

Target company The firm that is being solicited by an acquiring company.

Taxable transaction Transaction in which the form of payment is primarily something other than the acquisition of company stock.

Tax considerations Structures and strategies determining whether a transaction is taxable or nontaxable to the seller's shareholders.

Tax-free reorganization Nontaxable transactions usually involving mergers, with the form of payment primarily acquirer stock exchanged for the target's stock or assets.

Tax shield The reduction in a firm's tax liability due to the tax deductibility of interest.

Tender offer The offer to buy shares in another firm, usually for cash, securities, or both.

Term sheet A document outlining the primary areas of agreement between a buyer and a seller, which is often used as the basis for a more detailed letter of intent.

Total capitalization The sum of a firm's debt and all forms of equity.

Total consideration A term commonly used in legal documents to reflect the different types of remuneration received by target company shareholders.

Total purchase price The total consideration plus the market value of a target firm's debt assumed by the acquiring company. Also referred to as *enterprise value.*

Tracking stocks Separate classes of common stock of a parent corporation whose dividend payouts depend on the financial performance of a specific subsidiary. Also called *target* or *letter stocks.*

Two-tiered offer A tender offer in which target shareholders receive an offer for a specific number of shares. Immediately following this offer, the bidder announces its intentions to purchase the remaining shares at a lower price or using something other than cash.

Type A reorganization A tax-free merger or consolidation in which target shareholders receive cash; voting or nonvoting common or preferred stock; or debt for their shares. At least 50 percent of the purchase price must be in acquirer stock.

Type B stock-for-stock reorganization A tax-free transaction in which the acquirer uses its voting common stock to purchase at least 80% of the voting power of the target's outstanding voting stock, and at least 80% of each class of nonvoting shares. Used as an alternative to a merger.

Type C stock-for-assets reorganization A tax-free transaction in which acquirer voting stock is used to purchase at least 80% of the fair market value of the target's net assets.

Valuation cash flows Restated GAAP cash flows used for valuing a firm or a firm's assets.

Variable growth valuation model A valuation method that assumes that a firm's cash flows will experience periods of high growth followed by a period of slower, more sustainable growth.

Weighted-average cost of capital A broader measure than the cost of equity that represents the return that a firm must earn to induce investors to buy its stock and bonds.

White knight A potential acquirer that is viewed more favorably by a target firm's management and board than the initial bidder.

Zero-growth valuation model A valuation model that assumes that free cash flow is constant in perpetuity.

Index

Note: Page numbers followed by "*f*", "*t*" and "*b*" refers to figures, tables and boxes respectively.